THE WALLS
OF JERICHO

To David and Charlayne,

With my best wishes,
Robert Mann

Robert Mann

THE WALLS OF JERICHO

Lyndon Johnson,
Hubert Humphrey,
Richard Russell,
and the Struggle
for Civil Rights

A HARVEST BOOK
HARCOURT BRACE & COMPANY
San Diego   New York   London

For Cindy

Requests for permission to make copies of any part of the work should be mailed to: Permissions Department, Harcourt Brace & Company, 6277 Sea Harbor Drive, Orlando, Florida 32887-6777.

Library of Congress Cataloging-in-Publication Data
Mann, Robert, 1958–
The walls of Jericho: Lyndon Johnson, Hubert Humphrey, Richard Russell, and the struggle for civil rights/by Robert Mann.
p.   cm.
Includes bibliographical references and index.
ISBN 0-15-100065-4
ISBN 0-15-600501-8 (pbk.)

1. Civil rights movements—United States—History—20th century.
2. Afro-Americans—Civil rights. 3. Johnson, Lyndon B. (Lyndon Baines), 1908–1973. 4. Humphrey, Hubert H. (Hubert Horatio), 1911–1978.
5. Russell, Richard B. (Richard Brevard), 1897–1971.   I. Title.
E185.61.M296   1996
323'.0973—dc20   95-30058

The text was set in Fournier.
Designed by Linda Lockowitz
Printed in the United States of America
First Harvest edition 1997
A C E F D B

When the trumpets sounded, the people shouted,
and at the sound of the trumpet, when the people
gave a loud shout, the wall collapsed.

—JOSHUA 6:20

Justice is a machine that, when someone
has given it a starting push, rolls on of itself.

—JOHN GALSWORTHY

Great ideas may incubate in the House of Representatives,
but the size of that chamber muffles the voices of its members.
The Senate is small, intimate and obliged to listen
to every one of its members.

—ROBERT AND LEONA TRAIN RIENOW
Of Snuff, Sin and the Senate

The Senate is the last primitive society
in the world. We still worship the elders of the tribe
and honor the territorial imperative.

—EUGENE McCARTHY

The U.S. Senate—an old scow
which doesn't move very fast, but it never sinks.

—EVERETT DIRKSEN

CONTENTS

Black-and-white photos follow pages 182 and 374

THE WALLS
OF JERICHO

CHAPTER ONE

A Whirlwind
from Minnesota

AS HE APPROACHED the massive podium in Philadelphia's Convention Hall, Hubert H. Humphrey anxiously surveyed the boiling sea of perspiring, irritable delegates. On this rainy July afternoon, the last day of the 1948 Democratic National Convention, he would make history. In his hands, the lanky, black-haired mayor of Minneapolis clutched the text of a speech that in a matter of moments would propel him to instant celebrity and breathe life into his struggling cause.

As he stepped up to the microphone, Humphrey was understandably nervous. He knew that the stifling heat inside the convention hall—one reporter called it a "hot box"—had sapped much of the delegates' energy, leaving them restless and inattentive. Anticipating President Harry Truman's arrival, the Secret Service had sealed the building. Air circulation ceased. Although it was raining outside and in the low eighties, the temperature at the podium soared into the high nineties. Heightening Humphrey's anxiety was the knowledge that he had never addressed an audience of this size, which included millions outside the convention hall who followed the proceedings on radio and television.

The thirty-seven-year-old Humphrey was an ambitious, ebullient politician. He was well liked, always eager to make a new friend or win a new ally. A tireless worker, he often seemed to be juggling a hundred projects at once. "Hubert was like a whirlwind," said his friend, novelist Frederick Manfred. "He was everywhere at once, it seemed." But he felt deeply about *so many* issues. Consequently, he talked fast—and often too long. Humphrey could be eloquent at times. And when he cared deeply about an issue, he rarely failed to inspire his listeners with the intense passions and convictions that churned furiously inside him.

These qualities would serve him well. The coming moment would require all of his fire and eloquence.

The issue of civil rights compelled Humphrey to the podium. As a candidate for the U.S. Senate and vice-chairman of a new liberal organization, Americans for Democratic Action (ADA), Humphrey was among the most effective and ardent critics of an American social and legal system that had denied basic human rights to black citizens for most of the past hundred years. For too long, Humphrey and his ADA associates believed, Congress and leaders of both political parties had paid only lip service to the question of minority rights. In his first term, President Truman had courageously yet unsuccessfully fought to pass a civil rights program. Now he was tugged in opposite directions by liberals in his party who wanted a strong civil rights plank and conservative southerners who wanted none at all.

To Truman and his advisors, the dilemma begged for just the kind of compromise they had hatched: a simple reaffirmation of the moderate civil rights language the party had adopted four years earlier. In the days leading up to the convention, Truman's men hoped to strike this clever bargain with unruly liberals and conservatives. The platform committee agreed. A moderate plank, they believed, would keep the peace by mollifying liberals and discouraging restless southern delegations from bolting the party in the November election. Hoping to further ensure a placid convention, Truman's men made peace offerings to northern and southern delegates alike. To appease some southerners, the committee dropped a plank concerning offshore oil revenues. For northerners, it added language that urged stronger U.S. relations with the new nation of Israel.

Even if these machinations resulted in party unity, many delegates feared that the whole exercise—the whole convention, in fact—was a waste of time. Almost everyone attending believed that Truman could not be reelected. Absent harmony over civil rights, these Democrats—and almost everyone but Truman—believed that the president was certainly doomed.

Humphrey had given the party's bosses ample warning that he might force a showdown over civil rights. In March he and James Roosevelt, son of the late president, had written Democratic leaders urging them to embrace stronger language on civil rights. But many of those leaders—including Senate Whip Scott Lucas—spurned Humphrey, doubting not only his motives but his devotion to all-important party unity. Truman himself muttered to aides that Humphrey and his ADA followers were "crackpots" who cared not if southerners left the party. As a candidate for the U.S. Senate against incumbent Republican Joseph Ball, Humphrey had indeed assessed the personal and political benefits of his controversial stance. He had even briefly flirted with a bid for the vice presidential nomination. But those who knew him and his background understood that more than simple political advantage motivated him on this summer afternoon. His deep concern for his party's future and an unwavering commitment to human rights drove Humphrey toward the convention podium in Philadelphia.

Though concerned about the prudence of challenging his party's elders, Humphrey revealed none of his doubts in public. Days earlier, at a stormy platform committee meeting, he and former Wisconsin congressman Andrew Biemiller had implored committee members to strengthen the moderate civil rights language. To Humphrey, the proposed text was appallingly timid. Noting that Republicans had adopted a "forward-looking" civil rights plank at their national convention earlier that summer, Humphrey attacked the administration-approved plank as "a bunch of generalities" and "a sell-out to states' rights." As the platform committee deliberations stretched late into the night, tempers flared. Senator Lucas, appearing drunk, angrily asked "Who does this pip-squeak think he is?" and accused Humphrey of trying to undo the work of Franklin Roosevelt. Intense deliberations spanned almost two days. Finally, after considering several versions of a substitute plank, weary committee members overwhelmingly rejected Humphrey's arguments. Loyal to Truman, committee members ransomed civil rights for peace with southern delegations.

Exhausted and defeated, Humphrey and Biemiller trudged through the darkness to a nearby University of Pennsylvania fraternity house rented by the ADA. Joined by about 125 ADA delegates, they began plotting their next move. Despite their inexperience in convention politics, these liberals knew the slim odds of winning full-convention approval for a minority report. Not since delegates approved language urging repeal of Prohibition at the 1932 convention had delegates substantially amended a Democratic platform on the convention floor. With the president's men firmly in control and holding fast to their moderate language, Humphrey was caught in a thorny dilemma. If he forced the convention to consider an amended plank, delegates might dramatically rebuff the fledgling civil rights movement. Simply speaking out could anger party leaders and further complicate his hard-fought Senate race in Minnesota. Even if he prevailed, the political consequences might not be any brighter. A stronger civil rights plank would most certainly alienate southern delegates. It might even trigger a walkout or, worse, a rump party of disaffected southern delegates that would nominate its own candidate for president and lure away precious southern Democratic votes from Harry Truman.

In other words, if he carried his challenge to the convention floor and failed, he might become a laughingstock. But if he succeeded—if he won his fight to ennoble his party—Hubert Humphrey and other "impractical" liberals could be blamed for President Harry Truman's defeat.

Humphrey himself had little confidence in Truman's reelection prospects. Like many liberals, he despaired that Franklin Roosevelt's death in 1945 had left them listless, with no strong leadership and with little that resembled a unifying cause. Truman's progressive but often pragmatic policies did little to inspire Humphrey and other liberals. Leaders of Humphrey's own ADA had earlier formed a committee to draft General Dwight D. Eisenhower—whose political leanings remained a mystery—for the Democratic nomination. "The reelection of the president is a political impossibility," Humphrey declared in a letter to one friend. To another, he lamented that "we not only face defeat in November, we face the possible disintegration of the whole social democratic bloc in this country."

Humphrey certainly recognized the peril of pressing his case all the way to the convention floor. President Truman's representatives had explained the potential fallout to him in graphic, undeniable detail. Indeed, the collective leadership of the Democratic party worried greatly that civil rights might be an issue in the November election. They wanted the issue to disappear. And yet Humphrey—tenacious and stubborn with his threat of a minority platform plank—threatened to foil their plan.

Although Humphrey fretted over the consequences of his actions, the idea that the ADA might become a scapegoat after Truman's almost-certain defeat mattered little with the liberal ideologues who gathered in Philadelphia. "There was no question in the ADA fraternity house of going ahead," Humphrey's friend and ADA leader Joseph Rauh recalled. "Everybody there was [for] going ahead." But the final decision, said Rauh, rested with only one man. "That was Hubert Humphrey."

After discussing the question with his ADA associates, Humphrey returned to his fourth-floor room at the Bellevue-Stratford Hotel. There he spent an agonizing evening turning the issue over and over in his head. As Rauh recalled later:

> When you think of the pressure. Truman . . . is against the plank. [Senate Democratic Leader Alben] Barkley is gonna be nominated for vice president, is against [a] minority plank. Howard McGrath, the chairman of the National Committee, is against a minority plank. Dave Niles, Truman's civil rights guy, is against a minority plank.
>
> Dave Niles told me the next morning on the floor that I had ruined the chances of the best liberal product to come down the pike in years, and we wouldn't get fifty votes.

Even Humphrey's loyal labor friends gave him conflicting advice. They cared more, they told him, about economic issues.

Despite his confusion, Humphrey sensed that none of the party leaders who opposed the stronger civil rights language was a racist. "They were moderates who wanted to keep the party together and elect Harry Truman president," he later explained. "So did I." While he wanted the opportunity to present his case to the full convention, Humphrey needed reassurance. He took the question to his most trusted advisor—his father, H.H., who attended the convention as a South Dakota delegate.

"This may tear the party apart," H.H. finally told his son, "but if you feel strongly, then you've got to go with it. You can't run away from your conscience, son."

"What do you think will happen?" Humphrey asked.

"I don't know," H.H. said quietly, almost resigned. "But you'll at least have the eight votes of the South Dakota delegation."

Finally, Humphrey consulted his wife, Muriel. Her advice was resolute—"she assured me I was doing the right thing." Muriel calmed Humphrey's lingering fears. In the morning, he would take his fight to the convention floor. "For me personally, and for the party," he believed, "the time had come to suffer whatever the consequences."

The resolute convictions on civil rights that influenced Humphrey in Philadelphia were firmly grounded in his childhood. Born on May 27, 1911, above his father's drugstore in the small, windy prairie town of

Wallace, South Dakota, Hubert was the second of four children born to Hubert and Christine Humphrey. A smart, likable child, Hubert grew up emulating his father and his populist ideals. "My father was an intellectual prober, more interested in books and ideas," Hubert's sister Frances recalled, "while my mother wanted more practical things like rugs or dresses or pots and pans." It was his wife's desire for more of life's "practical things" that aroused H.H.'s ambition for a more lucrative business. In 1915 he moved his growing family to the larger town of Doland, thirty-five miles to the southwest, where he opened a drug store and ice cream parlor. In that store, Humphrey remembered, "I heard things that further shaped my life and attitudes toward people and ideas. At night, Dad would sit down with the local lawyer, the doctor, a minister, the bankers, and the postmaster, to discuss and argue the issues of the day." Folks in Doland often said about H.H., "He never sells you a pill without selling you an idea." While reading news stories about important national or world events, H.H. often paused to say, "You should know this, Hubert, it might affect your life someday." A devoted follower of the great populist William Jennings Bryan, H.H. regularly read Bryan's famous "Cross of Gold" speech to his children. "I heard William Jennings Bryan," H.H. once said, "and became a Democrat." Although he respected Christine's stubborn Republicanism—and told the children never to argue politics with her—H.H. could barely tolerate his wife's conservative views. "Sometimes," he told the children in all seriousness, "she's politically unreliable."

"Dad set high standards for me," Humphrey confessed. "The one fear I've had all my life was that I would disappoint him." Among the virtues the elder Humphrey taught his son were hard work, charity, an overflowing zest for life, and a strong sense of social justice. H.H. readily gave medicine and merchandise to needy customers and taught his children equal respect for all people, poor and wealthy. "My father did that kind of thing in a way that was not an act of charity—simply a matter of elemental justice and fairness," Humphrey recalled. "When the Depression hit, all people were equal," said Humphrey's sister Frances, "and Hubert remembers along with me that there were many men, businessmen, who got their meal at Humphrey's Drugstore when they didn't have any place else to go."

Like many children born into difficult times, Hubert often worked long hours after school. "He was popular, but he didn't participate in things too much," one of Hubert's teachers, Olive Doty, said. "That is, the fun that the kids had—he didn't have time for that because his father kept him so busy. He had to have help in the drugstore." While he played sports casually, Hubert excelled in academics and starred on the debating team. He made friends easily, even among the town's poor children. One particularly frigid day, Hubert appeared in the store with a friend. "Dad," Hubert said, "Jonathan here doesn't have any shoes, and his feet are so cold they're blue." Without hesitation, H.H. pressed his cash register's "No Sale" key, removed several bills from the drawer, and took the boy down the street to buy him a pair of warm socks and new boots.

Hubert learned more than generosity and justice from his father; as an alderman and then mayor of Doland, H.H. also taught his son about practical politics. Hubert watched as his father unsuccessfully fought the sale of Doland's city-owned power plant to a private utility. From the experience, he came to understand that personality could often transcend and soften partisan political differences. His father's good-natured independence, he said, "prevented controversy from becoming angry. Though he was a Democrat and a rebel in a politically orthodox town, people liked him enough to elect him mayor."

But the political success H.H. achieved in Doland brought him little financial reward. By 1927 an economic slump caused by severe drought and falling farm prices forced H.H. to sell the family's large, two-story house, one of the finest in Doland. For the first time in his life, Hubert saw his father cry. "It is something I have never forgotten," he remembered, "not just because it moved me deeply, but because what followed was so typical of my father's approach to life." H.H., he said, "showed not a discernible ounce of acrimony, apology, or defeatism, and I don't think he felt any. He plunged on." Although misfortune forced them into a small rented house, Humphrey said he never doubted his father would find a way to finance his college education. Sure enough, after Hubert graduated high school in 1929 (as valedictorian), H.H. found the money to enroll him in the University of Minnesota in Minneapolis.

Humphrey's university studies lasted no longer than his father's faltering Doland drugstore. In 1930, when the business failed, H.H. moved the family again—this time to Huron, South Dakota. Although saddened that his family would abandon his beloved Doland, Humphrey accepted his father's fate. More difficult, however, was his reluctant decision to leave the University of Minnesota and settle into the basement of his father's new store. Leaving Minneapolis meant abandoning a university education for a life in the drugstore, but Humphrey prepared to make the sacrifice for his father. The degree of that commitment was apparent in Humphrey's decision to enroll at a Denver pharmacy college in 1932. Not long afterwards, he returned to Huron with his pharmacy certificate, having completed two years' worth of course work in only six months.

Humphrey returned to take on greater responsibilities at the store, including helping in his father's new enterprise—peddling medicines that H.H. had developed for hogs. "I'll bet you I've vaccinated more hogs than any man in this audience," Humphrey once bragged during a campaign debate on farm issues. Though a druggist in his own right, he remained his father's eager student and admirer. Of the needy people put to work by Franklin Roosevelt's Works Progress Administration, H.H. told Hubert, "The only reason we're not on WPA is because other people are. They spend part of their income in our store and that's what keeps us going. I want you to have respect for them. We get ours in a second stage, but we're living off government help, too." Humphrey watched as his father bravely confronted impatient creditors, pleading for more time to pay. These financial difficulties did not embitter Humphrey, but they did leave lasting impressions: a deep suspicion of wealthy bankers, a fear of private debt, and a healthy respect for all people, regardless of their social or economic status. This period of his life, Humphrey said, taught him "how government can really affect the day-to-day lives of individuals for the better."

In 1932, Humphrey met Muriel Buck, an attractive student at Huron College who sometimes dropped by the drugstore for ice cream sodas and Cokes. He liked her immediately. "But dating was difficult in Huron," Humphrey said, "because there was almost nothing to do." Worse, the demands of the drugstore—usually working from seven in the morning to midnight—made romance almost impossible. On rare occasions, when his father gave him a Wednesday night off, Humphrey and Muriel went dancing. After two years of "serious" courtship, Humphrey bought a small diamond and proposed. They married in September 1936.

Like many young men his age, Humphrey yearned for more than Huron's dreary, small-town existence. While visiting his sister in Washington, D.C., in the summer of 1935, he had written to Muriel about new-found aspirations. "Maybe I seem foolish to have such vain hopes and plans," he wrote, "but Bucky, I can see how someday, if you and I just apply ourselves and make up our minds to work for bigger things, how we can someday live here in Washington and probably be in government, politics or service." The promise of public service, fostered by his father for so many years, had finally captured Hubert's imagination. Awestruck by Washington's marbled grandeur, he roamed the ornate halls of the Capitol for days and sat for hours in the House and Senate galleries, mesmerized by the debates.

Humphrey's ambitions soon clashed with his father's. After Hubert and Muriel married, H.H. assumed that life would return to normal: The couple would settle in Huron, and his son would continue helping run the store. H.H. even offered to make Hubert his partner. Had he accepted, it would have freed H.H.—now serving in the South Dakota legislature—to pursue his own political career and possibly run for governor or U.S. senator. But Hubert desperately wanted to finish college. "I can't stay," he finally told his father after a long evening drive outside Huron. "These dust storms—I just can't take them anymore. . . . The depression, the dust, the drought—they're wearing me out. I want to move along, to be on my own." H.H. sat silently for several moments. Finally he said, "If that's the case, we'll have to make other plans." The painful discussion ended with Hubert's decision to return to the University of Minnesota. His father's pursuit of higher office had ended.

Humphrey fulfilled his dream of a college education. In June 1939 he graduated *magna cum laude* from the University of Minnesota with a political science degree and a passion for the progressive New Deal politics of Franklin Roosevelt. With his sights on a post-graduate degree and a teaching position, he left Minneapolis for an unlikely locale— Baton Rouge, Louisiana—where he would pursue a master's degree in political science at Louisiana State University. He had never been to the South, but when offered a $450 fellowship to attend and teach at LSU, he accepted. He was joined later by Muriel and their new daughter, Nancy.

Life in segregated Louisiana quickly opened his eyes to the deplorable daily indignities suffered by Southern blacks. "When I discovered the WHITE and COLORED signs for drinking fountains and toilets, I found them both ridiculous and offensive," Humphrey recalled. "I remember my naive reaction: 'Why, it's uneconomic.' No one, I thought, could view black life in Louisiana without shock and outrage." Humphrey said the experience not only taught him about the evils of Southern segregation, "it also opened my eyes to the prejudice of the North." The man who would become one of the nation's leading advocates for civil rights confessed that his Louisiana experience gave "flesh and blood" to his previously "abstract commitment" to the human rights cause.

Humphrey soon befriended Russell B. Long, son of Louisiana's assassinated governor and U.S. senator, Huey P. Long. Years later the two men would joust over civil rights on the Senate floor. At LSU, however, they competed on the same side of the school's debating squad. As teammates in a match with Oxford University, they successfully argued against U.S. involvement to save Great Britain in the growing European war. In Baton Rouge, as in Minneapolis, Humphrey quickly gained a reputation as one of the political science department's most popular, energetic students. His mind was nimble, but his mouth seemed quicker. One professor reportedly told him, "If God had given you as much brains as he has given you wind, you would be sure to be another Cicero." That well-earned reputation for verbosity haunted Humphrey the rest of his life.

Humphrey spent only a year in Baton Rouge. With his master's degree in hand, he and Muriel returned to Minneapolis and the University of Minnesota for more post-graduate studies. But his college days ended permanently in 1941, when he accepted his first full-time job as a teaching supervisor for the WPA's Workers Education Service. Humphrey's outgoing personality and his leadership skills quickly caught the eyes of WPA administrators. By late 1942 he had ascended the ranks of wartime agency jobs to become regional director of the important War Manpower Commission—all by age thirty-two. The position gave him his entrée into the local politics of Minneapolis. Speaking often to civic clubs and fraternal organizations about WPA programs, he impressed listeners with his eloquence and passion for the job. Before long, some community leaders touted him as a mayoral prospect.

Although flattered by such talk, Humphrey worried that the city's reputation for political corruption would make the job impossible. But when approached by a group of political activists less than three weeks before the election, he jumped into the race and began assailing incumbent mayor Marvin Kline for the city's rampant crime problem. Cramming several months of campaigning into nineteen days, Humphrey was a ball of fire, seemingly oblivious of the enormous odds against beating an incumbent and six other challengers.

Kline tried to deflect Humphrey's spirited attacks on the city's inability to curb crime. When he suggested that "racketeers" were behind

Humphrey's campaign, Humphrey angrily barged into the mayor's office with reporters in tow. He demanded that Kline "name the racketeers." Dumbfounded by Humphrey's impertinence, Kline could produce only one name—a person with no connection at all to Humphrey's campaign. After the confrontation, a reporter suggested the two men shake hands for the cameras. "Well, you know Hubert," campaign aide Frederick Manfred recalled. "He never could carry a grudge longer than a minute or so." Humphrey joined hands with Kline as the photographer snapped the picture, diminishing the impact of the dramatic moment. On election day, Humphrey stunned Minneapolis, finishing second and qualifying for the general election against Kline. Although his campaign was poorly funded and judged amateurish by some observers, Humphrey showed surprising strength. He lost the general election by only 5,725 votes.

Humphrey was not finished with politics. For the next two years he worked tirelessly to build a strong base from which to run again. He played an instrumental role in the union of Minnesota's feuding but kindred Democratic and Farm-Labor parties, and he was now a leader of the newly named Democratic Farmer Labor (DFL) Party. He took a job as a local radio commentator and taught politics at St. Paul's Presbyterian Macalester College. In 1944 he attended his first Democratic National Convention as a delegate and later ran Minnesota's Roosevelt-Truman campaign.

Humphrey's next political opportunity came in the spring of 1945, when he challenged Mayor Kline again with a vow to "clean up this town and make it a decent city in which to raise our children." That promise, and the expectation that Humphrey meant it, propelled him into City Hall. This time, with strong support from organized labor, he trounced Kline by 31,114 votes, the largest winning majority in the city's history. At thirty-five, Humphrey became the youngest mayor ever to serve Minneapolis. "I considered my first job to clean up the city, to give it honest administration," Humphrey said of his first days in office. "And we did it."

Other than the right to appoint the police chief, the mayor of Minneapolis had few official powers in 1945. Humphrey understood that his success would depend mostly on his personal leadership and his powers of persuasion. And he knew that his selection for police chief would set the tone for his embryonic administration. He chose Ed Ryan, an FBI-trained police officer with an impeccable record of integrity. "[Humphrey] told me he wanted Minneapolis closed so tightly that [no one could] purchase a Coke after hours," Ryan recalled. With Humphrey's backing, Ryan shut down illegal gambling operations, closed dozens of bars that operated after closing hour, ended prostitution rings, and eliminated the police practice of entrapping restaurant owners to sell alcohol to minors. Humphrey settled several labor disputes and ordered his police officers to respect picket lines of striking union members. Whenever the city's charter prohibited him from acting to resolve a particular problem, Humphrey established a citizens' committee or advisory commission to recommend solutions.

With his official powers limited, the young mayor relied more on his engaging personality and boundless energy to lead Minneapolis into a new era of honest government. "Whatever the assorted personal opinions of Humphrey," a visiting journalist wrote in 1948, "Minneapolis concedes generally that his years as mayor have been the most exhilarating in the city's political history, replete with more roller-coaster dips and turns than any other six administrations." Eighteen-hour days were common for Humphrey. His staff turned away no visitor to his office. At night he often rode with policemen in their patrol cars to learn more about the city's crime problems. When a polio epidemic hit the city, he read the comics to quarantined children over the radio. He rarely missed the opportunity to address a civic club or association. He was not a perfect mayor, by any means. Sometimes he was poorly organized. He hated to delegate authority. He occasionally prowled his office after hours, riffling through employees' desks to inspect the progress and quality of their work. His propensity for verbosity, in conversation and in speeches, kept him constantly behind schedule. But many Minneapolis voters loved their progressive, energetic mayor. In 1947 they returned him to office by a record 52,000 votes.

Other than perhaps his crime initiative, nothing characterized Humphrey's tenure as mayor more than the way he reformed the city's official and unofficial discrimination against minorities. Less than a week after taking office, he went to Chicago to learn about that city's proposed fair employment practices ordinance; he returned to propose an even stronger ordinance for Minneapolis. An indifferent city council promptly rejected it, but the early defeat did not deter him. Instead, he created the Mayor's Committee on Human Relations chaired by Reuben K. Youngdahl, a highly respected Lutheran minister and brother of Minnesota's Republican governor. At Humphrey's direction, Youngdahl's committee embarked on a "self survey" of the city's racial attitudes and problems. Walking door to door, to factories and business, schools and churches, six hundred volunteers exposed areas of discrimination previously ignored by official Minneapolis. "The survey," said Humphrey staff member William Shore, "was not so much a scientific research into hidden facts, but a mirror that might get Minneapolis to look at itself."

One year after his initial defeat, Humphrey prevailed. The city council established the nation's first enforceable municipal Fair Employment Practices Commission, and doors of opportunity began opening to blacks, Jews, and Indians. Humphrey also prodded his police department to show greater sensitivity to minorities. He helped establish a human relations course for police officers at the University of Minnesota. He backed up his rhetoric on tolerance with decisive action. For example, when he learned that a police officer had called a traffic violator a "dirty Jew," Humphrey suspended the officer for fifteen days without pay.

Humphrey's vigorous support for civil rights matched his contempt for Communists and left-wing ideologues, who exerted growing influence in the labor movement and Democratic party politics in Minnesota after World War II. When radical members of his DFL party tried to seize control of the organization in 1946, Humphrey fought them ferociously. "You can be liberal without being a Communist sympathizer," he declared, "and we're a liberal progressive party out here." Despite Humphrey's fierce resistance, the leftists prevailed. "We had lost control," Humphrey remembered. "The left wing was on the move."

That defeat—coupled with rising Communist influence in other states—prompted Humphrey to join national liberal leaders who organized the Americans for Democratic Action, touted by Humphrey and others as "an anti-Communist liberal organization." At the ADA's first national convention in 1947, Humphrey dazzled the elite eastern liberals with a powerful and passionate call for action on civil rights. Eugenie Anderson, Humphrey's friend and political ally, recalled the immediate attraction Humphrey engendered among the ADA activists. "He had this, not just charm, but this ability to really command almost instant respect and affection." His performance so impressed delegates that they elected him vice-chairman. By 1948 the Minnesota ADA, led by Humphrey, was powerful enough to drive the pro-Communists from power. A fierce battle at the state convention of the Minnesota DFL Party ended when left-wing members stalked out of the convention, leaving Humphrey's forces in control. Exhilarated, the remaining delegates nominated Humphrey, their triumphant leader, for the U.S. Senate.

One month after his victory at the DFL convention, Humphrey left for Philadelphia to spar not with Communist sympathizers or the incumbent Republican senator but with the leaders of his national party. No matter how they tried, Humphrey knew he could not allow these leaders to intimidate him into quietly walking away from his platform challenge. His father, the romantic populist from whom he had inherited his respect for the dignity of all people, had not raised a quitter. If he lost—well, there was nothing ignoble about losing a fight over social justice. And if he won, the party would simply face the consequences of its courageous stand.

Humphrey, Rauh, and Biemiller worked all night plotting strategy and crafting the substitute language they would present to the convention in the morning. The civil rights plank that Humphrey wanted to amend was brief and recommended no specific congressional action. Using the exact language of the 1944 platform, it said, simply:

> The Democratic Party is responsible for the great civil rights gains made in recent years in eliminating unfair and illegal discrimination based on race, creed or color.
> The Democratic Party commits itself to continuing its efforts to eradicate all racial, religious and economic discrimination. We again state our belief that racial and religious minorities must have the right to live, the right to work, the right to vote, the full and equal protection of the law, on a basis of equality with all citizens as guaranteed by the Constitution. We again call upon Congress to exert its full authority to the limit of its constitutional power to assure and protect these rights.

The statement was bland and intentionally ambiguous. While a liberal might view "We again call upon Congress to exert its full authority" as a call to arms, a conservative southerner who believed Congress had no constitutional authority in civil rights might argue that it meant something else altogether.

In the morning, Biemiller sought out House Speaker Sam Rayburn, the convention chairman, to inform him of the ADA group's plans for a floor challenge and ask for a roll-call vote. In talking with Rayburn, Biemiller learned that former Texas governor Dan Moody planned to offer his own conservative plank on behalf of southern delegates. Rayburn assured both sides that he would give them roll-call votes at the day's afternoon session.

Back at his hotel, Humphrey, weary from the all-night meeting, took a nap. When he woke, he emerged to put the final touches on the platform language and begin working on his speech. Though the language Humphrey wanted to add to the platform was specific in its call for greater rights—it contained four points from the 1947 report of the President's Commission on Civil Rights—Humphrey was troubled. The text seemed to imply indolence by the party and Truman. Minnesota's national committeewoman, Eugenie Anderson, sensed Humphrey's concern. "He was trying to get some of these ideas he had through," she recalled. "It was a terribly tense moment. Everybody was sitting watching him." Anderson had a suggestion. Why not, she said, praise Truman's commitment to civil rights? Anderson's idea was just the nuance Humphrey had wanted. "Okay," he said, and the platform amendment language was ready. To the civil rights plank, the ADA would recommend adding:

> We highly commend President Harry Truman for his courageous stand on the issue of civil rights.
>
> We call upon the Congress to support our President in guaranteeing these basic and fundamental rights: (1) the right of full and equal political participation, (2) the right of equal opportunity of employment, (3) the right of security of person, and (4) the right of equal treatment in the service and defense of our nation.

Humphrey next turned to composing the speech he would deliver after Biemiller formally presented the amendment to the full convention. Working with Milton Stewart, leader of New York's ADA chapter, Humphrey dictated his thoughts about the speech. "The good phrases were his," a charitable Stewart remembered. As Stewart labored to put meat on the notes he had taken, Humphrey dressed.

Meanwhile, on the convention floor, Humphrey's ADA associates frantically lobbied for their amendment's passage. Joseph Rauh presented delegates who worried about a massive southern defection with a simple argument: "You want to build a [Henry] Wallace movement?" Wallace, the radical former vice president running on a third-party ticket, had embraced a strong civil rights program that threatened to peel away substantial liberal Democratic support from Harry Truman in the November election. "Henry Wallace was willing to say anything on civil rights," Rauh said. The specter of Wallace, he explained, "was our secret weapon in this fight."

Finally Stewart finished the speech. Pleased with the result, Humphrey left for Convention Hall. Shortly after he arrived, the convention began its debate over the states' rights substitute. Humphrey took his place on the platform behind the large dais and discovered that he was seated next to Ed Flynn, the powerful Bronx political boss. Almost sheepishly, he slipped the speech into Flynn's hands.

"Look," he told Flynn, "here's what we're asking. It isn't too much. We think we ought to make the fight. I'm sure we don't really have much chance to carry it, but we ought to make the fight. We surely would welcome your advice."

Flynn read the amendment.

"You go ahead, young man," Flynn finally said. "We should have done this a long time ago. We've got to do it. Go ahead. We'll back you."

As Humphrey waited his turn to speak, Flynn commanded his forces into motion. Humphrey and Biemiller watched in awe while the Bronx boss summoned Illinois state chairman Jacob Arvey, Pennsylvania leader David Lawrence, and New Jersey boss Frank Hague. Flynn urged them to deliver their delegations' votes for the ADA language. Flynn even converted the platform committee chairman, Senator Francis Myers of Pennsylvania, who had strongly opposed Humphrey only days earlier. Myers astounded Humphrey by stepping forward to say he would vote for the amendment.

Now it was Humphrey's turn at the podium. Throughout his career, Humphrey rarely delivered a speech without departing from his prepared text. This time—to the amazement of his friends and aides—he read his speech, forcefully and slowly.

"I realize that in speaking in behalf of the minority report on civil rights by Congressman Biemiller of Wisconsin that I am dealing with a charged issue," he began, "with an issue which has been confused by emotionalism on all sides of the fence. I realize that there are here today friends and colleagues of mine, many of them who feel as deeply as I do about this issue and who are yet in complete disagreement with me." Humphrey praised those friends for "the sincerity, the courtesy and the forthrightness with which they have argued in our discussions." He made clear "this proposal is made for no single region. Our proposal is made for no single class, for no single racial or religious group in mind." And he paid tribute to the convention's keynote speaker and eventual vice presidential nominee, seventy-year-old Alben Barkley of Kentucky, the Senate Democratic leader who had evoked Thomas Jefferson's words about the "equality" of men in a rousing speech.

Gradually the emotion and sincerity in Humphrey's voice swept over the now-attentive delegates like a swelling wave.

It seems to me that the Democratic Party needs to make definite pledges of the kind suggested in the minority report, to maintain the trust and confidence placed in it by the people of all races and all sections of this country. Sure, we are here as Democrats, but, my good friends, we are here as Americans; we are here as the believers in the principles and the ideology of democracy, and I firmly believe that as men concerned with our country's future, we must specify in our platform the guarantees which we have mentioned in the minority plank.

Yes, this is far more than a party matter. Every citizen in this country has a stake in the emergence of the United States as a leader in a free world. That world is being challenged by the world of slavery. For us to play our part effectively, we must be in a morally sound position.

We cannot use a double standard. There is no room for double standards in American politics. For measuring our own and other people's policies, our demands for democratic practices in other lands will be no more effective than the guarantees of those practiced in our own country.

We are God-fearing men and women. We place our faith in the brotherhood of man under the fatherhood of God.

Friends, delegates, I do not believe that there can be any compromise of the guarantees of civil rights which we have mentioned in the minority report. In spite of my desire for unanimous agreement on the entire platform, in spite of my desire to see everybody here in unanimous agreement, there are some matters which I think must be stated clearly and without qualification. There can be no hedging—no watering down. The newspaper headlines are wrong.

There will be no hedging, and there will be no watering

down, if you please, of the instruments and the principles of the civil rights program.

My friends, to those who say that we are rushing this issue of civil rights, I say we are 172 years late!

By now, Humphrey had ignited hundreds of delegates, many of whom leapt to their feet and cheered his every phrase. What followed next was perhaps the most memorable and eloquent statement of his political career. For many delegates, it sealed their decision to support his cause:

> To those who say that this civil rights program is an infringement on states' rights, I say this, that the time has arrived in America for the Democratic Party to get out of the shadows of states' rights and walk forthrightly into the bright sunshine of human rights.
>
> People, human beings, this is the issue of the Twentieth Century, people of all kinds, and these people are looking to America for leadership and they are looking to America for precepts and example.
>
> My good friends and my fellow Democrats, I ask you for a calm consideration of our historic opportunity. Let us forget the evil patience and the blindness of the past. In these times of world economic, political and spiritual—above all, spiritual—crisis we cannot, and we must not, turn from the paths so plainly before us.
>
> That path has already led us through many valleys of the shadow of death, and now is the time to recall those who were left on that path of American freedom.
>
> To all of us here, for the millions who have sent us, for the whole two billion members of the human family—our land is now, more than ever, the last best hope on earth. I know that we can, I know that we shall begin here the fuller and richer example of that—that promise of a land where all men are free and equal, and each man uses his freedom and equality wisely and well.
>
> My good friends, I ask my Party, and I ask the Democratic Party to march down the high road of progressive democracy. I ask this convention to say in unmistakable terms that we

proudly hail and we courageously support our President and leader, Harry Truman, in his great fight for civil rights in America.

When he finished, hundreds of northern and western delegates erupted in a loud, boisterous celebration of support—"cheering like madmen," one observer wrote. In all, they had applauded his eight-minute speech no less than twenty times. Now the demonstration lasted as long as the speech. Some delegates called for music, but the house band remained silent. Undeterred, the delegates provided their own music: they began to whistle. As Humphrey surveyed the throng of shouting delegates, waving their states' banners as they weaved up and down the aisles, he began to sense how his words had affected the convention. Only the southerners seemed unmoved. Throughout the demonstration, the indignant delegates from Dixie sat stoically in their seats.

To Illinois delegate Paul Douglas, who would soon enter the U.S. Senate with Humphrey, the speech was "the greatest political oration in the history of the country, with the possible exception of William Jennings Bryan's 'Cross of Gold' speech." Humphrey, said Douglas, "was on fire, just like the Bible speaks of Moses. His face was glowing and his sentiments were marvelous." Others would compare the speech to Lincoln's Gettysburg Address. "It was a very exciting moment in American history," remembered William Shore, then a young aide to Humphrey's Senate campaign. "There was a totally new mood from that time on at that convention." Years later, many historians would consider it one of the most significant speeches of the century.

In the *Minneapolis Star* the next morning, political writer M.W. Holloran admiringly declared the speech "the most remarkable accomplishment of the convention" because it "lifted the Truman campaign out of the rut of just another political drive to a crusade." Holloran had never heard Humphrey "speak with more deadly effect. He spoke with a deliberation that is not his custom. His words rang out clearly and his arguments . . . hit the bell again and again." Back in Minnesota, Muriel had been listening intently to Hubert's speech over the radio. When he finished, she was in tears.

As many as seventy million Americans heard or watched Humphrey's emotional appeal on their radios or televisions. Years, even decades later, many would fondly remember Humphrey as the brave young man whose courage and eloquence made him the star of the 1948 convention. "Even though I feared we would still lose," Humphrey recalled, "I felt that the speech was reaching the heart of the Democratic Party."

After eight minutes of wild, spontaneous cheering, Speaker Rayburn ordered the lights dimmed. It was the only way he knew to force the emotional delegates back to their seats. It was now time to vote.

The conservative states' rights plank was first, and went down to a crushing defeat, 925 to 309. Minutes later—after some confusion over whether the "Biemiller resolution" was, indeed, the amendment for which Humphrey had spoken—the roll call began. The early tallies were not encouraging. Alabama, Arizona, and Arkansas voted "no." Three delegations had voted, and Humphrey was already losing sixty to nothing. But next came California. All but one of its fifty-four votes went to Humphrey's amendment, as did ten of Colorado's twelve and all Connecticut's twenty. Illinois' Arvey delivered his delegation's sixty votes. Lawrence's New Jersey delegation cast its thirty-six votes for the resolution. As he promised, New York's Ed Flynn did the same with his delegation's ninety-eight votes. Likewise for Hague's seventy-four Pennsylvania delegates. As the tally went painfully forward, the "yes" and "no" votes seesawed. Near the end, the secretary called for South Dakota's vote. Humphrey's father, H.H., rose to announce proudly, "I am Hubert Humphrey, Sr. I cast South Dakota's eight votes for the plank." That put the tally almost fifty votes short of the 617 votes needed to win. Finally, Biemiller's twenty-four Wisconsin delegates gave Humphrey the votes he needed. After several more minutes, Rayburn announced the results: Humphrey had carried the day, 651½ to 582½—a stunning, historic victory. "The South had not just been defeated," former Georgia Senator Herman Talmadge later observed, "it had been humiliated."

Rayburn moved quickly to prevent southerners from spoiling Humphrey's moment. He called for a voice vote on the entire platform. Delegates roared their approval. Furious, some of Alabama's twenty-six delegates prepared to relinquish their credentials, a prelude to stalking out of the convention. As delegates frantically waved the Alabama banner, Birmingham's police commissioner, Eugene "Bull" Connor, shouted to Rayburn for recognition. He wanted to announce his delegates' departure. Rayburn ignored them all. There would be no roll-call vote on the platform, no opportunity at this moment, at least, for Alabama's delegates to stage a dramatic walkout. Instead, Rayburn recognized

House Democratic Whip John McCormack, who moved for a ninety-minute recess. "We're not going to walk," Connor told a reporter during the recess. "We're going to fly." When business resumed, half of the Alabama delegation and all of Mississippi's delegates marched down the middle aisle and out of the hall in protest, leaving only the most unity-conscious southern delegates in the hall.

Despite the Alabamans' defection, this glorious July afternoon clearly belonged to Humphrey. With only an eight-minute oration, he had catapulted to a lofty stratosphere of national prominence that would eventually take him to the heights of American politics. His eloquence and passion had inspired millions of Americans and challenged the prejudices of millions more.

The now-celebrated civil rights challenge injected new vigor into Harry Truman's faltering reelection effort. With its new, bolder commitment to civil rights, the Democratic party took its first real steps into the warm glow of the symbolic "sunshine of human rights."

And Hubert Humphrey had led the way.

CHAPTER TWO

The Southern General

MORE THAN SIX HUNDRED MILES southeast of Philadelphia, U.S. Senator Richard Brevard Russell followed the convention with detached interest from his home in rural Winder, Georgia. Fifty years old, Russell had been his state's junior senator for fifteen years. And he felt no need to condone these proceedings by participating in the nomination of a president with whom he had grown so disillusioned.

A dignified and reserved man, who some considered too serious and aloof, Russell commanded enormous respect among his Senate colleagues—liberals and conservatives, Democrats and Republicans. Physically, Russell was an impressive man. Although he was bald, his patrician nose, brooding eyes, and courtly poise gave him a noble, self-assured demeanor that some women found enormously appealing. Yet he was a bachelor, married to the Senate, an institution he loved dearly for its rich traditions, colorful history, and unique role as "the world's most deliberative body."

For more than any other senator of his time, Russell's life was his work. He knew many of the issues—his specialties were foreign and military affairs and agriculture—better than any other member. More importantly, Russell understood the Senate's complex parliamentary rules and precedents better than anyone—without exception. Armed with an encyclopedic knowledge of the rules and an unparalleled ability to employ them in debate, Russell had become the Senate's most effective opponent of civil rights legislation. Others, like Mississippi's James Eastland and Theodore Bilbo, were often more outspoken and shrill.*

---

*Once during a particularly contentious civil rights debate, Bilbo referred to a colleague as a "nigger-loving senator" (Tames OH, USSHO).

But Russell, the calm, steady rock of the Senate, carried the most weight on civil rights among southerners.

Russell believed deeply in the righteousness of the southern way of life—a manner of living that bestowed upon white citizens an undeniable social and economic superiority while imposing harsh, sometimes inhumane limits on the rights of black citizens. "Any attack on Georgia, her institutions, or the South always struck a raw nerve in Russell," his biographer, Gilbert Fite, wrote. "He never let slurs or insults against his beloved South go unanswered. As far as he was concerned, Southern society might not be perfect, but it was the best in the nation. Anyone who thought otherwise had better be ready to do battle with Dick Russell."

Fealty to the Old South ran in deep currents through every corner of Russell's beloved region. To many white southerners, legends of the Civil War were not simply stories from the gray, lifeless pages of history books. The thrilling tales of the heroism and brilliance of their Confederate forebears were like family heirlooms, proudly displayed and cherished for generations. Revisionist history made this worship of the Confederacy more palatable by maintaining that the war was not, in fact, fought over slavery.

By the time of Russell's birth in 1897, bitter memories of the war and its Reconstruction aftermath still haunted every Georgian over the age of 30. In the words of one historian, the state "was exhausted and clubbed to her knees." Impelled by congressional Republicans, federal authorities imposed military rule on Georgia three times and treated former Confederate states like conquered territory. Meanwhile, white citizens throughout the South—their economy devastated, their way of life overturned—began the slow, painful adjustment to a postwar, post-slavery order. Poverty was rampant as southerners struggled to rise from the aftermath of the bloody war. Ruled only briefly by federal troops, southern governments quickly fell to the control of "radical" Republicans—coalitions of blacks, progressive whites, and northern "carpetbaggers."

In this atmosphere, former slaves registered to vote in vast numbers and, in turn, elected blacks to political offices. The right to vote did not, however, ensure the right to serve. In 1868 white Georgia legislators exercised what power they had to expel twenty-eight blacks from their ranks. But those actions merely prolonged the pain of Reconstruction and delayed Georgia's reentry into the Union. The Republican-controlled Congress stubbornly refused to admit the state back into the Union until the legislature restored the black lawmakers to office.

Aided by the Fourteenth and Fifteenth amendments, which guaranteed full citizenship and voting rights, southern blacks achieved significant social and economic gains in the years after the war. Many left the plantations and moved to the cities, where they established small, sometimes profitable businesses. Those who stayed on the land became tenant farmers with greater, if not complete, control of their destinies. Though not equal with whites, southern blacks—for at least a fleeting, glorious moment in history—had made a quantum leap in status. Most white southerners, however, never accepted this "dreadful" new social and economic order imposed by the northern victors. The period became, in the words of former Tennessee senator Albert Gore, Sr., "emblazoned in the white Southern memory and psyche as an era of unparalleled and unmitigated oppression and corruption." To whites, Republicans and blacks were largely to blame and were hated equally with a red-hot intensity that blazed for generations after the war.

Reconstruction came to an official end in 1877, when Republican Rutherford B. Hayes—a former Union major general—narrowly won the presidency with the disputed electoral votes of several southern states. A conciliatory Hayes not only withdrew federal troops from the South but refused to support the aggressive enforcement of the Fourteenth and Fifteenth amendments. Thus, by the late 1870s, the legal disenfranchisement of blacks throughout the South had begun in earnest. Using political skill, guile, intimidation, and threats of violence, the Democratic party—now the official party of the white man—slowly regained control of the levers of governmental power in the South. "Eventually," historian Alan Conway concluded, "the only victor in the South was the new breed of politician dedicated to the twin creeds of keeping the Negro down and the Republicans out."

By the 1890s southern Democrats had imposed repressive laws, illegal state constitutions, and informal codes that dragged blacks almost completely back into their former slave status. The Jim Crow laws, named after a popular black-faced minstrel character who came to symbolize the new southern apartheid, gradually made all blacks half-citizens—more than chattel but less than sovereign individuals. Powerless to resist the mighty forces of white retribution, blacks were enslaved again, this time by a social system that existed only for the pleasure and enrichment of white power brokers. Complex voter registration laws, poll taxes and white-only primaries prevented most from voting and, therefore, from holding public office. In Louisiana, in 1896, more than 130,000 blacks were registered to vote. Two years later, the white-supremacist constitution of 1898 effectively disenfranchised most blacks, Republicans, and populists. By the time white leaders fully enforced Jim Crow eight years later, only 1,342 blacks remained on Louisiana's voting rolls.

Sanctioned by the 1896 Supreme Court ruling in *Plessy v. Ferguson*, which legalized "separate-but-equal" facilities for blacks, segregation was firmly rooted in every corner of the South by 1900. Under the laws and customs that made up Jim Crow, blacks entered a white man's home only through the back door. They addressed whites formally; the use of first names was forbidden. Whites, however, freely addressed blacks—regardless of their status—as "boy" and "girl" or, if elderly, as "uncle" and "aunty." Blacks and whites were segregated in almost every way. Rest rooms, water fountains, hospitals, schools, public transportation, theaters, and housing—all were separated by race. Black schools and hospitals were funded poorly, if at all. Many "teachers" had not even completed their elementary education. Most southern and western states outlawed interracial marriages.

A 1929 examination of the state of black America by author Scott Nearing painfully illuminated the deplorable existence for blacks in the South, virtually unchanged in the fifty-four years since the end of the Civil War:

> The churches and lodge rooms which are used for Negro schools are chiefly old, dilapidated buildings, unfit for teaching purposes. In some cases, they have no means of getting light; often there are no desks. In most of the churches and lodge halls, the children sit on plank benches which sometimes have no backs to them. In some counties there is not a single school building for colored children.

Living conditions described by Nearing were no better:

> The Negro shanties, built of logs in a few cases and of wood in most instances, are usually unpainted, old, out of repair, squalid, lacking modern conveniences, unsupplied with the simplest necessaries such as running water, adequate toilet facilities, heating facilities, and the like.

If there was any white guilt over these shameful conditions and social codes, it was often dismissed with the irrelevant explanation that blacks wanted their own schools and preferred socializing and living among "their own kind."

Another salve for white guilt was the misguided belief that northern states were as hostile to blacks and just as likely to ignore or trample their rights. Southerners argued that because some northern liberals did not carry the "burdens" of large black populations, they were free to criticize the South's transgressions. The truth was, these southern leaders maintained, the North was as racist as the South, differing only in the amount of hypocrisy northern whites brought to the civil rights debate. Southern leaders who believed such myths were either disingenuous or woefully misinformed. Northern states did not segregate whites and blacks on trains and buses. There were no strict social customs governing black-white relations. And blacks voted. The difference, in reality, was that the South usually wrote its bigotry and intolerance into law and enforced it relentlessly. Northerners were often no more enlightened on racial matters than southern whites, but their prejudice was far less entrenched and was usually transcended by ambivalence or ignorance about blacks.

The renowned economist Gunnar Myrdal, in his exhaustive 1944 study of American race relations, *An American Dilemma,* noted that in "social relations" the "average northerner does not think of the Negroes as former slaves." He was therefore "likely to let the Negro alone unless in his opinion they get to be a nuisance." For northern blacks, the major barriers were in public housing and schools. In New York City, for example, poor blacks could find housing only in the ghettos of Harlem, the East Bronx, Brooklyn, and other poor sections of the city.

Pulitzer Prize–winning journalist Ray Sprigle, who spent four weeks in the South posing as a black man, characterized the difference in his 1949 book *In the Land of Jim Crow,* a chilling firsthand account of white racism in Georgia, Mississippi, and Alabama:

> Discrimination against the Negro in the North is an annoyance and an injustice. In the South it is bloodstained tragedy. In the North the Negro meets with rebuff and insult when he seeks service at hotels and restaurants. But, at least in states like Pennsylvania and others, he can take his case to court and he invariably wins . . . In short, discrimination against the Negro in

the North is usually in defiance of the law. In the South it is enforced and maintained by the law.

As every black person knew, cruel social customs and white neglect were not the only enemies of southern blacks. In the South, they were three times as likely to be jailed as in other regions and were usually given harsher sentences than whites for the same crimes. All-white juries determined their guilt or innocence. White judges presided at all trials. Lynchings, many for petty offenses, were not uncommon at the turn of the century. Some states used vagrancy laws to force blacks into jobs. The laws of some states made it a crime for a farm laborer to leave his job during the crop year. Meanwhile, the Ku Klux Klan, whose violence and terror had hastened the emergence of Jim Crow, meted out its own brand of brutal justice, while many white authorities feigned an inability to protect the rights of blacks.

But the South *had* changed since the days of Russell's youth. Lynchings rarely occurred in 1948. Other violent acts against blacks, though not entirely eradicated, grew rarer. Time had indeed erased much of the savagery and terror of Jim Crow. In its place, however, remained many of the humiliating social and political rules of that terrible, hateful era. Most blacks were still unable to exercise their tenuous right to vote. Those with sufficient courage to register often could not pay their state's poll tax or pass its stringent literacy and civics tests. In 1948, the Gallup polling organization estimated that the total number of eligible voters not registered because of the poll tax "and other local reasons" was 7.7 million. When blacks did manage to register in significant numbers, city leaders often gerrymandered their neighborhoods out of the city limits.

A comfortable night's stay in a white hotel or a meal in a white restaurant were fantastic dreams even for those who could afford such luxuries. Public transportation, rest rooms, and water fountains remained segregated. "When I was growing up in the South," Georgia senator Herman Talmadge recalled, "it probably would have come as a shock to ninety-five percent of the white people and a substantial majority of the blacks to learn that some folks thought it downright immoral for persons to prefer associating with others of their own race. To us in the South, that seemed about as natural as chitlins, okra, and country music." But, as Talmadge admitted, "any honest person would have to admit that from the time of Reconstruction on, segregation had often been used as a means to assure the inequality of blacks."

Indeed, the belief that blacks were inherently "inferior" to whites was woven deeply into the fabric of southern life. Therefore, the purity of the "white race"—especially the precious virtue of white women—was guarded religiously, and violently, by its male leaders, many of whom took a lesson from the Roman Empire's downfall. Rome had been destroyed, they believed, by racial amalgamation. Many whites feared that if blacks and whites married, a "mongrelization" of the white race would occur. As documented by Myrdal's study, these fears grew from and were sustained by many widely accepted myths about blacks: they were lazy and grew sleepy when they worked heavy machinery; they lacked the mechanical aptitude necessary for most skilled labor; they were less intelligent than whites and, therefore, unqualified for most jobs that required mental exertion; their moral character was inferior; they had tendencies toward criminal activity; and their "hircine odor" justified the denial of most intimate social contacts, including their exclusion from white restaurants, rest rooms, and the white sections of buses and theaters.

In 1947 a special committee appointed by President Truman revealed the extent of the South's antipathy toward blacks. Despite finding "considerable progress" toward ending forced segregation, the committee documented deep veins of racial discrimination running through two important strata of southern life—education and housing. Separate facilities for blacks and whites left southern black students with pitifully substandard schools and with teachers who often earned less than half what their white counterparts were paid. Widespread use of "restrictive covenants"—in large northern cities as well as in the South—kept many blacks out of white neighborhoods and confined to the slums and ghettos.

It was this kind of South—still romantically attached to its brutal, racist past—that Russell defended so effectively on the Senate floor.

By the common definition of the word, Russell was indeed a racist; that is, he believed in white superiority. But despite his fierce hostility to black demands for civil rights, he was no radical. Unlike many southerners, he did not base his opposition on any visceral hatred of blacks. Rather, he simply believed blacks were inferior to whites. Intermarriages, or "mongrelization," would eventually destroy both races, he maintained. "He wasn't a lyncher," said his friend, Harry McPherson, "but he was certainly country bigoted in his views of blacks." Russell wanted blacks to succeed. Indeed, he had supported many federal programs that provided economic and educational assistance to citizens of all races. But the success that Russell tolerated for black citizens was acceptable only if it transpired in a strictly segregated environment. His views on race, McPherson observed, were "very much of a paternalistic land holder who wants to take care of his colored people but sees them very much apart and is terribly annoyed when they rise up and demand their rights annually." To Russell, the civil rights legislation that Harry Truman wanted was oppressive and unconstitutional. It violated the right of states to govern their own affairs. It would, he believed, undoubtedly wreak havoc in the South and would cause more, not less, civil unrest.

But unlike more-strident southern Democrats, Russell frowned on attempts to split the party over this one question. On most issues, he strongly agreed with the majority of his Democratic colleagues. As an ally and friend of President Franklin Roosevelt, he had supported most New Deal programs. Russell's leadership was largely responsible for the passage of the national school lunch program in 1946—an accomplishment he would always consider among his most important in public life. On programs like agriculture, public power, labor relations, and education, Russell was usually a Democratic stalwart. He disliked being labeled a conservative simply because he was a southerner and opposed civil rights. "It's a mistake to lump all of us southerners together," he once said, "just as it is wrong to expect people from any one section of the country to think alike." The only issue uniting southerners, Russell maintained, "is on the question of racial equality."

What he saw as liberal attempts to impose a new, alien way of life on southern states deeply offended Russell. For the past three years, nothing had commanded more of his attention than his determined struggle to stop President Truman's civil rights proposals. Over the years, Russell had gradually assumed greater leadership among his southern colleagues on civil rights. In March 1948, this position became official when twenty-one of his southern colleagues met to declare themselves under his "generalship." By summer, however, his able leadership in the Senate was simply not enough for his friends and admirers. They now pressed him to challenge Harry Truman for the Democratic nomination at the Philadelphia convention. Strom Thurmond had asked him to run, as did other southern leaders who promised to raise "incredible sums of money" if he would lead a third-party ticket.

Despite his passionate opinions about the perils of civil rights,

Russell did not want to abandon his party over this issue. But he was sympathetic to arguments that southern delegations—unable to stop Hubert Humphrey's liberal civil rights platform substitute—at least deserved to "have someone for whom they could vote." From Winder, he finally signaled his reluctant assent. As delegates prepared to vote on their nominee, Russell gave his supporters permission to place his name in nomination.

Only hours earlier, Hubert Humphrey had stormed the walls of his party from its left flank. And now, charging timidly at Truman from the right, was an unlikely and uncomfortable challenger from Georgia.

Russell was born on November 2, 1897, in the sleepy northeast Georgia farming town of Winder, about 50 miles from Atlanta. R.B., as his family and friends knew him in childhood, was not Richard and Ina Russell's first child; three daughters had preceded him. As the elder Russell began to fret that he might never have a namesake, even the family physician needled him about his seeming inability to father a male child. "You'll never have any Russells," the doctor reportedly said. "You'll have Mrs. Smith, and Mrs. Brown and Mrs. Jones in the family, but you won't have any Russells." Some recalled that when the doctor emerged with the newborn R.B. in his arms, Russell gleefully slapped the doctor's back so hard that he almost dropped the baby. The joyous new father then celebrated the great event by firing both barrels of his shotgun in the air. In all, Richard and Ina would have thirteen children: seven boys and six girls. "When a new child came along," Russell's mother once explained, "I just made some more gravy."

R.B.'s father was prosperous, at least by Winder standards. He owned a large white-frame house on a thousand-acre farm at the outskirts of town. The elder Russell, an attorney, rarely shied from controversy. The conservatives of the rolling hills of northeastern Georgia even regarded him as something of a liberal. "My father was a much more liberal man than I am in a great many respects," Russell said many years later, remembering his father's advocacy of state-funded college tuition for disadvantaged youth. "He was bitterly attacked editorially as being a Socialist," Russell said, admitting his own doubts about the wisdom of his father's proposal. That liberal streak did not, it appears, extend to matters of equal rights for black citizens. "They were servants and we treated them as servants," Russell's sister Patience recalled.

A lawyer, businessman, and former state legislator, Russell had his sights on Georgia's Western Judicial Circuit, to which he was elected the year after R.B.'s birth. He would eventually become chief justice of the Georgia Supreme Court. But he never realized his lifelong dream of serving as governor or United States senator, despite campaigns for both offices. Gradually he would transfer much of his political ambition to R.B. After losing the 1911 election for governor—his third statewide political race—Russell confessed that he would never be governor. But R.B. might. And so he admonished him, "Be a *man* and you can be a governor, but if you never are a governor be a man, dear boy."

Russell's grand dreams for R.B. prompted him to send his thirteen-year-old son to Georgia's renowned Gordon Military Institute in 1911. Far more than discipline and a superior formal education drew Judge Russell to the school. At Gordon, he hoped his son would meet boys from Georgia's most prominent families and build friendships that would eventually pay political dividends. "If he ever wants to go into politics," the judge said, "he will have met a good many people from over the state, different people." These friends would become political allies, he explained, "because there's no friendship that lasts as long as the friendship that forms when a person is young, especially in school."

Although R.B. was a devoted son who wanted to please his parents, his record as a student was far from exemplary. Like many young people, the temptations of an active social life—girls, drinking, smoking cigarettes and even cigars—often won the struggle for his attention. Constant letters from his father, while filled with admonitions to devote himself to his school work, were actually passionate ruminations about R.B.'s political possibilities. Pleadings to "carry on my work and fulfill what I leave undone" and "carve out your own destiny" were common. "The idea that young Russell should become famous and enhance the family name," wrote biographer Gilbert Fite, "had become almost an obsession with the elder Russell."

Dick, as his friends now called him, graduated from Gordon in 1915. He had recorded mostly mediocre grades. "I guess you'd say I was quiet [in school]," Russell observed years later. "I enjoyed my college life. I had a good time. I wasn't any flaming student. As a matter of fact, I didn't try to break any records." Later that year, he enrolled in the only school his father had ever seriously considered for him—the Lumkin School of Law on the campus of Judge Russell's alma mater, the University of Georgia, in nearby Athens. Russell did not excel at his law studies, but he finally graduated in 1918 after a very brief stint in the Navy. The new lawyer went back to Winder to begin the practice of law with his father, from their office in the People's Bank building.

Russell did not wait long to embark on the political path his father had planned for him. Less than two years after returning to Winder, he ran for the Georgia House of Representatives in the all-white Democratic primary election. In declaring his candidacy, Russell made a refreshingly simple pitch: "I will appreciate the support and influence of every white voter and, if elected, I pledge to serve you acceptably." This Spartan platform had its appeal. Russell beat his opponent, an elderly newspaper editor, by 671 votes out of almost 2,000 cast. He was twenty-two.

Though Russell was part of a group of reformers determined to take control of state government from the older Bourbons, he rarely assumed the lead on controversial issues. Instead he concentrated on building a political base within the House, winning friends and a reputation for honesty and fairness. Reelected without opposition in 1922, Russell's budding political career was enhanced by his father's election that year as chief justice of the Georgia Supreme Court.

But his father's undying ambition for higher office also had its drawbacks. In 1926, Judge Russell coveted the U.S. Senate seat held by incumbent Democrat Walter George, an icon of Georgia politics. The campaign was a painful, awkward experience for Dick. The elder Russell had already waged two unsuccessful statewide races for governor in 1906 and 1911. Now, as Dick and his allies in the legislature planned a race for House speaker, family loyalties forced him to join his father's campaign against the extremely popular Senator George.

Russell agonized over his father's quixotic race. "[Dick] helped him in every way he could," his sister Mary said, "but I can remember how he would dread to have to go out and make these speeches around in Georgia in different towns, begging the people to vote for his father for the Senate, when, in his heart, he was so sorry his father was running." Judge Russell's attacks on George's support of the League of Nations, the World Court, and other U.S. internationalist involvement did not sway large numbers of voters to abandon the incumbent. George beat Russell by more than two to one. The judge quietly returned to his seat on the Supreme Court.

With the distractions of the Senate campaign behind him, Russell entered what would be the most accelerated period of political activity in his career. During his six years in the House, his quiet manner, even temper, and reluctance to rush headlong into controversial issues had won Russell many friends and admirers among young and older members of the House. Not long after the legislature convened in June 1927, Russell announced his candidacy for the speakership. When his only opponent withdrew from the race, House members unanimously elected Russell to the office. He was twenty-nine, serving under a seventy-one-year-old governor. Despite Russell's pleas for bipartisan consideration of Governor L. G. Hardman's agenda, bitter acrimony marked his first legislative session. Lawmakers squabbled for months before reaching agreement on financing several major programs, including education and highway construction. Remarkably, his inability to quell the bitterness did not impair Russell's reputation as an effective leader. Collegues admired his subdued, noncombative style.

By 1930 Russell accurately sensed that Georgia was ready for more youthful leadership. In April he announced his candidacy for governor, declaring he would govern Georgia honestly and economically, independent of machines and factions. He also pledged a government that would operate "on a strictly business basis." The foundation of Russell's campaign was a grassroots operation that relied on his friends in the legislature. "Now, we'll stop at this next little town," he often told his childhood friend and sometimes driver, Mark Dunahoo. "I have a friend there who I served in the legislature with. We'll go by his house and maybe he'll give us [a] bed."

Russell was a tireless campaigner. He often woke farmers at two in the morning to ask for a vote, as he recalled in a 1970 interview:

> I would stop my car and give the customary, "Hello. Hello." That's what you'd do when you want to wake somebody up at night. The man would come out sticking his nightshirt in his overalls and—or his britches—and I'd apologize for waking him and tell him this was the only means I had of getting to him. I had a little five-minute speech I gave as to why I ought to be elected governor and I'd thank him for getting up and go on. But it was amazing the effect that had. I never did have a man . . . resent my calling him and waking him up and getting him down there and urging him to vote for me.

Russell was a superb campaigner, an excellent speaker with an amazing memory for names and faces. "Dick had a wonderful knack of magnifying issues—getting to the roots of them," recalled Dunahoo.

"He could eliminate the chaff from the grain about as quick as any man I've ever known."

Besides his age, there was only one aspect of Russell's personal life that posed a potential problem—his bachelorhood. Despite an active social life, full of dates with young Atlanta women, Russell had never shown any desire to settle down. When a woman displayed more than passing interest in him, Russell usually ended the relationship. In this respect, Russell's father may have influenced him greatly when he advised him, "I hope you won't ever want to get married because you can do better by yourself." Whatever Russell's reasons for staying single, some voters disliked the notion of a bachelor in the governor's mansion. Russell was ready with a simple but deceptive answer. "When I get to be governor," he told campaign audiences, "Mrs. Russell will be right in the mansion." Russell's sister Mary explained: "He meant Mother." The answer seemed to put the issue to rest.

On election day, Russell finished first, ahead of his four opponents, but his vote was not enough for an outright victory. Secretary of State George Carswell forced him into a runoff. Three weeks later, Russell won the Democratic nomination by a landslide, the largest majority in any governor's race in Georgia's history. Race had entered the campaign only once, briefly and without consequence. While the episode did reveal some of Russell's racism, it also illuminated his lifelong distaste for race baiting.

The editor of a black newspaper, the *Atlanta Independent*, had endorsed Russell, praising him for representing the attitude that "Democrats of Georgia are breaking away from their suicidal policy of factionalism and race prejudice." In another editorial, the writer defended Russell against assaults from the "ringsters, factional leaders, and special interests." Though white editors had defended him in similar fashion, Russell was far from flattered by the endorsement. Carswell pounced on the editorial as evidence that Russell was less than committed to white supremacy. Russell responded that "Carswell's crowd" had hired "this Negro" to write the endorsement in order to hurt Russell's campaign.

Russell, of course, did not want or need the support of black voters in an all-white Democratic primary. Yet he seemed to have resisted the urge to raise the stakes by making a naked racial appeal in his rebuttal of the endorsement. In campaign speeches, he did not rail against blacks at all, much less call them "niggers." He rarely used the term throughout his life, and then only in private conversation. Although he was a steadfast believer in white supremacy, Russell displayed no overt signs of animosity or hatred for blacks. He believed it was inappropriate for white politicians to exploit racial fears for political gain.

Chief Justice Richard Russell administered the oath of office to his son in Atlanta on June 27, 1931. At thirty-three, Russell became the youngest governor in the state's history. In the sweltering Georgia heat, before a crowd of five thousand, Russell called for an end to "petty factional or partisan politics." But his promise to balance the state budget attracted the most enthusiastic applause. Despite the economic hardships of the Great Depression and an $8.9 million deficit, Russell pledged he would find money to improve the state's highway and educational systems. He would finance his program, he soon revealed, by cutting state employees' pay as much as 10 percent. He would also undertake a massive reorganization of state agencies and would propose property tax reform.

In almost every way, Russell's first and only legislative session was an enormous success. While lawmakers rejected his proposal to slash state employees' salaries, they did approve his plan to reorganize state government. He slashed the number of state agencies from 102 to 17 and cut state expenditures by 20 percent. After a year and a half as governor, Russell had not only balanced the budget but had honored $2.8 million in delinquent state obligations. His promises to improve education and highways were more difficult to keep, limited by his self-imposed budget pressures. Nonetheless, reviews in and out of Georgia were almost unanimous: Russell had performed exceptionally well as Georgia's new governor. A second term seemed a certainty.

The sudden death of U.S. Senator William J. Harris in April 1932 changed Russell's life forever. As governor, Russell was obliged to appoint Harris's successor until voters elected a permanent replacement. Resisting suggestions that he appoint himself, Russell instead named John S. Cohen, a friend and publisher of the *Atlanta Journal*. Then, only eighteen months into his term as governor, Russell made a bold decision. He would seek election to the remainder of Harris's Senate term. His opponent would be Congressman Charles R. Crisp, a veteran politician who had represented a south Georgia district since 1912. Crisp was well known, popular, and just as conservative as Russell. But Russell had several advantages: a well-oiled state organization, overwhelming name recognition, and the good will of Georgia's electorate. While Crisp remained in Washington to emphasize his national experience, Russell campaigned vigorously across the state, portraying his opponent as an old, privileged politician who was out of step with his Depression-plagued constituents.

Crisp fought back. His long experience and his many contacts won him endorsements from all but a handful of Georgia's daily newspapers and several out-of-state papers, including the *New York Times* and the *Washington Post*. By election day, both candidates had resorted to personal attacks. Crisp supporters charged that Russell was a tool of special interests and that he had "sold" the Senate seat to Cohen for the support of the *Atlanta Journal*. Even Russell's marital status became an issue when Crisp suggested that a bachelor would find it impossible to resist the temptations of Washington's social scene. Russell was no more inclined to take the high road. He responded that Crisp had abused congressional mail privileges and had placed relatives on his Washington staff. Russell's strength on election day astounded the many observers who had predicted a close race. He won overwhelmingly, with 58 percent of the vote. He was thirty-four.

Russell arrived in Washington confident—and prepared. He had memorized not only the Declaration of Independence and the U.S. Constitution but all forty of the Senate's rules of procedure. Soon he learned that these rules were not nearly as important as the massive volume of precedents that guided the Senate's actions in debate. He borrowed the book from Senate parliamentarian Charlie Watkins and studied it intently.

Russell understood that getting the right committee assignment was just as important as knowing the Senate's rules. Shortly after he was sworn into office in January 1933, he brashly informed Majority Leader Joseph T. Robinson of his desire to serve on the powerful Appropriations Committee. Robinson thought the request was outrageous and politely explained that most freshmen waited the obligatory four to five years before they considered themselves eligible for a significant committee post.

But Russell had important insight into the majority leader's thinking, which he used to his advantage: He knew that Robinson and other senior senators would watch to see whether he would align himself with Louisiana's Huey P. Long. A brash, radical former governor who had recently arrived in the Senate, Long had made Robinson's life miserable with his populist antics and stubborn refusal of committee assignments. Russell cleverly told Robinson, "Senator Harris was on the Appropriations Committee and I'm succeeding him, and [my constituents] expect me to be on there. And if I can't be on the Appropriations Committee, I don't want to be on any committee." Russell was careful to avoid mentioning Long. But he knew that Robinson would realize the implied association. "With the reputation I had in those days," Russell recalled, "I guess I was a pretty two-fisted man on the stump. And he decided that he'd buy his peace with me and he went to those other senators and finally got them all to agree to let me go on the Appropriations Committee."

On Appropriations, eventually as chairman of its agriculture subcommittee, Russell became known for fiercely guarding Georgia's farming interests. On his other committees—Naval Affairs, Immigration, and Manufactures—he worked quietly to build a solid reputation as a studious, dedicated senator more interested in legislation than press releases. He studied bills—actually read hundreds of pages of complicated legislation—before he formed an opinion. Each day, aides insisted, Russell devoured the previous day's *Congressional Record* from cover to cover. He also found time to read his mail and personally sign every piece of outgoing correspondence. He was still a bachelor, a circumstance that seemed to pose no threat to the performance of his senatorial duties. Indeed, the absence of familial obligations freed Russell to devote his full energies to the Senate. "If there ever was anyone who gave his life to an institution," said his longtime Senate colleague J. William Fulbright of Arkansas, "I would say Russell gave it to the Senate."

Russell was once engaged to a young woman, but differences over the faith of any children—she was Catholic—caused the relationship to sour. Though he later dated and maintained a steady relationship with one woman for many years, he never again considered marriage. "He was very human," Mark Dunahoo remembered. "He could become emotional with women and did become emotional with them—involved with them—but when they became serious, that was the end of him." Russell acknowledged his wariness of women had begun when he was governor. "I couldn't decide in many instances whether the young ladies I'd meet were interested in me or the governor," he said. "I got so interested in my work that I'm afraid I would have made a very poor husband and father."

When he was not at work, Russell usually sought the refuge of his small Washington apartment. He eschewed most social functions, attending only those that absolutely required his presence. His only real interests outside of work were baseball and reading—especially books on Civil War history, which he read with passion.*

Russell plowed through books by the bundle. Dozens of volumes borrowed from the Library of Congress usually littered a large table in his Senate office. And his mind was amazingly retentive. Herman Talmadge, who would later serve with Russell as Georgia's junior senator, estimated that his senior colleague could read a thousand words a minute "with almost total recall." His remarkable powers of retention applied to baseball and football as well. He was a storehouse of information and statistics about teams and individuals.

Russell's willingness to forsake the social and marital demands other politicians took for granted only made him a better senator. He worked hard, he was dependable and honest, and his colleagues liked him. Though he would not always be known for his fealty to Democratic party programs, Russell was one of Franklin Roosevelt's most loyal supporters during his early Senate years. Throughout the Depression, he supported almost every piece of New Deal legislation in the belief that government intervention was the only way to alleviate the nation's suffering. "If the country's in bad shape," he said at the time, "why I'll resort to drastic means. If the country's in good shape, I don't see any necessity for tinkering with the system."

With his reelection in 1936—he defeated Governor Eugene Talmadge, the father of his future Senate colleague—Russell's position in the Senate seemed secure. As in his governor's campaign, Russell's bitter race against Talmadge illuminated the difference between his "dignified" brand of white supremacy and Talmadge's hateful racist appeals. Talmadge tried to brand Russell soft on racial issues, suggesting, among other offenses, that he had voted to confirm "niggers" to federal positions. Russell detested such race baiting. He had little choice but to respond to Talmadge's smears. The charges were false, Russell said. He added that America "is a white man's country, yes, and we are going to keep it that way." To even "insinuate that I stand for political and social equality with the Negro," Russell said, was an insult to the people of Georgia. In another speech, however, Russell attacked Talmadge's emphasis on race. "When a politician runs out of arguments, when he hasn't any more soap and knows that in the minds of the people he is

---

*Russell, however, was loath to use the term *Civil* to describe America's great military conflict, which he always called "the War Between the States." Using the term "Civil War," one aide recalled, was "the cardinal sin to him."

convicted of pure cussedness in keeping the old people of Georgia from getting their pensions, then he comes in hollering, 'nigger, nigger, nigger.' "

To some northern observers, Russell's defeat of Talmadge signaled the end of southern demagoguery. Although he had defeated a race baiter, his steadfast support of New Deal programs meant even more to many Democrats in Washington. In this area, however, Russell would not long be Roosevelt's dependable ally. In 1938 he parted painfully with the president over the administration's attempt to defeat several conservative Democrats who had opposed much of the New Deal. One of the targets of White House wrath was Russell's senior colleague, Walter George, who went on to defeat the anointed Roosevelt candidate. Expecting Russell to oppose George—who had come to Russell's defense in the race against Talmadge—was folly on Roosevelt's part. The episode cooled their previously warm relationship.

Another break with the president came over civil rights. With Russell's enthusiastic involvement, southerners had defeated an administration proposal in 1935 to outlaw lynching. Like most responsible southern leaders, Russell believed lynching was a heinous crime. But he also believed that the states, not the federal government, should decide the question. When the issue arose again in 1937, Texas senator Tom Connally, the leader of the southern forces, called on Russell and his encyclopedic knowledge of the Senate's rules. Serving as Connally's lieutenant, Russell performed effectively. His well-organized speech was among the highlights of the southern opposition to the proposal, which failed when supporters could not end a southern filibuster in January 1938.

Even the advent of American involvement in World War II—and the prospect that black soldiers would die to preserve rights they did not yet enjoy as citizens—did not disabuse Russell of his racist beliefs. "Just carve on my tombstone," a black soldier once said sarcastically, " 'Here lies a black man killed fighting a yellow man for the protection of a white man.' " The tragic irony in that statement may have never occurred to Russell. Though the war would eventually afford black citizens many new rights and economic opportunities, Russell used his status as a senior member of the Armed Services Committee to thwart this progress.

Although more than 1.1 million black Americans joined the military during the war, Russell adamantly opposed the pleas of black civilians for fair employment practices in war industries and apprenticeship programs. More sympathetic, President Roosevelt finally acquiesced in 1941. He issued an executive order—the first on civil rights since the Emancipation Proclamation—which banned such discrimination and established a Fair Employment Practices Commission (FEPC) to enforce it.

The FEPC sent Russell and his southern colleagues into a sputtering rage. Alarmed by the prospect of the federal government dictating hiring policy to private businesses, Russell declared the FEPC to be the "most dangerous force in existence in the United States today." A product of Roosevelt's expansive wartime powers, the agency sparked vigorous debate in both houses. Russell and his southern colleagues resolved to destroy it at the first opportunity.

Their opening came in 1944, when Russell sponsored legislation to halt spending for any agency established for more than one year without Congressional approval—in other words, the FEPC. As Congress considered Russell's legislation in early 1945, a dying Roosevelt begged lawmakers to continue the FEPC's funding. But Congress approved Russell's amendment anyway, and the FEPC suspended operations in June 1946. The new president, Harry Truman, tried to revive it, but the iron jaws of the Senate southern filibuster devoured it each time.

Despite Russell's success in opposing the government's fair employment effort, the war had spurred the growing demands for greater economic rights for blacks. New military and civilian facilities had appeared throughout the South, especially in Russell's Georgia, creating vast new opportunities for skilled black employment.

Perhaps an even greater impetus for civil rights was the growing realization that well over a million black citizens had joined the war effort in civilian and military roles. If blacks were brave enough, competent enough, and patriotic enough to join the struggle to save democracy halfway around the world, how could their government deny the rights of that democracy when they returned home? It was a difficult and embarrassing question that shamed growing numbers of white Americans. But the matter was not trying for Russell and his Southern colleagues in the House and Senate. At war's end, Russell held fast to his unassailable belief that blacks were socially and intellectually inferior to whites. Battlefield valor changed nothing in his eyes.

By 1945 Russell had gradually supplanted Tom Connally of Texas as leader of the southern anti–civil rights forces. An irascible man, Connally was often abrasive and sarcastic with his colleagues in debate.

Connally "was past his prime," recalled Louisiana Senator Russell Long, who maintained that the difference between Russell and Connally's effectiveness "was like the difference between A and Z." Russell was the consummate southern gentleman. He knew the Senate's rules and precedents better than any other senator. And despite his racist views, most senators saw him as a moderate. The South and its way of life were under fierce attack by northern liberals. Even some prominent southerners—such as Arkansas congressman Brooks Hays and Russell's friend, Ralph McGill, editor of the *Atlanta Constitution*—had begun to challenge southern racial attitudes. Faced with these threats—especially from the growing numbers of congressmen and Americans repulsed by the social and economic conditions imposed on southern blacks—southern senators instinctively looked to Russell for leadership.

And then there was Harry Truman, Russell's former Senate colleague, who was pushing civil rights legislation with more vigor than any previous president. For most of his life, Truman's views on racial matters had differed little from Russell's. Raised in rural Missouri, Truman came of age afflicted with many of the racial biases and beliefs that still possessed Russell. But Truman outgrew much of his bigotry. He now challenged many of the racial notions of his youth.

Relying on the 1947 report of his Civil Rights Commission, the president outlined an ambitious civil rights program in his 1948 State of the Union address. He challenged the Republican-controlled Congress to outlaw lynching, protect black voting rights, and abolish poll taxes in the seven southern states that still imposed a voting levy as a voting qualification. Furthermore, Truman wanted to establish a permanent Commission on Civil Rights, another FEPC, a Joint Congressional Committee on Civil Rights, and a civil rights division in the Justice Department. And he wanted to end discrimination on all modes of interstate transportation—bus, rail, and airplane. As commander in chief, he would instruct his Secretary of Defense to investigate how to abolish discrimination in the armed services. The cruel irony that the southern states still treated returning black soldiers as second-class citizens struck Truman as particularly unfair. When several Southern senators urged Truman to moderate his view on civil rights, Truman replied in writing that "my very stomach turned over when I learned that Negro soldiers, just back from overseas, were being dumped out of army trucks in Mississippi and beaten. Whatever my inclinations as a native of Missouri might have been, as president I know this is bad. I shall fight to end evils like this." Truman said he would transmit all his proposals to Congress in a special message on civil rights, the first formal communication from a president on that issue.

Truman's agenda angered Russell. "Mr. Truman's misnamed civil rights program is strictly a political gesture, bidding for the radical vote," he wrote, adding that "this uncalled-for attack on our Southern civilization has made me sick at heart." In a news release, Russell said that Truman's proposal "shows that the president is the political hostage of the lunatic fringe." Russell saw Truman's effort to make lynching a federal offense not as an attack on a brutal form of murder but as an assault on states' rights and Georgia's sovereignty. "I cannot support legislation to bring the federal government into the enforcement of the murder laws of my state in crimes of this nature unless they are to apply to all other types of murders in all of the other states," he said in a letter to a constituent. "To do so would be to admit that my state was more barbaric and incompetent than other states, and I do not believe this to be the case."

Truman's bold attempt to reverse racial discrimination was a call to arms for Russell and his southern colleagues. On March 6, senators from the eleven former Confederate states—with the sole exception of Florida's Claude Pepper—gathered in the office of Virginia's Harry Byrd to map their strategy. These men considered Truman's civil rights program an act of aggression against the South. As they girded for battle, they elected the man under whose "generalship" they would fight Truman and his liberal congressional allies. Richard Russell was already their leader. The meeting only formalized his predominance among the southerners.

With Russell at the helm, the southern bloc would enter its most active and effective period. He was now, as one journalist put it, "the big bear standing in the forest path, amiable enough if not aroused. He could be gotten around, sometimes, but one had to go slow and do maneuvers. It was safest to negotiate." From now on, "General" Russell would always have at least one southern sentry in the Senate chamber to guard against surprise attacks by pro–civil rights forces. The southerners would also take their case to the American people over the radio airwaves. "Our back is to the wall in this thing," Russell told reporters, "but I haven't surrendered yet." If the southerners lost, he said, "it will be only after we have exhausted every source at our command." Within days after Russell's elevation to southern leader, he demanded and re-

ceived equal time to rebut civil rights arguments on the Mutual Broadcasting System. Normally averse to national exposure, Russell delivered
a major speech on civil rights to a national audience in late March.

Allied with conservative Republicans, the Senate's southern bloc was
a powerful force. With their ability to filibuster and prevent a vote on
any civil rights proposal—the rules then required a vote of two-thirds
of those present and voting to shut off debate—they were virtually
unbeatable. Though almost always fighting from a defensive position,
they were able to block all of Truman's legislative proposals in 1948.
The Senate dropped the poll tax ban in August. The FEPC and antilynching bills were never even considered. In June senators rejected an
amendment to outlaw lynching of military personnel. Two days later
they rejected a proposal to allow military draftees and enlisted men to
serve in segregated or integrated units.

Despite his failures in the Congress, Truman still had one potent
weapon at his disposal—the executive order. In July he used it, issuing
two sweeping mandates. The first began the dismantling of segregation
in the military services. The other barred discrimination in the hiring
and management practices of the federal work force and established a
Fair Employment Board in the Civil Service Commission to handle complaints. Southerners were outraged. Now a prominent member of the
newly created Armed Services Committee, Russell branded Truman's
plan to desegregate the military "a threat to the morale and efficiency
of our National Defense establishment at one of the most critical periods
in history."

To Russell, the presidential foray into civil rights suggested that
Truman stood little chance of winning the November election. With
Truman heading the national ticket, Russell and other southern members
of Congress feared their constituents would abandon the party in November. Some, such as Alabama senators John Sparkman and Lister Hill,
voiced these concerns publicly. Sparkman said he would be "very happy
to see Truman step out" in favor of General Dwight D. Eisenhower.
Russell had already voiced his concern that Truman's advocacy of civil
rights might cost the Democratic party the South. Even his own Georgia
delegation to the convention wanted Truman out. Meeting shortly before
leaving for Philadelphia, the delegates called on Truman to step aside
in favor of Eisenhower. And the Georgians wanted Russell as Eisenhower's running mate, a move Russell firmly resisted.

But when Humphrey's tough new platform language on civil rights won approval by the full convention, alarmed southern leaders phoned Russell in Winder. They argued that southern delegations—some on the verge of bolting the party—desperately needed a conservative Democrat they could support. No one thought Russell stood a chance of beating Truman. But his presence on the ballot would at least allow the southerners to voice their dissatisfaction with Truman in a constructive manner. Russell reluctantly agreed.

Placing his name in nomination, Russell's friend Charles Bloch reassured the delegates that the Georgia delegation had no intention of bolting the convention. But he attacked Truman's civil rights program with strong language and praised Russell for his valiant attempts to defeat it. "He has fought courageously, and thus far successfully, against having any such [civil rights] program crammed down the throat of the South at the behest of well-organized minority groups." Bloch issued an ominous, grave threat. "The South," he said, to applause of southern delegates, "is no longer going to be the whipping boy of the Democratic Party and you know, or if you don't know you can learn here and now, that without the votes of the South you cannot elect a president of the United States." Borrowing a memorable phrase from William Jennings Bryan's "Cross of Gold" speech to the 1896 convention—ironically one of Hubert Humphrey's most beloved orations—Bloch shouted, "You shall not crucify the South on this cross of civil rights!"

South Carolina Governor Strom Thurmond seconded Russell's nomination. Russell, Thurmond declared, "has done everything to preserve the state. He stands as a shining beacon to those who believe in constitutional government and who want to see our American way of life preserved." Southern delegations staged a wild demonstration for Russell. Waving Confederate flags, they paraded around the convention hall for ten minutes. Just as the demonstration began to die, the band struck up and played *Dixie*. Suddenly revived, the demonstration went on for another ten minutes.

The anticlimactic nomination vote was no surprise. Truman won the nomination on the first ballot with 948 votes to Russell's 263. Russell received near-unanimous southern support. With Mississippi's delegates absent, nine of eleven Southern delegations voted solidly against Truman. North Carolina was the only southern state to give him any votes.

Before the convention nominated Senate Democratic leader Alben Barkley as Truman's running mate, Russell's name was again placed in nomination—this time for vice president. An obscure delegate from

Alabama, George C. Wallace, rose to nominate Russell and employed the now-familiar refrain that Russell was "the man who will see that the South will not be crucified upon the cross of so-called civil rights."

Despite the overwhelming vote of Democratic party loyalists, almost no one predicted that Truman could overcome the dissidents in his own party to win the election. Former Vice President Henry Wallace had challenged him on the left, running on the Progressive party's ultra-liberal platform. And now abiding anger over the party's civil rights platform plank seemed about to spawn a southern challenge from the right.

But the array of opponents only seemed to embolden the president. Feisty as ever, Truman had no plans to retreat. Though his representatives had opposed Humphrey's stronger civil rights language, he now had little choice but to embrace the platform plank as his own. In his early-morning acceptance speech to the convention, Truman boldly renewed his call for a strong civil rights program.

"Everybody knows that I recommended to the Congress the civil rights program," Truman said. "I did so because I believe it to be my duty under the Constitution. Some of the members of my own party disagree with me violently on this matter. But they stand up and do it openly. People can see where they stand."

Truman had wisely avoided a fight with Russell and other southern Democrats.

"But the Republicans," he continued, "all profess to be for these measures. But the Eightieth Congress failed to act."

Then, Truman dropped his bomb. He would summon the Republican-controlled Congress back into session with a challenge to pass the housing, education, and civil rights legislation its leaders professed to support.

"Now, my friends, if there is any reality behind that Republican platform, we ought to get some action from a short session of the Eightieth Congress, and they could do this job in fifteen days, if they want to do it."

Almost overnight, the speech put the Republicans on the defensive and breathed new life into Truman's campaign against New York governor Thomas Dewey. Historian James MacGregor Burns compared Truman's gutsy performance to the French general who had cried, "My left flank is in ruins, my right flank is retreating, my center is caving in. Good! I shall attack."

As the convention broke up, hundreds of disaffected southern Democrats streamed toward Birmingham, Alabama, for an impromptu gathering of a States' Rights party, formed to nominate a southern challenger to Truman. But attendance at the convention would not reflect a unified South. Only two senators would participate. No one would represent Louisiana or Georgia. Florida would send only seven delegates. Nonetheless, Mississippi governor Fielding Wright, who had led his delegation out of Philadelphia's convention hall before the nomination balloting began, hoped that a strong challenger would emerge. Eager to generate enthusiasm for the rump gathering, Wright sent telegrams to undecided southern leaders. "The chips are down," he said. "The die is cast. We must make Birmingham the beginning of our Electoral College fight to save the South."

Although no formal surveys were conducted of southern delegates to determine whom they wanted to lead them, delegates clearly favored Russell, indisputably the most popular and respected southern leader. As he approached the pinnacle of his influence in Washington, Russell was not being wooed by the white, southern mainstream of his party. His courtiers were boisterous malcontents who detested the liberalism of Harry Truman with a passion so fierce that they hoped to cripple their own party in pursuit of white supremacy.

For Russell, the question was not whether he would assume his role as the leader in the South's fight against civil rights. The real question was: *Which* South would he lead?

CHAPTER THREE

A Born Apple-Polisher

LYNDON JOHNSON WAS WEARY. Even if he had wanted to attend the Democratic National Convention in Philadelphia, there was simply no time. The forty-year-old congressman was entering the final days of an exhausting race for the U.S. Senate. For months he had been a political tornado, whirling his way all over Texas in a frenzied quest for votes. He had narrowly lost his first Senate race in 1941. He did not intend to let another victory slip from his grasp by relaxing now—not for even one moment.

The physical toll of the long, arduous race was apparent. Johnson's crippled throat uttered the faint, raspy croak that afflicts those who abuse their vocal cords. Dark bags hung under his tired brown eyes. He had lost considerable weight. One observer remarked that "his face seemed to be skin stretched over long bones."

With the election so close, leaving for a national convention was out of the question. Besides, everyone knew that President Harry Truman was sure to lose in the November general election. Any association with an unpopular president's unpopular program could only hurt Johnson's chances. In May, as he kicked off his campaign, he was careful to distance himself from Truman with a robust attack on the president's civil rights program. Truman's liberal proposals were, he said, "a farce and a sham—an effort to set up a police state in the guise of liberty." At his first campaign rally, in Austin, Johnson declared that states had the constitutional right to run their own elections. "I am opposed to the antilynching bill because the federal government has no more business enacting a law against murders [sic] than against drunks," he said. "I am against the FEPC because if a man can tell you whom you must hire, he can tell you whom you cannot employ."

Despite this harsh rhetoric, Johnson had never been a race baiter. While he had voted against every civil rights bill during his ten years in the House, he had nonetheless earned a reputation as someone concerned about minorities. "I will say that civil rights was not one of my priorities in those days," Johnson later explained. "I had other concerns." As the representative of a moderate-to-liberal district in the scrubby hill country surrounding Austin and the vast prairie stretching east toward Houston, Johnson had enjoyed considerable support among his district's relatively small population of black voters.

But black votes—many of them bought by payments to black leaders—had never been that important to Johnson. "His part of Texas," explained his friend William S. White, a *New York Times* reporter, "was not really southern. The war there, if anything, was the war with Mexico." Even so, civil rights was as much a litmus test for statewide candidates in Texas as it was for politicians in other southern states. "One heroic stand," Johnson later wrote, "and I'd be back home, defeated, unable to do any good for anyone, much less the blacks and underprivileged."

A tall, slender, earthy man, Johnson was consumed by ambition for power. In pursuit of the Senate seat, he had worked painfully long hours and driven himself and his staff relentlessly. "I think the first impression I had of him," said White, "was of furious, almost incredible energy." Johnson could be charming, rude, eloquent, profane, generous, and selfish—seemingly all at the same time. "Both his faults and his virtues were on a very big scale," observed his friend Katherine Graham. As *Time* magazine would explain years later, Johnson was "an anthology of antonyms."

His temper was legendary. And the term "son of a bitch" seemed to fall effortlessly from the lips of those who knew him well. "He may have been a son of a bitch," said his long-time press secretary, George Reedy, "but he was a colossal son of a bitch. By sheer size alone he would dominate any landscape." Said aide Gerald Siegel: "He was sometimes a mean sonofabitch. He was petulant. He was capable of childish temper tantrums." Moments later, however, he could smother the object of his wrath with warmth and affection.

To most, Johnson was almost entirely one dimensional, caring only about politics and power. "The thing that made Lyndon different from other people, I suppose," said his friend Virginia Durr, "was that when he started doing something, he poured every ounce of his energy into it and it became the great overriding thing of his life. He didn't hold anything back. He just pounded and pounded and pounded." Said boyhood playmate Sherman Birdwell: "His regular work was politics and his hobby was politics; his life was politics."

This passion for politics and power did not extend to matters of legislation. In more than ten years in Congress, Johnson had introduced only seven bills. Only two of his bills had ever become law, and those mattered only within the confines of his congressional district. He rarely spoke out on legislation. Colleagues never seemed to know where he stood on important issues.

Nonetheless, he was a dogged, effective advocate for his constituents. No letter went answered. No constituent problem was too small or insignificant for his attention. As a supporter of President Franklin Roosevelt's New Deal, Johnson had parlayed his White House relationship into money and public works projects for his constituents. In fact, the crowning achievement of his congressional tenure had been the acquisition of a different sort of power: electrical power. Nothing had meant more to the forgotten rural people of the hill country than the electricity he brought them with a loan from the Rural Electrification Administration (REA) in 1938. That loan had financed the extension of power lines to the remote reaches of his sprawling district. Electric power had brightened and simplified their dreary, rugged lives. Johnson's role in persuading President Roosevelt and the REA to approve the loan had won him their undying gratitude.

In the Senate race, Johnson's campaign themes were austere and sufficiently ambiguous: peace, preparedness, and progress. Though he opposed Truman's civil rights program, he rarely mentioned the issue in stump speeches. He told audiences that he opposed socialized medicine and supported the antilabor Taft-Hartley legislation "with the utmost enthusiasm." Early on, he had ignored his major opponent, Coke Stevenson, the conservative and popular former governor who had campaigned in the plodding, dignified manner befitting an old-fashioned Texas statesman. But when Stevenson finished ahead of him in the first primary, forcing a runoff for the nomination, Johnson was desperate. He attacked.

At first his campaign put considerable energy into spreading rumors that Stevenson had entered into a "secret deal" in which he would oppose Taft-Hartley. Later, only weeks before the election, Johnson unleashed a furious frontal assault on Stevenson. Seizing on Stevenson's stubborn refusal to endorse Taft-Hartley, Johnson's campaign blanketed Texas with propaganda about Stevenson's "unwillingness" to support the bill. Taft-Hartley—enacted over Truman's veto in 1947—was popular with the mostly antilabor voters of Texas. And Johnson missed no opportunity to cast doubt on Stevenson's position. "Do you want to vote for a man who won't tell you where he stands?" Johnson asked at almost every stop in the final weeks of the runoff election.

There were other issues, Johnson implied, on which Stevenson refused to state a position: the Marshall Plan to rebuild war-torn Europe, cost-of-living increases for the elderly, farm subsidies, rural electrification, and hospital construction. But Johnson's charges on Taft-Hartley hurt the most. As governor, Stevenson never had the opportunity to vote for the bill. Now, under the crushing weight of Johnson's attacks, Stevenson found his cherished reputation for integrity being questioned as much as his support for Taft-Hartley. "His refusal to be forthright made him appear unsure and vacillating," Johnson's friend Jake Pickle recalled. "Either way, Coke looked unsure, and people back home began to question his qualifications on the national scene." Late in the campaign, when Stevenson finally endorsed the bill, he could not repair the damage. Although victimized by the unfair implications of Johnson's attacks, Stevenson was not exactly a paragon of political virtue. He had unfairly implied that Johnson was indifferent to communism.

By election day, Johnson and his men were hopeful. The relentless attacks on Stevenson seemed to hit their mark. As the returns came in, however, Stevenson led by more than 2,000 of the 939,000 votes counted. But then his lead disappeared. By the next day, Johnson led by 693 votes out of 979,000. About 11,000 votes remained uncounted. The next day, Stevenson regained a slim, 119-vote lead, that grew to 349 a day later. When the Texas Election Bureau finally announced its unofficial tally on September 2, Stevenson's lead held at a mere 362 votes.

After thousands of miles and months of campaigning, Johnson's campaign—and his political career—had seemingly ended in a narrow, demoralizing defeat.

The Texas hill country of Lyndon Johnson's youth was not merely the far western end of the Confederacy; it was a world apart from the lush, rolling hills of Richard Russell's northeastern Georgia. Although settlers from places like Georgia and Alabama began to populate the region in the mid-1800s, their lives eventually took on the character and routines of the rugged American Southwest. "There were no 'darkies' or plantations in the arid hill country where I grew up," Johnson wrote in 1971. "I never sat on my parents' or grandparents' knees listening to nostalgic tales of the antebellum South. In Stonewall and Johnson City I never was a part of the Old Confederacy. But I was part of Texas. My roots were in its soil." The soil, with its abundant grass and its promise of good grazing land for cattle, had drawn the first settlers, including Johnson's paternal great-grandfather from Georgia. But the lure of this outwardly fertile land soon proved nothing more than a mirage. The land was mostly limestone covered by a thin, fragile layer of topsoil that washed away after cattle devoured the anchoring grass. What seemed at first seemed to be paradise quickly revealed itself a barren land, inhospitable to the settlers.

Lyndon Baines Johnson was born into this harsh environment on August 27, 1908, the son of Sam and Rebekah Baines Johnson, near the small town of Stonewall. Like Russell and Humphrey, Johnson was born into public life. His father—a hard-drinking former schoolteacher and sometime rancher and farmer—was a member of the Texas House, where he had earned a reputation for uncompromising integrity. "Sam Johnson," went the saying in Austin, "is straight as a shingle." Rebekah's side of the family was even more prominent. Her grandfather had been president of Baylor College. Her father, Joseph Wilson Baines, had been Texas secretary of state and had also served in the legislature.

But Sam Johnson's celebrated reputation for honesty brought him little reward. He routinely rejected the many financial "opportunities" available to less-scrupulous legislators. His refusal to sell his vote meant that when he left the legislature for a ten-year hiatus in 1908, he had no financial security. Farming and ranching produced little income for the family, and Sam was always only one step ahead of his creditors. But the hardships of hill country life were most difficult on Rebekah, a refined, intelligent college graduate and former newspaper reporter. Virginia Durr believed those hardships gave birth to Johnson's "passion against poverty and this passion for electricity. He did remember his mother doing all this hard, heavy work, and it did hurt him, and he did want to see her life made easier and he wanted to see the life of women like her made easier."

As much as he respected—and sometimes feared—his father,

Lyndon most often sought Rebekah's favor. "One of the things I used to like about him," Hubert Humphrey once said, "was that he would get tears in his eyes when he talked about his mother." To Johnson, Rebekah "was everything—religion, character, right and wrong." She was, he declared, "the greatest female I have ever known, without any exceptions."

At school, Lyndon impressed his teachers with a quick mind. Arriving unprepared at school did not bother him. When caught off-guard, childhood friend Joe Croft recalled, he employed diversionary tactics. "He'd come up with just any number of things and even have the teacher so interested that before you'd know it, the period had gone by, and the rest of us would sit there like a bunch of birds on a telephone line wondering what was taking place." But he was also an unruly boy. He constantly called attention to himself with pranks and mischief, and even the way he dressed. He frequently disobeyed his parents, resulting in many thrashings with his father's razor strap. In high school his attendance was poor—and when he did go, he seemed always to be in trouble.

At home, Sam did his best to instill in Lyndon a healthy respect for politics and a keen interest in public affairs. At the dinner table, the conversation was rarely lighthearted. Sam often led the family—Lyndon's two brothers, two sisters, and various guests—in deep discussions on issues ranging from government railroad ownership to the League of Nations. He drilled the children with spelling quizzes and mathematics problems.

When Sam returned to the legislature in 1918, Lyndon delighted in accompanying his father to Austin, as he later recalled: "I would sit in the gallery for hours watching all the activity on the floor and then would wander around the halls trying to figure out what was going on." Sam's determination to resist the influence of special interests in Austin had not waned during his absence from the House. To some, it almost seemed that he enjoyed championing lost or unpopular causes.

Soon after his return to Austin, he waded into the debate over a bill that pandered to anti-German sentiment in Texas by making it a crime to criticize America's war effort. Sam not only delivered a passionate speech against the bill on the House floor, he lobbied his colleagues to delete a provision that would have given any Texan the power to make citizen's arrests.

Nothing, however, revealed his independence more vividly than his vocal condemnation of the Ku Klux Klan. He knew the racist group was popular with many—perhaps most—of his House colleagues. But he supported a 1921 resolution denouncing the Klan, anyway. Lyndon's brother, Sam Houston Johnson, recalled the death threats his father received after he criticized the Klan in a highly publicized speech. "Now, listen here, you Kukluxsonofabitch," their father shouted into the phone when he received a threatening call one night, "if you and your god-damned gang think you're man enough to shoot me, you come on ahead. My brothers and I will be waiting for you out on the front porch. Just come on ahead, you yellow bastards." His father and his uncles—guns at the ready—waited on the porch until dawn. "And the Kukluxson-ofabitch," Sam Houston said, "never showed up." Lyndon, fifteen at the time, later said he was "fearful that my daddy would be taken out and tarred and feathered."

Despite his success in the House, Sam's personal fortunes sagged. Mounting debts forced him to sell his farm in 1922. Even with the proceeds from the sale, he remained heavily in debt. Giving up politics in 1923, Sam went looking for full-time work. When he finally found employment—as a lowly game warden—the job paid only two dollars a day. The Johnsons had become, as biographer Robert Caro wrote, "the laughingstock" of Johnson City.

In 1924, at age fifteen, Lyndon graduated high school in Johnson City. Though his parents hoped he would immediately enroll in college, Lyndon had little or no desire to continue his formal education. But after an impulsive trip to California and several years of working at various jobs, Lyndon finally agreed to enroll at Southwest Texas State Teachers College in San Marcos, where he would major in history. He wasted no time making himself known in his new environment. His assertive, friendly nature won him friends and detractors in almost equal numbers.

"Words won't come to describe how Lyndon acted toward the faculty," one disapproving classmate said, "how kowtowing he was, how suck-assing he was, how brown-nosing he was." Classmates remember that Johnson was full of big talk about his father's political influence and outright lies about his ancestors' role in Texas history. He introduced himself as "Lyndon Johnson from Johnson City," seeming to imply—falsely—that his family had founded the town. His manner was so grand, his personality so forceful and overbearing, that students began to derisively call him "Bull" Johnson. "Everybody called him Bull," recalled fellow student Joe Berry, who added that Johnson was "a real bullshitter if there ever was one." "That was what we called him to his face," remembered another classmate. "That was what he was generally called. Because of this constant braggadocio. Because he was so full of bullshit, manure, that people just didn't believe him. Because he was a man who just couldn't tell the truth."

Johnson began to hone the techniques of flattery he would later employ to build relationships with powerful men like Senator Richard Russell, House Speaker Sam Rayburn, and President Franklin Roosevelt. At San Marcos he focused his attention most sharply on the school's president, Dr. Cecil E. Evans, and one of its leading professors, Dr. H. M. Greene. As roommate Alfred "Boody" Johnson recalled, Lyndon told him "the way you get ahead in this world, you get close to those that are the heads of things. Like President Evans, for example."

Johnson had always tried to ingratiate himself with older men and women. As a teenager he showered attention on the elderly women of Johnson City and politely asked the older men about their views on various issues. Now, as a writer for the college newspaper, Johnson went out of his way to praise Evans in editorials. He systematically found ways to catch the president's eye, finally winning a job as his office boy. In short order, Johnson made himself indispensable. He flattered Evans shamelessly, gladly ran his errands, accompanied him to the state capital, drafted letters to lawmakers, and wrote reports to state agencies.

By the summer of 1928, Johnson had completed enough course work to earn a two-year certificate qualifying him to teach grade school. He left San Marcos for the small town of Cotulla, ninety miles south of San Antonio, to serve as teacher and principal at a school attended almost exclusively by Mexican-Americans. "Few of them could speak English, and I couldn't speak much Spanish," Johnson recalled many years later. "My students were poor and they often came to class without breakfast, hungry. They knew even in their youth the pain of prejudice. They never seemed to know why people disliked them. But they knew it was so, because I saw it in their eyes. I often walked home late in the afternoon, after the classes were finished, wishing there was more that I could do. But all I knew was to teach the little that I knew, hoping it might help them against the hardships that lay ahead." The experience had a lasting impact on Johnson. "Somehow," he said, "you never forget what poverty and hatred can do when you see its scars on the hopeful face of a young child."

By all accounts, Johnson was an extraordinary teacher. He prodded his students to excel. He made them speak English—because they would not be admitted into high school unless they could. He taught them to sing. He organized a band, a volleyball team, a baseball team, a basketball team, a debating team, and a literary society. Because school buses were not then available to Mexican-American students, he persuaded parents with automobiles to drive the debating team to its out-of-town competitions. In his spare time, he even taught the school's janitor to read.

Johnson returned to San Marcos in the summer of 1929 to complete his college studies. By August 1930 he had his degree and, shortly after that, a job as public-speaking instructor at Sam Houston High School in Houston. One student remembered him as a "human dynamo." When told by the principal that no money was available for an out-of-town trip because "it had never been done," Johnson shot back, "Yes, but you've never had a teacher like me." Almost singlehandedly, he revived the school's moribund debating program. Out of sixty-seven debates during Johnson's tenure, the Sam Houston team lost only one.

Johnson made his first political speech in 1930, when he attended a political gathering near the town of Henly. He had come to hear former governor Pat Neff, who was running for reelection to the state's powerful Railroad Commission. When Neff failed to show, the master of ceremonies asked for volunteers to speak for him. Lyndon came storming through the crowd. "By God," he said, "I'll make a speech for Pat Neff." His ten-minute speech, said one observer, was a "stem-winding, arm-swinging" defense of Neff. When asked why he had volunteered, Lyndon replied: "Governor Neff once gave my daddy a job when he needed it, so I couldn't let him go by default." Welly K. Hopkins, a state Senate candidate, was so impressed by Lyndon's speech that he quickly hired him to manage his campaign in Blanco and Hays counties, "and he did a magnificent job."

Johnson next caught the eye of Congressman Richard Kleberg, a multimillionaire rancher who owned a portion of the famous King Ranch. Elected to Congress from Texas's Fourteenth District in 1931, Kleberg needed a secretary—then the top position on a congressional staff—to run his Washington office. On the advice of his campaign manager, he offered the position to Johnson, who readily accepted.

Before long Johnson realized that Kleberg, despite his honesty and kind nature, was mostly a playboy who had no interest in the day-to-day service of his constituents. "Mr. Kleberg doesn't spend an hour a day there and then only signing letters," Lyndon complained in a letter to his mother. Johnson often worked twelve hours a day, seven days a week, fighting to keep his head above the flood of letters that poured into Kleberg's office. "In a very real sense," said staff member Luther Jones, "[Johnson] was the congressman." He drove the staff—who knew him not as Lyndon but as "Chief"—relentlessly to answer each letter promptly and to give maximum effort to each constituent request. "He took each case personally," remembered Gene Latimer, a Kleberg staff member and former Johnson debating student. "He wouldn't take no." Said another staff member of Johnson: "It's fantastic how absorbed he was in that job . . . even to the extent of writing personal letters to Dick Kleberg's mother."

Mastery of Kleberg's office was challenging, but not enough. Johnson soon set his sights on the association of congressional secretaries known as the "Little Congress." Members fancied themselves a microcosm of the House of Representatives, conducting debates on issues under rules of the House. But the group was stagnant. It was, recalled Kleberg staff member Russell Morton Brown, "sort of dull, and the membership had fallen." After attending only one meeting, Johnson decided to take it over. By tradition, the group chose its "speaker" by seniority. But Johnson reasoned that so many new secretaries had recently arrived on Capitol Hill that their votes alone could override the seniority system. Working only by telephone, Johnson secretly wooed the new secretaries. When he learned that everyone on the House legislative payroll—not just the secretaries—could apply for membership, he urged staffers to join and vote for him.

On the night of the election, Johnson stampeded the shocked handful of old regulars. The crowd of new members was so large it overflowed into the hallway. Johnson filled the room and seized control of the Little Congress. As speaker, he turned the organization into a vital, influential group. He invited prominent congressmen and senators to speak. Although he raised the profile of the association, Johnson's real purpose was to polish his own image on Capitol Hill. "It gave him an excuse to go and see [Louisiana senator] Huey Long or [Texas senator] Tom Connally or a Texas congressman who was head of a committee he thought he might need for something, and invite them to speak,"

Latimer observed, "and once he got in to see somebody, the Chief, being the way he was, could make them remember him."

Overpowering, boisterous, audacious—even at age twenty-six—Lyndon was impossible to ignore. When he met Lady Bird Taylor in the fall of 1934, he asked her to marry him on the first date. Initially, Lady Bird found Johnson "quite a repulsive young man." But upon closer examination, she "realized he was handsome and charming and extremely bright." Meeting Johnson, she said, "was just like finding yourself in the middle of a whirlwind." Lady Bird was twenty-one. Born Claudia Alta Taylor in the northeastern Texas town of Karnack in 1912, she was a shy, pretty woman who captivated Johnson from the moment they met in Austin, where she attended the University of Texas. The daughter of a well-to-do merchant, Lady Bird was not ready to marry. "He came on very strong," she said, "and my instinct was to withdraw." But Johnson persisted with dozens of desperate phone calls and letters from Washington. Finally, still unsure of the wisdom of her decision, she capitulated. "I knew that nothing this exciting would happen to me again, probably," she explained. They married on November 17, 1934, in San Antonio, in a small ceremony attended only by friends.

Back in Washington, Johnson continued to hone his sycophantic powers, so well developed at San Marcos. He now fawned over elder men of influence like Sam Rayburn of Texas, then chairman of the House Interstate Commerce Committee. A bald, short and stocky man, Rayburn was going places on Capitol Hill, and Johnson went to great lengths to win his friendship. As former speaker of the Texas House, Rayburn had been a periodic ally of Johnson's father. "I'm Sam Johnson's boy," he reminded Rayburn on their first meeting. Although Rayburn's grim, forceful personality intimidated many on Capitol Hill—including some House members—he took a liking to Johnson, greatly impressed with his intelligence and energy. One House member, Lyle Boren of Oklahoma, remembered the budding relationship in an unflattering way: "Lyndon would jump when Sam said 'Frog.' " Lady Bird perhaps had the most influence on the relationship. Johnson began inviting Rayburn—a confirmed bachelor—to his home for dinner, where Lady Bird prepared his favorite foods and quickly won his heart. As Rayburn became a regular visitor to the Johnson home, their relationship was cemented.

By 1935, Johnson—who at twenty-six had almost singlehandedly reelected an absentee playboy congressman—was hungry for a new challenge. With Rayburn's assistance, he won appointment as Texas director of the National Youth Administration, a New Deal agency established to keep young people in school by giving them jobs. In August Johnson left Washington for Austin as the nation's youngest NYA director, confident he would soon return to the nation's capital. "When I come back to Washington," he told one friend, "I'm coming back as a congressman."

Johnson attacked his new job with ferocious intensity. By November Johnson announced that he would enroll 20,000 Texas youth in school or in work on NYA projects. Omitted from this public announcement was the fact that Johnson would include all young people—including Mexican-American and black youths—in the NYA's Texas programs. He went out of his way to meet with black leaders to inform them of his plans, and he conferred with presidents of the state's black colleges on their students' participation. One NYA associate said that Johnson never asked about a student's race. "If we had the money, we hired the kids. It was as simple as that."

Johnson's willingness to hire black youths impressed black leaders in Texas and in Washington. "As far as most agencies were concerned, the Negroes weren't even considered, but this guy in Texas was giving them and the Mexican-Americans a fair break," recalled Robert C. Weaver, who later became Johnson's Housing Secretary. "That made quite an impression on me." The bursar of one black college could not have paid his faculty without help from Johnson. "He'd send us our quota of money," the bursar said. "Then, off the record, he'd say, 'I've got a little extra change here. Can you find a place for it?' We could always find a place."

Johnson's willingness to help blacks and Mexican-Americans, albeit surreptitiously, was not lost on the black leaders whose political help he might someday need. "It sorta sold us on him before he ran for elective office," the college bursar said. However, Johnson resisted directives from Washington to hire blacks for his NYA office staff, though he did establish a separate black advisory council.

Johnson's two-year tenure as Texas NYA director was an unqualified success. He was so effective that the national NYA director, Aubrey Williams, sent directors from other states to Texas to learn from Johnson. "He fought for those kids to get them all he could," Williams remembered, "he even fought me to get things and money for them."

Texas Congressman James P. Buchanan's death in February 1937 was the political opening Johnson needed and marked the end of his NYA service. With $10,000 borrowed from Lady Bird's father, he plunged into the race with his usual vigor and determination. Campaigning tirelessly, he stressed his support for President Roosevelt's scheme to overcome opposition to New Deal programs by expanding the Supreme Court. At campaign rallies he desperately tried to connect with voters, even if it meant stretching the truth about his upbringing:

> Don't you remember what cotton was selling at when Mr. Roosevelt went into office? Don't you remember when it was selling at a nickel? Don't you remember when it was cheaper to shoot your cattle than to feed them? Don't you remember when you couldn't get a loan, and the banks were going to take your land away? I'm a farmer like you. I was raised up on a farm. I know what it's like to be afraid that they're going to take your land away. And that's why I'm for Mr. Roosevelt.

Johnson was the youngest of eight candidates in the race, but his unabashed support for the popular president seemed to be the most sincere. He was also willing to work harder than his opponents. Recalled Johnson's friend and aide Sherman Birdwell:

> He was energetic, had long legs, he'd cover lots of territory. He went all over every town, every community, and every hamlet shaking hands, "I'm Lyndon Johnson. I want to be your congressman." He'd look them in the eye. He liked to press the flesh . . . He'd be going down the road, and he'd see a farmer over there plowing—several rows over, it wasn't just right at the fence. He'd stop the car and get out and go over there and stop the guy plowing with the team, you know, and say, "I'm Lyndon Johnson. I want your help."

At first Johnson had not wanted to attack his opponents, but when his advisors argued that he could not separate himself from the crowded field without taking the offensive, he reluctantly replied, "Well, if it's absolutely necessary—let's mix up a little mud." Johnson's relentless campaigning—including his unfair suggestions that none of his opponents supported Roosevelt—succeeded. He was elected on April 10, 1937. He polled 3,000 more votes than his nearest opponent.

While Johnson received a sizable white vote, it is possible that black voters provided a large portion of his winning margin. Biographer Robert Caro, in *The Path to Power,* suggested that Johnson's campaign engaged in the traditional southern practice of making payments to black leaders to deliver votes to their candidate. But Johnson's courtship of the black vote appears to have gone beyond simple vote buying. On occasion, after campaign rallies, he reportedly shook hands with blacks—no insignificant violation of the day's social customs. Johnson also met privately with Austin's black leadership. "He made a statement that there was some things he wanted to do that he couldn't do," recalled one man who attended, "and if we'd stick by him, 'I think I can help you.' " Another person who attended the meeting said that Johnson "went on to tell that if he got to Congress he could do such things as recognizing the Negroes for their votes, we together could recognize their voting rights. He spoke of the hot lunch programs. He was very favorably disposed toward us, and he was askin' for our help."

When Johnson returned to Washington as Congressman Johnson, he took to heart the advice of his friend and mentor Sam Rayburn, now the House majority leader. To Johnson and another freshman colleague, Rayburn said: "I want you two to keep your mouths shut on the floor. You won't know what the score is for a long time. Also remember, don't get involved in broad issues, because you have to get reelected; and if you get into the big issues, the voters will think you aren't taking care of your district's problems." Johnson also followed the counsel of another political friend, former Texas senator Alvin Wirtz, who told him, "I'd rather be a live congressman than a dead hero."

While eschewing floor speeches and legislation on broad issues—Johnson's practice during his entire House career—he redoubled his courtship of those in power. Now he directed his obsequiousness not only at Rayburn and other House leaders but at Roosevelt. As a candidate for the House, Johnson had made certain the president heard about his strong support for New Deal programs. Shortly after the election, Johnson finally got his chance to meet Roosevelt, who had docked in Galveston after a fishing trip. When invited by Governor James Allred to help him greet the president, Johnson jumped at the opportunity. Lady Bird said that "Lyndon was there with his eyes out on stems, taking in every word and every gesture."

The next morning, the president invited the new congressman to accompany him on a train trip to College Station, Texas. Roosevelt was impressed. He suggested that Johnson might be "just the person" for an appointment to the House Naval Affairs Committee—which he later received—and he gave him the phone number of an aide, Tom Corcoran. "I've just met the most remarkable young man," Roosevelt told Corcoran. "Now, I like this boy, and you're going to help him with anything you can." "By the time Lyndon arrived in Washington," Corcoran later recalled, "the word had gone out: 'Be nice to this boy.' " In no time at all, Johnson had courted and wooed his way into another relationship—with the nation's most powerful man. "He could always get to the president," Corcoran said, "and this information got around. He found other congressmen were asking him for favors; his prestige on Capitol Hill was sky high."

Corcoran was one of Washington's most experienced and savvy operators. But even someone of his superior political skills was impressed by Johnson's mastery of the art of bootlicking:

> He was smiling and deferential, but, hell, lots of guys can be smiling and deferential. Lyndon had one of the most incredible capacities for dealing with older men. I never saw anything like it. He could follow someone's mind around, and get where it was going before the other fellow knew where it was going. I saw him talk to an older man, and the minute he changed subjects, Lyndon was there ahead of him, and saying what he wanted to hear—before he knew what he wanted to hear.

Johnson, said his future Senate colleague Russell Long of Louisiana, was "a born apple-polisher." In the House, his courting of the Democratic leaders was shameless. Sometimes he tried charming them by sitting on the floor at their feet, a prostrate supplicant who eagerly devoured the wisdom fed to him. Though this practice usually had its intended effect on the elders he courted, it did not endear him to some contemporaries, who derisively called Johnson "the professional son."

Johnson was also now part of Sam Rayburn's inner circle, known to other House members as the "Board of Education." In the late afternoons, after the House had adjourned for the day, these men gathered in Rayburn's Capitol hideaway office to imbibe and discuss the day's events. An invitation to join this elite group was among the most coveted in Washington. Johnson soon became a regular attendee, a reward for his relentless courtship of Rayburn. Before long, he began to talk of Rayburn as a father figure. Sometimes he even made a grand production of planting a kiss on Rayburn's bald head when they met in a hallway.

Another authority figure who found a willing supplicant in Johnson was Congressman Carl Vinson of Georgia, the autocratic chairman of the Naval Affairs Committee. As junior committee members, Johnson and colleague Warren Magnuson of Washington curried "Admiral" Vinson's favor with a passion. Vinson, who left the House late each afternoon to tend to his invalid wife, returned to work each morning thirsty for news of House activities in his absence. Johnson and Magnuson were all too ready with a vivid report of the previous day's events, including, Magnuson said, "dirty jokes and the details of amorous escapades, which [Vinson] enjoyed with real vicarious pleasure."

Although Johnson assiduously courted House leaders, there is little doubt that Franklin Roosevelt was the prime object of his attention and loyalty. When Roosevelt wanted Vinson to quash a potentially damaging investigation of a friend—an influential columnist who supported the president's military and foreign policies—he called on Johnson. Johnson sided with Roosevelt, and talk of the investigation died. When Roosevelt needed money to boost the campaigns of his House allies, he leaned on an eager and effective Johnson for important fund-raising work. When the president craved information about the Texas delegation, Johnson was his detective. And when the work was dirty—even when it called for confrontation with Rayburn—Johnson was always at his president's service.

In 1939, Roosevelt forced Johnson into a painful fight with Rayburn over Vice President John Nance Garner. Roosevelt wanted to dump Garner for a more compatible running mate in 1940, but Garner had persuaded Rayburn to ask the Texas delegation to issue a resolution supporting him. On orders from Roosevelt, Johnson refused to sign. In a dramatic showdown before the Texas delegation, Rayburn said sternly, "I'm looking you right in the eye." Unfazed, Johnson shot back: "And I'm looking you right back in the eye."

Johnson's fealty to Roosevelt was equaled by his ambition for greater power and higher office. After all, to Johnson the House was only a stepping stone to the U.S. Senate—a goal more likely realized with Roosevelt's backing. Johnson knew that the president's enormous political influence and his long coattails were far more valuable than any alliance with Rayburn, even in Texas.

Johnson's opportunity to draw on his goodwill account with Roosevelt came in June 1941 in a special election to fill the unexpired term of Senator Morris Sheppard, who had died in April. With Roosevelt's implied endorsement, Johnson announced his candidacy from the steps of the White House. He was one of twenty-nine candidates who sought the seat, but his toughest opponent was the popular governor of Texas, Pappy O'Daniel. A flour salesman from Kansas, O'Daniel had a flamboyant style of selling—with a hillbilly band and a blatant religious appeal—that had won him hundreds of thousands of adoring customers and fans. As he had done during his first House race, Johnson strapped himself to Roosevelt's program. His campaign slogan was concise: "Roosevelt and unity." He supported parity for farmers, old-age pensions and federal controls on oil production—his only significant departure from the Roosevelt agenda. As for the brewing world war, he announced to wild cheers, "If the day ever comes when my vote must be cast to send your boy to the trenches, that day Lyndon Johnson will leave his Senate seat and go with him."*

The election ended in disappointment for Johnson—the only election loss of his career. With a 5,000-vote lead the day after the election, Johnson was eager to declare victory. He urged his supporters in several rural counties to release their vote totals, but he did not anticipate that O'Daniel's supporters would try to steal the election from him. Suddenly, boxes from east Texas began pouring in—with lopsided totals for O'Daniel. O'Daniel beat Johnson by a scant 1,300 votes out of 575,000 cast. The experience taught Johnson a lesson he would remember well during his next Senate race. When Johnson returned to Washington, Roosevelt lectured him over the loss. "Lyndon, apparently you Texans haven't learned one of the first things we learned up in New York State, and that is that when the election is over, you have to sit on the ballot boxes." The election contained another important lesson for Johnson: absolute loyalty to the New Deal was not the best route to political success in Texas.

Johnson could have responded to defeat by immersing himself in the affairs of the House and striving to build a record of legislative achievement. Instead he was, as described by reporters Rowland Evans and Robert Novak, "a shadowy, unmemorable figure in the House itself, known well only to his fellow Texans, to members of the Naval Affairs Committee, and to a few others." Meanwhile, to escape the debt that landed on him when his father died in 1937, he dedicated himself to

---

*When the United States declared war against Japan, Johnson artfully dodged his pledge. He spent most of the war evading combat and the rest of his career misleading voters about his very minor, and largely ignoble, war record.

building a personal fortune. In 1943, using Lady Bird as a front, Johnson bought an Austin radio station for $17,500. His behind-the-scenes influence soon turned the fledgling business into a highly profitable enterprise. Within five years, Johnson bragged to friends that his family's net worth was one million dollars. The financial backing to foster his political career was now secure as well. With Johnson's help, his friends George and Herman Brown won a government contract to build a dam in his district. The Browns in turn provided him with campaign money—a lot of it—and became his ambassadors to the important and influential Texas oil industry.

Although the death of Franklin Roosevelt in 1945 freed Johnson from his vows of loyalty to the New Deal, it also meant the end of a powerful White House alliance. Johnson knew Harry Truman slightly, but now his concerted attempts to court Truman bore no fruit. Even Truman's intimate friendship with Rayburn provided little entree to an Oval Office that Johnson had once found so accessible. The reason for Truman's coolness was simple, according to Congressman Richard Bolling, a fellow "Board of Education" member. Truman had witnessed Johnson's fawning behavior toward Rayburn and "knew exactly what Lyndon was doing. And so it didn't work." Truman's daughter, Margaret, confirmed Bolling's conclusion. She explained that because her father had observed Johnson's behavior around Rayburn, "he never quite trusted him." Once a regular and welcomed caller to the White House, Johnson visited Truman only once during all of 1945.

The absence of a presidential friendship showed in Johnson's voting record. He drifted toward the right, opposing most of Truman's ambitious Fair Deal programs. Johnson even seemed to suggest, in one interview, that he had never been a New Deal supporter. "I think the term 'New Dealer' is a misnomer," he told an Associated Press reporter. "I believe in free enterprise, and I don't believe in the government doing anything that the people can do privately. Whenever it's possible, government should get out of business." Only someone ignorant of Johnson's record of support for Roosevelt would have believed him. On at least one issue, however, he did have a point.

He had never supported one piece of civil rights legislation. While his actions as a teacher, congressional aide, and NYA director had shown compassion for minorities, his voting record in Congress was "unblemished" by even one vote in favor of civil rights. He had voted against the antilynching bill in 1937 and again in 1940. In 1942, 1943, and 1945, he had opposed legislation to abolish the poll tax. In 1946 he had opposed an amendment to deny funds under the school lunch act to any state or school that discriminated on the basis of race. The same year, he voted to adjourn the House rather than consider legislation concerning a Fair Employment Practices Commission.

In his congressional campaigns, he had never played on racial fears to win votes. He had paid perfunctory lip service to segregation, but had not made the issue a central theme. And unlike some southern members of the Congress, he made no speeches to the House about the dangers that civil rights and racial integration posed to the Republic— a practice then widely known as "talking Nigra." Incredibly, Johnson never once discussed the issue of civil rights on the House floor during his twelve years as a congressman. "Except for his nay votes," journalist Leonard Baker said, "the issue might not have existed for him."

To staff member and longtime friend John Connally, Johnson was "far more liberal than he voted. But he recognized that to be an effective politician you have to survive." He was more than effective. He was, in those years, the perfect politician for his district. He worked hard to bring home all the dams and public works projects he could find, while assiduously avoiding any discussion of civil rights. Politically, the strategy was sound. But for Johnson's more liberal associates and friends— chiefly his longtime friend from Alabama, Virginia Durr—his silence was not enough. She wanted action and would sometimes "bitterly" reproach him about his opposition to civil rights. Johnson always quieted her anger with a reassuring hug and the admonition, "You're dead right! I'm all for you, but we ain't got the votes. Let's wait until we get the votes."

As Johnson prepared to run again for the Senate in 1948, he drew on the lesson of one of his heroes, Texas congressman Maury Maverick, who had lost his House seat in 1938 after his support for liberal causes ran afoul of his conservative constituents. When Jim Rowe urged Johnson to take "some position which I thought was more liberal," Johnson reminded him of Maverick. "I can only go so far in Texas," Johnson told Rowe. "Maury forgot that and he is not here." And Johnson added, "There's nothing more useless than a dead liberal."

But beneath Johnson's abundant caution—according to many friends and observers—was a real and growing conviction that short of enacting civil rights laws, government should indeed act to improve the economic and living conditions of blacks and other minorities. "These feelings were always in him," according to John Connally, "and yet he picked his times and his places to voice them."

As he demonstrated on several occasions, when he had the chance to prove his sympathies for minorities in private—and sometimes in public—he rarely failed to act. Shortly after his election in 1937, Johnson not only supported legislation providing low-rent housing to the poor, he also lobbied Austin's city government to become the first city in the nation to join the program. "Now, look," he told local leaders, "I want us to be first in the United States if you're willing to do this, and you've got to be willing to stand up for the Negroes and Mexicans."

By the end of the year, the first three program awards went to New York, New Orleans, and Austin. When the city became the first in the nation to complete and lease housing units—albeit segregated—under the 1937 Housing Act, Johnson proudly posed with the Mexican-American families who would occupy the homes. "This country won't have to worry about 'isms' when it gives its people a decent, clean place to live and a job," Johnson declared. "They'll believe in the government—they'll be willing to fight for it." Sam Rayburn's aide, D. B. Hardeman, recalled that Johnson often boasted about the project "in places where it couldn't have done him the slightest good, only the opposite." John Connally agreed that the "political gain was nearly zero. Few urban blacks and Mexicans ever registered to vote. Many could not pay the poll tax."

Shortly after his election to Congress in 1937, Johnson had called on President Roosevelt to complain that minorities in his congressional district were not receiving benefits from the Agricultural Adjustment Administration. Roosevelt's first reaction to Johnson's complaint was "Now, this is a smart politician." But then it hit Roosevelt—Texas still held an all-white primary election! Roosevelt, according to an aide, realized that "contrary to the idea of adding votes or aiding the political career of Congressman Johnson, this might even backfire on him."

Although those who attended his campaign rallies during his 1948 Senate race sometimes heard diatribes against the passage of Harry Truman's civil rights program, Johnson was sending different signals to potential supporters in private conversations. Galveston banker Walter Hall, an outspoken liberal, recalled Johnson's comforting promises that, campaign rhetoric to the contrary, he was actually a liberal on the major issues of the day:

I've always felt he was telling me the truth. I think he had a burning compassion for unfortunate people, irrespective of their color. I think that he wanted to do something about it. He was confronted with the problem of how he could go about that. He dealt with this very frankly. How could he go about that, coming from a state that as yet had shown no signs of being as liberal or progressive as he would like to see it? . . . He convinced me, though, that if he ever got in a position of real power to where his own political life would not be sacrificed on the altar of liberal legislation, he would act. I am too pragmatic to expect *any* politician to sacrifice himself—I've known too many of them. After all, you can't do anything unless you are in office. I was convinced that once that man got in real power, that he would bring into reality legislation that would deal with the problems that I felt were so basic to the welfare of this nation.

Publicly, however, Johnson pandered to the racist sentiments of white Texas voters. He attacked Truman's civil rights program and suggested that his opponents might be soft on the issue. But voters would not elect Johnson on his opposition to civil rights alone. His runoff opponent, Coke Stevenson, was also a staunch opponent of civil rights. There was almost no difference in their positions on the issue.

After election day, finding himself less than 400 votes behind Stevenson in the official election tally, Johnson realized that no issue—no matter how potent—could now save his political career. For months he had worked tirelessly, pushing mind and body to the limits of its endurance, in pursuit of the Democratic senatorial nomination. And now his dream, denied him once before by a painfully narrow result, had again been snatched from his grasp by an almost-infinitesimal margin.

Stealing the election seemed the only viable option. Johnson's supporters in Duval and Jim Wells counties manufactured the votes of 202 citizens who had not voted on election day. The amended returns, combined with vote "corrections" in other counties, gave Johnson an 87-vote victory. Despite a vigorous legal battle waged by Stevenson, Johnson prevailed, largely by keeping the list of the 202 voters—who had "signed in" alphabetically, in the same handwriting, with identical ink—out of court. He "won" the election by the narrowest and most tainted of margins.

Johnson's arrival in the Senate in early 1949 was overshadowed by the advent of a number of extraordinary new senators, all possessing more star power than he. Hubert Humphrey, the Minneapolis mayor, had rocked the Democratic National Convention with his civil rights platform plank and then defeated his state's incumbent Republican senator. The renowned liberal economics professor from the University of Chicago, Paul Douglas, would be there, too, as would be Russell Long, the thirty-year-old son of the controversial late Louisiana governor and senator, Huey P. Long. The millionaire oilman and governor of Oklahoma, Robert Kerr, and Truman's former agriculture secretary, Clinton Anderson, had also won their races, as did Estes Kefauver, a veteran House member from Tennessee. For all his experience, strong personality, and powerful intellect, Johnson went largely unheralded by the national news media. What headlines he garnered focused on allegations that he had stolen his election.

Washington and Texas now knew him—derisively—by a new name: Landslide Lyndon.

CHAPTER FOUR

The World's Most Deliberative Body

DESPITE TEMPTING OFFERS of "almost incredible sums of [campaign] money" if he would lead a third-party ticket, Russell really had little choice but to spurn all entreaties from the States' Rights party. Russell understood that a white supremacist rebellion would probably not achieve its goal of sending the election into the House of Representatives, where southerners held the balance of power. With much of the South already prepared to abandon Truman, and New York seemingly lost as well, Russell wanted no share of the blame for the anticipated Democratic debacle, especially if Truman's sinking ship pulled congressional Democrats down with him.

Even if prospects for a southern challenge had been more promising, Russell harbored no desire to weaken his party by contributing to an embarrassing electoral failure. He was a Democrat and proud of it. He could not simply walk away and relinquish his party to Harry Truman and the pro–civil rights liberals. As he later explained, he did not "propose to be driven from the house of my fathers merely because a group of Johnny-come-latelys had taken over its administration temporarily." While he would not actively support Truman's candidacy—although unopposed, he weakly explained that he was running his own reelection campaign—Russell maintained that bolting the Democratic fold was unwise. He cherished his lifelong association with the party and believed that he could, and should, try to effect change as an insider, not as a mutineer.

But more important motives kept Russell and other southern members of Congress within the Democratic ranks. As a senior member of the newly created Senate Armed Services Committee, Russell would invite retribution from Democratic leaders if he bolted the party to seek the presidency or support the States' Rights nominee. Other southerners possessed even more power by virtue of their seniority among House and Senate Democrats. Like Russell, few of them wanted to risk their positions by supporting a foolhardy presidential challenge. Patronage— the coveted privilege to recommend friends, associates, and supporters to federal positions in one's state—was also at stake. If he won, Truman would almost certainly remember with disdain, and possibly hostility, those senators and congressmen who abandoned the party when he needed them most.

Russell would not run. It was a wise decision for him and a fortuitous result for the States' Rights party—or, as the press eventually dubbed it, the Dixiecrats. It is clear that Russell's heart would never have been fully committed to the endeavor. The Dixiecrats needed a fiery leader. Russell—the cautious and courtly creature of the Senate— would have been poorly suited for the role of insurgent.

Ideally cast for the role was South Carolina governor Strom Thurmond. An astute, ambitious, and energetic politician, Thurmond was a physical fitness fanatic who professed to believe fervently in racial segregation. He chose Mississippi governor Fielding Wright as his running mate. Then he flung his rhetorical gauntlet before Truman. In Birmingham, he told cheering delegates that "there's not enough troops in the army to force the southern people to break down segregation and admit the Negro race into our theaters, into our swimming pools, into our homes, and into our churches." Asked why he led a rebellion against Harry Truman when Franklin Roosevelt had also proposed civil rights measures, Thurmond replied, "But Truman really means it." As Thurmond left Birmingham to prepare for battle with the trio of Truman, Republican candidate Thomas Dewey, and Progressive party candidate Henry Wallace, some southern opinion leaders scoffed at his campaign. Most southern leaders ignored him. To one editor in Richmond, the Dixiecrat convention was a demonstration of "bogus genuflections . . . at the shrine of Robert E. Lee." Another paper, in Raleigh, said Thurmond's campaign would result in "the destruction of the Democratic Party and the election of Dewey." Ralph McGill, the moderate editor of the *Atlanta Constitution*, attacked the Birmingham gathering as "the same sort of leadership that in 1860 pushed a South, reluctant to indulge in the civil war, into conflict with an unreasoning denial of history and reality."

In Washington, Truman summoned Congress back into the promised special session. He challenged Republicans to pass several of the bills they had endorsed in their platform. One of Truman's eight proposals was to abolish the poll tax as a voting requirement for federal elections. The same day, Truman announced that he had signed executive orders to end discrimination in the armed services and to create a fair employment commission for federal civil service. As he expected, the session produced almost nothing of consequence. Republican leaders never intended to act on his legislative agenda. The southerners, abetted by intransigent Republicans, killed the anti–poll tax bill with a filibuster. When the session ended, Congress had passed only minor housing legislation and approved money to build the United Nations building. Feigning disappointment, Truman knew that the unwitting Republicans had played into his hands. By their inaction, they exposed the party's hollow rhetoric about tackling civil rights, education, inflation, and social security. Truman attacked them relentlessly and with relish.

Although Russell carefully avoided any association with Truman's campaign, Johnson and Humphrey—both former critics of the beleaguered president—eagerly bounded aboard his bandwagon after the convention. While his friends worked on stealing the Senate election in Texas, Johnson boarded Truman's campaign train as it pulled into San Antonio on September 26. Those on board were startled by the sight of Johnson, haggard and spent after months of furious campaigning. Reporter Jonathan Daniels recalled that Johnson "came aboard, looking like the damnedest tramp I ever saw in my life. He couldn't have shaved in at least two days, and he looked sick as hell." Having assiduously resisted a relationship with Johnson, Truman now saw him as a far more dependable ally than the archconservative Coke Stevenson. Johnson proudly stood beside Truman at stop after stop that day, while the president told audiences, "My advice to you is to go to the polls on Election Day and send Lyndon Johnson to the Senate." Truman made no mention of Johnson's vehement attacks on the administration's civil rights program or his tepid support for the president's other legislative proposals.

Several weeks later, when Truman's campaign train arrived in Duluth, Minnesota, Humphrey, the Democratic Senate nominee, was waiting. Like Johnson, Humphrey eagerly put aside his differences with the president. As the two men rode an open car through downtown, a massive crowd of 60,000—almost half the city's population—greeted them. Later, at a rally in St. Paul, Truman delivered a stem-winding speech, among the best of his campaign. Before an enthusiastic crowd of 21,000, Truman summoned "all liberals and progressives to stand up and be counted for democracy in this great battle."

Thurmond, meanwhile, struggled to draw just enough electoral votes to throw the election into the House of Representatives. His strategy—to supplant Truman's name on the Democratic ticket in southern states—produced only mixed results. He failed in North Carolina, Texas, and Georgia. In four other states, his strategy worked: Alabama, Louisiana, Mississippi, and South Carolina chose presidential electors pledged to the Dixiecrats. Those states also bumped Truman and placed Thurmond's name at the head of the Democratic party ticket. Voters in Alabama had no opportunity to vote for Truman at all; state election officials banished his name from the ballot.

On election day, the southern revolt that most believed would seal Truman's defeat inflicted only minor damage. Truman overcame Thurmond's southern challenge and scored a stunning historic upset. Of fifty respected political writers polled by *Newsweek* in early October, not one had predicted Truman's victory. Through it all, Truman displayed remarkable confidence. When given the results of the magazine survey, he did not flinch. "I know every one of these fifty fellows," Truman told an aide. "There isn't one of them has enough sense to pound sand in a rat hole."

Truman carried 28 states. He won 303 electoral votes and beat Dewey by 2.1 million popular votes. Dewey carried just 16 states and won only 189 electoral votes. Thurmond and Wallace each polled more than a million votes. Wallace carried not one state. Thurmond won a mere 39 electoral votes and claimed only Alabama, Louisiana, Mississippi, and South Carolina—all states that had denied Truman his rightful spot on the ballot as the Democratic standard bearer. In southern states where Truman appeared on the ballot, he fared much better. He carried Arkansas by an overwhelming margin, defeating Thurmond by more than 100,000 votes. In Florida he beat Thurmond by almost 200,000 votes and Dewey by 90,000. He carried Georgia, North Carolina, Tennessee, Texas, and Virginia by large margins. The Dixiecrat challenge had hurt, but not much. Had Thurmond and Wallace not run, Truman's astonishing victory would probably have been a landslide, worth an additional 85 electoral votes.

Thurmond's unsuccessful campaign suggested to Herman Talmadge, Russell's future Senate colleague from Georgia, that despite the Democratic party's strong stand on civil rights, most southerners would remain loyal to the party of their forefathers. Furthermore, Talmadge realized that Democrats could be elected president without support from a solid South. To Talmadge, "the lesson seemed to be clear—the South could not elect an unpopular Democrat . . . or defeat a popular one." National Democrats, Talmadge concluded, now "thought they could ignore the South altogether."*

In the end, Truman embarrassed those who believed that his reliance on the Democratic party machinery and his dogged adherence to a progressive agenda—including civil rights—would seal his defeat. Far from alienating voters, Truman's feisty attacks on Republicans rejuvenated and united large groups of farmers, blue collar workers, and big-city residents—a voting bloc presumed dormant since Franklin Roosevelt's death. "The gutsy little man from Missouri," historian James MacGregor Burns observed, "had ridden these forces, even guided them, rather than being overwhelmed by them."

Black voters, energized by the president's seemingly genuine concern for them, turned out in record numbers to cast their precious ballots for Truman. The president's support for civil rights, said Senator Howard McGrath, the Democratic party chairman, "lost us three Southern states, but it won us Ohio, Illinois, would have carried New York for us if it had not been for Henry Wallace, and it was a great factor in carrying California." As one historian observed, Truman's decisive popular-vote victory—in the face of vigorous challenges from the left and right—proved that the "nation's center of political gravity had shifted several degrees to the left."

The congressional election results provided further encouragement. Truman's fiery attacks on the "Do Nothing" Republican Congress— and his brilliant special-session gambit that proved his point—helped Democratic candidates snatch control of both houses from Republican hands. These Democratic victors represented potential new votes for the president's programs. Joining the new Democratic majority would be Humphrey, who decisively defeated Republican incumbent Joseph Ball to become Minnesota's first Democratic senator, and Lyndon Johnson, the victor over Republican nominee Jack Porter. These men would join the renowned Class of 1948, which also included Clinton Anderson of

*Talmadge's analysis was indeed astute. The Democratic party's advocacy of civil rights would eventually drive the South from the Democratic fold—but not, ironically, until 1968, when Hubert Humphrey was the party's presidential nominee.

New Mexico, Paul Douglas of Illinois, Estes Kefauver of Tennessee, Robert Kerr of Oklahoma, and Russell Long of Louisiana. It was one of the most extraordinary and talented groups of new senators ever simultaneously elected to the Senate. Among them were leaders who would dominate the Senate, and Washington, for the next twenty years.

As Russell prepared to leave Winder for the first session of the Eighty-first Congress in 1949, questions about how this new class of senators might alter the Senate's balance of power undoubtedly tempered his satisfaction over the Democratic victory. His party had regained control, but would new members like Anderson, Douglas, Humphrey, and Kefauver make it easier to pass Truman's civil rights program? Probably not. But Russell at least understood that his effort to stop civil rights had not become any easier. Further complicating his life was the leadership void left when Alben Barkley of Kentucky, the Senate Democratic leader who would have been the new majority leader, instead became Truman's vice president. As head of the important southern bloc, Russell would play a prominent role in choosing a new majority leader. But whoever led his party in the Senate, Russell knew Truman's election meant that the calls for civil rights would only intensify. He was ready, as never before, to mount a vigorous defense of the South and its "way of life."

Russell began the Eighty-first Congress with a radical proposal to solve the civil rights problem. On January 27, 1949, he introduced a bill designed to move blacks to states with the largest percentage of white citizens. "It would be manifestly unfair and un-American for the rest of the country," Russell said, "to compel the white people of the South by Federal fiat to associate in the most intimate relations of life, and perhaps eventually absorb, a much higher proportion of Negroes than they themselves will have an opportunity to accept and absorb." Therefore, Russell proposed a federal commission to "encourage and assist" blacks "to relocate throughout the nation in such a way as to accomplish an equitable distribution of the largest racial groups comprising our population." Russell's bill would have empowered the commission to loan those who moved up to $10,000.

In Russell's view, white racism was not a problem for the South. Rather, blacks were burdens on southern states and ought to be spread equally among the forty-eight states. Though he knew the Senate would not seriously consider his proposal, he hoped to prove that many northerners were not only racists but hypocrites as well. Almost no one took the plan seriously, but Russell's proposal was significant in one respect. It was one of the few times in his almost two decades as southern leader that he would employ an offensive weapon—something other than the defensive filibuster—to fight civil rights.

Article I, Section 3 of the Constitution states that "each Senator shall have one vote." The Senate, Daniel Webster once declared, is a body "of equals, of men of individual honor and personal character, and of absolute independence." In a classic, civics-text Senate, Webster was correct. Each member was equal in his vote, his right to be heard on the Senate floor, and his ability to introduce legislation.

Yet the textbook explanation of the Senate's culture and procedures was often naive and insufficiently simple. In truth, the Senate more closely resembled what ultimately became of George Orwell's fictional *Animal Farm,* where "all animals are equal, but some animals are more equal than others." Lyndon Johnson would later observe that "minnows [and] whales populated the Senate." Regardless of the analogy, the Senate was, in truth, a body of *distinct* equals who possessed differing amounts of talent, power, and influence.

Among them stood two men who were decidedly *unequal*—Richard Russell and Robert Taft. As unquestioned chieftains of the Senate's two powerful factions, Russell and Taft were, quite simply, the most influential senators. While new floor leaders—Democrat Scott Lucas of Illinois and Republican Kenneth Wherry of Nebraska—headed the Democratic and Republican parties, the Senate's real power rested with an informal coalition of southern Democrats and senior Republicans.

The Republicans were led by their de facto commander, Taft of Ohio, the fiercely conservative, brilliant, and intrepid chairman of his party's policy committee. Although Wherry, a moderate, managed the day-to-day legislative mechanics for his party, Taft most often supplied the spiritual guidance for his Republican colleagues. Under his thinly veiled leadership, the Republicans almost always sided with southerners on questions involving civil rights. In turn, the southerners usually allied with Republicans to oppose President Truman's social and economic initiatives. This cooperation occurred despite the absence of a formal compact between the two groups. As Lyndon Johnson once observed, Russell and Taft simply ran the Senate "with a wink and a nod."

Within this informal but effective coalition, the southern bloc—held together by geography and the mighty glue of civil rights—was the more formidable force. Civil rights, explained Arkansas Senator J. William Fulbright, "was the critical and most sensitive issue during that period." Southerners "might differ widely on other issues," said Fulbright, but on civil rights "they felt the same." Through force of personality and by virtue of his status as southern leader, Russell was, in the words of *New York Times* reporter William S. White, "incomparably the most influential man on the inner life of the Senate." He "commanded" the "unquestioned allegiance" of the southern bloc, said freshman Clinton Anderson. "In terms of legislative achievement," observed Johnson's longtime aide George Reedy, it was "impossible to find a national leader of greater stature" than Russell. "With Russell's blessing, almost any measure could pass the Senate. Against his determined opposition, it was doomed." Among his colleagues, journalist David Leon Chandler later wrote, "Russell seemed to stand for something bigger than personal glory or temporary laws. He stood for the Senate itself."

Wise was the freshman who recognized and paid homage to Russell's supreme status, as Humphrey later recalled: "I used to wonder why [the press] never gave the rest of us [northern liberals] much of a break except to give us a rough time. But you were literally told by the press before you ever got into Congress that if you didn't behave, that the southerners would get you, so to speak; that the man that you had to pay your respects to was Dick Russell."

Other powerhouses rounded out the leadership of the southern bloc: the diminutive and provident Allen Ellender of Louisiana; the revered, stentorian-voiced Walter George of Georgia; the formidable and cantankerous former southern bloc leader, Tom Connally of Texas; and eighty-year-old Kenneth McKellar of Tennessee, the new president pro tempore.

In the Senate, the power and influence of these southerners flowed from several sources. They dominated the Senate's committee system. Well liked by most of their colleagues, their manner on and off the Senate floor was almost always friendly, dignified, and courtly. But most of all, their knowledge of the Senate's rules was superb; and their skill in using those rules to stall civil rights, by filibusters and other means, was matchless.

Idealistic liberals such as Douglas, Humphrey, and Kefauver arrived in the Senate full of hope and promise for the progressive agendas they had championed back home. Soon, however, they realized that the Senate was not unlike a riverboat poker game that northerners joined only after the southerners were dealt a full house. Of the Senate's fourteen standing committees, southerners or senators sympathetic to southern issues chaired ten. Douglas observed that "since the new northerners had to be given some committees, they were relegated to those of secondary importance. The two subcellar or ghetto committees were those for the District of Columbia and the Post Office and Civil Service. These were stuffed with liberals." But, as Douglas wryly noted, a southerner even chaired the Post Office Committee!

Even southerners usually found it impossible to bound onto a top-tier committee in their first years as a senator. But if they behaved and voted with Russell and his southern bloc, they usually received the plum committee assignment they wanted. Senate leaders rarely cultivated northern liberals in the same way. "In '49," Humphrey recalled, "you were either in or out. There was a little band of liberals over here, and they were looked down upon. . . . The civil rights issue we had brought to the forefront, and those of us that had been associated with it were anathema. We were looked on as wild men, as dangerous radicals. The wrong people had gotten into the club." It was indisputable: Nonsoutherners usually went to the best committees only after they proved that they were not radical liberals or that their commitment to civil rights was more rhetorical than spiritual.

The fact that liberals were usually treated kindly by the very southerners who withheld influence and access to power was all the more frustrating. Privately, in meetings of the powerful and mysterious Democratic Steering Committee—which dispensed committee assignments—the powerful southerners shunted liberals to committees where they could do the least harm. On the Senate floor, southerners summarily smothered or short-circuited their civil rights initiatives by clever parliamentary maneuvers. Only rarely were the southern leaders unkind to them in person. Like the southern gentlemen their mothers raised them to be, they almost always showed good manners and civility. After all, to these southerners, tying the liberals' hands behind their backs was just business, not a sign of personal animosity. They simply treated Senate liberals as they treated southern blacks. Depriving blacks of their basic civil rights did not prove hatred or animosity, they argued; they were merely fighting to protect the Constitution and their "southern way of life."

"On the surface, the southerners treated us with the formal courtesy that is the regional characteristic," Douglas remembered. "But there was always the ineradicable belief in the air that we and our ancestors had perpetrated the unpardonable wrong of freeing the slaves, winning the Civil War, and carrying Reconstruction." William S. White, whose 1956 book, *Citadel*, explored the customs and history of the Senate, regarded the southerners as "highly sophisticated" politicians who could gracefully wave away "mere political differences with an opponent, much as counsel or plaintiff and defendant often go out amicably to lunch together after hurling imprecations at each other through the morning session of court."

Yet for all their powerful committee positions, southern men did not rise to committee chairmanships on their courtly demeanor alone. Geography and good manners might have opened the committee doors to them, but once inside, seniority prevailed. In Congress, committees were almost always chaired by the member of the majority party with the longest service on the committee. A senator might be the most ignorant, least qualified member of his committee. But if his party controlled the Senate and he had more years of service on that committee than his colleagues, he became "Mr. Chairman."

Therefore survival, not southern heritage, was the real secret of southern success. And these southerners, from rural states where the Republican party was only marginally competitive, became the Senate's political porcupines—exceedingly formidable to any and all predators. Together they formed a citadel of continuity. Southern bloc members were rarely challenged and almost never defeated. Although the most dependable anti–civil rights southerners represented only about a fourth of the Senate's membership, their domination of the committee system was awesome and greatly out of proportion to their population. As Randall B. Ripley observed in his book *Power in the Senate*, southerners enhanced the inherent power of seniority "by their skilled and judicious *use* of seniority." Better than most, he wrote, the older southern hands like Russell "understood the dynamics of power and their own relation to changing circumstances in the Senate and the country at large." Faced with certain defeat, they compromised in order to preserve their influence. However, Ripley noted that "on matters in which their interests were deepest"—civil rights, for example—they almost always occupied the "most advantageous bargaining positions."

Greater than even seniority was the filibuster, the parliamentary device used to prevent a vote on a bill by prolonged debate. Derived from the Dutch word *freebooter,* meaning "plunderer" or "pirate," the word evolved into English as "filibuster." Nothing made Russell's southern troops more imposing on the Senate floor than their ability to pirate a debate, preventing any civil rights measure from coming to a vote. Though they used the tactic with skill, Russell's forces had not invented the filibuster; they merely adopted it from the Senate's liberals, who had made more frequent use of the weapon in pre–civil rights days.

For all of its negative connotations, the filibuster was actually a grand device steeped in Senate history and lore. The filibuster permitted the Senate to boast of its distinction as "world's most deliberative body." Legislation might be railroaded through the House, with its more restrictive rules of debate, but in the Senate cooler heads would ensure that most measures would not pass until properly and soberly considered. Until 1917, any senator with a strong will and a healthy bladder could wage a lonely battle against a bill he found offensive, unconstitutional, or dangerous to the nation. A crusading member, or group of members, could seize the floor and talk until exhausted. No Senate rule existed that could force them to relinquish the floor. Those senators from small states, with meager representation in the House, especially loved the filibuster. After all, the apprehensions of the smaller, rural colonies had led to the creation of the Senate—the Great Compromise—an institution in which all states had equal representation regardless of size or population.

For most of its 160 years, the Senate had functioned with no rule for *cloture,* the process of ending or limiting debate. In 1917, however, the Senate came under attack from President Woodrow Wilson after a filibuster killed a bill to arm America's merchant ships against the Germans. Enraged that a "little group of willful men" had "rendered the great government of the United States helpless and contemptible," Wilson shamed senators into enacting a cloture rule.

Since 1917, Senate Rule XXII had required a two-thirds vote of senators *present and voting* to impose cloture. But as one Senate historian noted, the rule "bore within itself the seeds of its own nullification." An accumulation of interpretations and precedents in the years following 1917—declaring that the Senate could end debate on measures but not on motions or procedural questions—had left the cloture rule largely impotent and meaningless. In other words, on the vital procedure that led to consideration of a bill or resolution, the motion to consider, unlimited debate continued to thrive.

Even if the Senate did jump that formidable hurdle and proceed to consideration of a measure, the cloture rule required sixty-four votes— provided that all ninety-six senators voted—to stop a filibuster. This in turn meant that the filibusterers needed only thirty-three votes to stop any measure from coming to a vote. And so Rule XXII, the impenetrable parliamentary fortress, protected Russell and his southern troops from the growing ranks of civil rights proponents.

This was the wall that President Harry Truman and the Senate's liberals proposed to weaken when the first session of the Eighty-first Congress convened in 1949. "Few recognized the prior need for a procedural change in Rule XXII," Paul Douglas wrote, "and it was hard to arouse the general public to a realization that the walls of Jericho could not be leveled by a mere blast of the senatorial trumpets."

A fifteen-year war over civil rights was about to begin.

Republican Senator Arthur Vandenberg of Michigan, the revered former Senate president pro tempore, had unwittingly sown the seeds for one of the most rancorous civil rights debates in the Senate's history. In August 1948, during the filibuster over Harry Truman's legislation to outlaw the poll tax, Vandenberg had ruled that a motion to consider the bill was not a "pending measure" as defined by the Senate's rules. The ruling was momentous. According to Senate Rule XXII, cloture could only be imposed on debates over a "measure." If a procedural motion —such as a motion to consider—was not deemed a measure, then a filibuster of that motion could not be forcibly ended. At the time, Vandenberg drew the obvious implication. "In the final analysis," he said, "the Senate has no effective cloture rule at all." As every member must have understood, the Senate could no longer ignore the issue.

Hopeful that the new Democratic Senate majority might provide the votes needed to reform Rule XXII, Truman demanded immediate action in his 1949 State of the Union address. "The civil rights proposals I made to the Eightieth Congress, I now repeat to the Eighty-First," Truman said. "They should be enacted in order that the federal government may assume the leadership and discharge the obligations placed upon it by the Constitution." House leaders, more liberal and therefore more receptive to civil rights, accepted Truman's challenge. Even before his speech, Speaker Sam Rayburn and Rules Committee Chairman Adolph Sabath pushed through reforms to prevent the Rules Committee—which set parameters for floor debate—from smothering legislation like civil rights with endless delays. From now on, if the Rules Committee held a bill hostage for more than three weeks, committee chairmen could take legislation passed by their committees directly to the House floor. Getting Truman's civil rights program onto the Senate floor would not be nearly as easy. As expected, Russell, his united southern forces behind him, was ready to fight. He declared that Truman's proposals "were conceived in politics and thrive on the misrepresentation and misunderstanding of the worst sort of propaganda."

Truman's problems began not with Russell but with his own Democratic Senate leadership—Majority Leader Lucas of Illinois and his whip, Francis Myers of Pennsylvania. As nominal leaders who supervised the Senate's routine business, neither man had enough influence to impose his will on the Senate. Nor had they displayed any intuitive understanding of the politics of civil rights at the 1948 convention. Lucas had angrily called Humphrey a "pip-squeak" at a platform committee meeting,* and Myers had opposed his civil rights plank until shortly before the vote.

Thus, leadership on the cloture question fell instead to Carl Hayden of Arizona, chairman of the Senate Rules and Administration Committee, and the Republican leader, Kenneth Wherry of Nebraska. Despite calls by Oregon Republican Wayne Morse and other liberals for cloture by a simple majority, Hayden and Wherry eventually proposed only a slight modification of Rule XXII. Cloture, they said, should be imposed on measures *and motions* by a vote of two-thirds of those present and voting.

On January 24, as the two men convened hearings on their proposal, the Senate's liberal faction fell strangely silent. After two days of testimony, not one Democrat had stepped forward to speak in favor of the Morse or Hayden-Wherry resolutions to liberalize cloture. The battle had begun. But the Senate's pro–civil rights liberals had apparently opted not to fight. Their absence from the Rules Committee hearings prompted an alarmed official of the National Association for the Advancement of Colored People (NAACP) to send an urgent telegram to the White House protesting the "strange apathy and silence of Democrats during hearings on amendment of Senate Rules." NAACP official Walter White complained to Truman that "not one Democrat has as

---

*That opposition to Humphrey's platform challenge played no small role in the election of Lucas, who probably could not have become majority leader without Russell's approval.

yet fought or even spoken out to end filibusters. We are perturbed."

While the liberals rested, Russell's southerners remained on full battle alert. Early on, Russell had convened the southern bloc to discuss how they would repel the liberals' attack on the filibuster rule. As twenty of his colleagues filed into his cluttered room in the Senate Office Building, Russell undoubtedly noticed the absence of two senators. Southern freshmen Lyndon Johnson and Estes Kefauver of Tennessee had spurned Russell's invitation to join the strategy session. Minutes after the meeting began, an Associated Press reporter encountered Johnson strolling down a hallway and asked why he was not at the meeting. Johnson refused to answer. He angrily scampered to his office, locked the door, and complained that the "goddam so-and-so" tried to embarrass him. Though no one had really expected the liberal Kefauver to attend, Russell could not have been pleased with Johnson's failure to meet with the southern caucus. One report of the episode described Russell as "visibly miffed" by Johnson's absence.

Of course, Johnson well understood the risks involved in his independence from the southern group. He would not leave Russell fretting for long.

The Hayden-Wherry proposal meant only a very minor change in the cloture rule. Filibusters could be ended on procedural motions, as well as measures. But to hear Russell talk, even the slightest liberalization of cloture would all but destroy the Senate as "the last citadel of free and full discussion where the rights of the [Senate] minority can be heard and fully protected." The woeful irony involved in fighting for the rights of a southern Senate "minority"—a term used often by the southern bloc—in order to preserve the oppression of the nation's black minority appears to have eluded Russell and other southerners.

In the parlance of southern conservatives, cloture was almost always known as a "gag rule," a device to destroy their right of free speech in Senate debate. Liberals, they charged, hoped to prevent a proper airing of the civil rights opposition. The argument was disingenuous. No responsible liberal had ever proposed using cloture to stifle debate or "gag" the southerners. Supporters of bills rarely, if ever, offered a cloture motion until weeks of debate had transpired. Even if the Senate invoked it, the rules gave each senator one additional hour to continue debating the issue. "I set my sights on the rules of debate," explained Clinton Anderson, who became the Senate's chief advocate of liberalized cloture, "not because I sought to inhibit free expression but because I wanted to weaken an instrument of obstruction."

After weeks of preliminary skirmishes, Truman advised Majority Leader Lucas to begin the battle over cloture. On February 28, with much of Truman's legislative agenda on hold awaiting the outcome of the cloture debate, Lucas moved to consider the Hayden-Wherry proposal. Russell left little doubt about his response. His southerners would filibuster the motion to consider the resolution, knowing that under the Senate rules as interpreted by Vandenberg, cloture did not apply to such a debate.

As he presented the committee resolution to the Senate, Lucas argued that the Hayden-Wherry proposal was a "very reasonable step" that posed no threat to the Senate's integrity. Quoting Alexander Hamilton, Lucas told the Senate, "The public business must in some way or other go forward." And he cited the late senator Henry Cabot Lodge, who had insisted, "If there is a conflict between debate and a time for voting, action is a higher duty than debating."

Russell's reply was simple and straightforward: "The [southern] Democrats are in favor of free speech; they are opposed to gag rulings."

But Wherry objected to Russell's characterization. A reasonable cloture rule, which simply applied to motions as well as measures, he said, was not a gag on debate. "I believe the senator from Georgia is hurting his own case when he says it is a gag rule when those of us who believe in cloture by a vote of two-thirds of the senators, after a thorough debate has been held for days on an issue, after an exhaustive and complete debate has been had, vote to adopt a rule." To Wherry, Lucas, and the Senate's liberals, the issue was simple. "The real question," Wherry said, "is not whether we believe in cloture by majority vote or by two-thirds vote; the real question is whether we want a rule at all."

Russell, however, saw the issue in broader, more historical terms. He declared that "the Senate of the United States is the last forum of free discussion on earth, the last citadel of individual rights, the last hope of the rights of the small states, the last refuge of oppressed minorities, and . . . there should be a right here to discuss matters before cloture or a gag rule can be applied."

On March 9, as Russell's southern forces continued to filibuster the Lucas motion, Lyndon Johnson rose to deliver his first formal remarks as a senator. It was a speech certain to please Russell and dispel any worries about the new senator's loyalties. The issue before the Senate, he observed in his hour-long address, was a choice "between the freedom to enact laws hastily and the freedom to speak." Should cloture apply to motions, Johnson warned, "the bridle will be upon the tongues of all minorities, and no mount is free, once the bit is in its mouth."

Some southerners, who vociferously denied that the issue was central to civil rights, concealed their opposition behind the disingenuous cloak of free debate. Johnson, however, acknowledged the obvious—that civil rights was a central motivation for his opposition to the cloture rule change. "When we strip away the trappings of rhetoric and theory and legend which surround the arguments here against the filibuster, we have left the simple fact that we are debating the so-called civil-rights legislation." But, as Johnson quickly added, he had great sympathy for the plight of minorities. "For example, I do not believe in the poll tax as a prerequisite for voting," he said, later adding, "I, like all other citizens, detest the shameful crime of lynching just as I detest the crime of murder in every form." But Johnson, like other southerners, stubbornly clung to the preposterous argument that "the Negro—as a minority group involved in this discussion of civil rights—has more to lose by the adoption of any resolution outlawing free debate in the Senate than he stands to gain by the enactment of the civil rights bills as they are now written."

Truman's civil rights proposals had no support from Johnson. The poll tax ban, the FEPC proposal, and antilynching legislation—in Johnson's eyes, they all were measures appropriately left to the states or, in the case of the FEPC, a dangerous intrusion into private business affairs. "We in the Senate should learn the facts of life," Johnson said. "We cannot legislate love. We can, and as a nation we do, work together." If Johnson did not remember or regret his next thought, he would—in years to come—forsake the sentiment that he so forcefully expressed: "I realize, Mr. President, that it is easy for a young man to say, 'We're going to roll up our sleeves and remake the world.' I know the temptation is great for young men to assume that speed and progress are one and the same thing; that if you move rapidly, you move forward. No nation, though, can long survive if its lawmakers legislate only from day to day."

Johnson's words struck a responsive chord with voters in Texas, who—along with Russell and the Senate's other southern barons—were the speech's intended audience. Constituents mailed him hundreds of letters, almost all in praise of his remarks. Not all of the response was positive. His liberal friend Walter Hall wrote that he was "sorry you think more of your right to speak without limit than you do another man's right to vote." Lulu White, executive secretary of Houston's NAACP branch, wired Johnson immediately after the speech: "The Negroes who sent you to Congress are ashamed to know that you have stood on the floor against them today. Do not forget that you went to Washington by a small majority vote and that was because [of] the Negro vote. There will be another election and we will be remembering what you had to say today."

Perhaps the most eloquent and stinging criticism of Johnson's position came before the speech from former Roosevelt advisor James Rowe, who had offered his assistance in writing Johnson's remarks but later reconsidered. "There is little I would not do for you, such as shooting Coke Stevenson, or bumping off Tom Connally, but this I can't do," wrote Rowe, who urged Johnson to take a broader view of civil rights. "The only way I can see of solving this problem, besides the passage of time which is helpful, is to have the younger leaders of the South, of which you are very much one, start to handle the problem." Rowe said if Johnson could help solve only 20 percent of the problem in the next twenty years "you will be one of the great men of American history."

After delivering his speech, Johnson responded to Rowe: "You and Humphrey may be right when you start on your thesis," Johnson wrote on March 15. "I think all men are created equal, I want all men to have equal opportunity. Yes, I even think your civil rights slogans are eloquent and moving. But when you and Humphrey—and others before you—reach the point of translating your humanitarian spirit into law you seem always to lose any sense of charity, faith in your fellow man, or reasonableness. The civil rights legislation brought to Congress is not benevolent; it is, if I may say so, almost sadistic." Johnson believed that liberals had no understanding of the ultimate consequences of the punitive legislation they pushed. "That may not register favorably with you, but at [the Democratic National Convention in] Philadelphia you saw two blind unreasoning minorities collide," he wrote. "Both of them, judging from what I know of their character, are cruel, ruthless, and vicious. Justice, to their way of thinking, carries a cat-o'-nine tails in one hand and salt in the other."

To Rowe and other old friends, Johnson's position must have seemed like a repudiation of the New Deal philosophy he had once so eagerly espoused. As biographer Merle Miller observed: "The young man who had thrown himself heart and soul behind his president, who had not wavered at the unpopularity of Roosevelt's court packing plan or his wartime wage and price guidelines, who had seen to it that black students were the equal recipients with white of NYA projects—that Lyndon was difficult to find in the man who stood on the floor of the Senate attacking Truman's civil rights program." But *that Lyndon*—the rabid New Dealer—had not existed for years. Johnson had begun to jettison his New Deal loyalties the moment they became political liabilities.

Nonetheless, his speech to the Senate was more a political statement—and a sign to Russell that he could trust him—than a heartfelt diatribe against civil rights. As Johnson admitted to Rowe, he had not wanted to side so publicly with Russell and the southerners. He was "fully aware that I would be indicted with 'guilt by association.' I did not relish such an indictment." But politically he had little choice. He had won—or stolen—his election by a mere eighty-seven votes. "He had to establish himself in Texas, which [was] on a very, very wild conservative swing at the moment," said longtime Johnson aide George Reedy. Walter Hall believed Johnson "felt that he would have to sacrifice the liberal . . . forces in order to better secure his own base of operations in the state."

To aide Walter Jenkins, Johnson expressed the philosophy "that any member [of Congress] had two responsibilities: one was his conscience and one was his electorate, and that he had to temper one with the other. If he didn't, he wouldn't come back." To Bobby Baker, the smart young page who would later become one of his most trusted aides, Johnson confessed:

> I got elected by just eighty-seven votes and I ran against a caveman. I cannot always vote with President Truman if I'm going to *stay* a senator. I am a Texan and I've got a southern constituency and so I'm going to be more conservative than you would like me to be or than President Truman would like me to be. President Truman's about as popular as measles in Texas, and you'll waste your time trying to talk to me when I know it would cut my own throat to help him.

Meanwhile, the southern filibuster over cloture raged on the Senate floor. With each day, the issue seemed to grow more bewildering and the positions of each side more entrenched. With liberals and southerners firmly in opposing camps, the balance of power now rested with moderate Republicans, many of whom were reluctant to embarrass Senator Vandenberg by negating his 1948 cloture ruling.

President Truman had greatly injured his own cause early in the debate when he clumsily observed that he would support a rule change that permitted cloture by a simple majority of a Senate quorum—as few as twenty-five out of forty-nine votes. Those comments signaled a dramatic shift in the president's position and all but shattered the liberals' hopes of winning. Their tenuous bid for moderate Republican votes collapsed. As Ohio Republican Robert Taft later observed, Truman's remarks "made the position of the southern senators still more unyielding because the adoption of the Hayden-Wherry resolution would have provided cloture to support a subsequent effort to change the rules to meet the president's demands for 50 percent cloture." Russell echoed Taft's assessment. "The president has now justified every statement that we have made, that all this campaign was but a step toward simple majority cloture. I saw in the beginning that they were opening a Pandora's box. It is now clearly opened."

On March 10, liberals presented their cloture petition to Vice President Alben Barkley, calling for an end to the filibuster on the motion to consider the Hayden-Wherry resolution. Predictably, Russell raised a point of order, arguing that cloture applied only to pending measures, not to motions. This was, after all, the ruling that Vandenberg had issued the previous year. But Barkley, loyal to his president, overruled Russell's point of order, noting that "a motion to proceed to the consideration of a bill is an absolutely indispensable process in the enactment of legislation." When Russell moved to overturn Barkley's ruling, the Senate—perhaps spooked by Truman's ill-timed call for simple majority cloture—sided with Russell. On March 11, senators voted 46-41 to overrule the vice president. Twenty-three Republicans joined with twenty-three southern and western Democrats to give Russell's southern bloc a crucial procedural win.

Russell's victory did not end the matter. The motion to proceed to consideration of the Hayden-Wherry rule remained the Senate's pending business. But now Russell clearly had the upper hand. The Senate had upheld his interpretation of the Senate's rules that cloture applied only to measures and not procedural motions. Best of all, he appeared to have many more than the thirty-three votes he needed to sustain a filibuster.

With so much in his favor, Russell saw no reason to yield. Majority Leader Scott Lucas admitted as much on March 17, when he told Russell and his Republican ally Senator William Knowland of California, "Gentlemen, as far as a change in the rules is concerned, you can write your own ticket." Fretting over the pileup of important legislation awaiting resolution of the cloture issue, Lucas simply washed his hands of the matter.

The sudden vacuum of liberal leadership extended all the way to the White House, where Truman—so eager to fight for his programs during the campaign—appeared unwilling to impose his will on Congress. "The administration doesn't know what it's going to do," Humphrey complained to a group of advisors who met in his office to discuss strategy. "Instead of coming out with a clear-cut statement, we sit around." With Lucas and the Democratic leadership all but absent from the battle, Russell seized the opportunity. He quickly struck a deal with the Republicans.

The product of that compromise was a new Hayden-Wherry-Russell resolution, which seemingly liberalized cloture: it applied cloture to motions *and* measures. In reality, however, it guaranteed that unlimited debate would be more secure than ever. The revised rule would increase the votes required to end debate from two-thirds of those *present and voting* to two-thirds of the *entire Senate*. This meant that no matter how many senators actually voted, no fewer than sixty-four votes would always be necessary to stop a filibuster. Furthermore, the compromise made it nearly impossible to liberalize cloture in the future. The new rule stipulated that cloture could not apply to future filibusters on motions to change any Senate rule.

Although Russell argued that his modified rule "tightens the rule of cloture," liberals recognized it for the Trojan horse that it was. "It seems to me that here we propose to operate in reverse, to go backward, to go downhill," Humphrey told the Senate. "By this proposal we shall not be making progress." Humphrey—who understood that passage of the rule meant the end of Truman's civil rights program during the Eighty-first Congress—scolded his colleagues. Some of them, he thought, regarded the Senate's rules as matters of personal privilege. "The rules of the Senate belong to the people," he said. "They do not belong to us. The Constitution is the mechanism by which the people of the United States can make their will felt in the processes of government. Sometimes I think we get so cozy, we become so secure when we get into our six-year terms, that we forget that there may be some people out in the country who are expecting things to be done."

Despite warnings from liberals that the rule would render cloture meaningless—and therefore kill Truman's civil rights agenda—the Senate overwhelmingly approved the new rule by a 63-23 vote. "The anti-filibuster people had won an ostensible battle only to lose a very real war," journalist William S. White observed. "Cloture was in practical fact at least as far off as ever, and the Senate in plain fact retained what amounts to unlimited debate."

Though Russell rightfully received credit for saving the filibuster, he was not the sole influence. The ineffectual party leadership of Lucas and Wherry left a vacuum that Russell had easily filled. Truman's inept and ill-timed call for cloture by simple majority further weakened Majority Leader Lucas. Moreover, Lucas and the liberals simply needed more votes from Republicans than were available. Vandenberg, the former president pro tempore, commanded great respect among his Republican colleagues. Although he told Republicans they should vote their conscience on the issue, few wanted to defy his earlier ruling. Finally, for the most conservative senators, civil rights was the only real motivation for opposing cloture's liberalization. But for other senators—from states whose mostly white populations had little or no interest in civil rights—loyalty to the Senate's grand tradition of free, unlimited debate was an equally powerful influence.

The defeat may not have surprised the liberals, but it certainly reinforced for them the difficulties and perils that awaited any group hoping to thwart Russell and his conservative Republican allies in the Senate. "The Senate was not like the Democratic convention," Paul Douglas later observed, seeming to imply that he and other liberals might have believed otherwise. "So we began to stress to Negro, civil-rights, labor, and religious groups the effect of Rule XXII."

For this small, idealistic band of Senate liberals, liberalization of cloture had become the holy grail of their civil rights movement. As they began to understand, change would not soon come from within the Senate. Russell's ranks were too large and committed to their cause. Instead, the liberals naively concluded that effective pressure for change would come only from the other side of the Senate's walls—from the nation. Thus, said Douglas, "a necessary education of the American people was begun."

Through their dejection, Douglas, Humphrey, and other liberals failed to understand that their fledgling movement for civil rights needed more than the weight and force of public opinion. In many ways, public opinion had already moved in their direction. The liberals needed more allies *in the Senate*. More importantly, they needed a strong, effective leader—someone who could unite and lead the Democratic moderates and liberals without driving Russell and his southerners into the arms of the Republicans.

Douglas and Humphrey did not know it at the time, but that leader—the answer to their dream of passing civil rights legislation—already walked among them.

CHAPTER FIVE

That Damn Fool

AS HE SAT IN THE SENATE GALLERY one day in early January 1949, looking down on the back-slapping camaraderie and friendly banter of the assembled senators, Hubert Humphrey felt lonely and ignored. The Eightieth Congress had assembled for its final meeting. For retiring and defeated members, it was their last official gathering. Down on the floor, many of the new senators, not yet sworn in, mingled easily with the veterans. Senator Lucas warmly introduced his new colleague from Illinois, Paul Douglas. And Senator Dennis Chavez presented his fellow New Mexican, Clinton Anderson.

As he watched from above, Humphrey looked around anxiously. Surely, he thought, Senator Ball, whom he had defeated, or Minnesota's other senator, Edward Thye, would appear and invite him onto the Senate floor for a formal introduction. But Humphrey was a Democrat, the first elected to the Senate in his state's history. Ball and Thye ignored him. As Humphrey rose to leave the gallery, Senator Lister Hill of Alabama—a respected member of the southern bloc with some liberal leanings—spotted him. Always the southern gentleman, the affable Hill scurried up to the gallery and courteously escorted Humphrey to the floor for the proper introductions. Offended that his recognition in the Senate had been an insulting afterthought, Humphrey nonetheless understood the reasons for his chilly reception. His fiery speech to the Democratic National Convention had branded him a dangerous radical. The speech was, he later said, "a political albatross."

The indifferent, sometimes hostile attitude of his new colleagues manifested itself in other ways. While the Senate gave most incoming freshmen temporary office space where they could begin assembling their staffs, the Democratic leadership left Humphrey to fend for himself.

Humphrey believed that Majority Leader Lucas, angry over losing the platform fight at the Democratic convention, "had still not forgiven me" for challenging the party's leadership. "The extra perks of office that he could deny, he did deny." For nineteen days, Humphrey occupied office space borrowed from a local attorney. With the lame-duck Congress in a brief special session, the departing senators still occupied their offices; Humphrey knew that locating temporary work space would be difficult. "But I couldn't understand why only I, of all the newcomers, had to work in an office downtown, away from everyone else and through the generosity of a private citizen."

Although hurtful, these affronts were mild compared to the personal insults Humphrey endured. The earliest, most painful incident occurred early in 1949 as Humphrey strolled into the Senate's Democratic cloakroom and encountered Richard Russell and a small band of southern senators. With not so much as a polite nod, the group silently brushed by him on their way to the Senate floor. Still within earshot, Humphrey overheard Russell's sarcastic remark to the group: "Can you imagine the people of Minnesota sending that damn fool down here to represent them?" The insult, Humphrey said, "hurt me more than anything in my private or public life, anything." He said he had never "felt so unwanted as I did during those first months in Washington. I was unhappy in the Senate, uncomfortable, awkward, unable to find a place." As he drove home that evening, Humphrey cried. Many years later, in a 1973 interview, the painful memories of his early Senate days remained vivid. "I was a very lonesome fellow there," he confessed. "This town of Washington seemed a very different place than Minneapolis."

Despite his cool reception under the Capitol dome, Humphrey's arrival in Washington attracted more enthusiasm elsewhere. *Time* featured him on its cover and labeled him "the most articulate spokesman of the Fair Dealers" among the Senate's freshmen. Organized labor loved him. Americans for Democratic Action elevated him to national chairman shortly after his election, enhancing his prominence as an important spokesman for liberal causes.

As the Eighty-first Congress convened, Humphrey—like most junior liberals—went to minor committees: Post Office, Government Operations, and Labor and Welfare. As for freshman Lyndon Johnson, his acceptance into the southern fold was reflected in his assignment to the more influential Armed Services Committee—where he would serve with senior member Richard Russell—and the Interstate and Foreign Commerce Committee.

Though the doors of the Senate's inner sanctum were closed to Humphrey, Harry Truman recognized a potentially loyal ally when he saw one and welcomed him enthusiastically into his Fair Deal fold. When Humphrey called on Truman at the White House after the election, the president volunteered to help in any way he could. "Mr. President," Humphrey replied, "the one thing that would mean more to me than anything political would be to bring my mother and father here to meet you when they come down for my swearing-in." Truman instructed his appointments secretary to make the necessary arrangements.

As Humphrey took his oath of office, H.H. and Christine watched proudly from their seat in the gallery. Humphrey later said it was the "was the fulfillment of everything [H.H.] wanted in life." Later that day, Humphrey proudly escorted his awestruck parents into the Oval Office to meet Truman. The president greeted them enthusiastically, praised their son, discussed world affairs, and then took them on a tour throughout the White House, including his private quarters. Although they spent less than an hour with Truman, Humphrey said that the president "handled the conversation with such grace that it seemed a neighborly afternoon visit that simply went too quickly." From that day forward, Humphrey—the man whose support for Franklin Roosevelt's political heir had once been lukewarm, at best—said of Truman: "He never could have done anything wrong as far as I was concerned."

Before he left town several days later, H.H. pulled Hubert aside and told his son that he did not expect to live much longer. Offering no details of his physical condition, he secured Humphrey's promise to care for Christine and the drugstore. Later that year, H.H. died of a cerebral hemorrhage. To Hubert, his passing was a crushing blow. "His death meant not only the loss of father and friend, but it took the one man with whom I could have freely counseled as I tried to understand what moved this new political world and who held the levers that powered its movements."

It is difficult to imagine that a freshman *southern* senator with Humphrey's engaging personality, superb political skills, boundless energy, and agile and fertile mind would not have been welcomed into the

Senate with open arms. Almost anyone willing to assess Humphrey objectively—a near impossibility among southern Democrats and conservative Republicans in 1949—would have found him enormously appealing. His bubbly optimism about government's ability to effect positive change charmed younger liberals. "He always believed that if you really put your mind to it . . . and brought a lot of bright people in, that you could solve anything, that there were no intractable problems," said his longtime aide William Connell. "He was never short of the energy he needed," said aide Rein Vander Zee. "He could wear out two or three staffs. He just had that kind of stamina." ADA colleague Robert Nathan recalled that Humphrey not only had boundless energy, but "there probably was no peer to Hubert in the breadth and variation and scope of the things that he was interested in."

As he arrived in Washington, Humphrey seemed to have the charming but naive belief that he could provide the needed impetus for civil rights. As his aide Max Kampelman recalled, Humphrey believed "it was the right thing to do, it was part of the American tradition, it was the direction American democracy had to take and, therefore, it might be a little slower, but you had to keep at it, you had to push for it and it would happen." To staff member William Shore, Humphrey was among a dying breed of political leaders who actually tried "to persuade people who disagree with him. Everybody else reads the polls. At the best, they are brave voters of their own conscience at the last minute. But almost none of them go into the camp of the enemy and try to persuade them that they're right and that the enemy is wrong." Humphrey did.

Paul Douglas, who barely knew Humphrey but had supported his platform challenge in Philadelphia, quickly became a soul mate and devoted admirer. A respected economist from Chicago, Douglas acquired a reputation as one of the Senate's most dogmatic and outspoken liberals. Highly intelligent and scrupulously honest—although some considered him annoyingly self-righteous—Douglas championed liberal causes while often spurning the Senate's obligatory niceties. And he was completely taken with Humphrey. Humphrey, Douglas marveled, displayed "more physical and nervous energy than any man I have ever known in political life." Douglas, in his mid-fifties and still suffering from a World War II arm injury, admired his new friend's ability to "simultaneously push scores of measures, tend to the personal and political chores of his office, do his committee work and speak wisely and almost incessantly both in and out of the Senate."

Friends and enemies alike acknowledged, however, that Humphrey had at least one glaring fault. He talked too much. "Hubert never followed a speech," said Robert Nathan. "I don't know that ever in all of his life he ever read a speech without adding on or detracting." William Connell recalled, "I would do something for him which was supposed to take thirty minutes, and he would deliver what I did for him in thirty minutes and then go on for an hour on his own." Yet Humphrey was one of the few politicians who could speak for an hour and usually not bore his audience. "The more Hubert extemporized," Nathan said, "the better he got because he threw his heart and soul in it." In Minnesota, as Humphrey once explained, voters could appreciate fervid, longwinded speeches. "In my part of the country, a speech is a social occasion," he said, adding that when the great populist senator Robert La Follette spoke in Minneapolis, "at the third hour he took his coat off."

The Senate, however, was not Minnesota. Senate leaders not only expected brevity from freshmen, they expected little or no speaking at all. "The long custom of the place impels [the freshman senator], if he is at all wise, to walk with a soft foot and to speak with a soft voice, and infrequently," William S. White wrote in *Citadel*. J. William Fulbright, who had preceded Humphrey to the Senate in 1947, knew what the Senate's elders expected of freshman: "Young members, both in the House and the Senate, it was the custom they didn't speak much their first year or two. They usually were very reticent about that. There was much greater respect for what was called seniority." Observed freshman Clinton Anderson, who knew Washington well as a former Agriculture secretary: "In the old days, you waited until Hiram Johnson of California spoke before you presumed to say anything. Walter George of Georgia was expected to be the last speaker in any debate, bringing to bear his accumulated wisdom on some given question." Humphrey, both prideful and insecure in his new surroundings, neither understood nor embraced the quaint notion of deference to elders.

For any freshman liberal in 1949, the Senate was a perplexing institution. To someone like Humphrey—with a progressive liberal agenda for which he demanded swift, affirmative action—it was downright hostile. In contrast, a conservative freshman—especially a southerner—usually found that the Senate was like a roomy and comfortable easy chair. He settled in easily. He saw little that needed changing, an attitude that naturally pleased the powerful senior members.

Reveling in its self-proclaimed status as "the most exclusive club in the world," the Senate was an intimidating place for many newcomers. It had, after all, been home to some of America's greatest statesmen: John Quincy Adams, Sam Houston, Henry Clay, John C. Calhoun, Daniel Webster, and Robert La Follette, Sr. Within this select body of ninety-six existed an exclusive and influential clique, an entirely informal and nebulous inner sanctum of the Senate commonly known as the Club or the Inner Club. No formal rites of passage for new "members" existed. The rules that governed members' conduct were widely understood yet unwritten. In the Club, personality overshadowed political ideology: Liberals were just as eligible for "membership" as conservatives, although not as likely to seek it. Though central to the Senate's being, the Club had no official name, no established hierarchy, and no roster of members.

Those who knew the Senate knew who belonged: Russell, the military affairs expert and southern general; Scott Lucas and Kenneth Wherry, by virtue of their roles as Democratic and Republican leaders; Tennessee's Kenneth McKellar, the Senate's oldest member and its president pro tempore; Ohio's Robert Taft, chairman of the Republican Policy Committee and de facto Republican leader; Massachusetts's Leverett Saltonstall, the popular Republican whip; Texas's Tom Connally, a senior member and a powerful voice among southerners; Colorado's Eugene Millikin, chairman of the Republican Conference and widely respected for his insight and intelligence; Georgia's Walter George, the revered Finance Committee chairman; Rhode Island's Theodore Francis Green, a devout and respected liberal in his eighties; and Arizona's Carl Hayden, a wise veteran who had served in Congress since 1912.

Like elder members of most proud institutions, Club members scorned and ostracized those who accosted the established traditions and rules of their venerable "upper House." New members who desired admittance to the tight-knit circle conformed to its unwritten code of conduct. As explained in Donald R. Matthews's landmark study, *U.S. Senators and Their World,* those expectations included: a period of apprenticeship; a dedication to the quiet, thankless legislative work of his assigned committees; a narrow focus on just those issues that fall under the jurisdiction of his committee or affect his state; an abundance of courtesy and deference to other senators (a trait for which southerners were particularly renowned); and a willingness to help colleagues with a vote whenever possible.

Perhaps most important to wide acceptance in the Senate was what Matthews called "institutional patriotism." "Senators," he maintained, "are expected to believe that they belong to the greatest legislative and deliberative body in the world." As William S. White once observed in the *New York Times,* the typical "Senate man" had "great hesitation about any kind of precipitate action and when it comes to the Senate's affairs he is seriously inclined to think that its rules and even its habits are superior to any substitutes that could be devised in this quite doubtful age." In his examination of congressional government, published in 1885, even Woodrow Wilson recognized this important aspect of the Senate's culture: "If a new Senator knock about too loosely amidst the free spaces of the rules of that august body, he will assuredly have some of his biggest corners knocked off and his angularities thus made smoother."

If observers like Matthews and White believed that acceptance within the Senate was predicated on a senator's willingness to cheerfully embrace the chamber's venerable traditions, others saw the matter in harsher, more political terms. Howard Shuman, an aide to Paul Douglas, believed that "if senators didn't join the coalition that existed at that time among Southerners, Westerners and trans-Mississippi Republicans, to protect segregation, to protect oil and gas, to protect public works, to protect cotton and tobacco and wheat and to give the water projects to the Western states, if they didn't join that coalition, they didn't get into the club." From Shuman's perspective, "the quid-pro-quo was that the southerners, with their lock on the committees and on the money, parceled out their goodies to the trans-Mississippi Republicans and the Western senators. That's how senators got into the club." And nothing was perhaps more important to Club membership than a senator's position on civil rights—or more precisely, cloture. "They didn't get there because they were nice fellows," explained Shuman. "They got there because they voted and worked for segregation when the chips were down. They didn't have to vote against the final passage of a civil rights bill, but they had to vote with the South on the procedural issues that prevented any civil rights bill from ever coming to a vote."

Anyone who believed Humphrey might entertain notions of joining the Senate's inner circle was mistaken. Far from seeking membership, Humphrey would unknowingly devote himself to violating almost all of the Club's unwritten rules.

Humphrey once observed that when he arrived in Washington in 1949, "I was looked on there as a political accident, a flaming liberal, a very dangerous fellow. I liked to get in there and mix it up . . . And, worst of all, I took Mr. Truman seriously." Only in office a few days, Humphrey stunned the Senate the afternoon that he and a black aide, Cyril King, appeared in the ornate dining room where senators entertained guests and staff members.* Severely embarrassed, the black headwaiter stopped them cold. The customs of the Senate, it seemed, permitted service only to whites. It had never occurred to Humphrey "that the color of a senator's guest was anybody's business." And he insisted that he and King be allowed to dine together. Humphrey won that skirmish and later remembered that "no guest of mine was ever again questioned." Humphrey knew that unwelcome freshmen were, at least, accorded great latitude regarding the Senate's customs. He had marched into the dining room armed with this understanding—and no small amount of boldness. The Club's elders might ignore and scorn him, but even Humphrey understood that they would not stop him from integrating their restaurant.

On the floor of the Senate, Humphrey remained mostly silent—at least in the beginning. As ADA chairman, he saved his rhetoric for speeches to groups in New York and Chicago. Two months into his term, Humphrey finally rose to speak in the Senate for the first time.

And it seemed that he never stopped.

His first formal remarks supported legislation to create a Missouri Valley Authority. Next he spoke in favor of liberalizing the Senate's cloture rule. As a member of the Labor and Welfare Committee, he swaggered into a committee hearing on the Taft-Hartley labor bill and traded barbs with its author, Robert Taft. At another Labor Committee hearing, he tangled with North Dakota Republican William Langer. In all, Humphrey made six major speeches and 230 remarks on the Senate floor in his first ten months. One speech, calling for repeal of the Taft-Hartley Act, lasted four and a half hours. And when he was not talking

*In 1975, King became governor of the U.S. Virgin Islands.

in the Senate, he darted around the country delivering speeches—an average of about one a week—in order to supplement his Senate income. "I never worked so hard," he told a friend.

He did not limit his prolificacy to speechmaking and debating. He introduced legislation—lots of it. In March 1949 he filed legislation to make lynching a federal crime. In April he offered a bill to establish a permanent Federal Commission on Civil Rights. He introduced legislation to abolish the Electoral College and a bill to extend Social Security coverage to federal and state employees. By the end of the year, he had introduced fifty-seven bills and joint resolutions as well as seventeen amendments. By contrast, Johnson introduced only twelve bills and joint resolutions and remarked on forty-six topics in his first year.

Former congressman Andrew Biemiller watched painfully as Humphrey "tried to take charge too early. He insisted on speaking on everything . . . And he was resented by the old-timers." Max Kampelman later admitted that Humphrey did not receive "a great deal of advice" about expectations of freshmen senators. "People who didn't know him didn't presume to advise him," said Kampelman. "The people around him, who did know him, were probably encouraging him a little in his ways."

Such frenetic activity by freshmen senators is now expected, or at least tolerated. In 1949, the thirty-eight-year-old whirlwind from Minnesota raised more than a few eyebrows around Washington. The *New Yorker* magazine featured him in a column entitled "Wind on Capitol Hill." The *Minneapolis Tribune* reprinted it—sparking an angry protest from Humphrey to the editor. The *Nation* concluded that Humphrey appeared to be "a moderate-sized man with an unfortunately self-righteous style of speaking." *Newsweek* reported that Humphrey "is slipping with his colleagues," some of whom had complained that he "talks too much on almost every subject that comes on the Senate floor." The *Saturday Evening Post*, in an October story headlined "The Senate's Gabbiest Freshman," chided Humphrey for his loquaciousness. One Washington journalist who had observed Humphrey in Minnesota said, "When you ask that guy a question, you get a one-man filibuster for an answer." The same story mentioned unnamed friends who had warned Humphrey that he might wear out his welcome with his new Senate colleagues. But his friend and aide Max Kampelman urged him to persevere:

He liked to be liked. And the fact that he was not liked by his colleagues troubled him very much. But you remember, at about that time he was elected the national chairman of ADA . . . I remember saying to him . . . "You know, given the situation for what it is, you can either play the role of a freshman senator with all of its limitations or you can remember that you are the national chairman of ADA, looked upon by . . . labor union members as a leader, and have a constituency which is not only Minnesota, but national." And I think that as he thought of himself in that role, it gave him some feeling of compensation.

Another friend who prodded Humphrey to resist becoming a comfortable, accommodating Club member was his ADA associate Joseph Rauh. A civil liberties and labor lawyer, Rauh urged Humphrey not to let 1949 pass without delivering a rousing civil rights speech in the Senate. In an October letter to Humphrey, Rauh mused:

> Is there any reason against giving this speech? Only the fact that a few people who now more or less control the Democratic Party won't like it because it will reflect no glory on them and because it will make Hubert Humphrey rather than they themselves the spokesman for civil rights. But in my book, Hubert Humphrey's future lies not in pleasing the powers that be in the Democratic Party at any given moment, but in becoming more and more America's great spokesman for liberalism.

Humphrey merely inserted into the *Congressional Record* the speech Rauh had wanted him to deliver, but his actions of 1949 proved that he had indeed embraced the advice offered by Kampelman and Rauh. Yet while his ADA associates helped Humphrey become an influential national voice for liberalism, they clearly misjudged the consequences of ruining Humphrey's effectiveness in the Senate. After all, the liberals had no need for *another* voice in the wilderness. They desperately needed more effective voices in the halls of Congress. By systematically thumbing his nose at the traditions governing the behavior of freshmen senators, Humphrey had ensured that his influence among his new colleagues would be negligible.

Nothing justified the animosity of the Senate's establishment against Humphrey more than his all-out assault on Virginia Democrat Harry

Byrd in February 1950. An icon of federal budget parsimony, Byrd's rigid notions of government economy, observed one former Senate aide, "reflected those of an eighteenth-century shopkeeper." Journalist David Leon Chandler said that Byrd personified "the old Virginia belief that the government shouldn't spend much on anything." Although liked by his colleagues, the aristocratic Byrd was by no means the most popular member of the Senate. But his crusade against waste in government, through his chairmanship of the Joint Committee on Reduction of Non-Essential Federal Expenditures, had made him something of a celebrity around the country. That resulted in a respectful deference among his colleagues. So secure was Byrd's position as chairman that Republicans had left him in charge when they briefly took control of the Senate during the Eightieth Congress.

Humphrey first learned about Byrd's influence in early 1950 when a Minnesota group claiming to represent his committee released figures totaling the potential cost of legislation Humphrey had introduced since arriving in the Senate. The implication was clear: Humphrey was a big-spending liberal. After the *Minneapolis Star and Journal* published the total—about $30 billion in new appropriations—a conservative Washington radio commentator aired the figure. Humphrey was furious.

His anger was only magnified when Minority Leader Wherry brandished the list on the Senate floor. As a member of the Government Operations Committee, Humphrey had recently objected to a Republican proposal to require the Truman Administration to slash federal spending across the board by 10 percent. When Humphrey filed a dissenting report to the proposal, Wherry responded by calling the Senate's attention to Humphrey's spending requests. Though he fended off Wherry's criticism, the episode left Humphrey angry and frustrated.

Humphrey believed that Byrd's committee was itself a waste of money. The Government Operations Committee's Subcommittee on Expenditures in the Executive Department, on which Humphrey served, was charged with essentially the same mission as Byrd's committee. It did not, however, share Byrd's passion for cutting government spending. That is, the committee did not seek to eliminate the *kind* of spending to which Byrd and his fiercely conservative committee members objected. Humphrey decided to take on Byrd and expose his committee's hypocrisy. On the advice of a Government Operations Committee staff member, and armed with statistics provided by the American Political Science Association, Humphrey rose on the Senate floor on February

24, 1950, and nearly committed political suicide. He introduced legislation to abolish the Byrd committee.

Humphrey cited the Legislative Reorganization Act of 1946, designed to reduce and consolidate the myriad committees with overlapping jurisdictions in the House and Senate. He said the Government Operations subcommittee already performed the same function as Byrd's committee. Therefore, he said, the committee's existence "is a violation of the spirit of the Legislative Reorganization Act, as well as a waste of the taxpayers' dollar." The committee the Senate created to weed out waste, he declared, "is a waste of the taxpayers' money and is a fundamental violation of the purpose of the committee."

Humphrey noted that the committee's mission was to compile "a full and complete study and investigation of all [wasteful] expenditures of the federal government with a view to recommending the elimination of all such expenditures." However, he said:

we find that it has devoted itself almost exclusively to personnel statistics, and that without any justification whatsoever it has regularly issued general statements calling for blanket reductions in federal personnel. Even the most naive management engineering firm would never think of making recommendations concerning personnel without submitting detailed reasons for such reductions consistent with disclosed facts and indicating where they should take place.

Humphrey said the committee "stands as the number one example of waste and extravagance which the joint committee itself should have recommended be eliminated. It is my firm conviction that this committee serves no useful purpose, and is merely used as a publicity medium." (Given Humphrey's own penchant for self-promotion, members of the Senate's old guard—including Byrd—found that statement more than a little ironic.)

Although his speech had been a well-delivered, mostly accurate analysis of the Byrd committee's value, Humphrey quickly realized he had committed the "egregious error" of introducing his bill when Byrd was away from the Senate visiting his ailing mother. "I don't think Humphrey particularly gave this decision enough thought," said Max Kampelman, who believed Humphrey should have fought for issues "that were more basic to [his] philosophy and a little less basic to procedural institutional things." While he had not attacked Byrd personally, one Humphrey biographer wrote that Humphrey "might just as well have slapped Byrd across the face with a wet towel."

Byrd held his fire for a week. But on March 2 the Virginian and a chorus of southern colleagues unleashed a withering, well-orchestrated response to Humphrey's attack. Byrd led the charge, citing "at least nine misstatements which require correction for accuracy." And he charged—correctly—that Humphrey had little passion for deficit reduction. As evidence of Humphrey's disregard for government economy, he noted that his Minnesota colleague had recently proposed a $250,000 study of the nation's "coal situation." Contrary to Humphrey's charges of the committee's indolence, Byrd maintained his panel had issued seventy-one monthly personnel reports and twenty-six "formal" reports that had resulted in fifty separate instances of reductions in federal spending for a total savings of $2.4 billion.* "These are documented in the public records of Congress," Byrd declared, looking at Humphrey, "which are available to all who would choose to have themselves advised as to the facts in this respect."

Warming to his subject, Byrd also noted that Humphrey had alleged that his committee was "merely used as a publicity medium." Byrd then observed:

> As the senator from Minnesota is a publicity expert himself, his statement, although not intended as such, could be regarded as a compliment from one who welcomes, and has been signally successful in creating publicity from himself and his objectives. I know of no senator who has more generously used the *Congressional Record* and other governmental facilities to promote his publicity. If he has ever hidden his light under a bushel, I am not aware of it. If he has ever run away from publicity, I do not know of it, and no one else does. I am not impressed by any I have observed indicating that he is of the shrinking-violet type evading publicity.
>
> The senator charges propaganda when the newspapers publish the reports of the committee in its efforts to promote sound

*Many of the committee's recommendations were actually more a matter of priority and philosophy than attacks on outright, undeniable waste. Largely, they reflected Byrd's hatred of the progressive policies of Roosevelt and Truman; his reports had included recommendations to dismantle several New Deal agencies and to gut many farm programs.

fiscal policies. But he continually strives to propagandize himself and those things he advocates as being proper and worthy.

More than an hour after he began, Byrd sat down. Following some respectful, albeit skeptical, questioning from Majority Leader Lucas, he began conducting an orchestra of praise for the work of his committee. First came Walter George of Georgia: "I wish to bear testimony to the fact that the distinguished senior senator from Virginia has done a magnificent job as chairman of this joint committee through the years." Then Hugh Butler of Nebraska: "I am impressed with the splendid work done by the chairman of the joint committee from a nonpartisan stand-point." Next James Eastland of Mississippi: "The distinguished senator from Virginia has performed a public service of the highest importance." Wherry of Nebraska: "I have used the statistics furnished by the Committee on Reduction of Non-Essential Federal Expenditures. They have been very helpful to me. I only wish the committee were larger." Stennis of Mississippi: "After looking into this entire picture, I am fully convinced that the powers of the committee ought to be enlarged and strengthened, and the committee members encouraged, rather than to have the committee outlawed and its members abused."

This humiliating parade lasted for several hours. It also included Williams of Delaware, McClellan of Arkansas, Martin of Pennsylvania, Cain of Washington, McKellar of Tennessee, Mundt of South Dakota, Ferguson of Michigan, and Tobey and Bridges, both of New Hampshire. One by one senators filed into the chamber, many of them more glowing in their praise of Byrd than his committee's usefulness. Meanwhile, slumped in his seat, Humphrey passively endured the verbal thrashing. Several times he rose to make vain attempts to gain recognition. Byrd only waved him off, yielding instead to other adoring allies. Finally exhausted of their praise for the Byrd committee—and their implied disdain for their Minnesota colleague—Byrd and his friends turned their backs on Humphrey as he rose to respond. And then they left the chamber.

Humphrey was typically unbowed. He revealed not an ounce of remorse or anguish at having so provoked the Senate's patriarchs. He noted that "when we talk about world peace senators are often too busy to be present to hear the discussion. But when there is an opportunity to attack the [Truman] administration, through one of the junior members of the administration, then the faithful are rallied and the reactionary coalition which operates in this Congress is present en masse. Then the big guns are wheeled out, and we hear the thunder of the artillery—the thunder against the president's program and against the budget." Humphrey acknowledged some of his advisors had told him his bill would "open up a hornet's nest and they are going to mow you down. Well, Mr. President, there has been some lawn mowing going on today, but the shrinking violet still has not been clipped." Although he apologized for having introduced his bill during Byrd's absence, Humphrey bravely repeated his conviction that the committee "is wasteful and extravagant." Only Paul Douglas, Millard Tydings of Maryland, and William Langer of North Dakota offered Humphrey a hand of friendship. Each cited instances of government waste that the Byrd committee had ignored.

Humphrey finally left the chamber to return to his office. As he boarded the elevator, he encountered a sullen Harry Byrd. "Senator," Humphrey said, cheerfully extending his hand, "I know when I've been licked." Only reluctantly did Byrd shake Humphrey's hand.

For Humphrey, the experience had taught him much, as he frankly admitted to the Senate. "I learned that when one attacks the old-guard coalition in the Senate, through one of its prominent spokesmen, a freshman senator is going to learn something." At least, Humphrey later explained with his usual optimism, "I found out where the power was in the Senate, and I also found out what you could expect when you challenge that power frontally." Because he indeed benefited from the experience, the cause of civil rights advanced greatly that March afternoon. At the time, however, no one—not even Humphrey—realized it.

CHAPTER SIX

Uncle Dick

HUBERT HUMPHREY ONCE SAID that Lyndon Johnson "came to the Senate knowing what I had yet to learn, that the Eighty-First Congress was really very conservative." Exulting in the triumph of 1948 that returned Harry Truman to the White House and Democrats to control of Congress, Humphrey and other liberals had been optimistic about enacting a civil rights program. As they soon learned, however, many of the new Senate Democrats felt only sporadic pangs of loyalty to Truman or his program. "Lyndon was well aware of that," Humphrey observed, "and he was, I think, biding his time and building his contacts."

From his first day in the Senate, Johnson dedicated himself to two goals: getting reelected in 1954 and establishing a reputation as a serious, hardworking representative for Texas. He was, in the words of former assistant Senate secretary Darrell St. Claire, "a man who was totally devoted to himself and to his political career and the ensconcement of it by any means whatsoever." He worked staff members like horses, often riding weaker ones until they collapsed or quit. "I don't believe I'd like to work under him," Louisiana senator Allen Ellender once said, recalling Johnson's reputation as "a slave driver." Added Ellender: "He didn't know when to stop." Not only was Johnson a tireless worker who demanded absolute loyalty and commitment from his staff, he was a perfectionist who expected faultless work from himself and those around him. "He burned a lot of midnight oil," said longtime aide Clifton Carter. "A lot of times when others were sleeping, he was working to anticipate what the problems of tomorrow would be, where he could take action rather than react after something was already done."

But hard work alone would not give Johnson all he needed to become an effective and powerful senator. Without the kind of mentor he had cultivated during his early House years, Johnson might remain just another conservative freshman. Instinctively, he recognized that one senator in particular was more important to his budding Senate career than all others combined. But Richard Russell, Johnson soon realized, might not be his easiest conquest. Johnson had wooed earlier father figures such as Franklin Roosevelt, Sam Rayburn, and Carl Vinson with ease, largely because they had so much in common. With Roosevelt it was a mutual love of partisan politics and Johnson's eagerness to perform menial political duties for his president. Rayburn shared Texas roots and had known Johnson's father during their days in the Texas House. And Vinson grew fond of Johnson during their years on the House Naval Affairs Committee.

But Russell was different. Since coming to Congress in 1937, Johnson had rarely encountered Georgia's junior senator. They had worked together briefly on rural electrification and shared an interest in military affairs, but not much more. Furthermore, Johnson would not be the only freshman vying for Russell's favor. Several other new members could conceivably assert legitimate and even greater claims to Russell's goodwill and friendship. Oklahoma's Robert Kerr had, like Russell, been his state's governor. They were contemporaries, both in their early fifties. Much younger, at thirty, was Louisiana's Russell Long; but Long was the son of the late Huey P. Long, whom Russell had admired as a fellow governor and Senate colleague. Two other relative newcomers—Mississippi's John Stennis and Arkansas's J. William Fulbright—were hardworking, devoted members of Russell's anti–civil rights coalition.

Judged by their contrasting styles and personalities, Johnson seemed one of the last freshmen to whom Russell might be attracted. Given those obvious obstacles, almost no one would have predicted an intimate friendship between a cautious and thoughtful man like Russell and a brash, ambitious upstart like Johnson. But Johnson had perfected his skills as a professional son during years of practice in the House. He knew Russell's favor was crucial to rapid advancement in the Senate. Whether he understood just how important Russell's patronage would become to him—how Russell would become his vital link and advocate to the southern conservatives—is unlikely. Yet he clearly understood, in the words of his future aide Harry McPherson, that Russell could be "the most important two hands serving as a stirrup for Johnson to mount into the leadership saddle." With his usual skill and discipline, Johnson put his heart into a senatorial courtship unparalleled in its intensity, cunning, and ultimate results.

"Johnson learned to observe amenities with Senator Russell," remembered Russell's aide Bill Jordan. "With other senators, [Johnson] would just walk right into their offices, wouldn't even say how d'ya do. He would just barge in single-mindedly. Amenities were not part of his relationships." But such "Old World" courtesies were important to Russell, Jordan said. "So Johnson learned. He always referred to him as 'Senator Russell' and always sent in a note from the outer office to say he would like to come in." Majority Leader Lucas, characterizing the Johnson of 1949, thought he observed a man far different from the obsessive, overtly ambitious congressman of a year earlier: "I found him at all times what I would term a gentleman of the old school." While Johnson's staff members may not have detected a change in their boss's style—said one, "he still had the same energy; he was just as vigorous, just as dynamic"—the Senate received a rather subdued introduction to Johnson's enormous political ambitions. Humphrey, who noted a calm, businesslike approach, said Johnson "wasn't pushing. He was working his way into the apparatus."

In Russell, Johnson perceived much more than a courtly elder who preferred deference from freshmen. As with Rayburn, Johnson saw a lonely bachelor in need of companionship. Johnson later explained:

> Richard Russell found in the Senate what for him was a home. With no one to cook for him at home, he would arrive early enough in the morning to eat breakfast at the Capitol and stay late enough at night to eat dinner across the street. And in these early mornings and late evenings I made sure that there was always one companion, one senator, who worked as hard and as long as he, and that was me, Lyndon Johnson. On Sundays, the House and Senate were empty, quiet and still, the streets outside were bare. It's a tough day for a politician, especially if, like Russell, he's all alone. I knew how he felt for I, too, counted the hours till Monday would come again, and knowing that, I made sure to invite Russell over for breakfast, lunch, brunch or just to read the Sunday papers. He was my mentor and I wanted to take care of him.

"Lyndon was smart," Alabama senator Lister Hill said admiringly. "He recognized what an able, outstanding man Dick Russell was, and

right away he began to play up to Dick." In time, Sunday lunches led
to drop-in weekday dinners at the Johnson home, where Lady Bird
served the southern dishes—fried chicken, black-eyed peas, turnip
greens, peach ice cream—that she had earlier employed to win Sam
Rayburn's heart. Johnson even prodded his daughters, Lynda and Luci,
to call Russell "Uncle Dick." When not working together or sharing a
meal, Johnson, who had no interest in sports whatever, often accompanied Russell on one of his favorite outings—to a Washington Senators
baseball game at nearby Griffith Stadium. "I doubt that Lyndon Johnson
had been to a baseball game in his life until he heard that Dick Russell
enjoyed the sport," said Johnson's friend John Connally.

In those early months and years, hardly a day passed that Russell
did not encounter the fawning persona of Lyndon Johnson, who, according to Bobby Baker, "flattered him outrageously." Johnson treated
Russell to the full measure of his hospitality during the 1949 Thanksgiving holidays, part of which Russell spent at Johnson's Texas ranch.
Johnson even presented Russell with small gifts—and sometimes more
extravagant ones, including a unique wristwatch with an alarm. The
flattery, companionship, and gifts had their desired effect, said Senator
Lister Hill, who concluded that Johnson "captured Dick." Russell became, in Lady Bird's words, "very much a part of our lives." Russell's
aide William Darden said the two men "just seemed to work hand in
glove from the beginning."

As for Russell, he did not seem to find Johnson's intense courtship
offensive or even unusual. "Because he was a new senator then, and I
had been there for years," Russell later explained, "he rather put himself
under my tutelage, or he associated with me, you might say." To Russell, Johnson must have seemed just another eager supplicant for the
favor and attention of a powerful senior senator. Such courtship was not
strange to Russell, explained J. William Fulbright, because Russell routinely "went out of his way, when new senators came in, to befriend
them, to offer to be of assistance, to give them advice on the personal
details of adjusting to the procedures and life of the Senate itself." In
almost every way, said Darden, Russell seemed enormously impressed
with his new colleague and "how well organized his office was, how
energetic he was, and how he just got started on the right foot and
seemed to know where the sources of power were and how to proceed."
According to Russell Long, "Dick Russell really came to love Lyndon
Johnson as though he were a son."

No matter how significant his personal courtship of Russell, nothing mattered more in the budding relationship than Johnson's success in winning a seat on the Armed Services Committee soon after his arrival in the Senate. "I knew there was only one way to see Russell every day," Johnson explained, "and that was to get a seat on his committee. Without that, we'd most likely be passing acquaintances and nothing more." Johnson's appointment to the sought-after committee was no small accomplishment for a freshman. Though he had lobbied Steering Committee members such as Walter George, Tom Connally, Kenneth McKellar, and Carl Hayden, it was Russell who exerted the most influence on Johnson's selection and was most satisfied when his new, young protégé became one of the hardest working members of the committee.

Donald Cook, who worked for Johnson on the Armed Services Committee, believed that Russell quickly "formed the opinion that here was a man of tremendous competence, ability, patriotism." As a new committee member, Johnson did not approach his duties meekly. In 1950, he aggressively lobbied for the chairmanship of a special subcommittee on defense preparedness. When the leadership granted his wish, Johnson used the position to gain national attention and an immeasurably higher profile among his Senate colleagues.

Johnson's quest for greater power and influence through relationships with Russell and other Senate barons was enormously effective, but the reviews of other colleagues, especially the liberals, were at times less dazzling. His vicious attack on Leland Olds, a Roosevelt appointee whom President Truman had renominated to the Federal Power Commission in 1949, particularly outraged many of his liberal colleagues and friends. Olds was an outspoken liberal who favored expanded federal control over the nation's private utilities. As chairman of the subcommittee with jurisdiction over the commission, Johnson helped orchestrate a chorus of attacks on Olds. When the nomination reached the Senate floor, Johnson called Olds an enemy of private power and hinted that he might be a communist sympathizer. Most agreed that Olds's nomination had been dead long before Johnson's assault. Liberals concluded that Johnson was actually burnishing his conservative credentials in Texas, separating himself from his former New Deal ideology, and winning favor with his state's natural gas industry—all at the expense of Olds's reputation.

The nomination fight—and his overkill tactics—earned Johnson more than a few enemies within Washington's liberal community. His behavior sickened Paul Douglas, an Olds defender. His ruthlessness disheartened his New Deal friends Tommy Corcoran and James Rowe. And Joseph Rauh—the influential civil liberties lawyer who had helped Johnson win the legal challenge to his 1948 Senate election—was transformed from a potential ally into a bitter enemy who would give Johnson no quarter on civil rights for most of the next fourteen years.

Johnson's maiden speech in March of 1949, in support of the southern filibuster over cloture, was another factor in his early alienation from the liberals. According to Humphrey:

> I was in with Paul Douglas, for example, and Clinton Anderson and Estes Kefauver, and people of that group—our little group of twenty-five or so liberal senators were very suspicious of Johnson in those early years, very suspicious of him! I was maybe the one man that looked on him with more friendship, more acceptance. I always felt that he was a lot more liberal, from my point of view, than he ever acted. I really felt that early.

But just when liberal critics prepared to dismiss Johnson as nothing more than a pandering, knee-jerk conservative, he surprised them by his sensitive response to the case of Felix Longoria, a Mexican-American soldier who died in the Philippines during World War II. In early 1949, when Longoria's family sought to have his body brought home for burial in the Texas town of Three Rivers, the local funeral home refused to handle the arrangements. When Johnson learned of the family's plight, he promptly arranged for Longoria's burial, not in Three Rivers but in Arlington National Cemetery. At Johnson's request, President Truman's military aide attended the service, which was fit for a hero. "At that time, what he did could only hurt him politically in Texas," Sam Rayburn's aide D. B. Hardeman concluded. "But what the people in Three Rivers did outraged him." Of course the incident could only raise Johnson's standing with his growing Mexican-American constituency. "He saw it right away," said aide Walter Jenkins, "as an opportunity to do something that showed how he felt about the Latins."

More than one liberal senator must have wondered: Who is this former protégé of Roosevelt who opposes much of Truman's legislative program, slanders his nominee in the Senate, and opposes meager steps toward greater civil rights for all minorities? And how can this man pretend he is no part of the southern bloc while shamelessly courting its leader?

"I don't think Lyndon was either a conservative or a liberal," said Luther Jones, an aide to Johnson during his early House years. "I think he was whatever he felt like he needed to be." To Humphrey, the matter was quite simple. He believed Johnson merely wanted to avoid becoming "a captive of the southern bloc." As Hardeman explained, "In his early days in the Senate, he was cut by the extreme conservatives on the one hand and the extreme liberals on the other. In fact, that was true from the day he came to the Senate until the end. It was tough to stay in the middle, a very difficult thing to manage, but he did. I don't know how."

Humphrey, who appreciated and accepted Johnson's pragmatism more than any other liberal, thought he understood Johnson's curious relationship with Russell's southern bloc: "He was trying to be a captain of them, rather than a captive."

While Johnson basked in the glow of his new and successful relationship with the Senate's most influential man and his near-total acceptance into the Club, Humphrey languished in his own private exile. As he later recalled, he was "very sad" during his early years in the Senate. He admitted that his "errors in judgment"—including the attack on the Byrd committee—alienated many colleagues. "It was a difficult time," Humphrey said, "when I despaired of ever functioning well in the Senate."

Casting about the chamber, Humphrey saw that other freshmen such as Long, Kerr, and Johnson were adapting well. "They had friends in the South," he explained. "That's all you needed. I had nothing. Absolutely nothing. No friends any place." Though he despaired in private, in public he always projected an optimistic outlook. With support from Muriel—"without Muriel, I might have given up"—and a renewed dedication to his senatorial duties, Humphrey resolved that if his colleagues would not like him, at least he would earn their grudging respect.

At first, inadvertently, he began to woo his detractors with his easy humor. A student trip to Great Britain sponsored by Humphrey's ADA had raised the ire of several Republicans, including Indiana's ultraconservative Republican, Homer Capehart. But when Capehart demanded to know "one thing" Great Britain had that America did not, Humphrey quickly responded, "Westminster Abbey." Senators and visitors in the gallery burst into laughter, and Humphrey's quip quickly deflated his critics. Moderate Republicans Arthur Vandenberg of Michigan and Charles Tobey of New Hampshire both approached Humphrey "gleefully." Vandenberg told Humphrey, "They'll respect you from here on out." Although the encounter did little to endear Humphrey to the conservative Republicans, he detected that "they treated me more carefully from then on."

At the behest of his former LSU debating teammate and current Washington neighbor, Russell Long, Humphrey also began reaching out to his colleagues on a social level. Sensing that the alienation from the Senate's powers was hindering Humphrey's effectiveness, Long urged his friend to begin eating lunch in the senators' private dining room. In that inner sanctum, around a large table, southern Democratic barons routinely broke bread, gossiped, and debated legislative strategy. In an adjoining room, Republicans dined around a similar community table— all in complete privacy, shielded from staff and visitors. Long told Humphrey, "You'd like those guys if you get to know them, and they'd like you."

Humphrey wisely heeded the advice. "Surprisingly," he said, "these men accepted me. I was frightened, wondering if I ought to be doing this, nervous that they'd leave me off in a corner." Conservative colleagues probably perceived Humphrey's prior avoidance of the private dining room and other personal encounters as a rejection of the Club's tribal rituals. He had signaled them, unintentionally, that he did not desire admittance into their fold. But when he entered the room for something as simple as lunch—to dine with Russell and his conservative brothers—the ice slowly began to melt away. "Mostly, I just listened," he said, "learning the mechanism that made the Senate work."

Within several years, Humphrey made friends with Vice President Alben Barkley, the respected former majority leader, who occasionally helped him "against the wishes of the leadership." Violating Senate protocol that favored more senior members, Barkley selected Humphrey for a Senate trip to Germany and Austria. He also helped Humphrey win a seat on the select Small Business Committee—an appointment the leadership had once denied. Barkley's willingness to cultivate Humphrey was very different from his original sentiments, summed up in a quip during Humphrey's early days in the Senate. It was a play on the names of Humphrey's Senate predecessor, Joseph Ball, and his Minnesota colleague, Edward Thye: "Minnesota is a great state—first they send us their Ball, then they send us their Thye, and now they've sent us their goddam ass."

It is ironic that nothing hastened Humphrey's acceptance among his Senate colleagues more than his robust, well-organized challenge in 1950 to one of the Senate's most respected members. Like many liberals, Humphrey believed the nation's tax code was brimming with loopholes, carved out for corporate interests by the Senate Finance Committee. Because Finance was so conservative, so inclined to sympathize with big business, liberals rarely sought membership. Early in their Senate careers, Johnson complained to Humphrey "that liberals all wanted to get on the Labor Committee where it was nothing but a veneer, whereas the ultimate power in society was determined by the Senate Finance Committee and no liberal was on it and didn't ask to get on it."

Humphrey had never sought appointment to the Finance Committee. His interest in tax legislation was sparked early in 1950 during a conversation with his friend, Walter Heller, a University of Minnesota professor and former Treasury Department official. Heller told Humphrey about the wartime tax bill of 1943, legislation passed by the Senate Finance Committee but vetoed by President Roosevelt because it was loaded with special exemptions for wealthy interests. As Humphrey investigated the Revenue Act of 1950, just reported out of George's Finance Committee, he concluded that the same forces of wartime profiteering were still at work. Because giants such as George, Harry Byrd, and Eugene Millikin commanded the committee, few colleagues questioned their judgment, especially on the intricate details of the tax code. "They had an absolute monopoly," said Heller. "They got things through, special-privilege measures that no one really understood."

But with American forces now involved in the Korean conflict, Humphrey concluded that he should scrutinize and challenge any legislation that encouraged profiteering. George's committee, he believed, must not railroad important tax legislation through the Senate without offering at least some defense for its more questionable provisions. "I wanted to know what built-in privileges were available to the businessmen but not to the working men," Humphrey said, "what was available to the doctor but not the schoolteacher."

Helped by his colleague Paul Douglas, an economist, Humphrey assembled a team of tax experts that included Treasury Department economist Joseph Pechman, tax lawyer Louis Oberdorfer, and House Ways and Means Committee counsel Charles Davis. For about a month, the team pored over the highly technical provisions of the bill, identifying the most egregious loopholes for a possible challenge by Humphrey and Douglas. Humphrey finally settled on twelve provisions that he would attempt to remove or amend during debate. Closing those loopholes, Humphrey claimed, would increase federal revenues by more than $900 million. Humphrey buried his head in reams of briefing materials in a headlong effort to learn about each tax provision he would oppose. Often working until two and three in the morning, Humphrey delved into the mind-numbing world of the oil depletion allowance, intangible drilling costs, family partnerships, gift taxes, and capital gains preferences. In a matter of days, he acquired a thorough, working knowledge of each provision. To Pechman, Humphrey was "the quickest study I ever met."

This time, Humphrey's challenge to the Senate's barons would be no foolhardy surprise attack. Before the debate began, Humphrey demonstrated that his pummeling at the hands of Harry Byrd had taught him an important lesson. He would not risk alienating George by springing his amendments unannounced. Instead, he called on the Finance chairman and explained exactly what he and Douglas planned. "Go right ahead," George responded. "That's what a senator is supposed to do." The visit, Humphrey later explained, assured George "that I was serious about debating tax policy and that I was not playing to the galleries."

For a week, Humphrey valiantly and ably debated the intricacies of his amendments. He addressed almost every major portion of the bill, which he characterized as a "big pork barrel" and a "smoke screen" for relief of the wealthy. "I urge that while GIs are dodging Russian bullets and ducking Communist bombs, we must not make it possible for a new crop of war profiteers to dodge their rightful share of federal income taxes." Despite that audacious assertion, Humphrey was never brash or scornful in his challenge of the Finance Committee. From the beginning, he worked at being humble, admitting that tax law "is a new experience for me" and expressing his "desire to know more about this important subject." On his feet for hours at a time, Humphrey displayed a remarkable understanding of legislation about which he had known almost nothing a week earlier. His good humor was showing, too. "I was on the floor, sitting next to Humphrey throughout that whole debate," recalled Max Kampelman. "I could see how impressed people like Walter George and Eugene Millikin, who ran the Finance Committee, were at the forceful but gentlemanly way he engaged in the debate and the respect he showed to the leadership." Soon, Kampelman said, "ridicule gave way to respect."

In the end, Humphrey lost all but one amendment—a proposal to strike a provision that reduced the holding period for long-term capital gains from six to three months. But the experience helped him shed his reputation as an impudent, grandstanding publicity seeker. Colleagues increasingly viewed him as a good-natured, effective advocate of liberal causes. Walter Heller described the debate as a "David and Goliath" encounter in which "David didn't win, but it had a long-run effect. That debate was a landmark in terms of establishing a proposition that someone who was not one of the monopolists, so to speak, or oligopolists of tax policy in the Senate, could challenge them."

At the debate's conclusion, after George and Millikin had easily vanquished their opposition, the two men strolled over to Humphrey. In an impressive demonstration of acceptance, the two men put their arms around Humphrey and embraced him. "Their gesture," said Kampelman, "was not lost on the rest of the Senate. It remains indelibly and emotionally fixed in my mind as a moment of historic change."

After almost two agonizingly frigid years in the Senate, Humphrey finally began to feel the warmth of a springtime of approval and admiration. Far from prostrating himself at the barons' feet, Humphrey had won their admiration with a vigorous but fair and good-natured challenge. For the first time, senators began to see the Humphrey they would grow to admire and appreciate for his integrity, compassion, and valor. On many issues, scores of conservative Republicans and Democrats would do battle with their Minnesota colleague, but this would not prevent them from admiring him—and immensely so. "What ultimately saved the day for me in the Senate," he later said, "was that I never let my politics get to the point where I had any personal animosity with the other man." Though Humphrey would still have an occasional clash with conservative colleagues—including a near-fistfight with the unpopular Homer Capehart in 1951—he was now making his peace with the Senate and signaling his regard for the institution.

Humphrey learned a great deal from the tax bill debate. One lesson, he said, was "that as long as you treated other senators as honest men, sincere in their convictions, that you could usually gain the tolerance, if not affection, of even those who disagreed strongly with you." As for Kampelman, he knew that Humphrey's acceptance into the fold was complete a year or two later when he ambled into the Democratic cloakroom as Walter George held court with several colleagues. They were discussing Humphrey. "That young fellow," George said in his deep, booming voice, "*really believes* what he's doing." It was, to Kampelman, a sign of ultimate respect for a southern conservative to acknowledge that principle and not politics motivated a liberal like Humphrey.

But Humphrey was still not a full-fledged member of the Club. While the tax bill debate had elevated him in the eyes of his colleagues and lunching in the private dining room had helped immensely, Humphrey remained just outside the Senate's legislative mainstream. His influence on legislation was marginal, at best. Like most other Senate liberals, he was simply too idealistic, often impractical, and generally ignorant of the Senate's rules and the other mechanisms that made up the Senate's legislative engines. But through his budding relationships with the elders around the Senate's dining table, Humphrey began to learn.

"And then," he said, "I found Senator Lyndon Johnson—or he found me."

Humphrey and Johnson had little personal contact during their first year in the Senate. But Humphrey knew about Johnson and observed him with interest and, often, envy. "He was a Democrat and a Texan," Humphrey said, "enjoying the benefits of southern hospitality, southern power, southern support, but who carefully avoided the liabilities of being clearly labeled a southerner." More significantly, Humphrey saw something else in Johnson: his mastery of the levers of Senate power. "He understood the structure and pressure points of the government, and the process and problems of legislation." And Humphrey noticed that Johnson had very important friends: Sam Rayburn, Richard Russell, Walter George, Harry Byrd, and Tom Connally. "He knew all these men. I didn't hardly know the way home."

Humphrey was not alone in recognizing Johnson's early acquisition of influence and stature. "He knew what caused different people to respond and exactly how to get most people to respond in the way that he liked for them to," said Russell's aide William Darden. Senator John

Stennis saw a man who "understood the art of bending without breaking." Most important, it seemed to Humphrey that Johnson

> knew all the little things that people did. I used to say he had his own private FBI. If you ever knew anybody, if you'd been out on a date, or if you'd had a drink, or if you attended a meeting or you danced with a gal at a nightclub, he knew it! It was just incredible! I don't know how he was able to get all that information, but he lived and breathed and walked and talked politics. That's all. He was just totally immersed in it. I found him a fascinating individual right from the beginning.

Johnson's climb up the Senate ladder was indeed breathtaking. By the 1950 congressional elections, with less than two years of Senate service, Johnson was poised to make his move. He had chaired two important subcommittees, demonstrated an ability to shepherd legislation, and established powerful friendships. Despite having opposed so much of President Truman's legislative program, Johnson even found himself frequently invited to join friendly poker games on the presidential yacht.

The defeat of the Senate's top leadership in 1950 threw the door wide open for Johnson. In the fall elections, Majority Leader Scott Lucas of Illinois lost to Republican Everett Dirksen. When Francis Myers, the Democratic whip, also lost his bid for reelection, the void was enormous. As the Democrats searched for a new majority leader, Richard Russell's name surfaced more than any other. Several colleagues urged him to seek the post, which probably would have been his for the asking. Russell was flattered but had no interest in the job. Russell maintained he could not accept because of his concern for the South's fragile national image. He told Alabama senator Sparkman that a southern majority leader "would cause criticism of his acts to fall upon the South as a whole rather than upon the individual involved, though this would, of course, be the case with a leader coming from any other section of the country." Actually, Russell—like many other powerful senators—believed the leadership position would limit his power and prerogatives. As Senate leader for a liberal president, Russell and other conservative Democrats would be constantly whipsawed between the interests of their president and their conservative constituents. Besides, as the defeat of Lucas and Myers had proved, a leadership position did little to bolster a senator's standing back home. "It's a tinsel job," Russell explained to the *Atlanta Constitution*. "It carries many advantages and some power—but it's not for me. I want to stay independent."

Russell threw his support to Arizona's Ernest McFarland, whose ambivalence about civil rights would cause southerners little anxiety. A lackluster leader, McFarland, in the words of William S. White, was known for an "unconquerable and overweening tolerance" for his colleagues. "There are not many times when a Senate leader can afford to 'get tough,'" White said. "To McFarland there was no time at all." Facing a difficult reelection campaign in 1952, McFarland was easily elected majority leader over Joseph O'Mahoney of Wyoming.

The real intrigue revolved around selection of the Democratic whip, the Democrats' second-in-command and a potentially important position given McFarland's dim reelection prospects. At first, a group of liberals touted Alabama's John Sparkman, a dependable liberal on many issues other than civil rights. Russell was cool to Sparkman's candidacy. But Robert Kerr, the influential freshman and millionaire oilman from Oklahoma, had another idea. Kerr—an ostensibly devout Baptist and audacious power broker who was driven alternately by his lust for larger fortunes and greater dominions—had initially wanted New Mexico's Clinton Anderson, Truman's former Agriculture secretary. When Anderson turned him down, Kerr's eyes fell on Johnson. "You could tell immediately," recalled Kerr's friend Allen Barrow, "that Kerr was most respectful of . . . Johnson as a senator; he considered him one of his sidekicks." Johnson reciprocated. Johnson "thought Bob Kerr was Jesus Christ," recalled Pennsylvania Senator Joseph Clark, who later observed the Kerr-Johnson relationship in its maturity.

Though Kerr respected Johnson's abilities, he saw him mostly as a rising star to which he could hitch his own ambitions. But to Russell, Johnson was much more. He was a promising new breed of southern politician with liberal *and* conservative credentials who might help transform regional stereotypes of the South. Russell's biographer, Gilbert Fite, believed that Russell saw Johnson as "someone who could bridge the gap between North and South" because of his ability to look moderate—sometimes almost liberal—while talking like a southern conservative. "I think Senator Russell recognized him as having everything that it took [to be president]," said Russell's aide William Darden.

In other words, Russell probably saw in Johnson a steadfast opponent to civil rights who could relate to and move among the Senate's liberal coalition in ways no other southerner could. Most important, perhaps, was that Johnson—always playing the role of a dutiful son—gave Russell every reason to believe he would remain exceedingly deferential to the elder Georgian. With McFarland and Johnson as the Senate's nominal leaders, Russell could remain confident that his de facto command of the Senate would be undiminished.

There is no evidence that Johnson himself, or even a surrogate, planted the idea in Kerr's head. However, Johnson's eagerness to assail Leland Olds, along with his crucial assistance to Kerr on a natural gas deregulation bill in 1950, certainly was enough to bring Johnson to mind. At first, Johnson was wary of the job. When Bobby Baker broached the subject with him, Johnson laughed and said, "You'll destroy me, because I can't afford to be identified with the Democratic Party right now." Any reluctance, however, was only temporary. After weighing the proposition, he concluded that the job might not only lead to greater power in the Senate, the national prominence it afforded might bolster his reelection chances in 1954. Johnson quickly informed Kerr and Russell that he wanted the job and, with their support, actively campaigned for it.

On January 2, 1951, Democrats elected Johnson as their whip by acclamation. At forty-two, he was the youngest man ever installed in the position. "At that time," recalled Sam Shaffer of *Newsweek*, "the assistant leadership was little more than an honorary degree. But to Lyndon, it lifted him out of the rut of freshman senator, and he would sit in the leadership councils until the majority leader was out on the hustings campaigning, making a speech, and then he would be in charge of the fort. He would be noticed. Other senators would be aware of him."

Although Johnson's election would provide an enormous boost to his standing in the Senate, the benefits of his growing prominence would eventually accrue to another senator as well. For Humphrey, still licking his self-inflicted political wounds, Johnson's election was a turning point.

CHAPTER SEVEN

The Art of the Possible

BY 1952 RUSSELL HAD REASON for confidence in his ability to thwart Harry Truman's civil rights initiatives in the Senate. The president's legislative engines had exhausted their steam. When liberals had mounted another drive to establish a Fair Employment Practices Commission in 1950, Russell used his new cloture rule to stop them at every turn. In frustration, Truman had finally rejected any compromise on the issue after his allies failed twice to bring the matter before the full Senate. Although the southern opposition sometimes fell appallingly short of reality—"there will not be found a scintilla of proof that there is discrimination in Mississippi," declared that state's James Eastland—they *always* had enough votes to prevail. The first cloture roll call, in May 1950, fell twelve votes shy of the necessary sixty-four. The second vote, the following month, revealed some southern erosion, but not enough: the liberals were still nine votes short. Meanwhile, Truman's noble efforts to desegregate the military, articulated in his 1948 executive order, fared no better. Legislation aimed at dismantling a generations-old system of segregation in the armed forces remained stymied in the House and the Senate.

The congressional elections of 1950, in which both of the Senate's Democratic leaders had been defeated, provided further evidence of the unpopularity of Truman's Fair Deal agenda. The Democratic party still controlled Congress, but the elections had diminished their numbers by twenty-seven in the House and by four in the Senate. Furthermore, Russell's forbidding cloture rule seemed as safe as his own Senate seat. Four proposals to liberalize cloture—one of them offered by Humphrey—remained buried and lifeless in the Rules Committee throughout 1951. Perhaps most satisfying to Russell was the growing realization that

Truman, widely regarded as a lame duck and immersed in the growing conflict in Korea, had effectively abandoned civil rights as a legislative priority.

What mattered now to Russell—and almost every national Democrat of any ideological persuasion—was the Democratic party's future. Weakened by an unpopular war, various scandals, and suggestions of communism in its ranks, the Truman administration was in trouble. Republicans finally believed they could recapture the White House after sixteen years in exile. Russell confessed to worrying that the Republicans' sudden competitiveness might spark a legislative bidding war by both parties for minority votes that, he said, "will destroy our institutions and way of life."

With Truman faltering, Russell perceived an impending power vacuum in the Democratic ranks and worried that the party might fall into the wrong—that is, liberal—hands. He was equally concerned that the continuous strife over civil rights only furthered the South's alienation from the rest of the nation. "In his view," George Reedy said, "the eleven states of the Confederacy had been segregated from the mainstream of American life far too long." Russell and other southerners feared that a repeat of the divisive 1948 convention, resulting in a stronger platform commitment to civil rights, might trigger an even larger southern defection. That meant not only losing the White House; significant losses were possible for congressional Democrats if angry southern whites abandoned the party's candidates from top to bottom.

Before 1936, southern leaders had little reason to fear that a wholly unacceptable Democrat might become president: Party rules had required a two-thirds majority for the nomination, meaning that southern delegates possessed a de facto veto over all potential nominees. But when Franklin Roosevelt abolished the two-thirds rule, he opened the door for the 1948 States' Rights challenge and other defiant acts by disaffected southern leaders.

By 1952, Russell and other southern leaders believed they had only one weapon to prevent liberals from seizing their party: the South must put forth its own candidate. This person would not, of course, win the nomination. Their candidate might, however, amass enough delegates to hold the balance of power at the nominating convention. With enough delegates, a southern candidate could play a role in selecting the party's nominees and exert a moderating influence over the platform's civil rights language. Most importantly, a southern candidate might prevent tempestuous southerners from bolting the party after the convention. "In Russell's eyes," said George Reedy, another third-party southern defection "would cost the South valuable allies in the Democratic Party and leave Dixie to the tender mercies of the Republicans whom he did not expect to be grateful." Any southern challenge, he knew, *must* come from within the party.

It was Russell, the most respected southern senator, to whom southern leaders now turned. Although Russell had refused their earnest appeals to challenge Harry Truman as a third-party candidate four years earlier, an intraparty struggle in 1952 presented far fewer political risks. If Russell lost the nomination—a near certainty—he would still declare his support for the victor and suffer little or none of the blame if and when the party lost the White House.

No southerner was better suited to play the dual roles of challenger and conciliator. As the new chairman of the Senate Armed Services Committee, Russell had become a prominent national figure, widely respected by leaders in both political parties. In 1951 he had masterfully presided over the Senate hearings on President Truman's controversial dismissal of General Douglas MacArthur. Russell's steady hand and his determination to conduct an exhaustive series of bipartisan hearings had helped assuage the potentially dangerous public outcry over MacArthur's firing and prevented cancellation of armistice negotiations. Russell was, except for his crippling views on civil rights, an extraordinary public servant. His leadership, legislative expertise, and thorough understanding of the nation's military and foreign affairs objectives were unsurpassed in the Senate. "I think that if he had had his residence in some place like Kalamazoo, Michigan, instead of Winder, Georgia," North Carolina Senator Sam Ervin once remarked, "he would undoubtedly" have been elected president. Russell was, Ervin said, "the best qualified man by natural talents, by experience in government for that job of any man of his generation in this country." Even Harry Truman confided to Russell, "Dick, I do wish that you lived in Indiana or Missouri. You would be elected president hands down."

After weeks of agonizing reflection, Russell made up his mind. He would run. On February 28, 1952, flanked by colleagues Russell Long, Burnet Maybank, and John Stennis, Georgia's junior senator embarked on his gambit to save the South from the Republicans and his party from the liberals. Announcing his candidacy for the Democratic nomination, he told reporters in Washington that he was a "Jeffersonian

Democrat who believes in the greatest practicable degree of local self-government." He said nothing specific about civil rights. Asked if he would support Truman if Democrats renominated the president, Russell answered, "I shall not answer that until he is and I see the platform." While many Southern leaders greeted his announcement enthusiastically, *Time*—which featured him on its March 10 cover—noted that his supporters understood "he has about as much chance of being nominated as a boll weevil has of winning a popularity contest at a cotton planters' picnic." Other observers, however, speculated that Russell would exercise significant influence over the convention and nominating process. Said *Newsweek:* "As a Southerner, his chances for the nomination are still slim. But he will go to the convention with at least 300, perhaps 350, delegates in his pocket." That bloc of delegates, the magazine concluded, "seems sure" to guarantee Russell "a voice in naming the ticket, a hand in writing the platform and a prominent role in Democratic Party councils after the convention."

Many of Russell's friends believed he entertained no illusions about his viability as a serious contender. Russell Long said that Russell's "view was that he really had very little chance to get the nomination." James Eastland said that he "never thought that [Russell] was serious about getting the nomination" but merely hoped to derail the candidacy of Tennessee's liberal senator Estes Kefauver. Russell himself admitted years later that he had entered the race only "on the theory it would be a holding operation for the conservative South until the campaign developed." To a television interviewer in 1970, Russell confessed, "Very frankly, I didn't think I had much chance. I was thrust into that campaign by the force of circumstance."

At the time of Russell's announcement, Truman had not formally announced his retirement. Kefauver, who had garnered national attention by chairing a special Senate investigation into organized crime in 1951, was the only other announced Democratic candidate in the race. Other possible challengers included Oklahoma's Robert Kerr and Illinois governor Adlai Stevenson. In March, after Kefauver beat Truman in the New Hampshire primary, the president finally announced what everyone had suspected for months: he would not seek reelection.

Despite his decision to run, Russell was a reluctant campaigner who believed he could forgo a grueling state-by-state crusade. Instead, he hoped to operate his Washington-based campaign at a more civilized pace, relying on political associates in and out of the Senate to win him delegates. By spring, however, he yielded to a group of Florida congressmen who pleaded with him to enter their state's May 6 primary in order to prove his primacy as a southern leader. On April 26, Florida senator George Smathers witnessed the extent of Russell's reluctance to campaign as the two men sat together on the platform during Russell's first campaign rally, in Gainesville. While the city's mayor introduced other dignitaries, Russell's stage fright startled Smathers. Not only was he sweating profusely, but his knees were "trembling so" that Smathers shielded his legs from the audience's view with an umbrella.

Despite early jitters, Russell proved an excellent, fiery campaigner. Throughout the ten-day Florida campaign, he ripped into Kefauver. He exploited their differences over civil rights and the Atlantic Union—a proposal to unify the foreign and defense policies of the United States, Canada, and western Europe. While his opposition to civil rights, particularly the FEPC, won him support among Florida's conservative voters, Russell's prominent association with the issue only hurt him over time. By making civil rights such a significant part of his Florida campaign, Russell laid the groundwork for his eventual failure, highlighting the very issue that would cost him votes in every other region.

Civil rights and the Atlantic Union were not Russell's only issues. Straining credulity, he stressed his ability to win the election, if nominated. Most polls, Russell said, suggested that presumptive Republican nominee Dwight D. Eisenhower would carry much of the North, the Midwest, and even the South against any Democrat—save one. In the South, only Russell appeared to have a chance to block Eisenhower. At almost every campaign stop, he hammered home that message: "In thirteen Southern states, I am the only Democrat who can win." Russell argued that he would win 146 electoral votes from a solid South. Needing "only" 120 additional votes from the remaining thirty-five states, Russell claimed that he could win the election. Even if he did not win, Russell maintained, the Democratic party could not afford to lose important electoral ground in the South. As *Newsweek* observed prophetically on May 12, staving off a Republican invasion was crucial to southern Democrats: "An Eisenhower victory in a few Southern states might give the Republican Party there such impetus, the South would never be solid again."

In Florida, although Russell won—with 367,000 votes to Kefauver's 285,000—he polled poorly in the state's larger, northern-oriented cities. The majority of his votes came from rural Florida, where Old South attitudes prevailed. Even the margin of his victory was somewhat dis-appointing in light of predictions by some prominent Florida supporters that he would "swamp" Kefauver two to one. Nevertheless, Russell's Florida victory kept his candidacy alive.

But the victory created at least two immediate problems. While Russell had laid legitimate claim to the crown of southern leadership, party leaders now viewed him as a sectional leader who, more than anything else, represented the South's rage over civil rights. In March, *U.S. News & World Report* concluded that Russell's candidacy "means that the South is preparing to fight to return to power in the Democratic Party and will no longer serve merely as a source of votes to keep the northern wing of the party in the White House." A writer for *Time* was more direct: "Florida showed that Russell is the candidate for the South; outside the South, he has almost no support and plenty of bitter opposition. There is no lesson of American politics clearer than that such a sectional candidacy has little chance of winning the presidency." That Russell publicly refused to rule out bolting the party if he lost the nomination—conjuring up images of Strom Thurmond's 1948 States' Rights challenge—did not help him shed the sectional label. "I don't foresee anything will cause me to leave the party," he said, but quickly added that "I'm not going to take any paralyzed oath not to bolt."

The other problem created by the Florida victory was the impact it had on the momentum of Russell's campaign. Now identified as the Great White Hope, Russell had little choice but to stump for votes in other states. Years later, he confessed it was the "one time my political wisdom, if I ever had any, failed me." At the time, Russell said he did not understand "that if I ran in Florida that there wasn't any way honorably for me to get out short of the convention."

In June Russell made a fifteen-day foray into the Midwest designed to prove that he could attract delegates outside the South. "I am an American before I am a southerner," he told audiences. In Omaha he declared, "I have never been a sectional candidate." But the trip failed to stir widespread enthusiasm for his candidacy. Despite his near-solid Democratic voting record in the Senate, Russell simply could not per-suade delegates to look beyond his vigorous opposition to civil rights. "Too bad," one Midwestern party leader told a reporter, "that he's not from some place like Ohio or Indiana."

Although Russell intellectually understood that a southerner couldn't be elected president at that time, he was emotionally unprepared to face the stark reality once he began campaigning outside the South. As George Reedy explained: "To hit this first in New Jersey and then in Pennsylvania and then in Ohio. To get all these northern Democratic leaders, every single one of them saying you are the best man—which he was. I don't think there's any doubt about that. But then, to be told that because he had been born two hundred miles south of a certain point [that] he could not be president, that is what embittered Russell."

By the time of the July convention in Chicago, Russell was an obvious sectional candidate with virtually no northern or western delegate strength. On the first ballot, he finished third behind Kefauver, who led with 340 votes to Adlai Stevenson's 273. Although Russell's showing on the first ballot was respectable—he received 268 votes— he gained only a handful of votes in the second round, as delegates began a decided shift to Stevenson. By the third ballot, Russell was completely out of the running. Stevenson won with 617½ votes, just enough to win the nomination. Russell's final tally was 261.

For Humphrey and other liberals, the convention was a great success. With almost no dissent, a civil rights plank—with much stronger language than in 1948—became part of the platform by unanimous vote. "Our country is founded on the proposition that all men are created equal," the platform read. "This means that all citizens are equal before the law and should enjoy equal political rights. They should have equal opportunities for education, for economic advancement and for decent living conditions." Humphrey "thought that was [a] tremendous personal vindication," said Max Kampelman. In a mere four years, Humphrey had helped to determine where the national party stood on civil rights.

Meanwhile, when some party leaders urged Russell to seek the vice presidential nomination, he "definitely and unequivocally declined." The vice presidency, he told one friend, "held no allure." He had hoped instead to amass enough delegates to deliver the vice presidential spot to Johnson, who had worked vigorously for his presidential campaign. "Irrepressible and overpowering," as Russell's aide William Darden described him, Johnson had combed the convention floor "buttonholing people" for Russell. But with so few delegates, Russell had no influence at all over the convention's proceedings. The vice presidential nomination went to Alabama Senator John Sparkman, a moderate southerner who had helped Humphrey pass the civil rights plank.

Russell endorsed the Stevenson-Sparkman ticket with only minimal enthusiasm. Stevenson's tentative support for changing the Senate's cloture rule, announced shortly after the convention, persuaded Russell that his initial belief that the nominee was "a middle-of-the-road candidate" had been wrong. "Now it appears," he said, "that he is being influenced strongly by the CIO Political Action Committee and the Americans for Democratic Action." After Dwight Eisenhower won the election in a landslide—carrying Florida, Tennessee, Texas, and Virginia—Russell boasted to friends that the Democrats would have received more electoral votes if he himself had been the nominee. Perhaps it was best for the South that Russell was not the Democrats' standard bearer. Georgia governor Herman Talmadge argued that if Russell had been the nominee and then lost to Eisenhower—as he surely would have—the result "would have been cited as additional evidence that the South was a liability to the Democratic Party."

Ultimately, Russell's failed candidacy demonstrated how completely the South had become isolated in presidential politics. Few men of his time were better qualified for the presidency than Richard Russell. Yet because of his position on one issue—civil rights—Democratic leaders in every region but the South summarily dismissed him as a viable candidate. While he had hoped to gain greater influence for the South in the nominating and platform process, Russell instead learned that many Democrats viewed him as an anachronistic Old South relic. The truth was now abundantly clear to Russell and other attentive southerners: No one who represented a former Confederate state could be elected president as long as he opposed civil rights.

Five years later, as the Senate debated the Civil Rights Act of 1957, the painful lessons of his 1952 campaign would guide Russell. His acquiescence to Lyndon Johnson's efforts to pass that bill was born out of the bitter memories of his own failed presidential bid. Russell's failure and Dwight Eisenhower's election finally led Russell to conclude that Johnson might be the *only* southerner with any realistic hope of becoming president in his lifetime. In Johnson, Russell now invested not only his presidential aspirations but his abiding desire to restore his beloved South to the mainstream of American politics.

The defeat of Senate Democratic leader Ernest McFarland of Arizona at the hands of Republican Barry Goldwater in November 1952 came as no great surprise to those in Washington. "As a rule back in those days," explained Mississippi's James Eastland, "the minority leader or the majority leader was always a candidate for defeat." No senator was surprised that Johnson wanted to lead the Senate's forty-six Democrats, now in the minority after losing control of the Senate to the Republicans. As usual, the leader's job was Russell's for the asking. John Stennis believed that if Russell "had just nodded his head, he would have been chosen." Herman Talmadge maintained that Russell could have been easily elected as minority leader. "He didn't even have to ask for it." This time, Russell not only decided that Johnson was ready for the job, he apparently concluded that Johnson was the logical choice to lead Senate Democrats.

Russell may have been largely alone in that conclusion. "I think about the only man who had confidence in [Johnson's] ability to handle it was Dick Russell," said George Reedy, "and Russell was right." As Reedy noted, the election of a liberal would have torn the party "to pieces." Other than Russell, no strident anti–civil rights southerner could be elected. In Russell's eyes, Johnson was the one senator with a southern background who would not offend the sensibilities of the northern liberals. "It wasn't quite the same thing," Reedy said, "as bringing in somebody from Louisiana or Alabama or Mississippi or South Carolina."

Accounts differ as to whether Johnson or Russell first proposed Johnson's candidacy. Reedy claimed that Russell phoned Johnson at his Texas ranch shortly after McFarland's defeat, but "Johnson at first dismissed the idea." Some people recall that Johnson first called to urge *Russell* to seek the post. "I'll do the work and you'll be the boss," Johnson reportedly argued. Others, however, remember a markedly different scenario—a much more familiar image of an ambitious, scheming Johnson, who was determined to capture the leadership by any means possible. Ernest McFarland recalled that on the night of his defeat, Johnson phoned and "had me call all my friends boosting him."

The next morning, Johnson phoned Bobby Baker, the young secretary to the Senate Democrats.

"How do things look for me?" he asked.

"It looks like you're the new leader," Baker replied.

"I don't know. The Democratic Party's in disarray. The Senate 'red hots' [liberals] probably wouldn't go for me. Even if I get elected, it might be like getting caught in a nutcracker."

Baker said that he "received the impression that Lyndon Johnson was eager to be persuaded otherwise, and I was happy to accommodate him."

"The math's in your favor," Baker assured him. "All you've got to do is convince one man and you're home free."

"You're talking about Dick Russell."

"Sure," Baker said. "We're gonna have forty-[six] Democrats in the Senate. And Senator Russell will pretty much control half or more."

Baker and Johnson quickly engineered a plan to force Russell into the open. Baker persuaded Senator Burnet Maybank of South Carolina to wire Johnson pledging his support if Russell decided not to run. When reporters learned of Maybank's telegram, Russell quickly announced he had no desire to become the Democratic leader.

Russell's friend John "Jake" Carlton, then an aide to Florida senator George Smathers, remembered a slightly different approach by Johnson. When Carlton returned to Washington after the elections in late 1952, he went to see Russell, hoping he would run for leader.

"You know I promised to support Lyndon Johnson," Russell informed him.

"Well, you know, he's a very young senator," Carlton replied. "There are an awful lot of people who feel like you should accept this responsibility."

"Well, Jake, you know, I was sort of on the spot about this because Lyndon came to me and asked me to support him, and he said, 'I don't believe I can be reelected to senator in Texas without the prestige of this office.' And so, I've committed myself to support him."

Regardless of how Johnson secured Russell's support, there is no question that he campaigned vigorously for the position once he had the southern general's vote in his pocket. Shortly after the election, during a dinner party at the home of columnist Drew Pearson, a group of liberal senators caucused about the leadership race and concluded that Alabama Senator Lister Hill was the only southerner who could block Johnson's election. But when they phoned him in Alabama, they were startled to learn that Hill had pledged his support to Johnson only minutes earlier. With the public support of influential senators such as Russell, Kerr, Earle Clements of Kentucky, and J. Allen Frear of Delaware, Johnson had rounded up at least thirty endorsements in a matter of days—more than enough to win on the first ballot.

By the time Johnson phoned Humphrey to enlist his support, a group of liberals had persuaded James Murray of Montana—a wealthy, aging liberal—to challenge Johnson.

"How are you going to vote on minority leader?" Johnson asked.

"I can't vote for you," Humphrey said, explaining to Johnson that he was unacceptable to liberals on several issues, including civil rights.

"Well," Johnson replied, "I'm sorry. You know I'm going to win. You liberals don't have any votes."

"I think maybe that's true," Humphrey said.

"You haven't got even as many votes as you think you have," Johnson said.

"Well, maybe so. Maybe we ought to talk about that."

"We'll do that," Johnson answered. Then, almost casually, Johnson dropped his bomb. "But I was interested in you being minority whip."

"Well," Humphrey answered, candidly, "I can't vote for you."

"At least you're honest," Johnson replied. "But I want to tell you something. Some of the people that are telling you that they're going to vote against me are going to vote for me."

Later, in Johnson's office, Humphrey and Johnson met again to discuss the race.

"Well," Johnson asked, "who are you going to run, you liberals?"

"We're going to run Jim Murray," Humphrey said. "Not that Jim's going to get elected. I know he's not going to get elected, but we thought we'd put up a good showing for Jim. It would be something he deserves. He's an old-timer around here, and he symbolizes a lot of the liberal spirit that we have amongst the liberals in the Congress."

"Well, who do you think is going to vote for him?" Johnson demanded.

As Humphrey ticked off his list of names, Johnson scoffed at each one. "He isn't going to vote for him. He isn't going to vote for him. He isn't going to vote for him." Finally, Johnson declared that all "these fellows are going to vote for me."

Humphrey refused to believe that Johnson had already locked up *that many* votes. "I'll never forget this," he said years later. "When we had our caucus, he was just as right as day. They voted for Johnson."

On the morning of January 2, 1953, Democratic senators gathered in Room 201 of the Senate Office Building to elect their new leaders. Russell nominated Johnson. Though no written record exists of his exact words to the caucus, Russell's handwritten notes show that he praised his Texas friend for his "courage, character, ability, experience, tolerance." He told his colleagues that Johnson "possesses [the] qualities we need in [a] leader . . . [a] high degree of courage, tempered with judgment against rash decisions, patience and tolerance." Johnson later recalled that Russell told the caucus: "Our leader should be the most able man on the Democratic side of the Senate. My nominee isn't the best orator, he isn't the best parliamentarian, he isn't the most personable, he doesn't have the best mind." At this point, Johnson began to fret, but was relieved when Russell concluded that "he is the best combination of all these qualities."

Not surprisingly, the caucus voted overwhelmingly for Johnson. Humphrey later said that he had moved to make the vote unanimous, primarily to avoid humiliating Murray, who Humphrey said received just three votes. (Others recollect that Murray received five.)

Shortly afterwards, Johnson summoned Humphrey to his office to chastise him for becoming "mixed up with people that didn't keep their word."

"Now," Johnson said, "I'm willing to talk with you. You've kept your word, and you told me what you were going to do. You're a damned fool for what you're doing, but at least I know where you stand."

Johnson invited Humphrey to name the liberals he should appoint to influential committees. Murray went to Steering, Herbert Lehman of New York to Judiciary, Paul Douglas to Finance. "And every single request that I made, he fulfilled." Although Humphrey had not supported the new leader, his honesty and pragmatism impressed Johnson. "Johnson, I think, saw in me a man that would keep my word, and I saw in him the same thing. And I used to fight with all my liberals all the time about Johnson, because they always figured he was a conniving, southern conservative, and I always figured that he was a rather clever, adroit, astute pragmatist."

Shortly after his election, Johnson moved quickly to solidify his position with freshman senators. Previously, new senators had been shuffled onto committees of only marginal influence, waiting years for an important assignment. Johnson changed that. From now on, the Steering Committee would appoint all freshman Democrats to at least one of the Senate's top committees: Albert Gore of Tennessee to Public Works, Mike Mansfield of Montana and Humphrey to Foreign Relations, Massachusetts newcomer John F. Kennedy to Labor and Public Welfare, George Smathers of Florida to Interstate and Foreign Commerce, Russell Long to Finance. But Johnson had more in mind than simply pleasing his freshman colleagues. By appointing Humphrey to Foreign Affairs— which required his resignation from the Labor Committee—Johnson slightly diverted his attention away from domestic issues. The liberal Gore wanted the Judiciary Committee, which handled civil rights legislation. Johnson sent him instead to Public Works. There, while he became immersed in overseeing the Tennessee Valley Authority, he had fewer hours to devote to civil rights.

Moreover, Johnson understood just how much his Democratic minority was split between the northern and western liberals and the southern conservatives. As a writer for *Time* noted, "Johnson's first problem is to keep the . . . party together." He was the leader, wrote his friend William S. White, "of a party that was in great difficulties." His top priority was unity—at all costs. Along with House Speaker Sam Rayburn, Johnson declared that "wherever possible" the Democrats in the Senate would cooperate with President Eisenhower, something that the new majority leader, Robert Taft, could not confidently say about his own party. "Do no more talking than is necessary, as this merely unites the Republicans," George Reedy advised in a memorandum after the election. He added that Johnson should "use the coming period as a means of uniting the Senate Democrats." In the years that followed, said Alabama Senator John Sparkman, Johnson "could very well have been dubbed Ike's leader in the Senate." Douglas Cater, a Washington reporter and later a White House aide to Johnson, observed that "during those Eisenhower years, I dare say that Congress would have been at a complete standstill" if not for Johnson's willingness to cooperate.

The Democrats' cooperation was especially valuable in foreign affairs, where Eisenhower often found himself painfully at odds with Republican leaders in both houses of Congress. As Reedy saw it, Johnson's support for the president's foreign policy "built up Eisenhower's obligations to Johnson and Rayburn, which meant that he could not deal too harshly with their legislation." Johnson, Reedy noted, "took advantage of this situation" to secure Eisenhower's support for housing and health legislation. Better, said Reedy, "it presented the public the spectacle of the Congressional Democrats acting like true patriots who were sacrificing partisanship for the good of the nation and helping out a Republican president when they thought he was right."

To further the image of Democratic unity, Johnson established a "unanimous consent rule" in the Democratic Policy Committee. Under the new procedure, Democrats would bring no proposal to the Senate floor unless at least 90 percent of the southern-dominated committee approved. This did not please liberals, whose initiatives, especially civil rights legislation, would almost never make it out of the committee. But Johnson believed the change made political sense. "I don't see any profit," Johnson told Bobby Baker, "in calling up bills so that Jim Eastland and Herbert Lehman can insult each other, or so that Paul Douglas or Albert Gore can exercise their lungs. Why should we cut each other up and then lose after the blood shedding?"

Throughout Johnson's tenure as Democratic leader, Harry McPherson believed, it was "the great trick of leadership" to persuade the southern Democrats "to cooperate to the extent possible, without making it an ideological issue." Later, after Johnson became the *majority* leader in 1955, his narrow one-vote majority made Democratic unity all the more important. But his bare majority also afforded Johnson a great deal of clout. Johnson often pleaded with his Democratic colleagues to maintain unity out of his fear of "Russell walking across the aisle and embracing" Republican leader Everett Dirksen. "He had to keep the southerners in camp," McPherson said. Largely unspoken, but understood by all, was that this argument also helped Johnson resist demands for progress on civil rights. Humphrey's friend, ADA leader Joseph Rauh, often criticized Johnson's pragmatism, but he marveled at his "knack for finding that middle formula that pleases no one but satisfies everyone. That was, I think, what he really did in the Senate—find some middle ground where he could get some right-winger and Hubert Humphrey to agree."

From his first day as leader, Johnson attacked the job with unprecedented vigor. He installed six telephones in his office and worked them all, making up to a hundred calls a day. As he immersed himself in his new duties, he drove his staff to the limits of exhaustion. "He was a driver, and I don't mean maybe," remembered Senate parliamentarian Floyd Riddick. "Whenever he asked you for something, he wanted it five minutes before he asked you." But Johnson drove himself hardest of all. Once, when a friend urged him to take a break to see a new movie starring Lana Turner, Johnson replied, "Who's Lana Turner?" Besides the long, stressful hours he spent on the job, Johnson abused himself in other ways. He devoured fattening foods in large quantities until he weighed more than 220 pounds. He drank alcohol, often to excess. Sometimes, he smoked three packs of cigarettes a day.*

---

*The physical self-abuse finally caught up with Johnson in July of 1955. A serious heart attack forced him to abandon his Senate leadership duties for the remainder of the year.

While his energetic work habits became legendary, Johnson's amazing skill at winning votes and building majorities ultimately distinguished him as the most dynamic and successful Democratic leader ever. "He was about, face to face, as persuasive a man as you ever met," James Rowe recalled. "More persuasive than anybody I ever met. And he was a dangerous man in that sense. He could convince you black is white if you gave him enough time." Russell Long was amazed that Johnson "could think of more reasons why you ought to vote that way sometimes than you could yourself." As he prowled for votes on and off the Senate floor, Johnson was relentless, crafty, and overpowering. Wyoming senator Gale McGee grew accustomed to Johnson's imposing frame "as he would tower over you and get his head down close to your nose, you know, and really work you over in terms of trying to convince you to take a position that he favored." The technique became known in Washington as "the Johnson treatment," because every encounter with Johnson over legislation was a physical as well as intellectual experience. Said *Washington Post* editor Benjamin Bradlee: "When Johnson wanted to persuade you of something, when you got the 'Johnson treatment,' you really felt as if a St. Bernard had licked your face for an hour, had pawed you all over." Humphrey said Johnson won votes "by whispering in ears and pulling on lapels, and nose to nose. You have almost got to see the man. He'd get right up on you. He'd just lean right in on you, you know. Your nose would only be about—he was so big and tall, he'd be looking down on you, you see, and then he'd be pulling on your lapels and he'd be grabbing you."

"Watching him go after a vote was one of the rare delights of the Senate," *New York Times* reporter Russell Baker later wrote. "It was a form of hypnosis by movement, which seemed to leave the victim pliantly comatose. He might saunter up to his man and begin by seizing his lapels. Then the big hands would start flashing around the fellow's ears and the leader would lean into him, nose to nose, talking constantly, pounding his fist into palm, kneading the victim's lapels, bobbing and weaving, withdrawing abruptly, then thrusting his face just as abruptly against the gentleman's own, forcing him to retreat in mental disarray."

Besides his imposing physical presence, Johnson seemed always to know *exactly* what argument to make or pressure point to apply with each colleague. "Johnson had almost everybody's number," marveled Howard Shuman, aide to Senator Paul Douglas. "He knew their weaknesses, whether it was women or drink, or whether they wanted a certain bill, a committee assignment or whether they wanted more office space. He knew what almost everybody wanted." Johnson's "intelligence organization," said Washington senator Henry Jackson, "covered the Senate like the morning dew. I must say that he was a master of the doctrine that you better have your facts first before you make a move." As part of Johnson's unending quest for information, Democratic Whip Earle Clements and other senators and staff members became an omnipresent spy network. The result, Clements observed, was that Johnson usually "knew what the other members' viewpoints were before [he] started trying to persuade them." Another member "with less willingness to understand the other individual's viewpoint," Clements believed, "probably couldn't have gotten them together as he did."

From civil rights to farm policy, Johnson seemed to lack any overriding ideology to guide his actions or pursuits. Passing legislation and accumulating power seemed his only passions. "He didn't care whether his votes came from Joe McCarthy or Wayne Morse or Hubert Humphrey," said George Reedy. "Johnson would forget any political differences at any moment if he could get something done." Reedy detected "very little ideology" in Johnson. "He never let ideology get in the way of something, of an objective, never."

At times—on issues like housing, education, and social security— Johnson seemed to be a powerful force for progressive Democratic policies. But on oil and gas, civil rights, and labor legislation, he proved a reliable friend of the southern conservatives. When the Senate divided badly on an issue, Johnson's political philosophy—if he had one—rarely entered the picture. Rather, said Herman Talmadge, "he would work toward an area of compromise. Then he would normally get some senator who was not broadly identified with either side of the issue [to] offer some conciliatory amendment, which would normally bring the opposing factions together and succeeded in getting the consensus of the Senate in passing legislation."

Another enormous factor in Johnson's success, said George Smathers, was his acute sense of timing. "He never wanted to get a bill defeated if he thought by playing it [at] the right time he could get it through," Smathers said. "He would wait 'till he heard that two guys were going to be out of town. Right away, that would go into Johnson's calculated mind and he would think: 'I'm going to bring up this vote at that time because those guys have already committed to make a speech at the University of Southern California on a certain day at ten o'clock. I'm not going to agree to any sort of date to vote on it. I'm going to bring it up then.' And he'd bring it up and pass it."

Typical was the day in 1955 when Johnson realized that Florida senator Spessard Holland, the chief opponent of legislation to increase the minimum wage, was absent from the Senate chamber. Late in the afternoon, Johnson looked around and said to Humphrey, "I think we'll pass that minimum wage bill now." After a brief quorum call, Johnson engineered a voice vote. The bill passed. Minutes later, when Holland came storming onto the Senate floor, "jumping, screaming, hollering and pounding the desk," Johnson said, "Well, Spessard, I had a little quorum call. If you fellows aren't on the job around here, I've got legislation to pass."

Never was Johnson's sense of timing more valuable than in late 1954, when a lame-duck session of the Senate censured Senator Joseph McCarthy. For years the Wisconsin Republican's reckless charges about communism in the federal government had ruined reputations and lives. Spooked by McCarthy's public support, Republicans and southern Democrats had done little to challenge him. Senate liberals, meanwhile, badgered Johnson relentlessly to launch a Democratic counteroffensive. Aware of the danger of taking on McCarthy too early, Johnson resisted. "If I commit the Democratic Party to the destruction of McCarthy," he told his friend William S. White, "first of all, in the present atmosphere of the Senate we will all lose and he will win. Then he'll be more powerful than ever. At this juncture I'm not about to commit the Democratic Party to a high school debate on the subject, 'Resolved, that communism is good for the United States,' with my party taking the affirmative."

A united Democratic party finally joined a fractured Republican majority to censure McCarthy in December 1954, thanks mostly to Johnson's skilled leadership. Even Paul Douglas grudgingly acknowledged Johnson's crucial role. "With the northerners it was easy," said Douglas, who credited Johnson with winning the votes of the southern "mossbacks." "He was magnificent in that fight," Douglas declared. "Just magnificent." James Rowe's wife, Elizabeth, had been one of the liberals urging Johnson to act well before he was ready. "You see," Johnson told her after the Senate censured McCarthy, "you always wanted me to hurry, to speed it up, but I kept telling you, you can't speed it up.

You have got to know when the time has come for you to win. Now, I was right, wasn't I? We've done it. We've got him. He's finished."

Timing and pragmatic vote counts were constraints that Johnson also applied to civil rights legislation. Early in 1953—with the old Congress in an abbreviated session before Dwight Eisenhower's inauguration—Senate liberals coalesced for another push to liberalize cloture. With surreptitious help from Alabama's John Sparkman, liberals Clinton Anderson and Herbert Lehman devised an inventive strategy to challenge one of the Senate's most enduring precedents: For as long as anyone could remember, tradition held that, as a "continuing body," the Senate had no obligation to ratify its rules at the beginning of each Congress.

The "continuing body" principle held that because only one-third of the Senate was elected every two years, the remaining two-thirds of its membership "continued" into the succeeding Congress.* The point was important. Under Russell's 1949 rules change, the Senate could not invoke cloture on a debate over changing any Senate rule. Therefore, the only way to force a vote on the issue was to assert the Senate's right to approve new rules at the beginning of each Congress. "Why," Lehman asked, "should it be considered that rules adopted by majority vote, in the first session of the Senate in 1789, are binding and in effect in the Senate without affirmative, majority action on the part of the Senate of 1953?"

In early January, the liberals had beseeched the new Republican majority leader, Robert Taft of Ohio, for his support. "You are the people who kept us [Republicans] out of office for twenty years," Taft caustically replied after impatiently listening to the group's arguments. "I am not going to cooperate with you. I am against the Anderson motion." The group had not really expected Taft's support, but they did have reason to expect that outgoing Vice President Alben Barkley—the liberal former Democratic leader from Kentucky—would rule in their favor. However, before Barkley could issue his ruling, Taft sidetracked him by moving to table Anderson's motion. What Anderson

---

*In his book *Citadel: The Story of the U.S. Senate*, William S. White explained why the "continuing body" principle was so revered: "It was so arranged that while the House of Representatives would be subject to total overturn every two years, and the Presidency every four, the Senate, as a Senate, could *never* be repudiated. It was fixed, through the staggered-term principle, so that only a third of the total membership would be up for reelection every two years. It is therefore literally not possible for the voters ever to get at anything approaching a majority of members of the Institution at any one time."

found "most disheartening" was that Taft made his motion "by pre-arrangement with his Democratic opposite number, Minority Leader Lyndon Johnson." "Johnson's first act," Joseph Rauh said bitterly, "was to protect the filibuster in *violation* of the Democratic platform" and "help Taft wreck a proposal" to change the cloture rule. Rauh maintained that Johnson's support of Taft's tabling motion—ratified by a 70-21 vote—set the stage for years of sometimes-bitter acrimony and suspicion between the Senate's most fervent civil rights proponents and the pragmatic leader from Texas.

More than almost any other member of the Senate, Johnson governed his actions by the firm belief that politics was "the art of the possible." Though the NAACP's Clarence Mitchell eventually came to appreciate this aspect of Johnson's thinking, he was initially annoyed when Johnson flatly rejected his pleas for movement on civil rights legislation. "He thought it was unwise to try to get it through Congress because it would split the Democratic Party," Mitchell said. "He thought that most of the Democrats were poor people and they needed legislation in the social welfare field." Mitchell was not easily persuaded. "Clarence," Johnson said more than once, "you can get anything that you have the votes to get. How many votes have you got?" Mitchell had to admit he did not have the needed votes. In time Mitchell began to understand Johnson's philosophy—and worked tirelessly to help him round up votes for civil rights bills. Joseph Rauh had similar encounters with Johnson. "The trouble with you guys," he told Rauh, "is you don't realize you can beat the filibuster. You can always beat the filibuster if you've got fifty-one strong people." Rauh dismissed the theory as "nonsense."

Johnson's cooperative relationship with Eisenhower also displeased liberals, particularly Rauh. "My opinion was that he was destroying the Democratic Party and not doing his job. His job was the opposition to the Eisenhower Administration and he didn't do it. They were playing hanky-panky with each other and there was really no Democratic opposition." But as John Connally argued, Johnson was not merely accommodating Eisenhower. He was filling a leadership void left by the president's "distaste for the tedium of governing." Despite the criticism of the liberals, Johnson believed that the times called for his kind of consensus politics. In Johnson's world, pragmatism prevailed. "I think the Eisenhower years would have been far more dismal without Johnson," said Edwin Weisl, Jr., who was often a friendly critic of Johnson's conservatism in the 1950s. "If he had simply attacked and proposed extremely liberal programs in those days it would have failed, of course, or been vetoed." Weisl argued that Johnson chose cooperative progress over "wonderful liberal rhetoric."

Constant grumbling by liberals that he should have seized the reins of national leadership from Eisenhower, but chose not to, greatly exasperated Johnson. "That's like putting me in the cabin of a four-engine jetliner and locking me out of the cockpit and telling me to fly it to Los Angeles," Johnson once complained. "There's only one man who can lead. That's the president."

Timing, votes, and Democratic unity were not the only factors in Johnson's stubborn opposition to civil rights. Most important was his symbiotic relationship with Russell. "Johnson wasn't in control of the Senate, Russell was," insisted Howard Shuman. "Johnson essentially could not do anything that Dick Russell and his group fundamentally disagreed with. He was incapable of doing that. He never did." Shuman's view was largely correct, especially during Johnson's early years as leader. Johnson did little to discourage speculation that he remained under Russell's tutelage. Shortly after his election as leader, he persuaded Russell to move his desk to the second row, next to the center aisle, directly behind the leader's position. The move was partly a symbolic tribute to Russell's immense influence in the Senate, but it also ensured that Russell would always be there to whisper advice in Johnson's ear when a parliamentary rumpus erupted.

At first, as William S. White observed, Johnson held his position primarily through Russell's "benevolent though admiring patronage." With liberals alternately suspicious and hostile to Johnson, Russell's southerners formed his essential base of power. Until he established himself—until he made his brand of leadership indispensable to *all* the Senate's Democrats—Johnson could not stray far from his Georgia patron, especially on civil rights. "Every now and then, Johnson and Dick would come to loggerheads about something," George Smathers remembered. "And invariably, Johnson would back off. The only guy that ever would make Johnson back off was Dick Russell."

Though Russell made a convenient culprit for liberals frustrated by Johnson's refusal to initiate action on civil rights, Johnson was hardly Russell's pawn. Johnson did not ask Russell's permission; he won and wooed his approval. He did not beg for Russell's support; he seduced him with powerful logic and great deference. To many liberals, the Johnson-Russell relationship was almost entirely a one-sided affair, with Johnson on the receiving end of Russell's benevolence. But they failed to realize just how much Russell had invested in Johnson. Having staked his reputation on Johnson's suitability as Democratic leader, Russell did not simply want Johnson to slavishly do his bidding; he wanted Johnson to perform so well that the job would propel him into the White House.

Except for Humphrey, most of the Senate's ardent liberals came to resent Johnson's domineering leadership. Many of them viewed Lyndon Johnson's Senate as little more than an autocratic plantation. "To Johnson," Paul Douglas maintained, "the Senate was a circus and he was the ringmaster, putting the animals through their paces by the lure of the carrot and the sharp crack of the whip. He seldom called party conferences. The party line was supposed to emerge from the Southern-dominated Policy Committee as interpreted by Johnson." When a senator displeased him, Johnson, in Russell Long's words, "would find ways to cause you problems." And he was not secretive about his retribution. From experience, Long learned that Johnson would tell an uncooperative senator, "Well, now, if you're setting my barn on fire, I can't put that fire out unless I do something to give you some problems, because as fast as I put that fire out, you light another fire. The only way I can get you to stop is to go set your barn on fire. Then, while you're putting your fire out, I can put my fire out." Long said that before long, "you would get the idea that unless you wanted to cooperate with him, that as long as you were making life difficult for him and making it hard for him to move along with his program, that you were going to find that things that you wanted didn't happen very easily, either."

Johnson's "style," observed Strom Thurmond, "was to gain all the power." Though some bristled at Johnson's tight reins, Thurmond noted that most senators "didn't say much, because he was in the position to help them get better committees if they wanted them, or to help them in various other ways, such as getting bills through the Senate."

After he left the presidency, Johnson reflected on the criticism his lobbying style had generated among the Senate's liberals. Johnson complained of "intellectuals, who can never imagine me, a graduate from poor little San Marcos, engaged in an actual debate with words and with arguments, yet debating is what those sessions were all about." Johnson believed "the Harvards" pictured his lobbying as "a back-alley job with me holding the guy by the collar, twisting his arm behind his back, dangling a carrot in front of his nose and holding a club over his head." The intellectuals, Johnson said:

> never take the time to think about what really goes on in these one-to-one sessions because they've never been involved in persuading anyone to do anything. They're just like a pack of nuns who've convinced themselves that sex is dirty and ugly and low down and forced because *they* can never have it. And because they can never have it, they see it all as rape instead of seduction and they miss the elaborate preparation that goes on before the act is finally done.

Years later, sizing up Johnson's complicated relationships with colleagues, Humphrey also used sexual language:

> Many people look on Johnson as a heavy-handed man. That's not really true. He was sort of like a cowboy making love. He wasn't one of those Fifth Avenue, Madison Avenue penthouse lovers. He was from the ranch. But what I mean is he knew how to massage the senators. He knew which ones he could just push aside. He knew which ones he could threaten and, above all, he knew which ones he'd have to spend time with and nourish along, to bring along, to make sure that they were coming along.

Johnson never enjoyed warm relations with the Senate's liberals, but he could not afford to dismiss them as irrelevant nuisances. He often needed their votes for legislation. If he could not claim their enthusiastic support, at least he could vie for their grudging cooperation to maintain peace among Senate Democrats.

The problem with the Senate's liberals, observed Johnson's New Deal friend Jim Rowe, was that although they were united in philosophy "they were not cohesive in the sense of action." In Johnson's view, Rowe said, "each one would want to amend the other fellow's thoughts, and if he didn't get his own amendment, he wouldn't play. Johnson, I think, had contempt for this point of view."

In Humphrey, Johnson found a pragmatic ally, a friend, and, most important, a bridge to the liberals. "My God," he once said of Humphrey. "If I could just harness that guy's energy." Johnson admired—some thought he envied—Humphrey's speaking abilities, his intellect, and the bubbly enthusiasm he brought to any endeavor. "When I picture Hubert in my mind," Johnson said many years later, "I picture him with tears in his eye; he was always able to cry at the sight of something sad, whether it be a widow with her child or an old crippled-up man."

Johnson also saw aspects of Humphrey's personality that he wanted to change. "The trouble is that he's never learned to put feelings and strength together; all too often he sways in the wind like a big old reed, pushed around by the pressures of staff and friends and colleagues." Johnson's biographer, Doris Kearns, said she believed Johnson seemed "almost sad" as he described Humphrey, "as if he wished that the very men who had submitted to his will had fought a little harder against him." Harry McPherson observed Johnson's "terrific impatience with Humphrey for what he regarded as his impracticality." "Your speeches are accomplishing nothing," Johnson once told Humphrey in the early stages of their friendship. "Support me and deliver your liberal friends. Otherwise, you'll suffer the fate of those crazies, those bomb-thrower types like Paul Douglas, Wayne Morse, Herbert Lehman. You'll be ignored and get nothing accomplished you want."

Johnson made the first overtures. Almost from the beginning, Humphrey said, he was friendlier and more accepting than other southerners:

> Lyndon Johnson was the first man of what we called the southern senators . . . that came on over to me, towering over me, just like, you know, you'd expect him to be, and looking down at me and asking me all kinds of questions about how I got elected and how it was to be mayor of Minneapolis—made me feel important. I liked him. I guess he was about the only one at that time that was really interested in my election.

"I always felt," Humphrey once said, "that Johnson was a pragmatic liberal." After the scuffle with Harry Byrd in 1950, Johnson found Humphrey and joked with him about the episode. "He said he wanted to crossbreed me with Byrd," Humphrey recalled. "If he could get two pints of Byrd's blood into me to cool me off, and a little of Russell's restraint, I'd be great." After work, Johnson began to phone Humphrey. He often invited him to his office for casual conversation and a drink. Johnson did not, as Humphrey recalled, "come at me head-on." His courtship was more subtle and gradual. Occasionally, when Humphrey declined Johnson's invitation with the explanation that he needed to get home to his family, Johnson sputtered: "Damn it, Hubert, you've got to make up your mind whether you're going to be a good father or a good senator."

More often than not, Humphrey came when summoned. Sometimes another colleague would join them. Often they would talk alone—about the Senate, how it functioned and who made it work. To Humphrey, these frequent meetings with Johnson had "a second value": they appeared to have Richard Russell's "tacit approval." In fact, Russell sometimes joined Johnson and Humphrey for their after-hour sessions. Despite their differing styles and ideologies, the three men—especially Humphrey and Johnson—shared common backgrounds. They were children of rural America. Their fathers were elected officials who had instilled in them an abiding respect for government service and a passion for politics. Each was elected to public office at an early age. They distrusted the eastern political "establishment." Johnson and Humphrey had been teachers and had gained important experience, prior to elective office, as administrators of New Deal programs.

"It was very early in the game that he had a real fondness for Hubert," said Humphrey's friend Andrew Biemiller, who observed that Johnson "occasionally would get mad at Hubert, but at the same time, he took an interest in him, and he was advising Hubert frequently." "Johnson," said Harry McPherson, "loved Humphrey, admired his articulateness a great deal, shared probably most of his views. [Johnson] was much more inclined to look for the middle-ground compromise right off the bat. Humphrey would often come to it, and would often be the bridge." Johnson sometimes used Humphrey "as a foil," McPherson said. "He could go to the conservatives in his own party and say, 'If we don't yield on this, Hubert's going to lead the pack and they're going to tear us up.' "

Through Johnson, Humphrey began to learn more about his southern colleagues and why they voted against civil rights. Johnson "did a great deal to bring me into a more tolerant and friendly attitude" toward the southerners, Humphrey admitted. Eventually, said Humphrey, because of Johnson, southern leaders like Russell and Walter George began to "look with some favor on me." George, a leading voice on foreign policy, discovered that their views on world affairs were almost identical. Even Harry Byrd, Humphrey's old nemesis, grudgingly confessed to Johnson, "Lyndon, I just don't understand how you got me to liking Hubert Humphrey so much." As for Russell, he and Humphrey became better acquainted and discovered that they shared much common ground—on issues such as agriculture, labor, wages, and rural electrification. As Johnson's aide Gerald Siegel observed, the two men began to develop a high degree of mutual respect—"so that when a civil rights bill came down the pike, they weren't drawing swords and muskets and standing off just firing at will. They were willing to talk with one another."

By 1953 the relationship had warmed to the point that Humphrey felt comfortable reprimanding Russell after the Georgia senator had dismissed an effort to reform the Senate's cloture rule as "goon squad tactics." In a letter, Humphrey expressed his "high personal regard" for Russell and his concern that "our tempers will undoubtedly be strained" in the coming debate. "But I trust," he concluded, "we will both assume that our differing positions are sincerely and conscientiously held." Less than a month later, he was bold enough to ask for Russell's support of two civil rights bills he had introduced. He closed a January 26, 1953, letter to Russell with an expression of "faith that men of good will can resolve many differences." Though Humphrey could not have expected Russell's support, his colleague's generous, albeit formal, reply must have pleased him: "You may be assured that I shall examine these measures carefully. I shall, of course, be glad to discuss this matter with you at any mutually convenient time."

Throughout his early years in the Senate, Humphrey was aware that Johnson was seducing him. "It was a very slow process of calling me in and talking to me and saying, 'Do you think you can help out amongst your liberal friends on this?'" In time, Humphrey said, he became Johnson's "bridge to the liberals." Johnson needed a liaison, Humphrey argued, simply because "Johnson didn't enjoy talking with the liberals. He didn't think they had a sense of humor . . . So he wanted someone in the liberal ranks for information and help. Perhaps he came to the conclusion I could be had. I never felt I was. I felt I was getting more than giving." Still, serving as Johnson's unofficial liaison was not an easy assignment, as Humphrey admitted:

> The liberals are very independent. They are willing to vote in bloc, but they don't do it under anybody's direction. They prefer to think it's ideology. And my kind of politics met with Johnson's in this sense—that while I was a man of liberal persuasion, I often knew that you couldn't get as much as you

wanted, and therefore I was willing to settle for less. This, of course, was considered to be heresy amongst the true liberals. I used to say that some of my liberal friends were never so happy as when they were unhappy. If they really succeeded in their total measure, it made them unhappy. And they look upon us that would take a foot instead of a mile as unprincipled compromisers . . . I felt that it was important that we inch along, even if we couldn't gallop along, at least that we trot a little bit. And Johnson felt that way. And Johnson maybe convinced me more than anybody else that we could make steady progress if we just didn't bite off too much. Yet, he also knew that sometimes you had to go the whole way.

Humphrey's constant appeals for cooperation with Johnson did not please liberals such as Douglas, Morse, and Joseph Clark of Pennsylvania who, Maine's Edmund Muskie believed, would sometimes "rather get shot down in flames than just to get a small step forward." Never averse to taking a principled stand on an important issue, Humphrey was nonetheless "not one of those to get shot down in flames on every liberal cause," said Muskie. But, he added, "other liberals felt otherwise."

Humphrey later said that he "learned early" that "liberals were always out speaking while the conservatives were in legislating." Douglas believed that Johnson eventually persuaded Humphrey to tone down his rhetoric and "not push the South too far." On important votes, said Douglas, "Humphrey always voted with us, but he did not initiate [civil rights] measures after 1952." Douglas was misinformed. Humphrey continued to introduce and cosponsor dozens of civil rights bills throughout the 1950s. In 1953, for example, Humphrey introduced legislation to establish a permanent Commission on Civil Rights, an idea later incorporated into the Civil Rights Act of 1957. Explaining the bill and its limited objectives to a friend, Humphrey acknowledged criticism "that I have yielded or compromised my views." But Humphrey argued against "an all-or-nothing approach," maintaining that "the time is at hand to get something done."

Writing in the *New Republic* in 1955, journalist Robert L. Riggs astutely observed that Humphrey "has not retreated one inch from the liberal side while establishing a beachhead among Southern conservatives." Far from becoming Johnson's captive, said Riggs, "Humphrey has bored from within to give liberals a means of presenting their demands to the leadership." Humphrey was stung by criticism that "I have become cool toward civil rights." And he sometimes reached out to reassure his friends in the civil rights movement. To NAACP leader Walter White, Humphrey protested in January 1955 that "I am no quitter and I don't want any of my friends spreading unfounded rumors to the effect that Hubert Humphrey is compromising or backtracking." When he introduced a package of eleven civil rights bills in early 1955, he wrote a liberal editor to defend his willingness "to accept any one or two or three" of the bills "so that we can get off dead center and begin to make some progress." Along with spirited defenses of his own actions, Humphrey defended Johnson, too. To Walter White, he insisted that "Lyndon Johnson has been the most cooperative [Democratic leader] with the so-called liberal wing of our party." But he promised "to keep pressuring Lyndon for favorable action."

Though Humphrey often urged liberals to accept less than everything, many believed that Johnson "never had to give anything to the liberals" for their support on crucial issues while compromising freely with southern conservatives. As Edmund Muskie maintained, Johnson "paid a very small price for liberal support." Among liberals, a common saying about Johnson was: "We gave him an orchard and he gave us an apple."* Johnson's uncomfortable relationship with the liberals meant that what support he received from them was usually given grudgingly. Humphrey recalled how he often argued vigorously with his liberal colleagues about Johnson:

> I said, "On the basic things that we need around here Johnson is with us" . . . And that just infuriated a number of my lovable friends—Paul Douglas and Herbert Lehman and men of that quality . . . But I said, "Look at Johnson. On minimum wage he's with us. On health measures, he's with us. On agriculture measures, he's with us. On all the public works programs, he's with us. On public employment measures, when we had recessions, he was with us. He was with us on the counter tax proposals to the Eisenhower efforts . . . And on all education measures, Johnson was with us."

*In later years, during the civil rights skirmishes of 1956 and 1957, Howard Shuman insisted that Humphrey was a poor advocate for the liberal cause. "Invariably, Hubert would come back having lost his trousers" (Shuman OH, USSHO).

Still, on civil rights and oil and gas, Johnson was elsewhere. For many liberals, that was more than enough to justify their antipathy toward him.

Humphrey, like Johnson, often ran into trouble with the liberals for supporting the Eisenhower administration. Particularly irked was Humphrey's old friend Joseph Rauh, who headed a group of liberal activists determined to turn Humphrey against Eisenhower. Humphrey became infuriated. "I don't know about you fellows," Humphrey said, "but I've only got one president at a time and my president today is Dwight D. Eisenhower. And as my president, I'll help him when I can."

As with most successful relationships, Johnson and Humphrey each profited greatly from their association. In Humphrey, Johnson gained a crucial liaison to the Senate's liberals. In Johnson, Humphrey found a teacher and an influential friend willing to help him shepherd legislation through the Senate. "You had to persuade both sides to give some," Harry McPherson observed. "And so [Johnson] found in Humphrey a sensible, attractive guy who was willing to talk, willing to deal, willing to try to make the arrangements necessary to permit the progressive Democratic Party to proceed." Of all the liberals, said McPherson, Humphrey "was the most political . . . the most gregarious."

Ultimately the two men, in Max Kampelman's words, changed "the chemistry of the body" and helped "open up the club." "Ideology and suspicion," said Kampelman, "gave way, to some extent, to understanding and trust."

CHAPTER EIGHT

To Hell with
the Supreme Court

BY REFUSING TO CARRY her exhausted body to the back of an Alabama bus on December 1, 1955, seamstress Rosa Parks sparked a grassroots movement among blacks to win in fact the civil rights they won in name eighty years earlier. Although the resulting citywide boycott of the Montgomery City Lines—led by twenty-six-year-old Baptist minister Martin Luther King, Jr.—was among the early stirrings of the modern civil rights movement, the constitutional and legislative questions about blacks and their rights as citizens had arguably been "settled," legally and constitutionally, for decades.

The Thirteenth Amendment to the Constitution, adopted in 1865, said:

> Neither slavery nor involuntary servitude, except as a punishment for crime whereof the party shall have been duly convicted, shall exist within the United States or any place subject to their jurisdiction.

The Reconstruction Act of 1867 gave freedmen the right to vote. The Fourteenth Amendment to the Constitution, ratified in July 1868, said:

> No State shall make or enforce any law which shall abridge the privileges or immunities of citizens of the United States; nor shall any State deprive any person of life, liberty or property without due process of law; nor deny to any person within its jurisdiction the equal protection of the laws.

In March 1870 the states ratified the Fifteenth Amendment, which strengthened the right to vote:

The right of citizens of the United States to vote shall not be denied or abridged by the United States or by any State on account of race, color, or previous condition of servitude.

Five years later, Congress passed a civil rights bill that declared:

All persons within the jurisdiction of the United States shall be entitled to the full and equal enjoyment of the accommodations, advantages, facilities, and privileges of inns, public conveyances on land or water, theaters, and other places of public amusement; subject only to the conditions and limitations established by law and applicable alike to citizens of every race and color, regardless of any previous condition of servitude.

In support of these measures, federal troops streamed into the South in the years following the Civil War. The rights of blacks were upheld, for a time, at the point of a gun. Gleeful with their newfound freedoms, most former slaves could not have imagined how the forces of Jim Crow would ultimately undermine their ostensible victories. In their euphoria, some black leaders even declared that the struggle for civil rights had ended. "We have not only abolished slavery, but we have abolished the Negro," one leader triumphantly asserted. "We have actually washed color out of the Constitution." Said another, "All distinctions founded upon race or color have been forever abolished in the United States."

As these leaders would soon learn, the postwar civil rights laws were, in the words of one historian, only "fragile legal props." The truth was that racism and white supremacy were not dead, only in hibernation. When they awoke, these forces lurched into motion and roared with a brutal and violent fury.

Ignited by white southern leaders and fueled by the U.S. Supreme Court, white supremacy blazed across the South. It gutted the laws and constitutional protections that had briefly recognized blacks as citizens of the United States. In 1873, the Supreme Court ruled that the Fourteenth Amendment applied merely to *states*—not to individuals. Ten years later the court held that, because of its reliance on the Fourteenth Amendment, the Civil Rights Act of 1875 was unconstitutional. In language strikingly similar to arguments later used against modern civil rights legislation, the court declared that blacks could no longer be considered "the special favorite of the laws." These rulings—and others like them—nurtured an explosion of Jim Crow laws throughout the nation.

Mississippi led the effort to obliterate the Fifteenth Amendment when its 1890 constitutional convention adopted a provision allowing local voting registrars to reject blacks if they could not "understand" or "give a reasonable interpretation" of the state's constitution. In a remarkably frank admission, a white convention delegate acknowledged Mississippi's official hostility to the Fifteenth Amendment. "Sir, it is no secret that there has not been a full vote and a fair count in Mississippi since 1875—that we have been preserving the ascendancy of the white people by revolutionary methods. In plain words, we have been stuffing ballot boxes, committing perjury and here and there in the State carrying the elections by fraud and violence until the whole machinery for elections was about to rot down."

Shown the way by Mississippi's "visionary" tactics, much of the South followed suit. Other states erected a variety of clever roadblocks to black voter registration, including literacy tests, cumulative poll taxes, and lengthened residency requirements. By 1900, black voters—once registered in greater numbers than southern whites—were almost nonexistent.

In 1896 the Supreme Court again proved a reliable advocate for the white man when it sanctioned, in *Plessy v. Ferguson,* "separate but equal" facilities for whites and blacks. "If one race be inferior to the other socially," Justice Henry Brown wrote for the majority, "the Constitution of the United States cannot put them upon the same plane." Only Justice John Marshall Harlan of Kentucky, himself a former slave owner, spoke out against the rising tide of racism now given legal sanction by the nation's highest court. Declaring that the Constitution was "colorblind," Harlan accurately predicted that the *Plessy* decision would open the way for states to "defeat the beneficent purposes which the people of the United States had in view when they adopted the recent amendments of the Constitution." Two years later, the court upheld segregation again. In *Williams v. Mississippi,* justices ruled that Mississippi's voting requirements "did not on their face discriminate between the races." Meanwhile Congress, which had passed the civil rights laws and sent the constitutional amendments to the states for ratification, retreated into a climate of hostility and indifference toward black suffrage and other rights. Some southern senators even demanded the deportation of blacks.

Lynching was common in the South and in states like Ohio, Illinois, and Indiana. From 1889 to 1918, more than 2,500 blacks and 702 others were reportedly lynched, many for minor offenses and "general principles." Grisly tales were common. In Georgia in 1918, a white mob hanged a pregnant black woman from a tree, soaked her with gasoline and motor oil, and then set her afire. As her charred body dangled from the limb, a white man stepped forward with a pocket knife and slashed open her abdomen. When a screaming baby tumbled out of her lifeless body, the man promptly stomped the child to death.

While such brutal lynchings declined rapidly in the 1920s, the social and legal barriers to black rights remained firmly in place throughout the South. Only the Supreme Court's 1944 ruling in *Smith v. Allwright*—declaring that the all-white Democratic primary in Texas was unconstitutional—provided the kind of sweeping change that helped blacks win back an important aspect of their citizenship. With the death of the white primary, the numbers of black voters exploded throughout the South. In 1940, before the ruling, an estimated 5 percent of the eligible black voters in the South were registered. By 1947 that figure had more than doubled to 12 percent. Five years later, it was 20 percent. Despite these enormous gains, black registration lagged far behind that of whites: white registration in southern states ranged from 60 to 70 percent in 1952.

Those who believed that increased black registration would result in greater attention and consideration from the white establishment were disappointed. Of an earlier era, black historian Lerone Bennett, Jr. had written: "They were a formless and shapeless mass, outgunned and outmanned, nine to one, by mean and determined adversaries who held all the high ground." Decades later, the conditions Bennett described seemed tragically immune to the march of time.

Frustrated at every turn by implacable white supremacist forces in the states and in Congress—particularly the Senate—civil rights advocates took aid and comfort where they could find it. After three successive Republican administrations had ignored cries to end segregation in Washington's federal offices, President Franklin Roosevelt finally abolished the practice. Roosevelt also began integrating the armed forces and demanded that wartime industry follow equal opportunity employment practices. During his first two terms, he appointed 103 blacks to federal positions—though these were mostly clerical and lower-level executive posts. Roosevelt's wife, Eleanor, was more outspoken about the need for civil rights and worked diligently to find federal jobs for blacks. She achieved impressive results. By 1946 the number of black federal workers had quadrupled since 1933. "The Negro had never before had this penetration into the government that he had under Roosevelt," said NAACP leader Roy Wilkins, "and he'd never had access to this many or this variety of government jobs that he had under Roosevelt."

Federal employment opportunities were fine, but they were insignificant when compared with the millions of black citizens straining under the weight of the South's oppressive segregation laws and customs. With the blessing of the Supreme Court, states erected all sorts of onerous restrictions on the rights and prerogatives of black citizens. Black children were among the most pitiful victims of these statutes. In 1951 the laws of twenty-one states—most of them southern—and the District of Columbia required or permitted segregated schools. A 1944 study of the segregated South concluded that Mississippi and Georgia spent *five times* more on educating whites than blacks. Other southern states, on average, were better; the money they spent on educating white students was only three times what they spent on black schools. Salaries for white teachers were 30 percent higher than those of black teachers.

With the president able to effect only incremental change and Congress unwilling to address the deplorable state of black America, civil rights advocates had only one branch of government to which they might turn. The once-hostile Supreme Court, they hoped, might possess the will to restore the constitutional rights that southern leaders had dismantled or ignored throughout the previous seventy-five years.

As director of the NAACP's Legal Defense and Education Fund, Thurgood Marshall saw the federal judiciary as a legal crowbar. Used properly, the courts could pry open the doors of the South's white-only schools, railroad dining cars, restaurants, and hotels.

Marshall and his legal team had been challenging specific violations of the Fourteenth Amendment throughout the country since 1936—with great success. He had argued and won the case that outlawed the all-white Texas primary in 1944. He had helped stop the use of racially restrictive housing covenants. In 1950, Marshall and his team had finally persuaded a more liberal Supreme Court to deal body blows to three aspects of segregation built upon the foundation of "separate but equal." In three cases handed down on the same day in June, the court held that physical facilities were not the only factors in judging the equality of a black law school; that universities could not deny their black students the free use of school facilities; and that segregation in railroad dining cars was unconstitutional.

The next year was a turning point. Marshall and his team finally found the cases they believed would revive the moribund Fourteenth Amendment. Consolidating five school desegregation cases from Kansas, Virginia, South Carolina, Delaware, and the District of Columbia, Marshall's team filed suit for a group of plaintiffs who maintained that segregated schools were unconstitutional. The cases became known as *Brown v. Board of Education of Topeka.* "The question," Marshall argued before the court, "is whether a nation founded on the proposition that 'all men are created equal' is honoring its commitments to grant 'due process of law' and 'the equal protection of the laws' to all within its borders when it, or one of its constituent states, confers or denies benefits on the basis of color or race."

On May 17, 1954, the Supreme Court, led by its new chief justice, Earl Warren, handed down a unanimous ruling:

> We conclude that in the field of public education the doctrine of "separate but equal" has no place. Separate educational facilities are inherently unequal. Therefore, we hold that the plaintiffs and other similarly situated for whom the actions have been brought are, by reason of the segregation complained of, deprived of the equal protection of the laws guaranteed by the Fourteenth Amendment.

The Supreme Court's imprimatur of racial segregation had suddenly vanished. Although it applied only to the segregation of public schools, *Brown* was an earth-shattering milestone in the nation's evolving civil rights movement. This monumental decison transformed race relations for the rest of the century. Blacks who marched for their rights became legitimate news makers who were treated respectfully by the national media. The decision was a powerful moral impetus for the desegregation of the nation's public schools. And it foretold of greater victories, holding forth hope to the embryonic civil rights movement that all forms of racial segregation and discrimination might eventually be hounded to extinction.

Perhaps no group of Americans understood the potential consequences of the *Brown* decision better than southern politicians. Among this group, in the halls of Congress and in southern state capitals, reaction was swift and furious. With few exceptions, southern leaders proved that their devotion to segregation and white supremacy was far greater than the patriotic allegiance they routinely professed to constitutional government. Mississippi's James Eastland, a fierce defender of segregation, warned that the South would not "abide by nor obey this legislative decision by a political court." Eastland defiantly warned that southern leaders would "take whatever steps are necessary to retain segregation in education." South Carolina governor James Byrnes, himself a retired Supreme Court justice, declared angrily that the court "didn't interpret the Constitution; it amended it" and implied the justices were tools of communism. Russell was more conciliatory. He seemed torn between his waning respect for the constitutional role of the Supreme Court and his alarm at the justices' willingness to overturn precedents "solely on the basis of the personal predilections of some of its members."

In a letter to Judge H. R. Wilson of Alpine, Texas, Johnson expressed his view that the court had based its ruling on "criteria other than law and equity." He assured the judge that "we will find a method by which no one will be forced into distasteful or unpleasant associations. There is a long gap between a Supreme Court decision and action to enforce a decision and within that gap I believe we can find the necessary elbow room." Publicly, however, Johnson—aware that he now spoke for both wings of his party—advised caution. "The decision is an accomplished fact," he said, adding that "our people [will] work this matter out within the boundaries of the Supreme Court decision and in a manner that will be satisfying to both races." Persuaded that any southern revolt against the ruling would merely split the Democratic party and further alienate the South, Johnson counseled that it was useless to cry "over spilt milk." He worked quietly to undermine legislative proposals aimed at weakening the Supreme Court's powers.

Beyond Washington, a nationwide battle over civil rights followed with dizzying speed. White Citizens Councils—some later called them "Ku Klux Klans without the sheets" or "white-collar Klansmen"— sprung up throughout the South and dedicated themselves to resisting the court's alarming attack on segregation. "We say to the Supreme Court and to the northern world," declared Mississippi Judge Tom Brady, "you shall not make us drink from this cup." Brady's biblical allusion to Christ's entreaty before his death was not accidental. Many southerners believed they were about to be crucified by northern liberals, whose latest pawns were the justices of the U.S. Supreme Court. Despite their vociferous protests, many southern leaders were much calmer than their strong rhetoric suggested; most doubted that the decision would ever result in integrated schools.

A year after its initial *Brown* decision, justices remanded the suits to lower courts with orders to oversee desegregation of public schools "with all deliberate speed." Many southern school districts interpreted "deliberate" to mean methodical defiance, and they invented various schemes to evade the court's decree. Virginia moved to replace its public schools with a system of private schools; the state would pay tuition for white students. Other southern states completely ignored the court's order. Some retrenched by adopting aggressive measures aimed at widening the scope of segregation. In the years immediately following the *Brown* decision, southern states enacted more than 450 laws and resolutions in reaction to the "repulsive" notion that black children might be worthy to sit beside white children in a public school classroom.

In some border states and in cities such as Washington, Baltimore, Louisville, and St. Louis, schools quickly integrated with little controversy. The deep South was a vastly different case. Throughout the region, but particularly in Mississippi, reaction to *Brown* was ugly, hateful, and violent. Three blacks were lynched in the state in 1955. Two NAACP leaders, Reverend George W. Lee and Lamar Smith, were killed for refusing to remove their names from Mississippi's voter registration rolls.

In August a fourteen-year-old black youth from Chicago, Emmett Till, was kidnaped and brutally murdered near Money, Mississippi, after he flirted with a white woman. It took just over an hour for the all-white, all-male jury to acquit the two white men accused of his killing. However tragic, the trial focused national attention on the South and its cruel treatment of blacks. The summary acquittals of the two defendants sparked outrage throughout the nation, particularly among the national news media, which had previously paid scant attention to the plight of southern blacks. More important was how the dramatic events of 1955 emboldened and aroused blacks across the nation, who finally began to believe that perhaps—just perhaps—they might soon enjoy the rights of full citizenship denied for so long.

Nowhere were black citizens more emboldened than in Montgomery, Alabama, where a court convicted Rosa Parks of violating the state's bus segregation law by refusing to surrender her seat to a white passenger. Parks's arrest was not the first time she had encountered trouble on the city's bus system. Ten years earlier, a driver had evicted her from a bus when, after paying her fare, she refused to disembark and board again through the rear entrance.

Like Parks, growing numbers of blacks in Montgomery grew weary of the indignities forced upon them each time they rode the city's buses. Expected to pay the same fare as white passengers, they were treated rudely by drivers, forced to sit in the rear of buses, and often had to relinquish their seats to white passengers. Montgomery's civil rights leaders immediately saw Parks's case as their best opportunity to win a legal challenge to the city's bus seating law. For many blacks, however, a drawn-out lawsuit seemed to fall considerably short of the kind of visceral protest they had in mind. "There had been so many things that happened," one woman later explained, "that the black women had been embarrassed over, and they were ready to explode." Thus was born the plan for a boycott of Montgomery's bus system. An estimated 30,000 to 40,000 black passengers boarded the city's buses each day—about three-fourths of the total fares. If blacks refused to ride the buses, the system could be crippled.

The emerging boycott drew its strength from the black community's natural center—its churches. As long as the city's black ministers supported the effort from their pulpits, tens of thousands of bus riders could be persuaded to avoid the buses. To lead the effort, activists chose the twenty-six-year-old pastor of the Dexter Avenue Baptist Church, Reverend Martin Luther King, Jr. A popular and eloquent minister, King had held his preaching position for only a few months and, according to one boycott leader, looked "more like a boy than a man."

King was the son and grandson of preachers. His academic credentials were impressive, with degrees from Morehouse College and Crozer Theological Seminary and a doctorate in theology from Boston University. A devoted student of the teachings of Reinhold Niebuhr, the renowned American theologian, and Mohandas Gandhi, the Indian nationalist leader who had ended British rule through nonviolence, King believed deeply that blacks could best achieve civil rights with a peaceful approach. "We are not here advocating violence," he declared at the first of many mass gatherings to build support for the boycott. "We have overcome that . . . The only weapon that we have . . . is the weapon of protest."

As the boycott enjoyed greater success—participants set up an impressive system of car pools to replace the buses—some of Montgomery's white radicals reacted violently. "Listen, nigger," said an angry caller to King one evening, "we've taken all we want from you. Before next week you'll be sorry you ever came to Montgomery." King was deeply troubled. He had not asked to lead the movement. He had not wanted to become a lightning rod for the wrath of Alabama's white racists. The role had been thrust upon him. Throughout a sleepless night, the young minister began to doubt himself. As he pondered his role in the boycott and how it could violently deny his wife a husband and his daughter a father, King felt his courage slipping away. At that dark moment, as he later described it, "I could hear an inner voice saying to me, 'Martin Luther, stand up for righteousness. Stand up for justice. Stand up for truth. And lo I will be with you, even until the end of the world' . . . I heard the voice of Jesus saying still to fight on. He promised never to leave me, never to leave me alone."

Three nights later, King's fears were realized. His home was bombed during a boycott rally. Far from intimidating King and his followers, the incident emboldened them and renewed their wavering commitment to their cause. For almost an entire year, Montgomery's resolute black citizens steadfastly refused to ride the city's buses. And they brought the Montgomery City Lines to its knees. Without its black passengers, the bus company lost an average of $3,200 a day and was forced to double fares for the remaining white riders. A year later, in December 1956, the U.S. Supreme Court upheld a lower court decision declaring Montgomery's bus-segregation law unconstitutional. The boycott was over. Thousands of triumphant blacks returned to the buses—and sat where they pleased.

Two peaceful days of integration were shattered violently in the early morning hours of Sunday, December 23, when the angry blast of a shotgun tore through the front door of King's parsonage. Later that morning, King calmly warned his terrified congregation that "some of us may have to die" in the fight for racial equality. "We have just started our work," he declared. "We must have integrated schools . . . That is when our race will gain full equality. We cannot rest in Montgomery until every public school is integrated." On that morning, with those words, King had transformed a simple, narrowly focused bus boycott into the first real battle of the modern struggle for civil rights. The historic boycott now represented not merely an end to bus segregation but the beginning of a popular national movement. Out of the innocent fatigue of a modest black seamstress, the nation's greatest civil rights leader had found his voice. The epic struggle for social justice was joined.

President Dwight Eisenhower's 1956 State of the Union message gave little comfort to Russell and his southern colleagues. "It is disturbing," Eisenhower told the House and Senate, "that in some localities allegations persist that Negro citizens are being deprived of their right to vote and are likewise being subjected to unwarranted economic pressures." Recommending an investigation of racial discrimination by a bipartisan commission, Eisenhower declared that "we must strive to have every person judged and measured by what he is, rather than by his color, race or religion."

Despite that seemingly enlightened statement, Eisenhower was a cautious moderate who believed in pursuing civil rights advances gradually. No racist, Eisenhower was nonetheless the product of racist environments. Born in Texas and promoted through the ranks of a segregated army, he viewed the nation's racial problems through southern-tinted glasses. His 1952 election, in which he carried four of eleven southern states, marked the first time a Republican presidential candidate had received substantial support in the South. Believing that black leaders often made unreasonable demands for civil rights, Eisenhower doubted that the federal government could eradicate prejudice by "compulsion." To an old friend he wrote that on all issues, including civil rights, he hoped to remain on "the path that marks the way of logic between conflicting arguments advanced by extremists on both sides."

The *Brown* decision and its potential to incite turmoil in the South had troubled Eisenhower and helped to destroy his previously "cordial relations" with Chief Justice Earl Warren. Many southerners blamed Eisenhower for the decision because he had appointed Warren. Worried that the *Brown* case would cause southern states to abolish their public school systems, as some had threatened, Eisenhower refused to endorse the decision or to urge southern states to comply with it. This total lack of presidential leadership on civil rights only comforted and encouraged the growing massive resistance movement in the South. On the most important social issue of the century, Eisenhower was speechless.

Any real progress on civil rights within the administration would come because of Eisenhower's attorney general, Herbert Brownell. A politically astute New Yorker, Brownell had been Eisenhower's campaign manager and chairman of the Republican party. He well understood the inherent political perils and benefits of advancing civil rights. In 1953 Brownell had been responsible for reviving two "lost" District of Columbia statutes making it a crime for a restaurant to refuse service to a black customer. He had also filed a friend-of-the-court brief with the Supreme Court in which he urged the justices to side with the plaintiffs in the 1954 *Brown v. Board of Education* cases.

On one hand, Brownell knew that a sympathetic stance on the issue might help stop the exodus of black votes from the Republican party that began during Roosevelt's New Deal. Going too far, however, might prevent Republicans from building on their southern successes of 1952. In April 1956, with Eisenhower's reelection campaign on the horizon, Brownell prepared to take the risky step of presenting to Congress the draft of a Justice Department civil rights program.

While Eisenhower did all he could to avoid civil rights, southern leaders were encouraged not only by the president's ambivalence but by the Supreme Court's unwillingness to demand immediate compliance with its *Brown* decision. Resistance to desegregation of public schools stiffened. In Virginia, Senator Harry Byrd outlined his "doctrine of massive resistance" to integration. Scores of segregationist groups sprouted throughout the South. By 1956, the Ku Klux Klan alone boasted membership of more than 200,000.

Besides passing new segregation laws, southern politicians revived constitutional challenges to *Brown* based on the philosophy of "interposition." A tenet of states' rights dogma, interposition was rooted in an interpretation of the Tenth Amendment's assignation to the states and the people of all "powers not delegated to the United States by the Constitution." Employed more than a hundred years earlier by South Carolina and Virginia in an attempt to restrain federal powers, interposition enjoyed a sudden revival in southern capitals. It was the "constitutional" device of choice that the legislatures of Alabama, Georgia, Louisiana, Mississippi, and South Carolina used to challenge federal attempts to segregate their schools. Wrapping themselves in the banner of states' rights, southern governments sought to interpose the Tenth Amendment between the federal courts and their segregated schools. "The decision won't affect us at all," the superintendent of a Mississippi county had boasted after the *Brown* ruling. "That's because we're not going to observe it in our county. It will be 'to hell with the Supreme Court' down here. Of course, we may all hang for it. But we won't hang separately. We'll all hang together."

A controversial document conceived by South Carolina senator Strom Thurmond in early 1956 gave segregationists in Congress their first opportunity to formally declare war on the Supreme Court and its supporters. Never temperate in his approach to segregation, Thurmond proposed that southern congressmen issue a formal statement articulating their objections to the Supreme Court's *Brown* decisions. Thurmond maintained the court had misinterpreted the Fourteenth Amendment and had relied more on "the opinions of modern-day sociologists and psychologists." Furthermore, he argued, the Constitution did not mention education. Therefore, because the Tenth Amendment reserved to states all rights not accorded the federal government, education was none of the court's business.

This, said Thurmond, meant that "public education is a matter for the States and the people to control." Thurmond wrapped all these sentiments into his draft. In a flourish, he concluded with eight declarations attacking the court. He extolled the states that resisted the *Brown* decision, protested judicial activism, and urged "equal protection" for "all citizens where separate but equal public facilities are maintained." Thurmond found an immediate ally in Virginia's Harry Byrd, who helped him prepare the language they presented to their southern colleagues.

Russell not only backed Thurmond's idea—he seized the initiative. Perhaps, as George Reedy later explained, Russell hoped "to head off" and soften Thurmond's extremist language. Assisted by Walter George of Georgia, John Stennis of Mississippi, Olin Johnston of South Carolina, and Sam Ervin of North Carolina, Russell drafted a statement that he hoped every southern senator would endorse. As he discovered, such unanimity was not likely. Some southerners were less than enthusiastic about associating themselves with the radical document. While his ad hoc committee worked to hone the draft, Russell complained to a friend that some of his southern colleagues "actually favor" the *Brown* decision. Others were apparently unwilling to label the decision "unconstitutional," as the Thurmond draft had done.

Initially, Russell obtained little more than a dozen commitments from within the southern bloc. To a friend he confessed that he contemplated dropping the project altogether, because "when you run into five or six who are unwilling to denounce the decision as illegal and unconstitutional it is discouraging." Several senators, including J. William Fulbright of Arkansas, Spessard Holland of Florida, and Price Daniel of Texas, told Russell that "the language I had originally suggested was, as one of them expressed it, 'too bitter.'"

To Johnson's aide George Reedy, Thurmond's initiative was a hostile reaction to the gradual realization that "a civil rights act was inevitable." Southerners, he said, were now engaged in "a number of rear-guard battles, battles either to postpone the dreaded day as long as they could or at least convince their constituents that they were going down fighting."

Albert Gore of Tennessee later recalled that Thurmond presented the text of the declaration to him on the Senate floor, "in full view" of reporters perched above in the press gallery. "I took one quick look at it and gave a flat 'No,' handing it back to him with some disagreeable emphasis because he already knew I would not sign it." Gore regarded the document "as the most unvarnished piece of demagoguery I had ever encountered." He said he sadly concluded that his southern colleagues "were deliberately and callously misleading their people, and that nothing but tragedy and sorrow could come of this open defiance of the law, this cheap appeal to racism."

On March 12, 1956, Walter George rose on the Senate floor to read the statement, which became known as the "Southern Manifesto." (Its more formal title was the "Declaration of Constitutional Principles.") After announcing that nineteen senators and seventy-seven House members, representing eleven southern states, had signed it, George began reading the manifesto in his baritone voice:

> The unwarranted decision of the Supreme Court in the public school cases is now bearing the fruit always produced when men substitute power for established law . . .
>
> We regard the decision of the Supreme Court in the school cases as a clear abuse of judicial power. It climaxes a trend in the Federal Judiciary undertaking to legislate, in derogation of the authority of Congress, and to encroach upon the reserved rights of the States and the people.

The original Constitution does not mention education. Neither does the Fourteenth amendment nor any other amendment . . .

Though there has been no constitutional amendment or act of Congress changing this established legal principle [separate but equal] almost a century old, the Supreme Court of the United States, with no legal basis for such action, undertook to exercise their naked judicial power and substituted their personal political and social ideas for the established law of the land.

This unwarranted exercise of power by the Court, contrary to the Constitution, is creating chaos and confusion in the States principally affected . . .

We decry the Supreme Court's encroachments on rights reserved to the States and to the people, contrary to established law, and to the Constitution.

We commend the motives of those States which have declared the intention to resist forced integration by any lawful means . . .

We pledge ourselves to use all lawful means to bring about a reversal of this decision which is contrary to the Constitution and to prevent the use of force in its implementation.

Moments after George finished, Thurmond rose to elaborate on the manifesto. He attacked "the propagandists [who] have tried to convince the world that the States and the people should bow meekly to the decree of the Supreme Court. I say it would be the submission of cowardice if we failed to use every lawful means to protect the rights of the people." According to Thurmond, "the people and the States must find ways and means of preserving segregation in the schools. Each attempt to break down segregation must be fought with every legal weapon at our disposal."

Liberals quickly assailed the declaration. On the heels of Thurmond's speech, Oregon's Wayne Morse fumed that "you would think today [John C.] Calhoun was walking and speaking on the floor of the Senate." Morse complained that "the South has had all the time since the War Between the States to make this adjustment [to desegregation]. That is why I am not greatly moved by these last-hour pleas of the South, 'We need more time, more time, more time.' How much more time is needed in order that equality of justice may be applied to the blacks as well as to the whites in America?"

As Morse finished, Humphrey rose to cast the issue in broader terms: America's promotion of worldwide democracy. "If we persist in the course of denying people in America equal rights," Humphrey said, "we shall bring down upon our Nation the wrath of the world . . . If America ever hopes to give world leadership, we must set the pattern here in America. We have to set it unmistakably in a firm belief in human equality and equal justice under the law."

Oregon Democrat Richard Neuberger echoed Humphrey's argument. "We live in a world most of whose people are of a different color than white," Neuberger said. "What are they thinking when members of the highest American parliamentary body announce themselves as against judicial decisions granting equality to colored people in America? How fares the Soviet Union in the propaganda war as a result of these developments?"

The most significant aspect of the Southern Manifesto was not who signed but who *did not:* Gore, Kefauver, and Johnson. The absence of Johnson's signature attracted the most attention. Shortly after Walter George read the manifesto to the Senate, Neuberger noted Johnson's decision. "If that is true, Mr. President, it is one of the most courageous political acts of valor I have seen take place in my life." An unabashed Johnson fan, Neuberger perhaps exaggerated the extent of his leader's valor. Johnson's decision was no surprise. Three days earlier, in a press statement, he claimed he had "neither seen this document, nor have I been asked to sign it." Because he was majority leader, Johnson explained, the manifesto's authors "did not want their statement to be constructed as an attempt to formulate senatorial or Democratic Party policy." He did not, however, denounce the manifesto or "the distinguished Senators" who signed it. "In my opinion, the solution of the problem cannot be found on the Federal level," Johnson said, "for it involves basic values reflected in the sovereignty of our states. It's my hope that wise leaders on the local level will work to resolve these differences."

Privately, however, Johnson had struggled with the manifesto and the way in which it threatened to disrupt Democratic senatorial unity. "I'm damned if I do and damned if I don't," he reportedly told Bobby Baker. "The Dixiecrats, and a lot of my people at home, will be on me like stink on shit if I don't stand up and bray against the Supreme Court's decision. If I *do* bray like a jackass, the red hots and senators with big minority blocs in the East and the North will gut shoot me."

Russell never pressured Johnson. Surely he realized that signing the document would destroy Johnson's chances for the presidency. "Russell was very determined to elect Johnson president of the United States," said George Reedy. "Obviously [he] knew that this would end it." In essence, Johnson's southern colleagues let him off the hook. John Stennis said that southerners wanted Johnson's support, but they recognized "that he wasn't just a senator from Texas, he was a leader and he had a different responsibility in that degree."

Later, Johnson often emphasized his refusal to sign when he complained to Humphrey about his poor relations with the Senate's liberals. "I know you think Bill Fulbright is one of the great liberals around here," Johnson told Humphrey. Then, voice dripping with sarcasm, he added, "You liberals. You all have got your big heroes." Johnson reminded Humphrey of the manifesto. "I want you to notice who signed the Southern Manifesto and who didn't. Now all your bomb throwers over there think I am the worst thing that came down here . . . But they're all cheering Bill Fulbright. Why do they cheer Bill Fulbright? Because he's got great connections overseas. He's a Rhodes Scholar, and he's got the Fulbright [foreign exchange student] Act." Finally, Johnson made his point. "He signed the Southern Manifesto. *I* didn't."

Johnson had several good reasons not to sign. As Reedy and others suggested, Johnson was already nurturing presidential ambitions. "There was no question whatsoever," Reedy insisted: anyone who signed the document "could never become president of the United States." In a memorandum to Johnson in June 1955, Reedy asserted "there is some evidence" that a southerner could be elected president, but not "if he were known as 'the Southern candidate.'" As Johnson surely understood, nothing would brand him an old-style southerner more than his signature on the radical Southern Manifesto.

Furthermore, Johnson seemed to believe that his position as majority leader required him to have a broader vision than when he represented only his state of Texas. As early as November 1955, while still recovering from his heart attack of the previous summer, Johnson had delivered a widely publicized speech in which he had unveiled his "Program with a Heart." The speech outlined a thirteen-point New Deal–style legislative agenda, including a constitutional amendment to outlaw the poll tax. Arkansas Congressman Brooks Hays, who later regretted signing the manifesto, believed Johnson would not have signed it, even if pressured by Russell, not only because of his "new sense of responsibility from the national standpoint," but also "in material thought." Humphrey agreed. "I knew he didn't want to classify himself in those days as a southerner."

Perhaps most significant for Johnson was his growing fear that passions over civil rights would rip his party apart—a disastrous result in a presidential election year. With Eisenhower's attorney general preparing to submit a civil rights program, Republicans were making their first tentative overtures for the black vote. In a hotly contested election, Johnson knew that the issue might not only influence who occupied the White House but determine which party controlled the Senate.

The Southern Manifesto was a dangerous and foolhardy attempt to defy the Constitution as interpreted by a unanimous Supreme Court. It further separated the South from the rest of the nation and permanently stained the records of those who endorsed its racist appeals. Yet it is possible to conclude that the manifesto actually aided the progress of civil rights. Its presentation in March 1956 marked the first time that Johnson publicly parted ways with Russell's southern bloc in a substantive sense. Johnson's refusal to sign the manifesto was no endorsement of civil rights. It did, however, mark the beginning of his long but steady voyage across the great philosophical divide that separated states' rights from civil rights.

CHAPTER NINE

Two Can Play
at That Game

AT AN INFORMAL WHITE HOUSE DINNER shortly before the 1954 *Brown* decision, Chief Justice Earl Warren sat beside President Dwight Eisenhower. Although the president did not discuss the impending court decision with Warren, he went out of his way to praise another dinner guest: John W. Davis, the 1924 Democratic presidential nominee and now counsel for the segregation states. Later, as the men retired from the room for after-dinner drinks, Eisenhower took Warren by the arm. Of the defendants in the *Brown* case he said, "These are not bad people. All they are concerned about is to see that their sweet little girls are not required to sit in school alongside some big overgrown Negroes."

Although Eisenhower's clumsy attempt to influence the decision failed, the incident typified the president's overwhelming ambivalence on civil rights. Until 1956, it appeared that Eisenhower's only meaningful contributions to the civil rights struggle would be his appointment of Warren to the Supreme Court—which he later regretted—and the incremental acts of ending official segregation on military bases and in Washington restaurants and government offices. Despite boasting about his commitment to civil rights in his first State of the Union address in 1953, Eisenhower had relied on his philosophy "that legislation alone could [not] institute instant morality" as an excuse for legislative inaction. He resented lawmakers who "habitually tacked anti-segregation amendments" onto important legislation "and thus ensured its death." For that reason, Eisenhower opposed school construction legislation in 1955 because an amendment would have denied funds to any state that did not comply with the Supreme Court's *Brown* decision. Eisenhower mistakenly believed that civil rights leaders wanted to legislate morality, when they really only expected the federal government to enforce the Constitution as interpreted by the nine justices of the U.S. Supreme Court. True to his belief in the futility of mandating tolerance, Eisenhower offered no civil rights legislation during his first three and a half years in office. Other than reaffirming his abstract hope that "every person" should be "judged and measured by what he is, rather than by his color," the president showed little interest or understanding of the issue until the tumultuous events of 1954–56 forced his hand.

Beginning with the 1954 *Brown* decision, a dizzying series of events began to fuel the fires of civil rights as never before: the national uproar over the 1955 murder of Emmett Till in Mississippi; a riot over the admission of a black student, Autherine Lucy, to the University of Alabama in early 1956; the success of the Montgomery bus boycott that same year; the bomb that damaged the home of the boycott's leader, Reverend Martin Luther King, Jr.; and the 1956 attack on black singer Nat King Cole by white supremacists in Birmingham. Growing national sentiment for a legislative remedy was reflected in Congress, where members introduced more than 110 civil rights measures in 1955 alone. Only one—a bill to permit federal employment of Mongolians—won House passage. It was, as usual, spurned by the Senate.

Overcoming his instinctive reluctance to meddle in the affairs of individual states, Eisenhower finally emerged from legislative hibernation in early 1956 to call for a bipartisan Commission on Civil Rights to investigate charges of racial discrimination and voting irregularities. However, his attorney general, Herbert Brownell, knew that a commission alone would not satisfy those who wanted aggressive action to end voting rights violations and other forms of discrimination. Ready to compete for the growing black vote, Brownell sought Eisenhower's permission to make a bolder move. He would propose something that Democrats had long promised but never delivered: a comprehensive civil and voting rights bill.

Brownell's idea was not new. In fact, his program would eventually fall far short of the kind of activist legislation Harry Truman had proposed as early as 1948. Nevertheless, if approved, the bill would become the first civil rights legislation enacted by Congress since 1875—and Eisenhower's party could claim much of the credit. As Brownell well understood, the Republican party already held tremendous advantages in large urban states in congressional and presidential elections. Attracting additional black support might help Republicans capture and hold dozens of marginal Congressional districts.

Brownell undoubtedly realized that if even his bill failed, Republicans stood to inherit a windfall of black ballots. George Reedy, for one, theorized that Brownell's real strategy "was to send Congress a bill which could not be passed no matter which political party was in control." Reedy suspected that Brownell—"the most partisan politician I have ever met in either political party"—planned to "go before the country and talk about a forceful civil rights bill which was proposed by a Republican President and rejected by a Democratic Congress."

Brownell's early drafts of the bill sparked a vigorous debate within the president's cabinet and among his advisors. At first the attorney general proposed legislation to make lynching a federal crime and to outlaw the poll tax as a voting requirement. But he quickly dropped those provisions after FBI Director J. Edgar Hoover told cabinet members on March 9 that racial tensions had worsened in the South. Trusting Hoover's grim assessment, Brownell concluded that the lynching and poll tax provisions would unnecessarily inflame southerners and might jeopardize the rest of the bill.

After discussing the matter further with cabinet members—including several who strongly opposed the bill—Eisenhower finally gave Brownell his hesitant approval to "test" his plan before Congress. In April 1956 Brownell unveiled a six-point legislative draft. He asked Congress to: create a bipartisan civil rights commission to investigate civil rights grievances; establish a civil rights division in the Justice Department; expand federal laws to prohibit the intimidation of voters in federal elections; authorize the attorney general to file civil injunctions for civil rights plaintiffs; permit individuals to take their civil rights complaints directly to federal courts; and allow the Justice Department to sue in cases of attempted jury or witness intimidation.

Because it would primarily employ *civil* penalties to protect voting rights, Brownell hoped his bill would not incur the wrath of southern lawmakers. He was disappointed. His efforts to protect voting rights and his opposition to the Southern Manifesto had already branded him a dangerous man in the eyes of southern leaders. This new proposal only generated more scorn. At an American Bar Association reception, for example, Brownell and his wife encountered the attorney general of

Georgia, Eugene Cook, and his wife. An indignant Mrs. Cook refused to shake Brownell's hand and muttered, "Nigger lovers." At school Brownell's children endured similar insults. Some liberals in the Senate were only slightly less hostile. Humphrey denounced the program as "lip-service by leap-year liberals." Oregon's Richard Neuberger complained that Eisenhower already had the power to establish a civil rights commission. "If he wants one," Neuberger said, "he should regard it as no less important than a commission on highways, which he has already set up."

As always, the House was more receptive to civil rights. By late April its Judiciary Committee approved a scaled-down version of Brownell's proposal, which included the civil rights commission, the Justice Department's Civil Rights Division, and provisions for civil action to protect voting rights. Over the protests of southern congressman who claimed the legislation was an assault on states' rights, the House moved toward passage of the bill, set for July 23.

On the other side of the Capitol, meanwhile, the Senate's Democratic leaders, especially Johnson, seethed over the administration's "transparent" attempts to court black voters just as the Senate prepared to adjourn for the Democratic and Republican national conventions. Debate of a controversial civil rights bill, Johnson believed, was only an impediment to passing other, more urgent legislation—including social security, housing, and foreign aid bills. If Eisenhower really wanted a civil rights bill, George Reedy told Johnson in a memo, he "would not have waited three and a half years to send [his] recommendations to Congress. All it has done is to toss into the closing days of the final session of the Congress a measure which cannot, at the present time, be passed but will tie the legislative process into a tight knot."

Johnson worried about much more than what Reedy called the Senate's "regular and orderly procedure." He complained privately that "we Democrats have prepared this product of civil rights, and I don't want to see the Eisenhower Republicans putting their trademark on it." Moreover, Johnson determined that he must maintain unity among the Senate's Democrats as they went into their national convention—something a civil rights debate would certainly destroy. On June 27, Johnson informed Russell, Kerr, and other members of the Democratic Policy Committee that the Republican-backed civil rights bill posed problems not just for southerners, but for all Democrats. "The Republicans," he said, "would like to see us at each other's throats." Russell agreed. He warned Johnson that "if we get into civil rights, we will have trouble even recessing over the convention."*

With so much at stake—including his own evolving presidential ambitions—Johnson knew he could not permit Douglas, Humphrey, and other liberals to force his hand on civil rights. Any move to consider the bill would spark an almost-certain southern filibuster and subject a divided Democratic party to national ridicule. The situation was guaranteed to please no one but partisan Republicans. Johnson saw only one solution: if the bill passed the House, he would squirrel it away in the Judiciary Committee, whose new chairman was Mississippi's James Eastland. A fierce segregationist and anti-Communist whom New York's Herbert Lehman had once described as "a symbol of racism," Eastland would never willingly let such a bill out of his committee. Johnson would rely on Eastland to save the Democratic party from itself! The strategy seemed flawless. Yet as the House prepared to vote on the legislation in late July, Johnson learned of a plan to undermine his tidy solution to the civil rights problem.† Douglas and Lehman had hatched a parliamentary maneuver to bypass the Judiciary Committee and place the bill directly onto the Senate's calendar.

Douglas and Johnson had never enjoyed particularly friendly relations during their seven years in the Senate. The Illinois liberal resented Johnson's conservatism and his loyalty to Russell's southern bloc. And Johnson disliked the bullheaded self-righteousness that Douglas often brought to civil rights debates. "He had a great deal of respect for Douglas," explained Johnson's aide Booth Mooney. "He just didn't understand him at all."

Unlike Johnson, Douglas was a bona fide war hero who had maneuvered his way into the Marines at age fifty. The winner of two Purple Hearts and a Bronze Star, Douglas still bore the scar of battle—a useless, shattered left arm. A renowned economist, Douglas had advised President Franklin Roosevelt and had helped design the nation's Social Security system. The former professor was so scrupulously honest that

---

*James Rowe, for one, believed that liberals such as Paul Douglas hoped for a divisive civil rights showdown that would "drive the South out" and turn the party sharply leftward. Rowe's suspicions about Douglas were astute. Several months later, as Congress prepared to convene for the 1957 session, the Illinois liberal confessed on national television that he "would be very happy" if southern conservatives "should leave the Democratic Party" for "their spiritual home of the Republican Party" (Reedy to LBJ, 4/4/56, Office Files of George Reedy, Box 420, LBJL; *Meet the Press*, NBC, 1/20/57, Political VI, Box 15, RBRL).
†Some liberals believed that the tip came from Humphrey.

he would not allow his secretary to tell callers that he was "out" unless he first stepped into the hallway. Douglas, one admiring journalist later wrote, "combined the moral rectitude of old New England, where he was born, with the crusading liberalism of the Middle West, where he spent most of his adult life." Passionate and self-righteous, Douglas neither was a member of the Senate Club, nor did he desire admission. What bothered Johnson most about Douglas, Booth Mooney recalled, "was that even when he was right, he didn't seem to care whether he really won or not." Observed Harry McPherson: "Johnson made progress, not issues; Douglas the reverse."

Johnson rarely negotiated directly with Douglas, Lehman, or other hard-core liberals. He usually dealt with them through Humphrey, with results that were often far short of their expectations. By 1956, the liberals were tired of waiting for their Democratic leader to initiate action on civil rights. It was, by now, a frustration that made Eisenhower's Republicanism a secondary consideration. "For the first time," said Douglas, "the Republicans were now our allies, instead of covert opponents." If the Republican president proposed a civil rights bill, the liberals—their prior criticism of Johnson's cooperation with Eisenhower notwithstanding—were prepared to enlist as allies.

The Douglas-Lehman plan was simple. Immediately after House passage of the civil rights bill, the two would invoke an obscure Senate rule that permitted the Senate to place a House-passed bill directly on the legislative calendar if a senator objected to its committee referral. On the morning of July 23, at the appointed hour of the House vote, Douglas and Lehman sat in the Senate chamber awaiting the bill's arrival from the House. They were eager to launch their surprise objection to its referral to Judiciary. Long minutes passed. No communication on the bill arrived from the other side of the Capitol. Finally, an impatient Douglas walked to the House chamber to investigate.

Arriving in the House, Douglas approached the clerk's desk. When he asked about the civil rights bill, a flustered House employee shuffled his papers and feigned ignorance of its whereabouts. Moments later, a sympathetic liberal congressman spotted Douglas and delivered the alarming news: the House had just passed the bill, 279-126. It was on its way to the Senate. Suddenly Douglas realized—Johnson had known of their plan! He had waited until Douglas left the Senate floor, and then he made his move. As Douglas had walked to the House, he had probably passed the reading clerk, Joe Barlett, who was hurrying to the Senate to deliver the civil rights bill.

Bolting from the chamber, Douglas ran through the corridors, colliding with tourists on his way back to the Senate. Out of breath, he burst into the Senate chamber and spotted Alabama's Lister Hill in the presiding officer's chair. Where is the bill? he demanded of his Alabama colleague. Hill blithely said that the Senate had just referred the bill to Judiciary. Later, Douglas discovered what had happened after he left for the House: Johnson had Lehman lured from the chamber long enough for Hill to orchestrate two readings of the bill and a quick committee referral. When Douglas angrily protested that Hill should have known that he would oppose such a maneuver, the Alabaman could barely contain his glee as he replied, "Paul, my dear boy, we move in accordance with the time-honored rules and procedures of the Senate."

Douglas was furious. Although he wanted to recall the bill from committee, he realized that, without unanimous consent, the Senate could not consider such a motion until a new legislative day had begun. In other words, Douglas could not ask for a vote on discharging the bill from Judiciary unless the legislative day ended—meaning that the Senate must *adjourn*, not simply *recess*. That evening, when Johnson moved to recess the Senate until the next morning, Douglas objected, to no avail. The next morning, as the Senate debated a foreign aid bill, Douglas sought to offer his motion despite the prohibitive Senate rule. When Douglas sought unanimous consent to introduce his resolution discharging the bill from committee, Russell stymied him and served notice that "I shall continue to object." About an hour later, Douglas tried again but encountered a renewed objection from Russell. "I find this proposal just as obnoxious as it was about an hour ago, if not more so," Russell said.

As described by his aide Howard Shuman, Douglas's path to discharging the bill was hopeless, a parliamentary minefield:

> A petition for discharge had to be filed in the Senate at the morning hour. It had to lay over a day. Then, it could be motioned up. A filibuster could apply to the motion to proceed to its consideration. Then, if it was motioned up, another filibuster could apply to voting on whether to discharge the committee [bill]. If that was successful ... the bill went to the

calendar. Then the bill had to be motioned up, a filibuster had to be broken and the Senate had to break another filibuster before there could be a vote on the bill.

As Shuman observed, Douglas faced "an impossible situation." To initiate any of the steps toward discharging the bill, the Senate must first adjourn. "If the Senate recessed," Shuman noted, "there was no morning hour, no new legislative day and none of these steps could take place." Johnson and Russell understood the Senate's rules better than Douglas. They could stymie him—and any consideration of civil rights—simply by refusing to adjourn the Senate until senators left for the national conventions.

Douglas was outraged that he could not even offer even his simple resolution. When his friend Humphrey, with Russell's consent, attempted to introduce a bill on Indian affairs, Douglas served notice that he would object to all such unanimous consent motions until the Senate agreed to consider his discharge motion. "If every resort is to be made to every technicality so as to prevent the Senate from registering its opinion in this matter," Douglas said, "then two can play at that game as well as one."

Douglas kept his word. When Wisconsin's Alexander Wiley sought consent to insert a statement in the *Record*, Douglas objected. Because the Senate leadership had blocked his attempts to bring up the civil rights bill, Douglas said, "I must reluctantly say that what is sauce for the goose is sauce for the gander, and that hereafter I intend to object to any such requests." Later in the day, Douglas objected to a request by South Dakota's Karl Mundt, who wanted to insert a simple newspaper article into the *Record*. That evening he objected again when Wiley sought to insert "certain matters." When Arkansas's John McClellan asked consent to report three bills from the Government Operations Committee, Douglas lodged an objection, as he did when Maine's Frederick Payne tried to insert a report by the Board of Visitors of the U.S. Merchant Marine Academy. Mundt attempted again to insert a letter to the editor. But Douglas stopped him. Later he objected when McClellan tried again to report the Government Operations Committee bills, and again when Maryland's John Marshall Butler rose to introduce a joint resolution.

Finally, late in the evening, Douglas escalated the hostilities. In ultimate defiance of the Democratic leadership, Douglas moved to adjourn the Senate—normally a sacred prerogative reserved by custom for only the Senate's majority leader. Although his allies were eager to fight the motion, Johnson calmly waved them off. "I should like to see how many members wish to have the Senator continue the course he has followed today," Johnson told the Senate before requesting a vote on the Douglas motion. Johnson knew he would receive overwhelming support on this procedural question because it involved his exclusive right to make adjournment motions. Though he could have easily stopped Douglas cold, Johnson seemed to want a vote because it would, in Joseph Rauh's words, "rub [Douglas's] nose in the dirt."

To no one's surprise, the Senate upheld its leader, voting 76-6 against adjournment. Johnson had not only foiled Douglas—he had humiliated him publicly in a roll call that exposed his embarrassing dearth of support. The defeat did not deter Douglas. He valiantly objected to three more routine unanimous consent requests before he finally fled the Senate chamber. "My head is bloody, but unbowed," he said as he bravely objected to the submission of a Public Works Committee report.

His protests to the contrary, the vote was a crushing blow. "Most of my liberal friends had deserted me," Douglas later said, noting that even Humphrey had sided with Johnson. As Douglas somberly left for his office, he and Howard Shuman approached the bank of elevators outside the Senate chamber. Glumly, Douglas muttered, "Let us punch the bells three times [the sign that a senator was calling] and pretend that I am a senator." When they reached the office and Shuman had left for the evening, Douglas confessed that he "shed tears for the first time in years." Later he admitted that it had been "a foolish idea" to attempt his scheme with such little support. Through his tears, Douglas admitted, he wondered whether the civil rights legislation for which he yearned would ever be a reality. "How many senators really care about civil rights, I asked myself. How could we ever reverse the tide, and what an imperfect and erring human instrument I was to fail in so crucial a moment."

CHAPTER TEN

Galloping with the Crowd

BY 1956 HUMPHREY HAD BLOSSOMED into a respected and influential member of the Club. He was, as journalist Robert L. Riggs observed, "sitting firmly in the lap of the Senate's leadership." Though some of his liberal friends might have felt that he was sitting obediently on *Lyndon Johnson's* lap, his relationship with the majority leader nonetheless made him first among equals in the liberal bloc.

His impressive record on the Foreign Relations Committee and his growing friendship with Walter George of Georgia, a senior committee member, had finally won him a chairmanship: the disarmament subcommittee was created for Humphrey in 1955. The next year, Humphrey was a delegate to the United Nations General Assembly for the 1956–57 session. Johnson even appointed him to the Democratic Steering Committee. The committee remained a conservative bastion dominated by Johnson and Russell, but Humphrey's appointment further evidenced his acceptance. Granted, not much of his legislation had become law. But that fact said more about Johnson's steely determination to maintain party unity than about Humphrey's stature in the Senate.

From this lofty new perch, Humphrey prepared to scale even greater heights—moving brazenly into the realm of would-be presidential kingmaker by inviting his liberal hero, Adlai Stevenson, to enter Minnesota's Democratic primary in March 1956. Stevenson seemed a clear favorite to head the Democrats' presidential ticket. Sensing an opportunity to become his running mate, Humphrey offered his early endorsement. He hoped that a big win in Minnesota would help Stevenson secure the nomination and that a grateful Stevenson would look favorably on him when the time arrived to pick a vice presidential nominee.

Something went terribly wrong on the way to the White House.

Estes Kefauver trounced Stevenson in the Minnesota primary, beating him by more than 50,000 votes. Humphrey was devastated and embarrassed. He had lured Stevenson to Minnesota, where a group of Democratic party mavericks and Republicans—permitted to cross party lines in presidential primaries—had handed the likable Kefauver a stunning victory. So humiliating was the defeat that Humphrey was not even elected as a delegate. Thinking his vice presidential hopes had ended—"I'm walking around in ashes and sackcloth," he confessed—Humphrey soon received the encouraging news that Stevenson believed he might make a "wonderful" keynote speaker for the national convention. Later, when the national committee met to choose the speaker, Stevenson cruelly dropped his support for Humphrey, who lost to Tennessee Governor Frank Clement by one vote.

Certain that any hope of joining the presidential ticket had vanished, Humphrey was stunned months later when Stevenson informed him that he was still on the short list of vice presidential possibilities. As Humphrey remembered the conversation, Stevenson said he "would choose me as his vice-presidential running mate" if Humphrey could certify his acceptance among southern leaders. Believing he had a "commitment" from Stevenson, Humphrey broke precedent and announced his candidacy for the vice presidential nomination. He quickly secured endorsements from influential southerners such as Johnson, Russell, Walter George, John Sparkman, Lister Hill, and Sam Rayburn. Stevenson's "condition," Humphrey recalled, was seemingly satisfied. Exceedingly confident of his nomination, Humphrey even began preparing an acceptance speech after he arrived in Chicago for the convention.

Yet Humphrey would endure another cruel disappointment. As he and his aides watched television coverage of the convention from their hotel suite, Stevenson shocked them by announcing he would not choose his running mate. He would leave the choice to convention delegates. Swayed by arguments that Kefauver or freshman senator John F. Kennedy might draw more votes to the ticket, Stevenson had not even extended Humphrey the courtesy of a phone call before announcing his decision. Stunned, and unprepared to fight for the nomination on the convention floor, Humphrey watched helplessly as Kefauver, Kennedy, and Albert Gore drummed up support for their candidacies. On the first ballot, Humphrey finished far out of the running. His brief but promising opportunity for national leadership was crushed. Adding to his humiliation, Humphrey was forced to decide the outcome by throwing his meager but crucial support to Kefauver—an obligation he felt because of Kefauver's Minnesota primary victory.

Adding to his disappointment was Stevenson's refusal to push for strong platform language on civil rights. While the platform supported the principles of the *Brown* decision, it specifically rejected "all proposals for the use of force" to implement them. The convention rejected stronger language that called for legislation to ensure and protect civil rights and to "carry out" Supreme Court desegregation decisions.

Though Humphrey buried his pride and valiantly campaigned for Stevenson in the fall election, Muriel later characterized the whole episode as her husband's "worst" defeat. "He felt he had been made a fool of. He never would talk about it." Johnson tried to console Humphrey. "You have certainly had a rough year and my heart goes out to you," he wrote from Austin in September. "There is only one consolation. I long ago realized that you were one of those bold spirits that is tempered rather than weakened by adversity and I know that you have the energy and the ability and the initiative that will be required to rise through the years." Although Johnson assured him that "nothing will ever affect your standing in my eyes," Humphrey was only months away from proving Johnson wrong.

The election of 1956 served as Lyndon Johnson's wake-up call. The inability of the Democratic-controlled Senate to address civil rights helped send record numbers of urban and middle-class black voters flocking to Dwight Eisenhower. Estimates varied, but most agreed that Eisenhower had increased his black support by almost 20 percent since 1952. The Gallup polling organization concluded that "of all the groups of the nation's population, the one that shifted most to the Eisenhower-Nixon ticket . . . was the Negro voter." More startling to Democrats was that Eisenhower carried *five* southern states while winning record numbers of black votes in a second landslide over Adlai Stevenson.

Democrats were most alarmed that Eisenhower had won those southern states with the help of black voters. In 1952 Stevenson's black support had been strongest in the South. Four years later, however, the shift of blacks to the Republican ticket was most abrupt in the South. Attorney General Brownell's gambit had paid great dividends. His dogged advocacy of civil rights had helped the Republicans in the North *and* the South. But Richard Nixon also deserved credit. In Harlem, the vice president had effectively appealed for black votes by arguing that the Republican party in Congress was "solidly behind" the administration's civil rights program. Nixon said if blacks supported Eisenhower "and elect a Republican Senate and House of Representatives, you will get action, not filibusters." At the Alfred E. Smith Memorial Dinner in New York, shortly before the election, Nixon declared that "most of us here will live to see the day when American boys and girls shall sit, side by side, at any school—public or private—with no regard paid to the color of their skin. Segregation, discrimination, and prejudice have no place in America." While Nixon, Brownell and other Republican leaders recognized the potential that black votes held for continued electoral success—perhaps enough votes to make theirs the majority party—the victory did not seem to whet Eisenhower's appetite in the same way. He appeared doubly resolved to pursue an incremental, self-styled policy of "steady progress without rashness."

Leaders of both political parties pored over the election returns with great interest. For Republicans, a stronger push for civil rights legislation in 1957 now seemed the clear path to greater victories in the future, perhaps even the key to winning control of the Senate in the midterm elections of 1958. For Democrats the results were more vexing. Despite the Republican presidential landslide, Senate Democrats had widened their slim majority by one vote—allowing Johnson to claim vindication for his often nonconfrontational legislative strategy. Yet a growing chorus of liberals ignored this minor triumph. They maintained that Johnson's refusal to challenge Eisenhower had, in fact, contributed to Stevenson's embarrassing defeat. Johnson and House Speaker Rayburn, they complained, had drawn no distinctions between the two parties and therefore had presented voters with no reason to reject Eisenhower.

Democratic National Committee chairman Paul Butler, an aggressive, sometimes-strident liberal from Indiana, was a leading proponent of this criticism. Frustrated that Johnson and Rayburn usually disregarded the party platform and marched to their own legislative beat, Butler became an assertive spokesman for the party's liberal wing. In late 1956, hoping to unify congressional Democrats with their national committee, noncongressional Democrats such as Adlai Stevenson, Dean Acheson, Eleanor Roosevelt, Arthur Schlesinger, and John Kenneth Galbraith joined Butler to form a group known as the Democratic Advisory Council. These Democrats did not create the organization simply to challenge Johnson's leadership. Among other things, Butler and others merely wanted to prod Johnson and Rayburn into more aggressive action on the party's agenda. In that spirit, Butler invited Johnson, Rayburn, and a host of House and Senate members to join the new group. Only two—Humphrey and Kefauver—accepted. Johnson and Rayburn "thought that the place for the Democratic Party to set policy was in the Congress," said Stevenson's campaign aide Newton Minow, "and that the best politics was to go along with Eisenhower whenever possible, and fight with him only when they thought it was very, very important." Butler and other more combative liberals abhorred that strategy. Even Humphrey, Johnson's faithful liaison to the liberals, concluded that congressional Democrats must shed their legislative lethargy and begin advancing an aggressive liberal agenda.

Although Humphrey had assured Johnson in a September letter that he expected to be "working *with* you" when the Senate convened in 1957, he was already preparing to side with Butler. Shortly afterward, a furious Johnson learned that Humphrey had not only joined Butler's advisory committee but had banded with other liberals to issue a sixteen-point "manifesto" containing the "new liberal program" they demanded of the Democratic leadership in the new Congress. Johnson angrily spread word among Senate Democrats that he no longer considered Humphrey a trusted member of his inner circle. In January, when Humphrey phoned to discuss routine Senate business, Johnson was distant. "You broke faith with me," he finally said. Humphrey protested. "Now, Lyndon, you know I wouldn't do that. You can get more votes out of this body than anybody can get. You are a great, great leader, Lyndon. I was simply trying to make you an even better leader."

An anonymous memorandum to Johnson from an aide, probably George Reedy, reflected the seriousness of the threat to banish Humphrey. The memo's author cautioned Johnson to give "very serious thought" before "cutting off Senator Humphrey completely from any but the most formal contacts with the leadership." While condemning Humphrey's willingness to break with Johnson, the aide reminded Johnson that, of all the liberals, "he is about the only one who can be worked with to any real degree." Humphrey, the aide concluded, "is too important a prize to be lost." In the end, it appeared that Johnson had merely succumbed to one of his occasional temper tantrums. Humphrey indeed played too vital a role to be cast aside so casually. Within weeks the two men had returned to their usual friendly relations.

Although he publicly denied it, the presidential election returns and the threat of a liberal revolt in his ranks *had* persuaded Johnson of the inevitability of some kind of civil rights bill. "One thing had become absolutely certain," Johnson later said. "The Senate simply had to act, the Democratic Party simply had to act, and I simply had to act; the issue could wait no longer." This realization did not mean Johnson had resolved the question of *how* he would finesse the issue without destroying his party or losing his majority leadership in an angry southern revolt.

The previous fall, during a small party at the house of his aide Gerald Siegel, Johnson revealed the level of his anxiety and uncertainty when Siegel insisted that Johnson himself should move for consideration of the bill. Johnson scoffed at that notion. "You're crazy," he said. "What do you want me to do? Just move it, [and] resign from the Senate the next day?" Supporting a civil rights bill would be a dramatic reversal of Johnson's consistent opposition since 1937. While he often protested—truthfully—that he cared more about blacks than his voting record suggested, Johnson was by no objective measure a civil rights liberal. "I think it is fair to say," Paul Douglas observed, "that when Johnson was in the Senate, he opposed all methods and all attempts to liberalize the position of Negroes and other minorities." Thurgood Marshall, whom Johnson later appointed to the Supreme Court, never regarded Johnson as a liberal senator. For most of his congressional life, he was—in the words of Aaron Henry, a black civil rights advocate in Mississippi—"pretty much galloping with the [segregationist] crowd."

That harsh view of Johnson, largely unchallenged, is primarily based on his congressional record and his public utterances. However, those who understood not only Johnson but the Senate itself knew that no amount of dogged, inventive liberal leadership would likely vanquish Russell's southerners if they resolved to filibuster. For a few liberals, this knowledge produced a kinder, more understanding view of Johnson's record, attitude, and motivations. One "understanding" liberal was the NAACP's Washington director, Clarence Mitchell, who met Johnson shortly after his election as Democratic leader in 1953. Mitchell found Johnson "very cordial." Johnson assured Mitchell that "he believed in civil rights legislation, but that it was unwise to try to get it through Congress because it would split the Democratic Party." Johnson argued that social welfare legislation, court decisions and executive action were the best ways "to avoid these party-splitting fights in Congress." Mitchell had heard this before. Although Johnson's logic did not persuade him, he said "it didn't annoy me either because I knew this was the standard Democratic party line. I also knew from the standpoint of the Democratic party that it made sense."

Like others who knew and worked with Johnson throughout the 1950s, George Reedy believed that Johnson "was for civil rights from the very beginning." Johnson's "capacity to do something, that's what increased," Reedy argued. As he advanced to the Senate and ascended to the leadership, his constituencies—and therefore his latitude—broadened. Then, Reedy believed, "you saw more and more of the real Johnson." Johnson aide Edwin Weisl, Jr., marveled at his "capacity to grow and change with the times," and concluded that he was never a committed racist. "I think he had to do what a southern congressman had to do to get reelected."

The *real* Johnson, said aide Booth Mooney, detested the strident racism and militant anticommunism of conservatives such as Mississippi's James Eastland, a radical segregationist whom Clarence Mitchell had once called the "chief microbe poisoning the bloodstream of the nation." While Johnson sometimes depended on Eastland to pass rural and agriculture legislation, he mocked his colleague's irrational, reactionary obsessions. "Jim Eastland could be standing right in the middle of the worst Mississippi flood ever known," Johnson once joked, "and he'd say the niggers caused it, helped out by the Communists."*

Even some of his most vocal critics acknowledged that Johnson was no racist. "I don't think he was in any way anti-Semitic or viscerally anti-black, in the way that Dick Russell was," maintained Howard Shuman. Joseph Rauh, often a harsh detractor, did not believe that Johnson was "a conservative or a radical or anything else. It was simply that he was trying to be all things to all people." To Mitchell, who had weathered the racist hostility of so many southern conservatives, Johnson seemed a diamond in the rough. "You immediately felt that here was somebody you could respect and would like to work with and would like to maintain their friendship," Mitchell said. "And we did continue to work together."

No longer content to wait for Johnson's cautious, deliberate leadership on civil rights, the Senate's liberals declared their intent to wage an all-out fight to liberalize cloture at the beginning of 1957. On January

*Eastland and his strident opposition to civil rights had become something of a rallying cry for Republicans in the 1956 elections. "A vote for any Democrat," Republicans insisted in an oft-repeated expression, "is a vote for Eastland" (Burns, *John Kennedy*, 200).

The Russell family in 1929. Judge and Mrs. Richard B. Russell, surrounded by their children at the family home in Winder. *Left to right:* Alexander, Richard Jr., Robert, Judge and Mrs. Russell, Henry, Walter, Fielding, and William.   RICHARD B. RUSSELL LIBRARY

The teacher and his Mexican-American students. Johnson with his fifth-, sixth-, and seventh-grade classes at the Welhausen Elementary School in Cotulla, Texas.   LBJ LIBRARY COLLECTION

The progressive young mayor. Humphrey at his desk in Minneapolis City Hall. His wall is adorned with photos of his hero, Franklin D. Roosevelt.   MINNESOTA HISTORICAL SOCIETY

Left: The newlyweds. Johnson and Lady Bird in Washington shortly after their whirlwind courtship and marriage in 1934.   JOHNSON FAMILY PHOTO, LBJ LIBRARY COLLECTION

Before the historic 1948 speech in Philadelphia. Hubert Humphrey Sr. counsels his son to press the
Democratic National Convention to adopt a stronger civil rights plank. AP/WIDE WORLD PHOTOS

The class of 1948. Senate President Pro Tempore Arthur Vandenberg swears in four of the new senators elected in 1948. *Left to right:* Vandenberg, J. Allen Frear of Delaware, Johnson, Paul Douglas of Illinois, and Robert Kerr of Oklahoma. AP/WIDE WORLD PHOTOS

"General Russell" and the southern bloc in 1953. Southern senators opposed to civil rights gather in Russell's office. AP/WIDE WORLD PHOTOS

Above: Alone in the chamber. Johnson stands at his desk on the Senate floor at the close of the 82nd Congress in August 1953. JOHNSON FAMILY PHOTO, LBJ LIBRARY COLLECTION

Left: Russell and Johnson face the press after a White House meeting with President Eisenhower in 1953. WHITE HOUSE PHOTO COURTESY RICHARD B. RUSSELL LIBRARY

As the Senate debates the 1957 Civil Rights Act, Russell, Johnson, and Republican leader William Knowland caucus outside the Senate chamber.   GEORGE TAMES, NYT PICTURES

3, just after the Senate convened, New Mexico's Clinton Anderson moved to consider adoption of the rules. Liberals had advanced the same argument in their 1953 challenge to the filibuster: the Senate was not a "continuing body." Therefore, they said, at the beginning of each Congress, a majority of senators had the absolute right to adopt new rules. Vice President Nixon, continuing to court black voters for his anticipated 1960 presidential campaign, rendered an "advisory opinion" supporting Anderson's motion. According to Nixon, "the right of a current majority of the Senate at the beginning of a new Congress to adopt its own rules . . . cannot be restricted or limited by rules adopted by a majority of the Senate in a previous Congress." Nixon believed that a provision added to the cloture rule in 1949—which held that cloture could not be imposed on filibusters against proposals to change the Senate's rules—"is, in the opinion of the chair, unconstitutional." Hoping to avoid a partisan showdown with Nixon, Johnson cleverly moved to table the Anderson motion rather than challenge Nixon's opinion directly. Supported by Republican leader William Knowland, Johnson's maneuver—having the Senate vote on a tabling motion rather than vote directly on Nixon's opinion—"let a lot of the Republicans off the hook," as Howard Shuman said. By a 55-38 vote, the Senate tabled Anderson's motion.

The strong-arm tactics Johnson employed to win votes on the cloture question infuriated liberals. Anderson later complained that Johnson had been "particularly cruel" with Rhode Island senator Theodore Francis Green, an eighty-nine-year-old icon about to inherit the chairmanship of the Foreign Affairs Committee. Green had coveted the position for years. Now, Johnson threatened to deny Green the chairmanship because of his diminished sight and hearing if he did not vote with the Southerners. When Green defected, Anderson said "most of us understood and sympathized with him."

Though the liberals had lost another round on cloture, the vote portended their ultimate success. The last time the Senate had decided the same question, in 1953, senators had voted 70-21 against Anderson's motion. That year, only five Democrats and one independent had joined fifteen Republicans in support of Anderson. This time, however, twenty-one Democrats voted with seventeen Republicans to support a change in cloture. In four years, the liberal movement had gained seventeen important votes. The additional support, Joseph Rauh believed, "began to be a tipoff to the southerners that if they gave us nothing, and they really filibustered the [civil rights] bill to death, we might beat the filibuster rule in '59." As George Reedy told Johnson in a memorandum, "the South must cold-bloodedly assess the situation . . . if it is to avoid punitive, vengeful and possibly even disastrous legislation." In another memorandum, Reedy was more direct: "If a reasonable bill is *blocked* in this session, the way will be paved to majority cloture and a really tough bill in the near future."

Though Johnson clearly accepted Reedy's arguments for southern compromise, both men may have doubted that Russell would filibuster civil rights this time. In the fall of 1956, while Russell and George Reedy attended a NATO conference in Paris, Russell had confided that "we can never make [Johnson] president unless the Senate first disposes of civil rights." Russell stopped short of saying that he regarded Johnson's presidential hopes as a greater priority than defeating civil rights, but he left Reedy with "the clear impression that such a thought was somewhere in his mind." More importantly, Johnson and Reedy now had good reason to believe that if Johnson could amend the bill to Russell's satisfaction, southern forces might wage only a perfunctory battle.

Johnson knew that Russell wanted to help elect him president, but what about other southerners who cared less about Johnson's presidential ambitions? If these men refused to wage a vigorous fight, and a civil rights bill passed, how would they explain their refusal to filibuster when they returned home? If the southerners remained unified and determined, they could forestall any motion to consider a House-passed bill. But in the face of growing public support for civil rights, were they willing to face the consequences of bringing down another civil rights bill? How long could eighteen southern senators prevent the Senate from acting on one of the most pressing national issues?

The answer, largely, depended on Russell.

Gambling that Russell's desire to see him elected president would be greater than his antipathy toward a weak voting rights bill, Johnson began to lay the groundwork for the first civil rights act in eighty-five years.

On June 18 the House passed Eisenhower's civil rights bill—almost identical to the 1956 legislation—by the overwhelming margin of 286-126. As the Senate awaited the bill's arrival, battle lines were drawn.

Russell, stalwart as usual, stood ready to lead his southern opposition in battle. As majority leader, Johnson quietly plotted his own legislative strategy. For now at least, he would adopt a furtive leadership role. Republican leader William Knowland would instead occupy the Senate's most visible position of leadership on civil rights.

Knowland headed an unprecedented coalition of moderate Republicans and liberal Democrats. Though Eisenhower's advocacy had sparked these Republicans' sudden willingness to support a civil rights bill, other forces were now at work. Historically allied with the southern opposition to Roosevelt and Truman's progressive agendas, some Republicans had wearied of the alliance. Said George Reedy: "They did not, as a whole, throb to flood control, rural electrification, public power and parity farm programs that were absolutely essential to states that based their economies on cotton, rice and tobacco." For Republicans from midwestern and northeastern states—whose small black populations posed inconsequential threats to the white majority—something vastly more significant overshadowed their old alliance with southerners against civil rights. They now worried more about the political fortunes of the national Republican party and its leader, Dwight Eisenhower. With dizzying speed, they abandoned their erstwhile southern allies on civil rights. In almost no time at all, Russell and the southerners had precious few allies outside the South.

Russell derisively dubbed the new coalition, led by Paul Douglas on the liberal Democratic side, as "the Knowland-Douglas axis."* A conservative, humorless man from California, Knowland was neither a skillful legislative strategist nor a strong, dynamic leader. He was, in the words of Johnson's aide Booth Mooney, "a nice, decent fellow, but sort of thick-skulled." Washington senator Henry Jackson remembered Knowland as "a bull in a china closet" during Senate debate. He often reminded Jackson of "an unguided missile, going off in all directions." When Johnson and Knowland confronted each other in debate, Johnson usually won. "Knowland was a real Republican elephant," Humphrey said, "and Johnson was a lion." Senator George Smathers said Johnson

---

*Douglas inherited the liberal leadership role by default. The respected chairman of the Judiciary Committee's subcommittee on constitutional rights, Thomas Hennings of Missouri, was an alcoholic. Douglas, not a Judiciary Committee member, became the liberal leader on the bill after Hennings went on a drinking binge, brought on by the pressure of the civil rights debate (Shuman OH, USSHO; McPherson, 36).

often "led [Knowland] around by the nose. And everybody used to laugh about it." Eisenhower worked "much more closely with Mr. Johnson than he did with Senator Knowland," recalled Eisenhower's press secretary, James Hagerty. Even Eisenhower himself once wrote of his Senate leader: "It is a pity that his wisdom, his judgment, his tact, and his sense of humor lag so far behind his ambition." Despite all their shortcomings as proven floor leaders, Knowland and Douglas had—at least for now—the numbers and the Senate's rules on their side.

And Douglas had grown wiser. Following the 1956 debacle, when Johnson had humiliated him for trying to place the civil rights bill onto the Senate calendar, Douglas vowed he would be better prepared in 1957. Two days after the House passed the civil rights bill, Knowland and Douglas launched their attack. They objected to the bill's referral to Judiciary. With the Senate version of the bill still bogged down in committee, Knowland and Douglas had every reason to fear that a referral of the House bill would only ensure the slow death of *two* civil rights measures. At last, Douglas said, the liberals planned "to use the rules" to force action on the issue "instead of having the rules of the Senate continuously used to prevent the Senate from considering important issues." On June 20, when Russell objected to the Knowland-Douglas interpretation, the Senate overruled him, 45-39. Under the rules, the bill could now become the Senate's pending business by a simple majority vote.

The roster of Russell's supporters on this vote was a curious collection of Republicans and Democrats, including several liberals and moderates: Clinton Anderson, J. William Fulbright, Albert Gore, Estes Kefauver, John F. Kennedy, Warren Magnuson, Mike Mansfield, Wayne Morse, James Murray, and Joseph O'Mahoney. Eisenhower snidely observed that those votes "struck me as rather odd" because the list included those who "normally proclaimed themselves champions of 'liberalism' and the 'little people.' "

One other moderate Democrat joined in voting to sustain Russell's point of order—Lyndon Johnson. Certain that Douglas and Knowland would win, he bought time with his conservative Texas constituents by siding with Russell. To a constituent in Fort Worth, Johnson insisted he was "working to prevent the passage of legislation that would allow the Attorney General to haul our people into a federal court and prosecute them without a jury trial." While the day might soon come when Johnson would vote for a civil rights bill, a constituent uprising would only distract him from the important task of finding a reasonable compromise.

As for the liberals and moderates who voted with Russell, some of their votes seemed to suggest a basic distrust of Republican leader Knowland. A former opponent of cloture, Knowland had few real civil rights credentials. His support for the bill seemed based entirely on the promise of a political windfall for his party. Among the most suspicious of Knowland was Clinton Anderson, who believed Knowland hoped the southerners would filibuster the bill to death. This, Anderson explained, "would permit him to blame the Democrats for its defeat and permit the Republicans, in future elections, to pose as defenders of the American Negro." Anderson and several other liberals wanted the bill to pass but were "wary" of what they believed were "Knowland's traps."

Another, more intriguing motivation led several western Democrats—Morse, Mansfield, Murray, O'Mahoney, and Magnuson—to vote with Russell to refer the bill. All five apparently traded their votes in a deal brokered by Johnson, whereby a group of southern senators agreed to support a controversial dam and hydroelectric project on the Idaho-Oregon border.

For years, proponents had wanted the federal government to construct the dam at a place on the Snake River known as Hells Canyon. Western Republicans, the Eisenhower administration, the private power industry, and many business organizations had always opposed the plan, arguing instead for construction of three smaller privately owned dams. In June 1956, with Johnson doing little to promote the project, the Senate had voted 41-51 to reject Wayne Morse's legislation to fund the Hells Canyon dam. At the heart of debate was the perennial question of public versus private power. For many western politicians it was the crucial and most emotional issue of the day—far more important than civil rights.

Johnson understood the issue's importance better than most. But he also knew that the day might soon come when he and Russell's southern troops would need the goodwill and support of western moderates. So, on June 21—the day after the six Democrats supported Russell's attempt to send the civil rights bill to Judiciary—Johnson called for a vote on the Hells Canyon dam. This time, five southern Democrats who had voted against the dam in 1956 staged a sudden, "unexplained" about-face. To the utter amazement of their colleagues and the press, Russell, George Smathers, James Eastland, Sam Ervin, and Russell Long reversed their previous opposition to the project.

Although he had won the early procedural skirmish, Douglas felt particularly betrayed by Morse's reversal. When he learned that his Oregon colleague would vote to send the bill to Judiciary, Douglas called a meeting of his northern and western colleagues. Before the group of about sixteen senators, Douglas angrily condemned Morse for his perfidy and scolded him for not forewarning the group of his change of heart. The tense confrontation ended when Morse angrily stalked out of the room. Douglas was furious that some westerners so eagerly sold out civil rights for a less-than-certain dam project. After the Hells Canyon vote, he sought out Frank Church, a freshman Democrat from Idaho elected on the promise to fight for the project's approval. "Frank," Douglas said, "I am afraid you Hells Canyon folk have been given some counterfeit money." Douglas predicted that the private power interests would prevail when the bill reached the House. The following year proved Douglas correct. Despite having sold their votes to Johnson and Russell, the westerners saw their beloved Hells Canyon project die a quiet death in a House subcommittee in June 1958.

However, the ultimate defeat of Hells Canyon would not come until well after the civil rights debate. Meanwhile, what Johnson had accomplished was nothing short of brilliant. He had banked a tremendous amount of goodwill with western Democrats. "He made himself some friends on both sides of the issue," admitted Russell Long, a southerner who reversed his Hells Canyon vote. Years afterward, Johnson explained that he "began with the assumption that most of the Senators from the mountain states had never seen a Negro and simply couldn't care all that much about the whole civil rights issue." They did care, however, about Hells Canyon. "So I went to a few key southerners and persuaded them to back the western liberals on Hells Canyon." In return, Johnson now had grateful votes in reserve. He would spend them judiciously to secure the eventual compromise that he hoped would ultimately save the civil rights bill from defeat.

All he needed now was a compromise.

CHAPTER ELEVEN

Half a Loaf

IN MARCH 1956, MEMBERS OF White Citizens Councils throughout Louisiana embarked on an ambitious program to purge blacks from the state's voter rolls. The project was urgent, as the councils warned registrars, sheriffs, and other officials in a pamphlet: "The communists and the NAACP plan to register and vote every colored person of age in the South." Nowhere was the effort more successfully and relentlessly carried out than in Ouachita Parish, in northeastern Louisiana. Aided by the parish registrar, council members compiled a list of more than 3,400 black voters and filed affidavits challenging the voting qualifications of each. Although the affiants claimed to have examined the files of those whose registrations they challenged, the parish registrar knew better. Council members had failed to conduct a thorough examination of the rolls, and their affidavits were not sworn before the registrar or his deputy, as required by law.

The results of the council's examination were even more suspect. Each of the 2,389 black voters in Ward Ten was challenged, yet none of the 4,054 white voters was targeted. In Ward Three, the council filed affidavits against 1,008 of the ward's 1,523 black voters but only 23 whites.

Upon receiving the affidavits, the registrar dutifully mailed citations to challenged voters, instructing them to appear within ten days to certify their qualifications. The response was overwhelming. Black voters turned out in large numbers during April and May, forming lengthy lines at the parish courthouse. Sometimes they began queuing up as early as 5:00 a.m. This massive response evoked little sympathy from the registrar's office, which allowed only fifty people to plead their cases each day. As a result, most challenged voters never got the chance to prove their qualifications. The registrar summarily struck their names from the voter rolls. Those who were fortunate enough to have a hearing were presumed unqualified unless they proved otherwise. Furthermore, they could not call as witnesses people who lived in another precinct, those whose own voting qualifications had been challenged, or those who had been witnesses for other challenged voters.

The result was a holocaust of disenfranchisement for the hapless black voters of Ouachita Parish. In March, 5,782 blacks had been listed as voters. On October 4, after the registrar issued his ruling, only 889 remained on the rolls.

Later that year, sixty miles to the south in rural Grant Parish, the White Citizens Council began another purge. This time they hoped to rid the rolls of at least 90 percent of the parish's black voters—just before the November 6 general election. The challenges were devious but effective. Applicants who registered to vote had been asked to complete this obtuse statement: "I am not now registered as a voter in any other ward or precinct of this state except _____." Black voters who had answered "Grant" instead of the correct "nine"—for their ward number—were removed from the rolls. Likewise, blacks who wrote "C" instead of "colored" when asked their race were purged. A local newspaper's examination of the registration forms for a hundred white voters in one ward of the parish revealed that only *one* voter could have survived a similar purge attempt. Segregationist leaders made no apologies for their ruthless actions. "From the long-range standpoint," declared state Senator W. M. "Willie" Rainach, "our only hope in this segregation fight is to clear our rolls of all illegally qualified voters."

Louisiana was not alone in its hostility toward blacks who wanted to vote. In one North Carolina county, the registrar gave literacy tests only to black applicants; the test required them to write the preamble to the U.S. Constitution using perfect spelling, punctuation, and capitalization. In another county the registrar required black applicants to answer a list of twenty questions. Among other things, they were required to name all candidates running for public office in the county, explain the meaning of primary and general elections, reveal their membership in the NAACP, and declare whether they would support the organization if it attacked the U.S. government. Some Alabama counties ordered blacks to calculate their age in years, months, and days. If they missed by one day, the registrars rejected their applications.

"The right to vote is the cornerstone of our representative form of government," Attorney General Brownell said as he presented the Eisenhower administration's civil rights bill to a Senate Judiciary subcommittee in February 1957. "It is the one right, perhaps more than any other, upon which all other constitutional rights depend for their effective protection." Despite his serious concerns over the White Citizens Councils' assaults on black voters, Brownell and his Justice Department attorneys had no legal remedies they could employ to stop the practice. Their hands were tied. By law, they could intervene *only* when a registered voter complained that his voting rights had been denied on election day.

There was much about the administration bill that southerners found objectionable. Even so, the fundamental right of adult citizens to vote —guaranteed by the Fifteenth Amendment—was not something Russell and his troops were eager to oppose on the Senate floor. "I had a sense that the southerners felt guilty about depriving the Negroes of voting," said George Reedy. "They didn't at all feel guilty about depriving them of jobs, they didn't feel sensitive about housing, but they were defensive about the vote. That they couldn't justify." Said Florida's George Smathers, a civil rights opponent whose state had 366,000 blacks eligible to vote but only 148,000 registered: "I would not condone, or protect, any official who in any way participated in depriving any citizen of his right to vote." Reedy was correct. Southerners treaded lightly around the bill. They would find other aspects on which to base their objections.

Almost a carbon copy of the administration's 1956 legislation, the new bill was divided into four parts. Although called a civil rights proposal, the bill created no new rights; it merely provided for more effective federal enforcement of laws and constitutional guarantees already on the books. Part I created a bipartisan civil rights commission, for a two-year life span, with the power to subpoena witnesses in its investigations of civil rights violations. Part II would give the Justice Department a new assistant attorney general who, Brownell pledged, would head a civil rights division. Part III would give the attorney general new injunctive powers to fight and prevent violations of voting rights and other civil rights. Part IV outlawed attempts to prevent individuals from voting in federal elections and empowered the attorney general to initiate civil actions for preventive relief.

While they opposed the entire bill, many southerners particularly abhorred Part IV, which denied jury trials for defendants charged in criminal contempt actions arising from the legislation. Russell was concerned about the jury trial issue. But he was more alarmed by Part III, which gave the attorney general enormous new powers to initiate legal action against those who sought to deprive a citizen of voting rights or any other civil right. To southerners, this meant aggressive federal action to enforce the desegregation of public schools—possibly at gunpoint. Despite Russell's suspicions, it had not been school desegregation that Brownell had in mind when he inserted Part III into the bill. The brutal murder of fourteen-year-old Emmett Till in Mississippi had demonstrated to Brownell "the lack of power of the attorney general . . . to act in matters of this kind." After searching the federal statutes, Brownell had been frustrated that his Justice Department was unable to identify any legal basis the federal government could use to "enforce the constitutional promise that had been made to our citizens" by the Fourteenth Amendment.

Liberals, on the other hand, found Part III weak. Under its provisions, the federal government could not intervene until aggrieved individuals filed their own private lawsuits. "This meant," said Paul Douglas, "that the relatively poor and disadvantaged would have the heavy burden of initial costs and the grave danger of losing their jobs and their incomes at the hands of white rulers of their communities. If the NAACP, through its legal fund, helped, the financial burden would be lightened, but local pressures against litigants would still be heavy." Class actions were not allowed. That meant the Justice Department could not employ sweeping legal measures to address wholesale civil rights violations. Despite all its weaknesses, however, Part III was a far more potent weapon for civil rights than anything in current statutes.

As it emerged from the House, the bill had remained virtually intact. While southerners had tried vainly to amend it to require jury trials for criminal contempt, few House members had complained about Part III and the vast new authority it gave to the attorney general. Ostensibly the provision merely gave the federal government injunctive power to stop illegal discrimination. "This seemed innocent enough," said Paul Douglas, who admitted wondering why Justice Department lawyers had put it in the bill. However, Douglas added, "Dick Russell knew what it meant."

On July 2, Russell rose on the floor of the Senate to speak on the civil rights bill that Knowland would call up for consideration in only a few days. His powerful speech would drastically alter the dynamics of the debate. From his first words, Russell sought to dramatize the importance of his remarks: "Mr. President, for the first time since I have been a member of the Senate, I respectfully request that I be not interrupted in the course of my prepared discussion." Standing erect at his mahogany desk—directly behind Johnson's—Russell declared that approval of the House-passed bill "will cause unspeakable confusion, bitterness and bloodshed" throughout the South. In his usual low voice, he said, "If you propose to move in this fashion, you may as well prepare your concentration camps now, for there are not enough jails to hold the people of the South who will today oppose the use of raw federal power to forcibly commingle white and Negro children in the same schools and in places of public entertainment." Russell's language was strong and inflammatory, but he had read and researched the bill thoroughly. He did not believe his words were hyperbolic. While proponents had characterized it as a right-to-vote bill, Russell asserted "it is as much of an actual force bill as the measures proposed by Sumner and Stevens in Reconstruction days in their avowed drive 'to put black heels on white necks.' The powers are there, even though more cunningly contrived than the forthright legislation aimed at the South in the tragic era of Reconstruction."

Furthermore and most significant, Russell explained, the Justice Department had grafted Part III to a provision of the civil rights laws that were enforceable by an 1866 statute empowering the president to use armed forces to "aid in the execution of judicial process . . . and enforce the due execution of the provisions" covered by the statute. "I unhesitatingly assert," he told the Senate, "that this section of the bill was deliberately drawn to enable the use of our military forces to destroy the system of separation of the races in the southern states at the point of a bayonet, if it be necessary to take this step. I assert that this bill vests in one man, the attorney general of the United States, greater powers over the American people than any other man, including the president elected by the people, has ever possessed." If the Senate persisted in retaining Part III, Russell hinted that he would lead a filibuster against the bill. "I say to all the other members of this body: If there should ever be presented here a bill which proposed to deal so harshly with the people of their states as this bill would deal with the people of my state, if they did not fight it to the very death, they would be unworthy of the people who sent them here."

Near the end of his speech, Russell unveiled an unusual proposal for one who prided himself on his dedication to Constitutional principles. He called for a national referendum on the civil rights question. "I am not afraid to have this issue submitted to the people of the North and West in a clear-cut and fairly presented plebiscite." His proposal could not have been serious. Even if such a referendum were constitutional, its wording would have provoked lengthy and rancorous debate in both houses of Congress.

The curiosity of the referendum idea aside, Russell's speech was a major news event. A front-page story in the next morning's *Washington Post* was headlined, "RUSSELL SAYS PRESENT CIVIL RIGHTS BILL WOULD BRING 'BAYONET RULE' IN SOUTH." The *New York Times* headline said: "RUSSELL DEMANDS CIVIL RIGHTS ISSUE BE PUT TO NATION." Inside the paper, the *Times* printed excerpts of Russell's speech that filled almost half a page. *U.S. News & World Report* reprinted five and a half pages of excerpts.

At a press conference the next day, reporters eagerly quizzed Eisenhower about Russell's charges. "Well, I would not want to answer this in detail," the president responded, "because I was reading part of the bill this morning and . . . there were certain phrases I didn't completely understand." Eisenhower said he planned to "talk to the attorney general and see exactly what they do mean." Attempting to clarify his motives for reporters, Eisenhower unwittingly played into Russell's hands. He insisted that he simply wanted the bill "to prevent anybody illegally from interfering with any individual's right to vote." But that was only part of what his bill was designed to accomplish.

It was not the first time Eisenhower had shown his ignorance about his own legislation. When asked a benign question about the jury trial issue at a May 15 press conference, he explained, "I am not enough of a lawyer to discuss that thing one way or another . . . You will have to go to the attorney general. He knows more about it than I do."

Although Russell was the first person to highlight the impact of Part III, its significance should not have been a surprise. As *New York Times* columnist Arthur Krock observed in a July 13 column, "anyone with time, diligence, and some legal training could have known in advance the issues over the administration's bill" that Russell had raised. Brownell and North Carolina senator Sam Ervin had discussed its provisions in several exchanges during the Judiciary Committee's hearings in February and March.

In the wake of Russell's assault, southerners pounced on the bill, invoking horrific images of a second Reconstruction. "It would make of the southern states conquered provinces," Judiciary chairman James Eastland declared. "In its essence, it would deny to the southern states the fundamental base of the American system of government—and that is the right of self-government." Always eager to tie civil rights to the communist threat, Eastland said the bill "borrows the very worst form of Stalin tyranny" and would result in "forced integration by the use of the bayonet." The southern onslaught had its desired effect. Said *Time:* "After a while, many a conscientious Senator could no longer see the facts for the smoke."

Aided by Eisenhower's feeble defense of the bill, Russell's attack on Part III carried enormous weight in the Senate. "We were sunk," Paul Douglas said. Douglas's aide Howard Shuman placed equal blame on Brownell and his lawyers, who had so "shrouded" the bill "in general language" that few understood its potential impact. "The Justice Department lawyers should have come at it directly. They outsmarted themselves." The way they concealed the real impact of Part III justified southern fears that, as a *Time* reporter put it, "the Justice Department was trying to sneak Part III past the Congress as a sinister stowaway aboard an innocent-looking vessel."

Despite his apparent tactical victory, Russell knew that his southern troops were still very much on the defensive. In a story the day after the tirade against Part III, the *New York Times* observed that it was a time of "melancholy and the inner knowledge of ultimate defeat" for Russell. The irony of Russell's life, the *Times* said, "lies in the fact that he can be a primary leader only in [a] cause that he knows already to be lost in the unfolding movement of history. His mission thus cannot be to win any fight but only to lose fights as slowly as possible, one by one, and so to hold back a little longer the oncoming certainty of [a] compulsory federal civil rights program in his native South." Russell had once acknowledged as much to a Georgia friend who chided him by saying, "You're just fighting a delaying action." Russell replied, "I know, but I am trying to delay it—ten years if I'm not lucky, 200 years if I am."

On July 3, the day of Eisenhower's press conference, fifteen members of the southern bloc gathered to discuss legislative strategy in Russell's office. Russell was realistic. He stated the obvious: Despite the improving prospects that the Senate would remove the most potent provisions of Part III, the southern bloc was still under siege. Their numbers had dwindled to a core of about eighteen dependable members. Their once-loyal allies, the Republicans, had defected to the other side. With that in mind, Russell favored a nonconfrontational strategy by which southerners would not engage in a futile attempt to defeat the bill. Instead, he believed, they should work to so weaken it with amendments that its impact in the South would be minimal.

Typically, Russell did not attempt to force his views on his southern colleagues. "Dick would more or less present the question to people and let them answer it for themselves," Louisiana's Russell Long recalled. "It never gave the appearance that he was coaxing people into doing what they didn't want to do." Said Mississippi's John Stennis: "He would always listen to everyone at the conference table. He didn't start out with a premise and try to drive everyone to it." Russell, said Long, "was a master of putting the matter to the people so that they weren't doing him a favor."

Although South Carolina's Strom Thurmond and Olin Johnston dissented, Russell deftly guided the discussion toward a compromise rather than a divisive filibuster. While they would continue to use the specter of "extended debate" as a bargaining tool, Russell and the wiser members of the southern bloc understood the consequences of preventing the Senate from passing legislation that a majority outside the South regarded as desirable and inevitable. "I told them," Russell later said, "I would not [filibuster] because the threat of a filibuster was really more powerful than a real filibuster would have been." As the meeting ended, Harry Byrd captured the prevailing sentiment of the group when he turned to Russell and said, "Dick, it's up to you." On Russell's recommendation, the group agreed to allow a vote on Knowland's motion to bring the bill up for consideration. "The extraordinary decision reached by the Southern group was made for a hard and simple reason," *Newsweek* observed. "They were licked from the start. Their only hope, they realized, was not to defeat the bill with parliamentary devices but to attempt to gain the best possible revision of the bill."

That decision was unwelcome news for Douglas and the Senate's more dogmatic liberals. If liberal and moderate Democrats and Republicans remained a cohesive group, they could force their southern colleagues to choose between capitulation and filibuster. Either alternative was acceptable to the liberals. If they forced the southerners' hand, the best result would be a strong, effective bill. Yet if Russell's bloc filibustered the bill to death, liberals knew that civil rights would be a powerful issue in the 1958 congressional elections, perhaps resulting in an electoral mandate for a strong bill. A compromise bill would blur the battle lines. The bill would be weaker, but it would allow the southerners to escape the wrath of most voters, even those who wanted stronger legislation.

After the southern meeting, Thurmond was the one member of the southern group most dissatisfied with Russell's strategy of compromise. A fervent believer in segregation, Thurmond seemed to neither grasp nor care about the dire political consequences of sinking a popular bill.* Thirty years later, Thurmond still seemed unable to comprehend the importance of passing a civil rights bill in 1957. He still believed that the southern group should have filibustered but had sacrificed their principles in order to elect Johnson president. "Johnson," Thurmond said, "had told them that to have a chance [at the presidency], he'd have to have a civil rights program and a civil rights bill."

As the Senate approached the day it would vote to begin debate on the bill, Part III—the heart and soul of the Eisenhower-Brownell legislation—was in distress. On July 10, while the Senate debated Knowland's motion to call up the bill, Russell went to the White House. "It was one of the most interesting conferences I ever had with a president," Russell later said of his fifty-eight-minute meeting in the Oval Office. "[The president] just sat there and poured out his soul about that bill and the Supreme Court and several other things." Russell said the candid nature of the conversation amazed him, until he realized that Eisenhower "just thought he was talking to a good friend." Russell emerged tight lipped from the meeting, telling reporters only that Eisenhower seemed "very determined" to pass the bill. They discussed no concessions on Part III, he said. Asked if he felt encouraged by his discussion with the president, Russell said, "I can't say that I do."

Later that day, Vice President Nixon gave the bill a stronger endorsement than Eisenhower when he predicted that it would pass the Senate without "compromise." Nixon told a group of House freshmen of his determination to see the bill enacted "no matter how long it may take." Those who were responsible for rounding up votes in the Senate,

---

*University of Wisconsin professor Carl Auerbach sat beside Humphrey one evening on the Senate floor as Louisiana's Russell Long delivered a spirited attack on the bill. As Humphrey and Auerbach left the floor after Long's speech, Auerbach quizzed Humphrey.

"Senator Long can't possibly believe all that he said, does he?"

"No," Humphrey replied, "I don't think he believes a word he said. But that s.o.b. Strom Thurmond does."

it seems, were blissfully ignorant of just how unpopular Part III had become. When New Jersey Republican Alexander Smith went to the White House to urge Eisenhower's chief of staff, Sherman Adams, to give up the fight, Adams exuded confidence. "We'll win on Part III," Adams reportedly replied. "We have our finger on the Senate pulse. We know what's going on."

House Judiciary Committee chairman Emanuel Celler knew better. Early on, he had realized that the heart of Part III was dead unless Eisenhower made an impassioned, articulate plea for its passage. That was something the president would not—or could not—do. "There seems to be no fight in the administration," Celler told reporters after the Russell-Eisenhower meeting. "The President bends with every wind. I can't see a Truman or a Roosevelt—Teddy or FDR—yielding so pusillanimously. We liberal [House] Democrats went out on a limb in fighting for this bill, a limb which the administration would cut off."

Eisenhower, the former Supreme Allied Commander, had never been a battlefield general. As chief executive he would govern as he had warred: by establishing general policy from his White House headquarters while aides devised and carried out the tactics to win his Congressional battles. Eisenhower "wouldn't twist anybody's arm," complained Republican Congressman Wesley D'Ewart of Montana. "He wouldn't be vindictive if a person didn't go along with him." The president, as always, would leave the intense lobbying to others.

In the Senate, meanwhile, Johnson exhorted his colleagues to meet the nation's lofty expectations. He avoided much of the preliminary debate, leaving the floor to Knowland and Russell, who led their respective coalitions in the early skirmishes over the bill. On July 12, Johnson began the Senate's day by paying tribute to the "high caliber" of debate on both sides. He also began to lay rhetorical groundwork for the ultimate compromise on Part III. "There will be some," he said, "who insist that it is little short of treason to dot a single 'i' or cross a single 't' in passing the civil rights bill. There will be others who will insist that it is the height of infamy to approve a single 'i' or cross a single 't.' But I think the American people have more sense than that."

For some time, Johnson had known what it would take to stop the southerners from filibustering. Russell had presented his terms with unmistakable clarity: the gutting of Part III and approval of an amendment to Part IV providing for jury trials in criminal contempt cases. This was the price for southern acquiescence—to render the bill a toothless voting rights measure.

Yet Johnson knew that he and Russell alone did not have the votes to pay this price. Most of the votes to kill Part III and amend Part IV would, of necessity, come from outside the southern bloc. Finding these votes would not be easy. Johnson would have to deal, call in favors, and issue threats. He would also have to keep the Senate debate dignified and, more important, civilized. Johnson feared that George Reedy's early assessment might be correct: "The thinking of both pro and anti-civil righters is so polarized that *one side cannot vote for anything* and *the other side cannot vote for anything but everything.* The only solution in such an impasse is for reasonable men to emerge with a measure which may not satisfy the pro and the antis but *which is so demonstrably reasonable that it will satisfy the country.*"

Achieving the compromise that Johnson and Russell needed—one that could muster a majority on the Senate floor—would require all of Johnson's immense powers of persuasion. In the Senate, every member had his or her own unique definition of *reasonable*. James Rowe, who volunteered his views in a July 3 memorandum, sized up the situation well when he observed, "This is Armageddon for Lyndon Johnson."

When he did speak in the Senate, Johnson almost never mentioned the legislation's details or the compromises he was seeking. Instead he merely appealed for reasoned, courteous debate that would honor, not shame, the Senate. In the words of one reporter, he hoped to persuade the southerners to "hold back their blood-and-thunder oratory." On July 9 he said: "All of us are aware of the fact that many people throughout the country consider this issue to be a test of our democratic processes. Personally, I have complete confidence in the ability of the Senate to measure up to any reasonable test." On July 10 he expressed hope for "a climate of reason within which the Senate can reach a meaningful conclusion." The next day he began with a call for the Senate to "continue to explore the issues in the current spirit" and voiced his "confidence that the Senate, with dignity and decency, will reach a very reasonable judgment." Again, on July 12, he said, "I think all of us realize that, in a very real sense, that the Senate is on trial; and the American people want us to win." Three days later, he opened the day's proceedings by congratulating the Senate for proving "that it is not in a strait-jacket, but can act according to its convictions as to the course that best serves the national interest." And he praised those senators, liberals and conservatives, for the quality of the amendments they would offer. "The proposals are the reaction of thinking men who realize that great issues must be met with reason, instead of blind dogma."

Russell, too, exhorted his troops to wage a temperate debate. "We've got a good case on the merits," he told them. "Let's keep the argument germane. Let's see if we can keep our speeches restrained, and not inflammatory." Neither side, it seemed, wished to create the kind of rancorous atmosphere that might spawn a southern filibuster. While he nurtured a spirit of compromise (by Russell's standards this meant the *liberals* would yield in exchange for no filibuster), Russell knew the southerners had to present a spirited challenge to the bill for at least two reasons: Many white southerners believed it was an unconstitutional intrusion into the sovereign affairs of their states, and southern senators needed to prove to constituents that they had attempted to defeat the bill.

As the debate began, Russell split his troops into sectors. North Carolina's Sam Ervin, a Judiciary Committee member who had sat through many hours of hearings on the bill, would be ready to debate all sections. Arkansas's J. William Fulbright and Alabama's John Sparkman, both known for their liberalism outside civil rights, would lead the arguments for a jury trial amendment. Alabama's Lister Hill, another progressive southerner, would attempt to summon organized labor to support the jury trial amendment. Arkansas's John McClellan would join Russell in driving home the extreme nature of Part III. Russell's Georgia colleague, Herman Talmadge, would lead the fight against the bill on radio and television forums.

On July 16, Johnson broke new ground. He rose to announce that he would support Knowland's motion to call up the civil rights bill. Yet he quickly added that he would also vote for three other motions: to refer the bill to the Judiciary Committee for seven days, to water down Part III, and to add a jury trial provision to Part IV. Although his position on the bill was not yet entirely clear—he insisted that his vote for Knowland's motion "should not be construed as a vote in support of the bill"—those who knew him understood exactly what he meant by the following admonition: "I think the members of this body should debate it, discuss it, amend it, improve it and then vote on it."

On July 16, 1957, the decades-old coalition of southern Democrats and conservative Republicans died. The Senate finally voted, 71-18, for Knowland's motion to begin formal debate on the House-passed bill. When the presiding officer announced the tally, Johnson and Knowland leaned across the narrow aisle that divided the Republican and Democratic halves of the chamber and shook hands. Meanwhile, eighteen lonely southerners—abandoned by their former Republican allies and now exposed as the last defenders of the Old South—had weathered the prevailing national winds by voting to deny the Senate the opportunity to debate the bill. Despite the overwhelming vote, Johnson knew that much of the bill's support rested on shifting legislative sand. Russell's rhetoric after the vote was evidence of the precarious situation. The southern leader kept up his steady drumbeat of opposition. He ominously warned that his troops were "prepared to extend the greatest effort ever made in history to prevent passage of this bill in its present form." Russell dismissed the lopsided vote. His forces, he declared beforehand, would "muster nothing like our total strength."

Johnson knew that Russell was at least partially correct. Although the southerners were massively outnumbered on civil rights, they held at least one significant advantage over the liberals: they were *united*, almost to a man, in their goal of weakening the bill. The liberals and Republicans, on the other hand, were anything but a cohesive group. Some Republicans—Irving Ives and Jacob Javits of New York, Clifford Case of New Jersey, and Charles Potter of Michigan—were prepared to resist any compromise at all. Others, such as Karl Mundt of South Dakota and Milton Young of North Dakota, seemed agreeable to almost any type of compromise proposal. In the middle were the vast majority of Republicans, open to compromise but unwilling to give the southerners *everything*. The nonsouthern Democrats were split, too. The dogmatic liberals led by Douglas equated compromise with treason, while western Democrats—such as Anderson, Kerr, Church, and O'Mahoney—were eager for a reasonable bargain.

With so many factions playing so many different political games, the southerners remained the Senate's most cohesive faction. If he could not find a way to resolve southern concerns over parts III and IV, Johnson knew that the fragile majority supporting the bill would run headlong into a powerful, well-oiled southern filibuster machine.

"I think there is a way that you can finally put the other provisions through, and then the other southerners would have no real reason to go on with their filibuster." Those words from New Mexico's Clinton Anderson were music to Johnson's ears. He knew that the Senate must drastically weaken Part III to prevent a southern filibuster. Now, here was a trusted member of the liberal bloc volunteering to lead the fight.

Anderson's civil rights credentials were impeccable, but he understood that the "best" legislation would have no effect at all unless it could win the votes for passage. For several days before the Senate voted to take up the bill, he had "glued" himself to his desk on the Senate floor, where he listened intently to the debate over Part III. Anderson concluded that "if you could just remove the southern fears that we would march an army into the South, it would be worthwhile." After a couple of days, Johnson sidled over to ask Anderson why he was so interested in this debate. When Anderson volunteered that he was considering an amendment to strike the most potent provisions of Part III, Johnson urged him to do it—and offered a suggestion. "He thought I should get a really good Republican to join with me." After surveying the Senate, Anderson found two respected Republican moderates: George Aiken of Vermont and Francis Case of South Dakota.

Johnson instinctively understood the benefit of a liberal westerner and two moderate Republicans proposing to gut Part III. Had Russell or another conservative southerner presented the same amendment, liberals would have held it up as a willful attempt to destroy the bill by eliminating its strongest provision. It would have been anathema to everyone but the small southern minority. (Sure enough, when Russell later announced his support for an amendment to clarify provisions in Part IV of the bill, Paul Douglas wryly commented, "I am reminded of the old saying, 'Beware of the Greeks bearing gifts' . . . I say we had better button up our pockets and look closely at the fine print in the bill.") For many liberals, an Anderson-Aiken-Case amendment was a different matter altogether. The liberal Democrats and moderate Republicans who supported Part III could not intimate that these men were allies of Richard Russell. Their amendment immediately disarmed liberal critics, making it exceedingly easier for Johnson to find the votes to pay the first installment of his agreement with Russell.

The unexpected assistance from Anderson, Aiken, and Case also complicated matters for Russell's southern bloc. His sudden inheritance of liberal and moderate support foreclosed Russell's ability to filibuster. "If you were going to filibuster," George Reedy observed, "it's one thing to filibuster when nobody is agreeing with you, when you're standing there with your back to the wall. But when you start getting some reason and some cooperation from the other side, that puts you on a bad spot. You can't really filibuster then." From that point on, Reedy said, the southerners "laid down and they played dead."

Nothing, however, furthered the effort to emasculate Part III more than Eisenhower's weak, faltering defense of his own bill. The day after the Senate voted to consider the bill, the president appeared before the White House press corps. At earlier meetings with the media, the president had undercut Knowland's leadership by admitting his ignorance of the House-passed bill. A question from reporter Rowland Evans sealed the fate of Part III. Evans asked if "it would be a wise extension of federal power" to permit the attorney general "to bring suits on his own motion, to enforce school integration in the South?"

"Well, no," Eisenhower responded. "I have—as a matter of fact, as you state it that way, on his own motion, without any request from local authorities, I suppose is what you are talking about?"

"Yes, sir," Evans replied. "I think that that is what the bill would do, Part III."

Through the fog of apparent ignorance of his bill, Eisenhower's signal was clear: He did not support Part III. From the Senate floor, Oregon's Richard Neuberger decried the president's ineffectual advocacy. "At two successive press conferences, the president has revealed that, first, he is not thoroughly familiar with the contents of his administration's civil rights bill and, two, that he is not enthusiastically in favor of what he does believe the bill to contain." Neuberger complained that although White House press releases "speak approvingly" of a bill with Part III, "these, even, are issued while the president is at the golf course." Blindsided again by Eisenhower's inept defense of the legislation, Knowland did what he could to absolve his president of the blame. He argued, weakly, that "the details of the bill belong to this body and to the other body of Congress."

With Knowland's leadership undercut by the White House, Johnson quickly moved to fill the void. He launched his strategy to weaken Part III and began rounding up the necessary votes to do it.

Meanwhile, hoping to head off the total enervation of Part III, Humphrey offered an amendment that repealed the Reconstruction-era law authorizing the use of federal force. "I felt," Humphrey explained to the Senate, "that troops and civil rights ought to be disconnected both in theory and in practice." The Senate approved the amendment by a 90-0 vote, but its addition to the bill did not have the desired effect. Humphrey had hoped that his amendment would provide the "calm" needed to move to consideration of other portions of the bill, but southerners would not settle for anything less than a thorough gutting of Part III.

By now Johnson had supplemented his daily exhortations for lofty, dignified debate with aggressive appeals for deleting the heart of Part III. "The vote on Part III is of crucial importance," he told the Senate on July 24. "It can well make the difference between achievement and futility." Minutes later, Johnson's brand of pragmatism prevailed. The Senate approved the Anderson-Aiken-Case amendment, 52-38. Part III was dead.

Besides winning the votes of liberal southerners such as Gore and Kefauver, Johnson now had the support of four senators beholden to him from the Hells Canyon vote: Church, Mansfield, Murray, and O'Mahoney. Aiken and Case also peeled away eighteen colleagues from Knowland's Republican ranks. Added to the votes of the solid South, Johnson and Russell had jumped their first major hurdle with relative ease. "I believe the bill was strengthened," Johnson told senators the next day.

To the contrary, the bill was weakened. Only its chances for passage had improved. Liberals correctly asserted that striking the core of Part III would weaken it considerably. Yet the strong bill that Douglas and Knowland wanted would have only ensured a southern filibuster and a bitterly divided Democratic party. The ease with which the Senate removed the Part III language caused George Reedy to speculate "upon the possibility that it had been put in only for trading purposes." Such a scheme, Reedy concluded, "would have required a level of cooperation between Johnson and President Eisenhower that I do not believe was possible." More likely was an extraordinary level of cooperation between Johnson and Russell—what Reedy called a "grand strategy" to produce a bare-bones bill.

Throughout the debate, Johnson showed many faces to many people. He soothed Russell with sympathetic language: "These Negroes, they're getting pretty uppity these days and that's a problem for us since they've got something now they never had before, the political pull to back up their uppityness." With other conservatives he tried a different approach: "If you don't pass this moderate bill, you're going to have a bill crammed down your throat because Richard Nixon is very smart politically and he is courting black people right now and you're going to get something that you can't live with."

Speaking to his friend Humphrey, Johnson ridiculed the ease with which northern liberals supported civil rights. "Hubert, it don't take any genius to be for civil rights from Minnesota," Johnson said. "How many black people you got in Minnesota?" "Well, we've got about 12,000," Humphrey replied. "Well," Johnson muttered, "you make me sick." With other liberals Johnson played an enlightened moderate who was forced to shoulder the embarrassing burden of his Neanderthal southern colleagues. Years after the 1957 Civil Rights Act became law, Harry McPherson still had vivid memories of the day Johnson burst into the Democratic cloakroom and said to Paul Douglas, "Paul, be ready. The civil rights bill, we're going to have it up at two o'clock. We got it worked out. You and your boys be there." Johnson left the cloakroom. Several minutes later he was back. This time he spotted Sam Ervin. "Sam," he said, "get everybody here at two o'clock. We're going to get the nigger bill up." McPherson thought Johnson's behavior was "appalling," but he understood Johnson's need to romance both sides. "This is a leader trying to keep everything in the air, keep it going, every day making a speech about how reasonable and moderate and modest" the bill was.

Although Johnson was desperately trying to win the votes necessary to pass the first civil rights act since 1875, Douglas and his hard-line liberals disapproved of the tactics he employed. Johnson aide Gerald Siegel recalled that while Johnson attempted to win over the liberals, "the liberals, unfortunately, closed the line between them and Senator Johnson." Siegel believed a stronger bill was possible with more liberal cooperation. "But they made it necessary for Senator Johnson to put together, in order to pass anything, a coalition of the more conservative members rather than the moderates and the liberals. And he simply had to include, in many instances, the southern senators." Although Johnson used the threat of cloture or stronger legislation to win the grudging cooperation of Russell's southerners, Siegel noted that the liberals "weren't scared of anything. They didn't have anything to lose, in a sense. They'd never passed a civil rights bill. There'd never been any progress, really, made except in the Court. So what could he tell them they might lose, except any bill at all?"

The bill that Attorney General Brownell had conceived, President Eisenhower had endorsed, and Knowland and Douglas had promoted in the Senate now belonged to Lyndon Johnson. With the destruction of Part III, no one was more important to the bill's success. No one had more to lose or gain by its failure or passage. Despite the ease with which the Senate weakened Part III, Johnson dared not celebrate his victory for long. He had satisfied only half of Russell's terms. Southerners still demanded a jury trial amendment to Part IV.

The question was vividly simple: Should those who were tried for criminal contempt actions arising from violations of the legislation be guaranteed a jury trial? The answer, however, was far from simple. Southerners claimed that the bill violated the constitutional guarantee of trial by jury. Liberals, however, feared that trials with all-white juries would never result in convictions. The successful attack on Part III was bad enough; a jury trial amendment, they believed, was worse. It would completely gut the bill. Liberals, George Reedy said, were not "going to permit the law to be nullified by what would have been routine acquittals of white offenders by Southern white juries."

When the "full scope of the dilemma" became apparent to Reedy, he believed that "the world was finally going to get an answer to the old conundrum of what happens when an irresistible force meets an immovable object. There was no apparent 'give' on either side." Southern senators, already concerned about how their white constituents would view their decision not to filibuster, could not support legislation that would allow judges to jail people without a jury trial. Liberals and the White House, who had already swallowed one dose of bitter medicine in the Part III debate, could not face losing the debate over another important provision.

In the House at least, opponents of a jury trial amendment appeared to have the numbers and the facts on their side. After a spirited struggle, liberals had rebuffed southern proponents of such an amendment, 251-158. But as always, the Senate was another story.

When viewed through the prism of the southern electorate, a jury trial amendment seemed certain to inhibit a judge's ability to enforce his decrees. Simply put, if blacks were not registered to vote, they could not be selected to serve on southern juries, even in federal courts.* All-white juries in 1957 were unlikely to convict any white person for violating the voting rights of a black citizen.

Early in the debate, on June 10, Douglas began building the case against the jury trial amendment with an impressive speech. In painstaking detail, he described the degree to which southern states denied blacks their voting rights and therefore the right to serve on juries. White jurors, Douglas said

> would find it very difficult to exercise their fair judgment in civil rights cases. They will be making decisions in many cases where there exists an atmosphere of tension, coercion, threats and intimidation. If they support a federal judge's order protecting the voting rights of Negroes, they know they will be exposed to economic pressure and possibly to physical violence ... The jury trial amendment, then, will nullify the protection of the right to vote in those areas where the right to vote most needs protection ... The right to a trial by jury means the right of those who have intimidated, threatened or coerced Negroes from voting to be tried by a jury composed of those whom they have not intimidated, threatened or coerced. The jury will be composed of those who can vote, but not composed of those who have been denied the right.†

To bolster their argument against jury trials, Douglas and Knowland trumpeted a statement presented to the Senate on July 27 and signed by the deans of eleven law schools and thirty-four law school professors. "While we fully support trial by jury in its proper sphere," the group said, "we fear that its unnecessary injection into this legislation will only hamper and delay the Department of Justice and the courts in carrying out their constitutional duty to protect voting rights."

To counter the arguments of legal heavyweights, southern supporters of the amendment had a remarkably simple argument, concisely

---

*Federal law stated that "any citizen" over twenty-one was eligible to serve on a federal jury, unless, among other things, he was ineligible to serve as a juror in state court. "In other words," Paul Douglas explained, "state standards for jurors determine federal eligibility."

†The statistics supported the argument against jury trials in criminal contempt cases: In Mississippi, for example, only 3.9 percent of registered voters were black. Fourteen counties did not have one registered black voter, and twenty-five counties had less than ten. In South Carolina, blacks made up 38 percent of the state's voting-age population but represented only 16 percent of voter registration (*CR*, 6/10/57, 8603-05).

summarized by Alabama's John Sparkman on a June broadcast: "Running all through our Constitution and all through our legal texture is the rule that facts ought to be determined by juries and not by judges, unless a defendant is willing to have a judge determine the facts." Russell, always sensitive to slights against his beloved South, insisted on a national television news show that it was "a flagrant insult to all of the people of the South to say that every white juror will forswear and perjure himself where a colored citizen is involved—and that is simply not true."

While southerners trumpeted their case for the amendment in various public forums, Johnson worked furiously in the background for its passage. "I remember, in those days," said Idaho's Frank Church, "that he would sit at his desk in the Senate and plot ways and means to attract the necessary votes to cut this Gordian knot." Johnson so dedicated himself to passing the amendment that he rarely left the Capitol during a two-week period, often relying on Lady Bird to bring him a fresh change of clothes. When he learned that Eleanor Roosevelt was in town, he dispatched his aide Grace Tully, a former FDR employee, to bring the former first lady to the Capitol. "I'm here every single night, all night, day and night," Johnson complained to Mrs. Roosevelt, an outspoken liberal advocate of civil rights. "But where are all the liberals?" Frustrated that he was being forced to shoulder the burden, and eventually the blame, for weakening the bill so that it could pass, Johnson's message to Roosevelt was clear: The liberals wanted a civil rights bill, but they would not engage in the unseemly compromises necessary to assemble a majority. Someone else—namely Johnson— had to do their dirty work so that they could maintain their principled, vehement opposition to anything that might weaken the bill. Although Johnson understood his role and accepted it willingly, he was nonetheless irked that many liberals viewed him, according to Frank Church, "as a kind of Machiavellian leader in the Senate who was doing his utmost to dilute and weaken civil rights legislation." That characterization, Church said, "was a great injustice to him, the kind of injustice that can only be done by those who take a self-righteous view of such issues."

Johnson's determination to pass the jury trial amendment—and therefore ensure passage of the bill—"may well have justified his entire career," George Reedy asserted, adding that he was absolutely determined that there would be a bill. He regarded the measure as a true starting point for reconciliation of North and South and he refused to move it from the floor—despite advice to do so from many of his colleagues. He pleaded and threatened and cajoled. He prowled the corridors of the Senate grabbing senators and staff members indiscriminately, probing them for some sign of amenability to compromise. He spent hours on the phone in nonstop conversations with the most ingenious legal minds he knew—[Tommy] Corcoran, [Jim] Rowe, [Ben] Cohen, [Clark] Clifford, [Abe] Fortas, [Dean] Acheson—pleading with them for something to break the log jam. Virtually single-handed, he kept a large body of very strong-minded and willful men concentrating on a purpose which most of them thought could not be achieved.

Finally, the means to cut the jury trial knot appeared in a liberal magazine, the *New Leader*. Essayist Carl Auerbach, a Wisconsin law professor and Humphrey's friend and advisor, defined the important differences between civil and criminal contempt in the federal judiciary. In his article, which Johnson ordered distributed to every senator, Auerbach argued that judges normally conducted criminal contempt proceedings when an individual ignored a court's order to comply with a federal law. In such cases, Auerbach maintained, the law had traditionally required jury trials.

Civil contempt proceedings were another matter. They did not deal with guilt or innocence; rather, they were held by judges seeking to enforce future compliance with a court order, not punish a past violation. Judges conducted these proceedings without juries because they could immediately dismiss a contempt citation whenever the defendant agreed to comply with the court's ruling. "So it is said in these cases," Auerbach wrote, "that the defendant 'carries the key of his prison in his own pocket.' He can open the prison door and walk out any time he pleases by obeying the court's order." Auerbach's conclusion was that "effective enforcement" of voting rights "can be secured through the civil-contempt proceeding" and its powers of coercion. When Johnson's New Deal friend Ben Cohen presented the article to him over lunch, the majority leader realized that the distinction between civil and criminal contempt might—in Frank Church's words—be "the key to the passage of the bill itself." "Lord, he understood!" recalled George Reedy. "He could have argued that before the Supreme Court."

Johnson's challenge now was to persuade a majority of the Senate that the bill's *civil* contempt provisions would be a potent weapon to prevent voting rights violations in the South. Invigorated by the rhetorical ammunition supplied in Auerbach's persuasive essay, he instructed staff members Cohen, Gerald Siegel, and Solis Horwitz— assisted by lawyer Abe Fortas and former Secretary of State Dean Acheson—to begin writing an amendment.

Ostensibly, the leader of the jury trial effort was Wyoming's Joseph O'Mahoney, a liberal constitutionalist who had announced his support for such an amendment in early July. "Senator O'Mahoney kept on introducing these various amendments, one right after the other," said Horwitz. "It got rather ridiculous in many ways, because we didn't know which one we were supporting on any particular day." As Humphrey complained on CBS's *Face the Nation* in late July, "there are more jury trial amendments than there are woodchucks in Rock Creek Park."

While Johnson's staff labored over the precise language of the amendment, he persuaded Estes Kefauver to join O'Mahoney in sponsoring it. As in the Part III debate, liberals took the lead—evidence of Johnson's deft but furtive efforts to avoid giving the amendment a hard, segregationist edge. While Siegel, Acheson, Fortas, and others fine-tuned the amendment's language, Horwitz undertook a mission of shuttle diplomacy between Russell and the amendment's liberal sponsors. "I suppose we drafted twenty-five or thirty different versions of this thing," Horwitz recalled, "and were constantly trying to satisfy both sides, something that would be acceptable to the liberals and, at the same time, would get assurance from Senator Russell that there would be no filibuster." The resulting amendment—the last of three presented to the Senate by O'Mahoney—simply amended Part IV to guarantee jury trials in all cases of criminal contempt, including labor disputes.

Eisenhower, Knowland, and most of the liberal bloc opposed all amendments to Part IV. That meant the critical work of rounding up votes to pass the amendment—and thus forestall a southern filibuster—fell, as usual, to Johnson. One by one, he focused on key senators. Often he picked them off so quietly that Knowland and Douglas were oblivious to the steady erosion of their ranks.

Rhode Island's Theodore Francis Green was particularly crucial to Johnson's success. A patriarchal, highly respected liberal, Green commanded great influence over two other senators—his junior Rhode Island colleague, John O. Pastore, and John F. Kennedy of Massachusetts. Having already twisted Green's arm to vote against consideration of the bill several weeks earlier, Johnson suspected that another approach might now be more appropriate. Persuading Green this time would require finesse and perhaps the counsel of an old, trusted friend. For this assignment Johnson enlisted Dean Acheson, a pragmatic liberal whose role in writing the jury trial amendment was not yet widely known. As Secretary of State under Harry Truman, Acheson had earned Green's trust and respect—a fact long ago stored away in Johnson's encyclopedic brain. He also knew that any advice from Acheson on the amendment would play no small role in Green's ultimate decision.

Acheson knew that a direct approach would only raise Green's suspicions that Johnson had sent him. What he needed was an accidental, chance encounter. Leaving Johnson's office, Acheson rode the subway to the Senate Office Building, where he pretended to be strolling aimlessly down the hallway in front of Green's office. When Green's secretary spotted him—as he had hoped she would—Acheson feigned surprise as he was promptly ushered into a seemingly inadvertent meeting with his old friend, who predictably raised the issue of the civil rights bill. Some senators, Green confessed, wanted to know how he would vote. What would you advise, he asked Acheson, particularly on the jury trial amendment? "If I were you, Theodore," Acheson replied, "I'd vote for the jury amendment. Yes, I surely would." Minutes later, Acheson found a pay phone and called Johnson. "Lyndon," he said, "don't ask me any questions, but you've got your three votes." Though Green's support may not have been the only factor, Johnson eventually won the votes of Kennedy and Pastore—two more crucial northeastern liberals.

Johnson was winning, but time was running out. On Sunday, July 29, Humphrey went on a national news show to proclaim confidently that the amendment's supporters "haven't got the votes." Knowland, equally confident of victory, was now aggressively pushing for a vote. On July 29, he taunted the southerners to begin their filibuster. "Let's have it now and fight it out," he said.

What Knowland did not know was that Johnson had gained a powerful new ally only the day before. At the Glen Echo amusement park outside Washington, one of Johnson's aides encountered Cy Anderson, the chief lobbyist for the twelve railroad brotherhoods. Because the amendment would require jury trials in all criminal contempt cases, including those arising from labor disputes, Anderson was a strong supporter. "Any labor skate who is against trial by jury ought to have his head examined," Anderson said as the two men discussed the jury trial issue. The offhand remark revealed another potentially important source of votes for the amendment, previously unknown to Johnson.

It was no coincidence three days later that Johnson announced on the Senate floor that the presidents of twelve railroad brotherhoods, all but two of them members of the influential AFL-CIO, had endorsed the amendment.* The announcement destroyed the image of labor's solid opposition. While the AFL-CIO's executive committee officially opposed it, the amendment had garnered sudden, unexpected support from railroad unions, fifteen postal workers' unions, and the influential United Mine Workers president, John L. Lewis. The Mine Workers had ample reason to endorse the amendment: A judge had fined their union $3.5 million in 1946—without a jury trial—for ignoring a federal court injunction to call off a coal strike. In the days leading up to the vote, lobbyists for Lewis and the other unions provided considerable persuasive force for undecided senators with large labor constituencies. The railroad lobbyists were particularly effective with midwestern Republicans.

Another important vote was Maine's Margaret Chase Smith, a Republican whom Johnson had courted much earlier when he restored federal funds to survey a tidal basin on the Maine-Canadian border. Important to almost no one but Smith, Johnson had immediately recognized the project's potential as an IOU—just as he had seen the value of the Hells Canyon project to the bill's ultimate success. In the end, Johnson would pick up Smith, along with six important supporters of the Hells Canyon project. While he likely won several more votes through similar deals—including new judgeships in Kansas and Maryland for senators Andrew Schoeppel and John Marshall Butler—Johnson did not confine his maneuvers to the Senate's back rooms. He was not above orchestrating a little theater in the Senate chamber.

---

*The railroad brotherhoods had other reasons to support the amendment. As *Newsweek* noted on August 12, legislation to grant a 15 percent increase in retirement benefits to the brotherhoods was awaiting action in the Labor Committee, chaired by Lister Hill of Alabama. In addition, a pay raise for postal workers was "pigeonholed" in the Senate Post Office Committee, chaired by Olin Johnston of South Carolina.

From the day he had voted for Clinton Anderson's cloture proposal in January 1957—against Johnson's wishes—Frank Church's relations with his leader had been strained. For six months Johnson had refused to speak to him at all. "I was *persona non grata* with Lyndon Johnson." Now that he was a cosponsor of the jury trial amendment, Johnson welcomed the Idaho Democrat back into the fold. Like Johnson, Church knew that the margin on the jury trial amendment would be razor thin, perhaps a mere two or three votes. As Church studied the politics of the amendment, he saw that the major obstacle for liberals was the expectation that southern authorities would not seat blacks on most southern juries. However, Church had an idea—a simple but brilliant addition to the amendment. It would permit blacks to serve on federal juries even if they were not registered to vote.

Johnson had been searching for some kind of sweetener that might entice the handful of Republican and Democratic moderates who were still undecided. Before Church made his proposal, he had considered two options: abolishing the poll tax or establishing a federal conciliation service to mediate race disputes. Church's new idea, however, was just the nuance he needed. With Russell's tacit approval, Johnson persuaded O'Mahoney and Kefauver to accept the amendment.

Needing a persuasive answer to the liberals' arguments concerning the problem of all-white juries, Johnson persuaded Church to hold his amendment until the debate reached a dramatic climax late on the evening of July 31. Knowing that most of his colleagues would be finished with dinner, Johnson initiated a quorum call to summon all senators to the chamber. With ninety attentive colleagues behind their desks, Johnson gave O'Mahoney the signal to begin his speech on the jury trial amendment. According to Johnson's elaborate choreography, after only a few minutes Church would interrupt his Wyoming colleague to offer the crucial amendment. Unfortunately Church missed his cue. While a frustrated O'Mahoney circled in a rhetorical holding pattern, Church sat impassively at his desk. Finally Johnson saved O'Mahoney. Rising from his desk at the front of the chamber and looking directly at Church, Johnson pointed to him, as Solis Horwitz recalled, "just like an orchestra leader." Taking the cue, Church came alive, leapt to his feet, and asked for recognition.

With the Senate in rapt attention, Church offered his amendment. He explained that it would quell concerns "that the efficacy of trial by jury in the federal courts is weakened by the fact that, in some areas, colored citizens, because of the operation of state laws, are prevented from serving as jurors." The amendment would "confer another civil right" on black citizens by allowing them to serve on juries in federal court, regardless of their status as voters. Church's cameo appearance in Johnson's theatrical production had its desired effect. Several liberals—including Democratic Whip Mike Mansfield, John F. Kennedy, Warren Magnuson, and Henry Jackson—signed up as cosponsors of the amendment.

About an hour later, Johnson heightened the evening's drama by orchestrating another speech—this one by John Pastore of Rhode Island, a flowery orator who planned to feign skepticism of the jury trial amendment. Gradually, as he spoke, Pastore's doubts would evolve into outright advocacy. "We didn't know what Pastore was going to do," Horwitz recalled. "[Johnson] did, because he said, 'Now you just watch the little Italian dancing master and see what happens here.'"

True to Johnson's prediction, Pastore began his speech insisting that "I have not as yet definitely resolved the matter in my own mind. I reserve the right to keep my mind open until such time as I am called upon to make a decision, at which time I shall make it known." Later, as he questioned O'Mahoney about the amendment, Pastore insisted again that "I have not completely made up my mind."

Skillfully, almost imperceptibly, Pastore began to dissolve his skepticism into outright support for the jury trial amendment. Finally, as he sparred with New York Republican Jacob Javits, Pastore revealed himself an enthusiastic proponent. "I cannot subscribe to the argument that if we provide for jury trials in criminal-contempt cases we would be emasculating the bill, that it would not be worth the paper it is written on." The impact of Pastore's performance was profound. He played the role of an earnest, undecided senator. But he had actually led his colleagues through a crafty, subtle argument for the amendment. The whole spectacle, Horwitz insisted, "had been preplanned. And [Pastore] did one of the most effective jobs that was ever done." George Reedy concluded that Pastore had "changed some votes."

The next day Johnson picked up another important vote from John F. Kennedy. "I consider it a mistake," Kennedy told the Senate on August 1, "to insist dogmatically on the purity of the original act at peril to its larger objectives." Kennedy's presidential aspirations may have exerted no small influence on his vote. Although he professed his support for the bill and had voted to retain Part III, he took great care to reject the argument that southern whites could not be trusted to obey the law. "I do not count myself among those who are cynical about the capacity of citizens in any section of the country to rise to the challenge of one of the highest responsibilities of free men—the preservation of law and a just social order."

Humphrey's was another vote that Johnson wanted to win on the jury trial amendment. He had good reason to believe he could. Not only was Humphrey a strong labor supporter and one of the more pragmatic liberals, but Humphrey's friend Carl Auerbach had written the magazine article on which much of the argument for the jury trial amendment was based. Humphrey had even summoned Auerbach to Washington to help Johnson build support for the amendment. Auerbach believed that Humphrey's pragmatism told him to support the amendment, but he recalled that when he arrived in Washington, "Humphrey told me that the liberals groups had put too much pressure on this issue." He would oppose the amendment. "I think that he did not go up in the estimation of LBJ as a result of this," Auerbach said, "because LBJ knew what Humphrey really thought about this issue."

Humphrey did attempt to soften his liberal friends on the issue of jury trials. But by this point in the debate, his influence with the most dogmatic liberals had waned. Howard Shuman explained that "we kept sending him back to meet with Johnson on Part III and issues like the jury trial amendment." Shuman complained that "*every* time Hubert came back he had lost. Johnson seemed to have his number." Humphrey later acknowledged that his attempts to peddle a compromise on Part III to the leadership "did not receive too much encouragement." Though he cheerfully attempted to serve as an intermediary between Johnson and the liberals, he knew he could not assume the unyielding position required to bargain on the liberals' behalf.

Humphrey played a minor role during the debate. Perhaps, as Shuman complained, he surrendered to or was overpowered by Johnson's pragmatism. Yet his voting record on important changes to the bill—Part III and the jury trial amendment—revealed no retreat from his desire for strong legislation. More likely was the influence of Humphrey's *evolving* pragmatism. While he was not yet prepared to enlist as a partner in Johnson's let's-make-a-deal approach to legislating, he knew that the inflexible doctrine that motivated Douglas and other dogmatic liberals was an impractical legislative strategy. Accepting less than what one hoped for, he told another friend, "is the essence of the legislative process." As early as January, Humphrey seemed to anticipate that some of his more liberal friends would eventually attack the bill as "meaningless." Such talk, Humphrey wrote to United Auto Workers president Walter Reuther, "only serves to weaken our cause and finally to destroy what we are out to do. A bill to protect the right to vote is not meaningless, and anyone who says that it is, is just playing to the galleries and being a demagogue."

On the evening of August 2, Johnson—finally confident of victory—was ready to vote. Yet Knowland, who had previously pressed for a quick vote, began stalling, the clearest indication to Johnson that his own side would prevail. Having once been confident of thirty-nine Republican votes against the amendment, Knowland now pleaded for two additional hours. He could only hope that two absent senators, Maine's Frederick Payne and Missouri's Tom Hennings, would arrive at the Capitol in time to cast their crucial votes.

Johnson received additional assurance of his impending victory from an unlikely source—Vice President Richard Nixon. Brushing past Johnson in a reception room just off the Senate floor, Nixon snarled, "You've really got your bullwhip on your boys tonight, Lyndon." Not only was Nixon resentful that Johnson had seized the bill from the Republicans, he also knew that Republicans and Democrats would now equally share credit for its passage. Furthermore, because Johnson had so skillfully negotiated compromises on the bill's most controversial features, even the militant southern Democrats had been neutralized, and Democratic party unity had been preserved. As Nixon stalked away, Johnson shot back, "Yes, Dick, and from the way you've been trying to drive your fellows, you must have a thirty-thirty strapped to your hip, but it's not doing you any good." Nixon replied with a veiled threat that Eisenhower might veto the bill if it contained a jury trial amendment.

As the debate began to lose its steam, Knowland ominously warned that passage of the amendment "will be a vote to kill" the bill. Johnson had the last word. After midnight, near the end of the day's fourteen-hour session, he declared: "I believe in the right to vote. I believe in strengthening that right. I believe further that most of our people share my belief or are at least willing to accept it."

When voting ended, Johnson had prevailed, 51 to 42. Instead of thirty-nine Republican votes, Knowland had only thirty-three. He lost twelve crucial Republicans, while Johnson forfeited only nine of his forty-eight Democrats. The next morning, Johnson triumphantly declared that "we have strengthened the bill and we have strengthened the confidence of the American people in its provisions. That alone would justify the action we took." In the *New York Times*, William S. White characterized the amendment's passage as a "heavy defeat" for Eisenhower but "a great victory for a bipartisan coalition composed of Western liberal Democrats, Southern Democrats and a handful of traditional Republicans" headed by Johnson. *Time* called it "a shrewd political blow" to Eisenhower and Knowland's "prestige."

Johnson deserved credit for winning the votes to pass the amendment, but he was greatly aided by Eisenhower and Brownell's ineffective advocacy. Remote and largely uninvolved in the details of the bill, Eisenhower left to play golf as the crucial negotiations over the amendment's final wording reached their climax. "Senators," columnist Doris Fleeson observed in the *Washington Evening Star*, "will not put more passion into his desires than he does." Making matters worse, Brownell departed for a bar association meeting in London during the most intense bargaining.

While Eisenhower declared that the bill was now "largely ineffective," he refused to say whether he would sign it if the final product resembled the Senate version. To Vice President Nixon, the amendment's passage was "one of the saddest day in the history of the Senate because this was a vote against the right to vote." Knowland said the amendment had "greatly weakened" the bill. Oregon's Wayne Morse called the amended bill "a corpse." Although sorely disappointed, Knowland's Republicans knew their only option was to support the bill and wait for a House-Senate compromise to restore the provisions they had lost to Johnson's coalition. To vote any other way was to invite near-unanimous condemnation from liberals, black leaders, and the news media.

To ensure that Knowland and other disappointed proponents of a stronger bill understood this, Johnson inserted a fusillade of media commentary into the *Congressional Record* in the days leading up to the bill's final passage: On August 3 the *Washington Post* asserted "it really was absurd for Senator Knowland to talk as if the civil-rights bill were dead." The paper noted that "no doubt some Republicans are disappointed that passage of the jury trial amendment has deprived them of the spectacle of the Democratic Party tearing itself apart in the Senate." Reporter David Lawrence observed in the *New York Herald-Tribune* that a "reported plan of House leaders to drop the measure at this session and try again next January is a piece of mistaken judgment which they some day will regret." The *Baltimore Sun* argued that adoption of the jury trial amendment was "a real step forward."

Eisenhower's veiled veto threats startled the Senate's liberals. Suddenly the "weak" bill they once derided took on positive qualities that were previously unrecognized. If Eisenhower wanted to wield his veto pen, Humphrey and Douglas knew they must not make the decision easy for him by echoing his administration's criticisms. "This was the tipoff that the Democratic Party leaders felt they had the Republicans in a hole," David Lawrence wrote. "For it could now be demonstrated that the Democrats from both the North and the South wanted the legislation to pass and only those 'narrowly partisan' Republicans . . . were standing in the way."

New York Republican Jacob Javits, a fierce opponent of the jury trial amendment, summed up the philosophical resignation of pragmatic liberals: "I'm disappointed in the bill as it is, but I want a bill and not a campaign issue." Indeed, the bill's utility, observed Ernest K. Lindley in *Newsweek,* was its spirit of honest compromise. "It is less than most of the northern Senators with large numbers of Negro constituents wanted or felt that they must strive for," Lindley wrote. "It is more than most of the southerners want—which is no bill at all. It is a compromise wrought chiefly by Senators who on this issue have some measure of political latitude."

August 7, the day of the final vote, was an auspicious one for two senators in particular. For Humphrey, passage of the bill was a day for which he had yearned since his arrival in the Senate in 1949. While he had relinquished floor leadership for the bill to Douglas, Humphrey clearly believed he had played an important role in its ultimate success. Recalling his anguished early days in the Senate, Humphrey reminded his colleagues that

I am no Johnny-come-lately to this area of legislation. I have, as a United States Senator, suffered the criticism of many of my colleagues and hundreds of editors and publishers and columnists, for many years, because I have supposedly been one of those Senators who has been defying the South and advocating proposals that would tear the Democratic Party apart.

His long history as a civil rights advocate, he believed, entitled him to take an indirect swipe at the Senate's Republicans and President Eisenhower:

> If the bill is an adequate advance for those of us who have had to fight the year-round fight in the winter and in the summer, for those of us who have had to do battle on the issue when it was very unpopular and when we did not have help in high places, it ought to be a tolerable advance for those who have come onto the bandwagon when victory was almost assured.

For Johnson, supporting any civil rights bill was an enormous political risk in Texas, a fact he acknowledged as he announced his support for the bill:

> I am aware of the implications of my vote. It will be treated cynically in some quarters, and it will be misunderstood in others. No Texas Senator has cast a vote to consider a civil rights bill or vote for a civil rights bill since 1875.
> But the Senate has dealt fairly and justly with this measure. This is legislation which I believe will be good for every state of the Union—and, so far as I am concerned, Texas has been a part of the Union since Appomattox.
> I could not have voted for the bill which came to the Senate, and I so told the Senate. But the bill now before the Senate seeks to solve the problems of 1957—not to reopen the wounds of 1865 . . . Therefore, I shall genuinely support this measure, secure in the belief that it represents progress and that it assures an advance in the rights to which all our people are entitled.

Later that day, after twenty-five long days of debate, the Senate made history. It passed the civil rights bill, 72-18. Five southern Democrats—Kefauver and Gore of Tennessee, George Smathers of Florida, and Ralph Yarborough and Lyndon Johnson of Texas—voted for it.

Important to passage was a last-minute endorsement issued by the leaders of sixteen liberal organizations, including the National Association for the Advancement of Colored People and the Americans for

Democratic Action. A day-long debate among the various leaders ended when Roy Wilkins, the respected chairman of the NAACP, finally concluded, "I can't see anything to do except say that this is better than nothing. Let's take it." Joseph Rauh—who admitted "I was so mad at Johnson I was speechless, for gutting the bill so much"—finally adopted a pragmatic attitude toward the Senate product. "The best we could get was what they gave us."

House Republican leader Joe Martin briefly suggested that he might insist that the Senate accept the more-liberal House-passed bill. He hinted that no bill at all would be "preferable" to the Senate version. However, the politics of the moment left disgruntled Republicans little choice but to search for a compromise between the two bills. Democratic Party chairman Paul Butler, for one, relished the chance to turn up the heat on House and Senate Republicans. He suggested that "some Republicans have decided that their best vote-hunting strategy is to try to block any civil rights bill from passage in this session of Congress and to make it a political football in the 1958 elections." Johnson had his own blunt response to those who derided the Senate bill as an ineffective voting rights tool: "What other powers of compulsion do the opponents now seek? Are they asking for the thumbscrew, the rack, and the red-hot pincers?"

Two weeks of negotiations produced a final compromise. House and Senate leaders, having wisely rejected a formal conference committee, presented Eisenhower with a slight modification of the jury trial amendment. In a phone call to Eisenhower on August 23, Johnson said, "I can get Ervin and the others to agree to a compromise of three hundred dollars and forty-five days." A short time later, Johnson went to the Senate chamber to explain the unique compromise that applied only to voting rights cases. It gave judges the right to act in criminal contempt cases without a jury. The accused could demand a new trial with a jury if his conviction would result in a fine of more than three hundred dollars or a forty-five-day jail sentence. On other aspects of the bill, primarily Part III, Eisenhower and the Republican leadership knew they had no choice but to capitulate to the Senate or face a certain filibuster by southerners. Although he insisted that they "unalterably opposed" the compromise, Russell said his troops would not filibuster the bill. On August 27, the House overwhelmingly passed the civil rights bill, 279-97.

The following day, as the Senate debated the bill, South Carolina's Strom Thurmond—opposed to the jury trial compromise and still frustrated by Russell's refusal to orchestrate a southern filibuster—unexpectedly took matters into his own hands. Well rested and armed only with a handful of malted milk balls and throat lozenges, Thurmond asked for recognition at 8:45 p.m. "Mr. President," he said, "I rise to speak against the so-called voting rights bill, H.R. 6127." And he then launched into a remarkable speech that lasted until 9:12 p.m. the next evening. Over twenty-four hours in length, Thurmond's talking marathon became the longest continuous oration ever delivered in the Senate.

Having argued that a filibuster would result in stronger civil rights legislation and possibly provoke the Senate into liberalizing cloture, southerners had withheld their heavy filibuster artillery. Thurmond's grandstanding speech sent Russell and other southerners into a "cold fury," George Reedy said. "They felt," wrote Jay Walz in the *New York Times*, "that Mr. Thurmond was leaving in the South a public image of a single Southern senator standing at barricades that had been deserted by the others." As Louisiana's Russell Long observed, the southerners believed Thurmond "was making a cheap campaign for his own reelection at the expense of the other guys." That, Long said, "caused [constituents] to say, 'What's the matter with you? That man's out there fighting for us and you're sitting on your ass [and] won't even help him.' "

Less than two hours after Thurmond left the Senate chamber, the Senate passed the Civil Rights Act of 1957 by a wide margin: 60-15. On September 9 Eisenhower heeded the advice of NAACP leaders and Reverend Martin Luther King and reluctantly signed the bill while on vacation in Newport, Rhode Island. Even Russell—who had expected the bill to pass overwhelmingly—was surprised by its final margin of victory. "With our Tennessee brethren [Gore and Kefauver] against us," he complained to a friend afterwards, "we are down to only six or seven states that are all-out against integration."

In the wake of the historic vote, Johnson received rave reviews for his amazing skill in herding the bill through the Senate without a southern filibuster. Paul Douglas called it "a triumph" for Johnson's "policy of moderation over the [southern] extremists." At the time, William S. White believed the bill's passage set the stage for Johnson to dominate the 1960 Democratic National Convention and perhaps even win the presidential nomination. It was, White later said, "the most skillful single legislative job of leadership I ever saw." Noting that negotiations over the bill had been conducted under "volatile" conditions, George Reedy maintained that without Johnson's leadership "there would have been no bill at all." In an effusive letter of praise Clark Clifford told Johnson, "There's no one else alive who would have stood the ghost of a chance to keep our party from splitting irretrievably." Johnson's performance did not please everyone. One constituent from Arlington, Texas, complained that "it looks like you and Sam Rayburn have sold Texas into the hands of the Civil Righters of the north and west." From one Houston resident came a more pointed observation in a September 23 telegram: "Nigger lover."

For Johnson, the bill was far more than a legislative triumph. It propelled him into a position of true national prominence. No longer did he wear the label of sectional leader. His informal alliance with Russell's southerners had seemingly ended when he voted for the bill's passage.

The bill had political implications for at least one other Democratic senator—John F. Kennedy. "It was curious," said Tom Wicker of the *New York Times*, "that both Kennedy and Johnson used that bill for their presidential purposes. And my recollection is that they did exactly the same thing for precisely the opposite purposes." Wicker was largely correct. Johnson had voted to delete Part III and to add a jury trial amendment; Kennedy, too, had supported the jury trial amendment, but had voted to *retain* Part III. Inherent in Johnson's efforts was his desire to become more acceptable to northern liberals. Kennedy, meanwhile, probably cast his vote for the jury trial amendment with an aspiring eye to the South. Kennedy "walked a teetering tightrope," observed James MacGregor Burns, who found himself fascinated by Kennedy's handling of the bill and its politics. "At the same time he was telling liberals of the effectiveness of a bill that included the [jury trial] provision, he was assuring worried Southerners that it was a moderate bill that would be enforced by *Southern* courts and *Southern* juries." While others, including Joseph Rauh, believed that Kennedy "hadn't quite made a final decision on where he was going" on civil rights, the 1957 bill was the beginning of a philosophical evolution that would eventually lead to his civil rights program as president in 1963. For Johnson as well, the bill meant that he was well on his way to outright advocacy of the same civil rights proposal.

While Johnson received many plaudits for his skill in guiding the legislation to passage, initial judgments of the bill itself were less than generous. Paul Douglas said that "it reminded him of Lincoln's old saying that it was like a soup made from the shadow of a crow which had starved to death." Most common was the view that the bill was only "half a loaf." To the NAACP's Thurgood Marshall, the bill was "just barely progress." Like many other liberals and black leaders, Marshall came to believe that "the smallest slice was good ... because it was a strictly political move of getting something done." Harris Wofford called the bill "less than half a loaf, but it was, you might say, bait. Johnson's theory was [that] Congress took that bait, and, to use another metaphor, broke the ice." The 1957 act was important, insisted NAACP leader Clarence Mitchell, "because not only did it have substantive value, but it also represented a breakthrough. Up until that time, it had been assumed Congress could not and would not pass any civil rights legislation. We succeeded in passing it and that helped to let people know it could be done." Even Strom Thurmond acknowledged the bill's utility in opening the door for future civil rights civil legislation in 1960, 1964, and 1965. "I think that [it] more or less breached the wall."

Back home, southern senators quickly noted that they had allowed a vote *only* after they purged the bill of its most egregious provisions. No one other than Johnson deserved more credit for amending the bill than Russell, whom Johnson had sought to please and whose enormous stature among southerners prevented a potentially deadly filibuster. But as Russell was quick to note, the bill was still too harsh to win his vote. At a States Rights' Council dinner in Atlanta, Russell declared that "it will be difficult a few decades from now for a reasonable man to understand how an organized minority could have so intimidated and frightened the political leaders of the two great political parties with the threat to control the Congressional election of 1958 and the presidential election of 1960 in the large key states, including New York, Illinois, Pennsylvania, Michigan, Ohio and California."

Despite his feigned inability to comprehend the powerful forces behind the legislation's passage, Russell knew full well that the civil rights bill could not have become law without his tacit approval. For now, he could only pray that his huge gamble—his decision to cooperate with Johnson—would yield the results for which he hoped: Johnson's election as president, the rehabilitation of the South, and an end to demands for tougher civil rights legislation.

As for Johnson, he was confident that he had turned in a splendid performance. "Maybe I voted wrong on some civil rights bills in the past," he confessed, "but I'm learning all the time. I got all I could on civil rights in 1957. Next year I'll get a little more, and the year after that I'll get a little more. The difference between me and some of my northern friends is that I believe you can't force these things on the South overnight. You advance a little and consolidate; then you advance again. I think in the long run my way may prove to be faster than theirs."

In retrospect, the Civil Rights Act of 1957 clearly failed to conquer the racism of southern leaders determined to deny blacks the right to vote. Ultimately it would take passage of the Voting Rights Act of 1965 to fully enfranchise southern blacks. Nevertheless the bill was *the* important first step in the evolution of modern civil rights legislation— and the starting point for the civil rights policies of presidents John F. Kennedy and Lyndon Johnson. "In real as well as in symbolic terms," Senator Clinton Anderson later observed, "I think it represented a genuine defeat for racism and the society of the Old South."

At the very least, it was a good beginning.

CHAPTER TWELVE

Lyndon, You'd Better
Adjourn This Place

THE INK ON THE CIVIL RIGHTS ACT of 1957 was barely dry when racially motivated violence threatened to erupt in Little Rock, Arkansas, in late September. Only weeks earlier, Russell had worried aloud that President Eisenhower might dispatch federal troops southward to desegregate public schools. Now the atmosphere of racial unrest in Arkansas barreled down a slippery incline toward Russell's once-implausible scenario. By year's end, the unrest in Arkansas would further polarize southern and northern members of Congress over civil rights, and much of the progress achieved by the century's first civil rights act would be lost in a dark cloud of bitterness and suspicion.

In early September, following a court-ordered plan to desegregate the city's public schools, the Little Rock school board prepared for the uneventful enrollment of nine black students at the city's Central High School. Sensing an opportunity to make political hay, Governor Orval Faubus—running for reelection the following year—elbowed his way into the controversy just as the school year began. Under the pretense of preventing violence, Faubus pandered to the most racist of Arkansas's white citizens when he ordered the state's National Guard to surround the school to bar the black students' entrance.* Overnight, Little Rock became the next potential flash point in the nation's civil rights struggle.

Painfully indecisive about any civil rights controversy, Eisenhower

---

*Until 1957 Faubus enjoyed a reputation as a moderate—one of the few southern leaders who had resisted the urge to attack the Supreme Court's 1954 *Brown* decision. Ultimately, however, political considerations prevailed. Observed Harry Ashmore, then editor of the *Arkansas Gazette:* "When he became convinced that he could not hold his rural support in a third-term race for reelection against a segregationist candidate, [Faubus] grabbed the doomed strategy the Citizens' Council leaders were pressing on him" (Ashmore, *Civil Rights and Wrongs*, 132).

initially refused to intervene. He calmly continued his vacation in Newport, Rhode Island, while aides kept him informed of all developments. But the president's indecision only allowed the crisis to worsen. By the time he became involved, nothing short of the U.S. Army could restore order in Little Rock.

Ten days into the tense standoff, Eisenhower reluctantly agreed to negotiate with Faubus. However, their meeting in Newport produced nothing but ambiguous and insincere promises by the governor that he would diffuse the situation. He removed his troops only when ordered by a federal judge and did nothing else to bring calm to the city. And he recklessly fanned flames of racism in Little Rock with extreme and demagogic language. On September 23, the passions he had exacerbated finally boiled over. An angry, screaming mob of several thousand white racists converged on Central High School to protest the scheduled enrollment of the black students. In the melee, two black reporters were attacked. As the mob spewed racial slurs and epithets, authorities quietly ushered nine terrified black children into a side door of the school to begin classes. When the crowd realized that the students were safely inside, they became even more enraged and rushed the building. Reporters heard cries of "lynch the niggers" from the mob. Finally, fearing for the black students' safety, Little Rock Mayor Woodrow Wilson Mann ordered city police to remove them from the school.

The next morning, a troubled Mann wired Eisenhower: "The immediate need for federal troops is urgent . . . People are converging on the scene from all directions. Mob is armed and engaging in fisticuffs and other acts of violence. Situation is out of control and police cannot disperse the mob." Several hours later, Eisenhower resigned himself to the inevitable: he would order federal troops into Little Rock to restore order. It was the first time a president had sent the U.S. military into the South for such purposes since Reconstruction. "Well, if we have to do this, and I don't see any alternative," he told Attorney General Brownell, "then let's apply the best military principles to it and see that the force we send there is strong enough that it will not be challenged, and will not result in any clash." By day's end, forty-six giant transport planes roared into Little Rock Air Force Base, carrying more than a thousand paratroopers of the Army's 101st Airborne Division—the "Screaming Eagles." The next morning the troops, assisted by a federalized Arkansas National Guard, began dispersing the mob. With dignity and aplomb, the black youngsters endured the jeers of angry white bystanders and marched through the protective rows of soldiers into the now-integrated Central High School.

Eisenhower had been loath to send troops into the South. As he stressed in a speech to the American people, he did so only to prevent violent opposition to a federal court order, not to enforce integration. Many white southerners, enraged by the president's actions, failed to understand the distinction. Furious over what he called "the tragedy of Little Rock," Russell lamented Eisenhower's change of heart regarding states' rights. "His advisors have evidently changed his mind for him," Russell said in an angry and sarcastic statement, "and he has kicked into the trash can his many fine pronouncements of his desire to restore the states to the rightful position contemplated by the Founding Fathers. This sort of totalitarian rule may put Negro children in the white schools of Little Rock. But it will have a calamitous effect on race relations and on the cause of national unity." (Russell had been more than a casual observer of the unfolding events in Arkansas. Several times during the escalating crisis, he offered Faubus legal advice. He even considered traveling to Little Rock to show his support for the Arkansas governor.)

Two days after his first public comments on the matter, Russell sent a lengthy, passionate telegram to Eisenhower and Defense Secretary Charles Wilson. He bemoaned "the highhanded and illegal methods being employed by the armed forces of the United States under your command who are carrying out your orders to mix the races in the public schools of Little Rock, Arkansas." Citing "reputable" news reports, Russell charged that the "troopers are disregarding and overriding the elementary rights of American citizens by applying tactics which must have been copied from the manual issued the officers of Hitler's storm troopers." As it turned out, the news reports of military brutality were wrong. Eisenhower's reply, while conciliatory, was firm and unyielding. "I must say," the president wrote, "that I completely fail to comprehend your comparison of our troops to Hitler's storm troopers. In one case military power was used to further the ambitions and purposes of a ruthless dictator; in the other to preserve the institutions of free government."

Russell's belligerent reaction to the Little Rock crisis demonstrated not only why he could never be elected president, but worse, why he may have been fundamentally unqualified for the office. Forced to choose between upholding the Constitution as interpreted by the U.S. Supreme Court or yielding to a white racist mob, Russell would apparently have sided with the reckless forces of southern defiance. His oft-stated loyalty to Constitutional principles had its limits.

Yet when judged by the rhetoric of other southerners, Russell's heated reaction to Little Rock was almost restrained. South Carolina's Olin Johnston declared: "If I were governor and he [Eisenhower] came in, I'd give him a fight such as he's never been in before. I'd proclaim a state of insurrection and I'd call out the National Guard and then we'd find out who's going to run things in my state." Russell's junior Georgia colleague, Herman Talmadge, seemed equally disrespectful of the commander in chief, whom he compared to the Soviet communists who invaded Hungary in 1956: "We still mourn the destruction of the sovereignty of Hungary by Russian tanks and troops in the streets of Budapest. We are now threatened with the spectacle of the president of the United States using tanks and troops in the streets of Little Rock to destroy the sovereignty of the state of Arkansas."

Southerners were not the only ones critical of the president. New York Governor Averill Harriman, echoing the criticism of many northern liberals, observed that Eisenhower "by his inaction, has contributed to the making of the present situation, and any trouble we have from now on can be laid at the door of the president's complacency and policy of appeasement of Governor Faubus while the crisis was developing." Although the president's indecision and vacillation had contributed mightily to the crisis, liberals were wrong to suggest that Eisenhower should bear responsibility for Faubus's racist opportunism.

The violence in Little Rock destroyed much of the progress and harmony achieved by the passage of the civil rights bill. Southerners, once willing to grudgingly permit the passage of weak civil rights legislation, would now be expected to aggressively challenge—even filibuster—the next civil rights proposal. While Eisenhower's use of troops was unrelated to the 1957 civil rights act, Russell's southerners risked looking like fools or traitors to their region if they dared to strike another moderate posture on the issue. Observed *Newsweek:* "Even the moderates, who had been persuaded by Johnson to go along with the civil rights bill, would now, for the sake of their political skins, have to turn their backs on moderation."

The synergy of the civil rights act and the Little Rock crisis produced even more pronounced intransigence in Russell and other southerners. With the inevitability of increased black voting and the integration of public schools staring him in the face, Russell resolved to yield not another inch. Over time, his strident opposition to the Supreme Court's civil rights decisions had turned into irrational, unbridled hostility. In a February 1958 speech to the Georgia legislature, Russell warned that the court was one of two great "threats" facing the nation. (The other was communism.) In a bitter diatribe, Russell attacked those justices who "profane the name of what was once our most respected institution of government" by "playing on unwarranted prejudice against the South and her white people." The Warren court, he charged, "is now seeking to impose [its] will and predilections upon the people without regard to a written Constitution which properly divides the powers of government and to remake our institutions in the image of their thinking."

A year after the violence in Arkansas, the Supreme Court upheld the lower court's desegregation ruling in Little Rock, asserting that "the constitutional rights [of the children] are not to be sacrificed or yielded to the violence and disorder which have followed the actions of the Governor and the Legislature . . . Law and order are not to be preserved by depriving the Negro children of their constitutional rights." Russell issued an angry statement claiming that "the action of the court is further evidence that it accepts the briefs and arguments of Thurgood Marshall and the NAACP as their supreme law rather than the Constitution of the United States, the constitution and law of once-sovereign states and the numerous decisions of real judges and lawyers who were their predecessors on the Supreme Court." In another statement, Russell bitterly attacked the NAACP, Attorney General Brownell, and Chief Justice Warren, who he said suffered from a "Messianic complex." Russell indirectly sanctioned continued defiance of the court's rulings when he warned that the South's white people would not "surrender to the dictates of the NAACP merely because this organization is able to use the present Supreme Court as its mouthpiece and the powers of the Attorney General of the United States as its tool."

In 1958 Russell's growing despair over the steady advance of civil rights led him to abandon his longstanding support for federal aid to education. His reasoning was simple: "I am completely confident that within a year or two at best we will be confronted with provisions on appropriations bills that will deny funds to states that do not integrate their schools."* His racial views also appear to have at least partially influenced his opposition to statehood for Alaska and Hawaii in 1958–59. In both cases, southerners generally opposed admission, believing that senators from both states would likely provide four additional votes for cloture and civil rights. Over Russell's opposition, Congress admitted Alaska as a state in July 1958. Hawaii would become the fiftieth state the following year.

Perhaps the most telling evidence of Russell's alienation from his party's mainstream was his announcement in December 1958 that he would soon reintroduce his legislation "aimed at bringing about a more equitable distribution of the white and colored races throughout the United States." Essentially the same bizarre bill that he had offered in 1949, the legislation was the manifestation of Russell's strange belief that racial discord arose not from white racism but from the presence of large black populations in the South. "If the Negro population were spread more evenly over all sections of the nation—thus giving each state an equal share of the race problem," he explained, "it would be a substantial contribution to the easing of racial tensions and to providing a permanent solution." Russell's objective—the massive relocation of southern blacks by a Voluntary Racial Relocation Commission—was an exceedingly unusual proposal by someone so thoroughly opposed to other social engineering proposals. Moreover, while the legislation called for nothing more than the voluntary movement of blacks, Russell's unfortunate choice of words—his expressed desire to search for a "permanent solution" to the Negro problem—conjured images of Nazi Germany's "Final Solution" to its own racial problems.

Despite his desire to guide the South back into the mainstream of American life, Russell was in fact prodding his region in the opposite direction. He and his southern colleagues were now as isolated as ever.

The true philosophical divergence of Johnson and Russell on civil rights became apparent after the Civil Rights Act of 1957. Johnson—who had engineered the bill's passage and later offered only muted criticism of Eisenhower's actions in Little Rock—seemed prepared finally to embrace black voting rights and to accept the Supreme Court's dictums on school desegregation.

*Russell's prediction was off by four years. Congress adopted similar provisions as part of the Civil Rights Act of 1964.

Russell knew that nothing was likely to halt the advance of civil rights, yet he remained defiant, hoping at least to slow its progress. While genuinely alarmed at the new momentum the issue had gained—thanks in great measure to his Texas protégé—Russell had not become disillusioned with Johnson, for whom he still harbored presidential hopes. Russell may have believed that Johnson required *some* civil rights credentials to capture the 1960 Democratic nomination. As the debate over a quasi–civil rights proposal in 1958 showed, Russell—when he could afford to—remained ready to surrender some of his antipathy toward civil rights for Johnson's political well-being.

In April 1956 yet another Supreme Court decision had aroused the ire of congressional conservatives. This time the court declared that Pennsylvania authorities could not prosecute a Communist party organizer for treason against the United States because federal legislation preempted the state's antisedition law. The decision was only the most recent in a series of controversial court rulings in civil rights and civil liberties cases that had begun with the 1954 *Brown* decision. In each instance, conservative Democrats and Republicans were incensed and alarmed by the court's continuing leftward tilt. Exasperated by what they considered brazen judicial activism, conservatives finally demanded legislation to restrain the justices in several jurisdictional areas. The rulings, said Johnson's aide Harry McPherson, created "a ready-made issue for Republicans worried about revolution, and for southerners concerned about race." Suddenly, in the words of New Jersey Republican Clifford Case, legislative attacks on the court "came thick and fast."

The results were several measures, two of which contained serious challenges to the court's independence. The first, commonly known as H.R. 3, was a House bill to prohibit federal courts from declaring that a federal statute preempted a state law *unless* Congress so specified or there was "a direct and positive conflict" between the two. The bill was pure states' rights. It could have wreaked havoc in scores of areas where federal statutes did not expressly supersede state laws. It would also, its critics said, invite states to pass laws invalidating rights granted by federal statute. The other legislation, reported by the Senate Judiciary Committee, was commonly known as the Jenner-Butler bill. It would have reversed six Supreme Court rulings concerning state and federal antisedition laws, the admission procedures of state bar associations, and contempt of Congress proceedings. Civil rights organizations worried that the bill, if enacted, would allow Southern bar associations to disbar attorneys who accepted civil rights cases. Civil liberties groups, meanwhile, feared that the legislation would weaken the Bill of Rights by limiting the court's independence.

Although H.R. 3 had cleared the House in July, Johnson staved off Senate action on both bills. But pressure from restive conservatives in both parties was growing. "Well, I'm going to have to let them have their day on this stuff," Johnson finally declared in August, after Humphrey and Thomas Hennings of Missouri, chairman of the Constitutional Rights subcommittee, assured him they could muster the votes to defeat both bills. On August 20, during the last week of the 1958 session, the Senate rejected an attempt by Republican Senator William Jenner of Indiana to attach the wording of his Butler-Jenner bill to minor legislation pending in the Senate. Senators tabled Jenner's motion, 49-41.

Throughout much of the debate, Johnson was away from the Senate floor tending to other Senate business and political duties. He had no reason for concern. Humphrey and Hennings had assured him they would defeat the bills. Believing he had just enough votes to kill the legislation, Johnson wished only to give conservatives the opportunity to go on record in support for the measures—and to conduct a calm, civil debate. "The situation was in hand," Harry McPherson said later, "or so I thought."

The satisfaction of the Jenner-Butler bill's narrow defeat was not sufficient for Paul Douglas, who unwisely provoked the Senate's conservatives shortly after Jenner's motion went down. Seemingly oblivious to Johnson's delicate strategy, Douglas rose to offer an amendment to affirm the Senate's "full support and approval" of Supreme Court rulings that held "racial segregation unlawful in public education and transportation." The motion was a legislative finger in the conservatives' eye. Although Johnson quickly sidetracked the Douglas amendment, it had nonetheless injected the passionate issue of civil rights directly into the once-calm debate. Inflamed conservatives were now able to generate enough votes for approval of a motion by Arkansas Senator John McClellan to attach the language of H.R. 3 to another pending bill. Late that night, on the first vote, conservatives rejected an attempt to table McClellan's amendment, 46-39. Minutes later they deflected another attack on the amendment, this time by a 47-40 vote. The conservatives had achieved a stunning, unexpected victory—largely thanks to Douglas's intemperance.

The liberals were aghast and the galleries abuzz with amazement. According to McPherson, "the press went berserk." The conservatives, Humphrey later said, "had us on the ropes." In the chaos of the moment, Johnson was dumbfounded and speechless.

All at once, he heard the calm voice of Richard Russell. Leaning forward over his desk toward Johnson, Russell said in a low voice, "Lyndon, you'd better adjourn this place. They're going to pass this goddam bill."

Even Russell, who had delivered a speech in favor of H.R. 3, was pragmatic enough to understand the havoc it would create if enacted. Russell knew that adjourning for the evening would freeze McClellan's momentum and give Johnson time to reverse the vote. Sitting alongside Johnson was McPherson, who recalled that his mouth "fell open" when he heard Russell offer Johnson advice on defeating a states' rights proposal. "When he did that, I thought, 'Holy Cass, what a man, what a guy!' "

At Russell's gentle prodding, Johnson leapt to his feet. "Mr. President, I move that the Senate adjourn."

Though such a motion was the traditional right of the majority leader, Jenner and McClellan demanded a roll call vote. It was a colossal act of impertinence. They were questioning the leader's time-honored prerogative to adjourn the Senate. As the roll call ensued, Johnson made a very elaborate show of pulling out a legal pad and scribbling down the name of each member who opposed his adjournment motion. It was a bit of subtle intimidation—and it worked. The vote was 70-18 in Johnson's favor.

As senators wearily filed from the chamber, Johnson stormed over to Humphrey. "I thought you had this beat. You boys screwed up. I don't know what you did, but you screwed up. You told me wrong." Humphrey was cowed and dejected as Johnson berated him in front of the reporters who had begun to stream into the Senate chamber. "I don't know all these people," Johnson barked as he led Humphrey out of the chamber and toward his office. On the way Johnson encountered Anthony Lewis, the Supreme Court reporter for the *New York Times,* and invited him to join the meeting.

For more than an hour, Lewis and George Reedy sat awestruck in the majority leader's office as Johnson and Humphrey discussed how to defeat the McClellan amendment the next day. It was actually, Lewis recalled, a monologue in which a manic Johnson consumed eight to ten scotch and sodas while lecturing Humphrey on why he should filibuster to stop the passage of H.R. 3.

"Now, I know you spent a lot of your time fighting the filibuster," Johnson said, as Humphrey sat silently. "But Hubert, you've gotta. This is make or break. You gotta stop this legislation. And, you know, when they shout at you, tell you that you've betrayed your principles, you've got to turn your other cheek." For emphasis, Johnson startled Humphrey by slapping his own cheek so hard, Lewis said, "it pained me to see it happen."

Johnson's performance, Lewis later speculated, was staged more for the reporter's benefit than for Humphrey's—"a display of his being on the right side of issues." More likely, said McPherson, Johnson saw the liberals' botched effort to defeat H.R. 3 as a delicious situation: "What an opportunity: to defeat a bad bill, save the Court, and win the embarrassed thanks of Senate liberals! It was worth doing." Of course Humphrey could never filibuster the bill, although such a tactic would have likely succeeded during the session's final hours. It would, as always, fall to Johnson to find a majority to save the liberals from the conservative assault on the Supreme Court.

What Johnson needed was a different approach: a vote not on McClellan's amendment but on a motion to return the bill to the Judiciary Committee. This meant that those who switched their votes could truthfully claim that they had voted not to kill the bill but only to return it to committee. That decided, he went to work changing votes. Ohio's Frank Lausche, a conservative Democrat, said he would switch, as did Johnson's good Republican friends Everett Dirksen of Illinois and George Malone of Nevada. Another Johnson intimate, Bob Kerr—who had voted with McClellan—said he would not vote at all. The most astounding turnaround, however, was Utah Republican Wallace Bennett, an ultraconservative who had enthusiastically voted for McClellan's amendment the day before. McPherson said he suspected that Johnson asked President Eisenhower to persuade Bennett to change his vote. Some speculated that railroad union leaders, influential in Utah, applied the pressure. Others suggested that Bennett simply voted with Johnson to spare Vice President Nixon, the party's presumptive presidential nominee for 1960, the necessity of having to break a 41-41 tie—which, no matter how he voted, would incur the wrath of powerful interests.

On the afternoon of August 21, Johnson again saved the liberals from themselves. The Senate voted 41-40 to recommit the bill to the Judiciary Committee. "What you are is a great American," Humphrey told Johnson afterwards. "FDR would have been proud of you. You have his touch and his political genius." Anthony Lewis, who considered his late-night audience in Johnson's office an off-the-record experience, did not report the incident to his readers. But in an August 25 story he paid tribute to Johnson's brilliance: "The Senate majority leader has never demonstrated greater mastery of the legislative process than in his handling" of the court bills.

For Russell, the late 1950s was often a period of disappointment. The passage of time and his failing health slowed him considerably. He had turned 60 in 1957. Still a bachelor, he lived alone in a small apartment—a cluttered warren filled with books, many of them from the Library of Congress. Sometimes he accepted invitations to dinner at the home of his Senate friends such as Johnson or J. William Fulbright. More often he eschewed social invitations. Occasionally—mostly on weekends—he sent an aide to buy him two steaks, which he and his girlfriend, Harriet Orr, cooked at his apartment. Most evenings, however, he preferred to be alone. He devoured civil war histories and other nonfiction as well as western novels. Harry McPherson recalled that Johnson, the social animal, was perplexed by Russell's solitary intellectual pursuits. "Nobody's around here when I need him," Johnson once complained during a late-night meeting. "Russell's home reading Plato, and Harry's off somewhere reading the Bible."

More than three decades of chain-smoking caught up with Russell in 1958. Doctors at the Walter Reed Army Medical Center discovered the cause of the respiratory problems that had plagued him for several years: He had emphysema, a progressive lung disease that caused labored breathing and increased his susceptibility to lung infections. After several fits and starts, Russell quit cigarettes for good, replacing tobacco with candy and peanuts. His other vice was bourbon, a pleasure he did not intend to forgo. At the end of the work day, Russell often enjoyed a swig or two of his favorite brand, Jack Daniel's. "He never offered me a drink in his office," recalled his aide and confidant Proctor Jones, adding that he never knew Russell to share "his supply" with a staff member. "That was his—*his* whiskey," explained another aide, Earl

Leonard. Yet no one worried that Russell might imbibe too freely for his own good. Staff members joked that their boss's innate frugality would keep his habit in check.

Physical ailments were not Russell's only worries. Legislative woes also loomed over his horizon. The congressional elections of 1958 proved a watershed year for liberals, with voters sending significant numbers of northern freshman Democrats into both houses of Congress. In just one election cycle, Senate Democrats increased their margin over Republicans by twenty-eight seats—from a narrow 49-47 edge to an astounding 64-34 advantage. In the House the results were equally spectacular. Democrats stretched their 234-201 lead over Republicans to 283-153.*

Historically, the party controlling the White House forfeited congressional seats in midterm contests. But this election was an unusually crushing one for Eisenhower's party. Several factors contributed to the dramatic swing: Senate Republicans had defended eight more seats—twenty-one to the Democrats' thirteen—and suffered from weakened party organizations in several states. Eisenhower had shown almost no interest in his party's electoral fortunes and offered little help to his beleaguered Republican congressional allies. The president—and by extension his party—bore ample blame for a severe economic recession, especially in agricultural states. Furthermore, Eisenhower's already sagging popularity slumped lower when his chief of staff, Sherman Adams, resigned under a cloud of scandal. "The responsibility for this disaster, when you come right down to it," said the *Wall Street Journal*, "must rest on President Eisenhower. It was he who had the sense of direction and lost it; it was he who should have nurtured a party to support his ideas and did not."

Southerners were especially despondent over the results. "Time is short," the *Dallas News* said in an editorial. "The forces of conservatism in Washington are dwindling [to] men like Harry Byrd, [Barry] Goldwater. When they are gone, we are all gone." Speaking to the Georgia General Assembly in February 1959, Russell warned his state's lawmakers that southerners "simply do not have the strength" to pass legislation

---

*One notable Democratic casualty was Arkansas Congressman Brooks Hays, a moderate who had resisted the temptation to exploit the school desegregation crisis in 1957. Hays tried instead to mediate the standoff between President Eisenhower and Governor Orval Faubus. Voters rewarded his courage by electing his opponent, a segregationist member of the Little Rock School Board.

to restore the Supreme Court "to its proper place in our scheme of government." The southern bloc, he said, had "not only lost the support of many of those from other sections on whom we once relied, but the representatives from the states of the old Confederacy no longer present a common front." Russell's anxiety may have been overwrought, but southern influence in the Senate *was* shrinking. Throughout the 1950s, the southern ranks had been about equal to that of northern Democrats. After the 1958 election, nonsouthern Democrats outnumbered southerners by a huge margin—42 to 22.

The election transformed the ideological complexion of the entire Senate Democratic caucus. Before 1958, nonsoutherners were a tidy balance of liberals such as Humphrey, Douglas, and Lehman with moderates such as Carl Hayden, Dennis Chavez, and Allen Frear. The historic 1958 elections swept ten new liberal-to-moderate Democrats into the Senate: Clair Engle of California, a seven-term congressman who filled the seat of Republican leader William Knowland (who had left to run—unsuccessfully—for governor); Howard Cannon of Nevada, who unseated two-term Republican George Malone; Thomas Dodd of Connecticut, a former congressman who defeated Republican William Purtell; Vance Hartke of Indiana, the mayor of Evansville, who filled the seat of retiring Republican archconservative William Jenner; Edmund Muskie of Maine, the first Democrat ever elected to the Senate from his state by popular vote; Philip Hart of Michigan, who beat incumbent Republican Charles Potter; Eugene McCarthy of Minnesota, a veteran congressman who defeated Humphrey's Republican colleague, Edward Thye; Harrison Williams of New Jersey, a former congressman; Stephen Young of Ohio, who defeated two-term incumbent Republican John Bricker; and Frank Moss of Utah, the Salt Lake County attorney who beat incumbent Republican Arthur Watkins.

The liberals were ecstatic. "The election results," said Pennsylvania's Joseph Clark, "exceeded our fondest hopes." Before 1958, Johnson had often regarded the liberals as a yapping collection of impractical, impetuous bomb throwers. No more. The midterm elections, argued Humphrey's top aide, William Connell, transformed the Senate into "a liberal institution" in which Humphrey would conceivably control as many votes as Johnson. "If not equal partners," said Connell, "Humphrey became more important to Johnson after the 1958 election."

Johnson now had a potentially unruly, restive majority to lead. "He was confronted with much more of the issue-oriented Senate than he had

had before—much more of a Paul Butler–national party kind of Senate," Harry McPherson said. It would now be more difficult, he knew, to build majorities around incremental initiatives by uniting southern and western Democrats and moderate Republicans. Instead of staving off liberals and conservatives with his middle-ground, compromise-as-you-go approach, Johnson knew that Democratic unity in the new, liberal Senate would be more difficult than ever. "I'd just as soon not have that many Democrats," Sam Rayburn told Johnson. "Believe me, they'll be hard to handle. It won't be easy."

On the other side of the aisle, Johnson now faced a dynamic new Republican leader—Everett Dirksen of Illinois. A pragmatic, skillful politician, Dirksen was the virtual antipode to his predecessor, William Knowland. "I am a man of principle," Dirksen once said. "And one of my basic principles is flexibility." Dirksen, said his biographer Neil Mac-Neil, "wanted power, influence and the prestige that comes with them, and he wanted to shape and temper the course of American political affairs." (That description could have comfortably applied to Johnson.) First and foremost, Dirksen was a master politician. He was the kind of man, recalled Utah's Wallace Bennett, "who was willing to sacrifice himself for the good of the party." A powerful and eloquent speaker, Dirksen occasionally resorted to excessively majestic verbiage, sometimes to his own embarrassment. Once, when defending the nomination of Clare Booth Luce as ambassador to Italy, his own oratory carried him away: "Why thrash old straws or beat an old bag of bones?" When his colleagues began to chuckle at the unfortunate choice of words, Humphrey, his friendly rival, rose to seize upon Dirksen's inadvertent slur. "I must rise to the defense of the lady." A very flustered Dirksen backtracked. "I am referring to the old bag of political bones," he said sheepishly, "those old canards." With Dirksen as his counterpart, Johnson would never again find it so easy to dominate his colleagues on the Republican side.

In January, Johnson moved forcefully to solidify his leadership and bolster his credentials with the burgeoning liberal bloc. The day before Eisenhower's annual State of the Union address, Johnson delivered his own speech to the Democratic caucus in which he outlined a bold, liberal New Deal–style agenda for the coming Eighty-sixth Congress. Johnson's laundry list included economic relief for depressed regions, water development projects for the West, and a housing and urban renewal program. He did not mention civil rights. Despite that one glaring omission, his progressive talk heartened the liberals. Johnson also moved to further separate himself from his former informal association with Russell and the southern bloc; he began attending meetings of the caucus of western Democrats.

Johnson's leftward, westward shift may have heartened the Senate's liberals, but not for long. As the new Congress opened for business on January 7, liberals such as Douglas, Anderson, Humphrey, and New York Republican Jacob Javits were eager to test the strength of their swelling ranks. As in previous years, they planned to propose the adoption of new rules. The argument was familiar: The Senate was not a continuing body, and therefore it had the right to adopt its rules by majority vote at the beginning of each new Congress. But before Anderson and his allies could rise to make their motion, Johnson sideswiped them. Exercising his right as majority leader, Johnson captured the floor only minutes after Vice President Nixon convened the Senate. "From that moment on," reported *Time*, "it was all over but the shouting— and there was plenty of that." Hoping to head off the liberal efforts to relax the cloture rule, Johnson offered a moderate proposal of his own. Cosponsored by the Democratic and Republican leadership, Johnson's measure enabled two-thirds of senators *voting* to invoke cloture on any measure, including rule changes.* Ostensibly, Russell and his southerners opposed any rule change—although Russell had proposed the same language as a compromise made the previous year. Privately, however, Russell knew that Johnson's proposal was a good deal, perhaps the southerners' only hope of heading off more stringent constraints on filibusters by the newly empowered liberal majority. While the southerners would not vote to liberalize cloture, they were realistic. Russell's bloc would not filibuster Johnson's motion.

The Johnson resolution was just the kind of gradual modification liberals had always abhorred. It was "a meaningless gesture," Paul Douglas complained. Nevertheless, Johnson knew he had the votes for his proposal, a fact that became evident when he "generously" expressed his willingness to permit a vote on Anderson's proposition. On January 9, the Senate tabled the Anderson motion, 60-36.

Despite this defeat, the liberals did not intend to retreat. On January 12 Douglas offered a substitute cloture rule that allowed a majority of

---

*The existing cloture rule required two-thirds of the entire Senate membership to stop debate. Furthermore, debate on motions to change Rule XXII were not subject to cloture.

senators to shut off debate fifteen days after the filing of a cloture petition. But Johnson still had his votes. The Douglas measure lost, 28-67. Later that day, the Senate finally adopted—with the grudging support of most liberals—Johnson's cloture modification, 72-22. "The South won a great victory," Douglas said on CBS's *Face the Nation* several days later. What bothered Douglas, he later said, was that "by acquiescence or otherwise, we may, somewhere along the route, be construed as having accepted the existing rules of the Senate." Moreover, he saw Johnson's cloture victory as an impediment to aggressive action on civil rights in 1959. "I think a majority of the country wants it," Douglas said, "but the power of the South to filibuster and the protection thrown around the filibuster by the small states and by the conservative Republicans, I am afraid, is going to be such as to prevent it from being passed."

Most observers interpreted the cloture-rule votes as ringing endorsements of Johnson's continued domination of the Senate, but closer analysis revealed widening fissures in his leadership. Although eight of fifteen Democratic freshmen—including liberals Dodd, Hartke, and Cannon—had supported Johnson on the tabling of Anderson's motion, seven of the new Democrats broke with the Democratic leader on their first important Senate vote. Risking reprisals, Engle, Muskie, Hart, McCarthy, Williams, Young, and Moss had joined other liberal veterans to support Anderson over Johnson. Those votes portended even more liberal defections—and growing difficulties for Johnson.

As always, freshman senators had been under intense pressure to support the leadership—if they knew what was good for them. Even the most uninitiated newcomer knew that Johnson, as majority leader, and Russell, as the most influential member of the Democratic Steering Committee, held absolute sway over committee assignments. Said Douglas's aide Howard Shuman: "I've never heard anybody say that [Russell] directly said to a new member, 'Vote with us or you don't get your [committee] choice.' But it was very clear what a new senator had to do." Muskie, whom Johnson later described as "chicken shit" for his leadership-defying vote, was relegated to two insignificant committees, while Johnson supporters such as Hartke got choice assignments. "The sugar plums," Paul Douglas observed, "went to the boys who went along."

Despite the liberals' harsh judgment of his heavy-handed methods, Johnson was not quite the southern sympathizer they suspected. According to aide Solis Horwitz, Johnson had attempted to enlist Clinton Anderson's support for the compromise rules change. In exchange, Horwitz said, Johnson had promised to support an Anderson amendment to lower the cloture threshold from two-thirds to three-fifths of those voting. "Johnson was perfectly willing to take 60 percent and get rid of the issue," said Horwitz. But Anderson and the liberals rejected Johnson's offer. In the end, after rejecting Anderson's motion, the Senate turned down a subsequent amendment to reduce the votes needed for cloture to three-fifths. None of this would have happened, Horwitz insisted, if Anderson and his liberal colleagues had followed Johnson's lead. "That was another case of the liberals beating themselves," said Horwitz. To their detriment, the liberals simply could not overcome their immense distrust of Johnson to accept, in good faith, his efforts to reform the cloture rule.

Another fissure in Johnson's leadership opened in February when Wisconsin Democrat William Proxmire—elected to the Senate in a special election in 1957—openly attacked his leader. In a Senate floor speech, Proxmire lamented that Johnson had grown so powerful "that the typical Democratic Senator has literally nothing to do with determining the legislative program and policies of this party." Although only Oregon's Wayne Morse publicly endorsed this harsh criticism, Proxmire did receive hints of support from Douglas, Joseph Clark, and Albert Gore.

Johnson would ignore the speech at his peril. Proxmire had expressed a growing sentiment among Democrats, many of whom were privately frustrated by Johnson's heavy-handed methods. "Other senators were very, very reluctant to become involved personally," Proxmire later said. "In fact, when they called me about my speech, they would call me at home. They wouldn't call me . . . in the office. They were afraid the lines might be tapped. There was a real fear of Senator Johnson as the leader." Harry McPherson believed there was "some justification" for Proxmire's criticism, even if Proxmire and other Johnson critics were often beneficiaries of his power. "Johnson's control of the machinery was complete," said McPherson. "When it was used to pass one's bills or to secure a choice committee assignment, it was welcome, but it was oppressive to those in opposition." Johnson's "constant pressure" for unanimous consent agreements, McPherson acknowledged, "often came close to harassment."

Proxmire's attack outraged and offended Johnson. Privately, he called his unruly colleague "Senator Pissmire." Although he would never voluntarily relinquish his control over the levers of power, Johnson did agree to one minor reform: Worried that Proxmire's complaints might gain currency if not addressed, he agreed to hold a Democratic caucus meeting upon the request of any member. "Johnson assumed, correctly as it turned out," wrote political scientist Michael Foley, "that it would be the liberal group which would require additional caucuses and that ultimately the liberals would be the only members present at such caucuses."

Publicly, Johnson responded that "this one-man rule stuff is a myth" and asserted that he had never tried to force his will on any senator. But he correctly suspected that Proxmire's attack was the early warning of more pronounced unrest among those in the liberal ranks who sought institutional reforms and more action on their legislative agenda—especially civil rights. Douglas, for one, had already confirmed this for Johnson in January, when he complained openly—albeit diplomatically—about the leader's ambivalence toward meaningful civil rights legislation. "This is the real world," he said on *Face the Nation*, "but I do think it is unfortunate that the image which the Democratic party gives to the country is the image created by the political necessities of Texas and the South."

Johnson hoped the Senate could avoid the divisive and tiring issue of civil rights for several more years. Eventually, his aide Horace Busby and former Secretary of State Dean Acheson persuaded him otherwise. Acheson argued persuasively that Johnson was "the one man in the Democratic Party whose rare gifts of leadership . . . make possible the solution of this seemingly insoluble problem." Gradually, Johnson came to realize that the relative impotence of the Justice Department under the 1957 act would inevitably spawn broader civil rights legislation by Senate liberals and the Eisenhower administration. Another civil rights bill, he realized, was a certainty. But the political questions facing Johnson were more vexing: Who would write the bill, how strong would it be, and who would receive the credit for its passage or failure? These were variables Johnson *could* control, but only if he took the initiative. If Johnson refused to take charge, he knew that a newly empowered coalition of liberal Democrats and moderate Republicans would almost certainly commandeer the civil rights issue—with uncertain and possibly dangerous results for the Democratic party.

Humphrey, meanwhile, continued to exist in the ideologically neutral zone between the liberal bloc and Johnson's leadership circle. During a September 27 appearance on *Face the Nation,* he expressed confidence in Johnson when moderator Stuart Novins asked, "Do you think Lyndon Johnson is dragging his feet on that right to vote?"

"No, sir," he replied.

"Do you think you will get that kind of legislation in the next session of the Congress?" Novins asked.

"Yes, sir."

On January 20 Johnson submitted his own civil rights legislation, hoping he could hurriedly pass a mild bill before the issue became embroiled in the politics of the 1960 congressional and presidential elections. Too strong for Russell's southerners yet much too weak for the liberals, the bill's main features were an antibombing provision that barred interstate transportation of explosives; an extension of the Civil Rights Commission created by the 1957 act; subpoena powers for the Justice Department in voting rights investigations; and establishment of a Federal Community Relations Service to mediate local disputes over segregation and integration.

The bill's centerpiece was the Community Relations Service, a compromise provision that fell far short of the aggressive federal action sought by liberals. Johnson's own aide, Solis Horwitz, acknowledged the provision's inherent weakness in a February 16 memorandum: "While the plan recognizes that the implementation of the Supreme Court decisions through the judicial process in the District Courts has not worked satisfactorily, it makes no change in existing law." The provision, Horwitz explained, "provide[s] an additional method which is non-coercive and wholly voluntary in character."

Not surprisingly, the NAACP's Roy Wilkins reacted coolly to the bill, charging, with some accuracy, that it was "an effort to block consideration of effective legislation in this field. We regard it as offering liniment to cure a tumor, for it omits entirely the paramount domestic issue of desegregation of the public schools." Calling for enactment of the 1957 act's erstwhile Part III provision, Wilkins said its omission from the Johnson bill "prompts the suspicion that it is a sugar-coated pacifier."

Not to be outdone, the White House offered its own bill. Similar to Johnson's legislation, the Eisenhower program—actually seven separate bills—contained an antibombing provision and an extension of the Civil Rights Commission. But Eisenhower went further. His legislation, sponsored by Dirksen and Arizona's Barry Goldwater, would have made it a federal crime to interfere with a federal school desegregation court order. The White House program would have also empowered the Justice Department to inspect local voter records and prohibited their destruction; authorized technical and financial assistance to areas with school desegregation problems; and provided emergency schooling for children of armed forces personnel if an integration dispute closed their public school.

The most extensive bill was, of course, offered by Douglas and a bipartisan group of seventeen senators. The chief provision of their legislation was the scuttled Part III provision of the 1957 bill, which empowered the attorney general to initiate civil suits for school desegregation on behalf of black students. The Douglas bill also authorized the federal government to develop and enforce school desegregation plans through the courts.

Russell, predictably, opposed all of the bills. But his words—"I shall oppose all of this political legislation to the limit of my ability"—had begun to sound tired, even hollow. By summer the fate of all three civil rights programs rested with the southern-dominated Senate and House Judiciary committees. In the Senate, a Judiciary subcommittee, after a squabble over the controversial Part III provision, approved only mild legislation to extend the life of the Civil Rights Commission and require state and local election officials to preserve voting records for federal inspection for at least three years.* By the time Congress adjourned for the year, in mid-September, the bill was moribund and hopelessly mired in committee. The only civil rights legislation to pass Congress was a last-minute measure to fund and extend the Civil Rights Commission until November 1961.

Johnson seemed unaware of the liberals' determination to pass another civil rights bill. The 1957 act had satisfied only those conservatives and moderates who viewed the issue as a nuisance, not a moral crusade. Moreover, the law was proving extremely difficult to enforce. Federal judges had dismissed Justice Department voting rights suits in Alabama and Georgia. In the Georgia case, Judge T. Hoyt Davis ruled that one provision of the bill, which empowered the attorney general to seek preventive relief in voting rights violations, was unconstitutional. Yet

---

*Although his Attorney General had proposed it in 1957, Eisenhower opposed the addition of Part III to the bill in 1959.

some civil rights advocates charged that the difficulties with enforcement did not rest entirely with the legislation's inadequacies or with unsympathetic southern judges. The Justice Department's ambivalence, they said, was to blame. Indeed, by the end of 1959 the Justice Department had filed only four lawsuits under provisions of the act: three to address voter discrimination and one against an all-white primary in Fayette County, Tennessee.

Even a simple extension of the Civil Rights Commission had been an uphill struggle. Johnson resurrected the legislation only when liberals hinted they would delay the Senate's adjournment by offering civil rights provisions as amendments to the Mutual Security Appropriations Bill. Moving to head off an embarrassing year-end deadlock over civil rights, Johnson and Dirksen reluctantly mollified the liberals by extending the commission.

The sputtering drive for a civil rights bill gained some impetus in early September. A Civil Rights Commission report on voter registration in the South revealed that in 1956 only a quarter of the nearly five million eligible Southern blacks was registered, compared with 60 percent of voting-age whites. "Some method must be found," the commission declared, "by which a federal officer is empowered to register voters for federal elections who are qualified under state registration laws but are otherwise unable to vote." In a five-to-one vote, the commission recommended a process by which the president could appoint temporary federal voting registrars.

Days later, in an important concession, the two Senate leaders promised to bring a civil rights bill to the floor early in 1960. On September 14, the day before adjournment, Johnson made the announcement: "I serve notice on all members that on or about twelve o'clock on February 15, I anticipate that some Senator will rise in his place and make a motion with regard to the general civil rights question." Privately, Johnson signaled liberals and conservatives that he would tolerate nothing stronger than a voting rights bill—in other words, he explained, "an effective bill that will satisfy the consciences of sixty-seven senators [the cloture threshold]."

Russell regarded Johnson's move toward civil rights with disgust. Publicly, at least, he blamed the liberals. The various bills introduced in 1959, Russell told a Lions Club meeting in Dawson, Georgia, in December, "vary only in the degree of their vindictiveness. All of them are hostile to our concept of government and contrary to the spirit and intent of the Constitution." The "ultimate price" of such federal inter-vention, he warned, "would be totalitarianism." The most extraordinary aspect of an otherwise conventional speech was Russell's absurd and naive assessment of race relations in the South, which he said "remain generally good. This has been brought about under our traditional social order which permits members of both races to live and work together in peace, harmony and mutual understanding."

Six weeks later the more authentic nature of southern race relations manifested itself in Greensboro, North Carolina. On February 1, 1960, four black freshmen from North Carolina A&T College peacefully en-tered a downtown Woolworth's store. As they settled onto stools at the white-only lunch counter, the black waitress refused them service. "Fellows like you," she angrily told them, "make our race look bad." Two days later, the impromptu protest blossomed. More than eighty A&T students, now coordinated by student leaders, were reserving times for their shifts in an organized sit-in at Woolworth's and the local Kress store. Similar protests quickly spread throughout the South. Within the span of three months, thousands of black and white students staged sit-ins at lunch counters in fifteen cities in five Southern states. At almost every site, students sat at white-only counters, demanded service, and left only when the store closed or when local police officers arrested them. While most of the demonstrations were peaceful, some resulted in violence.

The civil rights movement, previously a well-mannered cause led mostly by clergy and directed primarily at school desegregation and voting rights, was now awakened by the infusion of thousands of en-ergetic, indignant black college students who demanded their full rights as citizens. Astute politicians, including Russell, soon understood that this brewing unrest throughout the South would mean even greater pressure for tougher civil rights legislation in 1960.

Such a bill now seemed inevitable—as was the first personal strife between Russell and his protégé, Lyndon Johnson.

CHAPTER THIRTEEN

Let Me Have the Nomination

JOHNSON'S PROMISE TO TAKE UP a civil rights bill by February 15 was no idle threat. As the day approached, he reminded Russell of his plans. "Yes," Russell said, coolly, "I understand that you let them jockey you into that position. I understand." Later Johnson mentioned his promise again. "Yes, I know that," Russell replied. "Go ahead, do whatever your judgment tells you. That's your business, your responsibility. I'm not the leader."

With his 1960 reelection campaign on the horizon, Russell engaged in a complicated game of verbal gymnastics, declaring his unwavering opposition to legislation that he implied was inevitable. In an unusually vitriolic and defeatist speech to the Georgia Assembly on February 8, Russell declared: "The NAACP and the ADA and similar rag-tag, left-wing politicians and groups are pulling the strings on the puppet politicians and demanding passage of the most extreme and vicious legislation." Russell, who lamented that "a stable" of presidential hopefuls was "dancing to the tune of the pressure groups," insisted that the Democratic party "has virtually abandoned us." The party of "Jefferson and Jackson had become," Russell said, "the captive of a left-wing element that is barely Democratic in name, but which is trying to recast the party in its image. Many of this gang of phony liberals and party-wreckers have publicly advocated driving the South from the house of our fathers."

Back in Washington, on the same day, Republican leader Dirksen introduced Eisenhower's civil rights bill. Virtually identical to the administration's 1959 proposal, it had one additional provision—a plan for court-appointed voting referees to force the registration of blacks who

248 + *The Walls of Jericho*

were unlawfully disqualified or purged. The bill did not, however, contain several stronger provisions that liberals still regarded as crucial, particularly the Part III language from 1957.

The following day, on February 9, Russell again sounded the alarms in a speech to the States' Rights Council in Atlanta. In language that, if used on the Senate floor, would have violated the Senate rule against questioning the motives of a colleague, Russell said that the "sponsors of these mis-called proposals have not the slightest regard for the Constitution or for the rights of the states. They are interested only in currying favor with the pressure groups who purport to speak for a sizable bloc of minority voters in key areas of the nation." Russell said that Humphrey and other liberals "must be running a race to see who can introduce the greatest number of bills and the most ingenious means for punishing the southern people."

Russell was at least partially correct about the amount of civil rights legislation awaiting action. In addition to bills by Johnson, Eisenhower, and the coalition of Democratic and Republican liberals—all of which were carried forward from 1959—Humphrey and several other Democrats had introduced an alternative to Eisenhower's voting referee proposal. Humphrey's legislation and its companion bill in the House empowered the president, in certain cases, to appoint officials to register blacks for federal elections.*

On February 15, shortly after 11:00 a.m., Johnson surreptitiously moved to fulfill his promise to bring civil rights legislation to the Senate. Matter-of-factly, he asked for and received the Senate's unanimous consent to proceed to the consideration of a minor, noncontroversial House-passed bill, H.R. 8315. The legislation authorized the army to provide unused officers' quarters at a Missouri military base for students whose school had burned in 1959. Nothing about the legislation should have raised anyone's suspicions. Later that afternoon, however, Johnson's announcement almost jolted Russell out of his chair.

"Mr. President," Johnson said, addressing the presiding officer, "the unfinished business now before the Senate, H.R. 8315, relates to the leasing of a portion of Camp Crowder to a school district in Missouri.

---

*Those who favored the administration's referee proposal argued that it covered registration for all kinds of elections, not just federal. Moreover, it embodied Eisenhower's hands-off philosophy on civil rights, leaving its ultimate execution to federal judges and not the Justice Department. Proponents of the liberals' registrar plan argued that it was a more direct and expeditious way to register blacks because southern judges often moved too slowly, or not at all, in voting rights cases.

Because there is, as yet, no civil rights legislation on the Senate Calendar, this bill has been selected as the one on which, in fulfillment of the Senate's pledge of last year, to begin discussion of civil rights proposals in this chamber." Johnson then invited senators to propose civil right amendments. "I hope all interested senators will offer in a spirit of constructive, responsible, and nonpartisan dedication to human rights, the proposals they believe will best serve the ends of protecting the constitutional rights of American citizens."

Johnson's move was brilliant. Because he had opened a House-passed bill to civil rights amendments, Johnson had bypassed the Senate Judiciary Committee. In addition, as he knew, Senate amendments to a House-passed bill would return directly to the House floor, bypassing the Rules Committee. Johnson had given Russell plenty of warning that he would attempt to bring a civil rights bill before the Senate, but Russell never guessed that Johnson would go beyond a routine attempt to prevent referral of the bill to the Judiciary Committee. Russell expected that Johnson would merely offer a motion to take up the civil rights bill directly—which, of course, the southerners would filibuster. Weeks of debate on Johnson's procedural motion would occur, Russell assumed, before the southerners launched another series of filibusters over individual amendments.

Johnson's clever tactic carried the double indignity that legislation reported out of Russell's own Armed Services Committee would now be transformed into a civil rights bill. "I rise to protest action of this sort," Russell said angrily. Later, his voice dripping with sarcasm, he asked whether Johnson and Dirksen "proposed to boil us in oil, or to burn us at the stake, or to fricassee us on some new kind of rack or wheel or simply to stick a bayonet into our bodies." His strongest words came moments later, when he decried Johnson's move as "a lynching of orderly procedure in the Senate of the United States. In other words, the end justifies the means—'Let us at 'em, come the fifteenth day of February."

In an acrimonious exchange with Russell, Dirksen staunchly defended his Democratic counterpart's maneuver. "I had wished, of course, that a civil rights bill might be on the floor or that we might have had one out of committee." Sometimes, as Dirksen argued, "we have to pursue extraordinary procedure. In order to get the job done, I am willing to accept any castigation or blame for invoking an extraordinary procedure."

Although furious that Johnson's sneak attack might open the door for consideration of all sorts of proposals, Russell may not have been as adamantly opposed to civil rights legislation as he seemed in front of Georgia audiences or on the Senate floor. In early February Russell had confessed to Johnson's aide Gerald Siegel that the administration bill, then slowly working its way toward House passage, might be acceptable. In a February 2 memorandum Siegel reported the news to Johnson, adding that Russell "believes that bill should not be amended, or amended to no greater extent than adding whatever voting provisions the Senate selects." As for his choice between the administration's voter referee proposal and Humphrey's federal registrar bill, Siegel said Russell "appeared to prefer the referee" provision. For now, at least, the southerners would not allow Johnson, Dirksen, or anyone else in the Senate dictate the terms of a civil rights bill. They wanted instead to forestall Senate action until the House had a chance to pass the so-called "clean" administration proposal, without a Part III provision. Meanwhile the southerners had a problem. How could they kill time until the House acted?

The smell of filibuster was in the air.

In 1957, before the Little Rock crisis, most southern senators had believed that their decision to forgo a filibuster in return for a weak voting rights bill was thoroughly defensible. This bill was different. "One of the main reasons why we filibustered against that 1960 bill," Herman Talmadge later explained, "is that we had been burned badly in 1957. We had been talked out of blocking that earlier bill by assurances that federal troops would not be used to enforce court orders." After Little Rock, Talmadge said, he realized that "we were pretty naive to have believed that." By 1960 these southerners, stung by criticism that they had not fought hard enough to defeat the 1957 bill, found themselves corralled into a filibuster by their own doomsday rhetoric. For example, Russell called the bill "the gravest threat to free national elections in this country since the stolen presidential contest of 1876."* The legis-

---

*Perhaps the most controversial U.S. presidential election ever, the 1876 contest pitted Republican Rutherford B. Hayes of Ohio against Democrat Samuel J. Tilden of New York. Though Tilden beat Hayes by 250,000 votes, the electoral votes of three southern states remained in doubt when each state filed two sets of returns with opposite results. An electoral commission finally awarded the election to Hayes by the narrowest of margins—one electoral vote. That "stolen" election, however, resulted in the death of Reconstruction.

lation, Sam Ervin charged, would "single out certain groups of Americans on no basis but their race, and demand that they be given rights superior to those ever sought by or granted to any other Americans . . . in history."

On February 16, Russell moved to postpone consideration of the civil rights issue for a week. He lost overwhelmingly, 28-61. Later that day, Wayne Morse, an Oregon liberal offended by Johnson's unorthodox parliamentary maneuver of the previous day, moved to discharge civil rights legislation that the Senate had already referred to the Judiciary Committee. But Johnson and the liberals remained in firm control, and Morse's motion failed, 4-68. Finally the Senate rejected, by voice vote, Morse's motion to discharge from the Rules Committee Humphrey's bill that authorized federal registrars. The actual question of civil rights was finally presented to the Senate on February 17, when Dirksen offered the Eisenhower administration's seven-part bill as an amendment to the House-passed Missouri school bill. Their resolve now growing stiffer by the day, southerners refused to yield an inch of ground. They permitted no votes, objecting even when Dirksen asked for unanimous consent to consider the bill's seven parts "en bloc."

On Tuesday, February 23, after a week of running in place, Johnson knew it was time to spur the Senate to action. He announced that on the following Monday, February 29, the Senate would begin an around-the-clock, continuous session. If southerners wanted to prevent a vote, he would force them to wage a full-fledged filibuster—not the gentlemanly nine-to-five variety that had been the rule in recent years. If Johnson forced them to debate the bill for twenty-four hours a day, southerners could not claim that he had denied them ample time to air their views—a common argument against cloture. "Therefore," he told the Senate, "I think all members should be on notice that their presence may be demanded at any time during any evening, or the early morning hours of the morning, all night around the clock, every night next week or the following week, until a vote is obtained."

That day the filibuster began to take life. Although he said he was not complaining about "the very onerous schedule which has been outlined to us," Russell served notice on Johnson that "there are senators who know how to play that kind of game." Chief among the southern weapons, he announced, would be quorum calls "at awkward times" of the day and night. "We will resist to the limit of our ability, within the provisions of the rules," Russell added. "I think I can speak for the majority of those associated with me in resisting this legislation when I say that we will use every legal means at our command to undertake to prevent this legislation from being passed until it has been thoroughly and fully discussed and explored." To more than one discerning ear, Russell was announcing the beginning of a filibuster.

Johnson, meanwhile, hoped that the continuous session would force the southerners into an early capitulation. He did not, however, know that Russell and his troops were prepared to revolutionize the use of the modern filibuster.

For decades, a filibuster usually meant that a handful of outnumbered senators talked until they reached the limits of physical and emotional endurance. Such tactics were most successfully employed near the end of a legislative session, when their members were eager to depart Washington and thus more agreeable to compromise.

This filibuster was different. Staged early in the session, it would not benefit from the same time constraints. Furthermore, the southern group, which included many of the Senate's oldest members, was not likely to prevail in any confrontation where physical stamina was as important as oratorical skill.* Nonetheless the southerners at least knew that history favored their cause: the Senate had *never* imposed cloture on a southern filibuster in a civil rights debate.

Ostensibly concerned about the physical strain that around-the-clock sessions would impose on the Senate's older members, Florida's sixty-seven-year-old Spessard Holland attempted to lay the potential blame on Johnson and Dirksen. "The responsibility," he said, "for the lives and health of certain members of the Senate who are of age and in feeble health is upon the hearts and consciences of the two leaders of the Senate." Johnson adamantly refused to accept such responsibility. "I am not the one who prevents the majority of the Senate from expressing themselves," he replied. "I am not the one who says that the members of the greatest deliberative body in the world should not have a right to vote." Johnson noted that "if the majority want to adjourn at eight o'clock this evening, they can do so."

To prove his point—and to divest himself of responsibility for the possible collapse of an elderly senator—Johnson called the southerners'

---

*Filibusters were often physically taxing because of the Senate rule that required members to stand while addressing the Senate. Any member who sat or left the chamber without yielding temporarily to another member lost his or her right to the floor.

bluff. On February 26 he moved to adjourn the Senate the following Monday at 5:00 p.m. "I do not want to have on my conscience," Johnson said, "an individual decision that was not in accordance with the majority wishes of this body." Caught off guard by Johnson's sudden move, confused southerners began voting for adjournment. When Russell learned of Johnson's scheme, he moved quickly to deny the leadership a chance to display its true strength. Midway through the roll call, southerners stopped voting for adjournment and begin voting to remain in session. Although Russell described the 67-10 vote against adjournment as merely "a straw man," a satisfied Johnson declared himself merely an agent of the Senate's will.

Assured of twenty-four-hour sessions for at least two weeks, southerners began to discuss how they might sustain a lengthy filibuster without exhausting themselves in the process. What they needed were not eighteen marathon runners but a well-conditioned relay team. Russell's Georgia colleague, Herman Talmadge, had just the idea. Relying on his experience "standing watch" in the Navy, Talmadge devised a plan to "outfox" Johnson.

"Look, Dick," Talmadge said, "this is as simple as ABC. We've got nineteen [actually eighteen] senators on our side. That's one general and eighteen troops. You divide those eighteen troops into three platoons of six men each. A platoon will go on duty for a twenty-four-hour period. You divide each of those platoons into squads of two men each. Those two men will be responsible for filibustering for eight hours. They can take turns talking and resting. Then, when the eight-hour watch is over, another squad will replace them. That means that each of us will be on duty for eight hours and then have two days off."

Talmadge's proposal was brilliant. "I don't know why in the whole history of the country," he later said, "nobody ever thought of that before . . . It was so damn simple." In a meeting in Russell's office, at his large round table, the southern general gave the idea life and issued his marching orders. "Just remember," Russell told his colleagues, "that they didn't have any mercy on us and we won't have any on them." That, advised Russell, meant forcing Johnson and Dirksen to maintain a quorum to answer roll calls at every hour of every day. "Whenever you finish speaking," he said, "call for a quorum. Call for a quorum at the most inopportune time of the day for the great majority of senators." A very good time to demand such a roll call, Russell advised, "is dinner time in the evening, when the senators are scattered all over the District and enjoying their dinner." Another good time, he said, "is about one o'clock in the morning or three o'clock in the morning or five o'clock in the morning or seven o'clock in the morning. Just select one of those hours and stop speaking and call for a quorum."

But quorum calls were more than just dilatory and bothersome. Under the Senate's rules, each senator could deliver only two speeches during a single *legislative day*. And legislative days, unlike twenty-four-hour *calendar* days, ended only when the Senate adjourned. Therefore, quorum calls were vital because, without a quorum (less than fifty senators), southerners could force adjournment and the advent of a new legislative day. As Herman Talmadge explained, "The only way the opposition could hope to thwart us [short of cloture] was to keep the legislative day going until we all had given our two speeches. That meant preventing adjournment."

To make it difficult for Johnson and Dirksen to assemble a quorum, no southerners—except the filibustering senators on duty—would answer any quorum call. That would force the two leaders to draw at least forty-nine votes from their own ranks—a sometimes impossible task at 3:00 a.m.

In a matter of days, Russell succeeded in turning the tables on Johnson. Instead of wearing down the southerners, Russell's forces turned the pro–civil rights senators into a fatigued and grumpy collection of middle-aged and elderly men who were forced to find precious moments of slumber on dozens of uncomfortable army cots placed just off the Senate floor. At all hours of the night, southerners demanded quorum calls. Bells rang loudly. Groggy, red-eyed senators would emerge from fitful sleep, stagger onto the Senate floor, answer the roll call, and stumble wearily back to their cots for an hour or two of sleep before the bells rang again. "They smothered us with quorum calls," recalled Jacob Javits. "Sleep became the unifying force in the drama," reporter Thomas Wolfe wrote in the *Washington Post*. During early-morning sessions, as the southern sentries conducted their lonely "debate," Wolfe observed that "sleep hung in the air like nerve gas." Quorum calls become so incessant that New Jersey Republican Clifford Case one night woke from a dream in which he thought heard the bells signaling a quorum call. Hurriedly dressing, Case rushed to the Senate floor to find only a couple of filibustering southern senators engaged in a dreary colloquy.

New Hampshire Republican Norris Cotton captured the atmosphere of the Senate in a newsletter to constituents in which he described a "typical day":

11 p.m. Long of Louisiana having spoken ten hours drones on, reading voluminous court decisions. Senators huddle in the back of the Chamber waiting for the end of the speech and the inevitable quorum call which follows, before trying to snatch a few hours sleep.

12:30 a.m. The quorum call starts.

12:51 a.m. A quorum of 51 Senators is finally rounded up, and Sparkman of Alabama launches into a speech. He says he believes in freedom of speech and proceeds to prove it.

1:52 a.m. Another quorum call. Sleepy Senators stagger in to respond to their names and quickly head back for the cots and couches. Dignified Leverett Saltonstall is in Indian moccasins. Many are without ties. The required 51 is not mustered. A roll call follows on sending the Sergeant-at-Arms to bring more in. As it progresses, enough arrived to make the quorum.

4:50 a.m. Sparkman finishes. Another quorum call. Thirty minutes later enough Senators have shuffled in (and out again), and Smathers of Florida undertakes to keep the flood of words rolling on.

6:45 a.m. Smathers quits. Quorum call and roll call to bring in Senators consume 33 minutes. Then Stennis of Mississippi takes over. He says he has never seen "the Senate in better tradition or in better form."

9:30 a.m. Another quorum call. The ball is passed to Talmadge of Georgia, and so on throughout the daylight hours and into another night.

The southerners, meanwhile, were fresh and well rested. Because they purposely abstained from most quorum calls, all but a handful of them enjoyed a full night's rest throughout the filibuster. "We had a comparatively easy time," Sam Ervin recalled, "but the majority was run ragged." Said Herman Talmadge: "We beat them to death." The southerners were more than a little amused at how easily they had put their pro–civil rights colleagues on the defensive. "You'd be surprised how much physical strain we could put on the opposition," Alabama's John Sparkman bragged years later. Said Paul Douglas's aide Howard Shuman: "A senator who was filibustering didn't have to show except every third day and didn't have to speak except every sixth day. The people who were trying to break the filibuster had to be around, fifty-one of them, at all times, to answer the quorum calls . . . The effect of it was to wear out the people who were trying to break the filibuster, rather than to wear out the people who were filibustering."

Denying requests for unanimous consent was another dilatory tactic that Russell used skillfully to thwart the opposition. Under Johnson's regime, unanimous consent—a routine voice vote on noncontroversial matters—had become the bread and butter of the Senate's daily business. Russell now served notice that southerners would refuse almost all such requests for the duration of the filibuster. Like other weapons in the southerners' arsenal, this tactic was not simply an annoyance. Denying unanimous consent for routine motions—for example, to dispense with the reading of amendments or an entire bill—consumed time and gave the southerners a chance to rest their weary feet and voices. The southerners used other parliamentary weapons as well. They demanded roll calls on all sorts of procedural inquiries and posed convoluted questions to the presiding officer. To give a filibustering senator a brief respite or bathroom break, southerners sometimes posed questions lasting several minutes.

Throughout the filibuster, Johnson was on constant alert for surprise attacks from the southerners. If Russell or one of his men could catch the leadership dozing, they could do almost anything they wanted with a simple unanimous consent request. On one night in particular, Johnson suspected that Russell might attempt some parliamentary trick. Although he had placed a pro–civil rights senator in the chamber to guard against a southern surprise attack, Johnson worried that the senator might be caught off guard by Russell's suspected scheme. Sometime after midnight, Johnson dressed, put on his shoes, and walked over to the Senate chamber. "He looked around," Harry McPherson recalled, "and heard the southerners speaking and saw his watchman sitting there, his head nodding off. And at that very moment at the other end of the chamber he saw the door push open about two inches, and there was Dick Russell looking out, waiting for Johnson to pull a trick, cut this guy off and pass the bill."

By March 5, southerners had filibustered for 125 hours and 31 minutes. Except for a single fifteen-minute recess, the Senate had remained in session for its longest continuous period ever. All Senate committees had suspended hearings. During that time, the Senate had held only one substantive vote: On March 2, the Senate tabled an amendment proposed by Russell Long of Louisiana to the bill's first section.

The debate, though spirited, was surprisingly free of acrimony. And southern speeches were germane. There were, however, some tense moments. On March 4, when Oregon's Wayne Morse appeared in the chamber to invite senators to sign a cloture petition, Lister Hill protested. Denied unanimous consent to leave the petition on a table for signatures, Morse ignored Hill's objection. Defiantly, he placed the document on the clerk's desk and left the chamber. Moments later, Kentucky's Thruston Morton, a Republican civil rights advocate, snatched the document and dramatically ripped it into hundreds of pieces that he dropped into a trash can and a spittoon. Morse, he said, had been absent for most of the civil rights debate and was engaging in dramatic gestures to draw attention to himself. "Censure me if you will!" Morton shouted dramatically. "Do what you will. But if we're going to get this thing solved, we must leave partisan politics out of it."

On March 5, an exhausted Johnson finally relented. "Every man has the right to a Saturday-night bath," he said as he sent his weary allies home for the evening. To Russell and the southerners, the recess meant only that they were winning. "I think we could have carried on . . . for the rest of the session if necessary," Sam Ervin said, "because [Russell] had a very good system for conducting a filibuster." His troops, Russell told the press, were in splendid condition and there was "no area of compromise." Such talk, however, was merely for show. A compromise, Russell Baker reported in the *New York Times*, "is palpably in the air and everybody knows it." But as Baker correctly noted, when and if the Senate reached a compromise, it was likely to be the northern liberals—not Russell—who relented.

Three days later, a partial southern victory seemed assured. Johnson finally called off the continuous session when the bipartisan liberal group filed a cloture petition on March 8. Further evidence of the southerners' clout was the unsuccessful cloture vote on March 10. Johnson and Dirksen had both opposed cloture, arguing that they needed time "to find an area of agreement" that could "represent the views of sixty-seven members of the Senate [the two-thirds majority needed to impose cloture]." But Jacob Javits protested that Johnson should not force the Senate to wait until two-thirds of the body agreed. "The people of New York sent me here on the constitutional principle that it took a majority, not two-thirds, of the Senate to act." Douglas warned—accurately— that failure to impose cloture would send a signal that "strong measures" would never be part of the final legislation. "The result," he declared, "will be a truncated bill." The cloture vote that the liberals demanded only proved Douglas's point. A majority sided with Johnson and Dirksen. Senators rejected cloture, 53-42, opting to wait for an acceptable compromise.

The vote, the first on cloture since 1954, was a blow to the liberals. Gone was their argument that an outmoded cloture rule was preventing the Senate from acting. They had not even garnered a simple majority. Another defeat came quickly on the heels of the cloture vote, when senators approved Johnson's motion to kill a Part III amendment in a 55-38 vote.

As Johnson searched for a compromise, he faced the daunting challenge of appeasing at least two of the Senate's three competing factions: Russell's southerners, ostensibly opposed to all civil rights legislation but obviously willing to end their filibuster in favor of a mild, compromise version of the administration's bill; the Democratic and Republican moderates, led by Johnson and Dirksen, who supported the administration proposal but were willing to compromise on some provisions, particularly exclusion of the Part III language; and the Democratic and Republican coalition of liberals—led by Douglas, Clark, and Javits—who were pushing legislation to strengthen the administration proposal by attaching amendments supported by the NAACP and the ADA. The liberal group was itself divided: Some Democrats hoped that the proposed amendments would help erase the Republican fingerprints left on the bill by the administration's proposals.

Particularly dear to the liberals' hearts were proposals to permit the president to appoint federal registrars wherever the Civil Rights Commission certified that voting discrimination existed—a more aggressive approach to voting rights than the administration's referee provision. Oddly enough, the idea for registrars came not from within the liberal ranks but from Louisiana's Russell Long. A moderate southerner who occasionally expressed his belief in voting rights for blacks, Long gave Douglas some frank advice: "Douglas, you are never going to get anywhere on this tack. We will tie you up by delays of the [voter registration] law[s] and wear you out. The only way you are ever going to break through our defense is to give the federal government the power to send in marshals or legal officers who will directly register the voters themselves." Then, with a smile, Douglas recalled that his southern friend added, "Of course, I am opposed to all this; I will fight it with all the strength I have. But you damn-fool innocents should wake up if you are really in earnest." (Long, who later said he could not recall the conversation with Douglas, acknowledged that he subsequently had told President John F. Kennedy "that he should seek to pass a voting rights bill which would send registration officials down the roads and byways looking up black citizens who appeared to be literate and registering them.") Despite the surreptitious help from Long, the Senate tabled two registrar proposals on March 18 and 24.*

On March 4 the House finally began its long-awaited debate on the administration bill. On March 24, House members voted 311-109 to send a watered-down version of the bill to the Senate. It included a provision, added during floor debate, which provided for the appointment of voting referees—but only in areas where a federal judge determined that discrimination prevented black registration. The House had also eliminated the school desegregation and job discrimination provisions which southerners found most objectionable. In short, the House bill seemed just the kind of compromise that Johnson and Dirksen believed would short-circuit the southern filibuster.

On March 24 Johnson moved to abandon the Senate legislation and refer the House bill to the Judiciary Committee with instructions to report it to the Senate by March 29. Although Judiciary Committee chairman James Eastland protested that his committee needed more time to consider the referee provision, the Senate overwhelmingly sided with Johnson. By an 86-5 vote, senators gave the committee only five days to do its work.

In two days of hearings, Judiciary members recommended amendments to every section of the bill. On March 30 the Senate went into high gear. It voted 71-17 to begin consideration of the House-passed legislation. In rapid-fire succession, senators adopted eight amendments, most of them minor. Among the substantive changes, senators voted 68-20 to outlaw obstruction of *any* federal court order, not just those relating to school desegregation. Suddenly the bill had gained unstoppable momentum.

---

*"Five years later," Douglas wrote, "I had the happy experience of seeing the identical proposal embodied in the Voting Rights Act [of 1965]. It was highly praised by the same two men [Johnson and Dirksen] who had condemned and sidetracked it earlier, supposedly forever. They even posed as its originators."

The Senate's final product seemed to satisfy only the moderates. Russell said that the bill "flies in the face of the Constitution; it absolutely destroys due process so far as the local election official is concerned." Yet liberals such as Joseph Clark believed that southerners had successfully weakened a strong bill. Clark, who would reluctantly support it, waxed melodramatic. "Dick, here is my sword," he joked shortly before the final vote. "I hope you will give it back to me so that I can beat it into a plowshare for the spring planting. Surely in this battle on the Senate floor the roles of Grant and Lee at Appomattox have been reversed." Javits, another reluctant yes vote, called the bill "a victory for the Old South." For his part, Douglas told the Senate that the concluding lines of T.S. Elliot's poem "The Hollow Men" captured his feelings about the 1960 civil rights debate:

> *This is the way the world ends*
> *This is the way the world ends*
> *This is the way the world ends*
> *Not with a bang but a whimper.*

On April 8, before a virtually deserted gallery, the Senate made history for the second time in three years. It passed the Civil Rights Act of 1960 in a 71-18 vote. In contrast to 1957, the vote was almost anticlimactic. After fifty-three days of debate, both sides had long since exhausted their arguments. House members, meanwhile, were in no mood for a contentious conference to resolve differences in the bill's two versions. "We're tired of this thing," said House Republican leader Charles Halleck. "We want to get rid of it and do something else for a change." Two weeks after Senate passage, the House agreed to the Senate's amendments, 288-95. Eisenhower signed the bill on May 6.

Except for a few ideologues, the eighteen members of the southern group knew that Russell had negotiated a fair deal. In the Senate they had appeared reasonable, even progressive, for having "wisely" resisted the primal urge to continue their filibuster. At home, however, they were free to declare, as did Russell, that they had "defeat[ed] the most vicious schemes proposed by the South haters" and had "stri[cken] out or modif[ied] other unfair and inequitable features." Johnson, too, could claim victory. Again he had broken the debilitating civil rights gridlock. Cries of despair from the extremists on both sides seemed proof enough that he had performed well.

In the end the bill satisfied no one completely, least of all Russell.

He recognized the legislation for what it was—another step in the slow but steady march toward a comprehensive civil rights act. "He can slow the onward course of the opposition," William V. Shannon wrote in the *New York Post* in March. "He can avoid surrender. But he cannot ultimately win a total victory."

The civil rights debate in Congress was merely a sideshow to the real political spectacle of 1960: the race for the White House. With Vice President Richard Nixon virtually assured the Republican nomination, the contest among Democrats attracted most of the national headlines. The race was full, but not crowded with active candidates. All of them, however, were senators:

John F. Kennedy of Massachusetts was a charismatic second-termer who had almost been chosen as Adlai Stevenson's running mate in 1956. Although some branded him a liberal, he was actually a moderate. Mindful of potential southern delegates, he had displeased dogmatic liberals by his refusal to condemn Senator Joseph McCarthy's reckless pursuit of communists in the federal government. Worse, Kennedy's own brother Robert had served as minority counsel to McCarthy's investigative committee. On civil rights, despite his otherwise-impressive voting record, some liberals still bitterly remembered his vote to send the 1957 bill to the Judiciary Committee and his support for the jury trial amendment. Liberals also may have been aware that Kennedy counted among his southern supporters men like John Stennis and Herman Talmadge.

Kennedy's political strengths were not always evident when he strolled onto the Senate floor or arrived at a committee hearing. His appeal was with the larger American public, many of whom were captivated by his youthful good looks and his heroic wartime exploits as skipper of a sunken PT boat. Other than his age—he was only forty-two—one liability loomed large: He was Catholic, and no Catholic had ever been elected president. In the minds of most political odds makers, Kennedy's religion was a major handicap.

Unlike previous candidates who relied on support from state party leaders, Kennedy determined to ensure his nomination by entering a string of state primaries from Wisconsin to West Virginia to Oregon. If their candidate could rack up decisive victories in most or all of these states, Kennedy's advisors believed that his Catholicism would vanish as an issue with party leaders. Decisive primary victories might also create enough momentum to bring other state party bosses flocking to his bandwagon.

Another candidate was Stuart Symington of Missouri, a tall, elegant patrician who had been Harry Truman's Air Force secretary. Symington was a liberal, well respected by his colleagues and renowned for his defense expertise. Yet he was virtually unknown outside Washington and Missouri. Unlike Kennedy, Symington and two-time nominee Adlai Stevenson would not compete in the primaries. Remaining aloof from the rough-and-tumble, state-by-state battles, each hoped that a deadlocked convention would turn to him in the end.

As for Humphrey, he had been lusting for a spot on a national ticket since 1948, when his sudden prominence as a national ADA leader gave him the notion that he might be a suitable running mate for Harry Truman. In the two subsequent elections, he had caught Adlai Stevenson's eye but had never been chosen. The 1960 campaign, however, gave him pause. He might, he thought, sit this election out. That was until his European trip in December 1958 brought him face to face with one of the world's most powerful men, Soviet leader Nikita Khrushchev. After an historic eight-hour meeting with Khrushchev at the Kremlin, Humphrey became an instant worldwide celebrity and readily offered his insights about the enigmatic leader to an eager news media. The foreign trip gave Humphrey sudden confidence in his qualifications for the presidency. "I knew now that I was able to deal effectively with heads of state," he said.

When he announced his candidacy in December 1959, Humphrey said he believed he was "as competent as any man to be president with the exception of [Adlai] Stevenson." Even so, he put his chances at one in ten. "Still, there *was* that chance. And besides," he explained, "even if I didn't make it, I'd be able to do two things: first, condition the entire political climate of the campaign and then, second, *we* would write the platform, and whoever was the nominee, *he* would have to accept it. We'd make so much commotion that whoever got the nomination, our ideas would be accepted." And that, Humphrey boasted, "was a way of evening the score with the Dixiecrats. I'd been looking for it from the day when Harry Byrd and his fellows first jumped me when I came to the Senate."

Like Kennedy, Humphrey believed he must prove himself by competing in several of the nation's sixteen state primaries. "You are just not that well known," Jim Rowe advised Humphrey in late 1959, "and if you are going to have any chance at all, you are going to have to challenge Kennedy in the primaries." The first significant contest—his first direct challenge to Kennedy—would be right next door, in his neighboring state of Wisconsin.

Finally, there was Johnson.

Although he had insisted throughout 1959 that he was ambivalent about a presidential campaign, Johnson's friends had pushed him to declare his candidacy. In October Speaker Sam Rayburn and Texas governor Price Daniel announced the formation of an "unofficial" Johnson for President committee. In the spring of 1960, Johnson finally decided. He would run for president, but not like Kennedy and Humphrey. While his two Senate colleagues prepared to slug it out in half a dozen state primaries, Johnson would remain in Washington. As majority leader, he regarded the primaries as a distraction from more important duties in the Senate. Unlike Kennedy and Humphrey, who held no official leadership roles, Johnson could not leave Washington on a whim. Furthermore, he believed his leadership position would help prove his qualifications as a national leader. Therefore he would remain in Washington and work to pass progressive legislation through the Senate—including an increase in the minimum wage, medical assistance for the elderly, housing and farm legislation, and a school construction bill.

There was another important aspect to Johnson's strategy. Like Symington and Stevenson, he was betting that no candidate would receive a majority of delegates on the first ballot. A deadlocked convention might ultimately turn to him. Meanwhile he hoped to parlay friendships with influential senators into delegates from their home states. "For a long time," Harry McPherson recalled, "I thought Johnson truly believed that senators and representatives were major political forces in their states, that having their support meant capturing their delegations at the convention." "Johnson thought he could do it through the Senate," said Humphrey. "To him, the Senate was it. The Senate to Johnson was power." Johnson's rude awakening would come later. For now he seemed ignorant, Humphrey said, of the fact that "senators don't have much power, politically, back in their states . . . They don't run the state political apparatus. It's governors and national committeemen and chairmen."

Johnson even believed that he could rely on *Republican* colleagues for help in rounding up delegates. Early in his unusual quest for the nomination, he summoned Russell's good friend Milton Young to his desk on the Senate floor. "I want you to get some delegates for me in North Dakota."

Although Young admired Johnson greatly, he was doubtful of his ability to help. "How can I get delegates for you in North Dakota?" he protested. "I'm a Republican."

"That doesn't make a damn bit of difference," Johnson replied. "I want you to get some delegates."*

Booth Mooney, Johnson's longtime aide and political operative, believed that another important consideration precluded Johnson's entrance into the primaries. "I suspected," Mooney said, "that he doubted his ability to win them."

Ultimately, by stressing his role as Senate leader, Johnson only highlighted his reputation as a ruthless deal maker whose passion was the art of compromise. When Johnson did venture out from Washington, his unpolished and earthy speaking manner often failed to inspire audiences, especially when compared with the refined, urbane demeanor of Kennedy and Symington or the effusive eloquence of Humphrey. McPherson believed that Johnson's years of devotion to the Senate's arcane "procedural matters, and on building majorities behind other men who had detailed views on substantive matters . . . made him seem vague and elusive under questioning outside the Senate chamber." Explained Howard Shuman: "He knew Senate politics instinctively, but he didn't understand national politics, and he wasn't really attuned to national issues because of his focus on the Senate."

Johnson also waited too long to enter the race, telling too many people for too long that he would not run. Although he finally decided to enter the race in early 1960, he waited until just days before the July convention to formally announce his candidacy. The delay was very costly. Dean Acheson's predicament was typical. Earlier in the year, when called upon to support Johnson, Acheson reportedly replied, "I'd love to support him. I think he's the best man around. But the difficulty is that I was assured so many times that he wouldn't run that I finally pledged my support to Stu Symington and I can't withdraw it now." Later, when Johnson finally began plying the West for delegates, he

---

*One colleague who wanted to help Johnson but could not was Russell. Although he wished to endorse Johnson publicly and enthusiastically, he feared "any concerted action that would stamp Lyndon as the 'Southern' candidate." Such a designation had been Russell's fate in 1952. He would not help Johnson make the same mistake. Actively campaigning for his protégé, Russell said, would cause Johnson "a great deal more harm than good" (Fite, 376).

discovered that Kennedy had already built an insurmountable lead in several states. Ernest McFarland, formerly majority leader and now Arizona's chief justice, stood ready to help his old friend win his state's delegates. But Johnson, he complained, "wasn't an easy man to help, because he would never say that he was going to run."

Humphrey got his first full taste of Johnson's presidential ambitions when he visited Johnson's Texas ranch on December 4, 1959. During dinner, Johnson said that he wanted to win the nomination but his duties as majority leader would prevent him from entering the primaries. The next morning, according to a friend who accompanied Humphrey on the trip, Johnson woke everyone at 5:00 a.m.:

> He came into the bedroom carrying coffee and orange juice and a big wet towel to wipe our faces. We went down to breakfast, and Johnson took great pride in the fact that the honey came from the Johnson bees and the ham from the Johnson hogs and the eggs from the Johnson chickens. He waited until Hubert had a big mouthful of eggs, and then he said, "Hubert, are you going to do me out of the nomination?" Well, Hubert sat there chewing and thinking all the time, and then he said, "Lyndon, you have all *this*. Let me have the nomination."

For Kennedy and Humphrey, the primaries were the only route to the nomination. "If they could not at the primaries prove their strength in the hearts of Americans," journalist Theodore H. White observed, "the Party bosses would cut their hearts out in the back rooms of Los Angeles." Of the sixteen state primaries, Kennedy would enter seven and Humphrey five. Wisconsin's April 5 primary would be their first real battleground. In many ways the state should have been a natural stronghold for Humphrey. It was next door to Minnesota. Humphrey had good relations with the state's Democrats. Because Republicans had held both Wisconsin Senate seats for many years (until William Proxmire's election), Humphrey had often been introduced as the state's "third senator." The introduction became so familiar, Humphrey said, "that I began to believe it."

The reality of Wisconsin presidential politics was quite different from what Humphrey had imagined. "We thought of it as we would a campaign in Minnesota," Humphrey said, "a separate, local campaign. That was a mistake." After a few weeks of campaigning, he realized that his strength rested mainly in the sparsely populated western region of the state. Farther east, toward Milwaukee, his popularity and recognition were minuscule. Humphrey had also not anticipated the vast sums of money that such an endeavor required. He soon depleted his funds.

Kennedy was much better organized and vastly better funded. His campaign flooded the state with family and friends. While Humphrey's organizers struggled even to assemble small groups for meetings with their candidate, Humphrey recalled with some bitterness that "the Kennedys, with engraved invitations, were packing ballrooms" in Wisconsin's largest cities. "Mink never wore so well," he said, "cloth coats so poorly." Kennedy flew to events in his private Convair, the *Caroline*, while Humphrey's troupe chugged across the state in an old rented bus. On election day, Kennedy's 56 percent was not the decisive victory he had expected. To Humphrey, his 43 percent was all the encouragement he needed to fight on to West Virginia, the next big battleground state.

West Virginia seemed tailor-made for a Protestant, prolabor candidate like Humphrey. It was poor, rural, and only 5 percent Catholic. The state was dominated by the coal mining industry; its politics were, in turn, heavily influenced by the United Mine Workers of America. But campaigning in West Virginia was no different from running in Wisconsin in one important way—it required a large amount of money. Humphrey said that Kennedy "understood something that neither the press nor I fully grasped." A "political machine, usually the sheriff," controlled the Democratic party in each county. Most important, Humphrey said, these machines "could be 'bought,' county by county." Traditionally, local Democratic organizations merely handled the buying and selling of small, low-budget local and county races. The state had never held a presidential primary. Kennedy and Humphrey's foray into the state, and the prospect of a spending spree by both sides, must have thrilled the county bosses. But Humphrey was virtually broke. It was Kennedy, with his boundless family resources, who had plenty of money to shower upon the local leaders in almost every corner of the state. Still heavily in debt from his Wisconsin race, Humphrey would muster only about $25,000 for his West Virginia effort, a paltry sum even by 1960 standards. Kennedy, by contrast, spent $35,000 just on television advertising. His spending in one important county may have been as much as $100,000.

Even Kennedy's Catholicism did not seem to trouble many of the state's voters. Instead of trying to conceal his religion, Kennedy cleverly addressed the issue directly in television and radio commercials. "Is anyone going to tell me," Kennedy told one large rally, "that I lost this primary forty-two years ago when I was baptized?" Many voters, their religious bigotry challenged, apparently concluded that a vote for Kennedy was the best way to prove their tolerance. Kennedy's religion presented an almost impossible dilemma to Humphrey. If he highlighted his own Protestant background, Kennedy might accuse him of religious bigotry. But if he followed his natural instincts and stressed his firmly held, lifelong belief in racial and religious tolerance, he might be encouraging people to vote for his opponent.

Kennedy's operatives, meanwhile, did not appear to possess the same compunctions about ad hominem attacks on Humphrey. One prominent Kennedy supporter, Franklin D. Roosevelt, Jr., charged that Humphrey had avoided military service in World War II while Kennedy had distinguished himself as a patrol boat commander in the South Pacific. "I didn't expect it to become so bitter," Humphrey complained. "This is just cheap, low-down, gutter politics." Humphrey would never forgive Roosevelt for the attacks on his character. Neither would he forgive Kennedy's younger brother, Bobby, whom he suspected of prompting Roosevelt to make the charges. For his part, Humphrey responded with sharp criticism of Kennedy's spending. "I can't afford to run throughout this state with a black suitcase and a checkbook." Kennedy was incensed.

Kennedy decisively won West Virginia, 61 to 31 percent. Among the several humiliations of Humphrey's defeat was his poor showing among the state's blacks. One of the nation's most outspoken champions of civil rights, Humphrey lost heavily in areas with the largest concentration of black voters. Like many poor whites, black voters in West Virginia took their signals from county bosses whose support Kennedy had bought. After the votes were counted, Humphrey walked glumly through the rain toward Kennedy's hotel room to congratulate the victor. On his way, he stopped at his own headquarters to read a brief statement: "I am no longer a candidate for the Democratic presidential nomination."

Much later, Kennedy realized that he had been fortunate to have Humphrey's determined opposition in West Virginia. At first, Humphrey's dogged refusal to quit after his Wisconsin defeat had infuriated Kennedy's aides. Some of them even believed (erroneously) that Humphrey was merely a stalking horse for a stop-Kennedy campaign controlled by Johnson, whose hopes hinged on a deadlocked convention. After the Wisconsin primary, Kennedy's staff had pressured Humphrey's friends to urge their man to withdraw from the race, mostly to avoid a divisive confrontation over religion. "Yet it was Kennedy's ordeal and triumph there, on that issue, that overcame the chief obstacle to his nomination," his aide Harris Wofford argued. "If Kennedy had not had Humphrey to fight and beat . . . he might well have been stopped at the convention." Humphrey "transformed the primaries," argued Kennedy aide Richard Goodwin. "If Kennedy had won without significant opposition, his victories would have been meaningless." In heavily Protestant West Virginia, with Humphrey's crucial help, Kennedy closed the book on religion as an issue in presidential politics.

The next morning, reporters crushed around Johnson as he conducted his morning press briefing. He was, said Harry McPherson, "drawn and somber, his words low and almost inaudible." He rejected the notion that the West Virginia victory had sewed up the nomination for Kennedy. Kennedy was very popular, Johnson allowed. "They put a lot into the state, I understand, though I wouldn't know. I haven't followed it closely. I've been trying to get these bills through." That same morning, Humphrey returned to the Senate—dejected, beaten, and exhausted. Hoping to lift his friend's spirits, Johnson called up a minor, noncontroversial bill that Humphrey had sponsored. Although Johnson thought it would take about an hour to pass the measure, he was surprised when Karl Mundt of South Dakota and a group of Republicans rose to oppose it. A taxing eight-hour debate followed. Although the bill eventually passed, Humphrey regarded the opposition as "gratuitous" and remembered the day as one of his "few really unpleasant Senate memories."

Bitter memories of the hard-fought race still plagued Humphrey into the Los Angeles convention. Still stung by the attacks on his World War II draft record, Humphrey made it clear he wanted no spot on Kennedy's ticket, even if prominent liberals and labor leaders were urging Kennedy to choose him. "Frankly, I couldn't see the politics of it," Humphrey explained later. "I couldn't see why Kennedy would want me when we were both Northern liberals."

If not Humphrey, then who?

On June 9, Humphrey's fiercely loyal friend Joseph Rauh attended a fund-raising luncheon in Washington for Democratic Senator George McGovern of South Dakota. Kennedy, now the presumptive Democratic nominee, was a speaker. After lunch, Kennedy invited Rauh to share a taxi back to the Senate. Worried that the *New York Post* was about to publish a story alleging (correctly, as it was later revealed) that Kennedy suffered from Addison's disease, Kennedy asked for Rauh's help. Would you tell your friends at the *Post*, Kennedy asked, that I am completely healthy and able to do the job? Rauh agreed to relay the message.

Now it was Rauh's turn to ask a question. Whom did Kennedy have in mind for the vice presidential spot? Rauh wrote down Kennedy's exact words when he returned to his office: "It will be Hubert Humphrey or another Midwestern liberal."

"Well," Rauh replied with satisfaction, "I guess that relieves my fears about Johnson."

Kennedy was reassuring. "There's no need for fears."

CHAPTER FOURTEEN

Go Get My Long Rifle

BECAUSE OF AN INDIFFERENT, Washington-based campaign, Johnson never stood a chance of winning the nomination. His southern roots and his reputation as a conservative made his candidacy even more impossible. It mattered not that he was responsible for passing two civil rights bills, the first such legislation in the twentieth century. Many influential liberals did not trust him. Their memories of his fealty to Russell's southern bloc were too powerful, and a couple of incremental voting rights bills could not capture their hearts.

In early 1960 Johnson had traveled to New York to enlist socialite Mary Lasker in his campaign to win Eleanor Roosevelt's endorsement. If she supported Johnson, the former first lady would confer enormous legitimacy upon his candidacy and possibly bring along scores of other influential liberals. But when Lasker pleaded Johnson's case ("He's for civil rights"), Roosevelt scoffed. "He's from the South, and it's impossible." Lasker met with the same skepticism when she approached Dorothy Schiff, publisher of the New York *Post*. "It was very hard to convince people that he was a genuine liberal, as I was sure he was," Lasker recalled. Had Johnson spent more time courting liberals like Roosevelt and Schiff, Lasker believed that "he could have convinced them. But he was too busy as majority leader, and the convincing couldn't be done secondhand."

A significant part of Johnson's problem with Democratic liberals, then-Minnesota governor Orville Freeman later concluded, was that he "had simply no time for the people who wanted to talk a good game but never get anything done. He really held them in great repugnance . . . And so, sometimes he would . . . fail to communicate with them even when he had really a very excellent liberal record." Freeman, who later was agriculture secretary under presidents Kennedy and Johnson, admitted that he was among those who had believed that Johnson was too conservative. However, while traveling to the Democratic convention in Los Angeles, he began reviewing Johnson's voting record, and he was "astounded" to learn that Johnson was far more liberal than he had imagined.

Many liberals not only opposed Johnson for president but despaired at the thought that Kennedy might choose him as his running mate. One ADA leader, Robert Nathan, recalled that members of his organization opposed Johnson because he "was not 'all out,' that he was attempting to compromise and take what he could get, so to speak." Johnson would probably have agreed with Nathan's characterization, and that was the problem. The liberals did not want a compromiser; they wanted a *real* liberal. What they could not admit publicly was that Kennedy's *overall* record was barely more liberal than Johnson's.

Much of the problem was Johnson's reluctance to sell himself aggressively. Complained John Connally: "We ran a halfhearted campaign to win the nomination in 1960 because we had a halfhearted candidate . . . He wanted the nomination, but did not want to be tarred with having lost it. He would gamble on the win if he could avoid being responsible for the loss."

Not long after he arrived in Los Angeles, Johnson knew the race was over. At Kennedy's hands, he learned a hard lesson: his strength in the halls of Congress—his ability to forge compromises and build consensus—was no advantage in the presidential arena. Had his congressional colleagues possessed the power to choose the nominee, Johnson would have won hands down. But they did not have such authority; the more liberal Democratic activists did. In their eyes, Johnson was merely a southern wheeler-dealer and protégé of Richard Russell. Too many influential liberals, black and white, simply doubted his loyalty to their causes, particularly civil rights.

Kennedy, meanwhile, enjoyed generous support among blacks and civil rights activists. One advantage was his near-perfect voting record on civil rights during his thirteen years in the Congress. From his 1947 House vote for an anti–poll tax bill to supporting stronger amendments to the 1960 Civil Rights Act, Kennedy had been with the liberals on all but two major votes.

To bolster his standing among black leaders, Kennedy had enlisted Harris Wofford, a Notre Dame Law School instructor, former staff member of the U.S. Civil Rights Commission, and the first white man ever to graduate from Howard University Law School. Though originally hired to advise Kennedy on Asian affairs, Wofford now became the campaign's advisor on civil rights. "We're really in trouble with Negroes," Robert Kennedy confessed to Wofford in May 1960. "We really don't know much about this whole thing. We've been dealing outside the field of the main Negro leadership and have to start from scratch." Despite John Kennedy's uneasy relations with black leaders, his civil rights record was clearly superior to Johnson's—at least in the eyes of liberals and civil rights activists. As for Johnson, most black delegates regarded him as a halfhearted newcomer to the civil rights debate.

There were some notable exceptions to this view. NAACP Secretary Roy Wilkins confessed to Wofford that he regarded Johnson as a better friend of civil rights. "If you ask me who, of all the men in political life, I would trust to do the most about civil rights as president," he said, "it would be Lyndon Johnson." According to Wofford, Wilkins saw in Johnson a quality that eluded most liberals, "a deep, inner determination" about the need for civil rights "that stemmed from his intimate knowledge of the damage racial discrimination was doing not only to the South but to the whole country." Wilkins was correct. Despite all his dispassionate votes in favor of civil rights, Kennedy would never have Johnson's innate feel for the issue.

Yet Kennedy's fortunes with black delegates were not based solely on his Congressional voting record. His inadvertent support of a strong civil rights platform plank played an equally decisive role.

As chairman of the platform committee, Connecticut congressman Chester Bowles—a Kennedy advisor and former ambassador to India—had drafted a forceful and extensive platform plank on civil rights. Bowles first presented the civil rights language to Kennedy in mid-May, several months before the convention. Kennedy reviewed it, but only casually. The day before the final committee vote on the platform, Bowles again presented his draft. This time he gave it to the campaign manager, Kennedy's brother Robert. Like his brother, Robert Kennedy all but ignored the platform's wording.

"What Bowles may not have made clear to any of them," Wofford later suggested, "was that the draft on civil rights was a maximal position." At Bowles's direction, Wofford and two committee aides had composed two planks. The first draft was a liberal's dream come true: It embraced all the recommendations of the U.S. Civil Rights Commission and more. It was, Wofford believed, only a *starting point* from which to compromise. The other plank was "a minimal position, on which there should be no compromise." No one, Wofford said, expected that the maximal plank could win approval "with all the southerners on the committee." The most likely result was a compromise between the two versions.

Although Robert Kennedy had spoken about his general desire for a strong civil rights plank, he had failed to understand Bowles's maximal-minimal strategy. On the morning of the committee vote, the campaign manager stood on a chair and issued last-minute instructions to the Kennedy platform committee delegates. "And remember," he said as the meeting adjourned, "we're all out for the Bowles platform." Said Wofford: "He didn't know our strategy. And so the Kennedy delegates had spread the word that we're for the Bowles [maximal] platform before we knew it was being passed."

Imagine Bowles's surprise when committee members whom he had expected to propose or support weakening amendments either said nothing at all or actively supported the strong civil rights language. Southerners, suddenly outnumbered by the dutiful Kennedy delegates, made only minor changes. The committee adopted the maximal plank in a 66-24 vote.

The platform language that Robert Kennedy inadvertently endorsed was stunning in its commitment to bold action on civil rights. "The time has come," it declared, "to assure equal access for all Americans to all areas of community life, including voting booths, schoolrooms, jobs, housing, and public facilities." The platform pledged that a Democratic administration would use "the full powers" of the 1957 and 1960 civil rights acts to ensure the right to vote; "eliminate literacy tests and payment of poll taxes" as voting requirements; seek desegregation plans in "every school district" covered by the Supreme Court's school desegregation decision; empower the Justice Department to initiate civil suits "to prevent the denial of any civil rights"; make the U.S. Commission on Civil Rights a permanent entity; establish a Fair Employment Practices Commission; "use its full executive powers" to end racial segregation in the federal government; and end discrimination in federal housing programs, "including federally assisted housing."

"It was like a child in a candy store," Joseph Rauh later said. "They just gave me what I wanted, all the way on the plank. It was unbelievable. Then, Kennedy campaigned that way. If anybody looks at the

Kennedy campaign in 1960, you will see he just said any damned civil rights thing you suggested. I mean, it was perfect."

In 1948, and perhaps in 1952, such a liberal platform would have sparked an angry walkout of southern delegates. Not in 1960. Many southerners who supported Johnson knew they would likely hand the election to the Republicans if they abandoned the convention. Instead of walking out, the southern platform committee members—including Spessard Holland, James Eastland, John Stennis, Sam Ervin, and Russell's close friend Charles J. Bloch—filed a minority report. "There is no 'constitutional requirement that racial discrimination be ended in public education,'" the delegates asserted, clinging hopelessly to their threadbare massive resistance philosophy. "All that the courts have said on this subject is that if a state chooses to establish and maintain a public school system, the children in the schools of that system may not be segregated by the standard of race or color. If the people of any state choose to abandon their public schools rather than to integrate them, no court or Congress may compel the submission of any plan of compliance." Arguments like this, their passion and sincerity aside, only demonstrated the philosophical bankruptcy of the states' rights forces. When the platform reached the convention floor, southern opponents were in no mood for a spirited challenge. Although they offered their minority report as a substitute to the civil rights plank, southerners wisely declined a roll-call vote. Delegates quickly rejected the southern substitute by voice vote.

Such were the declining fortunes—and the increasing isolation—of the civil rights opponents. Several weeks later, the Republican National Convention that nominated Vice President Richard Nixon approved an equally forceful civil rights plank. "Although the Democratic-controlled Congress watered them down," the Republican platform stated in a partisan jab at Democrats, "the [Eisenhower] administration's recommendations resulted in significant and effective civil rights legislation in both 1957 and 1960."

Johnson, meanwhile, contended with his resistive supporters and allies, many of whom worried that Kennedy would offer him the vice presidency—and that Johnson might feel obligated to accept. Johnson was uniformly reassuring: He had no interest in becoming Kennedy's running mate.

Shortly before the convention, Georgia's Herman Talmadge encountered Johnson on the Senate floor. "Lyndon," Talmadge said,

"Kennedy's going to be nominated on the first ballot." Talmadge had another prediction. "If Kennedy's as smart as I think he is, he's going to offer you the vice presidency, and I hope you won't accept it."

"Good God, Herman," Johnson replied. "You know I've got no such idea of doing any such foolish thing."

In an appearance on NBC's *Meet the Press* the day before the convention began, Johnson insisted that he would not accept the nomination. "Most vice presidents don't do much," he told *Time*'s John Steele.

Wyoming's Gale McGee said he was so certain Johnson would refuse a spot on Kennedy's ticket that he personally reassured his state's delegation that "this was absolutely impossible, there would be no chance of its happening, that I knew Lyndon Johnson very well and that it should be understood by everybody that he would not and could not take that spot." To a group of southern governors, Johnson insisted he would not accept the nomination if Kennedy offered it.

Johnson's dismissing the idea of an offer from Kennedy made political sense at the time. He was still a candidate for the top spot, hoping for a deadlocked convention. He could hardly expect to remain viable if he announced his willingness to accept the vice presidency. Deeper, perhaps, was his repulsion at the thought he might be asked to take a back seat to the younger, more junior senator from Massachusetts. In casual conversation, Johnson often called Kennedy "the boy." Although he admired his opponent's eloquence and intellect, Johnson—the serious, hardworking master of the Senate—resented Kennedy's cavalier willingness to forsake Senate duties while campaigning for president. "Kennedy had been out on the hustings for three or four years making hay with the delegates and with the party leaders," said South Dakota Senator George McGovern, "while [Johnson] had been in Washington fighting for things like a stronger agricultural program and Medicare program and these things that would give a Democratic candidate appeal." While all the Democratic candidates privately complained that Kennedy was a spoiled child of privilege, *Time*'s Hugh Sidey recalled that Johnson's assessment of Kennedy was "the most vicious" and, he added, "that got quite violent at times."

When the end finally came, it was decisive. Kennedy beat Johnson by a two-to-one margin on the first ballot. "Well, that's it," Johnson remarked after Kennedy won the nomination. "Tomorrow we can do something we really want to do—go to Disneyland, maybe." That evening Sam Rayburn called. It was late and he was ready for bed, but he had some advice for Johnson: Something told him Kennedy would call the next morning to offer the vice presidency. Don't take it, he pleaded. Don't worry, Johnson replied, Kennedy won't offer. If he does, I won't give him an answer until I talk with you.

It was no secret that Kennedy *ought* to want Johnson as his running mate. He was, after all, the runner-up for the nomination. As the Senate majority leader, he was one of the party's most prominent and skilled leaders. In several southern states where Kennedy's Catholicism was a liability—in Texas, for example—Johnson could make the difference. As an astute politician, Kennedy understood that the electoral votes of Johnson's home state might give him the edge in a tight race with Richard Nixon.

On the morning of July 14, Kennedy phoned and invited himself to Johnson's suite. When the nominee arrived around 10:00 a.m., the two men retired to an adjoining room, where Kennedy offered Johnson the vice presidency. According to Johnson, he did not immediately accept Kennedy's offer. However, neither did he reject it, as he had assured so many of his friends he would. He told Kennedy that he needed time to think.

Kennedy's associates offered a different version of the same meeting. According to Robert Kennedy, the nominee did not believe that Johnson would accept the offer. "He thought that he should offer it to him," Kennedy said later, "but he never dreamt that there was a chance in the world that he would accept it." Robert Kennedy said that when his brother returned from his meeting with Johnson, he announced, "You just won't believe it . . . He wants it." Throughout that afternoon, according to Robert Kennedy, campaign advisors debated the advantages and liabilities of a Kennedy-Johnson ticket. Robert Kennedy claimed that when he called on Johnson later in the day, hoping to persuade him to withdraw from consideration, Johnson said tearfully, "I want to be vice president, and if the president will have me, I'll join with him in making a fight for it."*

Robert Kennedy was not the only member of Kennedy's staff opposed to Johnson's selection. Kenneth O'Donnell told Kennedy that Johnson's selection was "the worst mistake you ever made." Arguing

---

*John Seigenthaler, Attorney General Robert Kennedy's administrative assistant, believed that "the bad blood" that later existed between his boss and Johnson "started right there" with Kennedy's attempt to bump Johnson from the ticket (Strober, 16).

that despite Kennedy's promises to "get rid of the old hack machine politicians," his first decision after his nomination was to "go against all the people who supported you" by choosing Johnson. Kennedy reacted angrily to O'Donnell's lecture. "I'm forty-three years old, and I'm . . . not going to die in office," Kennedy said. "So the vice-presidency doesn't mean anything. I'm thinking of something else, the leadership of the Senate. If we win, it will be by a small margin and I won't be able to live with Lyndon Johnson as the leader of a small majority in the Senate. Did it occur to you that if Lyndon becomes the Vice President, I'll have Mike Mansfield [Johnson's whip] as the leader in the Senate, somebody I can trust and depend on?" O'Donnell recalled that after Kennedy's outburst, "I began to soften and see things differently."

With Congress set to return for a postconvention session in August—to consider housing, Medicare and civil rights legislation—Kennedy needed peaceful relations with Johnson and Sam Rayburn. "If Johnson and Rayburn leave here mad at me," Kennedy told O'Donnell, "they'll ruin me in Congress next month. Then I'll be the laughingstock of the country. Nixon will say I haven't any power in my own party, and I'll lose the election before Labor Day. So I've got to make my peace now with Lyndon and Rayburn, and offering Lyndon the vice-presidency, whether he accepts it or not, is one way of keeping him friendly until Congress adjourns."

Meanwhile, in Johnson's camp, few of his friends wanted him to accept. Lady Bird was opposed, as was Rayburn, Bob Kerr, and several Texas congressmen. Texas governor Price Daniel scoffed that a Kennedy-Johnson ticket would "have all its strength in its hind legs." In a phone conversation with Congressman Homer Thornberry, Johnson voiced his dilemma: If he turned down Kennedy and Kennedy lost, "they'll blame me for it, and then my position as majority leader might be in jeopardy." Yet if Kennedy won, "they'll say, 'He won without your help,' and then I'll have some problems." Ultimately, Johnson told Thornberry that "I may owe a responsibility to try to carry this country for the Democratic party."

Johnson may also have realized that his days as the Senate's dominant force were ending, given the number of restive liberals who now chafed under his leadership. Harry McPherson speculated that this realization weighed heavily on Johnson's mind. "Well, hell, I'm tired," McPherson imagined Johnson thinking. "I've been working hard as leader. I've had a heart attack. I think, instead of going through the frustrations and agonies of being on the short end of the stick down at the Hill and being kind of an errand boy for Jack Kennedy, I'll run with him. I'll be vice president and bide my time."

As Johnson mulled his options in a hotel suite full of aides and friends, Oklahoma senator Bob Kerr burst into the room. He was livid. His eyes immediately fixed on Johnson. According to Arkansas congressman Oren Harris, Kerr shouted, "Lyndon, they tell me that Jack Kennedy wants you to be his running mate. If you accept, I'll shoot you right between the eyes!" Tennessee governor Buford Ellington remembered Kerr's first words differently: "I know what's up, and I'll go get my long rifle. It ain't going to happen!" Before Kerr could say more, Sam Rayburn herded him into the bathroom. Now a supporter of Johnson as running mate, Rayburn reasoned with Kerr for several minutes. When the two men emerged, Kerr walked calmly to Johnson and said, "Lyndon, if Jack Kennedy asked you to be his running mate, and if you don't take it, I'll shoot you right between the eyes."

Later that day Johnson phoned Kennedy to inform him of his decision. Minutes later he stepped into the crowded corridor outside his hotel room and stood on a chair. "Jack Kennedy has asked me to serve," he announced. "I accept."

Johnson and Kennedy moved quickly to calm liberals and black leaders who were outraged by Johnson's nomination. "Just give me a chance," Johnson pleaded at a caucus of black delegates near the close of the Los Angeles convention. "I won't let you down. I'll do more for you in four years in the field of civil rights than you've experienced in the last hundred years." Civil rights activists were dubious. James Farmer, head of the Congress of Racial Equality, considered Johnson's nomination "a disaster, because of his southern background and his voting record on civil rights."

"Well, I'm here to tell you that all hell broke loose," Humphrey later said. Liberals such as Joseph Rauh and Michigan governor G. Mennen "Soapy" Williams "were just up in arms," said Humphrey, who was pleased with Johnson's selection. "I sat down and visited with [Johnson] a good long time," Humphrey said, "and then went to work amongst as many of the liberals as I could on his behalf." At the time, Humphrey said, few liberals were willing to voice their public support for Johnson. "All I know," grumbled Rauh about Kennedy's earlier pledge not to pick Johnson, "is that if a political promise is worth a damn, I had a broken promise." On the convention floor when he first heard the news of Johnson's selection, Rauh had grabbed an open microphone. To delegates and a national television audience, he bellowed, "Wherever you are, John F. Kennedy, I beseech you to reconsider." Johnson's selection disappointed Rauh's ADA board members so much that they later refused to endorse the whole ticket. Only Kennedy received the ADA's official sanction. Oklahoma Senator A. S. "Mike" Monroney said that Johnson's ties to the oil industry and his "questionable" support of civil rights conjured up horrific images in liberal minds. "You could almost picture that Simon Legree, at any moment, would walk on stage with his big black snake whip to beat down any civil rights movement."

More practical liberals recognized the brilliance of Kennedy's selection. "The Democrats never carried Texas," observed Connecticut governor Abraham Ribicoff. "If Texas did not go for the Democrats, they could not win the presidency. Johnson was the only one who could bring him something." Orville Freeman, a last-minute convert to Johnson's camp, argued "very strongly" with his liberal friends "that Lyndon Johnson had an excellent liberal record, and that basically he was a populist in his political and economic and social orientation." In what turned out to be a remarkably prescient assessment, the *New Republic* insisted that "by changing Lyndon Johnson from a Texas to a national politician, Kennedy frees him to take more liberal positions if, as Johnson's old friends in Washington have always vowed, those are the true beliefs of the inner man."

Voices of conservative dissent were heard as well. Influential columnist and newspaper editor James J. Kilpatrick, a staunch defender of the Old South, called Johnson a "Counterfeit Confederate" and wrote that Kennedy had "blundered" by putting him on the ticket. "If Mr. Kennedy sweeps the South, it will not be because of Lyndon, but in spite of him; for the Senator from Texas, however he may be respected on the Senate floor, is neither liked nor admired below the Potomac. In the South of 1960 as in the South of 1870, a carpetbagger may be bad, but a scalawag is worse." Johnson, Kilpatrick charged, had "turned his back upon the South."

Johnson clearly understood that his political future hinged on whether he could carry the South for Kennedy. One southern conservative in particular was on his mind in the days following the convention. Would Russell, who had not attended the convention and had openly worried about the leftward drift of his party, lend his considerable influence to a liberal ticket on which Johnson occupied the number-two spot?

Through his nephew Bobby, a Georgia delegate, Russell had advised Johnson to reject Kennedy's offer. He thought it unwise for Johnson to relinquish his majority leader's post for the ceremonial and powerless job of vice president. Russell also worried that Johnson's position on the ticket would amount to an endorsement of the liberal platform that he regarded as "a mess of unconstitutional vote bait."

For his part, Johnson believed that Russell's endorsement was crucial to the ticket's chances in the South. At a "unity meeting" of southern governors called at his behest by Tennessee's Buford Ellington, Johnson spotted Robert Troutman, a Georgia-born lawyer who was a friend to both Kennedy and Russell. Later that evening, Johnson pulled Troutman aside. He was "very depressed," said Troutman, that southern leaders had not yet endorsed the Democratic ticket. Please go to Russell and Herman Talmadge, Johnson implored, and remind them that Kennedy had chosen him "with the expectation" that he could deliver the South for Kennedy. Johnson, said Troutman, "felt that [Russell and Talmadge] were almost obligated" to publicly support him. In a rambling and emotional monologue, Johnson described the long and tangled history of his friendship with Russell.

Troutman did as Johnson asked. Shortly after the Nashville meeting, he drove to Russell's Winder home. To Russell's "amusement," he recounted the entire conversation with Johnson. Yet Russell remained "very bitterly" opposed to Johnson's acceptance of Kennedy's offer and told Troutman that he had already "done a great deal to show his friendship in times past." Troutman left with the distinct feeling that Russell "was gonna sit it out."

Russell indeed planned to watch the 1960 presidential race from the sidelines. He planned to lend Johnson two of his aides but nothing more. Although he personally liked Kennedy, Russell vehemently opposed the Democratic platform that promised to "implement these vicious [civil rights] provisions." On September 24 Russell issued a perfunctory and unenthusiastic statement: "On November 8, I shall vote the straight

Democratic ticket as I have always done." Several weeks later, he left for a three-week inspection of U.S. military bases in Europe.

Johnson, meanwhile, embarked on an old-fashioned whistle-stop tour of the South aimed at persuading the region's predominately Protestant voters to give a Catholic candidate a chance. At stop after stop through eight states over five days, Johnson recounted Kennedy's heroic exploits as commander of PT-109 during World War II: "When he was savin' those American boys that was in his crew, they didn't ask what church he belonged to."

Throughout the train trip, Johnson conveniently dispensed with his former identification as a southwesterner. On the LBJ Victory Special, Johnson was all southern. His drawl was deeper, and he laced his speeches with folksy adages. He was, he often noted, "the grandson of a Confederate soldier."

He met the issue of civil rights honestly and directly—almost. He rarely waited until questioned about the issue, broaching the subject himself in every major speech. "I say to you," he declared in numerous speeches, "we will protect the constitutional rights of every living American, regardless of race, religion, or region." Johnson's only acknowledgment of southern fears about civil rights was a promise that he and Kennedy would single out no "region"—meaning the South—for civil rights enforcement. In other speeches, Johnson replaced the word *region* with "where he lives" or "no matter . . . what section of the country he comes from." But the message was always the same: Jack Kennedy and the Democratic party would *protect* or *guarantee* the civil rights of every American. Yet Johnson made no mention of his and Kennedy's explicit endorsement of a platform that pledged aggressive action to ensure desegregation of schools and federal housing and employment.

Johnson's southern tour was a great success. As he attracted hundreds and then thousands of supporters at nearly every stop, state and local Democratic leaders began shedding their reluctance to support the ticket. In Florida the Democratic nominee for governor declared Johnson "immensely qualified." Governors Ernest Hollings of South Carolina and John Patterson of Alabama warmly embraced Johnson's candidacy, as did senators Talmadge of Georgia and Eastland of Mississippi. By the time Johnson's train reached its final stop in New Orleans, an impressive array of Democratic officials was waiting, ready to present Johnson their enthusiastic endorsements. The group included

Louisiana senators Russell Long and Allen Ellender and New Orleans Mayor deLesseps Morrison.

Besides helping blunt the issue of Kennedy's religion in the heavily Protestant Bible Belt, Johnson had also reassured many nervous southern Democrats that a Kennedy administration would not take a radical approach to civil rights. Yet it was just that question—how aggressively would Kennedy push for action on civil rights?—that plagued liberals and conservatives alike. Shortly after the convention, Johnson had advised Kennedy to be careful. To coax nervous southern states back into the Democratic column, Kennedy must play the issue with finesse. Kennedy was not so sure. While he wanted to avoid needlessly provoking white southerners, he understood that the growing black vote in the North and South would be crucial to his election. Kennedy, however, was unsure how to court black voters. The strong Democratic platform would help, but the Republican platform was just as forceful. A well-publicized meeting with prominent civil rights leader Martin Luther King, Jr., might help Kennedy prove his commitment to civil rights. However, the two men had been unable to agree on the time and place.*

Actually, many voters found it almost impossible to discern differences in the two parties' civil rights policies. A Republican president had proposed the civil rights acts of 1957 and 1960, but Democrats—minus their southern bloc—were the ones who provided the congressional leadership and the crucial votes to ensure their passage.

In the end, it was Martin Luther King's arrest in October—and Kennedy's inadvertent reaction to it—that would help transform the racial dynamics of presidential politics for the rest of the century.

On October 19 King joined black students in a peaceful protest at the all-white lunch counter of an Atlanta department store. Refused service, King and the students refused to leave and were arrested. Although police eventually released the students, King had more serious legal problems. In May he had been issued tickets for two minor traffic violations. He paid the $25 fine, but the infractions carried a one-year probationary period. During that time, if King violated any federal or

---

*Kennedy and King had met for the first time in June, before the Democratic convention. King later said that he detected in Kennedy "a long[-time] intellectual commitment" to civil rights. But, he said, Kennedy "didn't quite have the emotional commitment. He had not really been involved enough in and with the problem. He didn't have—he didn't know too many Negroes personally" (King OH, JFKL).

state law, he was subject to more serious charges. A segregationist judge in Atlanta was unmoved by King's protests that he had not known about the probation. He sentenced King to four months in prison.

In Washington, officials of Eisenhower's Justice Department briefly considered court action to rescue King. Instead Deputy Attorney General Lawrence Walsh merely drafted a sympathetic statement that Eisenhower declined to use. Richard Nixon's advisors also considered urging their candidate to express concern for King and his wife but concluded that this might alienate white voters.

In Washington, Harris Wofford, a friend of King, had monitored the Atlanta situation for Kennedy's campaign. He urged his Atlanta friends to get King out of jail. Already Wofford's interest in the case had drawn his candidate into the controversy—although Kennedy had not personally lifted a finger for King. When Atlanta's progressive mayor, William Hartsfield, engineered the release of the student protesters, he gave Kennedy the credit. Wire services carried Hartsfield's statement nationwide.

When Wofford learned of Hartsfield's statement, he protested to Atlanta lawyer Morris Abram: "But Kennedy knows nothing about my call. I told you I was acting on my own." Hartsfield himself tried to comfort Wofford, admitting that he "ran with the ball farther than you expected." But the mayor insisted that he was "giving [Kennedy] the election on a silver platter, so don't pull the rug out from under me." Scrambling to contain the controversy, Kennedy's campaign issued a brief statement claiming that the candidate had merely ordered "an inquiry" to obtain "the facts on that situation and a report on what properly should be done."

Now that King faced a four-month prison term, Wofford worried that Kennedy risked looking ambivalent and ineffective. He urged a stronger statement to increase pressure on Georgia authorities to release their prominent prisoner. Kennedy's Georgia leaders were much more cautious. Any further intervention by the Democratic candidate, they advised, might cost them Georgia and several other southern states. Finally Governor Ernest Vandiver, husband of one of Russell's nieces, promised to get "the son of a bitch" out of jail if Kennedy made no more public statements.

Three days after the students' release, as King languished in jail, a frantic Coretta King phoned Wofford. Frustrated that he could not reveal the governor's promise and that Kennedy "could not make any public comment on the case," Wofford only informed Mrs. King that he was "doing everything possible." After the call, Wofford confessed his frustration to Louis Martin, a black former newspaper publisher.

"Who cares about public statements?" Wofford complained. "What Kennedy ought to do is something direct and personal, like picking up the telephone and calling Coretta. Just giving his sympathy, but doing it himself."

"That's it, that's it!" Martin said. "That would be perfect."

That night the situation in Georgia worsened. Deputies awakened King abruptly at about 3:30 a.m., slapped handcuffs and leg irons on him, shoved him into the back of a car, and embarked on a harrowing two-hundred-mile trip to the Georgia state prison in Reidsville. When Wofford found out the next morning, he tracked down his close friend Sargent Shriver, Kennedy's brother-in-law and Illinois campaign manager. As luck would have it, Kennedy was in Chicago that morning. Wofford made his proposal: Kennedy should phone Mrs. King and express concern for her husband's safety. Shriver agreed and left immediately for Kennedy's hotel room. When he arrived, several other aides were in the room. One by one, they left. Finally Shriver and Kennedy were alone. "It was miraculous," he recalled, "because I had not wanted to bring up the idea of calling Mrs. King with the others there, because I knew it would precipitate a debate about the call's pros and cons."

Shriver broached the subject. "Jack, I have an idea that might help you in the campaign: Mrs. Martin Luther King is sitting down there in Atlanta, and she is terribly worried about what is going to happen to her husband. I have her home telephone number; I suggest that you pick up the phone, say hello, and tell her you hope that everything works out well."

Kennedy pondered Shriver's suggestion for about fifteen seconds. "That's a good idea," he said. "Can you get her on the phone?" Shriver placed the call and handed the phone to Kennedy, who spoke with Mrs. King for no more than three minutes. "I want to express to you my concern about your husband," he said. "I know this must be very hard for you. I understand you are expecting a baby, and I just wanted you to know that I was thinking about you and Dr. King. If there is anything I can do to help, please feel free to call on me." Before Shriver could report to Wofford, Coretta King called. "She was very moved and grateful," Wofford recalled. By day's end, she had given the story to the *New York Times*.

When he learned of the call, Robert Kennedy was furious. Shriver, Martin, and Wofford all received severe tongue-lashings. "You bomb-throwers have lost the whole campaign," Kennedy bitterly told Shriver. However, when he learned the circumstances of King's imprisonment, Kennedy was incredulous. "How could they do that?" he asked Louis Martin. "Who's the judge? You can't deny bail on a misdemeanor." By day's end—partly out of outrage, but also hoping to deflect attention away from his brother's phone call—Kennedy phoned the Georgia judge to urge King's release. "I called him," he later told Wofford and another aide, "because it made me so damned angry to think of that bastard sentencing a citizen to four months of hard labor for a minor traffic offense and screwing up my brother's campaign and making our country look ridiculous before the world." Shortly after Kennedy's call, the judge released King on $2,000 bond.

King told reporters he was "deeply indebted to Senator Kennedy." Although he stopped short of endorsing the Democratic candidate, King later praised Kennedy for having "moral courage of a high order." At a joyful gathering that night at King's Ebenezer Baptist Church, King's father, Reverend Martin Luther King, Sr., was effusive in his praise of Kennedy. "Jack Kennedy has the moral courage to stand up for what he knows is right." Elated by his son's release and the role the Kennedy brothers had played in it, "Daddy" King—a Republican—later announced he would vote for Kennedy, even though he was a Catholic. "I had expected to vote against Senator Kennedy because of his religion," Daddy King said in a statement. "But now he can be my president, Catholic or whatever he is. It took courage to call my daughter-in-law at a time like this. He has the moral courage to stand up for what he knew is right. I've got all my votes and I've got a suitcase and I'm going to take them up there and dump them in his lap."

With ten days left before the election, Wofford and Martin moved quickly to capitalize on the unexpected turn of events. Kennedy's intervention would likely generate some white backlash in the South, yet even Johnson was supportive. He told Kennedy, "Well, we'll sweat it out—but you'll have the privilege of knowing that you did the right thing." Because of the feared losses among southern whites, it was imperative to offset those votes with a large black turnout. In a day's time, Martin and Wofford found a way to spread the word of Kennedy's crucial intercession. They produced a small pamphlet with statements about Kennedy by the three Kings—Martin, Coretta, and Daddy

King—and other civil rights leaders. Martin and Wofford headlined it, "'NO COMMENT' NIXON VERSUS A CANDIDATE WITH A HEART, SENATOR KENNEDY: THE CASE OF MARTIN LUTHER KING." In the days before the election, Kennedy's black supporters distributed hundreds of thousands of the pamphlets in black churches and neighborhoods all over the country.

On October 30 Wofford met Kennedy at Washington National Airport as the candidate prepared to leave town on a final preelection campaign swing. He hoped that Kennedy would endorse a report by the Conference on Constitutional Rights, which the campaign had sponsored several weeks earlier. Kennedy read the detailed report carefully. It recommended action, Wofford said, in "practically every area of civil rights." Kennedy looked Wofford in the eye. "Tell me honestly whether you think I need to sign and release this today in order to get elected a week from Tuesday. Or, do you mainly want me to do it to go on record?" Wofford reluctantly admitted to Kennedy that the report would do little to win new votes.

"Then we can wait, and release it when I'm elected," he said. "You can consider me on record—with you."

As the two men walked toward the campaign plane, Kennedy turned to Wofford. "Did you see what Martin's father said?" Kennedy asked. It was the only time ever Wofford heard Kennedy discuss the King episode. "He was going to vote against me because I was Catholic, but since I called his daughter-in-law, he will vote for me. That was a hell of a bigoted statement, wasn't it? Imagine Martin Luther King having a bigot for a father!"

Then Kennedy grinned and added, "Well, we all have fathers, don't we?"

Back in Texas, Johnson was having a rough time. Granted, he had performed admirably across the South and had fortified Democratic support in several crucial states. Outside the South, especially in southern California, he had comported himself well. Even liberal leaders, impressed with Johnson's spirited attacks on Nixon and Eisenhower, were reassessing their opposition to his nomination.

But in Texas he was in trouble. The state was still not secure for Kennedy. Political experts polled by *Time* and *Newsweek* gave Nixon the edge in the competition for the state's twenty-four electoral votes.

If Johnson could not deliver Texas—the main reason for his selection —Nixon's election might not be the only consequence. Losing Texas would do irreparable harm to Johnson's own political fortunes. Although the state legislature had passed legislation allowing him to run for reelection to the Senate *and* for vice president, Johnson could ill afford to return to Washington as a majority leader unable to deliver his own state. With one week to go, Johnson returned to Texas, where he would remain until election day.

On his way to a November 4 rally in Dallas, the state's conservative Republican stronghold, Johnson got the break his Texas campaign desperately needed. As he and Lady Bird walked across a downtown street toward the Adolphus Hotel, an angry mob of Republican activists rushed them. Bruce Alger, the lone Republican congressman from Texas, led the unruly crowd and waved a placard with a portrayal of Johnson carrying a carpetbag and the message "He Sold Out to Yankee Socialists." As Johnson and Lady Bird tried to cross the street, a woman rushed forward, snatched Lady Bird's gloves from her hands, and threw them in the gutter. Furious at the harassment, Johnson immediately recognized the political implications of the incident. Aware that reporters would record the next few ugly moments and broadcast them throughout the country, Johnson asked his police escort to stand back. "If the time has come when I can't walk through the lobby of a hotel in Dallas with my lady without a police escort," he said, "I want to know it."

As Johnson and Lady Bird went through the hotel doors, they encountered another screaming mob. Someone hit Lady Bird over the head with a picket sign. Others spit at them. Lady Bird was frightened, but she was also angry. She began to answer one young woman. But Johnson stopped her, placed his hand over her mouth, and kept moving forward.

For thirty minutes the Johnsons inched their way through the mob. Johnson and Lady Bird could have easily walked through the lobby in five minutes. As D. B. Hardeman noted, Johnson took his time because he knew that "it was all being recorded and photographed for television and radio and the newspapers, and he knew it and played it for all it was worth."

The following morning, one Georgia newspaper reader who learned about the ugly incident was Richard Russell, just back from his tour of military bases in Europe. He was horrified, but not at how the crowd had assaulted Lyndon. It was Lady Bird—his beloved Lady Bird—for whom he really cared. For weeks Johnson had been trying, with absolutely no success, to lure Russell out on the campaign trail. Now, infuriated at Lady Bird's humiliation and more sympathetic to Johnson's desperate pleas, Russell relented. Soon came the wire from Georgia: Russell would join Johnson for the last two days of the campaign. The next morning, Russell arrived in Houston. He later confessed to a friend that when Johnson called him the third time "and said that he was really in trouble and I could help, I stopped weighing issues and went out." Discarding his vehement opposition to the Democratic party platform, Russell plunged into the campaign with a vigorous endorsement of the Democratic ticket. At a Houston rally attended by more than 50,000 supporters, Russell introduced Johnson enthusiastically. "This one man," he said, "in the last six years as Senate majority leader has had more experience in government than those other two (Nixon and running mate Henry Cabot Lodge) have had in all their lives."

On November 8, Kennedy was elected president by the razor-thin margin of 118,574 votes out of 68.3 million cast. More decisive was the Electoral College, where Kennedy defeated Nixon 303 to 219. In Texas, where more than two million voters went to the polls, Kennedy won by a margin of just 46,233 votes. It was the first time Texas had gone Democratic since 1948. Johnson won two elections that day, also beating Republican nominee John Tower by 364,000 votes to win reelection to his Senate seat.

Johnson's presence on the ticket, and his vigorous campaigning across the South, were at least partly responsible for an impressive string of southern victories. Seven former Confederate states fell to the Democrats: Alabama, Arkansas, Georgia, Louisiana, North and South Carolina, and Texas. The rest of the South went to Nixon—except for Mississippi, whose voters gave a plurality to a segregationist candidate. Without Johnson as his running mate, said Mississippi's James Eastland, "Kennedy would not have carried any Southern state." House Republican leader Charles Halleck put it bluntly: "I don't think Jack Kennedy could have been elected if he hadn't had Lyndon Johnson with him."

Difficult to imagine was a Kennedy victory without a southerner on the ticket. More difficult to imagine was anyone whom southerners would have found more acceptable than Johnson—progressive enough to appease disgruntled liberals and blacks yet conservative enough to calm uneasy white Democrats. In retrospect, Kennedy's controversial decision seemed brilliant.

Now that Kennedy had won, southerners worried. What would Kennedy do on civil rights given the activist agenda outlined in the party's platform? "I am afraid that I go too much on personalities," Russell confessed to a friend several days after the election. His last-minute support for the Democratic ticket may have been hasty, but Russell could not resist Johnson's pleadings. "On reflection," he rationalized, "I guess it is for the best for I am confident that [Johnson] will be a power in the next administration. If he has any sense of loyalty (and I am sure that he does), he and Kennedy both will appreciate the fact that they would have been signally defeated without the South."

In the end, two Georgians had helped Kennedy and Johnson considerably—Martin Luther King by going to jail, and Russell by going to Texas. How would the new president and vice president express their gratitude? For the moment, no one was certain.

CHAPTER FIFTEEN

How Did We Let This Happen?

FROM THE MOMENT HE BECAME vice president, Lyndon Johnson was a miserable man. "Lyndon looked as if he'd lost his last friend on earth," recalled journalist Margaret Mayer. "Every time I came into John Kennedy's presence," Johnson later said, "I felt like a goddamn raven hovering over his shoulder . . . I detested every minute of it."

Partly to preserve some semblance of his former power and importance, Johnson was reluctant to relinquish his role as Senate potentate to Montana's Mike Mansfield, the Democratic whip who was about to replace him as majority leader. Even the trappings of his former office were impossible to surrender. Normally Mansfield would have occupied the majority leader's roomy and lavishly decorated suite of offices in the Capitol, derisively known around the Senate as the "Taj Mahal." But Johnson retained the space, leaving Mansfield with an office only half the size of Johnson's.

When Johnson confessed to Bobby Baker that he and Mansfield had agreed that Johnson would become chairman of the Senate Democratic Caucus—and therefore its presiding officer—Baker was "both astonished and horrified." Johnson had not fully understood how many of his colleagues yearned to be free from the constraints of his oppressive rule. "Under Johnson, it was like a Greek tragedy," said Howard Shuman, Paul Douglas's longtime aide. "Nothing went on in the Senate that hadn't happened off the floor beforehand." Even Johnson's former whip, Florida's George Smathers, acknowledged the obvious: "Johnson had just thwarted the democratic concept of the Senate, because he was so powerful and worked so hard at it." To Harry McPherson, Johnson had been the right man for the times. But times changed. "Johnson was the ideal opposition leader," McPherson explained. "Mansfield would be the perfect team player." Many Democrats, especially the liberals, were thrilled to be playing for a new coach.

Mansfield was very different from Johnson in almost every way. A quiet, passive man, he was content to allow legislation to take its course. To Mansfield the leadership was "a moral post," said George Reedy. His philosophy, according to Gerald Siegel, was "It's my role as leader to make it possible for every senator to do what he wants." Said Rein Vander Zee, an aide to Hubert Humphrey:

> The way Mansfield read the Johnson years was that the committee chairmen were rankling somewhat, they didn't particularly like to be steamrollered. They didn't like to have their staff people [forced] to move stuff out of committee when they weren't ready . . . Mansfield thought it would be a good idea for him to go back to where the old committee chairmen were almost autonomous in their domain. So he reextended them that type of courtesy—if that's the proper word. And I guess they *loved* it!

Unlike Johnson, Mansfield rarely pressured his colleagues for their votes. "He was perfectly willing to explain a bill," recalled J. William Fulbright of Arkansas, "but he very rarely asked you, 'Say, would you please vote for a certain bill?' " Said Herman Talmadge of Georgia: "Mansfield was a moderator and not a leader."

Mansfield was not only reluctant to lead but reluctant to become the leader at all. Booth Mooney, a former Johnson staffer, encountered the leader-apparent after the 1960 Democratic National Convention. "Well, senator," Mooney said jovially, "I guess you're going to be the majority leader." Tugging on his trademark pipe for a moment, Mansfield finally declared woefully, "I don't *want* to be majority leader."

On January 3, 1961, less than three weeks before Johnson would be sworn in as vice president, Senate Democrats met to choose their new leaders. Mansfield made his proposal, one that would effectively make the majority leader a deputy to the vice president of the United States. For a moment, utter silence reigned. Finally Albert Gore spoke up. He was angry. "We might as well ask Jack [Kennedy] to come back up and take *his* turn at presiding." Another Johnson critic, Joseph Clark, also objected. At first red with embarrassment, Johnson's face turned ashen. He was astonished. Old cronies like Willis Robertson of Virginia, Olin Johnston of South Carolina, and Clinton Anderson of New Mexico rose to speak against Mansfield's proposal. They argued that the arrangement would violate the Constitution's separation of powers.

Although most senators said nothing, the smattering of vehement opposition threatened to embarrass Mansfield just minutes into his term as majority leader. Worried about a larger revolt, he threatened to resign unless the caucus upheld him. The Democrats grudgingly approved his motion, 46-17, but their message was clear: Despite his "victory," Johnson knew the arrangement could not work. As Bobby Baker said, "They were inviting [Johnson] out of their Senate inner circle." Although the Constitution made him the Senate's president, Johnson's legislative powers had vanished. "He was no longer the majority leader," explained William Proxmire, "and there was no way he could discipline anybody. And I think it took a little while for people to really appreciate and understand that, they were so used to giving Johnson what he wanted."

As he angrily left the meeting, Johnson reportedly snarled, "I now know the difference between a caucus and a cactus. In a cactus all the pricks are on the outside."

Absent Johnson's smothering influence, the Senate blossomed in a springtime of openness, freedom, and fresh air.

About a month after the inauguration, Harry McPherson saw the new vice president strolling through the Democratic cloakroom. In the past, McPherson recalled, Johnson's mere presence had released "an electric charge" into the air. Lounging senators straightened up. Conversation ended. All eyes fixed on Johnson. But now Johnson was vice president, occupying a ceremonial and largely powerless office. As he entered the room, McPherson noticed that "nothing happened." No one stood up. Conversations continued. His former colleagues, McPherson said, still found their former leader "quite acceptable, but he was no longer a member of the Club. It was a very subtle thing, but you could feel it."

The White House staff greeted Johnson with even greater indifference. Given oversight of the U.S. space program and appointed by Kennedy to chair the President's Committee on Equal Employment Opportunity, Johnson found little else of substance to consume his time and his enormous energies. He was uncomfortable around the urbane, well-educated hotshots on Kennedy's staff, and their disrespectful practice of calling him "Lyndon" offended Johnson. Most of Kennedy's aides and advisors—especially Attorney General Robert Kennedy—scorned the vice president. Johnson returned their scorn in kind. "His complaints against Bobby Kennedy," said Bobby Baker, "were frequent and may have bordered on the paranoiac." Johnson's friend William S. White of the *New York Times* recalled that "Kennedy's people fell into two sets. There were those who were associated with Bob Kennedy who had a violent and irrational dislike of Johnson, always tried to cut him down, just to cut him down. Then, there was another set of Kennedy people, I think, who received him with more objectivity, but who had a belief that Johnson was bad for Kennedy, that he was associated with the South and oil and what not."

Despite the humiliation and isolation of his new job, Johnson remained exceedingly deferential to Kennedy in public. Conscious of the "provocations" at the hands of Robert Kennedy and others, James Rowe, for one, marveled at Johnson's restraint. "I thought his conduct was exemplary all through that period." White found Johnson "almost excessively correct" around Kennedy. "He would not get into a picture with the president unless he was asked by the president. He would not go near the White House socially on any occasion unless he was asked."

Although Kennedy publicly portrayed his relationship with Johnson as intimate, the two men had at best an uneasy, distant arrangement. "They abided each other," said George Smathers, a friend to both men, "but they didn't like each other, really." Nonetheless, Kennedy always treated Johnson with respect and even reprimanded staff members who failed to do the same. "He understood Lyndon like the back of his hand," said Kennedy's appointments secretary, Kenneth O'Donnell. "[Johnson] was an insecure fellow and as long as you treated him right, he was all right."

Yet Kennedy rarely discussed major decisions with his vice president, and Johnson almost never volunteered his opinion or advice unless Kennedy asked. "The president wanted to consult him," maintained Assistant Attorney General Burke Marshall, head of the Justice Department's civil rights division. "He just had a hard time getting the vice president to [speak up]. The vice president was very reluctant to tell the president what to do." At meetings with the cabinet or congressional leaders, Johnson sat silent and desultory. When asked his opinion, he was often a mumbling, muted shell of his former self. Rowland Evans and Robert Novak speculated that Robert Kennedy and other younger administration officials "misinterpreted" Johnson's silence during White House meetings "as a sign of inability to cope with the great problems of the day." Johnson's towering accomplishments as majority leader, they noted, were either unknown, forgotten, or dismissed. Johnson therefore "began to be marked down in a grossly unfair and wildly uncorrect appraisal as a lightweight." Johnson knew that he had become the butt of jokes around Washington. "Whatever happened to Lyndon?" was a common question. Such derision is standard fare for vice presidents. For someone of Johnson's enormous ego and hypersensitivity, however, the humiliation was almost unbearable. Johnson fell into a deep and conspicuous funk.

Perhaps what made Johnson most unhappy was Kennedy's inexplicable refusal to use him as an administration lobbyist on Capitol Hill. As *Wall Street Journal* reporter Allen L. Otten noted in a July 1961 story, "Rather than applying his well-known legislative skill to pilot President Kennedy's program through Congress, [Johnson] is operating mainly as part of the policy-making apparatus within the executive branch." Noting that "at least a half-dozen" cabinet and staff members were more influential than Johnson, Otten observed that Johnson had "largely abandoned" the role of a legislative strategist "that everyone expected [him] to continue in the vice presidency." Perhaps Kennedy understood better than Johnson how the vice president's intimate involvement in legislative affairs would have ruffled the feathers of some congressional leaders. As one senator confided to Otten, "The Senate is a club and there's a thick curtain between active members and retired members."

No matter the reason, Johnson's reaction to his sudden estrangement from the legislative process troubled Kennedy. "I cannot stand Johnson's long, damn face," Kennedy complained to George Smathers one day in 1960. "He just comes in, sits at the cabinet meetings with his face all screwed up, never says anything. He looks so sad." To *New York Times* columnist Arthur Krock, Kennedy confided, "I don't know what to do with Lyndon. I've got to keep him happy somehow. My big job is to keep Lyndon happy." At Smathers's suggestion, Kennedy eagerly agreed to send Johnson on a foreign trip so that, as Smathers said, "he can get all of the fanfare and all of the attention and all of the smoke-blowing will be directed at him, build up his ego again, let him have a great time." Most of Johnson's friends, while sympathetic, were not surprised by Johnson's despondency. Explained columnist Drew Pearson, "You transpose a man from [majority leader] to the job of Vice President, where he has only one official duty, presiding over the Senate, which is very boring, and another unofficial duty, waiting for the President to die, which is disagreeable, and you have normally an unhappy man."

While Johnson languished in his sudden obscurity, Humphrey flourished in newfound prominence.

In December 1960 Humphrey went to New York to persuade Adlai Stevenson to become Kennedy's ambassador to the United Nations. At the apartment of former Connecticut senator William Benton, Humphrey beseeched Stevenson—who wanted to be Secretary of State—to accept Kennedy's offer. "Adlai, you've got to take it, you don't have any choice," Humphrey argued. "The president has asked you to do something and you may be responsible for this man's election. What makes you think that you can turn it down?" As the three men conferred, Johnson phoned Humphrey with a proposal. He urged him to return to Washington immediately to discuss how Johnson and Mansfield, with Kennedy's blessing, might engineer Humphrey's election as Democratic whip.

After Johnson's call, it was Humphrey's turn to vacillate. Stevenson and Benton both advised him to decline Johnson's offer, arguing that "if you take that job of majority whip, you're not going to be free, you can't speak out as you'd like, call the shots. This, in a very real sense, will limit your possibilities of ever becoming president." But after an hour of debate, Humphrey concluded that he should accept the whip position for the same reason he had urged Stevenson to become U.N. ambassador: "I think that I've got the same obligation that I told you that you have. If they want me for majority whip, I'm going to be majority whip. We've got to make this administration the best one that we can." To his liberal friends, Humphrey offered a simple explanation: "I have made mud pies and built dream houses long enough. Now I want to do something."

With Johnson's generous assistance, Humphrey was elected Democratic whip on January 3, 1961. Now, suddenly, their roles were reversed. Humphrey was in; Johnson was out. A fiery, liberal outsider, once scorned and ostracized by the Senate Club, Humphrey now stood near the pinnacle of that body's power and influence. He was now the Senate's number-two Democrat and a leading member of his party's steering and policy committees. Furthermore, his leadership role and his twelve years of seniority afforded him a new degree of legislative preeminence on three of the Senate's most important committees:

Foreign Relations, Agriculture, and Appropriations. As a top congressional leader, he would now be an advisor and lieutenant to the president. He would meet with Kennedy often and would be a participant in the Wednesday morning congressional leadership meetings. "I would now be having regular policy discussions, the privilege of sitting with the man who, more than anyone else, shapes the world today," Humphrey explained at the time. "It was a chance to speak my mind in his presence, and it was a chance no man could turn aside."

Humphrey won the whip job for several reasons. Of all the senior liberals, he was the most pragmatic, the person most able and willing to trim his sails to achieve legislative victories for the new president. Because of his powers of persuasion, he could occasionally persuade even the more dogmatic liberals to acquiesce to their president's wishes. In addition, despite his liberal credentials on civil rights, Humphrey enjoyed cordial relations with almost every member of the Senate. His natural "warmth and his human qualities," said Harry McPherson, even appealed to conservatives like Russell and Kerr. "It would be impossible for any of those people, being men of quality themselves, to remain cold to Hubert Humphrey." Humphrey actually *cared* about his colleagues. Said his longtime aide David Gartner:

> He would spend long, long hours in the Senate on the floor talking to his colleagues, not necessarily about the legislation at hand or what the president wanted or what Humphrey wanted or the administration wanted, but he took a very deep interest in each of his colleagues, in their family life, in the things that they themselves wanted on a legislative basis . . . Whenever Humphrey would go to somebody really wanting something, he really had a very definite advantage because he was in a position, not only to be nice and decent to them, which he always was anyway, but to do things for them that they wanted. So they would be inclined to go along with Humphrey unless they felt extremely strong about a matter.

Nothing, however, made Humphrey an effective leader in the Senate more than Mansfield's virtual abdication of the traditional leadership role of majority leader. "He tried to be effective without being oppressive," Humphrey said, diplomatically, of Mansfield. Because Mansfield was so passive, so unwilling to twist arms or lead his colleagues in the traditional manner of Johnson, or even Rayburn and Dirksen, the duty fell to Humphrey. He viewed his job not simply "as a creature of the Senate," but "as a sometime-extension of the administration." As one liberal Democratic senator said in April 1961, "Mike Mansfield is a fine, sweet, lovable guy, but when you want something done in the Senate nowadays, you go to Hubert."

Humphrey attacked the job with typical enthusiasm and good humor. Only three months after becoming the whip, his tally of legislative accomplishments included a minimum wage increase, an aid to education bill, and a compromise on Kennedy's farm program. By year's end, Kennedy adopted and Congress enacted a pet project of Humphrey's— the Peace Corps. Just as impressive was the skillful way Humphrey persuaded liberals to drop their opposition to the appointment of John Connally, Johnson's old friend, as secretary of the navy. He also kept southern conservatives from thwarting the confirmation of a black man, Robert Weaver, as administrator of the Housing and Home Finance Administration. In time, in the words of one *New York Times* reporter, Kennedy had "no more trusted ally on Capitol Hill." Dismissing the bitterness of their 1960 primary contests, Kennedy and Humphrey developed a warm and easy friendship. "It was kind of a fun relationship," Humphrey's aide, David Gartner, recalled. "They deeply respected each other, but on the other hand they just got along well." Humphrey was one of the few advisors who regularly teased the president.

One illustration of Humphrey's usefulness to the White House— and his willingness to forge a compromise when necessary—is found in his handling of Kennedy's legislation to provide aid to economically depressed areas. Although President Eisenhower had vetoed the bill twice, the legislation took on new life under Kennedy. Paul Douglas introduced the bill early in the 1961 session. But conservatives soon threw up objections over the legislation's funding mechanism—directly through Treasury instead of the yearly appropriations process. When Kennedy caved in to the conservative objections, Douglas's resolve stiffened. He refused to support the compromise Humphrey had crafted. Finally, in frustration, Humphrey told Douglas, "I'll bargain for you. I'm not so pure." With Humphrey's aggressive lobbying, the bill passed the Senate and the House. Kennedy signed it on May 1. The result was creation of the Area Redevelopment Administration.

Humphrey firmly believed that his new job required him "to cajole and to persuade" in order to build "a consensus or majority to support a program." Yet some of his old liberal allies, especially those in the

ADA, worried that Humphrey had become far too willing to compromise. "You can get away with a few things," one ADA leader complained in April 1961, "but it's going to catch up with Hubert if he keeps it up." Howard Shuman recalled that "Humphrey almost never failed to vote with us and support us on the crucial issues, but he was not as strong in his negotiating situation as we would have liked." Humphrey offered no apologies. "I don't have to prove I'm a liberal," he said the day after his election as whip. "After twenty years of sincere and conscientious effort, there is nothing more I can do. I don't have to tell people I didn't sell out. I won't waste my time talking to them if they think that."

Harris Wofford had been standing on a Washington street corner one August morning in 1960 when John Kennedy spotted him. Kennedy pulled up in his red convertible and said, "Jump in." As the two men rode toward the Capitol, Kennedy instructed his civil rights advisor, "Now in five minutes tick off the ten things a president ought to do to clean up this goddamn civil rights mess."

Wofford had several ideas. First, the next president should sign an executive order ending racial discrimination in federally assisted housing. Only the previous year, Wofford had helped his former boss, Civil Rights Commission member Father Theodore Hesburgh, in the drafting of such a proposal. The commission had unanimously urged President Eisenhower to take that action, but the order laid dormant and unsigned as the president prepared to leave office. As Kennedy and Wofford drove across town, Wofford ticked off several more proposals, all of them recommendations by the commission or commitments in the Democratic party platform plank on civil rights. "But the main theme," Wofford recalled, "was the great unused potential for executive action." As an up-close witness to the Eisenhower administration's inaction on civil rights, Wofford longed for a president who was willing to use "the enormous power" of the White House to effect change. Wofford believed "if you could get a president who really would use that power, it could make a major change and could open the way to legislation."

Despite his seeming ambivalence and uncertainty about civil rights, Kennedy was not without feeling for the plight of black Americans. In his first debate with Richard Nixon, he displayed a profound *intellectual* understanding of the impact of racial discrimination. A black child, he said, has about one-half as much chance of completing high school as a white baby born on the same place on the same day, one-third as much chance of completing college, one-third as much chance of becoming a professional man, twice as much chance of becoming unemployed, about one-seventh as much chance of earning $10,000 a year, a life expectancy which is seven years shorter, and the prospects of earning only half as much.

In the second debate, Kennedy used a line that Wofford had supplied during their car ride in August. If elected president, he would, "by one stroke of the pen," issue the housing order that Eisenhower had refused to sign.

On inauguration day, January 20, 1961, Wofford and millions of other hopeful Americans were stirred by Kennedy's eloquent speech in which he declared "that the torch has been passed to a new generation of Americans." Kennedy's support for a strong United Nations and his promise to help "break the bonds of mass misery" around the world was exactly the vision Wofford had hoped Kennedy would present. But Wofford was not so pleased by Kennedy's brief, almost cryptic mention of civil rights. Only the day before, Wofford had protested that the draft of Kennedy's speech did not mention civil rights, the nation's most divisive and controversial social problem. "You can't do this," Wofford said, mindful of the peaceful lunch-counter sit-ins that had begun in Virginia that very day. Kennedy's speech would lament human rights struggles in foreign counties, but he would not discuss the civil rights movement in his own nation. "You have to say something about it," Wofford insisted. "You have to."

Kennedy relented. To his declaration that the United States would remain opposed to human rights violations "around the world," Kennedy added only three words. Now the sentence would assert that America was "unwilling to witness or permit the slow undoing of those human rights to which this nation has always been committed and to which we are committed today *at home and* around the world."

Though Kennedy had avoided inaugurating his presidency with a vibrant call for action on civil rights, discrimination appalled him when he encountered it personally. For example, just a few hours after his brief, reluctant reference to civil rights—after the final float in the inaugural parade had passed the president's reviewing stand—Kennedy sought out his new assistant special counsel, Richard Goodwin.

"Did you see the Coast Guard detachment?" Kennedy asked.

Goodwin was puzzled. He had no idea what Kennedy meant.

"There wasn't a black face in the entire group," the president said. "That's not acceptable. Something ought to be done about it."

Goodwin took the "observation" as "an order." Minutes later, he called incoming Commerce Secretary C. Douglas Dillon to convey Kennedy's wishes. By summer the Coast Guard Academy had hired its first black professor. The next year the academy enrolled four black cadets.

In the early days of Kennedy's presidency, episodes like these only served to raise puzzling questions in the minds of civil rights leaders, congressional liberals, southern segregationists, and Kennedy's own staff. Was Kennedy *completely* committed to civil rights? Would he support legislation or simply follow the less-confrontational path of executive action? In the end, they wondered, would he live up to his promise of courageous, visionary leadership?

So far, judging by his conflicting actions and statements, no one knew for sure.

John Kennedy entered the White House having made thirteen separate promises of action on civil rights. Among other things, he had pledged to

- push for enactment of the "Part III" legislation giving the attorney general full powers to enforce all civil rights;
- "continue and strengthen" the U.S. Civil Rights Commission;
- end discriminatory poll taxes and literacy tests;
- "pass effective antibombing and antilynching legislation";
- issue "the long-delayed" executive order on housing; and
- enforce school desegregation orders.

His rhetoric in support of these proposals had not been tentative. Candidate Kennedy had firmly declared that the next president "must give us the legal weapons needed to enforce the constitutional rights of every American. He cannot wait for others to act. He himself must draft the programs—transmit them to Congress—and fight for their enactment." At a September press conference, Kennedy had gone a step further, asking Pennsylvania senator Joseph Clark and House Judiciary Committee chairman Emanuel Celler to draft legislation "embodying our platform commitments for introduction at the beginning of the next session" of Congress. "We will seek the enactment of this bill early in that Congress," Kennedy declared unequivocally.*

Now that Kennedy was president, millions of black Americans eagerly awaited the "moral and persuasive leadership" that he had promised. Despite all the rhetoric about action and his early indignation over segregation in the Coast Guard, Kennedy was far from committed to an all-out drive to fulfill his promises on civil rights. He was hesitant to dive headlong into a divisive fight over the issue in his administration's early months. His narrow election had been no mandate. Though he had often promised action on civil rights—and black votes may have guaranteed his razor-thin margin of victory—the issue had not been central to his campaign. Believing he had little popularity to spare in a divisive civil rights fight, Kennedy focused on other important issues such as tariffs, taxes, unemployment, education, the minimum wage, and depressed areas.†

In May White House press secretary Pierre Salinger suddenly disavowed the bills introduced by Clark and Celler, which had been created at candidate Kennedy's request. The bills, he announced, "are not administration-backed bills. The president does not consider it necessary at this time to enact new civil rights legislation." That announcement "floored" NAACP executive secretary Roy Wilkins, "because it amounted to telling the opposition, for example, in football analogy, that you weren't going to use the forward pass." Wilkins believed the time had come to "charge the opposition."

Besides the normal hostility of southern conservatives, any Kennedy-sponsored civil rights bill would face other formidable institutional barriers. The cloture rule still required a daunting two-thirds vote—sixty-seven, if all 100 senators voted—to end a filibuster. Despite a Democratic platform pledge to liberalize Rule XXII, Kennedy believed that he could not afford to antagonize conservatives by taking sides in the biannual cloture fight in January.

---

*Actually, Republicans had forced Kennedy's hand during a "rump session" of Congress in August. When Republican leader Everett Dirksen and ten other Republicans called on Johnson and his Democratic colleagues to enact two civil rights proposals, embarrassed Democrats tabled the measures to prevent a preelection revolt by southern Democrats. Hoping to mitigate the debacle, Kennedy promised to push the Celler-Clark program if elected.

†Kennedy may have commanded more public support than he first realized. In a May 1961 Gallup Poll, 83 percent of those surveyed approved of Kennedy's performance as president—a higher approval rating than Eisenhower had ever achieved (*U.S. News & World Report*, 5/15/61).

Furthermore, despite the recent influx of new liberals into the body, southerners continued to chair most of the Senate's committees. While civil rights advocates and some congressional liberals viewed the world through the lens of one issue, Kennedy believed he was obligated to govern in a broader, more pragmatic fashion. He feared that alienating important southern committee chairmen by offering a volatile civil rights bill might be disastrous for civil rights and everything else Kennedy wanted from Congress. As one Kennedy aide explained to Anthony Lewis of the *New York Times*, "Suppose the president were to send up a dramatic message on civil rights and alienate enough southerners to kill his economic program in Congress? Would the Negro be better off or worse off? I think he'd be worse off." A disappointed Roy Wilkins believed that Kennedy's strategy demonstrated a poor understanding of Congress: "In the first place, any history would show that the opponents of civil rights legislation didn't give a hoot whether you introduced it or didn't introduce it as far as their attitude toward the major legislative proposals are concerned. They weren't going to let the major legislative proposals go through because the president did not introduce civil rights legislation out of their great gratitude and compassion and so forth, nor were they going to attack the proposals just because he introduced civil rights legislation."

Kennedy's reluctance on civil rights was more deeply rooted in his own political insecurity. Because he had defeated Richard Nixon by so narrow a margin, Kennedy was unsure of his ability to bend members of Congress to his will. "He didn't feel he had a mandate," explained Assistant Attorney General Nicholas Katzenbach. The advice congressional leaders gave Kennedy reinforced this assessment. House Judiciary chairman Emanuel Celler believed "the climate wasn't ready yet" for civil rights. There remained, he said, "a great deal of brush work to cut down the stumps of opposition." Kennedy received similar advice from Lyndon Johnson, Majority Leader Mansfield, and Bobby Baker, secretary to the Senate majority.

At the time, Kennedy's tentative approach to civil rights deeply troubled Civil Rights Commission member Theodore Hesburgh. With more than thirty years of perspective, however, Hesburgh appreciated Kennedy's political dilemma. "I think the bottom line on Jack is that he's the same as any other president we ever had," Hesburgh said. "The day they walk in that front door of the White House, their next thought is, 'How am I going to stay here for eight years?' " Hesburgh speculated that Kennedy understood "as a northerner, that if you really wanted to commit political suicide, as a Democrat who'd been elected by a small handful of votes, the easiest way to do it would be to come out strongly on civil rights."

To civil rights leaders, Kennedy was honest to the point of being blunt. "Nobody needs to convince me any longer that we have to solve the problem, not let it drift on gradual[ly]," Kennedy told Martin Luther King. "But how do you go about it? If we go into a long fight in Congress, it will bottleneck everything else and still get no bill."

As Kennedy's civil rights advisor, Harris Wofford was caught between restive civil rights leaders calling for swift congressional action and a president who wished to avoid a futile confrontation. As Wofford explained, it was not

> that [Kennedy] had lingering doubts about whether you ought to end segregation or integrate schools or get, above all, get voting rights. He had a very early conviction that the strategy of civil rights should be to do an end run around Congress and use federal power to the maximum extent to break barriers in employment, to use the voting rights laws that were put on [the books] to bring voting rights suits. He believed that the voting rights front . . . was the least divisive strategy. It was where you could win a majority of the South most clearly . . . He felt that the school desegregation process should go forward, I think with some moderation.

Moderation meant no legislation, only executive orders to initiate or expand enforcement of existing civil rights statutes. Kennedy, said Wofford, "loved the idea of executive action." The absence of a legislative program led some to question whether Kennedy's commitment to civil rights was sincere. "I don't read it that way at all," Wofford insisted. "I think John Kennedy was inhibited, intimidated by Congress. He wasn't a real insider. He didn't feel confident in dealing with Congress. He estimated the opposition in Congress as very dangerous on civil rights."

Wilbur Cohen, an assistant secretary of Health, Education and Welfare, described Kennedy's reluctance to prod the Congress, especially on civil rights and federal aid to education, as "a process of putting his big toe into cold water every morning and seeing what he could probably make out of it." When Kennedy pressured Cohen repeatedly to persuade a particular member of the House Rules Committee to support the administration's education bill, an exasperated Cohen finally responded, "Why don't you get them? I mean, why ask me to get them? You get them!" Recalled veteran Louisiana senator Allen Ellender, "I've served under many presidents since 1937 . . . and I don't know of any who were less aggressive" with Congress than Kennedy.

Another, more compelling explanation for Kennedy's reticence is that his "commitment" to improving the lives of black Americans had not yet grown beyond an intellectual distaste for segregation and discrimination. "Jack was not passionate about anything," Wofford asserted, including civil rights. Burke Marshall believed that Kennedy approached civil rights in the cool, analytical way he dealt with every other important issue. Kennedy supported civil rights, his close friend George Smathers said, "but it was strictly an intellectual matter of being fair with him, it wasn't a burning need." Historian James MacGregor Burns, who spent considerable time pondering Kennedy's approach to civil rights, concluded that the president would not "have done what his heroes in *Profiles in Courage* did." Kennedy "could never throw himself into some cause blindly," he said. "There would always be part of him sitting back and watching with some detachment." Like other pragmatic liberals—including Johnson—Kennedy would wholeheartedly support civil rights legislation *only* when he believed the political climate was ripe for its passage. "Everyone down in Congress," Burke Marshall said, "told him that he couldn't pass a civil rights bill. So, he had a choice of not pushing one or pushing one but ending up with the defeat and wasting a lot of time, goodwill to some extent."

Executive action—the exercise of presidential authority already approved by Congress—ruled the day. In contrast to the lethargy of the Eisenhower years, the Kennedy administration, led by Attorney General Robert Kennedy, launched aggressive action on several fronts:

In March the president issued an executive order merging two former executive committees—the president's committees on Government Contracts and Government Employment Policy—into the President's Committee on Equal Employment Opportunity. "I intend to insure that Americans of all colors and beliefs will have equal access to employment within the government," Kennedy announced, "and with those who do business with the government." With Lyndon Johnson as chairman, the committee was empowered to fight discriminatory hiring practices by the federal government and by private companies with government con-

tracts. Although Johnson adamantly pushed his committee staff to identify and weed out job discrimination, some critics contended that
Johnson leaned toward a more polite cajoling of businesses, while Robert
Kennedy and other administration officials supported greater initiative
and more aggressive action.

Nonetheless Johnson was not hesitant to summon business leaders
who held government contracts and demand explanations for their poor
minority hiring records. In May 1961, spurred by complaints from the
NAACP, Johnson's committee pursued and won its first big case—a
broad antidiscrimination agreement with a Lockheed Aircraft Corporation plant in Marietta, Georgia. Through the efforts of Richard Russell
and House Armed Services chairman Carl Vinson, the government
had awarded the California-based corporation a $1 billion contract to
assemble giant C-141 transport jets. Afraid of losing its lucrative government contract over the simple matter of a segregated work place,
Lockheed capitulated. Down came the "white" and "colored" signs on
bathroom doors. Segregated water fountains and the white-only cafeteria
were abolished. The company agreed to hire more blacks (then only
450 employees out of 10,500) and train them for skilled positions.

Kennedy's own hiring policy led him to appoint several blacks to
high positions, including Robert Weaver to head the Housing and Home
Finance Administration. A fifty-three-year-old, Harvard-educated civil
rights activist, Weaver had served as national chairman of the NAACP,
New York State's rent administrator, and vice-chairman of the New
York City Housing and Redevelopment Board. Not surprisingly, southern conservatives opposed his nomination. Mississippi's James Eastland charged that Weaver had been associated with several subversive
organizations, describing him as "a man who has a pro-Communist
background" and "belonged to half a dozen Communist-front organizations." On January 22 Louisiana's Allen Ellender declared that he had
seen "some of the proof," supplied by the House Un-American Activities Committee, of Weaver's alleged Communist affiliations. Those
charges lost their steam, however, when committee chairman Francis
Walter announced the next day that no committee evidence linked
Weaver to Communist activities. The Senate finally confirmed Weaver
by a voice vote in early February.

Kennedy appointed other blacks to government positions: George
Weaver as assistant secretary of labor; Carl T. Rowan as assistant
secretary of state for public affairs; Andrew Hatcher as associate press

secretary; Lisle Carter as deputy assistant in the Department of Health, Education and Welfare; and Frank Reeves to the White House staff. He named blacks to ambassadorial posts, including Clifton Wharton as ambassador to Norway, the first black to represent the United States to a predominantly white country. For the first time, two blacks—in San Francisco and Cleveland—were appointed as U.S. attorneys. "It got to be a kind of *sub rosa* joke around Washington, even among Negroes," recalled Roy Wilkins, "that Kennedy was so hot on the Department heads [to hire blacks] . . . that everyone was scrambling around trying to find himself a Negro in order to keep the president off his neck."

Kennedy also named blacks to the federal bench, including the now-legendary NAACP lawyer, Thurgood Marshall, to the Second Circuit Court of Appeals. Judiciary chairman James Eastland held up Marshall's nomination for many months. Eastland relented only when Kennedy agreed to appoint his law school roommate, Harold Cox, to a federal district judgeship. "You tell your brother," Eastland reportedly told Robert Kennedy, "that when I get Cox, he gets the nigger."

Although the Democratic platform had promised "whatever action necessary" to eliminate literacy tests and poll taxes, Kennedy proposed no legislation in 1961. Attorney General Robert Kennedy announced he would instead aggressively enforce the 1957 and 1960 civil rights acts, which gave him the authority to seek injunctions against voting rights violations. "We will enforce the law, in every field of law and every region," the attorney general bravely declared to a University of Georgia audience in May. "If the orders of the court are circumvented, the Department of Justice will act." The speech was Kennedy's first formal address as attorney general. Although not one prominent Georgia public official was present, the crowd of 1,600 alumni and students applauded Kennedy enthusiastically when he finished.

In April his department filed its first voting rights suit, against voting officials in Dallas County, Alabama. By year's end he would file fourteen voting rights suits; by mid-1963, forty-two. (Eisenhower's Justice Department, by comparison, had filed only nine suits since the passage of the Civil Rights Act of 1957.) Even Martin Luther King argued that "suffrage" was the "central front" of his Southern Christian Leadership Conference. "If we in the South can win the right to vote, it will place in our hands more than an abstract right. It will give us the concrete tool with which we ourselves can correct injustice."

As for school desegregation, the Democratic platform had promised to give the Justice Department new legislative authority—the language gutted from Part III of the 1957 act—to file suits against deprivation of *any* civil right. In this area as well, Kennedy would pursue no legislation—for now. Instead the Justice Department quickly entered a desegregation dispute in New Orleans, suing Louisiana officials for refusing to release federal school funds to the New Orleans School Board. Kennedy also sued the Louisiana legislature to prevent lawmakers from interfering with New Orleans school officials' desegregation efforts. With little fanfare, Kennedy sent Burke Marshall and other Justice Department lawyers to almost every school district slated for desegregation. Marshall offered to assist local officials in complying with court orders, and he established important lines of communication with political and community leaders throughout the South.

All of this was appallingly insufficient to many liberals. Civil rights advocates suggested that the law did not require the government to wait until private citizens sued. The administration, they said, already had the legal authority to initiate school desegregation suits on its own. At his first press conference, on April 7, Robert Kennedy rejected the notion of a more direct approach. "I don't believe we do have that power," he argued. As for legislation to secure such authority, Kennedy said that he had not yet made "a final determination as to exactly what we will do."

"You did get more vigorous action under [the Kennedy] administration, many suits filed by the Justice Department, more in a few months than the predecessor administration filed in several years," Martin Luther King later acknowledged. King and others were not satisfied. "I don't think that his leadership really, at this point, grappled with the magnitude of the problem." Joseph Rauh, then general counsel for the United Auto Workers and a staunch Kennedy supporter, found himself sorely disappointed at the pace of civil rights action. "I feel that he was going too slow," said Rauh. Unimpressed by executive action and appointments of blacks to government posts, Rauh concluded—correctly—that the daunting challenge of negotiating with Congress intimidated Kennedy. "That is the political way," he said. "Do a lot of administrative things, but stay away from Congress."

In February 1961 Rauh joined a group of ADA board members to visit Kennedy at the White House. Economist Robert Nathan, a long-time Humphrey advisor, began the discussion with a pitch for increased government spending to achieve full employment. "Of course, there will be a fifty-billion [dollar] deficit to get full employment," Nathan asserted. Leaning back in his chair, Kennedy challenged Nathan. "Well, the difficulty with your proposal," he said, "is that 93 percent of the people in this country are employed. That other seven percent isn't going to get enough political support to do it." Kennedy did not believe such deficit spending would be possible. "But I want you to keep this up," he told Nathan. "It's very helpful now for you to keep pushing me this way."

Kennedy's amiability encouraged Rauh to speak up for civil rights. "Well, Mr. President, I hope the spirit with which you have treated Bob's pressure from the left, on the issue for which he speaks for the ADA, will go equally for the issue on which I speak for the ADA—civil rights."

In an instant, Kennedy's mood darkened.

"Absolutely not," he snapped. "It's a totally different thing. Your criticism on civil rights is quite wrong."

As Kennedy listed the names of blacks he had appointed to government posts and the voting rights suits the Justice Department was preparing to file, Rauh thought to himself, "Oh, shit. Oh, shit. Nothing is going to happen. How did we let this happen?"

Looking back, Rauh later concluded that Kennedy had taken the reproach over civil rights as "a kind of moral criticism," while Nathan's reproving on employment had been received "as a matter of judgment." As usual, Rauh said, "I was the skunk at the garden party." Rauh believed Kennedy's angry response was the product of "a kind of guilty conscience because he felt that he wasn't doing enough in there, that this was a moral issue, that he didn't know just how to confront it." In another interview, many years later, Rauh seemed to sympathize with Kennedy's dilemma. "I think he should have done it," Rauh maintained, but "one can certainly understand the feelings he had when the civil rights thing was really thrown in his face."

Another visitor to Kennedy was Father Theodore Hesburgh, president of Notre Dame University and a member of the U.S. Civil Rights Commission. When Hesburgh urged Kennedy to initiate a thorough integration of National Guard and reserve units, Kennedy protested. Events in Berlin, where Soviet authorities had built a wall to stem a mass exodus into West Berlin, had become, in Kennedy's words, "the great testing place of Western will and courage."

"Look," Kennedy told Hesburgh, "I have serious problems in

West Berlin, and I do not think this is the proper time to start monkeying around with the army. I don't think we'll have to call these southern reserve units or National Guard units, but if we did, I'd like to make sure that everything was in order and they could move immediately and that we weren't in the middle of a real problem here." Despite Kennedy's reluctance to aggressively act on civil rights, Hesburgh was impressed that Kennedy seemed "enormously informed" about the slow pace of college desegregation in the South.

Kennedy also seemed to understand the importance of a strong Civil Rights Commission—although its reports and recommendations sometimes caused considerable consternation at the White House. "In part because of Kennedy appointments," *New York Times* reporter Anthony Lewis wrote in October, "the commission has made a startling change from a prolix debating society to a firm advocate of prompt justice for the Negro." In a flurry of reports in 1961, the revitalized commission urged Congress to give every segregated southern school district six months to develop a desegregation plan; proposed an end to literacy tests for voting registration by requiring a sixth-grade education as proof of literacy; and urged Kennedy to issue an executive order ending discrimination in all federally aided housing.

In their early months in the White House, Kennedy's people hoped they could contain and manage the building pressure for action on civil rights. They simply would not permit civil rights to intrude on more pressing domestic and international concerns. Instead Kennedy would rely on a deliberate, well-managed program of executive orders, Justice Department suits on voting rights and school desegregation, appointments of blacks to federal positions, and conciliatory meetings with civil rights leaders. He promised to do more—but only when the political climate improved.

His incremental policy of slow but steady action would never completely satisfy congressional liberals and civil rights advocates. The politician in Kennedy understood that. However, because he primarily saw the issue in intellectual and political terms, the president seemed to underestimate the brewing forces of discontent among the downtrodden black citizens of the South. Before long, Kennedy began to learn something about the determination of black activists and their willingness to risk their lives in challenging segregation in the South.

In May 1961, the civil rights movement shifted from the peaceful resistance of lunch-counter sit-ins to more aggressive action. That month, groups of black and white college students left Washington and Nashville on buses bound for southern cities. These "Freedom Riders," some of them well trained in nonviolence, would goad southerners to violence in order to illuminate the failure of the southern states to comply with a 1960 Supreme Court decision outlawing segregation of public facilities in interstate commerce. At each bus terminal, they would attempt to integrate all-white waiting rooms, restaurants, and rest rooms—all in violation of unconstitutional local and state segregation statues. "We can take anything the white man can dish out," one rider said bravely, "but we want our rights. We know what they are—and we want them right now."

As they made their way through Virginia, North Carolina, South Carolina, and Georgia, the nervous riders encountered little violence or resistance. Once they crossed into Alabama, domain of archsegregationist governor John Patterson, the climate changed. Angry, violent mobs accosted them at almost every stop. Near Anniston, a crowd of whites attacked the Greyhound bus, slit its tires, smashed the windows with pipes, and set it afire. Terrified and overcome by smoke, the riders found their way to a nearby hospital, where white attendants refused them medical treatment. A Ku Klux Klan–led mob attacked riders on another bus that managed to reach Birmingham. Local police waited a full ten minutes before they intervened. By then some riders were badly beaten.

In Montgomery, angry whites pummeled six riders with bricks and a garbage can. Others barely escaped serious injury by fleeing in taxicabs and private cars. In a rage, some in the white mob snatched the students' suitcases and smashed them against a wall of the bus station until their contents spilled out—and then they set fire to the heap of clothing and books. While trying to save one rider from the mob, the attorney general's personal emissary, administrative assistant John Seigenthaler, was beaten over the head with a metal pipe and kicked unconscious. Only when the Montgomery police belatedly fired tear gas into the crowd did the violence wane.

"Obviously," *Newsweek* reported, "this was a total breakdown of law enforcement in Alabama." But Patterson and other Alabama authorities, unaware they were playing into the Freedom Riders' hands, remained defiant. "We respond to calls here just like any place else," said Montgomery Police Commissioner L. B. Sullivan, explaining why his men waited so long to intervene. "But we have no intention of standing guard for a bunch of trouble makers."

Throughout the crisis, Attorney General Kennedy played mediator, working around the clock to persuade both sides to back down and leave the matter to the courts. Patterson's violation of his promise to protect the Freedom Riders outraged both Kennedys. With his racist white electorate in mind, Patterson was in no mood to compromise. "I'm getting tired of being called up in the middle of the night," he complained, "and being *ordered* to do this and *ordered* to do that." For two days, Patterson—the first southern governor to endorse Kennedy's candidacy—refused even to take phone calls from the president. "That Bobby Kennedy is just treacherous, that's what he is," Patterson complained to a reporter. "I don't trust him and he don't trust me."

The brutal response by locals and the negligence of Alabama authorities was *exactly* the reaction the Freedom Rides' organizers had hoped to provoke. The bloody violence made national news. Newspapers around the country—and as far away as Africa, Europe, and Asia—carried shocking accounts and photographs of the beatings. Said France's *Le Monde:* "The current toward racial integration has now acquired an irresistible force . . . Advocates of white supremacy . . . may retard evolution but they can't halt it." A *Daily Express* reporter told readers in London that the Kennedy brothers had proved to the world "that they are as ready to defend the ideals of individual liberty within the borders of the United States as they are to act outside." In the United States, public sentiment for legislative action on civil rights grew with every angry blow and racial slur hurled at the students. Governor Patterson deserved much of the credit. "If he had kept his mouth shut and accepted his responsibility to maintain law and order," *Time* observed, "the Freedom Riders would probably have passed through Alabama with little incident—just as they had passed through Virginia, North Carolina, South Carolina and Georgia."

The Freedom Riders hoped that the crisis they provoked would move Kennedy to support comprehensive civil rights legislation. "I think we knew we were testing this new administration when we decided on the Freedom Rides," said John Lewis, a rider who was beaten by white thugs at a South Carolina stop. "I think it was right to test this young president early. The people associated with Kennedy gave us a lot of hope; there was something about the man that was the embodiment of change."

Whatever encouragement the riders got from Kennedy was mostly inadvertent. At first unaware of the riders' plans, both Kennedys worried that the whole exercise would cast the United States in a bad light. It was not the kind of distraction the president needed as he dealt with the crisis in Berlin and prepared for a momentous summit with Soviet leader Nikita Khrushchev in Vienna. "These things," Nicholas Katzenbach said frankly, "were seen as a pain in the ass."

"Tell them to call it off!" John Kennedy bellowed to Harris Wofford in a phone call. "Stop them!"

"I don't think anybody's going to stop them right now," Wofford responded.

Unable to persuade local and state officials to protect the Freedom Riders, Robert Kennedy finally ordered hundreds of federal marshals into Montgomery.

As the marshals prepared to move in, more violence threatened to erupt at Reverend Ralph Abernathy's First Baptist Church in Montgomery, where Martin Luther King arrived on May 21 for a massive rally. King and his mainstream Southern Christian Leadership Conference had not been responsible for the Freedom Riders' foray into the South.* But now that this dynamic new assault on segregation had been unleashed, there was no turning back. King and other black leaders embraced the riders' cause. Even Thurgood Marshall, soon to become a federal judge, acknowledged that the pace of the civil rights movement had not been fast enough. "These kids are serving notice on us that we're moving too slow," he said. "They're not content with all this talking."

In his speech to more than a thousand people, King demanded aggressive federal intervention to end segregation. "Unless the federal government acts forthrightly in the South to assure every citizen his constitutional rights," King declared, "we will be plunged into a dark abyss of chaos." Robert Kennedy could not have been pleased to learn that King had called for "a full-scale nonviolent assault on the system of segregation in Alabama," including a voter registration drive and attempts to integrate public schools, lunch counters, public parks, and theaters. "In short, we will seek to mobilize thousands of people, committed to the method of nonviolence, who will physically identify themselves with the struggle to end segregation in Alabama."

As King spoke an unruly mob gathered outside and began pitching rocks and bottles at the church. Undeterred by tear gas released by the

---

*The more confrontational, New York–based Congress of Racial Equality (CORE) had organized the rides.

federal marshals, the mob seemed on the verge of storming the church. One person shouted, "We'll get those niggers!" Another cried: "We want to integrate, too!" Trapped inside, the terrified congregation waited until the crowd finally dispersed early the next morning.

Now the Freedom Riders were even more determined to press on. They ignored desperate pleas from Robert Kennedy to call off their mission in exchange for Kennedy's abstract promise of assistance. "People were going to be killed," Kennedy feared. But there were no more beatings, only arrests. When another group of fearless riders arrived in Jackson, Mississippi, Governor Ross Barnett avoided violence not by restraining angry whites but by promptly arresting all twenty-seven riders on charges of disorderly conduct. "I feel wonderful," Barnett bragged once the riders were behind bars, twenty-two of them choosing to remain in jail rather than pay a $200 fine. "I'm so happy that everything went off smoothly. The nation had its eyes on Mississippi today, and I think we showed them that we could handle our own affairs in an orderly manner."

In the Senate, reaction to violence against the Freedom Riders was swift and emotional. Majority Leader Mike Mansfield said the incidents in Alabama "should cause us—as a Nation—to hang our heads in shame." Humphrey called it "a sad day for Americans when some of our citizens are set upon as if they were enemies or as if they were not even human beings." The violence, Humphrey added, has "made a mockery of our democracy and of our national purpose, for the outbreaks have evidenced disorder and violence unworthy of a great nation. This problem is not confined to any particular area; it is a national problem."

Southern conservatives condemned the violence but made it clear that they blamed the Freedom Riders and their provocations. "The self-styled freedom riders set out deliberately to create trouble at all costs," Strom Thurmond told the Senate. "Their avowed purpose, publicly expressed, was not to work toward the creation of better race relations, but to incite incidents." Thurmond cited *Washington Star* columnist David Lawrence, who maintained that "what happened in Alabama . . . reveals clearly that incitement to riot is the fundamental cause of the trouble." That attack on the Freedom Riders prompted New York's Herbert Lehman to respond, "I have yet to hear any excuse for the anarchy and the refusal or failure to take authoritative state action in terms of protecting the lives of citizens and enforcing the laws and

Constitution of the United States." Thurmond bitterly replied that he "did not expect" Lehman to agree with Lawrence "or with the Constitution of the United States."

On May 24, when New York's Jacob Javits proposed a resolution commending Kennedy for his efforts to "enforce the Constitution," Russell objected. "I have deplored all the acts of violence," Russell told the Senate, "not only because they were against the law, but also because they ran counter to the best interests of the people of the South—and I refer now to the white people of the South—whose interests have been at stake in the legislative battles we have waged on this floor." Russell said that Alabama citizens "made a mistake when they permitted themselves to be provoked into violence." He quickly added what he regarded as a reasonable explanation for the violence: "The so-called freedom riders, I understand, had no difficulty anywhere they traveled until they did associate young white girls with Negro males, and that did bring forth these lawless acts. I deplore every one of them even though I realize the extent of the provocation."

Perhaps the most shameful and hysterical response to the violence against the Freedom Riders came from Judiciary Committee chairman James Eastland. In a lengthy speech full of "exhibits" and other purported evidence, the Mississippi Democrat attacked the Congress of Racial Equality (CORE), which had sponsored the riders, as a communist-front organization. "Since its inception," Eastland said of CORE, "its creed has been lawlessness and its tactics have followed the pattern set by Communist agitators the world over." Eastland said he had been "informed" that the Freedom Rides were "devised deliberately as a prelude to various high-level meetings in Europe, as a propaganda method to embarrass the government of the United States in the handling of international affairs." CORE, he declared, "is carrying on the fight for a Soviet America."

By the summer, Robert Kennedy responded to the Freedom Rides —but not with a civil rights bill. Under intense pressure from the Justice Department, the Interstate Commerce Commission ordered the desegregation of all interstate bus terminals, and the Justice Department began enforcing the order. (In 1955 the ICC had banned segregation on buses and trains and in railroad stations but had done nothing about segregation in bus terminals.) By year's end, all forms of segregated interstate transportation were abolished.

The ICC's order was an unmistakable victory for Kennedy's administration, but it did little to improve the president's standing with civil rights activists and other liberals. Although the president had helped to finally end segregation in interstate travel, the Freedom Riders and King had seen Kennedy as a reluctant and mostly silent supporter of their cause. Despite constant prodding by Wofford and others, Kennedy had stubbornly refused to issue a strong declaration of support for the riders.

Days after racists in Alabama pummeled the riders, Kennedy had appeared at a Joint Session of Congress on May 25 to deliver his second State of the Union address of 1961. Though he declared in the speech that "we stand for freedom," he had refused entreaties by Harris Wofford and Burke Marshall to speak about the freedoms denied black citizens in the South. Instead Kennedy asserted that the "great battleground for the defense and expansion of freedom today is the whole southern half of the globe—Asia, Latin America, Africa and the Middle East—the lands of the rising peoples. Their revolution is the greatest in human history. They seek an end to injustice, tyranny, and exploitation. More than an end, they seek a beginning." During the lengthy speech, Kennedy did not mention the civil rights struggle in the American South. As Wofford explained, the president undoubtedly suspected that Robert Kennedy's "actions had spoken louder than words, and he feared a white backlash in the South."

As 1961 ended, Congress had little to show for its efforts on civil rights. Kennedy's proposal to elevate the Housing and Home Finance Administration to cabinet status ran up against a wall of southern opposition. The agency's administrator, Robert Weaver, was black—and would thus become the nation's first black cabinet official. Moreover, he was an outspoken advocate of integrated housing, or "open occupancy."

In the Senate the venerable filibuster remained as strong as ever. As the session came to a close in September, senators rejected a proposal to lower the threshold for imposing cloture from two-thirds of those voting to three-fifths. An attempt to force a vote on the motion by invoking cloture failed miserably, 37-43. By year's end Congress had enacted only one civil rights measure—legislation extending the life of the U.S. Civil Rights Commission for two years. The Senate soundly defeated efforts to make the commission permanent.

As the commission issued its mammoth, five-volume report for the year—offering recommendations on voting, education, employment, housing, and the administration of justice—veteran commissioner Theodore Hesburgh added a separate dissenting statement. It was a stinging, albeit indirect, rebuke of Kennedy's emphasis of foreign affairs over important domestic issues such as civil rights:

> Americans might well wonder how we can legitimately combat communism when we practice so widely its central folly: utter disregard for the God-given spiritual rights, freedom and dignity of every human person . . . Personally, I don't care if the United States gets the first man on the moon, if while this is happening on a crash basis, we dawdle along here on our corner of the earth, nursing our prejudices, flouting our magnificent Constitution, ignoring the central moral problem of our times, and appearing hypocrites to all the world.

CHAPTER SIXTEEN

You'll Never Get a Civil Rights Bill

THE EARLY 1960S WERE BLEAK TIMES for Richard Russell. Civil rights was on the march—literally—and Russell had little stomach for the momentous social changes he knew were inevitable. "We have come to evil days," he told a friend. "He was," observed longtime aide Proctor Jones, "out of step with what was likely to happen."

With its bold commitment to civil rights legislation, Russell's beloved Democratic party had veered sharply to the left in the 1960 election. "My party had deviated from the past and has gone off and left me," he had complained during the presidential contest. In the Senate, Lyndon Johnson was gone, and Russell was no longer a hidden hand behind the leadership. Two liberals, Mike Mansfield and Hubert Humphrey, ran a much more progressive Senate. Mansfield, while always friendly and courteous, was not Russell's protégé and owed him no special debt. Russell's once-fearsome domination of the steering and policy committees had been eroded by Johnson's departure and by the addition of liberals such as Mansfield, Humphrey, Michigan's Philip Hart, Maine's Edmund Muskie, and Pennsylvania's Joseph Clark. The southern bloc that Russell led was shrinking—and aging. Of the bloc's eighteen members, more than half were sixty or older, and four were over seventy.

As chairman of the Armed Services Committee and a senior member of the Appropriations Committee, Russell still wielded enormous power, but only within certain realms—defense, agriculture, and, to a rapidly declining degree, civil rights. Furthermore, because of age and his deteriorating health, Russell had simply lost some of his enthusiasm for waging legislative battles. He had rarely if ever been an offensive combatant in the fight against civil rights, but now he seemed more defensive and fatalistic than ever. He was afraid, he wrote to himself in 1960, that "my leadership has lost inspiration."

None of this meant that Russell would ever capitulate to demands for civil rights. In early 1961 he led a surprisingly spirited fight against liberalization of the cloture rule and threatened a filibuster against the proposal. With no real support from the Kennedy White House, the rule change died.

Except for agricultural policy, Russell found himself at odds with every major legislative initiative proposed by President Kennedy. His relationship with Lyndon Johnson was not much better. As vice president, Johnson now wholeheartedly supported Kennedy's program of executive action on civil rights. One of his first acts as chairman of the President's Committee on Equal Employment Opportunity had been to force the desegregation of the Lockheed plant in Russell's home state. Russell had hoped that Johnson, the southern moderate, would exert a moderating influence on the liberals in Kennedy's White House. He was mistaken. To the extent he had any influence, Johnson seemed to have become an all-out civil rights liberal.

Russell, quite naturally, felt betrayed.

One Saturday afternoon, probably in 1962, Buddy Darden witnessed Russell's growing disillusionment with his former protégé. A Capitol elevator operator under Russell's patronage, Darden (later a congressman from Georgia) was walking toward Russell's office when Johnson's chauffeur-driven limousine pulled alongside him.

"Hey, boy," Johnson shouted, "is Dick in?"

"Well, yes, sir," Darden replied.

"Well, tell him I'm out here in the car and I want to see him."

Darden scurried inside to deliver the message, but Russell was in no mood for Johnson that afternoon.

"You just tell the son of a bitch I'm not here. I don't want to fool with him today."

Darden was petrified. "Here I was, just walking in off the street, carrying a message from the vice president of the United States to the chairman of the Armed Services Committee, and I was supposed to go back and tell him that he wasn't in—yet I had already told him he was in." Not knowing what to do, Darden shuffled his feet and remained in Russell's outer office, hoping, he said, "that something would happen."

Before long, an impatient Johnson burst through the door and barged into Russell's office, where Russell received his old friend warmly. Darden said when he realized the two men "weren't going to come to blows, I exited and wasn't around there anymore."

As few but Darden understood, the Russell-Johnson relationship was evolving.

Demands for progress on civil rights only intensified in 1962. "The president of the United States," New York Republican Jacob Javits declared from the Senate floor in January, "has apparently adopted the calculated policy of avoiding the Congress at this session on civil rights, and it cannot be done." By March Javits's frustrations boiled over. He finally gave public voice to a growing sentiment among civil rights advocates. "In my view," he told the Senate, "the President is appeasing southern members of his party who are in powerful committee positions, by his attitude on civil rights legislation, and as a result many parts of the administration's own program are getting absolutely nowhere." Javits's harsh criticism was close to the mark. It would have been difficult to imagine much of Kennedy's program faring any worse in Congress—even if he had introduced a strong legislative proposal on civil rights. Administration bills to create a Department of Urban Affairs and a Medicare system were stalled in committee, as was legislation to provide federal aid to education.

Humphrey bravely defended Kennedy's civil rights policies, despite his personal concerns over Kennedy's reluctance to embrace the bold, comprehensive program he had promised during his campaign. On May 29, 1962, Humphrey rose in the Senate to deliver a lengthy defense of every portion of Kennedy's domestic and foreign policies. He passionately challenged those who claimed that Kennedy "has not even requested civil rights legislation or issued an Executive order ending racial discrimination in federally assisted housing." As Humphrey noted, Congress had extended the Civil Rights Commission in 1961 and was near enactment of a constitutional amendment banning the poll tax in federal elections. Furthermore, Humphrey declared,

> the Kennedy administration has accomplished far more than its predecessor through administrative action—through lawsuits to compel voter registration, through negotiations on the successful integration of schools, through increased employment by federal agencies and federal contractors, and through action to end segregation in bus, airline and train terminals.

At least one Kennedy-backed legislative proposal was making progress. Since 1949, Florida senator Spessard Holland—a tough, somewhat pedantic, seventy-year-old conservative—had bravely and repeatedly introduced a constitutional amendment to ban the poll tax. Once widespread, the poll tax was now an endangered species. Only Alabama, Arkansas, Mississippi, Texas, and Virginia still imposed a yearly tax as a voting requirement. But Holland, who wanted it completely abolished throughout the South, made destruction of the tax a personal crusade. In years past, both houses of Congress had approved some version of a ban, but they had never agreed on whether statute or constitutional amendment should end it.

By 1962 the times were finally catching up with the Florida Democrat. Desperate for *some* legislative progress on civil rights to appease restless liberals, Kennedy and Majority Leader Mansfield happily lent their support. On March 14 Mansfield called up a minor bill to establish the former home of Alexander Hamilton as a national monument. This legislation, he told the Senate, would serve as the vehicle for Holland's amendment. Russell's southerners, of course, objected. While he said he held "no brief for the poll tax," Russell complained that a constitutional amendment had no business as a rider to such a bill. The Senate disagreed. By a 58-34 vote, senators rejected Russell's constitutional point of order.

Passage of Holland's amendment was virtually assured. After all, the Senate had approved a poll tax ban in 1960 by a wide margin. (The House failed to act on the measure, favoring legislation over a constitutional amendment.) This year the only questions were how long the southerners would stall a vote and how strident they would become in defense of a decaying device of southern white supremacy. Past debates usually found southerners opposing civil rights legislation as unconstitutional infringements on the sovereign rights of states. Change the Constitution, they cried, but don't pass unconstitutional laws. Now Holland's amendment had called their bluff—and forced them to defend not the Constitution but the poll tax itself. In the end, much of the debate served only to portray the southerners as antiquated and ridiculous relics of the Confederacy.

Mississippi's John Stennis, one of the more respected southern members, was most pitiful when he explained that the poll tax was only "misunderstood." Voting, he declared, "is a privilege; it is not a right.

It has never been a right. I hope that in our form of government it will never be a pure right." As if some in the chamber might have misunderstood him, Stennis repeated his point, the Fifteenth Amendment notwithstanding. "The casting of a vote is a privilege," he stubbornly insisted, "and that privilege arises from the states of the Union, not from the Federal government."

Russell's arguments against the amendment did little to enhance his reputation for statesmanship. On March 14 he permitted Paul Douglas to lure him into a bizarre discussion over the wisdom of the Fifteenth and Nineteenth amendments and of the South's conduct in the Civil War. Asked by Douglas if he favored the Nineteenth Amendment, which required states to grant suffrage to women, Russell replied that he would not support repealing the amendment. "But I am frank to say that, since the states had the power to grant women the right to vote, if I had been a member of the Senate at the time I might have voted against the amendment." While saying that he would not vote to repeal the Fifteenth Amendment and its voting protections, he admitted, "I am not enthusiastic about the amendment." Seeming to forget that the Civil War had ended almost a hundred years earlier, Russell said:

> That amendment was written in the blood of the Civil War* and was inevitable after Appomattox and the South is reconciled to it. We were not happy about it, but it was written in blood, by the bayonets of the soldiers of our friend from Illinois and other states who overpowered us in the most calamitous and fratricidal strife this nation has ever seen . . . But if the Senator is going to try to get me to apologize for the Civil War at this late date or to get on my knees any further than was necessary at Appomattox, I shall not do it. I am proud of our part in it, though it was one of the greatest tragedies this country was confronted with. I am proud of the record the people of my blood made in it, and men of my clan shed their blood on battlefields from Gettysburg to Brice's Crossroads.

On March 27, after a ten-day quasifilibuster, the Senate finally approved Holland's constitutional amendment, 77-16. Four southerners— Louisiana's Russell Long, Tennessee's Estes Kefauver, Florida's George

---

*An unusual slip by Russell, who rarely used that term in describing the conflict.

Smathers, and Texas's Ralph Yarborough—joined Holland in supporting
the amendment. Several other previously loyal allies abandoned the
southern coalition on the vote, including West Virginia's Robert Byrd
(a former Ku Klux Klan member) and Oklahoma's Bob Kerr. Every
Republican but Lyndon Johnson's successor, John Tower, supported the
measure. On August 27, the House approved the amendment, 295-86.
Many House members had preferred a legislative ban instead of a constitutional amendment. In the end, however, they supported it because
it was the only measure that could pass the Senate. "I am a pragmatist,"
House Judiciary chairman Emanuel Celler declared. "I want results, not
a debate. I want a law, not a filibuster. I crave an end to the poll tax,
not unlimited, crippling amendments. I say to you gentlemen and ladies,
stretch your feet according to your blanket." In January 1964, upon
ratification by the thirty-eighth state, the proposal became the Twenty-
fourth Amendment to the Constitution.

Kennedy applauded the congressional vote and was happy to count
the poll tax amendment as a civil rights victory for his administration.
However, the vote had never really been in doubt. Once a burning
issue, the poll tax ban was now among the civil rights movement's lowest
priorities. When ratified, it would have only minimal impact on black
voting rights.

More important was another civil rights measure that Kennedy supported. With administration backing, Majority Leader Mansfield and
Minority Leader Dirksen introduced legislation based on a 1961 Civil
Rights Commission recommendation to establish a sixth-grade education
as proof of literacy for voter registration in states that employed literacy
tests. According to a commission report, about one hundred counties in
eight southern states excluded blacks from voting in "substantial numbers" because of their race. A "common technique" of barring black
voter registration, the commission reported, was the "discriminatory application of legal qualifications for voters." White officials typically required would-be black voters to read and write, offer a "satisfactory"
interpretation of the U.S. Constitution, calculate their ages to the day,
and prove that they were of "good character." In one case cited by the
commission, a registrar rejected a black schoolteacher for mispronounc-
ing "equity" while reading a long passage. Commission member Theodore Hesburgh, in a 1960 speech, had painted a particularly pitiful
portrait of the humiliation suffered by thousands of blacks who attempted to exercise their Fifteenth Amendment rights:

They would go down to the courthouse and instead of going in where the white people registered, they would have to go to a room in the back where they would stand in line from six in the morning until two in the afternoon, since only two were let in at a time. Then, people with Ph.D.s and the master's degrees and high intelligence would sit down and copy like a schoolchild the first article or the second article of the Constitution. Then they would be asked the usual questions, make out the usual questionnaires, hand in a self-addressed envelope and hear nothing for three months. And then they would go back and do it over again, some of them five or six or seven times, some of them standing in line two or three days until their turn came.

Mansfield monitored the political climate in the Senate. He doubted that a majority of his colleagues would support a literacy proposal that contained mandates on state and local elections. So, unlike the Civil Rights Commission's proposal, the Mansfield-Dirksen bill would apply only to *federal* elections. Under the legislation, registration officials could still use arbitrary literacy standards to exclude citizens seeking to vote in nonfederal contests.

In January, despite liberal protests, Mansfield sent his bill to the Judiciary Committee for hearings. Sensitive to concerns that Chairman James Eastland would "pigeonhole" the bill, the majority leader promised to attach the bill to a House-passed measure if the committee did not report it within sixty to ninety days. Sam Ervin's constitutional rights subcommittee held hearings in March and early April. Then, true to form, Eastland and Ervin sat on the bill and refused to report it out. As promised, Mansfield moved to bring the legislation to the floor. On April 24 he told the Senate he would attach the literacy legislation to a minor House-passed bill.

Mansfield's move sparked an immediate filibuster. The southern opposition featured the standard bombast about the evils of cloture and the dangers of unconstitutional federal usurpation of the right of states to establish voting qualifications. Typical was Virginia's Willis Robertson, who maintained the issue was "whether Congress can say, *ipse dixit*, 'No matter what kind of dumbbell you are, if you stay in school through the sixth grade, mister, you qualify to vote.' "

On May 2 Eastland may have established the all-time standard for irresponsibility in debate when he unleashed a spiteful attack on the

Supreme Court. The court, he charged, had "infringed, invaded and usurped" congressional powers. "The court must be restricted," he declared. "Unless it is, it will not only snap and bite, but will tear to pieces and devour constitutional government." To prove his point, Eastland offered detailed "box scores" of court decisions "involving communism or subversion" in which he believed justices had voted "in favor of the position advocated by the Communist Party." Explaining only that his staff had determined the "pro-Communist" standards, Eastland asserted that Justice Hugo Black, a former Alabama senator, had voted the "communist" position in each of 102 decisions. Chief Justice Earl Warren and Justice William Brennan, he claimed, had sided with the Communists in a majority of decisions.

Humphrey and others vigorously attacked Eastland's offensive remarks. "It is a disservice to the cause of constitutional government," Humphrey said the following day, "and it cannot be justified." New York's Jacob Javits labeled Eastland's remarks "tommyrot." California Republican Thomas Kuchel called the speech "pitiful, puny . . . shocking and evil." Reaction to Eastland's performance might have provided momentum for supporters of the bill, but Mansfield refused to force the issue. For two weeks he allowed southerners to wage what one *Congressional Quarterly* writer described as "a rather leisurely filibuster" in which neither side strictly enforced the rules of debate. Respecting his colleagues' aversion to the marathon debates of the 1950s, Mansfield ran the Senate more like a bank. The Senate convened, usually at noon, debated the bill—and other matters—for no more than six hours, and usually adjourned before 6:00 p.m. He ordered no weekend sessions. "The leadership gave up," said Pennsylvania's Joseph Clark. The debate, said *Time*, "had all the conviction of a professional wrestling match: everybody played his role for the crowd, but nobody got hurt."

It was Mansfield's legislative judgment, not his accommodating leadership style, which deserved the most criticism. Before a May 10 cloture vote, Mansfield told the Senate that if the cloture motion failed, he would move to table the bill. It was a tactical error Johnson would never have committed. In making the announcement, Mansfield revealed his hand. Wavering moderates in both parties were off the hook, knowing that they could placate both sides by opposing cloture and then voting against Mansfield's tabling motion. Absent the knowledge of an impending tabling motion, the cloture question would have been all-important—a vote for or against the literacy bill. Now it was just a procedural question for those moderate Republicans and Democrats who hoped to appease the powerful southerners still chairing the Senate's most important committees. The cloture motion failed as expected, 43-53. Twenty-three Republicans joined twenty-three southern Democrats and seven northern Democrats in supporting the filibuster. True to form, moderates of both parties effortlessly switched sides when Mansfield moved to table the bill. With even Mansfield voting against it, the tabling motion failed, 33-64. In other words, an overwhelming majority of senators supported legislation on which they were unable or reluctant to allow a vote. "This is the damnedest thing I ever saw," a reporter scoffed. "That bill hasn't got a chance and everybody knows it. Yet everybody's getting fat off of it." Mansfield tried—and failed—again on May 14 to get cloture.

When critics suggested that the Senate leadership had bungled the bill, Mansfield countered that liberals and the Kennedy administration were more to blame because they were unwilling to aggressively fight for its passage. While New Jersey Republican Clifford Case took Mansfield to task for his failure to force the issue on the Senate, he reserved equal criticism for Kennedy—who, he said, "gave the matter a very low priority." Mansfield said that when he secured Kennedy's unenthusiastic support for the bill, he found little fervor for it among liberal organizations. "The liberal groups came in after ten days of doing nothing to ask me what they could do and I said in effect, 'You're too late. You could have helped before, but it's gone too far now.' And we were defeated."

During the debate, on May 8, Humphrey had delivered one of the more eloquent appeals for the legislation, drawing on his enduring theme of America's tarnished image around the world:

> People are speaking up for their rights, here at home as well in Africa, in Latin America, in Asia, and everywhere else.
>
> They are demanding the right to vote.
>
> I am happy to say that people behind the Iron Curtain are speaking up for their rights . . . All over the world people are demanding that they be treated as human beings, with the qualities of dignity and decency to which humanity is entitled . . .
>
> Democracy is under attack today, every hour of the day and night. A world of coercion, of tyranny, confronts our world of free choice.

But democracy can be sapped from within as well as besieged from without.

Democracy is an end, or objective, but it is also a means. It must work as a means by which people can meet their problems, or its survival as an end is less than certain . . .

The preacher and poet John Donne once said: "Any man's death diminishes me, because I am involved in Mankinde; And therefore never send to ask for whom the bell tolls; it tolls for thee."

Liberty is just as indivisible, democracy is just as indivisible. If the bell tolls against democracy in any corner of our country; if citizens are denied the vote without just cause, it tolls for us here in Washington, in our respective States, and here in the Chamber of the Senate, too.

The failure to muster the votes to pass even an incremental, seemingly innocuous civil rights measure was a sobering defeat that only reinforced the perception—at the White House and now in the Senate—that civil rights was an impossible hurdle. Consulting with Mansfield after the vote, Assistant Attorney General Burke Marshall asked, "What should we tell people about the prospects for civil rights in the Senate?" "Tell them the truth," Mansfield replied. "What is the truth?" Marshall asked. Said Mansfield: "That you'll never get a civil rights bill with a Democratic president." A Democratic president, Mansfield believed, could "never persuade that many Republican senators to vote for cloture," even if he decided to "become involved" in the fight.

Given the legislative record of the previous five years, few could argue with Mansfield's logic. Congress had enacted civil rights measures in 1957 and 1960 because a Republican president, with considerable help from a strong majority leader, had assembled a coalition of northern and western Democrats and moderate Republicans. By themselves—without public support and White House leadership—the northern Democrats were powerless to enlist ambivalent western Democrats to join a civil rights coalition. Likewise, Republicans were unlikely to support civil rights bills that enjoyed only mild popularity and that the president himself was unwilling to actively champion. The failure of the literacy bill persuaded Marshall that "nobody cared" about a bill "that shouldn't have been controversial at all." The plight of black Americans,

Marshall concluded, was "still pretty invisible to the country as a whole."

While the civil rights filibuster thrived in the Senate,* Kennedy's Justice Department continued waging its quiet war against voting rights violations and school segregation throughout the South. In June 1962 Robert Kennedy announced that the department had initiated investigations and legal actions in almost one hundred southern counties under provisions of the 1957 and 1960 civil rights acts. (One was Sunflower County, Mississippi, the home of Senator James Eastland.) Kennedy's department also actively encouraged civil rights organizations to undertake voter registration efforts. Assured that the federal government would protect their workers, Southern Regional Council established the Voter Education Project, an outgrowth of Kennedy's determined belief that the power of the ballot would be far more effective than marches, sit-ins, and Freedom Rides. "If enough Negroes registered," he maintained, "they could obtain redress of their grievances internally, without the federal government being involved at all."

Meanwhile, officials at the Department of Health, Education and Welfare began an effort aimed at the gradual desegregation of public schools in the South. Relying on two 1950 laws, the administration said it hoped to establish desegregated schools in areas "impacted" by federal military or civilian activities. HEW Secretary Abraham Ribicoff announced in March that the administration might begin implementing provisions of the 1950 laws that allowed the federal government to establish on-base schools when no "suitable" schools were otherwise available for children living on federal property. The definition of "suitable," said Ribicoff, would now include "desegregated." At the same time, the Justice Department signaled its willingness to expand the scope of federal intervention by compelling desegregation of local school districts receiving federal impact funds. That, reasoned Burke Marshall, might lead to even more aggressive federal action. "If we have the power to bring suits to compel the desegregation of impacted area schools, it follows that within the limits of staff and time we are going to desegregate all impacted schools."

---

*The Senate invoked cloture for the first time since 1927 in August 1962 when it voted, 63–27, to break a *liberal* filibuster against Kennedy's communications satellite bill.

While southern members of Congress opposed Ribicoff's plans, many of them could never have imagined just how far Kennedy and his Justice Department would carry their efforts to desegregate educational facilities in the South. The first bloody confrontation would occur, not surprisingly, in Mississippi.

The crisis began when the NAACP's Legal Defense Fund took up the cause of James Meredith. A twenty-nine-year-old black Air Force veteran, Meredith had first been rejected by the University of Mississippi in Oxford in 1961. With the NAACP's help, Meredith sued the school. He lost, but in June the Fifth Circuit Court of Appeals overturned the district court ruling and ordered the school to enroll Meredith. The decision set Meredith and the federal government on a collision course with Mississippi governor Ross Barnett, a firebrand segregationist who had campaigned for office on a pledge to keep the state's schools "segregated at all costs." With his political fortunes sagging midway through his four-year term, this was a promise Barnett meant to keep—and exploit.

In September Barnett placed himself squarely in the middle of the controversy when he persuaded the university's trustees to appoint him as "special registrar" so that he could personally reject Meredith's admission. On September 20, shortly after Meredith arrived on campus, Barnett defiantly sent him away. The school's trustees were not so resolute. When threatened with federal contempt charges, they capitulated and agreed to enroll Meredith. Barnett, who instinctively understood the political benefits of his opposition to Meredith's enrollment, stood firm. On September 25 he physically blocked Meredith and two Justice Department officials from entering the offices of the state's college board in Jackson. "I hereby finally deny you admission to the University of Mississippi," Barnett announced after refusing to receive a federal court order enjoining him from further interference in Meredith's registration. As Meredith left the building, a gaggle of state legislators cheered Barnett and jeered Meredith and his entourage. According to one state senator, Barnett's defiant stand had been "the most brilliant piece of statesmanship ever displayed in Mississippi."

The following day Meredith was thwarted again, this time by Lieutenant Governor Paul Johnson, who stepped in when inclement weather grounded Barnett's airplane. Bolstered by twenty highway patrolmen and a dozen Mississippi sheriffs, Johnson planted himself in the middle of the main road leading into campus. After a brief but tense confrontation, Mississippi authorities again turned away Meredith and the Justice Department officials. In Washington an exasperated Attorney General Kennedy, who had been prodding Barnett by phone for days, pledged to do "whatever is necessary" to enroll Meredith—including, he said, sending in "federal troops."

On September 26, accompanied by twenty-five unarmed federal marshals, Meredith approached the town of Oxford to make his fourth attempt at the court-ordered enrollment. This time the opposition to Meredith's enrollment would be a contrived confrontation, choreographed by Kennedy and Barnett during intense phone negotiations. The plan was simple: By refusing to enroll Meredith, Barnett would defend Mississippi's "honor" and keep his campaign promise to resist the forced integration of the state's schools. As part of the plan, two dozen U.S. marshals, one of them with his gun drawn, would then force Barnett to back down.

The deal was really no more than a tenuous agreement. Neither side trusted the other, especially Barnett, who wanted Kennedy's men to employ greater force. "We got a big crowd here, and if one pulls his gun and we all turn, it would be very embarrassing," Barnett explained to Kennedy. "Isn't it possible to have them all pull their guns?" Kennedy demurred. He would make only one promise: "I am just telling you," he told Barnett, "that we are arriving and we are arriving with force."

All over Mississippi, but especially in Oxford and Jackson, emotions ran violently high. On Saturday, September 29, Barnett addressed an agitated crowd of 46,000 during halftime of the Ole Miss-Kentucky game at Jackson's Memorial Stadium. "I love Mississippi!" he shouted from a microphone on the field. "I love her people!" With a clenched fist held high, Barnett left the crowd in a racist fury, declaring, "I love our customs!" The whole scene, one student later said, "was like a big Nazi rally."

The next day, as Meredith and his escorts drove toward the campus, word came that an unruly, possibly violent mob of twenty-five hundred citizens and about five hundred state police officers had gathered on campus. Barnett pleaded with Attorney General Kennedy to call Meredith off. "There is liable to be a hundred people killed here," he said. Kennedy relented and ordered Meredith to turn back. He could not enroll Meredith, he announced, "without major violence and bloodshed for the citizens of Mississippi."

Failing to get "satisfactory assurances" from Barnett that he would enroll Meredith, President Kennedy had already federalized the Mississippi National Guard and placed federal troops on standby in nearby Memphis, Tennessee. Finally, after Attorney General Kennedy threatened to reveal the details of Barnett's secret negotiations with the White House, the governor signaled his willingness to back down. The next day—Sunday, September 30—Barnett would allow Meredith on campus. Barnett and the university would ostensibly bow to the superior and overwhelming federal forces. That evening four hundred federal marshals led by Deputy Attorney General Nicholas Katzenbach escorted Meredith onto the Ole Miss campus for his registration the next morning.

In Washington, meanwhile, at about 10:00 p.m., President Kennedy went on national television and radio with a plea for respectful obedience of the law. He regretted, he said, that executive action was necessary to ensure Meredith's enrollment. "But all other avenues and alternatives, including persuasion and conciliation, had been tried and exhausted." Then Kennedy spoke to the university's students. "You have a great tradition to uphold, a tradition of honor and courage, won on the field of battle and on the gridiron as well as the university campus."* But Kennedy noted that the "eyes of the nation and all the world are upon you and upon all of us, and the honor of your university and state are in the balance. I am certain the great majority of the students will uphold that honor."

Minutes later, Barnett released the alarming news to his citizens: Federal authorities had "overpowered" state forces at Ole Miss. By the time Kennedy finished delivering his speech, an ugly and bloody riot engulfed the university. Realizing that Meredith was now on campus, rioters began attacking the Lyceum, an impressive antebellum building that had once served as a hospital for wounded Civil War soldiers and now housed the school's administrative offices. For most of the evening, the mob mistakenly believed Meredith was inside. Actually he was in another part of campus, under heavy guard and sleeping fitfully in a dormitory room as the violent unrest unfolded.

As federal marshals and highway patrolmen stood guard, the mob began shouting, "Go to Cuba, nigger lovers, go to Cuba!" Some threw rocks at the marshals and slashed the tires of nearby army trucks. As

---

*Kennedy's admonition to Mississippians to "uphold" their state's "great tradition" offended Martin Luther King and other civil rights leaders.

the rioting intensified, Barnett deplored the violence but did little to stop it. He and other state authorities stood by idly as most of the local police and highway patrolmen slowly disappeared, some of them derisively dismissing the federal marshals as "Kennedy's Koon Klan." The evacuation left four hundred marshals to stave off an angry mob of twenty-five hundred, and it left the campus gates unguarded. As the local authorities abandoned the school, a hodgepodge of unsavory, enraged adults and students from other colleges—from states as far away as Georgia, Texas, Arkansas, and Florida—streamed onto campus. Until now the marshals had held their fire, calmly withstanding the barrage of rocks, eggs, and verbal taunts. However, when a two-foot piece of lead pipe came shooting out of the darkness and struck a marshal on the side of his helmet, chief U.S. marshal James McShane gave the word: "Let 'em have it. Gas!" he ordered, as the marshals donned their masks and began firing tear gas canisters into the crowd.

Choking and cursing, the crowd dispersed, but only temporarily. Retired major general Edwin A. Walker, an erratic racist who had commanded the army troops sent into Little Rock by Dwight Eisenhower in 1957, was on the scene. Standing at the foot of the school's rebel monument, he rallied the students for a counterattack. "Don't let up now," he cried. "You may lose this battle, but you will have to be heard . . . You must be prepared for possible death. If you are not, go home now." Their courage revived and their anger intensified, the students began streaming back toward the Lyceum, shouting, "You goddam Communists!" and "You nigger-lovers, go to hell!" Many of them wielded shotguns, rifles, bats, clubs, bricks, and hunks of concrete. Some came charging with firebombs made from Coca-Cola bottles.

"There were a lot of people going 'squirrel hunting' that night," Katzenbach later recalled. In their mad attempt to get at Meredith, the rioters even commandeered a fire truck, and later a bulldozer, hoping to storm the Lyceum. Marshals repelled them with tear gas and, later, with the only federal gunfire of the evening: When the students aimed their firehoses at the building, marshals responded by shooting up the hoses. Despite the relative success of the tear gas, casualties mounted. Dozens of marshals were wounded by bullets and flying debris. Finally, a worried President Kennedy—who had, ironically, declared in 1960 that "there is more power in the presidency than to let things drift and then suddenly call out the troops"—ordered in regular army units from Memphis and the local Mississippi National Guard unit. Among the

National Guardsmen—commanded by the nephew of Oxford's most famous citizen, the late novelist William Faulkner—was Barnett's own son.

By dawn the rioters had gone, but not until they had inflicted heavy casualties and wreaked warlike havoc on campus and in town. Two people—a French newspaper reporter and a local jukebox repairman— were dead. Another 166 federal marshals had been wounded, 28 of them by gunfire. Forty soldiers and National Guardsmen were injured. "We brought in too many troops, too late," Katzenbach later said. "In retrospect, there should have been more decisive action. The Kennedys just didn't understand Barnett's weakness." Later that morning Meredith, unharmed and escorted by federal marshals, registered and began attending classes. As he headed for class, Meredith endured the taunts of white students: "Hey, James, how you like seeing what you did to your campus, nigger?" and "That blood is on your hands, nigger bastard!"

As the campus emerged from its violent stupor, twenty-three thousand federal troops poured into Oxford to maintain order, imposing what *Newsweek* called "an undeclared state of military rule." Although Barnett was clearly responsible for having allowed the highway patrolmen to withdraw at a crucial moment, the governor shamelessly pointed his finger at the Kennedy administration and "inexperienced and trigger-happy" marshals. The violence, he declared, had been "deliberately flamed in order that the resulting resistance can be cited as justification for military force against the people of the sovereign state and the crushing of the rights of all the states."

Among southern members of Congress, there was little support for Meredith and even less for President Kennedy's decision to send in troops. Louisiana's Allen Ellender declared his "full sympathy" with Barnett, who, the senator explained, "is doing his utmost to fulfill the campaign pledges and the will of the people of his state." Meredith had received "better offers from other schools," Ellender reported to the Senate. "His idea is to enroll in a strictly white school and it strikes me that his motives should be closely scrutinized." While deploring the violence at Ole Miss, North Carolina's Sam Ervin blamed Meredith for much of the unrest. "It seems to me that those who are engaged in fomenting litigation which has such a tragic aftermath might well meditate upon the words of St. Paul when he said: 'All things are lawful unto me, but all things are not expedient.' " In Birmingham, just days before the violence, Russell had voiced his enthusiastic support for "the great and courageous governor of Mississippi." Were he governor, Russell told a meeting of Alabama Democrats, he would take the same stand as Barnett. For good measure, he attacked the nation's highest court. "It is regretful," he said, "that we have no one in the Supreme Court that recognizes the fundamentals of democracy."

More responsible leaders backed Kennedy. Days earlier, Dwight Eisenhower had deplored Barnett's refusal to admit Meredith as "absolutely unconscionable and indefensible." In the aftermath, Harry Truman tartly declared that Kennedy "is doing the right thing." Ohio's Democratic senator, Stephen Young, insisted that "there just cannot be any compromise on civil rights." New York Republican Jacob Javits, a sometime critic of the president's lethargy on civil rights, strongly supported Kennedy. He told the Senate that while the nation was "grief-stricken by the unbelievable stupid violence and tragic casualties, we can only hope the lesson that reckless defiance of the law only breeds anarchy will at last be learned in Mississippi."

Internationally the incident was another human rights embarrassment for the United States—and for the administration's attempts to foster freedom and democracy around the world. In France, *Le Monde* noted that "each time the resistance [to desegregation] appears more anachronistic and more odious." State radio in Moscow solemnly observed that Meredith's registration at Ole Miss would not erase the "national shame" over segregation. The foreign critics were correct. America could hardly champion human rights abroad when the enrollment of a black citizen in a public university sparked a violent uprising that bordered on open rebellion. It is impossible, *New York Times* columnist C.L. Sulzberger argued in an eloquent October 3 essay, to defend "the downtrodden overseas while permitting a second class of citizens at home in the land of liberty." Those who hinder social progress, said Sulzberger, "serve only to aid our enemies and to inspire resentment among those who would be our friends."

The consequences of the Oxford riot were not all negative. Ole Miss, after all, had been integrated—finally. Thanks to courageous federal judges—particularly those on the Fifth Circuit Court of Appeals—and the Kennedy Justice Department, whites in Mississippi and other southern states were beginning to realize that the Constitution would henceforth be applied to every citizen. "No American need be ashamed of the 'Oxford incident,'" a Massachusetts man insisted in a letter to the editor of *Time*. The bloodshed and violence, he argued, had overshadowed the fact that "the basic rights of one American—one quiet, unassuming citizen—were being infringed upon, and as a result of this infringement, the entire power, might and prestige of the U.S. Government went to his assistance . . . Americans abroad and at home need not hang their heads in shame. This was a proud day for Americans."

President Kennedy's pledge to sign an executive order barring discrimination in public housing—"by a stroke of the pen," he had once declared—haunted him into the fall of 1962. Two years after his election as president, Kennedy stood accused of the same reluctance to act that had afflicted his predecessor. For months supporters of the long-promised order had ridiculed Kennedy's unfulfilled rhetoric by mailing thousands of ink pens to the White House. Not particularly amused, Kennedy ordered the pens piled in Harris Wofford's office. For the first twenty-two months of Kennedy's term, federal housing remained a bastion of racial discrimination, tacitly sanctioned by the federal government and practiced in virtually every American city.

Kennedy had several persuasive reasons to delay issuing the order. As with other civil rights proposals, Kennedy hoped to avoid antagonizing the southern Democrats whose support he needed on a host of other domestic initiatives, including his plan to create a Department of Housing and Urban Affairs. Kennedy's advisors believed that the ultimate success of that proposal hinged on the tenuous, dwindling goodwill of southerners. If Kennedy won approval for the new department, Robert Weaver—head of Kennedy's Housing and Home Finance Administration—would become the first black person nominated to head a cabinet department. According to Burke Marshall, Kennedy concluded that the daunting task of winning approval for the new department, with Weaver as secretary-apparent, "would be much more difficult" if he issued the housing order first. Yet Congress had now rejected the proposal twice. By late 1962 creation of the new cabinet-level department appeared hopeless, effectively removing at least one of Kennedy's rationales for continued delay.

There were more reasons as well. Other civil rights issues—the Freedom Rides, the Ole Miss crisis, school desegregation, and voting rights—also demanded Kennedy's time and attention. "We were up to our necks in civil rights," Robert Kennedy later observed, adding that "the amount of good that was going to be accomplished by [the housing

order] was marginal." By the summer of 1962, the approaching congressional elections only complicated matters. Issuing the controversial
directive before the November elections would likely infuse a highly
emotional civil rights question into the campaigns of southern Democrats, who were already on the defensive over Kennedy's other domestic
programs.

Finally was the question of the order's exact wording. Though it
would clearly prohibit discrimination in federally owned or operated
housing and housing built with federal loans or federally secured loans,
other issues were not so clear. Should the nondiscrimination order apply,
as the Civil Rights Commission recommended, to conventional loans
and mortgages made by financial institutions that the federal government
merely regulated? And should the order be retroactive—that is, should
housing already built with federal money be included, or should the
order simply apply to all such housing built in the future? Kennedy's
advisors even debated whether the president should take the more dramatic step of demanding that the Federal Deposit Insurance Corporation
and the Federal Home Loan Bank Board force its member banks and
savings and loans to comply with the order. Kennedy doubted his ability
to persuade the institutions' conservative board members to follow his
lead, and he worried about the economic impact of such a sweeping
order. A broad, retroactive directive, he feared, might dampen housing
starts at a time when his priority was ensuring greater economic growth.
"And the president finally decided," said aide Theodore Sorenson, "that
we should make the order as broad as we were certain our writ would
run and no further."

On November 20, two weeks after the congressional elections and
twenty-two months into his term, President Kennedy signed the long-
awaited order. Its announcement—dispensed along with the dramatic
news that Soviet bombers were leaving Cuba and another pronounce-
ment on an Indian border dispute with China—was not a major news
story. Limited in scope and not retroactive, the order required federal
agencies to take all legal steps to prevent racial discrimination in the
selling and leasing of federally owned or operated housing. Also covered
was housing built with federal loans—including senior and community
facilities and college housing—and single-family and apartment dwellings insured by the Federal Housing Administration or the Veterans
Administration. "It is neither proper nor equitable," Kennedy said, "that
Americans should be denied the benefits of housing owned by the federal

government or financed through federal assistance on the basis of race, color, creed or national origin."

While the presidential directive was welcome news to liberals and civil rights leaders, it failed to satisfy those who expected more of Kennedy. As Martin Luther King acknowledged, presidential leadership on civil rights was now much greater than under Eisenhower and Truman. "But that didn't mean," King added, "that [Kennedy] was giving the kind of leadership at that time that the enormity of the problem demanded." The violence sparked by the Freedom Riders in Alabama and James Meredith in Mississippi had given Kennedy grand opportunities to display support for basic civil rights, but his refusal to press the Congress for a comprehensive legislative remedy fed the lingering questions about the degree of his sincerity and the strength of his commitment. To critics and even allies, Kennedy seemed to pay attention to civil rights only when an issue or a crisis imposed itself on his administration.

Active and eloquent on so many other fronts, Kennedy drifted aimlessly in the sea of civil rights, tossed back and forth by the rolling waves of competing interests and ideologies. The seas, meanwhile, only grew more tumultuous.

CHAPTER SEVENTEEN

"Wait" Has Always Meant "Never"

AFTER TWO YEARS IN OFFICE, President Kennedy still had no comprehensive civil rights program and no prospects for one. Even if he overcame his hesitancy to send Congress a legislative proposal, his dismal record on Capitol Hill made passage an unlikely prospect at best. The president, said one senate aide, "couldn't buy a bill out of Congress." While Kennedy and his men temporized and worried about alienating southern congressmen, events in the South spun out of control. The Freedom Rides, the violence at Ole Miss, and other ugly incidents slowly awakened the slumbering national consciousness and dramatized the plight of southern blacks.

In February 1963, a Kennedy-requested Civil Rights Commission report, "Freedom to the Free," supplied another call to action, graphically documenting the pitiful progress of civil rights in the hundred years since Abraham Lincoln had signed the Emancipation Proclamation. Citizenship for blacks was not "fully realized," the commission declared. Blaming southern leaders for their dogged "resistance to the established law of the land and to social change," the commissioners reported that "subtler forms" of discrimination still existed in vast areas of the North: the "gentlemen's agreement" barring blacks from housing outside ghettos, discriminatory employment practices that kept blacks in menial jobs, and overburdened neighborhood schools that resulted in inadequate educational opportunities. Kennedy tried to put the best face on the damning report, and weakly pointed to the modest civil rights progress of the previous fifteen years. Despite "setbacks," Kennedy admitted that "we still have some length to go." To many, that was a vast understatement. Georgia activist Julian Bond and his coworkers on the Student Nonviolent Coordinating Committee believed that Kennedy was "cowardly in enforcing existing civil rights laws, cautious in seeking new, stronger legislation from Congress, and too eager to trade justice for order when racist whites threatened violence against civil rights forces in the South."

Attorney General Robert Kennedy, meanwhile, was far more energetic. He aggressively touted the administration's achievements in "every area of civil rights—whether voting, transportation, education, employment or housing." The attorney general insisted that 1962 had been "a year of great progress in civil rights." Yet sadly, despite the administration's otherwise truly remarkable record of executive action, the crisis at Ole Miss was symbolic of Kennedy's passive approach to civil rights: aggressive enforcement of impotent laws and failure to propose new, stronger statutes. The Ole Miss debacle had only highlighted Kennedy's sometimes-painful inability to tackle the intransigence of southern officials with anything less than military might.

On civil rights the young president resembled a fire chief who waited until a situation burst into flames before acting. "Events," said Ramsey Clark, then a young Justice Department official, "outran leadership." Although Kennedy refused to admit it, the vigorous enforcement of powerful, comprehensive civil rights legislation—not yet on the books—was the only means to begin curbing the nation's escalating social unrest. There were simply not enough assistant attorneys general to shuttle between cities and disarm brewing racial violence, not enough federal troops to keep or restore the peace in dozens of southern locales. Executive action and military coercion were weak substitutes for strong, enforceable civil rights statutes. Absent tough federal laws, the Kennedy Justice Department was a only minor combatant in the civil rights fight. The struggle was, instead, waged in the streets and in federal courtrooms throughout the South. The NAACP sued. The courts ruled, and southern authorities often defied those decrees. In the worst of cases, the president finally dispatched U.S. marshals or federal troops to ensure compliance or quash the resulting violent uprisings.

Even the federal courts were not always reliable on civil rights. Despite Kennedy's efforts to nominate liberals to judgeships, southern senators often foisted their segregationist friends on the president. "We came out with some bad appointments in the South," Nicholas Katzenbach admitted. Walter Gewin, appointed to the Fifth Circuit Court of Appeals from Alabama, strenuously opposed the court's decision to order desegregation of schools in Birmingham. E. Gordon West, appointed to a district judgeship in Louisiana, had once assailed the *Brown* decision as "one of the truly regrettable decisions of all time." Another Kennedy appointee in Louisiana, Frank B. Ellis of New Orleans, upheld the constitutionality of a state law requiring disclosure of a candidate's race on election ballots. In Mississippi, William Harold Cox—James Eastland's college roommate—dragged his feet on voting rights cases and denied several Justice Department requests to order the compliance of state officials. During his first voting rights case, Cox had attacked the black plaintiffs as "a bunch of niggers" who were "acting like a bunch of chimpanzees." In Georgia, another Kennedy-appointed judge, J. Robert Elliott, dragged his feet on two important civil rights cases. Before his appointment, Elliott had defended Georgia's county-unit system, which ensured the primacy of rural counties, by declaring, "I don't want these pinks, radicals and black voters to outvote those who are trying to preserve our segregation laws and other traditions." NAACP leader Roy Wilkins was one of many civil rights leaders who worried that Kennedy's "obeisance" to southern senators hindered the civil rights movement. "They should have said, 'We want judges that are going to carry out the Constitution of the United States as it is interpreted by the Supreme Court and by most of the people of this country, and we want people who are going to do that, and those who aren't, we don't want.' They didn't say this."

Kennedy's cautious deference to southern members of Congress yielded him little legislative success. Most southerners opposed his domestic policies and vigorously protested his response to the unrest in Alabama and Mississippi. Kennedy's cautious, incremental approach seemed to please no one in the South, nor did it serve to calm racial tensions. Several cities appeared ready to ignite at the slightest spark. The growing disquiet in the South, George Reedy advised Vice President Johnson in a memorandum, was "spreading and a number of northern cities are dry tinder—ready to burst into flames at the least spark." After two years of delay, almost everyone but Kennedy's White House advisors understood that the president's policy of caution and executive action had failed—rather miserably. It was time for aggressive action.

Yet no civil rights bill, however popular, stood a chance of becoming law until Kennedy and Senate liberals found a way to deprive the southerners of their most potent weapon—the filibuster.

The biennial clash over cloture began on January 14 with Clinton Anderson's proposal to lower the cloture threshold from two-thirds to three-fifths of senators present and voting. Humphrey also entered the debate, filing a statement on behalf of fifty-one senators—thirty-six Democrats and fifteen Republicans—who wanted cloture invoked by "a lesser number" of votes. The southerners, of course, filibustered the motion to consider Anderson's resolution. In a debate on the motion, which lasted for twenty-four days, Russell and other southern leaders worked feverishly to stave off cloture. (The cloture rule, as amended in January 1959, no longer excluded from cloture those filibusters designed to stop proposed rule changes.) Freshmen senators eager for certain committees and veterans who longed for better committees found that Russell and other conservative steering committee members refused to make assignments until the Senate resolved the cloture question. "This," complained Pennsylvania's Joseph Clark, "held the sword of Damocles over the heads of all Senators" hoping for better committees. Russell also "reasoned" with small-state senators, persuasively arguing that the filibuster was their only protection from the tyranny of the majority.

Meanwhile, as the Senate's presiding officer, Johnson refused liberal entreaties for a ruling on the constitutionality of changing the Senate's rules by majority vote. Liberals wanted the vice president to rule that the Senate was not a "continuing body" and could therefore rewrite its rules by a simple majority vote at the beginning of each new Congress. Had Johnson ruled in their favor—as Richard Nixon did in 1959 and 1961—a simple majority of senators *might* have voted to uphold the ruling, clearing the way for another vote on lowering the cloture threshold. Johnson refused to take sides. He testily explained, "that is a question for the Senate itself to decide." Senators, not the vice president, he said, must rule on the constitutionality of changing the rules by simple majority.

Harry McPherson, who assured Johnson that he had no right to make such a ruling, said he feared that if the vice president intervened as the liberals wanted, "Russell, old as he was, might climb right over [Senate parliamentarian] Charlie Watkins's wispy head and seek to throttle him." On January 31, with Majority Leader Mansfield on the sidelines, the Senate declined, 53-42, to consider the constitutional question as propounded by Johnson. One week later, in a cloture vote, senators refused to end the southern filibuster. Liberals fell 10 votes short of cloture, 54-42.

Russell had won. The filibuster seemed safe, and civil rights only a faint hope.

In that vote, however, Russell could see his ultimate defeat. After the southerners prevailed, Joseph Clark ambled over to Russell. "Dick," he said, "here's my sword again. I guess fate has cast me in the role of Robert E. Lee and you as Ulysses S. Grant." Smiling sadly, Russell replied, "Dammit, Joe, it's beginning to look like I'm Lee and you're Grant. You're slowly eroding us away." As Russell understood, the fifty-four votes marked the first time liberals had mustered a majority for cloture. It was only a matter of time until, as one *New York Times* reporter wrote, the "irresistible current in national attitudes" caused ten more senators to support cloture. Like General Lee, *Newsweek* observed, Russell was now "burdened with a lost cause and a tragic destiny: to throw his monumental talents against the relentless mainstream of history."

Leaders of both political parties sensed the shifting political sands on civil rights. Growing numbers of voters, in the North and South, wanted Congress to act—some because they believed in equal rights for black citizens, others for fear that the violent social unrest in Alabama and Mississippi might soon engulf their peaceful cities.

On January 31 a large group of House Republicans led by New York's John Lindsay introduced a surprisingly strong civil rights bill. Accusing Kennedy of failing to honor the Democratic party platform, Lindsay declared his legislation was "designed to pass," unlike the Democrats' "public relations" attempts. Lindsay's potent bill made the Civil Rights Commission permanent and empowered its members to investigate election fraud. Furthermore, the bill created a federal commission for Equal Opportunity in Employment to investigate job discrimination by government contractors, authorized the Justice Department to initiate lawsuits in school desegregation cases, and made a sixth-grade education the standard for proof of literacy in voting registration. In the Senate, meanwhile, a bipartisan group of liberals led by Joseph Clark introduced school desegregation legislation. Kentucky Republican John Sherman Cooper and Connecticut Democrat Thomas Dodd also introduced a measure requiring states to impose uniform voting requirements to prevent the arbitrary and discriminatory application of voting laws.

The very fact that Republicans had beaten the Democratic president to the punch on civil rights was more than a little embarrassing to Democratic liberals. Kennedy still had no bill, not even a weak one. Morale was low among members of the Civil Rights Leadership

Conference. One day when NAACP lobbyist Clarence Mitchell arrived for a meeting of conference members, someone asked, "Can you cheer us up?" Mitchell responded, "Certainly. The Republicans are going to introduce some bills."

President Kennedy finally joined the legislative debate over civil rights on February 28, sending Congress a voting rights bill with minor education provisions and a four-year extension of the Civil Rights Commission. But the bill's primary aim was to correct "two major defects" of the 1957 and 1960 civil rights acts: "the usual long and difficult delays" in obtaining court judgments in voting rights cases and the laws' failure to address the "abuse of discretion" by local voter registrars "who do not treat all applicants uniformly." In addition to permitting federal judges to appoint referees before the conclusion of a voting rights case, the bill required courts to give "expedited treatment" to voting rights cases; prohibited "the application of different tests, standards, practices or procedures" for different prospective voters in federal elections; and established a sixth-grade education as proof of literacy in voter registration. Kennedy's bill also created a program of technical and financial assistance for school districts implementing desegregation plans.

The president's acknowledgment that his bill would not "constitute a final answer to the problems of race discrimination in this country" was clearly an understatement. As a voting rights measure, it was a moderate proposal; as a civil rights program, it was a pitiful substitute for aggressive legislative action. Martin Luther King, Joseph Rauh, and other civil rights advocates were dejected by Kennedy's refusal to offer a stronger, more comprehensive program. King told a friend that the Kennedy bill only strengthened his view of the president's "schizophrenic tendency" on civil rights. To Rauh, the bill was so "inane" it made civil rights activists "feel that it wasn't worth going for." NAACP leader Roy Wilkins saw little value in the Kennedy bill. "They were putting a toe in the water but they didn't dive in at all," Wilkins said. The bill was useful, he added, only because "it finally signaled that the administration recognized the necessity and efficacy of legislation."

Although civil rights leaders viewed the bill as only a weak voting rights measure, Russell declared that it encroached on "almost every phase of social and racial relations." In a relatively mild attack, the Georgia senator unveiled a new criticism of the administration's attempts to desegregate restaurants, hotels, bus stations, airports, and other public accommodations. The fault, he asserted, rested not with white racists but with the unacceptable nature of blacks. "Not on a single occasion," Russell said in a prepared statement, "has the president called upon any of the members of such groups to make any effort whatever to improve themselves so that they will be more acceptable to other citizens who may have certain standards for their associates." Russell offered no advice on how blacks might better themselves, but he clearly spoke for many southern racists when he asserted that whites should grant full citizenship only to those blacks whom they found "acceptable." John Stennis was more severe in his assessment of the bill. The Mississippi Democrat branded its provisions "so extreme and unconstitutional that Congress should not seriously consider them." Mississippi congressman John Bell Williams was even more explicit and outrageous: "The whole kit and caboodle is nothing more or less than an attempt to turn the government over to the NAACP."

Perhaps the most damning criticism of the bill came not from liberal Democrats or southern conservatives but from Republicans who, for now, were sponsors of the only comprehensive civil rights proposal before the new Congress. Gleeful at yet another opportunity to exploit divisions over civil rights within the Democratic ranks, Lindsay and other Republicans derided Kennedy's bill as a "thin" proposal. New York governor Nelson Rockefeller—whom Kennedy regarded as a prime contender for the 1964 Republican presidential nomination—dismissed the legislation as too little, too late. He noted that it addressed only five of the twenty-eight proposals recently made by the Civil Rights Commission. The real problem, said Rockefeller, was Kennedy's reluctance to fight for stronger legislation, which he said could pass "if the necessary leadership were forthcoming."

The obligatory partisan swipes at their civil rights proposal did not alarm Kennedy's men. Far more troublesome was the restlessness in the Democratic ranks, especially in the Senate. To dejected liberals such as Douglas, Humphrey, and Clark, the Republican initiative seemed more than a little enticing. At weekly leadership breakfasts, Humphrey had become a minor nuisance with his constant pleas for strong civil rights legislation. Kennedy rebuked Humphrey on at least two occasions, but Humphrey stood firm. "The leadership for civil rights," he told Kennedy, "either has to take place in the White House or it is going to take place in the streets." For now, at least, Humphrey and the other liberals would grudgingly yield to White House pressure to support Kennedy.

In Birmingham, meanwhile, Martin Luther King's followers prepared to take to the streets in fulfillment of Humphrey's ominous warning to Kennedy. By nature a moderate, conciliatory man, King had become the nation's leading voice for civil rights as president of the Southern Christian Leadership Conference. In the nine years since the Montgomery bus boycott, King's SCLC had become the preeminent civil rights organization in the South. King himself had become something of a living martyr of the civil rights movement. Racist white authorities had arrested and jailed him several times. His home had been bombed. In New York in 1958, a deranged assailant had stabbed him in the chest.

In 1963, King's aide Wyatt Tee Walker finally persuaded the civil rights leader to consider a dramatic showdown on civil rights. Only the year before, the SCLC had reluctantly abandoned a frustrating year-long desegregation project in Albany, Georgia. King failed because Albany's white leadership, although racist and intransigent, was not dumb. Led by the town's savvy police chief, Laurie Pritchett, Albany had responded to King's demands with a firm yet nonviolent no. A dedicated white supremacist, Pritchett had learned the unmistakable lessons of the Freedom Rides and Ole Miss: if he prevented violence, he could avoid federal intervention in his town. As Pritchett no doubt understood, refusing black civil rights demands became untenable only when violence resulted in the unkind glare of national news attention. King's Albany protest finally fizzled in September 1962, largely because of Pritchett's determination to arrest black protesters with minimum incident and no brutality. The events in Albany had never generated sensational front-page news in the *Washington Post* or the *New York Times*.

Old-fashioned nonconfrontational protest had proved ineffective. And King and his advisors knew that their movement could ill afford another failure like Albany. "To take a moderate approach hoping to get white help, doesn't work," Walker insisted to King. "You've got to have a crisis." King and his aides finally acknowledged the folly of fighting local disputes with narrowly focused goals. What they needed, in the words of one historian, was "an American Bastille," the kind of confrontation that could result in a symbolic victory with national repercussions. As King's friend Bayard Rustin observed, "protest becomes an effective tactic to the degree that it elicits brutality and oppression from the power structure." In Birmingham, King's men gave the effort the appropriate name of Project C—for *confrontation*. In early March, several weeks after the Kennedy administration presented its civil rights program to Congress, King arrived in Alabama to organize a series of mass demonstrations aimed at desegregating several downtown department stores, a group of federal buildings, and a suburban shopping center.

King's choice of Birmingham was significant. Among dozens of racially oppressive southern cities, none was more segregated and officially hostile to its black citizens. In the previous six years, Birmingham had suffered eighteen racially motivated bombings and fifty cross burnings. City parks had been closed since 1962, when local officials refused to heed a court order mandating integration of all public playgrounds. Birmingham officials had even abandoned their minor-league baseball franchise rather than compete against integrated teams. In almost every way, the city's white community clung desperately to the South's racist traditions. It was, in King's opinion, the best place in the South to make a dramatic statement about the evils of racial segregation. Yet despite the severe nature of its racial divisions, the city was no caldron of black anger and resentment. In the words of a *Time* reporter, Birmingham's blacks were "docile" and "they knew their place: they were 'niggers' in a Jim Crow town, and they bore their degradation in silence."

Viewed from another perspective, Birmingham's blacks were not willingly pacific but fearfully cowed into submission by the city's public safety commissioner, Eugene "Bull" Connor. A brutish racist, Connor had long ignored, perhaps even encouraged, violence against black leaders. Although he had recently campaigned for mayor and lost to a more-moderate opponent, Connor remained in complete control of the city's fearsome, all-white police force. With an eye on statewide office, the commissioner could not allow King and his black followers to humiliate or intimidate his department before all of white Alabama. He would hold the line. The defense of his city's racist mores would be forceful and unrelenting.

On April 3, the day after Birmingham's mayoral election, King and local minister Fred Shuttlesworth set their plan in motion: a gradual, deliberate escalation of organized protest. That day police arrested twenty black demonstrators at white-only lunch counters at four stores. The next day authorities apprehended several more in similar lunch-counter protests. King then declared that the foundation of the effort would be a widespread black boycott of Birmingham's white-owned department stores. Until these stores desegregated their lunch counters and hired more blacks in responsible positions, black shoppers would make their not-insignificant purchases elsewhere. "The Negro has enough buying power in Birmingham," King observed, "to make the difference between profit and loss in a business."

A simple economic boycott would never give King what he wanted most—a dramatic confrontation with Bull Connor. Although the boycott held firm, Project C unfolded in near oblivion for almost a week. Most local black leaders, resentful of King's "outsider" status, initially wanted no part of his movement or the uproar it might bring to their peaceful and comfortable lives. King was resolute. He upbraided more than a hundred black ministers for "riding around in big cars, living in fine homes" yet refusing "to take part in the fight." Those unwilling to "stand up with your people," he declared, "are not fit to be a preacher." Despite King's passionate appeal, only a handful of the local pastors offered their enthusiastic support.

Just as Project C appeared doomed at the hands of black apathy, Bull Connor came to its rescue. At the end of the first week, the police commissioner committed the first of many tactical blunders. On April 7 his officers arrested Reverend Shuttlesworth and forty-two others who joined a small band of peaceful black marchers on their way to City Hall. The next day, King's brother, A.D.—a local Baptist minister— led another small march from the Sixteenth Street Baptist Church toward downtown. Connor's men were on the scene again, now reinforced by a pack of vicious police dogs. This time an indignant crowd of black citizens lined the street in support of the marchers as the officers began making their arrests. When an onlooker charged at a dog with a knife, the dog attacked. Within minutes, other officers—some with dogs, other with clubs—turned on the crowd. Most of the terrified onlookers scurried for safety.

Wyatt Tee Walker instantly understood the significance of the brief scuffle. From now on King would stage all demonstrations to provoke a brutal response from Connor, which would in turn attract national attention and create an outpouring of sympathetic outrage. He encouraged those unwilling or unable to march to lend their moral support by lining the streets as the protesters passed.

On April 12 King defied a local court order and led a small march—supported by more than a thousand black spectators—from the Sixteenth Street Baptist Church. King had hoped the day's march would end in his arrest, thus ensuring wider popular support and notoriety for his cause. His wish was fulfilled. Police rounded up King and fifty of his followers after they marched only four blocks. King's arrest—he was placed in solitary confinement—finally began to focus the glare of the national news media on Birmingham. From his cell he answered his critics in the city's white religious community, who had condemned him as a troublemaking "outsider." In his now-legendary "Letter from a Birmingham Jail," King wrote:

> For years now I have heard the word "Wait." It rings in the ear of every Negro with a piercing familiarity. This "Wait" has always meant "Never." It has been a tranquilizing thalidomide, relieving the emotional stress for a moment only to give birth to an ill-formed infant of frustration. We must come to see with the distinguished jurist of yesterday that "justice too long delayed is justice denied." We have waited for more than three hundred and forty years for our constitutional and God-given rights.

In his letter, King acknowledged that his protest movement in Birmingham "seeks to create such a crisis and establish such creative tension that a community that has consistently refused to negotiate is forced to confront the issue. It seeks to dramatize the issue so that it can no longer be ignored."

King languished in jail for more than a week. By the time he posted bond and resumed leadership of Project C on April 20, his movement was in crisis, sputtering toward a complete standstill. Almost a thousand protesters languished in the city's jails or were out on bond. Among participants on the outside, morale was low. Precious few demonstrators were joining King's ranks. To make matters worse, neither Connor nor the city's white business leadership had shown even the slightest willingness to accede to the demonstrators' demands. President Kennedy helped increase national awareness of the situation briefly when he phoned King's wife, Coretta, to express his concern during King's imprisonment. But Kennedy's involvement appeared only to have resulted in permission for King to phone Coretta. Again, the national news media—after a brief spurt of attention—largely ignored the story.

"We had run out of troops," Wyatt Walker later explained. "We had scraped the bottom of the barrel of adults who could go. We needed something new." Finally King and his aides settled on a highly controversial and potentially dangerous strategy. Sometime in late April, King reluctantly approved a plan to enlist thousands of teenagers for the front lines of the protest movement. Organizers littered the city's black high schools with leaflets urging the students to "FIGHT FOR FREEDOM FIRST THEN GO TO SCHOOL." The youngsters responded, enthusiastically, by the hundreds. On the day of the first march, Birmingham's black schools were left virtually empty.

On Thursday, May 2, just before noon, a large crowd of black onlookers gathered outside the Sixteenth Street Baptist Church. Nearby, Bull Connor's menacing forces assembled and waited for the anticipated march, which would—unbeknownst to Connor—forever change the nature and course of the nation's civil rights movement. Inside the church were the newest soldiers in the civil rights struggle, young people whose lives King would risk for the cause of freedom. Suddenly the students burst through the front doors of the church. They sang, shouted, and danced as they made their way toward downtown. They did not march far. Connor's men promptly arrested most of them, five hundred in all, without incident. Again, as King had hoped, Birmingham began to make national news.

The next day, before a large crowd of black onlookers and scores of newspaper and television reporters, a new corps of brave teenage marchers left the church in several waves as they chanted "We Want Freedom" or sang the hymn "We Shall Overcome." This time, one of Connor's captains commanded the youngsters to stop. Still chanting, the students ignored the order and marched headlong into the phalanx of officials, which now included fire fighters equipped with high-pressure water hoses. As tensions mounted, onlookers shouted insults at the assembled police officers. Then bricks and bottles rained down from the roof of a nearby building. Two firemen and a news photographer were hit. In response, Connor called up police dogs to force back the encroaching throng of onlookers. Frightened by the snarling animals, the crowd edged nervously backwards. Others ran away. One nightstick-wielding officer on a three-wheel bicycle pursued fleeing protesters who ran from the scene. Stragglers were struck. "Look at 'em run!" Connor yelled gleefully. When he noticed that his officers were holding back a curious crowd of whites, Connor ordered them brought forward for a better view. "Let those people come to the corner!" he shouted. "I want 'em to see the dogs work. Look at those niggers run." Finally Connor called in the water hoses. Fire fighters pummeled the protesters with streams of water under enormous pressure. The water toppled protesters like dominoes. Several were injured. A few brave souls got up and charged again, only to have a crushing blast of water knock them off their feet. The relentless pressure violently ripped clothes off the backs of some. In less than thirty minutes, the confrontation was over. The protest was quashed. Police had arrested 250 students—including a six-year-old girl.

That night at a church rally, King implored his followers to continue the fight. "Don't worry about your children who are in jail," he cried. "The eyes of the world are on Birmingham. We're going on in spite of dogs and fire hoses. We've gone too far to turn back." King's emotional plea struck a chord. Day after day, hundreds of enthusiastic children appeared at the church, eager to march and well aware that they faced arrest or injury. On Friday less than five hundred students marched out of the church before authorities sealed the doors. By day's end police had arrested more than 250 people after dispersing the marchers with water and dogs.

Some of the worst violence occurred on Tuesday, May 7, when twenty-five hundred black protesters swarmed out of the church and caught Connor's men by surprise. As the lounging officers scrambled into formation, the protesters broke through their lines. They surged into nearby Kelly Ingram Park and headed toward downtown, where they ran into department stores, singing and chanting. As police rounded up the demonstrators, an ugly confrontation unfolded in the park near the church. As hundreds of blacks lobbed bricks and bottles at them, police officers responded with blasts of water. This time firemen trained their hoses on one of the protest's top leaders, Reverend Fred Shuttlesworth. Shouting defiantly at the officers as he stood in front of the church, Shuttlesworth was pounded by a bone-crushing blast of water that slammed him into the side of the building. Later, when Connor learned that Shuttlesworth had been carried away in an ambulance, he responded: "I waited a week down here to see that, and then I missed it. I wish it had been a hearse."

Later that night, after city officials threatened to impose martial law, top business leaders and protest organizers began negotiating in earnest. Assistant Attorney General Burke Marshall assisted them. On Thursday they announced the terms of their agreement. Demonstrators would cease marching if business leaders would promise to begin desegregating downtown stores and end discriminatory hiring practices. King hailed the settlement. "This day," he said, "is clearly a moment of great victory."

The spirit of harmony lasted barely two days. Radical whites denounced the accord, and Connor called for a boycott of the white stores whose owners had agreed to the deal. Alabama governor George Wallace scoffed at the agreement, declaring that he would never "be a party" to any compromise on segregation. On Saturday, May 11, after a large Ku Klux Klan rally, the bombing of Reverend A.D. King's parsonage shattered Birmingham's uneasy peace. Neither King nor his family was injured. Minutes later several bomb explosions rocked the Gaston Motel, which served as Martin Luther King's Birmingham headquarters. Four blacks were hurt. Presumably the target of the blasts, King was out of town. The bombings sparked a round of riots that raged throughout the city for hours. Rioters burned houses and other buildings. Fifty policemen and rioters were injured in the violence. By dawn, a nine-block section of town was smoldering, virtually destroyed in the previous night's mayhem.

The violence in Birmingham, especially Bull Connor's clumsy and ruthless tactics, made for sensational news on television and in newspapers across the country. "DOGS AND FIRE HOSES ROUT 3000 NEGROES," said *The Boston Globe* on May 4. The paper, like most others in the country, prominently featured shocking photographs of firemen blasting children with water hoses and a policeman gripping a stunned black youth while a menacing dog lunged at his exposed torso. "DOGS AND HOSES REPULSE NEGROES AT BIRMINGHAM," announced the *New York Times*. In the *Los Angeles Times*, a front-page story was headlined "NEW ALABAMA RIOT: POLICE DOGS, FIRE HOSES HALT MARCH." *Time* and *Newsweek* devoted extensive coverage to Birmingham for several weeks. Said *Newsweek* on May 17: "The blaze of bombs, the flash of blades, the eerie glow of fire, the keening cries of hatred, the wild dance of terror in the night—all this was Birmingham, Ala." Overseas the headlines were worse. London's *Daily Mirror:* "RACE CLASH—1,000 CHILDREN JAILED." Moscow's *Pravda:* "MONSTROUS CRIMES OF THE RACISTS IN THE UNITED STATES." *Liberation* in Paris: "SAVAGES IN ALABAMA."

In the Senate, southern segregationists loudly decried perceived violations of the Constitution. "None of us should be content to sit idly by in the face of this direct threat to historic constitutional principles," Mississippi's John Stennis declared. Of course, the constitutional principles about which Stennis and other southerners cared so deeply were the rights of *states*—not the obvious violations of individual civil rights. Stennis had no complaints about Alabama authorities, who he said had functioned "fully and effectively." Later in the day, Oregon's Wayne Morse took the floor with a passionate rebuttal. "I say to my good friend from Mississippi," Morse said, "he need only turn the pages of *Life* magazine of last week for pictorial proof, if he is not already aware of it, of the shocking, inhumane, atrocious, horrendous conduct of the so-called Alabama state law officials and municipal law officials, bespoiling the precious liberties of supposedly free Americans but of colored skin . . . There is no place in America for inhumanity to man."

The resulting media coverage elated King. As Wyatt Tee Walker later explained, the blustering, uncompromising Bull Connor had been "a perfect adversary." In Walker's opinion, "Birmingham would have been lost if Bull had let us go down to the City Hall and pray; if he had let us do that and stepped aside, what else would be new? There would be no movement, no publicity. But all he could see was stopping us before we got there. We had calculated for the stupidity of a Bull Connor." Said CORE's James Farmer, "People . . . all over the U.S. sat in their living rooms, just finishing dinner or eating dessert and drinking coffee, and watched those abysmal scenes. [And they thought:] Those scenes are horrible; those little children—they haven't hurt anybody—those women. Bull Connor's a beast, we have to get rid of him; we have to put an end to this thing. This is not American. Give us some laws; let's have some laws. Laws that can be enforced and get this problem behind us . . . After Birmingham, the majority was with us; their consensus had arrived."

President Kennedy, who had threatened to send in the National Guard to quell the May 11 violence, urged Birmingham's white leaders to give some ground. On Capitol Hill, Humphrey must have found the president's words satisfying—yet maddeningly overdue. "There is an important moral issue involved of equality for all of our citizens," Kennedy said at a press conference. Until whites treated blacks as full citizens, Kennedy said, "you're going to have these difficulties . . . The time to give it to them is before the disasters come." It was precisely the point Humphrey had made to the president weeks earlier.

From the beginning, King had hoped that the events in Birmingham would force Kennedy's hand by creating "such a crisis in race relations that it was an issue which could no longer be ignored." Perhaps, King later mused, Kennedy "came to see in a way that he had probably never seen—and in a way that many other people finally came to see—that segregation was morally wrong and it did something to the souls of both the segregationist and the segregated." Birmingham, Roy Wilkins observed, showed the White House "that perhaps the attack agreed upon was not as adequate as the president had thought at the outset." Most important, the alarming news stories and graphic images from Birmingham had awakened the nation to the brutal treatment that southern blacks usually encountered when they demanded their constitutional rights.

"Blacks," Arizona congressman Morris Udall said later, "simply weren't going to shuffle along the dark side of the sidewalk anymore." At the urging of King and other leaders, blacks in Birmingham and elsewhere had taken to the streets, chanting "Freedom! Freedom! Freedom Now!" By the end of May, civil rights demonstrations had broken out in dozens of cities in Maryland, Illinois, Pennsylvania, North Carolina, New Jersey, and New York. But exactly what did King and his new legions of emboldened followers mean when they demanded their immediate "freedom"? "If the Negroes wanted something specific, the federal government might be able to find specific remedies," George Reedy told Johnson in a May 24 memorandum. "But the Negro revolt is not directed against the federal government. It is directed against the white governments they know—right in their own communities." There was, however, one "common denominator" among blacks and white supremacists, Reedy accurately argued. It was "a belief that the United States—in the person of the president himself—has not made a real moral commitment to the cause of equal rights and equal opportunity." By now it was clear to everyone that Kennedy's February legislative offering was woefully inadequate. No one could deny that the volatile situation now called for a much stronger, comprehensive package of legislative proposals. By May, Burke Marshall said, Kennedy himself arrived at that conclusion "without having a meeting or discussion about it."

Yet most of the president's advisors were far from enthusiastic about the prospect of their leader embarking on a controversial crusade for civil rights only seventeen months before the 1964 presidential election. Kenneth O'Donnell opposed it, as did congressional liaison Larry O'Brien. Ted Sorenson was described as "dubious." Majority Leader Mansfield and Bobby Baker doubted they could ever break a southern filibuster. Even Marshall, the Justice Department's top civil rights official, was hesitant. Kennedy would be making civil rights *his* issue. "And doing that in 1963," Marshall said, "with the southern control of a third of the Senate, was a very, very serious undertaking." The bill "would tie up the Congress for months, for a year, maybe more than a year, making it impossible for him to get other legislation through." Marshall also worried that a strong civil rights program "would focus national attention on it, so that the failure to pass a bill would have been a failure of the Kennedy presidency" just before the 1964 presidential election. To Marshall, introducing a new civil rights bill was noble, but it amounted to Kennedy "betting" his presidency on one polarizing issue. Almost no one who understood the dynamics of Congress believed that Kennedy would ultimately pass a strong civil rights bill. "I'll give you fifteen to one," Theodore Hesburgh said many years later, "that he couldn't have got [a bill] through Congress."

Attorney General Robert Kennedy believed that, despite the forbidding odds, the president had no choice but to submit a comprehensive bill. Those who knew the president's pragmatic, often impulsive brother were not surprised by the advice he offered. Once he decided that the nation's racial problems could no longer be managed by executive action, the attorney general eagerly advocated altering the administration's course. As the president's brother, Kennedy had wide latitude. No other attorney general would have begun drafting a controversial civil rights proposal without the president's express permission. But on May 17, Robert Kennedy and Burke Marshall ordered a draft of the bold legislation that the attorney general knew his brother would eventually offer to the Congress. Several days later, at a May 22 news conference, the president confirmed reports that he was considering a new civil rights plan "which would provide a legal outlet" for blacks. Kennedy was vague about the legislation. "I would hope that we would be able to develop some formulas so that those who feel themselves barred, as a matter of fact denied equal rights, would have a remedy."

As Justice Department attorneys began drafting the bill—in consultation with Kennedy's White House advisors—several provisions quickly emerged. The bill would almost certainly allow the federal government to withhold federal money from any discriminatory program or activity. It would create a Community Relations Service to help resolve local racial disputes and would establish a sixth-grade education as proof of literacy in voting registration. The bill would also provide for preferential and expedited treatment of voting rights suits and court-appointed voting referees in some pending voting rights cases.

These provisions, however, would not make up the heart and soul of Kennedy's bill. Two others would be more important—and far more controversial.

Justice Department lawyers had drafted a provision to permit the attorney general to initiate and file desegregation suits aimed at public schools and colleges. This was, in essence, the controversial Part III of the 1957 act. If included in the bill, this provision threatened to revive the kind of bitter opposition that erupted in response to the 1957 bill. "If [the administration] supports the [Part III] proposal," columnists Rowland Evans and Robert Novak wrote on May 24, "it may kill all chances for a civil rights bill this year, even though the climate, on the heels of Birmingham, is ripe." Robert Kennedy was determined to draft this provision so narrowly that it would calm all fears of a reckless, vindictive attorney general given free rein to harass local school boards. According to Deputy Attorney General Nicholas Katzenbach, Kennedy and others believed "you shouldn't try to give the Department of Justice authority that it couldn't possibly enforce." Therefore, he said, the provision's language "was more specific in terms of just what kinds of suits you could bring up, what evidence was needed on these, and something [on which] we felt the staff could do a reasonable job."

Perhaps the bill's most controversial section was one that historians and southern blacks would come to view as the core of the legislation—a provision to require "equal access" to all public accommodations, including hotels, restaurants, theaters, and stores. It was the part of the bill for which President Kennedy had the most passion and enthusiasm. "He thought it was just outrageous to refuse to serve people because of their race," Burke Marshall recalled, adding that Kennedy "couldn't understand why that was a big issue." Kennedy told Ted Sorenson that reaction to this provision would be mild compared to other parts of the bill. Of course, because Kennedy was not a southerner, he failed to understand that the public accommodations provision would be the *most* disputed provision in the bill. As Richard Russell would later assert, with passion: "The fact that every citizen has the same right to own and operate a swimming pool or dining hall constitutes equality. The use of federal power to force the owner of a dining hall or swimming pool to unwillingly accept those of a different race as guests creates a new and special right for Negroes in derogation of the property rights of all of our people to own and control the fruits of their labor and ingenuity."

Kennedy was firmly persuaded that the public accommodations section was an essential part of the bill. More vexing, however, was the constitutional basis for such a provision. Would it be grounded in the language of the Fourteenth Amendment, which prohibited a state from denying any of its citizens "the equal protection of the laws"? Or could Congress assert its power, under Article I, Section 8, "to regulate commerce . . . among the several states." The question was the most hotly debated aspect of the public accommodations section. The president favored the more straightforward language of the Fourteenth Amendment. Justice Department officials disagreed. In enacting the Civil Rights Act of 1875—identical to the proposed public accommodations language in many respects—Congress had used the Fourteenth Amendment as its source of legislative authority. Eight years later the Supreme Court declared the law unconstitutional because, it said, the power of Congress under the amendment was limited to enforcing prohibitions against discriminatory actions by *states*. In a document prepared for the Senate Commerce Committee in 1963, Justice Department lawyers noted that "the *Civil Rights Cases* [of 1883] were decided 80 years ago and have never been questioned in subsequent opinions of the court. An expansion of the concept of State actions has occurred, but the basic 14th amendment distinction between governmental and private action has been consistently observed down to the present day."

Finally, at Burke Marshall's urging, the president agreed that the administration should construct the bill's language on a more solid foundation: the Constitution's commerce clause. Thus discrimination in public places or businesses would be outlawed if goods, services, or accommodations were provided "to a substantial degree" to interstate travelers; if a "substantial portion" of the goods sold to the public had moved in interstate commerce; or if a business's activities "substantially affect" interstate commerce. Discriminatory practices in these businesses, the administration maintained, "obstructs interstate travel and the sale of related good and services [and] restricts business enterprises in their choice of locations for offices and plants, because of their inability to obtain the services of persons who do not wish to subject themselves to segregation and discrimination." Actually the administration would also apply the Fourteenth Amendment's prohibition on state-sanctioned discrimination. Segregation or discrimination in public accommodations would be specifically outlawed if carried out "under color of any law, statute, ordinance, or regulation; or . . . under color of any custom or usage required or enforced" by state or local officials.

One other aspect of the bill sparked considerable debate among Kennedy's advisors. Although the president had already endorsed equal employment opportunity legislation in the House—similar to the FEPC of the 1940s—Humphrey and other liberals strongly urged him to include the provisions in the administration's bill. Kennedy refused. "We were all conscious of the fact that some kind of [fair employment] provisions . . . were terribly important," said Nicholas Katzenbach, who quickly added that Kennedy's advisors were virtually "unanimous" in believing the provisions would be "impossible to enact." The only employment provisions added to the bill authorized the President's Committee on Equal Employment Opportunity to stop discrimination by the federal government and its contractors. To Katzenbach, that language was only "window dressing."

On May 24, as Justice Department lawyers continued to work on the bill, Vice President Johnson gave further rise to expectations that the Kennedy administration was about to make a significant and momentous proposal on civil rights. Johnson had become an outspoken and enthusiastic proponent of a comprehensive civil rights bill. His rhetoric was combative. In Detroit, in January, he told a university audience: "To strike the chains of a slave is noble. To leave him the captive of the color of his skin is hypocrisy." Several weeks later, speaking before the Cleveland Urban League, he declared that the next hundred years "demand of us that we resolve the problems left unresolved when the Emancipation Proclamation freed the slaves." In mid-May, in a speech to the Capital Press Club in Washington, he said, "It seems to me that in the field of human rights, we are well past the stage where half a loaf will do."

On May 30, in an eloquent Memorial Day speech at Gettysburg, Pennsylvania, Johnson hit a rhetorical crescendo in a speech that Hubert Humphrey or Paul Douglas could have easily delivered. In a way, the speech was a watershed in Johnson's evolution as a civil rights proponent and was the strongest pro–civil rights statement he had ever made in a public forum:

> One hundred years ago, the slave was freed. One hundred years later, the Negro remains in bondage to the color of his skin. The Negro today asks justice. We do not answer him—we do not answer those who lie beneath this soil—when we reply to the Negro by asking, "Patience."

It is empty to plead that the solution to dilemmas of the present rests on the hands of the clock. The solution is in our hands. Unless we are willing to yield up our destiny of greatness among the civilizations of history, Americans—white and Negro together—must be about the business of resolving the challenge which confronts us now.

Our nation found its soul on these fields of Gettysburg one hundred years ago. We must not lose that soul in dishonor now on the fields of hate.

To ask for patience from the Negro is to ask him to give more of what he has already given enough. But to fail to ask of him—and of all Americans—perseverance within the processes of a free and responsible society would be to fail to ask what the national interest requires of all its citizens . . .

In this hour, it is not our respective races which are at stake—it is our nation. Let those who care for their country come forward, North and South, white and Negro, to lead the way through this moment of challenge and decision.

The Negro says, "Now." Others say, "Never." The voice of responsible Americans—the voice of those who died here and the great man who spoke here—their voices say, "Together." There is no other way.

Until justice is blind to color, until education is unaware of race, until opportunity is unconcerned with the color of men's skins, emancipation will be a proclamation but not a fact. To the extent that the proclamation of emancipation is not fulfilled in fact, to that extent we shall have fallen short of assuring freedom to the free.

At first Johnson had wanted to decline the invitation to speak at the ceremony commemorating the hundredth anniversary of the great Civil War battle. His personal secretary, Juanita Roberts, refused to let him. "I can't [decline] this one, yet," she told her boss in a memorandum. As Roberts explained to Johnson, "The distinguished grandson of distinguished Confederates giving, on the 100th anniversary of the Gettysburg battle, a speech that could be HIS Gettysburg address—a masterpiece to be remembered by." With Roberts's help, Johnson not only recognized the possibilities for such a forum—he rose to the occasion, delivering a forceful and passionate call for national unity on civil rights. Not once, however, did he mention specific legislative proposals Kennedy might offer. "The law cannot save those who deny it," he said, "but neither can the law serve any who do not use it. The history of injustice and inequality is a history of disuse of the law."

In the White House, meanwhile, the history of the Kennedy administration was the disuse of Lyndon Johnson. "It was a time of deprivation," Harry McPherson recalled. "He grew very fat and drank a lot." Clearly unhappy with the unimportant and ceremonial duties that made up the vice presidency, Johnson was never the asset on Capitol Hill some had expected. He rarely participated in discussions to set the administration's legislative strategy. "I had the feeling," said Texas congressman Homer Thornberry, "that his talents were not being utilized to the fullest." Although Kennedy respected his vice president for his intellect and "his obvious ability," Robert Kennedy maintained that it was Johnson who "wasn't helpful at times that he might have been helpful." He was always a loyal soldier, Kennedy said, "but he never gave any suggestions or ideas on policy." This criticism may have been accurate on other aspects of Kennedy's legislative programs, but not on civil rights. To the contrary, Johnson had developed strong and definite ideas about the politics of Kennedy's impending legislative proposal.

And he yearned to play a role.

CHAPTER EIGHTEEN

A Bill, Not an Issue

JOHNSON HAD STRONG FEELINGS about civil rights and the legislative strategy Kennedy ought to pursue. Making certain that Kennedy heeded his advice—or even heard it—was another matter. White House staff members often ignored him, and they severely limited his access to the president. Despite a presidential order to include Johnson in every White House meeting on civil rights, Lee White, Kennedy's civil rights assistant, sometimes forgot. "Now look, you work with Lyndon Johnson and make sure that he knows about all of these things," Kennedy ordered. "I want him here. I think he can do a lot. First of all, he's pretty damned smart; and second of all, he's a southerner and he has got a better speaking voice for a lot of these people than I have got. Third of all, I think we ought to have the whole panoply of presidential executive branch superstructure. And besides that, let's keep him involved in this." Despite the unmistakable nature of Kennedy's feelings about Johnson's involvement, White admitted that of eight meetings held by the White House and Justice Department staff to discuss civil rights, "there must have been two or three when I just clean forgot about the vice president—just forgot!" Of course, Johnson, extremely sensitive to such slights, did not attend any meeting to which Kennedy's men did not invite him.

Gradually, as the civil rights bill began to take form, Johnson became more outspoken. Yet when he asked appointments secretary Kenny O'Donnell for fifteen minutes with the president to discuss the issue, Kennedy responded by sending over Burke Marshall to hear his thoughts. Johnson talked with Marshall not about legislative strategy but about the importance of addressing the economic hardships endured by black citizens. Johnson never "came down hard one way or another" on whether Kennedy should offer a tough, comprehensive civil rights bill, Marshall said. "He'd talk around it, about the economic problems and his own experience with the [NYA] in the thirties, and so forth."

Following his meeting with Marshall, Johnson again pressed O'Donnell for an audience with the president. This time, on June 3, Robert Kennedy dispatched Norbert Schlei––the assistant attorney general in charge of drafting the legislation––to see Johnson. An agitated vice president "absolutely poured out his soul" about the bill, Schlei recalled. Ignoring the substance of the legislation, the vice president instead offered his strategic and tactical advice on the bill's presentation to the nation and its passage through the Congress. Later that day Johnson received a phone call from another administration aide, Ted Sorenson, a top advisor to the president who doubled as a speech writer.

By now, although he still had not seen the bill, Johnson vaguely understood the legislation Kennedy was prepared to submit to Congress; his information came mostly from a newspaper account. In a lengthy conversation with Sorenson (recorded by Dictaphone), Johnson repeatedly advised caution: "I think that we got to do our homework before we send a message, one, and we can't do that unless we spend some time on the message. Two, I think we ought to exchange some viewpoints on what legislation we can get." The president, Johnson counseled, should unveil his proposal in the South. As for the message Kennedy would eventually deliver to the nation, Johnson suggested that he declare:

> Now, I don't want to come here without talking about our constitutional rights. We're all Americans. We got a Golden Rule, 'Do unto others as you would have them do unto you.' Now I'm leader of this country. When I order men into battle, I order them men without regard to color. They carry our flag into foxholes. The Negro can do that, the Mexican can do it, others can do it. We've got to do the same thing when we drive down the highway at places they eat. I'm going to have to ask you all to do this thing. I'm going to have to ask the Congress to say that we'll all be treated without regard to our race.

Johnson told Sorenson that such a message would "run some of the demagogues right into the hole." He remained doubtful of Kennedy's ability to sell it to Congress.

I think we run the risk of touching off about a three- or four-month debate that will kill his [legislative] program and inflame the country and wind up with a mouse. I don't think that means that a legislative proposal ought to be abandoned. I think it means that some specific proposals have to be weighed a lot more carefully than I've been able to weigh them, then reach a conclusion as to all of us lining up on this play that's going around the right end . . . I know the risks are great and it might cost us the South, but those sort of states may be lost anyway. The difference is if your president just enforces court decrees, the South will feel it's yielded to force. But if he goes down there and looks them in the eye and states the moral issue and the Christian issue, and he does it face to face, these Southerners at least respect his courage. They feel they're on the losing side of an issue of conscience.

Reflecting counsel he had received in a memorandum from George Reedy a week earlier, Johnson told Sorenson that southerners of both races shared "one point of view that's identical":

They're not certain that the government is on the side of the Negroes. The whites think we're just playing politics to carry New York. The Negroes feel and they're suspicious that we're just doing what we got to do. Until that's laid to rest, I don't think you're going to have much of a solution. I don't think the Negroes' goals are going to be achieved through legislation and a little thing here on impact area or voting or something. I think the Negro leaders are aware of that. What Negroes are really seeking is moral force and to be sure we're on their side and make them all act like Americans. And until they receive that assurance, unless it's stated dramatically and convincingly, they're not going to pay much attention to executive orders and legislative recommendations.*

Despite his doubts about the efficacy of Kennedy's proposal, Johnson believed that "he's got to have his bill." Referring to Kennedy's modest civil rights proposal in February, Johnson said:

---

*Johnson, when he became president, heeded his own advice by issuing strong, eloquent declarations about the federal government's firm commitment to securing civil and voting rights for all Americans.

He's sitting over here, we've got six months, we haven't passed anything! I think he ought to make them pass some of this stuff before he throws this thing out. This is just what the Republican Party, if I was their manager, this is what I'd recommend they do. And this is what they're doing. They're sitting back giggling. Here Javits gets Humphrey souped up; they put on a few terrible demonstrations; we get a civil war going on in the South; they move Kennedy in and they cut off the South from him and blow up the bridge. That's what they want to do.

If I were Kennedy, I wouldn't let [the Republicans] call my signals. I'd pass my program, make them stand up and vote for it. While I was doing that, I'd go into the South a time or two myself. While I was doing that, I'd put the Republicans on the spot by making them buy my program.

Yet Johnson again advised caution, especially regarding the administration's relations with Congress. "We better just see what we want to do and be sure that everybody wants to do it and then go ahead," he said. "I don't think we're at that stage now. I told the Attorney General that, and I tell you that. Now, if you are at that stage [ready to introduce the bill], I'm making it abundantly clear I'm on the team and you'll never hear a word out of me."

Still, Johnson complained about the frustrating White House practice of excluding him from the decision-making process.

Now, I want to make it clear, I'm as strong for this program as you are, my friend. But you want my judgment now, and I don't want to debate these things around fifteen men and then have them all go out and talk about the Vice President and how he is [not supportive], because I haven't talked to one southerner about this. I haven't been able to talk to one executive man about it except the attorney general and you and Ken [O'Donnell] very briefly this morning. I haven't sat in on any of the conferences they've had up here with the senators. I think it would have been good if I had. I don't care. I'd just as soon be included out on all these things, but if at the last minute I'm supposed to give my judgments, I'm going to do it honestly as long as I'm around here and I'm going to do it loyally.

I think that [Kennedy will] be cut to pieces with this and I think he'll be a sacrificial lamb. I think his program will be hurt, if it's not killed. I don't want to be extreme. We may be able to pass it. But I think he's entitled to more support than he's got to go in with or that he'll get after he does.

In Johnson's view, Kennedy's men had done little to build support among moderate Democrats, especially those from western states. "He got Humphrey," he told Sorenson. "What the hell is Humphrey? He's a wonderful man, but we know he's like Bob Taylor's goat—he's done voted. We got to get some other folks in this thing to get that cloture. You got to get a good many of your westerners. You got to sit down with them, help them have a reason" to support the bill.

Johnson again complained about being excluded from strategy sessions. "I don't know who drafted it. I've never seen it," he told Sorenson. "Hell, if the vice president doesn't know what's in it, how do you expect the others to know what's in it? I got it from the *New York Times* and from that message of yours this morning. I've never seen anything else." Recalling southern outrage over Part III of the Civil Rights Act of 1957, Johnson noted, "That's the way Eisenhower took Part Three and [Richard] Russell just ran him out of the White House balcony, because he said, 'I never heard of it, didn't know what was in there, they slipped it in on me.'"

Johnson suggested Russell should be among the first members of Congress consulted. "Let him advance every argument he can and be sure he got the answers," Johnson advised. "Then go on and send the bill if you want to. But I would make them show every card they got." Furthermore, Johnson argued, the White House should also consult congressional Republicans,

> because while you get your message off tomorrow, my friend, probably Everett Dirksen and Dick Russell will be sitting around next Sunday over a mint julep with an understanding that they're going to do a good deal more—Dirksen is—than you've asked, and that he hadn't been consulted and he's got a right to offer more than you've asked and that will be defeated and then he won't go along. Then he'll go along with Russell. And he's made a book against you. I'd make a book with him instead of Russell making it with him.

In his 1965 memoir of the Kennedy presidency, Sorenson painted a different portrait of the administration's attempts to curry congressional favor for the bill. Sorenson accurately recalled that Kennedy and his aides "consulted frequently" with leaders of both political parties, but he gave Johnson no credit for having forcefully advocated this part of the president's strategy, and he did not mention his own lengthy discussion with Johnson. In an oral history interview with the John F. Kennedy Library in 1964, Sorenson claimed "the vice president had a major role in the formulation of the legislation," a statement that Johnson might have disputed. Robert Kennedy was more forthcoming about Johnson's late involvement in the process. Johnson, Kennedy recalled, argued "that we should do some work in Congress before the legislation was sent up, and that was a very wise suggestion." Heeding Johnson's advice, the attorney general met with Russell twice to explain the president's legislation. The president himself even talked with Russell. Courteous as always, Russell firmly informed both men that he would not only oppose the bill but would work vigorously to defeat it. Of course no one had expected that Russell would endorse the legislation. As Johnson understood, if the White House properly briefed Russell, he could not rise on the Senate floor—as he had in 1957—to accuse the Justice Department of subterfuge and deceit.

Johnson was not the only member of Kennedy's administration who worried about the bill's ultimate impact on Kennedy's reelection in 1964. "If I had been the president," Burke Marshall later said, "I would have thought it was a very—and I think he thought—that it was a very risky bet, politically." Marshall was certain that Kennedy knew "perfectly well, that in the short run, that the solid, white South that had voted for the Democratic party nationally would be lost."

On June 11, hours after Alabama became the last state in the nation to desegregate its state university, President Kennedy appeared on national television and radio to announce his civil rights legislation. Although Kennedy had planned a televised address only if violence erupted in Alabama, he abruptly decided to announce his program while the nation's attention was focused on civil rights. Kennedy's decision sent Ted Sorenson into a last-minute speech-writing frenzy. Sorenson did his best, even though the bill's exact language was not complete and would not be ready for submission to Congress for another week. Just minutes before the broadcast, Kennedy still did not have the final draft of Sorenson's text. Sitting before the camera in the cabinet room, accompanied only by his brother Robert and Burke Marshall, Kennedy scribbled his own speech notes. "Come on. Come on now, Burke," he said, half joking, "you must have some ideas." Kennedy knew what he wanted to say. "But it was a very, very close question whether the whole speech was going to be more or less extemporaneous," Marshall said. "The last part of it was anyway."

At eight o'clock, Kennedy began his historic speech to the American people. The nation, he said, was

> confronted primarily with a moral issue. It is as old as the Scriptures and is as clear as the American Constitution. The heart of the question is whether all Americans are to be afforded equal rights and equal opportunities; whether we are going to treat our fellow Americans as we want to be treated.
>
> If an American, because his skin is dark, cannot eat lunch in a restaurant open to the public; if he cannot send his children to the best public school available; if he cannot vote for the public officials who represent him; if, in short, he cannot enjoy the full and free life which all of us want, then who among us would be content to have the color of his skin changed and stand in his place?
>
> Who among us would then be content with the counsel of patience and delay?
>
> One hundred years of delay have passed since President Lincoln freed the slaves, yet their heirs, their grandsons, are not fully free. They are not yet freed from the bonds of injustice; they are not yet freed from social and economic oppression.
>
> And this nation, for all its hopes and all its boasts, will not be fully free until all its citizens are free . . .
>
> The fires of frustration and discord are burning in every city, North and South. Where legal remedies are not at hand, redress is sought in the streets, in demonstrations, parades and protests which create tensions and threaten violence—and threaten lives.

Kennedy described the legislation he planned to send Congress. Nearing the end of his speech, and out of prepared text, he improvised:

> We have a right to expect that the Negro community will be responsible, will uphold the law. But they have a right to expect that the law will be fair, that the Constitution will be

color blind, as Justice [John M.] Harlan said at the turn of the century.

That is what we're talking about. This is a matter which concerns this country and what it stands for, and in meeting it I ask the support of all our citizens.

Those who hoped that Kennedy's speech might calm racial strife in the South were shocked later that night by the cold-blooded murder of the NAACP's Mississippi field secretary, Medgar Evers. A tall, impressive-looking World War II veteran, Evers had recently gained prominence as the inspirational leader of several sit-ins and demonstrations in Jackson. That evening, just before midnight, as he entered his home, the crack of a high-powered deer rifle shattered the late-night silence. Evers lay wounded and bleeding in his driveway. His wife and three children rushed out of the house. "Please, Daddy, please get up!" his children cried. Evers died an hour later.

Russell reacted to Kennedy's speech with predictable outrage and sorrow. "The outstanding distinction between a government of free men and a socialistic or communistic state," he said in a statement the day after Kennedy's speech, "is the fact that free men can own and control property, whereas statism denies property rights to the individual." Not content to suggest only socialist and communist tendencies in Kennedy's bill, Russell went one reckless step further. "Marxism has not worked and can never work because it does not take human nature into account." Russell declared that he would oppose Kennedy's bill "with every means and resource at my command."

Russell knew that he was fighting a losing battle. His southern bloc was shrinking and aging. In the coming months their public image would be unmistakable: graying Confederates waging a fierce battle not to win the war but only to stave off defeat as long as possible. Russell could not even be certain that he still had the overwhelming support of southern whites: In August a poll by Louis Harris showed that 54 percent of white southerners favored legislation to open public accommodations to blacks.

Russell's only real chance of winning was to compromise or offer a reasonable alternative to Kennedy's legislation. Russell seemed to consider neither. As *Wall Street Journal* reporter Jerry Landauer observed in a June 19 column:

Richard Russell can summon a parliamentary precedent at the snap of a finger, yet there are some among his warm admirers who believe his 30 years in the Senate blind him to what's going on outside. Certain friends fervently hope that he will now bend somewhat to what they think is the Nation's mood for action.

But as the great struggle over minority rights looms, the senator from Georgia seems to be thinking far harder about the use of legislative machinery to block the president's plan than he does about the social revolution sweeping North and South. He has no alternatives to offer the impatient Negro. He denounces certain northerners for riding the race issue for votes but says nothing publicly about southern politicians who do the same.

Russell assured his colleagues and constituents of his determination to fight. The whole matter, he told a friend in an August 16 letter, "is shot through and through with politics." Although the president had not wanted to propose a civil rights bill during his first term, Russell believed that "when the agitations started, the attorney general convinced the president that he should go all out to force through a civil rights bill and get it through this year so that the southern people would have become accustomed to it and follow their customary Democratic voting tradition in '64." Russell maintained that "all" of Kennedy's political advisors "are convinced that he can be reelected by carrying all the big-city states where the Negro vote is a balance of power, and they have decided to gamble on the South and let it go down the drain if necessary."

In Congress, Kennedy's bill would encounter many skeptics and enemies. None would prove more formidable than Russell. It was, for several reasons, a prospect that Kennedy and other admirers of the senior Georgia senator did not relish. In January, during a lengthy Oval Office meeting with *Atlanta Constitution* editor Ralph McGill, Kennedy had openly pondered Russell and his stubborn opposition to civil rights. "I don't know any person that puzzles me more than Senator Russell," Kennedy confessed to McGill. "Here's a man of great gifts and great capacity for friendships and loyalties. The whole world is changing, and the whole nation is changing. And yet this gifted man remains adamant and defiant in the matters of any measures which tend to enter the field of race—civil rights." Others shared Kennedy's concern about Russell's inability to evolve with the times. His loyal aide Proctor Jones believed that most of Russell's staff members regarded their boss's racial attitudes as antiquated. In an interview with the *New York Times*, Humphrey predicted that Congress would eventually enact a civil rights bill over Russell's opposition. "I only wish," Humphrey lamented, "that Dick Russell could have put his God-given talents to work on the side of constitutional guarantees of civil rights."

Few northerners who despaired over Russell's intransigence fully understood the political mentality of the average southern politician. To many northern liberals, civil rights was one of many issues about which they felt strongly. For southern politicians, particularly those of Russell's generation, support for civil rights was not only political suicide—it was flat wrong and immoral. "It was just a very deep underlying conviction of his, a sincere conviction," said Ivan Allen, the progressive mayor of Atlanta, who doubted that politics influenced Russell's opposition to civil rights. Jimmy Carter, then a moderate Georgia state senator, also admired Russell because "he accurately mirrored the feelings of the Georgia people, [and] the southern people." CBS correspondent Roger Mudd said of Russell: "He was protecting and defending a way of life that he had been reared in and the majority of his people had been reared in, the majority of his constituents had been reared in, and that's what a man is sent here for—to defend the way of life that most people who sent him here enjoy. So I never faulted him for that."

Whatever his motives, Russell vowed that he would oppose Kennedy's civil rights bill to "the last ditch." In the end, White House congressional liaison Larry O'Brien said, "we will just have to place the prestige and power of the president into the scales to see if they can outweigh Dick Russell."

The prospects for Kennedy's bill, in the Senate at least, were grim. On June 27 Majority Secretary Bobby Baker reported to Majority Leader Mansfield that his "poll" of senators showed "conclusively that it is virtually impossible to secure fifty-one senators who will vote for the president's bill." Even if Kennedy found "a formula" on public accommodations acceptable to three key Republicans—Minority Leader

Dirksen, George Aiken of Vermont, and Bourke Hickenlooper of Iowa—the chances for cloture were "50-50," Baker concluded.

In the House, meanwhile, Robert Kennedy had not helped his cause. On June 20, during his first day of testimony before a House Judiciary subcommittee, he brusquely dismissed a Republican civil rights bill by telling New York Republican John Lindsay he had not found time to read it. That admission was unfortunate. With southern Democrats in opposition, the White House would need substantial Republican support in the House and Senate to pass the bill. "If we become too partisan," Baker had warned Mansfield, "we have no chance of passing a bill in the foreseeable future."

Republicans held the key to the bill's passage, and many of them sincerely wanted to play a meaningful role in the process. Yet some of them were reluctant to support the bill's strongest provisions as long as they suspected that Kennedy might trade them away to gain the support of moderates in the Senate. That was no idle suspicion. Administration strategists—including Kennedy and Johnson—initially believed that several unspecified House provisions could be cast aside as the bill moved through the Senate. The Republican most leery of this strategy was William McCulloch of Ohio, a senior Judiciary Committee member who had aided passage of the 1957 and 1960 civil rights bills. Widely respected among congressmen of both parties, McCulloch was his party's point man on civil rights in the House—and one of the administration's best hopes for a bipartisan agreement. Following secret negotiations between McCulloch and Burke Marshall, the president agreed to two important conditions in exchange for crucial Republican support: First, the administration would oppose any attempts by conservative senators to weaken a House-passed bill and would not agree to amendments until McCulloch approved them. Second, Kennedy would publicly praise Republicans for their role in passing the bill. While the bargain buoyed hopes for House passage, the deal suddenly forced Justice Department officials to view their bill in a new light. Deputy Attorney General Nicholas Katzenbach and others now realized that the White House was unlikely "to get anything in the House of Representatives unless we were prepared to fight for it in the Senate." That realization, Katzenbach said, prompted them "to think more seriously of cloture than we ever had before."

At the White House, President Kennedy launched a full-court press to generate public support for his bill, meeting with representatives of many civic, political, and religious organizations. On June 13 he conferred with nearly three hundred labor leaders. Most of them endorsed the bill. Five days later, he met with two hundred fifty religious leaders. The meeting was a first. Never before had a large group of American religious leaders gathered to plot strategy for a major legislative initiative. Kennedy also lobbied a group of eight governors, more than two hundred prominent attorneys, and representatives of a hundred women's organizations.

On June 22, three days after formally submitting his bill to Congress, Kennedy convened a White House meeting of the major civil rights groups. Although the president had not solicited advice from black leaders in drafting the legislation, he now asked for their support. In explaining the congressional maze that the bill must negotiate toward passage, Kennedy emphasized the difficulty of stopping the anticipated southern filibuster. Cloture would be impossible, he said, without the votes of midwestern Republicans. A proposed march on Washington, he told them, would only complicate matters and make it more difficult to win the support of ambivalent senators. "Some of those people are looking for an excuse to be against us," Kennedy said. "I don't want to give any of them a chance to say, 'Yes, I'm for the bill but I'll be damned if I will vote for it at the point of a gun.' " Johnson, normally reticent at such gatherings, spoke up. He agreed with Kennedy. To win about twenty-five crucial swing votes in the Senate, he explained, "we have to be careful not to do anything which would give those who are privately opposed a public excuse to appear as martyrs." Martin Luther King, A. Philip Randolph, and James Farmer disagreed. A mass demonstration in the nation's capital, King argued, "could serve as a means through which people with legitimate discontents could channel their grievances under disciplined, nonviolent leadership."

As if to dramatize the serious nature of his own commitment to the issue, Kennedy pulled a piece of paper from his pocket. On it, he declared, were fresh poll numbers showing that his national approval rating had sunk from 60 percent to 42 percent in the days since he unveiled his bill. "I may lose the next election because of this," he insisted. "I don't care." No one ever found the figures he had cited, said Joseph Rauh, but Kennedy's point was clear: "It was a moral issue. It was a great speech he made to us. I felt from that moment he was terribly committed."

Kennedy made another effective point during the meeting. He chided those who had harshly condemned Bull Connor's brutal tactics in Birmingham. "I don't think you should all be totally harsh on Bull Connor," Kennedy whimsically advised, revealing that he had fully understood the goals of the Birmingham demonstrations. "After all, he has done more for civil rights than almost anybody else."

The unusual debut of Kennedy's program in the Senate spoke worlds about the treacherous journey it faced. On June 19 Majority Leader Mansfield submitted Kennedy's entire civil rights program in one bill. Cosponsored by thirty-seven Democrats and nine Republicans, it was promptly referred to the legislative domain of Judiciary Committee chairman James Eastland, one of the bill's most vociferous opponents. Although the legislation that Mansfield introduced contained public accommodations language, the majority leader immediately moved to assuage Republican leader Everett Dirksen. A vocal opponent of the public accommodations provision, Dirksen had refused to cosponsor the entire Kennedy program. Therefore Mansfield joined Dirksen as a sponsor of another bill that was identical to Kennedy's proposal in every way except public accommodations.

Dirksen was not the only powerful senator whom Mansfield courted. He joined Commerce Committee chairman Warren Magnuson in the introduction of a separate bill containing *only* the public accommodations section. Because it would regulate interstate commerce, the bill went to Magnuson's Commerce Committee, a more liberal and accommodating panel than Eastland's very conservative Judiciary Committee. In the House, meanwhile, Judiciary chairman Emanuel Celler, who had already begun hearings on the bills, introduced Kennedy's entire program on June 20.

As the legislation began its deliberate pilgrimage, Kennedy and his aides worried that persistent outside pressure might complicate the task of selling their program to Congress. Despite the president's attempts at dissuasion, a group of ten national civil rights, labor, and religious organizations continued planning a massive civil rights rally in Washington for August 28. To the White House, the "March on Washington for Jobs and Freedom" would not build public support for the bill. It would instead threaten congressional passage. Although CORE leader James Farmer never heard Kennedy's people demand the march's cancellation, it was clear to him that "they wanted it called off" because they feared "that there would be violence and it would turn into a riot and so forth." Kennedy also worried that the march, with its implicit pressure on Congress to pass the administration's civil rights bill, might alienate some House and Senate members. Kennedy not only rejected addressing the rally—fearing an "adverse reaction" from the crowd— he wisely turned down a meeting with march leaders before their rally at the Lincoln Memorial. Suspecting they would present him a lengthy list of demands that the administration could not honor, which would turn the march into an anti-Kennedy protest, the president instead welcomed the leaders to the White House following their rally.

On the day of the march, official Washington was a ghost town. Fearing violence, most government workers stayed home. By late afternoon more than two hundred thousand people, including an impressive percentage of whites, gathered peacefully at the foot of the Lincoln Memorial and spilled alongside the enormous reflecting pool that stretched east toward the Washington Monument. With the brooding figure of Lincoln the Emancipator over their shoulders, speaker after speaker demanded freedom and greater economic opportunities for black Americans. For Humphrey the day was enormously uplifting. "If I had to pick one day in my public life when I was most encouraged that democracy could work, when my spirit soared on the wings of the American dream of social justice for everyone, it was that day," he insisted. In the Senate, Humphrey had been one of the march's most outspoken supporters:

> There is no sense of threat or intimidation among these people. They are not traveling to Washington to disrupt the established legislative procedures followed by the Congress in considering the civil rights legislation. But they are coming to express their deep convictions that the president's legislation should be enacted promptly.

Later, Humphrey and his Minnesota colleague, Eugene McCarthy, joined marchers in their walk to the memorial grounds. By the time Martin Luther King delivered his historic "I have a dream" speech, Humphrey said it finally seemed possible to him that Congress might pass the president's bill. Originally organized to highlight the need for greater economic opportunities for blacks, the march instead gave voice to the growing public support for Kennedy's civil rights program. When more than seventy senators and House members appeared on the memorial steps, shouts of "Pass the bill! Pass the bill!" greeted them. The event became, said march leader Bayard Rustin, "a call for the passage of civil rights legislation."

In the House, meanwhile, Judiciary Committee chairman Emanuel Celler lost control of Kennedy's bill. Ignoring advice from the White House on what kind of legislation could muster cloture in the Senate, Celler stubbornly clung to his own strategy. Goaded by the NAACP and the Leadership Conference on Civil Rights, Celler reported a much stronger bill out of his subcommittee. Laded with provisions he believed he could use as "trading chips" with southern Democrats and conservative Republicans in full committee, Celler ignored the advice of more pragmatic legislative strategists.* "We'd lost him," Robert Kennedy later said. The White House had, for now at least, also forfeited the crucial support of William McCulloch. "It's a pail of garbage," McCulloch muttered. He predicted that the full committee would never approve the stronger provisions written in subcommittee.

In an ironic twist, southerners cleverly seized Celler's subcommittee bill in hopes they could muscle it through the full committee and onto the House floor—where it would face almost certain defeat. Celler's clumsy miscalculation now placed the White House in the awkward position of publicly demanding milder legislation. "What I want is a bill," Robert Kennedy told the full Judiciary Committee in October, "not an issue." Although some civil rights groups accused Kennedy of a "sellout" to House conservatives, the president held firm to his original legislation. His goal was not just a bill that could pass the Judiciary Committee but one that could pass the gatekeeper for all legislation on its way to the House floor—the crucial Rules Committee, controlled by archconservative Howard Smith of Virginia. "Can Clarence Mitchell [the NAACP's Washington lobbyist] and the Leadership [Conference on Civil Rights] group deliver three Republicans on the Rules Committee

---

*Among other things, the subcommittee bill applied the administration's voting rights provisions to federal *and* state elections; widened the administration's public accommodations provision to outlaw discrimination in *any* accommodation that operated under state authority or license; gave the attorney general much broader authority to initiate lawsuits in civil rights cases (the long-desired Part III language); made the U.S. Civil Rights Commission permanent; and established an Equal Employment Opportunities Commission with powers to end discriminatory hiring practices in all but the smallest businesses.

and sixty Republicans on the House floor?" Kennedy angrily asked his aides. "*McCulloch* can deliver sixty Republicans. Without him it can't be done."

After lengthy negotiations, and with Johnson's assistance, Kennedy persuaded Celler to alter his strategy in favor of a bipartisan approach and then wooed McCulloch back into the fold. On October 29 the Judiciary Committee rejected Celler's subcommittee legislation and reported the bipartisan product to the full House by a 23-11 vote.* Robert Kennedy hailed McCulloch and House Minority Leader Charles Halleck for having saved civil rights from defeat in committee, but the experience left some civil rights leaders feeling betrayed. "Today's events are no cause for rejoicing but a challenge to work to strengthen the bill," NAACP leader Roy Wilkins declared, seemingly oblivious to the fact that Celler's subcommittee bill would have certainly died in full committee. "It wouldn't have gotten through the House," Burke Marshall flatly declared. "We would have lost the Republicans, and we had to have them to pass it."

As both Kennedys learned, enmities with southern conservatives were sometimes preferable to their maddening alliances with civil rights proponents and impractical congressional liberals. Robert Kennedy later said that some liberals would

> rather lose the whole bill and lose the legislation than to make the kind of effort that *we* wished, the course of action that we wished to follow. I just thought an awful lot of them . . . were in love with death . . . I think that's why so many of them just think that Adlai Stevenson is the Second Coming, because, I mean, he never quite arrives there; he never quite accomplishes anything. That's a terrible way of putting it, but I think . . . they like it much better to have a cause than to have a course of action that's been successful.

Russell knew that the coming debate would be the fight of his life. His troops, as always, would be well prepared for battle. In early August he had summoned eighteen of his southern colleagues to the Armed Services Committee Room to begin mapping strategy. "Well, gentle-

---

*The committee bill, although weaker than the subcommittee legislation, was stronger and broader than Kennedy's original proposal. It included creation of a Fair Employment Opportunities Commission.

Senate leaders. Johnson met his match in Republican leader Everett Dirksen.

Above: A handful of civil rights bills. Shortly after the Senate began debate over the 1960 Civil Rights Act, Russell displays the numerous civil rights proposals introduced in Congress. He vowed to fight them all. AP/WIDE WORLD PHOTOS

Left: President Kennedy, Vice President Johnson, and Senate Democratic Whip Humphrey at the White House. WHITE HOUSE PHOTO COURTESY MINNESOTA HISTORICAL SOCIETY

The March on Washington. Humphrey carries his state banner prior to the historic rally at the Lincoln Memorial. MINNESOTA HISTORICAL SOCIETY

Right: Late-night strategy session. Humphrey and his Senate staff discuss ways to break the marathon southern filibuster over the Civil Rights Act of 1964. FRANCIS MILLER, LIFE MAGAZINE

Below: Lyndon Johnson presents ink pens to Humphrey and Dirksen after signing the Civil Rights Act of 1964. He is flanked by dozens of civil rights leaders, cabinet members, and congressional leaders. WHITE HOUSE PHOTO COURTESY MINNESOTA HISTORICAL SOCIETY

The Democratic ticket. Johnson and Humphrey at the LBJ Ranch following the 1964 Democratic
Convention.   WHITE HOUSE PHOTO COURTESY MINNESOTA HISTORICAL SOCIETY

Right: Russell receives the "Johnson treatment" in the Oval Office.   WHITE HOUSE PHOTO COURTESY RICHARD B. RUSSELL LIBRARY

Below: The Voting Rights Act of 1965 becomes law. Johnson with congressional leaders after the signing ceremony in the U.S. Capitol. *Left to right:* Majority Leader Mansfield, Humphrey, Minority Leader Dirksen, Johnson, and Speaker John McCormack. YOICHI R. OKAMOTO, WHITE HOUSE PHOTO

After he signs the Voting Rights Act, Johnson congratulates civil rights leaders Ralph Abernathy, Martin Luther King, and Clarence Mitchell.   YOICHI R. OKAMOTO, WHITE HOUSE PHOTO

Triumph for freedom. Johnson addresses members of Congress in the Capitol Rotunda on August 6, 1965, before signing the Voting Rights Act. The nation, he declared, would insist that all Americans "have the same right as all others to share in the process of democracy." YOICHI R. OKAMOTO, WHITE HOUSE PHOTO

Chairmen's conference. Senate Finance chairman Russell Long of Louisiana and Armed Services chairman Richard Russell discuss legislative strategy with Johnson in his White House study in February 1966. WHITE HOUSE PHOTO COURTESY RICHARD B. RUSSELL LIBRARY

men," Russell said as he took his place at the massive rectangular table. "Let's get under way." For ninety minutes they reviewed the legislation they expected from the House and discussed how they would employ the filibuster, their only real weapon. As in the debate over the 1960 Civil Rights Act, the southerners would split themselves into three teams. While two-thirds of the southerners rested, one team would handle the day's debate. This highly effective tactic had broken the back of Lyndon Johnson and the northern liberals once before, and Russell expected it would work again. "We were not without hope," Russell said after the meeting, declaring the mood of his colleagues was one of "grim optimism."

Though eager to fight the bill, Russell had begun to reveal the slightest amount of resignation. In an August interview, he acknowledged that he could never reverse or stop the coming social changes. And "the Negro," he admitted,

> *has* been imposed upon. He *has* been subjected to indignities. But we shouldn't upset the whole scheme of constitutional government and expect people to swallow laws governing their most intimate social relations. The tempo of change is the crux of the whole matter. Any realist knows that the "separate but equal" doctrine is finished. There has been assimilation in the larger towns, but it is just hitting the rural areas. I don't think it is fair or just to ask these people to make these additional changes at the same time.
>
> Every Negro citizen possesses every legal right that is possessed by any white citizen, but there is nothing in either the Constitution or Judeo-Christian principles or common sense and reason which would compel one citizen to share his rights with another race at the same place and at the same time.

Some observers applauded Russell for his calm and reasoned opposition to Kennedy's civil rights bill. After all, as *Newsweek* noted, Russell "scorns the crudity of depicting the civil rights movement as a Communist plot or a concoction of 'outside agitators.' His arguments are far more sophisticated and plausible." Russell may have avoided calling the proponents of civil rights communists, but he had no compunctions about tossing around words like *Marxism* and *socialism* when discussing their legislative product. As for Russell's "sophisticated" arguments against civil rights, his ridiculous statement of June 12 would hardly have qualified under even the most generous definition of the term: "If the Commerce clause will sustain an act to compel the white owner of a dining hall to accept a Negro against his wishes, it can be used to sustain the validity of legislation that will compel his admittance into the living room or bedroom of any citizen."

Like many southern politicians of his generation, Russell was still a philosophic captive both of his archaic racist beliefs and of the notion that his constituents would never accept the social changes that John F. Kennedy had in mind. Yet other southerners had reached different conclusions. Two of the nation's most prominent Georgians had now publicly endorsed Kennedy's bill. Secretary of State Dean Rusk declared that the bill's failure would cause the rest of the world to doubt the "real convictions of the American people." Besides, Rusk said, "racial discrimination is wrong." More significant was the support of Atlanta mayor Ivan Allen, who endorsed the bill in late July. When asked by Kennedy to testify before the Judiciary Committee, Allen hesitated. Black leaders in Atlanta urged him to remain quiet out of fear an endorsement would result in his defeat. Allen was almost certain that his city's voters would not reelect him if he endorsed the bill. (He was mistaken.) Yet he summoned the courage to speak out—and did so forcefully. Segregation, he told the committee, was "slavery's stepchild." Failure to enact public accommodations legislation, he said, "would amount to an endorsement of private business setting up an entirely new status of discrimination throughout the country. Cities like Atlanta might slip backward." Businesses and rural communities ought to be given some time to desegregate voluntarily, but he stressed that "now is the time for legislative action."

Of course, Rusk and Allen were not the most prominent southerners supporting the bill. That distinction went to Lyndon Johnson. In the White House and in the Senate, Johnson had awakened from what many people believed was a political hibernation. Civil rights appeared to be the issue that had triggered his resurrection. From his intense strategy discussions with Burke Marshall and Ted Sorenson to his active involvement in White House negotiations with the House Judiciary Committee, Johnson became a forceful, useful, and wise advisor and legislative strategist.

He was also, it appears, a true believer in the need for a strong civil rights bill.

Harry McPherson recalled the first time he witnessed "the real sense of Johnson's commitment" to civil rights—"one that didn't have anything to do with getting a bill through for either the prestige or the political gain that that entailed." Not long after Kennedy's bill was introduced in Congress, McPherson sat with him one afternoon as Johnson presided over the Senate. As he and Johnson discussed the civil rights bill and its prospects for passage, Mississippi's John Stennis rose from his desk and walked toward the door. Johnson called him over.

"How do you like that Title II of the civil rights bill, John?" asked Johnson, referring to the section covering public accommodations.

"Oh, Lyndon," Stennis said, "well, you know our people just can't take that kind of thing. It's just impossible. I mean, I believe that a man ought to have the right—if he owns a store or owns a cafe—he ought to have the right to serve who he wants to serve. I mean, people don't want to associate that way and that sort of thing. Our people just never will take it."

"Then, you don't think you'll support it?"

"Oh, no, Lyndon. I don't think I'll support it at all."

Johnson moved in for the kill.

"Well, you know, John, the other day a sad thing happened. My cook, Zephyr Wright, who has been working for me for many years—she's a college graduate—and her husband drove my official car from Washington down to Texas, the Cadillac limousine of the vice president of the United States. They drove through your state and when they got hungry, they stopped at grocery stores on the edge of town in colored areas and bought Vienna sausages and beans and ate them with a plastic spoon. And when they had to go to the bathroom, they would stop, pull off on a side road, and Zephyr Wright, the cook of the vice president of the United States, would squat in the road to pee. And you know, John, that's just bad. That's wrong. And there ought to be something to change that. And it seems to me that if people in Mississippi don't change it voluntarily, that it's just going to be necessary to change it by law."

"Well, Lyndon," Stennis replied, "I'm sure that there are nice places where your cook and . . ."

But Johnson ignored Stennis, looked away vacantly, and said, "Uh-huh, uh-huh. Well, thank you, John." As Stennis walked away, Johnson turned to McPherson and winked.

Johnson's encounter with Stennis may have been contrived, but the story was real. Johnson had long ago learned from his domestic employees about the indignities blacks endured in the South. In 1951, Johnson asked Gene Williams and his wife, Helen, to drive his car and his beagle to the LBJ Ranch in Texas. Williams, in a rare moment of defiance, demurred. Driving Johnson's car between Washington and Texas had been a yearly chore, but he refused to take the dog. Johnson demanded to know why. Williams finally replied, "It's hard for me to get a place to stay, much less the dog."

The incident apparently had a profound impact on Johnson and enhanced his understanding of the daily difficulties of black life in the South. In his 1971 memoirs, *The Vantage Point,* he began the chapter on civil rights with the account of Williams and the beagle. Johnson ended the story by declaring, "So there was nothing I could say to Gene. His problem was also mine: as a Texan, a southerner and an American."

That Johnson cared about his black employees was clear. That he wanted to help Kennedy pass a civil rights bill was evident. Little of this, however, mattered to most black leaders. Lyndon Johnson—prominent southerner, former Senate majority leader, and now vice president—was one of the most powerless people in the government. Most civil rights groups ignored him or took his support for granted. Some suspected that his motives for supporting civil rights were more political than personal. In any event, there was simply not much he could do for their cause.

After November 22, 1963, however, every civil rights leader and congressional liberal—indeed every black American yearning for freedom—suddenly saw Lyndon Baines Johnson in a brand new light.

CHAPTER NINETEEN

Tell Him to Cry a Little

THE NEWS OF PRESIDENT KENNEDY'S MURDER hit Washington during the
lunch hour. When Russell heard the first reports, he went directly to
the ornate Marble Room, just off the Senate chamber. Several minutes
later, CBS correspondent Roger Mudd found him there, hunched over
the Associated Press and United Press wire machines. Mudd was moved
by what he saw: Russell, tears streaming from his eyes, reading the news
aloud to a stunned group of senators and staff members. Later Russell
joined Majority Leader Mike Mansfield in the radio-TV gallery—a rare
appearance for the camera-shy Georgian. "It was very hard for Dick to
get through it," Mudd recalled. "And he damn near didn't get through
it." Mudd said it was a scene he would never forget. "Considering how
stately and self-collected Dick Russell always was, he just really came
apart that afternoon."

Later that day, in his office and surrounded by his staff, Russell's
thoughts turned to his friend and protégé—the new president. "Well,
Lyndon Johnson has all of the talents, the abilities and the equipment
to make a very good president of this country, a very good president."
Then Russell added, "And of course old Lyndon is going to enjoy being
president. He'll enjoy every minute of it, every hour of it."

Across town, Humphrey and Muriel had been attending a luncheon
at the Chilean Embassy. Standing alone in the embassy's library, Humphrey received the news in a phone call from White House aide Ralph
Dungan. Humphrey tried but failed to fight back tears. Struggling to
regain his composure, Humphrey numbly staggered into the dining
room, where he delivered the dreadful news to the assembled guests
before the tears engulfed him. Leaving the embassy, Humphrey and
Muriel headed straight for the White House. As they rode through the

Washington streets, Humphrey could not accept the reality of the tragic event. He muttered to himself several times, "John Kennedy is dead. John Kennedy is gone." Arriving at the White House, Humphrey spotted Kenny O'Donnell, perhaps Kennedy's closest aide—and burst into tears again. Humphrey gained control of his emotions only after a lengthy, solitary walk in the Rose Garden.

That evening, when *Air Force One* touched down at Andrews Air Force Base bearing Johnson and the casket with Kennedy's body, Humphrey was waiting for his old friend, the new president. As Lady Bird disembarked, she greeted Humphrey and Muriel warmly with a kiss. "We need you both so much," she said quietly. Later that evening Humphrey and other congressional leaders huddled with Johnson in the Old Executive Office Building, where Johnson simply and humbly asked for their help and guidance. When the meeting ended, Humphrey lingered for a moment, "to assure President Johnson privately of my desire to be of all possible assistance." Johnson wrapped an understanding arm around him. He needed Humphrey, he said, "desperately."

It was understandably the most overwhelming day of Johnson's life—a day when he would need the advice, counsel, and comfort of his oldest friends and advisors. Stepping onto the tarmac at Andrews, he had searched the crowd for his mentor from Georgia. "Where's Dick?" he asked. Russell had avoided the chaotic airport scene. Johnson phoned him several hours later, and the two men talked for ten minutes. The next day Johnson summoned Russell to the White House for lunch. During the meal, Russell continually addressed his old friend as "Mr. President." Johnson found Russell's deference awkward. He insisted, "Call me Lyndon as you used to. After all, we've been together all these years." Russell steadfastly refused. "No, Mr. President, now you're the president of the United States. You, to me, are Mr. President." No one ever again heard Russell address Johnson by his first name.

In the days following the assassination—in discussions with friends, associates, and former adversaries—Johnson was modest and deferential. In conversation after conversation, meeting after meeting, he reached out for help and guidance. He asked Kennedy's grieving staff, as well as his cabinet, to stay on board. He made amends with his old friend Jim Rowe, with whom he had quarreled during the 1960 campaign. He renewed friendships with former advisors and associates such as Clark Clifford, Dean Acheson, and Adlai Stevenson. Most of all, Johnson was humble. In phone conversations on the night of the assassination with

Justice Arthur Goldberg and Allen Hoover, son of former president Herbert Hoover, Johnson insisted that he was "inadequate" for the job.

Yet he was *more than adequate*. He was arguably the most qualified vice president ever to assume the office upon the death of a president. No person had ever inherited the presidency with more experience, more confidence, and a better understanding of the nature of power and how to use it. From the moment of John F. Kennedy's death, Lyndon Johnson was in complete control of the federal government. He did not waver. He did not hesitate to issue orders or make decisions. He was now the nation's chief executive, and he used the powers of his office to the fullest extent. Gardner Ackley, then a member of the President's Council of Economic Advisors, watched Johnson dominate a November 25 meeting called to discuss economic matters. "To me," Ackley wrote in his notes of the meeting, "the most impressive thing was the confident way in which he approached the whole problem—not necessarily implying that he knew the answers, but he knew the score, and that the problem could be solved." From the beginning, Johnson made it clear that he would finish what Kennedy had started. That meant, among other legislative priorities, a civil rights bill. "The first priority," he told Jack Valenti and Bill Moyers, "is passage of the civil rights act." On the night Johnson became president, he told Valenti he was eager "to get civil rights off its backside in the Congress and give it legs."

As he prepared for his speech to a joint session of Congress on November 27, Johnson telephoned several civil rights leaders. He was, he assured them, sincerely devoted to their cause. To National Urban League director Whitney Young, Johnson confided that he would challenge Congress to pass the civil rights bill. Young was pleased, saying, "I think you've just got to make a date for [its passage] and point out that out . . . hate that goes unchecked doesn't stop just for the week."

Johnson enthusiastically seized Young's point. "Dedicate a whole page on hate, hate international, hate domestic and just say that this hate that produces inequality, this hate that produces poverty. That's why we've just got to have civil rights. It's a cancer that just eats out our national existence." Perhaps most encouraging to Young was Johnson's rock-solid determination to push for the bill's passage. Although Johnson cautioned, "let's not move with that ball until we know where we're going," he exuded a resolve and tenacity that must have delighted Young. "Let's go and go right on through the goal line . . . [We] might get run out of bounds a time or two—but [we'll] keep coming." The situation, Johnson said, reminded him of the person who asked, "What's the difference between a Texas Ranger and a Texas sheriff?" The answer was, Johnson said, "Well, when you hit a Ranger, he just keeps coming. So, that's kind of the fight we want to get in. We want to just keep coming when we start." The next day, when Martin Luther King told him that passage of Kennedy's "great progressive policies" would be "one of the greatest tributes that we can pay" to the late president, Johnson replied, "Well, I'm going to support them all and you can count on that and I'm going to do my best to get other men to do likewise and I'll have to have ya'll's help . . . I never needed it more than I do now."

Under Kennedy, civil rights leaders had been supplicants who struggled to win the president's tentative support for their cause. Now, under Johnson, the same men became lieutenants and advisors in a newly energized crusade. In an Oval Office meeting with NAACP leader Roy Wilkins, Johnson could not have been more emphatic. "I want that bill passed," he said. Wilkins believed him.

Johnson's demeanor with King, Wilkins, and Young was no patronizing bluster. From the beginning he believed passage of a civil rights bill would require a fierce and protracted legislative battle. On November 25 he told his economic advisors, "The only way you could lick this was to stay in continuous session . . . It's too bad that the deliberative process has to come down to an endurance contest, but that's the way it is." Within days of assuming office, Johnson began devising his legislative strategy for the Senate, even though the civil rights bill was still mired in the House Rules Committee. When he first quizzed Marshall about the legislative strategy, Marshall confessed, "I didn't have the foggiest idea how we were going to get it through the Senate, though I was sure, and I told him I was sure, we could get it through the House." When the bill arrived in the Senate, Johnson wondered, would the liberals would be on their mettle for a fight with the southerners? "Some of the liberals make a few good speeches on the floor," Johnson remarked on November 25, "and then run off to make speeches and collect their honoraria."

For now Johnson had a speech of his own to deliver. Appearing before a joint session of the House and Senate, he would reassure a nervous world and a grieving nation. He would challenge Congress to help him finish the domestic and foreign policy initiatives that Kennedy had started. Johnson had first enlisted two Kennedy associates, speech writer Ted Sorenson and Ambassador to India John Kenneth Galbraith, to compose the message. But the night before the speech, over dinner with Humphrey and Abe Fortas, Johnson handed the draft to the two men with instructions to produce a more "suitable" speech. Humphrey and Fortas went to work immediately. They put their final touches on the rewritten text at around 2:30 a.m.

The next day at noon, on the eve of Thanksgiving, Johnson stood at the rostrum in the House of Representatives. He spoke softly and deliberately. Some congressmen in the back of the chamber could barely hear him.

> All I have I would have given gladly not to be standing here today.
>
> The greatest leader of our time has been struck down by the foulest deed of our time . . .
>
> And now the ideas and the ideals which he so nobly represented must and will be translated into effective action . . .
>
> We will carry on the fight against poverty and misery, and disease and ignorance, in other lands and in our own.
>
> We will serve all the Nation, not one section or one sector, or one group, but all Americans. These are the United States—a united people with a united purpose . . .
>
> On the twentieth day of January, in 1961, John F. Kennedy told his countrymen that our national work would not be finished "in the first thousand days, nor in the life of this administration, nor even perhaps in our lifetime on this planet. But," he said, "let us begin."
>
> Today, in this moment of new resolve, I would say to all my fellow Americans, let us continue.*

Having now wrapped himself in the mystique of the Kennedy legend, Johnson launched his own pitch for civil rights:

> First, no memorial oration or eulogy could more eloquently honor President Kennedy's memory than the earliest possible passage of the civil rights bill for which he fought so long. We have talked long enough in this country about equal rights.

---

*"Let us continue"—perhaps the most memorable line of the speech—was one of Humphrey's contributions to the text and one in which he took enormous pride.

We have talked for one hundred years or more. It is time now to write the next chapter, and to write in the books of law.

I urge you, as I did in 1957 and again in 1960, to enact a civil rights law so that we can move forward to eliminate from this Nation every trace of discrimination and oppression that is based upon race or color. There could be no greater source of strength to this Nation both at home and abroad . . .

We meet in grief, but let us also meet in renewed dedication and renewed vigor. Let us meet in action, in tolerance, and in mutual understanding. John Kennedy's death commands what his life conveyed—that America must move forward. The time has come for Americans of all races and creeds and political beliefs to understand and respect one another. So let us put an end to the teaching and the preaching of hate and evil and violence. Let us turn away from the fanatics of the far left and the far right, from the apostles of bitterness and bigotry, from those defiant of law, and those who pour venom into our Nation's bloodstream.

When Johnson finished his speech, the House chamber erupted in boisterous, sustained applause. Even the southerners joined the standing ovation. (Most of them, including Russell, had refused to applaud Johnson's call for a civil rights bill.)

The speech was enormously reassuring to uneasy liberals and civil rights leaders. As black comedian Dick Gregory quipped afterwards, "As soon as Lyndon Johnson finished his speech before Congress, twenty million of us unpacked." Paul Douglas viewed the speech with bittersweet irony: "It remained for Lyndon Johnson, who as senator had been the most subtle and determined opponent of all civil rights legislation, to become, as president, the evangelist for the movement." Although Douglas vastly exaggerated the president's former opposition to civil rights, Johnson's passionate embrace of Kennedy's civil rights proposal was not enough to persuade some liberals of his sincerity. Johnson knew that the most dubious liberals would ultimately respect only accomplishments, not words. For now many of them remained wary of their new president. The reaction of Ruby Martin, a staff attorney for the U.S. Civil Rights Commission, was typical: "I was probably as distressed as any black person in America at the time at the thought of a . . . southerner ascending to the presidency . . . All of the things that we were looking forward to under Kennedy seemed to have [been] killed with him in Dallas."

Many southern conservatives were not as doubtful about Johnson's determination to enact a tough civil rights bill. "People were probably a little more fearful," said Mississippi lieutenant governor Paul Johnson. "They were fearful because they knew that Lyndon Johnson was probably a hundred times smarter than Jack Kennedy was—smarter from the standpoint of being able to handle the Congress." Yet strangely, Johnson's speech did not alarm or shock most of the southerners. After all, it was the first presidential call for civil rights ever uttered in a bona fide Dixie drawl. "The essential difference in Johnson's civil rights approach," observed journalist Tom Wicker, "was in the overtures he was able to make to the South *at the same time*. Kennedy could not have done that, nor Nelson Rockefeller, and perhaps not even Dwight Eisenhower; certainly not Barry Goldwater."

In the days and weeks after Kennedy's death, Johnson reached out to prominent liberals, many of whom had distrusted him well before he engineered the compromises of the 1957 Civil Rights Act. Johnson asked Walter Heller, the liberal chairman of the Council of Economic Advisors, to "Tell your liberal friends . . . that I am an old-fashioned FDR liberal and that I want to work with them, and that they will have an ally here in the White House." In early December Johnson began courting Joseph Rauh, one of his most dependable, longtime critics. When New York senator Herbert Lehman died, Johnson invited Rauh to accompany him to the funeral on *Air Force One*. Throughout the early months of his administration, Johnson consulted civil rights leaders— who were generally more eager than their white liberal counterparts to believe that the new president would back up his strong rhetoric with equally decisive action. "I had always said I always felt," Whitney Young recalled, "that if ever I turned on the radio and heard the president of the United States speaking with a deep southern accent that I would panic. But I did not feel that way at all. I felt by that time that Lyndon Johnson would do exactly what he did."

On the opposite end of the civil rights spectrum, Russell supported Johnson's call for a strong national defense, a sound dollar, and economy in government. Of course he was unmoved by the president's emotional appeal for civil rights. "My reason for opposing the so-called civil rights bill are the same," he said in a prepared statement. "It is still the same vicious assault on property rights and the Constitution. It is still fraught with many more liberty-destroying provisions than ever it could create. It still proposes to take away from our society the oldest of our rights—that of freedom of association and the right to do business with whom one pleases."

Though disappointed in his old friend, Russell was not surprised that Johnson would push for enactment of Kennedy's civil rights program. He was, however, shocked and dismayed at the way Johnson suddenly drafted him into service on the blue-ribbon commission to investigate the Kennedy assassination. Worried that neither Texas authorities nor the FBI would have the credibility to calm rampant speculation about foreign plots and even Johnson's own complicity, the president appointed the "Special Commission to Investigate the Assassination of President Kennedy." It later became known as the Warren Commission, so named because of its chairman, Chief Justice Earl Warren. From the beginning, Johnson recruited only men of the highest stature and credibility: House Democratic leader Hale Boggs of Louisiana, Kentucky Republican senator John Sherman Cooper, Republican Michigan congressman Gerald Ford, former CIA director Allen Dulles, and banker and diplomat John McCloy of New York. Warren was not an easy sell, but Johnson finally persuaded him that the assignment was his patriotic duty. Persuading Russell to serve was another matter entirely.

Shortly before 9:00 p.m. on November 29, Johnson phoned Russell in Winder to tell him that he had already announced his appointment to the commission. (This was not exactly the case: the announcement had been drafted but not yet released to the press.) "I just can't serve on that commission," Russell protested, explaining that "I don't like" Earl Warren. Johnson firmly rejected Russell's protests. "You've never turned your country down," he said sternly. "This is not me. This is your country . . . You're my man on that commission and you're going to do it and don't tell me what you can do and what you can't. Because I can't arrest you and I'm not going to put the FBI on you, but you're goddamned sure going to serve. I'll tell you that."

Russell was distraught. "I don't know when I've been so unhappy about a thing as I am this," he told Johnson's friend A. W. Moursund, who came on the line briefly until Johnson seized the phone.

"Your president's asking you to do these things," Johnson argued, "and there are some things I want you in besides civil rights, and by

God, you're going to be in them because I can't run this country by myself."

Russell shot back. "You know damned well my future is behind me and that is not entering into it at all."

"Well, your future is your country and you're going to do everything you can to serve America."

"I can't do it," Russell protested. "I haven't got the time."

"All right. We'll just make the time."

Later in the conversation, when Russell complained that "you're taking advantage of me," Johnson stopped him cold.

"No. No. No. I'm not taking advantage of you. I'm going to take a hell of a lot of advantage of you, my friend, 'cause you made me and I know it and I don't ever forget. And I'm going to be taking advantage of you a good deal. But you're going to serve your country and do what is right and if you can't do it, you get that damned little Bobby [Russell's nephew Robert Russell] up there and let him push your tail and put a cocklebur under it."

Johnson's hectoring worked. Russell softened. "I'm at your command," he finally said. "And I'll do anything you want me to do."

"Well, you damned sure going to be at my command," Johnson replied. "You're going to be at my command as long as I'm here."

Finished with his hard sell, Johnson now moved in deftly with flattery and soft words.

"Nobody ever has been more to me than you have, Dick, except my mother."

Russell laughed.

"No. No. That's true. I've bothered you more and made you spend more hours with me telling me what's right and wrong than anybody except my mother . . . I just want to counsel with you and I just want your judgment and your wisdom. 'Cause I haven't got any daddy and you're going to be it."

Russell served on the Warren Commission, but only reluctantly. "You destroyed me, putting me on this commission," he complained to Johnson on December 7.

Russell attended only a few of the commission hearings (although he claimed to have read "every line of testimony") and tried to persuade Johnson to relieve him of the assignment in a February 1964 letter. Johnson ignored Russell's request. "I was badly overloaded," Russell later said, "undoubtedly more so than any other man on the commission." The coming fight over civil rights, his day-to-day Senate duties, the commission assignment, and his continued failing health would make 1964 one of the most miserable periods of Russell's life.

Johnson's immediate concern was the House, which was still in session at the president's behest despite the approaching Christmas holidays. There the civil rights bill, H.R. 7152, was stranded in the Rules Committee, the domain of "Judge" Howard Smith, an eighty-year-old veteran from Virginia. A segregationist and fierce opponent of civil rights, Smith steadfastly refused to grant a rule for the bill's floor debate. Smith's intransigence sent Johnson into a rage. "There's all this stuff going on [protests] and we've been talking about this for one hundred years," Johnson complained in a phone conversation with former Treasury secretary Robert Anderson. "Looks like about time we stopped talking. And I just think that we're going to have [black protesters] out in the streets again if we don't make some little progress. Yes, but Howard has just gone off to his farm and tells the Speaker, 'I won't even give you a hearing on it' . . . Says, 'Hell, no. Go eat cake, goddamn it. Don't mess with me until next year.' "

Johnson was equally irked by Republicans who refused to sign a discharge petition, a parliamentary device to bypass Rules and force the bill onto the House floor. He mused about issuing these Republicans a challenge: "Now, you're either for civil rights or you're not. You're either the party of Lincoln or you ain't. And this, by God, put up or shut up. This is it. If you are, sign the petition to consider it. If you're not, why just get over there, by God, with Jim Eastland and Howard Smith and stay. And I believe that we can dramatize it enough that we can wreck them."

Johnson, the legislative strategist, understood why the discharge petition could become so important to the bill's ultimate success in the Senate. As he explained to *Washington Post* publisher Katherine Graham on December 2, "If we could ever get that signed, that would practically break [the southerners'] backs in the Senate because they could see that here is a steamroller that could petition it out. And they will put cloture on and the psychology would be just like [the University of] Texas won every game this year—that they are a going [successful] outfit."

Although he quietly pushed for the bill's speedy consideration in the House, Johnson was quick to caution Graham to avoid optimistic expectations. Kennedy had tried for almost a year without success, he said. "Now, I hope in twelve months I can be, but he tried since May on civil rights and he hasn't been successful, so they better not be too quick to judge it. If this Mickey Mantle that's got a batting average of .500 and is the star of the Yankees—if he couldn't do it, how do you expect some pug-ugly from Johnson City to come in and do it pretty quick?"

Meanwhile Johnson wisely handed over tactical control of the bill to Attorney General Robert Kennedy, Deputy Attorney General Nicholas Katzenbach, and Assistant Attorney General Burke Marshall. "I'll do on the bill just what you think is best to do on the bill," Johnson told Kennedy. "We'll follow what you say we should do on the bill." While Kennedy appreciated Johnson's willingness to rely on the judgment of Justice Department attorneys, he suspected an ulterior motive. Johnson, Kennedy suggested, "didn't want President Johnson to be the reason, to have the sole responsibility" if the bill failed. If Kennedy plotted the bill's strategy and Johnson only followed instructions, Kennedy reasoned that Johnson "could always say that he did what we suggested."

In the end Johnson was spared a fight with Chairman Smith over his refusal to report the bill out of the Rules Committee. Public opinion, largely driven by the emotional reaction to Kennedy's death, finally forced Smith's hand. Polls showed that more than 60 percent of the nation supported the bill. Johnson himself enjoyed an impressive 79 percent approval rating. Smith had no choice. "You'll have to run over us," he defiantly told the bill's supporters when he finally called for hearings on the bill. Smith knew the ultimate outcome. "We know we'll be run over."

On January 30 Smith's committee voted, 11-4, to send H.R. 7152 to the House floor under an "open rule." House members could offer amendments to every section. During floor debate, Judiciary chairman Emanuel Celler and his Republican counterpart, William McCulloch, held their ground. Bolstered by vocal support and active lobbying from the White House, the Justice Department, the major civil rights and religious organizations, and organized labor, the bill emerged intact. Southern opposition was surprisingly listless and unorganized. During nine days of debate, southern opponents failed to add even one major weakening amendment to the bill.

The bill that passed the House on February 10—by a 290-130

vote—was much broader and more potent than President Kennedy could have ever imagined. The "Part III" and fair employment provisions added by the Judiciary Committee remained, as did provisions on public facilities and the withholding of federal funds from discriminatory programs.* It was, in the words of *Congressional Quarterly*, "the most sweeping civil rights measure to clear either house of Congress in the 20th Century."

The House victory invigorated Johnson. Minutes after its passage, he phoned two of the bill's chief lobbyists, his old detractor Joseph Rauh and the NAACP's Clarence Mitchell. As Mitchell recalled:

> When we got the bill through the House, Joe Rauh and I were in a foot race over [to] the Senate to start work there. You know there are certain details you have to get squared away. The phone rang in one of those booths over there in the House wing and to our amazement it was the president calling. I don't know how he ever managed to get us on that phone, but he was calling to say, "All right, you fellows, get on over there to the Senate and get busy, because we've got it through the House and now we've got the big job of getting it through the Senate." Well, this was really a fascinating thing to me, that the chief executive of a country could have followed this legislation so closely that immediately on the passage of it by the House, he knew how to get the fellows who were working over there on a pay phone.

The Senate, as usual, proved a curious beast. Like the body that Johnson commanded during the 1957 civil rights debate, the Senate of 1964 divided into three distinct groups: pro–civil rights Republicans and Democrats, Russell's southern Democrats (joined by far-right Republicans John Tower of Texas and Barry Goldwater of Arizona), and moderate Republicans. By themselves, the pro–civil rights forces could produce the fifty-one votes needed to pass a civil rights bill. But unless they found sixteen additional votes to invoke cloture, their bill would never come to a vote.

---

*The fair employment section was one of the bill's strongest. Omitted from Kennedy's original civil rights program, Title VII established a five-member Equal Opportunity Employment Commission empowered to prevent and eliminate workplace discrimination by employers, employment agencies, and labor unions. After a three-year phase-in period, the provision would apply to all businesses and unions with at least twenty-five employees or members.

It was the support of the third group—moderate, mostly midwestern senators who made up about two-thirds of the Senate's thirty-three Republicans—that the Senate's liberals desperately needed to pass civil rights. On their own, Mike Mansfield's Democrats were dead. With a two-to-one advantage—at 67 to 33, their largest majority since 1939— the Democrats could conceivably invoke cloture anytime, but *only* if they voted as a bloc. With Russell's southerners in their ranks, that would never happen. During the forty-seven years of the cloture rule's existence—in eleven separate votes—liberals had never forcibly ended a southern filibuster of a civil rights bill.

With precious little hope that the Senate could stop a southern filibuster, Johnson gambled on an audacious strategy. He approved the Justice Department's plan for a bold, frontal assault in the Senate. The administration would neither seek nor entertain any compromise with southerners and conservative Republicans. "It would be a fight to total victory or total defeat without appeasement or attrition," Johnson later said, explaining that the "slightest wavering" on the bill "would give hope to the opposition's strategy of amending the bill to death." As Johnson and his Justice Department advisors knew, any agreement that weakened the bill in the Senate would probably result in its defeat once it returned to the House. William McCulloch would make certain of that. When asked about possible weakening amendments in the Senate during Rules Committee hearings, McCulloch replied, "I would never be a party to such a proposal. My head is still bloody from 1957. I feel very strongly about this."

In many respects, Johnson had become the most unlikely proponent of a no-compromise strategy. After all, striking legislative bargains had been his stock in trade, the primary coin of his realm. As president, however, Johnson realized that his constituency no longer was Texas, nor was it the southern Democrats who had been the backbone of his support as majority leader. He was now, as he later explained, the leader of an entire pluralistic nation. Politically he could now afford to take a principled and courageous stand. Philosophically he was freed from the shackles of his Texas roots and his House and Senate voting records. Now, when he looked at civil rights, he no longer viewed the issue through the lenses of the parochial South or the clannish Senate. "When you have the responsibility for fifty states," he later said, "it is different than responsibility for one. I'm sure the county attorney doesn't feel the same depth and breadth of the nation's affairs as much as the attorney general does. Now I'm sure the local district judge or county judge doesn't feel it as the Supreme Court justice and if there's anything that makes a person realize what his conscience and soul ought to be, [it] is being president of the United States. And he's president of *all* the people and he's the one they have to look to and it's a lot different from representing the little isolated district in one corner of one state."

Furthermore, Johnson knew that he could not maintain his credibility as a strong and true advocate of civil rights if he began consorting with Dirksen or Russell to weaken the bill simply to avoid a filibuster. "I knew that if I didn't get out in front on this issue, [the liberals] would get me," he later said. "I couldn't let that happen. I had to produce a civil rights bill that was even stronger than the one they'd have gotten if Kennedy had lived. Without this, I'd be dead before I could even begin." The matter was simple: There was no room for compromise. The strategy was not only sound legislative politics; it had now become a matter of principle.

Johnson's strategy neither surprised nor disappointed Russell. As Russell told reporters, Johnson really had no choice. The president's robust advocacy of civil rights seemed not to affect Russell's affection for the president. They maintained their intimate friendship. Barely a day passed when they did not talk by phone several times. Many evenings found Russell at the White House enjoying a cozy dinner with Johnson and Lady Bird followed by several hours of easy conversation. Russell was no longer Johnson's means to power in the Senate. He was a trusted, valuable friend and arguably Johnson's most intimate advisor.

On civil rights, however, Russell offered no advice. His views were well known. Likewise, Johnson did not try to dissuade his old friend from organizing a filibuster to stop the administration's civil rights bill. Apparently neither man feared that their differences on this issue would harm their friendship. "There will be times when my convictions on issues will conflict with his views and purposes," Russell told an Atlanta church on January 5, "and he would not expect the intimate friendship we have enjoyed through the years to in any wise restrain me in fighting for those things in which I believe." Three days later, in reaction to the president's renewed call for civil rights in his State of the Union address, Russell made his position clear. He regretted, he said, that Johnson "has embraced in toto the far-reaching program of the left-wing groups that is erroneously called the civil rights bill."

Despite their disagreement over the issue, Russell understood—even reluctantly accepted—Johnson's embrace of civil rights. He told Johnson's aide Bill Moyers, "Now you tell Lyndon that I've been expecting the rod for a long time, and I'm sorry that it's from his hand the rod must be wielded, but I'd rather it be his hand than anybody else's I know. Tell him to cry a little when he uses it." As Russell explained to a *Business Week* reporter in April, "President Kennedy didn't have to pass a strong bill to prove anything. President Johnson does." To another reporter in May, Russell confided, "If Johnson compromises, he will be called a slicker from Texas."

For the first time, finding sixty-seven votes for cloture on a civil rights bill was not a hopeless objective. By Nicholas Katzenbach's informal count, liberals might have as many as seventy-four votes. Johnson was not so sure. At best, he estimated, there were fifty-eight votes—nine short of cloture. Katzenbach bluntly told the president, "If you do anything publicly but indicate that we're going to get cloture on this bill, we can't *possibly* get cloture on this bill. And the only way we can get it is for you with your experience to express absolute confidence, publicly and privately, that we're going to get cloture on this bill." Katzenbach also reminded Johnson that several conservatives had abandoned their absolute opposition to cloture in 1962 when they cast their first-ever votes to shut off a filibuster (waged by liberals during debate over the communications satellite bill). They can't oppose cloture on principle any more, Katzenbach explained, expecting to gain "some additional votes" from the conservative ranks.

Johnson endorsed the Justice Department's cloture strategy, but he continued to urge Majority Leader Mansfield to turn up the heat on southerners by holding the Senate in around-the-clock sessions when the expected filibuster began. Mansfield knew that this strategy was unwise. In 1960, that approach had failed to exhaust the southerners, enhanced their leverage, and resulted in passage of a weakened civil rights bill. During that debate, Mansfield explained, "it was not the fresh and well-rested opponents" of civil rights "who were compelled to the compromise. It was, rather, the exhausted, sleep-starved, quorum-confounded proponents who were only too happy to take it." As White House aide Mike Manatos explained to Larry O'Brien, Johnson's chief congressional lobbyist, "Night sessions make it necessary for at least fifty proponents to be within a few minutes of the Senate chambers while only three to four southerners need be on hand."

Mansfield was rarely a headstrong man. On this point, however, he would not be bullied by Johnson or the civil rights activists. He feared that twenty-four-hour sessions would kill some of the Senate's older members. More important was the Senate's image. "This is not a circus or a sideshow," he declared. "We are not operating a pit with spectators coming into the galleries late at night to see senators of the Republic come out in bedroom slippers without neckties, with their hair uncombed, and pajama tops sticking out of their necks." As for Russell, he and his troops had no reason to fear a continuous session. "We will be there twenty-four hours a day," he promised.

Mansfield prevailed; there would be no "circus." As Johnson later declared, the eventual administration strategy was simple and straightforward: "We would win, by securing cloture, or we would lose."

Although Mansfield helped set the overall tone for the coming debate, he remained a reluctant leader. He had no interest in assuming the day-to-day duties of managing the bill during floor debate. He awarded that role to Humphrey. Honored and somewhat overwhelmed to be entrusted the fate of legislation he had championed for so long, Humphrey realized the coming debate "would test me in every way." As he already knew, his performance on civil rights would serve as an audition for the role of Johnson's running mate in the fall presidential elections. As the Senate leader for civil rights, Humphrey would be thrust into the national limelight as never before. In the coming months, his vice presidential ambitions and the fate of civil rights would be inextricable.

"What is going to be important," Humphrey's aide, Rein Vander Zee, wrote in a December 1963 memorandum, "is a man's proven experience and ability in the federal government." Vander Zee's advice was blunt. If Humphrey wanted to be vice president, he should strive to be

> a constructive middle of the roader doing everything possible to help President Johnson get his program across. Don't let the ultra-liberal wing or a bunch of political faddists isolate you in left field because, when it is all said and done after the Democratic convention a meager six months from now, the Irish Catholics, the ultra-liberals, and all the rest will be on the team because, as always, they have no place else to go.

Johnson gave Humphrey little or no advice about how to campaign for the vice presidency, but he had plenty of ideas about how to pass civil rights. Early in the year Johnson summoned Humphrey to the White House for a pep talk. "You bomb-throwers make good speeches, you have big hearts, you believe in what you say you stand for, but you're never on the job when you need to be there. You spread yourselves too thin making speeches to the faithful." Humphrey later said that Johnson's diatribe would have offended him "if he hadn't been basically right and historically accurate." Humphrey said he knew that Johnson "had sized me up. He knew very well that I would say, 'Damn you, I'll show you.' One thing about Johnson was that even when he conned me I knew what was happening to me. It was kind of enjoyable. I mean I knew what was going on, and he knew I knew." Johnson gave Humphrey another piece of important advice. "Now you know that this bill can't pass unless you get Ev Dirksen. You and I are going to get him. You make up your mind now that you've got to spend time with Ev Dirksen. You've got to let him have a piece of the action. He's got to look good all the time."

Humphrey took Johnson's advice to heart. In a March 8 appearance on NBC's *Meet the Press,* Humphrey heaped generous praise on the Republican leader. "He is a man who thinks of his country before he thinks of his party. He is one who understands the legislative process intimately and fully, and I sincerely believe that when Senator Dirksen has to face that moment of decision where his influence and where his leadership will be required in order to give us the votes that are necessary to pass this bill, he will not be found wanting." Watching Humphrey's interview was Johnson, who called him afterwards. "Boy, that was right. You're doing just right now. You just keep at that. Don't you let those bomb throwers, now, talk you out of seeing Dirksen. You get in there to see Dirksen! You drink with Dirksen! You talk to Dirksen! You listen to Dirksen!"

As everyone in Johnson's White House well understood, Dirksen was the key to beating the southern filibuster. "We knew we could not pass it with Democratic votes," Nicholas Katzenbach argued. "We could not pass it with Democratic votes, plus liberal Republican votes. We *had* to have the leadership of the Republican party with us in order to get that legislation passed." The path to the votes to enact civil rights, said Humphrey's aide Raymond Wolfinger, "went through Dirksen."

Before 1964 virtually every civil rights filibuster was strictly a one-way affair. Russell's southern troops engaged in lengthy monologues and colloquies while proponents of civil rights watched from the sidelines. Occasionally they sparred with the southern conservatives. Usually they relinquished the Senate chamber, appearing only for quorum calls and roll-call votes. Every time, the southern troops were more organized and better versed in the details of the legislation.

This time Humphrey meant to alter that equation. Working closely with Minority Whip Thomas Kuchel—a California liberal whom Dirksen had appointed Republican floor manager for the bill—he devised a system by which the proponents of civil rights would aggressively challenge, refute, question, and debate the southerners on every major point. Toward that end, Humphrey appointed rotating four-member groups of senators—known as the Civil Rights Corporals' Guard—to remain always in the Senate chamber. "We determined early not to let the Southerners occupy the press," Humphrey recalled. "So, in the very opening days, starting with the March 9 motion to take up [the bill], we proceeded to debate the Southerners. We took the offensive and we were able to get good press . . . In other words, we were active, at no time passive, and at all times challenging the opposition."

For each of the bill's major titles, Humphrey appointed a floor captain to organize and lead the response to the southern opposition: Joseph Clark would defend the fair employment practices provision, Commerce Committee chairman Warren Magnuson the public accommodations section, and Michigan's Philip Hart the voting rights section. As Humphrey explained, "When each senator has had a chance to debate the bill, title by title, they also had an opportunity to get some press for themselves, to be known as part of the team fighting for civil rights. This was not only good for the issue itself, but also for the senators and their public relations and they seemed to like it." Humphrey even suggested radio and television programs on which senators might argue the merits of the bill.

Each morning Humphrey, Kuchel, their floor captains, and a Justice Department official—usually Nicholas Katzenbach—met in Humphrey's Capitol office to discuss and coordinate the day's tactics. At least two days each week, Clarence Mitchell and Joseph Rauh joined them. The results were impressive. In April Murray Kempton reported in the *New Republic* that "one result of this concern for detail is that for the first time in memory a civil rights debate has turned out to be almost lively; and at the very least Humphrey and Kuchel have improved the theater available to the visiting schoolchildren. At the most they have made the filibuster an inconvenience for those who practice it."

To build solidarity among the civil rights proponents, Humphrey published a bipartisan civil rights newsletter. Every morning each pro–civil rights senator received a summary of the previous day's debate, complete with responses to the most recent attacks leveled by the southerners. "For the first time, we are putting up a battle," Humphrey bragged to the Senate after John Stennis demanded to know "who writes these mysterious messages?"

The April 9 newsletter was typical. It alerted senators that "Title II, the public accommodations section, will be discussed by proponents of the bill. Senators Magnuson and Hruska have been assigned responsibility for this title. Floor captains for the day will be: Democrats: Clark (10 a.m. to 1 p.m.); Bayh (1 to 4 p.m.); Muskie (4 to 7 p.m.); Moss (7 p.m. to recess). Republicans: Javits (all day); Allott (all day)."

Making the Humphrey-Kuchel coalition even more impressive was its sophisticated system for answering quorum calls. For years the suggestion of the absence of a quorum had been the southerners' favorite way to harass the majority. Quorum calls gave the filibusterers time to sit and rest their feet and voices. They also served an important parliamentary purpose. Under the Senate's rules, each senator could deliver only two speeches per subject in a legislative day. If Humphrey and Kuchel failed to muster fifty-one senators, the Senate could adjourn and a new legislative day would begin, allowing the southerners to make more speeches. Failure to produce a quorum might also suggest that Humphrey's side lacked the resolve needed to beat the filibuster. As Humphrey knew, many undecided senators would stop thinking about a compromise with Russell only when liberals proved that their determination to endure was greater than that of the southerners. That meant aggressively debating the southerners, voting down their weakening amendments, and, most importantly, appearing for every quorum call.

Humphrey addressed the quorum problem by taking a page from the southern playbook. He divided his Democratic troops into two platoons, each with about twenty-five members. Each day Humphrey notified members of one platoon that their names were on the duty roster. They were expected to answer all quorum calls. Added to their total were Humphrey, his floor captains, the few Southern Democrats who were always in the chamber and Kuchel's reliable but less-structured

Republican forces of about sixteen. With Humphrey in charge, answering routine quorum calls took on the air of a track meet. Each day's bipartisan newsletter scored the previous day's success: "Quorum scoreboard: There were two quorum calls yesterday," he wrote on April 10. "The first one took nineteen minutes and the second was made in twenty minutes." Throughout the months of debate, Humphrey's platoon system failed only once to muster a quorum when called.

In the early weeks of the debate, Humphrey also enlisted the active participation of the nation's religious leaders. Prominent Protestant ministers, Catholic bishops and priests, and Jewish leaders were influential with undecided senators, and their active support was instrumental in transforming the political issue of civil rights into a moral question. "THE CRUCIAL SENATE FIGHT IS ABOUT TO BEGIN," two officials of the National Council of the Churches of Christ told their members in a March 6 letter. "THE EFFORTS OF THE RELIGIOUS FORCES OF OUR NATION WILL AGAIN BE THE DECIDING FACTOR . . . THE BATTLE AHEAD OF US WILL ONLY BE WON AS WE CONVINCE OUR SENATORS THAT WE ARE DEEPLY COMMITTED TO THIS CIVIL RIGHTS BILL AS AN IMPORTANT STEP ON THE ROAD TO FREEDOM AND JUSTICE FOR ALL AMERICANS." Protestant, Catholic, and Jewish clergy planned a prayer vigil at the Lincoln Memorial for April 19. It would continue twenty-four hours a day until the Senate passed the bill. Other religious leaders prepared for a national convocation at Georgetown University on April 28. "It was the first time," said James Hamilton of the National Council of Churches, "that I ever recalled seeing Catholic nuns away from the convents for more than a few days. There was an agreement among religious groups that this was a priority issue and other things had to be laid aside." Commenting on the unprecedented convocation, the ecumenical publication *Christian Century* rejoiced, "The unequivocal stand taken by the religious leaders encourages the hope that the church at large is at last beginning to wake from its long slumber and assume its duty in solving the nation's racial problem."

Because of Humphrey's imagination and legislative skills, the civil rights forces were organized as never before. From the beginning it was evident that his appointment as floor leader had been a wise one—for several reasons. Well respected for his intelligence and his understanding of the legislative process, he was the most eloquent and passionate spokesman for the cause of civil rights in the Congress. Furthermore, Humphrey was enormously popular with his colleagues. Even the most racist of southern conservatives found it impossible to dislike him. "Everybody liked Hubert," declared William Hildenbrand, secretary of the Senate from 1961 to 1981. "If you opposed him, you didn't do it with a great deal of fervor. You just voted no and that was the end of it. You didn't really get up there and try to embarrass him or anything like that."

While the southerners prepared to launch their longest filibuster ever, Humphrey underwent one last bit of preparation. As he confessed:

> I had to make up my mind as to my mental attitude and how I would conduct myself. I can recall literally talking to myself, conditioning myself to the long ordeal. I truly did think through what I wanted to do and how I wanted to act . . . I made up my mind early that I would keep my patience. I would not lose my temper and that if I could do nothing else, I would try to preserve a reasonable degree of good nature and fair play in the Senate . . . I knew that if the southerners could get the pro–civil rights people divided in fighting among themselves that the opponents would win."

Mike Mansfield could not have placed civil rights in better, more capable hands.

Russell and his southern forces comforted themselves with the knowledge that liberals had never invoked cloture on a civil rights bill. History was on their side—but not much else.

"No person . . . could have carried more on his shoulders in a period of a year than Senator Russell carried in 1964," said Bill Bates, Russell's press secretary. He was sixty-six, and his emphysema had worsened. Besides the usual duties of his office, he was saddled with two monumental tasks—service on the Warren Commission and the civil rights debate. Yet he did not publicly grumble about his enormous responsibilities. "Whenever the bell rings I'll come out," he told a *Washington Star* reporter in March. "A man who has been in fifty prizefights does not mind another."

Russell's strategy for the coming debate was simple. Knowing he could never defeat the bill outright, he declared that he would still fight it "to the last ditch." He would not repeat his success in winning backroom concessions from Lyndon Johnson, as he had in 1957. This time, he knew, compromise would come only if he sustained a filibuster through the summer. On CBS's *Face the Nation* in early March, Russell dismissed any suggestion of negotiating with Humphrey's liberal forces. "It seems to me," he said, "that we are just about to come to a state where it will be necessary for us to fight this bill to the bitter end." Russell's Georgia colleague, Herman Talmadge, explained the strategy differently: "We knew that there was no way in hell we could muster the necessary votes to defeat that civil rights bill, but we thought we could filibuster long enough to get the other side to agree to amendments that would make it less offensive."

Russell could always hope that the filibuster—"extended debate," as he called it—would enlighten the American public to the "evils" in the bill. Several months of illuminating debate—combined with spreading racial violence and the increasing volume of protests around the country—might turn public opinion around and evaporate support for civil rights. That scenario was far-fetched. It was certainly nothing around which to construct a winning legislative strategy.

Russell's strategy of delay was about all he had. There were no attractive alternatives to his last-ditch resistance. Even if he could negotiate a compromise with Dirksen, such an agreement guaranteed him the support of only a handful of Republicans. Unless he lured more Republicans to his side, he would still fall short of the thirty-four votes needed to sustain the filibuster. Yet any compromise on civil rights might leave Russell vulnerable to mutiny from incendiary southerners such as Thurmond and Eastland. Russell had only one hope for at least a partial victory: He must filibuster indefinitely and hope that an impatient White House and exhausted Senate liberals would eventually plead for a truce.

Besides himself, Russell had nineteen soldiers: eighteen southern Democrats and Republican John Tower of Texas. He would divide them into three platoons of six, led by Allen Ellender, John Stennis, and Lister Hill. Each platoon would see action every third day of debate. Each member would be responsible for talking only four hours a day—which, as a *New York Times* reporter observed in February, "is a mere throat-clearer for an accomplished southern orator."

Just below the surface, Russell was in serious trouble. He knew that he could sustain a filibuster only if he prevented Johnson and Humphrey from seducing Everett Dirksen—and that Humphrey was already courting Dirksen with a shameless, religious fervor. "I was his Jiminy Cricket," Humphrey later said, "visiting with him on the floor, in the cloakroom, in the corridors and on the elevators. I constantly encouraged him to take a more prominent role, asked him what changes he wanted to propose, urged him to call meetings to discuss his changes."

Russell had other woes. Some members of the southern bloc, it seemed, were less than passionate about the strategy of fighting civil rights "to the last ditch." Talmadge, Long, Fulbright, and Smathers were not in the same league with segregationists like Russell, Eastland, Stennis, and Thurmond. Younger, less regional in their view of the nation, these more moderate southerners would dutifully deliver their speeches and otherwise feign a passionate fealty to the spirit of an Old South that they knew was dying. However, they would do little else to help Russell. Some of them were tired of being outcasts in the Democratic party and weary of swimming against the tide of history. Others realized that their opposition to civil rights was no longer a surefire way to win elections. As Russell Long—always refreshingly frank about his political motives—explained many years later:

> That black vote was getting to be a very significant vote and I was getting it all. Now, you read those speeches, I don't think you'd find anything in there where a person could stir up blacks to get angry at me. I think I said that these people deserve a better break than they're getting and I want to see them have it, but I don't think this is the way to do it . . . I didn't want to say anything that was going to alienate the blacks or do anything that was going to alienate the blacks because they had always been for me.

Analyzing the younger, moderate southerners, journalist Murray Kempton called it a case "of age resisting youth; and a cause is hardly healthy when the realistic young think of a separate peace and only the principled old think of resistance to the end."

Giving Russell even more reason for distress were adverse political developments back home. In January, when he learned that the Georgia Senate had approved legislation to abolish the state's poll tax, Russell announced to his colleagues that the vote was "a source of humiliation to me." Those who supported the amendment in Georgia belonged to a "pernicious drive to enforce coercion and conformity" on other southern states. In a March 1 appearance on *Face the Nation,* Russell acknowledged "an increase in sentiment" favoring civil rights in Georgia. "My people are not immune from brainwashing," he explained. "A great many of them have been brainwashed and they have forgotten the first constitutional principles and have failed to see the dangers of passing legislation on the threat of demonstrations."

In April, when Russell again proposed legislation to subsidize the relocation of southern blacks to other states, the *Atlanta Constitution* ridiculed him for "expos[ing] for all the nation to see an image which Southerners are trying to overcome, the callous attitude that Negroes can be moved about like chess pawns." The proposal even emboldened one member of the legislature to openly criticize Russell. State Senator Lamar Plunkett observed that "the people of Georgia are now going forward with a little different beat of the drum. Those who are not thoroughly conversant with it may lose the beat." As journalist Meg Greenfield wrote in the *Reporter*, Russell's behavior "go[es] a certain way to disprove a current theory that [he] is only leading the fight against the administration's civil rights bill in the Senate to make a show for the folks back home. If anything, political wisdom would seem to dictate a little more circumspection on Russell's part."

But Russell believed his cause was just. "I realize there is a group in the South and in some places in Georgia that is yielding to overwhelming force even if they don't like the trend," Russell said in March. "They think it is not worth it to carry on the fight. They've quit fighting. I haven't." As for why he was leading a losing battle, in April Russell told *Business Week:* "I'm not an anthropologist, but I've studied history. And there is no case in history of a mongrel race preserving a civilization, much less creating one."

Russell lost his first skirmish of 1964 early in the debate. On February 26 the Senate rejected his objection to placing H.R. 7152 directly on the Senate calendar. Using the same rule that liberals had employed to bypass the hostile Judiciary Committee in 1957, Majority Leader Mansfield easily won in a 54-37 vote.

On March 9, after almost two weeks of mostly lackluster debate, Mansfield made his next move. He propounded a motion to begin formal consideration of the civil rights bill. "I implore the Senate," Mansfield said, "when this bill is taken up, to debate it, to debate it as long as is necessary for views to be presented and argued. But then, Mr. President, I implore the Senate to vote on it, to do whatever is necessary so that, in the end, it may be voted up or down." Although they insisted they were not yet filibustering the bill, southerners delayed the vote on Mansfield's motion for more than two weeks.

From the first days of debate, southern rhetoric took on an air of excited desperation. On March 21 Eastland told Humphrey that the bill "takes us back to Stalin, Khrushchev, Nasser, Hitler and a dictatorship."

"What is closer to Stalin and Hitler and Khrushchev," Humphrey replied, "is discrimination on the basis of race."

"I know of no discrimination on the basis of race," Eastland angrily shot back. "I disagree with the Senator on the definition of discrimination, of course." Minutes later, Eastland charged that the legislation "amounts to a destruction of the American system of government."

Eastland was not alone in making wild, irrational statements that could only erode southern credibility. On a CBS news program in March, Strom Thurmond told Humphrey that "such a law would do nothing more than enslave a minority. Such a law would necessitate a system of federal police officers such as we have never before seen. It will require the policing of every business institution, every transaction made between an employer and employee."

Despite his reputation as a dispassionate and dignified debater, Russell was not immune to hysterical rhetoric, especially regarding the equal employment opportunity provision. "This is mere socialism," he declared to the Senate on April 20. "Anybody who is familiar with the operations of state machinery in lands where all industry has been taken over by the government knows that the state tells the individual whom he must hire, whom he must promote, who shall be laid off, who shall fill that position. Then it cannot be long until the government takes over the remainder of the operation of the business." While Russell said he would not allege that the "well-meaning" supporters of the bill "are all Socialists," he noted that "every Socialist and Communist in this country has been supporting the proposed legislation since it was first dreamed up and submitted to the Congress."

There *were* substantive arguments made against the bill. Americans, the southerners argued, had a constitutional right to rent or sell their property, merchandise, or services to those of their choosing. "Americans now possess the liberty to consider the matter of race, and even to prefer persons of their own race over members of another race, in their business dealings with others," North Carolina's Sam Ervin told the Senate on January 29. This bill, Ervin and others maintained, was unconstitutional because it conferred upon blacks new "privileges superior to those ever granted to any other Americans in history." As Russell argued on March 9, there could not be "any such thing as compulsory equality. To attempt to bring it about is to curtail the talented without assisting the stupid. The attempt to mold every American into a common form, if it succeeds, can only curse us forever with the drabness of forced similarity."

Furthermore, the southerners claimed, basing the bill's public accommodations section on the Constitution's commerce clause was unsound. "Clearly," Alabama's John Sparkman insisted, "Title II is not a regulation of commerce between the states, or even with the Indian tribes. Rather, this proposal invades the domain reserved to the states by the Tenth Amendment. This type of police regulation is one which, without a doubt, should be left to the state and local governments."

As for the fair employment provisions, Russell argued that they gave the federal government too much authority over the hiring practices of private businesses. "I state unhesitatingly that no member of the Reconstruction Congress, no matter how radical, would have dared to present a proposal that would have given such vast governmental control over free enterprise in this country so as to commence the processes of socialism."

Even when southerners tried to offer their most earnest arguments against the bill, they often appeared as mossbacks. Lister Hill's speech against the public accommodations section on March 9 was typical. Once the bill became law, Hill said,

> if Mr. Jones wishes to go out to dinner with people of another race he is free to do so. Presumably government cannot prohibit him from doing so and cannot prohibit a restaurant from serving the group. If Mr. Smith wishes to go out to dinner with people of the same race he likewise may do so free of any official restraint and may select an eating place for that purpose. In other words, government now stands neutral in both situations.
>
> This bill, however, would deprive Mr. Smith of his present freedom; it would do this by forbidding any eating place from serving clientele of one race only. There would then be no eating place to which Mr. Smith could go with any assurance of associating only with those with whom he wants to associate.

On March 26, after what *Time* called "sixteen days of drone-and-drawl talk," the civil rights bill finally became the Senate's pending business. Russell realized that a continued filibuster of the motion to consider the bill might only provoke the Senate to impose cloture. Without further ado, he permitted a vote. Mansfield's motion to take up the legislation passed, 67-17.

Oregon's Wayne Morse then moved to refer the bill to the Judiciary Committee until April 8. "This bill is going to remake the social pattern of this country," Everett Dirksen said in support of Morse. "Nobody should be fooled on that score." Mansfield was more persuasive. He argued that when the Judiciary Committee returned with the bill, it would no longer be the Senate's pending business. Instead it would go back on the Senate calendar, where a motion to call it up would be debatable—and therefore subject to another filibuster. "How many days would we have to repeat the ordeal of the last two-and-a-half weeks?" Mansfield asked. By a 50-34 vote, senators rejected Morse's motion. "We lost a skirmish," Russell said after the two votes. "Now we begin to fight the war."

"This is no longer a battle of the heart for [the southerners]," Humphrey told a reporter after the debate began. "They simply have to die in the trenches; that's what they were sent here for. They're old and they haven't any recruits. They know it—one of them said to me, 'You simply have to overwhelm us.' And so we have to beat them to a pulp. No one can make peace. They have to be destroyed."

Thus began the longest debate in the Senate's history.

CHAPTER TWENTY

An Idea
Whose Time Has Come

SHORTLY AFTER NOON ON MONDAY, March 30, 1964, Humphrey stood at his mahogany desk in the Senate chamber and began the long-awaited formal debate on the civil rights bill. Although reporters, staff members, and tourists packed the galleries, only a half-dozen senators were present as Humphrey launched a comprehensive discussion of the bill. His speech was long, even by Humphrey's loquacious standards. He talked for three and a half hours.

"We are participants," he said, "in one of the most crucial eras in the long and proud history of the United States and, yes, in mankind's struggle for justice and freedom which has gone forward since the dawn of history. If freedom becomes a full reality in America, we can dare to believe that it will become a reality everywhere. If freedom fails here in America, the land of the free—what hope can we have for it surviving elsewhere?"

Discussing Title II, the public accommodations section, Humphrey offered his colleagues a graphic yet tragic example of racial discrimination in the South. He quoted from two travel guides. One listed motels and hotels in the South that accepted pets; the other listed establishments that accepted black guests. "It is heartbreaking," he declared, "to compare these two guidebooks. In Augusta, Georgia, for example, there are five hotels and motels that will take dogs and only one where a Negro can go with confidence. In Columbus, Georgia, there are six places for dogs and none for Negroes. In Charleston, South Carolina, there are ten places where a dog can stay, and none for a Negro."

To Humphrey, the bill was "moderate" but "long overdue." Yet he insisted that "moderate as it is, it insures a great departure from the misery and bitterness that is the lot of so many Americans." It was a misery, Humphrey lamented, that "has found remarkably quiet methods of expression." Far from faulting blacks for their urgent demands for strong civil rights legislation, Humphrey said he "marve[led] at the patience and self-control of Negroes who have been excluded from the American dream for so long."

> But the passive stage is ending in the history of the American Negro. Within the past few years a new spirit has arisen in those people who have been so long denied. How will we respond to this challenge? The snarling dogs of Birmingham are one answer. The force of equality and justice is another. That second choice is embodied in the bill that we are starting to consider . . .

The civil rights act of 1964, Humphrey said, "has a simple purpose":

> That purpose is to give fellow citizens—Negroes—the same rights and opportunities that white people take for granted. This is no more than what was preached by the prophets, and by Christ Himself. It is no more than what our Constitution guarantees.
> One hundred and ninety years have passed since the Declaration of Independence, and one hundred years since the Emancipation Proclamation. Surely the goals of this bill are not too much to ask of the Senate of the United States.

Humphrey directed his passionate speech at every member of the Senate, but Everett Dirksen—sitting quietly at his desk—was his primary target. To move Richard Russell or any one of the southern bloc would have been nothing short of miraculous. It would not happen. But to win Dirksen's heart—now that was a real possibility!

Even as he plotted to lure Dirksen to his side, Humphrey realized that he must first persuade his own troops to stay in the battle.

On Saturday, April 4, Humphrey suffered an embarrassing setback: His side failed to assemble a working majority when the southerners suggested the absence of a quorum only forty minutes after the day's opening gavel. When the clerk tallied the roll, only forty-one senators were present. The civil rights forces fell ten short of a quorum. Of the fifty-nine absentees, seventeen were Republicans, seventeen were southern Democrats—but *twenty-five* were northern Democrats who claimed to support the bill. The Senate was unable to function because the bill's own proponents refused to show.

The situation elated the southerners. Although Russell could have moved to adjourn, he did not, leaving it to Mansfield to pick up the pieces. The normally tranquil majority leader was livid. He angrily denounced the truancy as "a travesty on the legislative process" and moved to recess the Senate until the following Monday morning "in order to prevent this situation from turning into a farce." Although Mansfield and Humphrey had strongly urged their colleagues to attend the Saturday session, many had gone home to campaign for reelection; others were out of town delivering speeches.

Humphrey moved quickly to embarrass the absentees. Over the weekend he made certain that the news media knew and published the names of those senators who had failed to attend the Saturday session. "I'll bet there are so many senators here on Monday," he told the *New York Times,* "that you will think each state sent four." Later, Humphrey observed, "That was the end of that . . . We had the problem licked."

By April 11 Humphrey could count on the regular attendance of a solid, dependable majority. On that day he produced a quorum in less than ten minutes. By then the civil rights proponents were organized so well that Humphrey, Mansfield, Dirksen, Russell, and several other senators confidently left the Capitol on April 13 to attend the Washington Senators' first home baseball game. If the southerners suggested the absence of a quorum, Humphrey knew that his aide, David Gartner, would phone the stadium's manager. Humphrey had even composed the message for the public-address announcer. Barely three innings into the game, Gartner called. "Attention, please," the announcer said, "there has been a quorum call in the United States Senate. All U.S. senators are requested to return to the Senate chamber immediately." As Humphrey, Mansfield, Dirksen, and others scurried for the exits—where a police escort awaited them—one senator remained immersed in the game between the Senators and the Los Angeles Angels. Russell, said a colleague, "never moved."

Humphrey's determination to keep at least fifty-one senators within twenty minutes of the Senate floor did more than prove the iron will of the civil rights proponents; it also magnified the antagonism these senators had for the southerners. "This made them all the more unhappy when the filibuster was under way," Humphrey said, "because it meant they had to be away from their duties back home and be present in

Washington only to answer quorum calls and, frankly, to get very little else done." If the southerners used the filibuster to foment public outrage over the supposed evils of the bill, Humphrey would play the same game. He would attempt to "arouse the public" over the way the southerners had hijacked a popular civil rights bill, "to create a sense of wrath and indignation in the public, and also in the Senate."

After this brief brush with defeat, Humphrey's troops never again fell short on a quorum call.

No senator was more valuable to Humphrey than Dirksen. Renowned for his legislative and political artistry, Dirksen was, in many ways, a Republican version of Lyndon Johnson. Few members of the Senate were more pragmatic and flexible in their approach to legislation. "I am not a moralist," Dirksen once explained. "I am a legislator." On most major issues, Dirksen's had his terms. At some point, Humphrey suspected, he would be ready to bargain for the best possible deal. Humphrey knew something else about his colleague: The Illinois senator was an eloquent, theatrical orator who relished the starring roles made possible by his leadership post. "He was the greatest actor I had ever seen in or out of the theater," observed Georgia's Herman Talmadge. "He was one of the few senators who could draw a crowd of other senators just to hear him speak." Dirksen was happiest when at the center of a grand drama such as the civil rights debate would provide. To win his crucial support, Humphrey knew that he must address Dirksen's substantive concerns about the bill while guaranteeing Dirksen a share— perhaps more than his share—of the glory and acclamation for the bill's passage. As one aide to the Democratic leadership confided to a reporter, "We are carving out that statesman's niche and bathing it with blue lights and hoping that Dirksen will find it irresistible to step into it."

Mansfield made no secret of Dirksen's importance to the bill's passage. "The key is Dirksen," he said flatly, echoing the sentiments of Johnson and Humphrey. Even the *Washington Post* adopted that theme. It argued in a February 20 editorial that Dirksen "has it in his power, through generous cooperation with the Administration, to bring about an expeditious and healing resolution of the civil rights controversy." "I know the White House is saying that about me," Dirksen said, "I wish they wouldn't." Dirksen's discomfort had nothing to do with any hesitancy to step into the spotlight. He worried that he might not persuade enough Republican votes for cloture. "Getting cloture is going to be as difficult as hell," he confessed. "I don't know that we can do it."

In truth, Dirksen and his Republican colleagues had plenty of compelling reasons to support the bill. According to at least two national opinion surveys, more than 60 percent of the nation supported the House-passed legislation. Even without polling data, Dirksen could discern the political wind direction as well as any member of the Senate. In a presidential election year, he knew that his party could suffer significant losses if the public viewed Republicans as obstructionists or, worse, as racists. After all, Republicans were the party of Lincoln, inheritors of a grand legacy that Dirksen knew he could preserve or destroy. "He knew that the majority of Americans were eager to see a civil rights bill become law," Herman Talmadge explained, "and he wasn't about to let the Republicans be on the wrong side of history." Moreover, Dirksen's hands were tied by the knowledge that any substantial weakening of the bill would almost certainly result in fierce opposition from William McCulloch and his liberal Republican colleagues in the House. Dirksen had very little latitude on civil rights. Other than endorsing the bill, his options were scarce.

At heart, Dirksen was a conservative. From the beginning he had candidly acknowledged his qualms about the bill, particularly its public accommodations and fair employment sections. Although President Kennedy had once endorsed a separate fair employment bill, he had not included those provisions in his 1963 proposal—largely out of deference to Dirksen. The Republican leader had reciprocated by joining Mansfield as cosponsor of a pared-down Senate bill without fair employment or public accommodations language. If he could, Dirksen wanted to make the bill more palatable to his conservative Republican colleagues. On April 7 he submitted forty fair employment amendments to members of the Republican policy committee. The next day he shared the amendments with the entire Republican caucus. The changes he sought to Title VII, the equal employment opportunity provisions, were severe. They would prohibit the proposed Equal Employment Opportunity Commission from seeking court injunctions to end discriminatory hiring practices and would allow state fair employment agencies to preempt the federal EEOC. Harsh as they were, Dirksen's proposals were music to the fiercely conservative ears of Bourke Hickenlooper of Iowa, chairman of the Republican policy committee. Like Russell and the southern conservatives, Hickenlooper believed that Title VII gave the EEOC too much power over private businesses. He also believed that it would create serious conflicts with the twenty-five states that had fair employment laws—including Dirksen's state of Illinois. "This is a vulnerable section," Dirksen told a press conference. "I'd like to strike it altogether." As for how he would amend Title II, the public accommodations section, Dirksen was mum.

Dirksen's remarks about Title VII and his laundry list of amendments sparked a vigorous debate among the liberals, moderates, and conservatives who made up the thirty-three-member Republican caucus. "My gracious sakes alive," liberal Republican Clifford Case of New Jersey protested on *Face the Nation*, "the Republicans are letting themselves be put in a position which is really not an accurate position when it looks as though they are opposing a strong civil rights bill." Dirksen insisted that he was trying to save the bill, not kill it, by attracting Republican votes through weakening amendments to the fair employment provision. "I have a fixed polestar to which I am pointed," Dirksen declared, "and this is: first to get a bill, second to get an acceptable bill, third to get a workable bill, and finally to get an equitable bill."

Dirksen cautiously waded into the debate on April 16 when he presented ten Title VII amendments to the Senate. Dirksen's effort must have disappointed Russell. The Republican leader's amendments fell far short of his earlier stated desire to eliminate Title VII altogether. The proposed changes did not seek to eliminate the EEOC's injunctive powers, nor would they give state fair employment agencies preemptive powers over federal law. Instead Dirksen proposed only minor modifications to the bill, one of which stipulated that only aggrieved parties or an EEOC member could file fair employment complaints.

Humphrey responded to Dirksen with patience and deference. When he first learned of Dirksen's lengthy list of proposed amendments— during a meeting with Burke Marshall, Joseph Rauh, and Clarence Mitchell—he remained calm. Don't be antagonistic, Humphrey advised the group. "The Republicans must carry the fight," he explained. "Let the Republicans argue it out with their own leader. Dirksen told me that if he did not get support, he would retreat." Humphrey's initial appreciation of Dirksen's situation was wise and correct. The Republican leader, at Humphrey's quiet urging, had unceremoniously retreated from at least forty of his amendments—some of which would have gutted Title VII. What remained was a collection of minor proposals.

As usual, some dogmatic liberal Democrats failed to comprehend the sagacity of Humphrey's deference to Dirksen. "You're manager of the bill," they argued. "We're the majority party. Why don't you call Dirksen to your office?" Humphrey replied, "I don't care where we meet Dirksen. We can meet him in a nightclub, in the bottom of a mine or in a manhole. It doesn't make any difference to me. I just want to meet Dirksen. I just want to get there."

As the southern filibuster droned into its fourth week, a vital new force entered the civil rights debate. A continuous prayer vigil by Catholic, Protestant, and Jewish seminarians had begun at the Lincoln Memorial on April 19. Students from seventy-five seminaries from around the country made a pilgrimage to Washington to pray for the bill's passage. On April 28, sixty-five hundred people from various faiths gathered in support of civil rights at a National Interreligious Convocation at Georgetown University. Then, over the next few days, the religious leaders fanned out over Capitol Hill to lobby members of Congress.

Humphrey not only understood the potential of the religious organizations and their sprouting political involvement; he also helped to guide it. For example, religious leaders had organized the Georgetown convocation at his suggestion. "The secret of passing the bill is the prayer groups," Humphrey confided to Joseph Rauh and Clarence Mitchell. To a reporter, he boasted: "Just wait until [senators] start hearing from the church people."

Actually some religious groups had been laboring for the bill for many weeks. At the behest of the National Council of Churches—which would spend $400,000 in its grassroots lobbying effort—clergy from all over the nation had been writing letters to House and Senate members. Some scheduled appointments with senators who came home during the Easter recess. Spearheaded by the council's Commission on Religion and Race, the lobbying effort was based primarily in midwestern states whose congressmen and senators were uncommitted and represented only negligible numbers of black constituents. Although these states had no natural constituency for civil rights, the religious organizations created one. In Nebraska, Iowa, and Minnesota, commission staff members taught church leaders and members how to lobby their members of Congress for support.

During the House debate, the gallery sometimes seemed to overflow with ministers, priests, and rabbis—most of them voluntary watchdogs, or "gallery watchers," who tracked the votes and other activities of House members. Rauh, who spent many hours with Mitchell observing the debate from their perch in the gallery, recalled, "You couldn't turn around where there wasn't a clerical collar next to you . . . This was kind of like getting an army with new fresh guns, fresh rations, ready to take the place of the others. It made all the difference in the world."

The clerical network was effective. On Saturdays and Sundays the rabbis, ministers, and priests sermonized in favor of human rights. By week's end senators received hundreds, sometimes thousands of letters urging them to support the bill or vote for cloture. While the public outpouring might not have made immediate converts in the Senate, undecided senators could no longer ignore the issue. Father John Cronin, a staff member of the U.S. Catholic Conference of Bishops, worked especially hard to recruit clergy for the civil rights cause, calling many bishops across the country. One such phone call went to a bishop in South Dakota, home of Republican Karl Mundt. "Oh, there's a priest in the office and he's a high school classmate of Senator Mundt," the bishop volunteered. "I'll have him get in touch with Senator Mundt." When Mundt finally supported the civil rights forces on a key vote, he reportedly emerged from the Senate chamber and grumbled, "I hope that satisfies those two goddamned bishops that called me last night." The influence of these clergymen was profound, Rauh insisted. "It was one thing for these guys to brush past Clarence [Mitchell] and me and vote against us, but it was another thing to brush past the high church and vote against them." Celebrating the powerful new unanimity among religious leaders, the national Catholic weekly *America* noted "the great and cheering fact" that "the Christian churches and the synagogues are, with only a few lamentable exceptions, speaking with a single voice. Is it any wonder that so many members of Congress have been impressed?"

Russell complained that the National Council of Churches was not speaking for him. Support for civil rights, he explained on *Face the Nation*, was "more at the top than it is throughout the church. Of course, these preachers are men who boast of their high ideals, and they do have high ideals and noble principles, but sometimes they are very impractical." Among more than four hundred "impractical" Presbyterian ministers, educators, and laymen from the South who signed a May 7 letter to the Senate in support of the bill was William D. Russell, a minister from Decatur, Georgia—and nephew of Richard Russell. "Contrary to the argument of some members of the Senate," the Presbyterians wrote, "there is genuine support of the civil rights bill in the communities of the South. The voice of the filibuster has for too long been regarded as the most authentic southern voice. It is not. The South's most authentic voice is the voice of conscience and of faith."

By late April Humphrey thought that he had gained the upper hand. Senators and the American people were growing tired of the southern talkathon. "No one can justify the filibuster," Humphrey indignantly declared on *Face the Nation* on April 26. "What is going on now demeans the Senate, insults the American citizens. And the American citizen is going to ask his senator and the Senate of the United States to stand up and to be counted on this vital issue of our time."

Just as Humphrey began to detect a growing national impatience with the filibuster, groups of black militants began undercutting the bill's support. In New York, the Brooklyn chapter of CORE announced that its members would disrupt the opening day of the World's Fair, where Johnson was scheduled to deliver a speech. The CORE members said they planned to jam the Long Island Expressway with hundreds of "stalled" automobiles. Elsewhere other militants engaged in senseless and destructive protests. Radical black protesters entered an Atlanta restaurant and urinated on the floor. That act prompted a speech by former mayor William Hartsfield entitled "Is Urination Nonviolent?" In a Berkeley, California, supermarket, demonstrators piled groceries into shopping carts and then abandoned them. A New Orleans CORE official publicly warned of dire consequences if the civil rights bill died: "It is frightening to think of what will happen. There might be armed rebellion—and I wouldn't say one word to discourage it."

National civil rights groups—including the NAACP, CORE, and the Urban League—recognized the potential for a white backlash against the bill and strongly condemned the militants. CORE suspended its Brooklyn chapter and forced it to cancel the threatened "stall-in." At the White House, Johnson was quick to speak out. "We do not condone violence or taking the law into your own hands, or threatening the health or safety of our people." Humphrey and Kuchel, equally distressed over the radical nature of the protests, issued a joint statement: "Civil wrongs do not bring civil rights. Civil disobedience does not bring equal protection under the law. Disorder does not bring law and order." The "unruly demonstrations," they said, "are hurting our efforts in Congress to pass an effective civil rights bill."

If such protests continued, Humphrey knew that the southerners would begin exploiting them to heighten white anxiety over the bill. In his April 26 *Face the Nation* appearance, he tried to neutralize the militants' impact by sympathizing with their frustration while condemning their actions. Furthermore, in talking about the "stall-in," he noted that some southerners were just as guilty of their own brand of obstructionism:

> When you wake up with this hangover of disobedience and violence and disorder that you witness, just put yourself in the other fellow's place. Think of the generations of injustice and abuse and denial of opportunity that the American Negro has had to face. Think of the indignities that he has had to suffer. Is it any wonder, therefore, that some of the more—well, the more radical people, or those who want to take things in their hands, their own hands, gain control of certain groups?
>
> But let the record be clear that the responsible leaders in the civil rights movement did not advocate the stall-ins. They did not participate in these sort of activities that we have criticized. And I finally say that the Senate of the United States is not setting a very good example. We are talking in, while some other people are stalling in. The difference is that they called off their stall-in, and we have not called off our talk-in. And I suggest that the answer to the stall-in is to stop the talk-in.

Thirty-seven days after they began their filibuster, the southerners finally made a tactical move on April 21. Herman Talmadge called up his amendment to require jury trials in criminal contempt cases arising from any provision of the bill. Suddenly the debate shifted from the larger civil rights question to the venerable jury trial issue—a reprise of the most contentious portion of the 1957 act. The Talmadge amendment did more than simply narrow of the debate. It lured Everett Dirksen into direct negotiations with the Democratic leadership.

Three days later, on April 24, Dirksen made his first substantive movement toward cooperation with the pro–civil rights forces. He and Mansfield offered a substitute to Talmadge's amendment. They proposed limiting the bill's penalties for criminal contempt to thirty days in jail or a three-hundred-dollar fine, unless a jury convicted the defendant. Russell was unimpressed with Dirksen's effort at compromise. The amendment, he told reporters, imposed an arbitrary limit on criminal contempt proceedings that would guarantee only partial constitutional rights to defendants. Dirksen's proposal was "just a mustard plaster on a cancer," he said.

The importance of Dirksen's amendment lay not in its impact on jury trials but in the fact that Dirksen had begun cooperating with the civil rights proponents. He was finally mapping strategy with Mansfield and Humphrey. By April 29 he was voicing frustration with Russell's absolute refusal to permit votes on *any* amendments. Dirksen told the Senate that if the southerners did not loosen their grip on the bill, he would join Mansfield in seeking cloture on the jury trial amendment.

Mansfield, while still opposed to around-the-clock sessions, had nonetheless begun turning up the heat on the southerners. Gone were the usual banker's hours. Now Mansfield convened the Senate at ten in the morning and usually held it in session until midnight. The always-bubbly Humphrey was also becoming irritated by the filibuster. "When we get around to the latter part of April," he told reporters, "we'll start spelling 'filibuster' in capital letters."

Humphrey and Mansfield's increasing impatience with the filibuster did not surprise Russell. Dirksen's sudden restlessness, however, was more troubling. Although any chance that Dirksen would ultimately side with the southerners on cloture was fading fast, Russell knew not to give up all hope. He quickly announced that a cloture vote might not be necessary. Emerging from a meeting with Russell on April 29, Dirksen told reporters that Russell would probably allow the Senate to vote on the jury trial amendment by May 6.

While taking his first tentative steps toward direct negotiations with the Democratic leadership, Dirksen still hoped for an even better deal—some kind of sweeping compromise with Johnson. Rumors of such a deal swirled around the Capitol. Perhaps Alabama Governor George Wallace's unexpectedly strong showing in the Wisconsin Democratic primary meant that support for the bill was waning and that Johnson would be eager to strike the best possible bargain for quick passage of the bill.* After all, how could the Great Compromiser resist the primal urge to broker an agreement that would ensure passage of a bill of such enormous importance?

---

*Campaigning vigorously against the civil rights bill, Wallace received 264,000 votes against 511,000 for Johnson's stand-in, Governor John Reynolds. The governor had unwisely dismissed Wallace's candidacy by insisting that if he received 100,000 votes it "would be a catastrophe." Arguing that the results suggested that many northerners were against civil rights, Wallace said, "Well, I guess we've got two catastrophes."

He could, and he would. "I had seen this moderating process at work for many years," Johnson later said, conveniently omitting any mention of his role as a facilitator of that very "process." "I had seen it happen in 1957. I had seen it happen in 1960. I did not want to see it happen again." That meant no compromise, no deals, and no high-profile involvement by the president. Johnson explained that while he "gave to this fight everything I had in prestige, power and commitment," he had "deliberately" toned down his personal involvement "so that my colleagues on the Hill could take tactical responsibility—and credit; so that a hero's niche could be carved out for Senator Dirksen, not me."

Believing that his special relationship with Johnson might lure the president into direct negotiations, Dirksen scheduled an April 29 meeting at the White House in order to make his case. Continued pursuit of a bill with no substantive changes, he would say, would almost certainly result in the bill's defeat in the Senate. If Johnson would only agree to bargain, Dirksen believed he could deliver as many as twenty-five votes for cloture. "Now it's your play," he would tell the president. "What do you have to say?" Dirksen expected that Johnson, the pragmatist, would have no choice but to deal. Yet when he met with the president, Dirksen found him strangely unwilling to negotiate. Humphrey had strengthened his resolve the previous day. "Victory was in sight" and "lay down the law," he told Johnson with great effect. Dirksen left the Oval Office disappointed and empty-handed.

Johnson's refusal to negotiate forced Dirksen to face grim reality. Unless he was willing to join Russell's filibusterers—a politically unattractive option—there appeared to be no chance for a grand compromise, no watered-down bill to resolve his dilemma. In a matter of weeks, Dirksen's thirty-two Republican colleagues would choose between the positions of the racist, intractable southern filibusterers and the supporters of a bill so popular that it was a memorial to a martyred president. In the end the decision would not be difficult for a man with Dirksen's acute sense of history and intuitive feel for politics.

All the while, Humphrey kept the pressure on Dirksen to come to the bargaining table. "Well, Dirk, when do you think we ought to meet and talk over some of your amendments?" Humphrey asked.

"Well, give me a couple more days. It isn't time yet."

By Tuesday, May 5, Dirksen was ready. That morning he finally began full-scale negotiations with Mansfield and Humphrey. They were joined by Robert Kennedy and Nicholas Katzenbach from Justice, Commerce Committee chairman Warren Magnuson, and Republican senators Kuchel, Hickenlooper, and Aiken. Dirksen entered the room well armed. His aides lugged in their notebooks full of research and copies of the bill that Dirksen had carefully annotated during a lengthy hospital stay in February. Although he initially shocked Humphrey and Mansfield with the number of his requests—about seventy amendments—the two men soon realized that most of what Dirksen wanted were face-saving technical alterations to the public accommodations and fair employment sections.

Dirksen did propose some substantive changes. For example, he wanted to amend the public accommodations and fair employment sections to limit the attorney general's power to intervene in cases of discrimination. In fair employment cases, he proposed giving state agencies at least thirty days to act before federal intervention. In both sections, Dirksen wanted proof of a clear "pattern or practice" of discrimination before the Justice Department acted. After the first meeting, Dirksen explained to reporters his sudden willingness to negotiate: "I'm trying to unscrew the inscrutable." As Elizabeth Drew noted in the *Reporter,* the meeting initiated "a process almost unprecedented in the annals of legislative history." The fate of the civil rights bill was not in the hands of a formal Senate committee. Instead it was entrusted to "a sort of ad hoc committee of senators with an interest, senators who were friends of the senators with an interest, senators' aides, and Justice Department officials."

As Dirksen and the Democratic leadership inched toward a deal, Russell temporarily dropped his objection to votes on southern amendments. On May 6, in five roll calls, pro–civil rights forces turned away two alternatives to the Mansfield-Dirksen jury trial substitute. Just when the Senate's pace quickened, Russell applied the brakes. Later that day the debate halted. With several southerners leaving town to tour poverty-stricken areas of Appalachia with President Johnson, Russell made it clear that the day's votes were the extent of his accommodation.

Russell's turnabout infuriated Humphrey. "The whole procedure is disgusting," he complained after the filibuster—by now almost seventy calendar days—had become the longest in the Senate's history. "All that is being accomplished here is a display of adult delinquency. Any intransigent minority can run the Senate if a majority stands around with jelly for a spine." As he made clear, Humphrey was not simply angry with the southern "obstructionist tactics" that he said "were to be expected." He was angrier at those who professed to support the bill but continued to withhold their votes for cloture. The usually mild-mannered Mansfield agreed. "We are witnessing a travesty on the legislative process," he growled. "The majority is being told what it can do and what it cannot do." The *New York Times* lent its voice, reprimanding both the "arrogant" southern refusal to allow votes and "the spinelessness of Democrats and Republicans from outside the South" who were permitting "the Dixiecrat minority to frustrate action indefinitely."

The debate exhausted Mansfield's abundant patience. On May 11 he announced that he would turn up the heat on Russell's troops. The Senate would "stay in session if it takes all year" to pass a bill. He would also resume holding the Senate in session until midnight. Russell was defiant. "That doesn't scare us," he replied. "We're ready for it."

Off the Senate floor, in Dirksen's office, the ad hoc civil rights group moved steadily toward a compromise. After four intense meetings, they neared an agreement, finding common ground on many substantive issues and purely technical points. "The trick was to be sure you got it agreed to before too much bourbon was drunk," Katzenbach recalled with a laugh, "or else you had to do it again the next night." The group's fifth meeting, on May 13, was the turning point. Only two major differences remained. Dirksen was still holding out for further weakening amendments to the fair employment section. He also wanted to eliminate the Civil Rights Commission's authority to investigate voting fraud. On this point Robert Kennedy said that he agreed with Dirksen—the provision should not have been added to the bill—but he had promised William McCulloch that it would remain. Removing it now might jeopardize support for the bill in the House.

On the fair employment changes, Humphrey knew that he must hold the line. To strengthen his hand he choreographed a bit of minor drama for Dirksen's benefit. At Humphrey's direction, Joseph Clark protested vociferously about Dirksen's proposals to gut the fair employment provision. Stomping out of the room in what only Humphrey knew was mock anger, Clark complained, "It's a goddam sellout!" Humphrey turned to Dirksen. "See what pressure I'm up against? I can't concede any more on this point." Humphrey's ploy worked. Dirksen reluctantly dropped his demands. By day's end the group emerged from Dirksen's office to announce an agreement.

Standing before the assembled reporters, Dirksen gleefully took the lead. "We have a good agreement," he declared. Robert Kennedy concurred. "This bill is perfectly satisfactory to me." Humphrey added, "And it is to me, too." The changes to which they had agreed "would not weaken the bill," Humphrey insisted. "We have done nothing to injure the objective of this bill."

The major changes to the House bill were:

• elimination of the attorney general's unfettered authority to initiate court action in public accommodations and fair employment cases; the Justice Department could only sue when the attorney general had "reasonable cause to believe" that a "pattern or practice" of violations existed;

• in the thirty-four states with public accommodations and fair employment laws, the bill would require that complaints first be filed with state or local authorities;

• in the school desegregation section, the bill would specify that it did not authorize federal courts or officials to order the busing of school-children to eliminate de facto segregation;

• the cutoff of federal funds to discriminatory programs would be limited to the particular political subdivision "or part thereof" in which a violation took place.

Most of Dirksen's amendments were to the fair employment section: Employers with seasonal workers would be exempted; American Indians on or near reservations could discriminate in favor of hiring Indians (the leaders wrote this amendment to secure the tenuous support of South Dakota's Karl Mundt); no outside groups, such as the NAACP, could file complaints for a worker; and courts would be required to rule that defendants had "intentionally" discriminated before granting relief.

Dirksen was satisfied with his product. The House bill, he believed, had given the attorney general too much discretion over the bill's enforcement and would invite the Justice Department to involve itself in local disputes and harass small businesses. Because of his changes, the Justice Department would be restrained. Even the attorney general agreed that the House bill gave him more enforcement powers than he wanted.

The Dirksen amendments, though far from meaningless, would neither cripple nor substantially alter the bill. Joseph Rauh, not entirely pleased with Humphrey's willingness to deal with Dirksen, later admitted that the modifications were "minor face-saving changes" designed to give the impression that Dirksen had exacted major concessions from the liberals. The vast majority of Dirksen's amendments, Rauh noted, "were 'ands' and 'buts.' " "Dirksen came out just about where he went in," one of his aides told the *New Republic,* explaining that Dirksen viewed public accommodations and fair employment problems as local issues. "When the bill first reached the Senate, the specifics of what he wanted to do hadn't crystallized in his mind. The problem with the negotiations was that they were like labor negotiations. Everyone started out in adversarial positions and overstated their cases. It took some time for it to become clear that they really weren't so very far apart." Journalist Murray Kempton noted that "Dirksen had done no small thing. He had acted out the ritual of initial distrust, long deliberation and final acceptance for all the dubious Republican senators who have appointed him their agent." Kempton marveled at Dirksen's ability to persuade some Republicans that his amendments "were substantive changes even while he was converting them into refinements of punctuation."

Dirksen's role in the compromise made him an instant hero—just the role Johnson and Humphrey had first envisioned for him in February. To *Time,* the bill was now "Ev's Law." Reporters who had previously ridiculed Dirksen for his lack of principles now viewed the Republican leader as a statesman. Russell, who had hoped to exploit Dirksen's doubts about the bill, saw no heroic qualities in his colleague. "He is without doubt the most accomplished thespian who has ever trod this floor," Russell told the Senate. "Ordinarily, I can see him in a Shakespearean role. This time, however, he has gone beyond that." Noting that Dirksen had waxed eloquent about having "grasped lightning," Russell said, "That is going pretty far." He added that the bill now stood "stripped of any pretense." The remaining compromise was "a punitive expedition into the southern states" that he deeply resented. "Unless I am badly fooled," Russell added, Dirksen has "killed off a rapidly growing Republican Party in the South, at least so far as his party's prospects in the presidential campaign are concerned."*

*Despite Russell's dire prediction, Dirksen's support for civil rights would not destroy the Republican party in the South. Arizona Senator Barry Goldwater, the 1964 Republican presidential nominee, was one of six Republicans to oppose the bill in the Senate. Goldwater carried five southern states.

Downplaying the hero's role yet relishing the praise and attention it generated, Dirksen insisted that civil rights was only one in a long series of inevitable social reforms. At a May 19 meeting with reporters, he quoted Victor Hugo, who Dirksen claimed had written in his diary on the night he died: "No army is stronger than an idea whose time has come." Actually no diary of Hugo's exists. The quotation, from Hugo's *Histoire d'un Crime*, was different from Dirksen's version: "A stand can be made against invasion by an army; no stand can be made against invasion by an idea." Nevertheless, Dirksen had chosen an appropriate axiom, which he eventually adopted as his own. "Let editors rave at will and let states fulminate at will," Dirksen later said, "but the time [for civil rights] has come, and it can't be stopped." As for criticism by Russell and some reporters that Robert Kennedy had duped him, Dirksen responded, "Dick Russell says that the attorney general has nailed up my skin on the barn door to dry. Well, nobody had hung up my conscience and my sense of duty to dry."

Most of the Senate's thirty-three Republicans quickly fell in line behind their leader. "Dirksen was the darling of the conservatives within the Senate," recalled William Hildenbrand, then secretary of the Senate. "So when he took that kind of position, it made it extremely hard for the others to take a different position." Not all conservatives were persuaded. Policy committee chairman Hickenlooper complained that the amendments "don't go far enough to meet the real evils of this bill." Wyoming's Milward Simpson compared Dirksen's effort to hash. "They've just warmed it over," he said, "to make it more palatable."

Liberals weren't particularly overjoyed by the product of Humphrey's negotiations with Dirksen, but as a White House aide bluntly told *Newsweek*, "Where the hell else can they go? We're about ready to come out with a good bill."

On May 26—after three months of seemingly endless floor debate—Mansfield, Dirksen, Humphrey, and Kuchel introduced a seventy-four-page substitute bill containing the Republican leader's amendments. "I doubt very much whether in my whole legislative lifetime any measure has received so much meticulous attention," Dirksen observed. Humphrey announced that a cloture vote would finally occur, probably on June 10. Dirksen stared, "I believe we can get cloture. And I think we have to have cloture now." With imposition of the dreaded "gag rule" staring him in the face, Russell was suddenly willing to allow more votes on jury trial amendments. On June 2 Russell gave Mansfield all of twenty minutes notice that he was ready to begin voting. Mansfield saw Russell's announcement for what it was: a ploy to relieve the growing pressure for shutting off debate. Confident of victory, Mansfield told Russell that he was "talking to the winds." Despite Russell's charge that the liberals were now engaged in a time-killing filibuster of their own, Mansfield held firm. "Why does he wish to go over until next week?" Russell asked the Senate. Acknowledging that the civil rights leadership was not prepared to vote, Humphrey replied, "Simply because we need more time to nail down those cloture votes."

Part of the problem was a minor mutiny in Dirksen's Republican ranks, led by policy committee chairman Bourke Hickenlooper. Dirksen's refusal to seek modifications to several of the bill's provisions displeased Hickenlooper. Humphrey suspected less-noble motivations. "He was resenting the publicity and the play that Dirksen was getting," Humphrey said. Hoping to undermine Dirksen's position, Hickenlooper had convened several furtive meetings of conservative Republicans, at least one while Dirksen was at home ill. Concerned about reports that Hickenlooper might be "picking up strength," Humphrey went to Dirksen. Don't worry, the Republican leader told Humphrey. He was certain that he still had at least twenty-six votes for cloture.

On Friday, June 5, Hickenlooper—claiming the support of seventeen to twenty Republicans—came out in the open and listed his demands. He wanted cloture moved back by one day, to June 10, to accommodate senators who would attend a governors' conference in Cleveland. Next he wanted votes on three key changes to the bill: an amendment by Thruston Morton of Kentucky to give all criminal contempt defendants (except in voting right cases) the right to a jury trial; an amendment by Norris Cotton to limit the application of the fair employment section; and an amendment of his own to eliminate training for school personnel in desegregation cases. While Humphrey predictably opposed the weakening amendments, he was still short of the sixty-seven votes he needed for cloture. An agreement with Hickenlooper might help him pick up a few more votes. First, however, he demanded solemn assurances from Hickenlooper that three Republicans—Mundt, Cotton, and Roman Hruska—would vote for cloture. With those votes duly promised, Humphrey approved the deal. It was a good bargain. Morton's jury trial amendment narrowly passed, 51-48, and Humphrey agreed to substitute it for the Mansfield-Dirksen jury trial amendment.

In two other roll calls, the leadership easily mustered the votes to defeat the Cotton and Hickenlooper amendments. Humphrey maintained that his willingness to satisfy the last-minute requests by conservative Republicans "brought us the extra votes we needed for cloture."

Humphrey's bargaining with Hickenlooper struck Russell as unfair. After all, the goal of the southern filibuster was to force liberals to deal with Russell. In earlier days, when the alliance between southern Democrats and conservative Republicans was still intact, Russell would have undoubtedly been part of Hickenlooper's negotiations. By 1964, however, the two groups no longer fought civil rights in concert. Humphrey said that Russell complained "quite bitterly" that the civil rights leadership had refused to cooperate with him only days earlier when he had wanted to vote on jury trial amendments. "Well, Dick," Humphrey replied candidly, "you haven't any votes to give us in cloture and these fellows do."

Now Humphrey knew he would have the votes to shut off debate. On the evening of Tuesday, June 9—the night before the scheduled vote—Humphrey phoned Johnson to give him the news: He had sixty-six votes for cloture, with two or three more senators in reserve if needed. Johnson seemed doubtful of Humphrey's count. "I told him I was sure of it," Humphrey said. Despite abundant optimism, Humphrey continued lobbying past midnight. He rounded up three more votes.

That evening at 7:38, West Virginia's Robert Byrd, a former Ku Klux Klan member and future majority leader, stood on the Senate floor to begin what would be a fourteen-hour, thirteen-minute speech. The bill, Byrd defiantly declared, "would impair the civil rights of all Americans. It cannot be justified on any basis—legal, economic, moral or religious." Byrd ended his speech at 9:51 a.m. on June 10. Nine minutes later, the Senate's leaders began their final remarks on the cloture vote.

Mike Mansfield went first, reading a letter from a twenty-nine-year-old constituent in Montana. Near the end of her long, poignant letter, the woman wrote:

> At night, when I kiss my children good night, I offer a small prayer of thanks to God for making them so perfect, so healthy, so lovely, and I find myself tempted to thank him for letting them be born white. Then I am not so proud, neither of myself nor of our society, which forces such a temptation upon us . . .
> I am only one person, one woman. I wish there was some-

thing I could do in this issue. I want to help. The only way I know how to start is to educate my children that justice and freedom and ambition are not merely privileges, but their birthrights. I must try to impress upon them that these rights must be given, not held tightly unto themselves, for what cannot be given, we do not really have for ourselves.

Russell was next. Despite his strong opposition to cloture, he seemed to have little passion left for the fight. It appeared, one observer said, "that we were witnessing the end of an era." Ridiculing Mansfield's emotional appeal for the bill, Russell insisted the legislation had "no more emotional appeal than that which could be made for a purely socialistic or communistic system that would divide and distribute among all our people every bit of the property and wealth of the people of the United States." He derided the immense influence that religious leaders had exerted throughout the debate. "I cannot make their activities jibe with my concept of the proper place of religious leaders in our national life . . . They have sought to make [the bill's] passage a great moral issue. But I am at a loss to understand why they are 200 years late in discovering that the right of dominion over private property is a great moral issue." Russell knew that he was about to lose, but he bravely made one last appeal. He urged senators to reject "this gag rule" and "rise above the pressures to which they have been subjected and to reject this legislation that will result in vast changes, not only in our social order, but in our very form of government."

As Russell slumped into his seat, Mansfield yielded two minutes to Humphrey. Buoyant as usual, sporting a red rose in his lapel, Humphrey was a changed man. He had worked so hard during the arduous debate that he lost twenty pounds. His skillful management of the bill since February 26—through more than three months of debate—had transformed him into a national figure; he was now the leading prospect for the Democratic party's vice presidential nomination. Characteristically, he chose to view the day and the impending cloture vote in the most optimistic light. Cloture would signal not merely an end to southern domination over civil rights in the Senate, but the dawn of a new day for the United States. "I say to my colleagues of the Senate that perhaps in your lives you will be able to tell your children's children that you were here for America to make the year 1964 our freedom year. I urge my colleagues to make that dream of full freedom, full justice, and full citizenship for every American a reality by their votes on this day, and it will be remembered until the ending of the world." It was perhaps the shortest formal speech Humphrey had ever delivered on the Senate floor. But it may have been the most satisfying.

Finally it was Dirksen's moment. Weakened by a peptic ulcer that had plagued him throughout the debate, Dirksen showed the strain of the long hours he had spent in negotiations with Humphrey and Mansfield. He rose slowly from his seat and removed his glasses. "His face," one observer noted, "looked like a collapsed ruin, drawn and gaunt." Paraphrasing Victor Hugo again, Dirksen declared, "Stronger than all the armies is an idea whose time has come. The time has come for equality in sharing in government, in education and in employment. It will not be stayed or denied. It is here."

Before Dirksen could complete his speech, presiding officer Lee Metcalf of Montana rapped his gavel. The hour had arrived for the vote. It was 11:00 a.m. As Dirksen took his seat, Humphrey stepped across the aisle to shake his hand. Then Metcalf propounded the question: "The chair submits to the Senate, without debate, the question: Is it the sense of the Senate that the debate shall be brought to a close? The Secretary will call the roll."

Before a packed gallery, Secretary of the Senate Felton Johnson began the historic roll call. "I never heard the chamber so silent," Mansfield said later. "Mr. Aiken. Mr. Allot. Mr. Anderson. Mr. Bartlett. Mr. Bayh . . ." Senators responded with either "aye" or "no." When Johnson arrived at the name of Clair Engle, all eyes fell upon the frail, wheelchair-bound Democrat from California whom aides had escorted into the chamber. Crippled by two brain operations, Engle had not appeared in the Senate since April. Everyone knew he was dying from a brain tumor. Engle tried to answer the roll, but he could not speak. Finally he struggled to lift his partially paralyzed left arm. He pointed to his eye. "Aye!" declared the clerk. The scene moved many senators to tears. As Engle slowly left the chamber, the roll call continued.

As the clerk reached the name of John Williams, Republican of Delaware, the count stood at sixty-six votes for cloture, twenty against. When Williams softly answered "aye," another senator exclaimed, "That's it!" Mansfield relaxed. Russell frowned and began scribbling on a yellow legal pad. Humphrey stuck his tally sheet into his mouth, bit down, and beamed. To a *Life* reporter, he looked "like a schoolboy who had just scored 'A' on a tough exam."

Suddenly Arizona's Carl Hayden emerged from the Democratic cloakroom. Hayden was eighty-six, the dean of the Senate and its president pro tempore. The beginning of his service in Congress predated the 1917 cloture rule. In his long Senate career, he had never voted for cloture. But now he was grudgingly prepared to give Lyndon Johnson and Mike Mansfield his vote. As Hayden hobbled down the aisle, Mansfield intercepted him. "It's all right, Carl. We're in." Relieved, Hayden voted no.

By the time the roll call ended, the tally stood at 71-29. Forty-four Democrats and twenty-seven Republicans had supported cloture. Only twenty-three Democrats, most of them southerners, joined six Republicans in opposing the historic motion. It was the first time the Senate had invoked cloture on a civil rights bill.

Russell was a sore loser. He bitterly informed senators that he would now insist on calling up hundreds of southern amendments that were still eligible for roll call votes under the Senate rules. Later, as the Senate began voting down the amendments—southerners had submitted about 560 before the cloture vote—Russell complained angrily, "We are confronted with the spirit of not only the mob but of a lynch mob in the United States. Senators are paying no attention to what they are doing . . . There is no need for us to expect any fairness." Contrary to Russell's regrettable and intemperate assertion, senators knew *exactly* what they were doing. They had spent more than three months debating a single bill. They were more than a little frustrated by Russell's dilatory tactics, and they were eager to vote on final passage.

While Russell fumed, Humphrey staggered numbly through the last few days of debate. Two days before the historic vote, misfortune struck the Humphrey household. On the afternoon of June 17—just after the Senate had approved a motion to substitute the Mansfield-Dirksen amendment for the House-passed bill—Humphrey left the Senate floor to take an urgent phone call from Muriel. One of their sons, Robert, had recently entered a Minnesota hospital for tests after complaining of swelling in his neck. When Humphrey answered the phone, a tearful Muriel gave him the awful news. Robert had a malignant growth in his neck. He would undergo immediate surgery. "It was exactly as if I'd been hit in the head with an iron hammer," Humphrey said. As he sat crying in his whip office, Joseph Rauh and Clarence Mitchell burst into the room, joyous over the overwhelming 76-18 vote on the substitute amendment. "Their joy disappeared as they shared my gloom and fears," Humphrey recalled. "Three grown men trying to savor the fullness of our success after decades of failure were instead sharing bitter tears."

Humphrey was torn. Should he rush to Robert's side or fulfill his duty to the Senate and the nation? Consumed by "a kind of selfish guilt," Humphrey knew that if he left the Senate "we might lose the legislation." More than two hundred amendments were pending. "I was the only man who knew the whole story of the bill, knew all the amendments—and one little slip and we'd be gone." Perhaps Humphrey recalled Johnson's question to him early in his Senate career: "Hubert, do you want to be a good family man or a good senator?" Robert's operation was a success, and he enjoyed a full recovery. But the ordeal dampened Humphrey's joy over what would become his greatest legislative triumph. "So much pleasure on top of so much pain," he later said. "It sharpens both—brings out the tartness of life."

On June 19, after 106 roll call votes on southern amendments— Senate leaders accepted only a handful of minor changes—the Senate adopted the civil rights bill, 73-27. The vote came almost four months after the debate had begun—and exactly one year after President Kennedy's civil rights program had first been submitted to Congress.

After a brief debate, House members accepted the bill, voting 289-126 on July 2 to approve the measure as amended by the Senate. Later that day Johnson staged a nationally televised signing ceremony in the East Room of the White House. "We believe all men have certain unalienable rights," Johnson said, "yet many Americans do not enjoy those rights. We believe all men are entitled to the blessings of liberty. Yet millions are being deprived of those blessings—not because of their own failures, but because of the color of their skin . . . Our Constitution, the foundation of our republic, forbids it. The principles of our freedom forbid it. Morality forbids it. And the law I will sign tonight forbids it."

Humphrey called the bill's final passage "the culmination" of his fifteen-year struggle for civil rights and of "a lifetime in politics in which equal opportunity had been *the* objective above all others." To many observers—despite Dirksen's heroic leading role—Humphrey deserved most of the credit for the bill's passage. As Democratic whip and as one of the nation's most prominent liberals, he had been the perfect choice to manage the bill in the Senate. His legislative skills had proved superb. The liberals were never so well organized and disciplined. Furthermore, Humphrey's good humor and boundless optimism had been a priceless resource. "There were many times when less patience and good humor on Humphrey's part might have changed the situation," *Congressional Quarterly* observed. True to his pact with himself, Humphrey never allowed the debate to dissolve into personal recriminations. He and Mansfield had wisely resisted the advice of Johnson and many liberal leaders to play hardball with the southerners by holding the Senate in around-the-clock session. Humphrey's conduct and demeanor impressed even Russell, who told NAACP lobbyist Clarence Mitchell that "if it had not been for Senator Humphrey's fairness in giving a full opportunity to the opposition to present its view," the bill would not have passed.

While Humphrey may have been the big winner, no one's loss seemed greater than Russell's. His thirty-two-year fight against civil rights had ended in total, humiliating defeat. Russell had opted for a risky all-or-nothing strategy—and lost everything. *Newsweek* observed, "Had Russell not played for time—banking on his mistaken belief that the Senate would not vote cloture—the Southerners probably could have softened the bill." Russell's purely defensive strategy puzzled Humphrey. "Frankly," he said, "I was rather surprised at the Southerners' tactics. I never could quite understand why they didn't let us vote more often because they had so many amendments in. If they had done so, they could have insisted that the legislative process was working, that amendments were being voted on. Instead of that, they just kept talking and talking. It seemed to me that they lost their sense of direction and really had little or no plan other than what they used to have when filibusters succeeded." By the time the Senate imposed cloture, it was too late for compromise. Russell's bargaining power had vanished. He watched helplessly as the Senate defeated hundreds of southern amendments in lopsided roll calls. "Dick Russell just couldn't believe that so many of his friends would desert him," said an aide to one southern senator.

Russell's strategy had been curious. Having privately acknowledged the bill's inevitability, why did he choose an unimaginative filibuster over conciliation and quiet negotiation aimed at softening the bill's most "egregious" provisions? Perhaps he hoped that Humphrey's liberal coalition would fall apart as the debate dragged on. He may also have anticipated that Dirksen would do the dirty work of compromise for him and negotiate amendments to substantially weaken the bill's public accommodations and fair employment sections. Russell may have gambled that Dirksen would never compromise with Humphrey and Mansfield—or that, if he did, he would be unable to persuade more than a handful of his Republican colleagues to follow his lead. Perhaps Russell, fully aware of the bill's inevitability, fought mostly for show. He reportedly told Clarence Mitchell "that if the opponents had not put up the fight they had, the bill would never have been enforceable in the South." Exactly what Russell might have meant by that assertion is not clear. Humphrey, however, speculated that Russell "thought it was important to have satisfied the people of the South that everything that could have been done had been done in opposition."

If Russell was putting on a show, it was too often a bad one. Throughout the debate, the usually dignified Georgian had presented the most unattractive sides of his personality. He was sarcastic, shrill, and arrogant—sometimes all at once. When the bill became law, however, he was his usual responsible and gracious self. "I have no apologies to anyone for the fight that I made," he said. "I only regret that we did not prevail. But these statutes are now on the books, and it becomes our duty as good citizens to live with them." When Johnson read Russell's conciliatory comments, he praised his old friend effusively: "As the acknowledged leader of the opposition to the Civil Rights Bill, your reputation and your standing could not be higher in those areas where the adjustment to the bill will be the most difficult. Your call for compliance with the law of the land is, of course, in keeping with your personal code and I am confident it will have a great impact. It was the right and courageous thing to do."

Russell and the southerners were not the only losers in the debate. One of the bill's most prominent Republican opponents was Arizona senator Barry Goldwater. As the presumptive presidential nominee, Goldwater had been under tremendous pressure from Dirksen and others in his party to support the legislation. "Barry, this is a dreadful mistake," warned Jacob Javits after Goldwater's Senate speech attacking the bill. Most agreed that Goldwater's vote against the bill showed, in the words of *Time,* "just how far he is removed from the mainstream of U.S. and Republican Party thinking." While Goldwater's opposition to the Civil Rights Act of 1964 only exacerbated his image as a philosophical extremist, the vote helped him and his party considerably in the South. As John Kennedy, Lyndon Johnson, and Burke Marshall had known, civil rights marked the beginning of the end of the Democratic party's dominance in southern presidential politics. Before 1964, Republican presidential candidates had carried southern states only 7 percent of the time; from 1964 to 1992, Republicans would win southern states 70 percent of the time. Johnson remarked to an aide shortly after he signed the bill into law, "I think we delivered the South to the Republican Party for your lifetime and mine."

Although many credited Dirksen and Humphrey for the bill's passage, Russell thought it was Johnson who "had more to do" with the bill's success "than any other man." In a way he was correct. More than anyone else, it was Johnson who had skillfully transformed the bill into a memorial to his slain predecessor. Without his effective, dogged leadership and his steadfast refusal to compromise with Everett Dirksen, the debate would almost certainly have dissolved into partisan bickering. In highlighting his commitment to the passage of civil rights, Johnson had also put his legislative agenda on hold for more than three months while the Senate debated the bill. His patience and determination paid off. His wisest decision had been to leave the day-to-day negotiations and the lobbying for the bill to Robert Kennedy, Humphrey, Mansfield, and Dirksen. Becoming actively involved, he knew, would only inject presidential politics into the debate and complicate Humphrey's efforts to reach a bipartisan agreement. Therefore Johnson played only a minor public role in the debate, periodically issuing strongly worded statements in support of the bill's overall objectives.* Privately, however, Johnson had been an enthusiastic strategist. He talked with Humphrey by phone constantly. Every week, over breakfast with the congressional leaders, he eagerly discussed legislative strategy. His aides constantly fed him information about the debate.

In the end, Johnson had made the most arduous of philosophical journeys. As Humphrey noted, it was Johnson who—as Senate majority leader—had wisely allowed the southerners "face-saving victories while he established the principle of federal intervention." Because of Johnson's leadership in the 1950s, Humphrey explained, "the most venomous" southerners had been isolated, and the southern bloc began falling

---

*One of Johnson's statements in support of the bill was to the Georgia legislature on May 8. He declared, "Because the Constitution requires it, because justice demands it, we must protect the Constitutional rights of all our citizens . . . No one of us [is] fully free until all of us are truly free, and the rights of no single American are truly secure until the rights of all Americans are secure" (Speech Files, RBRL).

apart "with its own help." Johnson's leadership in shepherding through the 1957 and 1960 civil rights bills, though not landmark achievements, had paved the way for passage of the 1964 legislation.

As Johnson put his pen to the bill during the East Room ceremony, he thought of Gene Williams, his black employee, who had once been reluctant to drive Johnson's pet beagle back to the Texas ranch. As he noted later, "That had been the day I first realized the sad truth: that to the extent Negroes were imprisoned, so was I. On this day, July 2, 1964, I knew the positive side of that same truth: that to an extent Negroes were free, really free, so was I. And so was my country."

CHAPTER TWENTY-ONE

Do You Want
to Be Vice President?

AFTER ONLY ONE DAY IN OFFICE, Lyndon Johnson had begun contemplating whom to choose as his running mate for the 1964 election. In a phone conversation with Johnson on November 23, 1963, Florida senator George Smathers stressed the importance of nominating a liberal. Smathers mentioned only one name. "Most of the southerners," he advised, "would be for Hubert."

Humphrey himself began entertaining thoughts of the vice presidency, a position he had wanted as early as 1948, soon after Johnson took office. Only hours after Kennedy's death, Humphrey's friends began calling to urge him to seek the vice presidency. His answer, he said, had been brief: "I had no plans; whatever Lyndon Johnson wanted, Johnson would get." Humphrey tried to remain a passive participant in the draft-Hubert movement, at least in the months immediately following Kennedy's death. When several friends began meeting at Max Kampelman's home to map strategy, Humphrey was aware of their activities but stayed away. "Our goal," Kampelman explained, "was not so much to win a competition with other people, but to elevate Humphrey beyond competition. Our purpose was not to make him first among equals, but without an equal, and thus the only possible choice for Johnson."

Ted Van Dyk, a brash, young public affairs officer for the European Common Market, outlined Humphrey's chances to become vice president. In an unsolicited memorandum presented to Humphrey, Van Dyk argued that Humphrey must persuade Johnson that he "would be the best president in the event of tragedy." Humphrey's image needed an overhaul, he advised; the senator seemed a "little too much like my neighbor down the street."* To be seriously considered for vice president, Van Dyk argued that Humphrey should portray himself as "an experienced leader in Congress . . . the sort of man to count on should, God forbid, anything happen to President Johnson." That prospect was not a farfetched one. After all, of the four men who preceded Johnson as president, two (Roosevelt and Kennedy) had died in office and one (Eisenhower) had suffered a serious heart attack. "To put it coldly and bluntly," said Clark Clifford, an advisor to several Democratic presidents, "it was well known that President Johnson had had a serious coronary attack years before, so I think the job [of vice president] was eagerly sought."

While Humphrey played a passive role, his friends were not at all shy about promoting his candidacy to Johnson. United Auto Workers president Walter Reuther and Supreme Court justice Arthur Goldberg voiced their support of Humphrey directly to the president, as did some of Humphrey's Senate colleagues. When one senator informed Johnson that as many as twenty of his Democratic colleagues wanted to express their support for Humphrey, the president exclaimed, "Not in a delegation!" Asked by Johnson to name his top three choices for vice president, AFL-CIO president George Meany replied, "I have only one choice—Hubert Humphrey." Governors Harold Hughes of Iowa, Richard Hughes of New Jersey, Edmund Brown of California, John Reynolds of Wisconsin, and Edward Breathitt of Kentucky all urged Johnson to choose Humphrey, as did the four living former chairmen of the Democratic party.

Viewed objectively, a Johnson-Humphrey ticket made perfect sense: Johnson, a son of the South and former leader of the Senate establishment, and Humphrey, a fiery northern liberal admired and respected by liberals and conservatives alike. Johnson enjoyed good rapport with the nation's business chieftains; Humphrey had excellent support among labor leaders. Of course other men with similar voting records or liberal credentials were available—most notably Robert Kennedy, Humphrey's Minnesota Senate colleague Eugene McCarthy, Connecticut senator Thomas Dodd, and Peace Corps director Sargent Shriver (brother-in-law of the late president). None, however, approached Humphrey in his almost unique combination of celebrity, legislative accomplishment, and friendship with Johnson. Yet Humphrey could afford to take nothing

*Shortly after Van Dyk submitted his memo, Humphrey hired him.

for granted. "The capricious part of Johnson's nature," Max Kampelman observed, "made it impossible for Humphrey ever to relax about the relationship."

From the earliest days of 1964, Humphrey understood that his management of the civil rights bill would be a test of his leadership and his worthiness for the vice presidency. Throughout the months of debate, Johnson closely watched and measured him. In the spring Johnson first broached the subject of the vice presidency, telling Humphrey that he would choose him "if nothing arose that put an obstacle in his way." However, Johnson quickly added, nothing was certain. Ironically, Johnson repeated almost exactly what Adlai Stevenson had told Humphrey in 1956. This time Humphrey was wiser. He would not delude himself. "If it comes, it'll come," he said, almost nonchalantly, after his discussion with Johnson.

Another strong indication of Johnson's interest in Humphrey came from Jim Rowe, a friend of both men, who came to see Humphrey early in 1964. "Are there any skeletons in your closet?" Rowe asked Humphrey. Humphrey replied that nothing in his past would embarrass the president. As Ted Van Dyk put it, Johnson had issued Rowe "a hunting license" to find a candidate. Rowe told Humphrey that Johnson expected him to build support for his candidacy. "If he could prove himself an asset to the ticket, and so on, he'd be considered," Van Dyk said, adding that Johnson "was going to offer the same choice to others." Remembering Humphrey's bitter disappointment in 1956, Rowe was careful not to leave the impression that Johnson was offering the nomination. "I was more cautious in talking to Humphrey," Rowe said later, "than Johnson had been in talking to me."

Heeding Johnson's instructions, Humphrey quietly began seeking support for his candidacy among labor and political leaders, journalists, and influential businessmen. Kampelman's group routinely sent favorable articles and polls to party leaders, labor officials, and potential convention delegates. Dwayne Andreas, a wealthy businessman and Humphrey's close friend, helped him build stronger relationships with the business community. Humphrey's aides funneled information about all of his activities to the White House.

Humphrey's effort was working, especially with some leading businessmen. "If I had to name one of a half-dozen people in Washington who would have been against us," said New York Stock Exchange president Keith Funston, "Hubert Humphrey would have been at the head of the list. But I found out a couple of years ago he was a real capitalist. The business community had the wrong picture of him." *Forbes* magazine publisher Malcolm Forbes observed that "while [Humphrey's] liberal convictions have not melted, he himself has mellowed, matured."

Throughout the spring and early summer, Johnson floated several trial balloons concerning other possible nominees. Each only added to Humphrey's anxiety. At one White House dinner, Johnson leaned over and playfully whispered to Humphrey that he planned to "drop Mike Mansfield's name into the hopper," explaining that besides flattering Mansfield, "it will give a lot of people something to talk about." In a matter of days Washington was abuzz with rumors of Mansfield's candidacy. The speculation amused Mansfield, who quickly disclaimed any interest in the position. Johnson continued dropping names, including those of New York mayor Robert Wagner and California governor Edmund Brown.

In his search for a running mate, Johnson cast a wide net. He discussed the selection with dozens of cabinet members, governors, political consultants, and party officials. He consulted public opinion polls. Finally, he reached two conclusions: First, every potential running mate only weakened the ticket; Johnson would have been strongest running alone, if he could. Second, although Humphrey ran behind other contenders in the polls, he was the most popular second choice. "I had the feeling most of that summer," Humphrey later recalled, "that I would most likely make it. But I also knew that Johnson was a very pragmatic man and that if it looked to him like I couldn't be of any help to him or might be a hindrance to him or a load to carry, I don't think he'd have hesitated a minute to have said, 'Good-bye Hubert.' "

For a brief while, Johnson insisted that he wanted to balance the ticket with a Catholic, preferably Shriver or McCarthy.* During a meeting in the spring of 1964, Johnson convened a group of aides and advisors to discuss the vice presidential nomination. At Johnson's direction, an aide produced a poll. "It was just made up in their office about fifteen minutes before," insisted Kenneth O'Donnell, a former Kennedy aide who had remained on staff to help Johnson. According to the "poll,"

---

*Although his friendship with McCarthy would later dissolve, Johnson and Lady Bird were particularly fond of the junior Minnesota senator, as was Johnson's most trusted aide, Walter Jenkins.

Johnson might lose to presumptive Republican nominee Barry Goldwater if a Catholic was not on the Democratic ticket.

As Johnson debated the respective qualities of McCarthy versus Shriver, he turned to O'Donnell. "What do you think about it?"

"Mr. President," O'Donnell replied, "I thought we licked that in West Virginia—religion. I never voted for anybody for their religion in my life, and do you know what? I don't know any Catholic in the country that gives a damn where the guy goes to church. Whoever gave you that poll, you ought to get your money back. Because personally, I'm for Hubert Humphrey. He deserves it. He has worked hard for the party all these years, and you cannot pick the junior senator [McCarthy] over the senior senator. If you pick him just on religion alone, which will be written in every paper in the United States of America, you will blow the election. I think I would be totally opposed to it."

Johnson turned to Jim Rowe. "My hands are not clean," Rowe confessed. "I'm for Hubert Humphrey. I've been for Hubert Humphrey for years and years, so I happen to agree with Kenny, but I'm not going to say anything."

Johnson consulted several more advisors. All expressed support for Humphrey. "Now Lyndon was furious, furious!" O'Donnell recalled, adding that except possibly one person, "everyone in the room was a Catholic."

Following the meeting, Johnson pulled O'Donnell aside: "All right, you've got him and you can go leak it if you want. I'm committed to Humphrey. So forget it."

In August, when Humphrey arrived in Atlantic City for the Democratic National Convention, he was the acknowledged front-runner. Johnson had eliminated most other candidates, including Attorney General Robert Kennedy, with his declaration in late July that he would not consider cabinet members for the job. The only two men now in serious contention were Minnesota's two senators, Humphrey and McCarthy. After Humphrey appeared on NBC's *Meet the Press* with McCarthy on the Sunday before the convention, Jim Rowe told him, "I can't predict what Johnson is going to do for certain, but it looks like you're the man."

Just as Humphrey began to savor the impending realization of his longtime dream, Johnson threw up another potential obstacle. He wanted Humphrey to play mediator in a credentials dispute over which group of delegates would represent Mississippi at the convention—the all-white delegation led by Lieutenant Governor Paul Johnson (who had once joked that the NAACP stood for "niggers, alligators, apes, coons and possums") or the mostly black Mississippi Freedom Democratic Party. The black delegation, claiming to represent 450,000 black Mississippi citizens who had been systematically denied the right to vote, demanded that the convention seat its members instead of the state's all-white "official" delegation. Johnson gave Humphrey his charge: use your considerable influence with the civil rights community to head off a potentially embarrassing fracas. "I always had the feeling, and it was implicit," said Ted Van Dyk, "that if Humphrey messed this up, Johnson was not going to make him the running mate. It was a kind of test for Humphrey . . . If he couldn't do it, so much for Humphrey." Humphrey's role in the settling the dispute was ironic, and more than a little uncomfortable. After all, his dogged advocacy of a strong civil rights platform at the 1948 convention had catapulted him into national prominence. Sixteen years later, as an established national leader, his political future hinged on his ability to diffuse a potentially embarrassing confrontation over the same issue.

To help with the negotiations, Johnson sent Humphrey White House aide Walter Jenkins and Washington attorney Thomas Finney. Humphrey also summoned two trusted friends of his own, Minnesota attorney general Walter Mondale and UAW president Walter Reuther. After several days of difficult negotiations among members of the Mississippi Freedom Party, the official state delegation, and the credentials committee, Humphrey announced a compromise that failed to delight anyone: The credentials committee would seat only those delegates willing to take an oath pledging support for the ticket in the fall election. Two Freedom Party delegates would be seated with the Mississippi delegation, each with one vote. The convention would seat the rest of the black delegates on the floor as "honored guests." The agreement also included a rule, applied to future conventions, that would bar the seating of any state delegation that excluded blacks. The agreement "wasn't a bad offer," acknowledged Joseph Rauh, who had represented the Freedom Party in its negotiations. In protest, the Mississippi and Alabama delegates walked out of the convention hall. Yet Humphrey's negotiating skills and his stature as a strong advocate of civil rights had averted a larger southern walkout and a potentially embarrassing floor fight over credentials.

Rauh was most impressed with Humphrey's unwillingness to urge his liberal friend to capitulate. "Five times I saw him and five times he would have had a chance to say, 'Joe, moderate your views, give in for me.' Never once, when the president of the United States was pushing Hubert to push me, never once did Hubert ever, ever ask for any concession on this basis . . . All I can say, for a guy who wanted to be vice president never once to ask for anything in that regard, I consider about as fine a thing as could have been done." More difficult to understand was Rauh's apparent unwillingness to help his loyal friend achieve a lifelong dream. Although Humphrey never publicly complained about Rauh's stubborn reluctance to compromise, he did lament the way that liberals took him for granted. "Nobody has to woo me," he told the *New Republic* in July. "I'm old reliable, available Hubert."

The morning, after the compromise was sealed, Eugene McCarthy withdrew his name from consideration. Soon Jim Rowe arrived with more good news. Johnson wanted Humphrey in Washington later that day so that he could formally offer him the vice presidency. As Humphrey began preparing for the flight, however, he encountered one last maddening obstacle. Rowe told Humphrey that Connecticut senator Thomas Dodd would accompany him to Washington. The news took Humphrey by surprise.

"What? Is Tom Dodd being considered, too?" he asked Rowe.

Rowe assured him that Dodd's presence was "just a cover" and a way to keep the press "off balance." As Oklahoma senator Mike Monroney explained, "People were restless and there hadn't been much of a show [at the convention]. And if the Democrats don't have some kind of a fight, they're unhappy . . . [Johnson] was just trying to put a little bit of life in the convention."

When the two men arrived at the White House, around 5:00 p.m., Johnson kept them waiting in the White House Cadillac for almost twenty minutes. Humphrey, who fell asleep, was awakened by a sharp tapping on the car window. "Hubert," said Johnson as he peered inside the car, "come on in." Surrounded by a crush of reporters, Johnson, Humphrey, and Dodd walked into the White House. Johnson talked with Dodd first, while Humphrey waited nervously in the Cabinet Room, browsing through a book on Thomas Jefferson and Alexander Hamilton.

Finally it was Humphrey's turn. After only a few pleasantries, Johnson asked simply, "Hubert, do you want to be vice president?"

"Yes," Humphrey answered.

"Why would you want to have the job? You know it's a thankless job."

Humphrey said he could overcome the job's "thanklessness." Furthermore, he could help Johnson with liberals, blacks, labor, and voters in the large industrial states.

Johnson was frank. He noted that most presidents and vice presidents "just don't hit it off. There is something about the jobs and the responsibilities that seem to get in the way of those friendships and understanding." The office, Johnson said, not only would require complete loyalty, it would "require that you not be out front, that you not be in the headlines." Johnson prophetically warned Humphrey "that all the people associated with the president will look down on you. They're not interested in you and they'll try to stir up difficulties between the president and the vice president." If Humphrey disagreed with administration policy, Johnson insisted that he state his objections privately. "I don't want any open disagreements," Johnson said, "because that will be very destructive."

Humphrey and Johnson left the White House for the trip to Atlantic City. Humphrey was sworn to secrecy. Observant reporters, however, could smell the news. Humphrey's face told the story. He "seemed happier than a bouncing beagle," George Sperling wrote in the *Christian Science Monitor*. Arriving at Andrews Air Force Base outside Washington, Johnson finally broke his silence in an impromptu news conference. "Boys," he said, "meet the next vice president." Humphrey beamed.

Many delegates agreed that Humphrey's acceptance speech, with its robust attacks on Goldwater's conservative voting record, was better than Johnson's lackluster effort. To the enthusiastic cheers of the partisan crowd, Humphrey declared:

> During the last few weeks, shrill voices have tried to lay claim to the great spirit of the American past, but they long for a past that never was. In their recklessness, in their rationalism, they distort the American conservative tradition. Yes, those who have kidnaped the Republican Party have made it this year not a party of memory and sentiment but one of stridency, of unrestrained passion, of extreme and radical language . . .

Most Democrats and Republicans in the Senate voted for an $11.5 billion tax cut for American citizens and American business, but not Senator Goldwater. Most Democrats and Republicans in the Senate—four-fifths of the members of his own party—voted for the Civil Rights Act, but not Senator Goldwater . . .

Yes, yes, my fellow Americans, it is a fact that the temporary Republican spokesman is not in the mainstream of his party. In fact, he has not even touched the shore.

By his own admission, Humphrey enjoyed "every exhausting moment" of the campaign. For the first time in his political career, Humphrey traveled in style—crisscrossing the country in a four-engine Electra, which his campaign dubbed "The Happy Warrior." "He went out and sang the liberal line and attacked Goldwater as an extremist and loved it," said Van Dyk. Years later, Van Dyk said, people often asked him, "What was the high point of Humphrey's vice presidency?" His answer was always the same: "It was the night he was nominated. Everything from there went downhill."

Hoping to limit Democratic losses in the South, Johnson sent Lady Bird on an eight-state, twelve-hundred-mile whistle-stop tour from Virginia to Louisiana. Accompanied by her daughters, Lynda and Luci, Commerce secretary Luther Hodges (a former South Carolina governor), and House majority whip Hale Boggs, the first lady bravely faced crowds of hostile southerners still angry over Johnson's support for the Civil Rights Act. Some crowds were worse than others. South Carolina and Georgia were the meanest. At the last whistle stop in New Orleans on October 9, the president joined Lady Bird for a rally at the city's train station. Johnson told tens of thousands of supporters, including many blacks, "I am going to repeat here in Louisiana what I have said in every state that I have appeared in, and what I said the night that I walked to the White House to take over the awesome responsibilities that were mine: As long as I am your president, I am going to be president of all the people." At a fund-raising dinner that night, Johnson refused to paper over his support of civil rights. To prolonged, enthusiastic applause, he declared:

Whatever your views are, we have a Constitution and we have a Bill of Rights, and we have the law of the land, and two-thirds of the Democrats in the Senate voted for it and three-fourths of the Republicans. I signed it, and I am going to enforce it, and I am going to observe it, and I think any man that is worthy of the high office of President is going to do the same.

To the dismay of his staff and many of his southern supporters, Johnson departed from his prepared text and recalled the story of a young Sam Rayburn and his visit to a dying Texas senator, Weldon Bailey. As Johnson told the story, Bailey, a Mississippi native, said, "Sammy, I wish I felt a little better. I would like to go back to [Mississippi] and make them one more Democratic speech. I just feel like I have one in me. The poor old state, they haven't heard a Democratic speech in thirty years. All they ever hear at election time is 'Nigra, Nigra, Nigra!' " At first many in the audience were stunned. "It was a physical thing," recalled Johnson's aide Jack Valenti. "Surprise, awe; ears heard what they plainly could not hear, a cataclysmic wave hit everyone there with stunning and irreversible force." What followed was a full five minutes of enthusiastic applause.

On election day the Johnson-Humphrey ticket piled up what was then the largest victory ever in American presidential politics. Johnson won 61 percent of the vote and carried 44 states and the District of Columbia. In the South, Johnson's results were mixed. He won Arkansas, Florida, North Carolina, Tennessee, Texas, and Virginia. In the Deep South, however, he fared badly. Of the six states Goldwater carried nationally, five were southern: Alabama (where officials kept Johnson's name off the ballot), Georgia, Louisiana, Mississippi, and South Carolina. In Mississippi, where most blacks could not vote, the Johnson-Humphrey ticket suffered its worst defeat: The president received 53,000 votes to Goldwater's 360,000. Outside the South, Goldwater's only victory came in his home state of Arizona.

In 1957 Richard Russell's covert compromises with Lyndon Johnson had resulted in passage of the first civil rights bill of the twentieth century. Russell had hoped that a civil rights bill would release Johnson from the shackles of his heritage and hasten the day when a southerner— preferably Johnson himself—could be elected president of the United States. Now, almost eight years later, when fate presented Russell with the historic opportunity to help his protégé achieve that goal in his own right, he had demurred. In spite of pressure applied by some Georgia

Democratic leaders, Russell told constituents that "I do not intend to take any part in the national campaign."

Despite his earlier exhortations to constituents to peacefully obey the civil rights law, Russell explained that he could not bring himself to actively support a presidential ticket that pledged support and enforcement of what he called "the Federal Force Bill of 1964." To Georgia state senator Jimmy Carter, who had written urging Russell to participate in the campaign, Russell replied that even his friendship with Johnson would not lure him onto the stump. "I do not believe that even he would ask me to stultify myself by getting out now and supporting a campaign platform endorsing and assuring enforcement of a system which changes the form of government that we have heretofore known in this country." Furthermore, Russell said, he could not support Humphrey because the nominee had consistently opposed the cloture rule. "He is one of the most attractive personalities I have ever encountered and I know of no man who is a more fluent and eloquent speaker—in fact, he can 'charm the birds right down out of the trees'—but the fact remains that his philosophy is different to mine and is contrary to that the president always expressed as a member of the Senate." Goldwater, on the other hand, was "a real states' righter who believes in integration but thinks that it is a matter that should be determined by each state."

Despite his historic landslide election elsewhere in the country, Johnson lost Georgia by 94,000 votes out of more than 1.1 million votes cast. Although Johnson apparently had never asked Russell to lend his considerable influence to the campaign, Lady Bird had. On three separate occasions Russell politely rejected the first lady's entreaties to join her campaign swing through Georgia. His objections to Humphrey's liberalism, he explained, were simply insurmountable. When the Johnson-Humphrey ticket won, Russell seemed almost dispirited by the outcome and by the overwhelming endorsement of Johnson's liberal platform implicit in the election returns. While he blamed the most "radical" portions of the party's platform on Humphrey, Russell surely understood that virtually no word of the document would have been included without Johnson's support.

Most likely, it was neither the election nor the platform that really bothered Russell. He was still smarting from passage of the civil rights bill and resentful that Humphrey, the bill's chief proponent and floor manager, was now the vice president. "The political wounds inflicted by the overwhelming forces, not only in the Senate, but in the communications media and throughout the land, led by vice president–elect Humphrey, were still bleeding," he later admitted. The prospects for 1965 and later were even more appalling. To his friend Senator Willis Robertson of Virginia, Russell confessed, "They have overtaken and overwhelmed us."

CHAPTER TWENTY-TWO

We Are Demanding the Ballot

FOR YEARS SOUTHERN MEMBERS OF CONGRESS fought to defeat civil rights measures by arguing that such pernicious legislation would inevitably lead to violence and dangerous social upheaval in the former Confederate states. The balance between whites and blacks, they argued, was simply too delicate to alter suddenly with sweeping federal legislation.

The passage of the Civil Rights Act of 1964 proved what many liberals had suspected: Such arguments were not based on legitimate concerns about maintaining peace and harmony; they were merely insincere excuses for preserving the South's brutal status quo in race relations. Those who had accepted the threadbare southern arguments against the bill must have been greatly surprised by southern reaction to the legislation's passage. While Democrats suffered significant electoral losses in the South, the five southern states that Goldwater carried hardly qualified as the electoral disaster predicted by Russell and others. Furthermore, response to the dreaded public accommodations provisions was surprisingly benign: An extensive fifty-three-city survey conducted by the Community Relations Service found "widespread compliance" with the bill's provisions. "What is most important," Johnson said in reaction to the report, was that "it shows the law is being obeyed in those areas where some had predicted there would be massive disobedience." In New Orleans two hundred business leaders—including the manager of the well-known Roosevelt Hotel—put their names on a newspaper advertisement urging compliance with the law. Elsewhere in New Orleans, blacks quietly and peacefully desegregated downtown movie theaters and dined at French Quarter restaurants for the first time. The Jackson, Mississippi, Chamber of Commerce called on its members to obey the law "pending tests of its constitutionality in court." In Birmingham, where Mayor Albert Boutwell refused to use the city's resources to enforce the act, blacks and whites ate together in several downtown restaurants; the city's hotel and motel associations said they would obey the law. Holiday Inns of America told its 488 motels to observe the law. The South's largest cafeteria chain, Morrison's, announced it would do the same.

There was resistance. The city of Greenwood, Mississippi, drained its white and black community swimming pools rather than allow blacks and whites to swim together. Despite the peaceful integration of three hotels in Jackson, the Robert E. Lee Hotel closed its doors on July 6, four days after the bill became law. The Mississippi state legislature unanimously praised the hotel's owners for their "courageous" decision.

There was scattered violence. In Moss Point, Mississippi, a sniper's bullet wounded a nineteen-year-old black girl as she sang the civil rights anthem "We Shall Overcome" at a voter registration rally on July 7. That day, in Bessemer, Alabama, a band of white men wielding baseball bats assaulted a group of blacks who asked for service at a department-store lunch counter. The most prominent resistance to the bill came on July 3 in Atlanta by Lester Maddox, owner of the Pickwick Restaurant. Aided by angry white customers waving ax handles, Maddox produced a revolver and chased three blacks from his establishment. Three days later, when another black bravely demanded service, Maddox again refused. He called the police, who took away the would-be patron.

In late July a three-judge panel in Atlanta ordered Maddox to obey the law, a decision that was affirmed by the U.S. Supreme Court in December. In writing for the 9-0 majority, Justice Tom Clark said that Congress possessed clear constitutional authority to enact laws removing obstructions to interstate commerce. "How obstructions in commerce may be removed—what means are to be employed—is within the sound and exclusive discretion of the Congress," Clark wrote.

For Maddox, the unfavorable Supreme Court ruling was not a total defeat. He became a hero among Georgia's white racists. In 1966 the voters of Georgia—aided by the state legislature—rewarded his contempt for the law of the United States by electing him governor.

As the Supreme Court ruling of December had shown, the Civil Rights Act's public accommodations provision had sharp teeth. By contrast, the act's voting rights provision proved a toothless, ineffectual instrument to guarantee black voting rights. Despite three separate acts—the 1957, 1960, and 1964 civil rights bills—Congress had so far been unable to break down the barriers to significant and widespread registration of blacks in the South. Under Dwight Eisenhower, the Justice Department had often been hesitant to employ the meager legal weapons issued by the Congress in the 1957 act. As the Kennedy administration proved with its more determined enforcement of the 1957 and 1960 acts, assertive executive action was severely limited without potent legislation. Because the Justice Department could enforce these laws only through the federal courts, hostile or indifferent southern judges controlled the fates of many voting rights cases. "The avenues for opposition through litigation were so manifold," observed Stephen Pollak, an attorney in the Justice Department's Civil Rights Division, "that the pouring of the Civil Rights Division's total resources into voting discrimination" had resulted "in only minuscule advances." The existing voting rights statutes, Nicholas Katzenbach said, "were all sort of hopeless, the way judges down there were reading them and administering them. It just never got anybody registered." Katzenbach, now attorney general, quickly learned "that you're never going to get anywhere going case by case."

The voting rights provisions of the 1964 act were designed primarily to accelerate the consideration and appeals of voting rights cases. Voting rights suits would be heard expeditiously by a three-judge panel and could be appealed directly to the Supreme Court. The bill also prohibited the unequal application of voter registration laws, outlawed disqualification for insignificant errors or omissions, and stipulated that a sixth-grade education was adequate proof of literacy. But the law applied only to voting in federal elections.

Despite these stronger provisions, black registration in November 1964 was much lower than white registration in every southern state. Across the South, only 43 percent of eligible blacks were registered, compared to 73 percent of eligible whites. The greatest disparities existed in Mississippi, where 70 percent of eligible whites were registered but only 6.7 percent of eligible blacks; in Alabama, with 71 percent of whites registered to 23 percent of blacks; and Louisiana, with 80 percent of whites and 32 of blacks.

This deplorable state of black voter registration had lured about nine hundred idealistic college students from northern campuses to Mississippi during the summer of 1964. Under the auspices of the Council of Federate Organizations (COFO), an association of major civil rights groups, the students came flocking southward to participate in a voter education and registration effort known as the Freedom Summer Project. Led by Robert Moses of the Student Nonviolent Coordinating Committee (SNCC), the students—mostly whites—went door to door in rural Mississippi, hoping to persuade nonvoting blacks to attend voter education seminars at local churches. After being educated in the art of passing a voter registration test, the would-be voters—at least those with enough courage—were ready to present themselves to the county registrar.

For most of the students, Freedom Summer was no vacation. Resistance among black citizens was high—and rightly so. As Civil Rights Commission member Theodore Hesburgh later remarked, "In some areas, just attempting to vote is tantamount to suicide." Freedom Summer exacted an awful toll: six murders, thirty homes and buildings bombed, thirty-five churches burned, thirty-five shooting incidents, eighty beatings, and thousands of arrests. The events of the hot Mississippi summer not only highlighted the near-impossibility of black voter registration but exposed the woeful inability of the federal courts and the FBI to register and protect blacks in the South.

From the White House, Johnson watched the Mississippi summer with concern and dread—fearing that events might force him into another divisive civil rights battle in the new session of Congress. If necessary Johnson would be ready with a bill. At his behest, Attorney General Katzenbach had begun drafting voting rights legislation just days after the Civil Rights Act had passed. "I could have shot him," Katzenbach later said. "I was so tired of being down in the halls of the Congress on the '64 act." The charge from Johnson: "I want you to write me the goddamndest, toughest voting rights act that you can devise." After all, it was Johnson's sincere belief that ballots paved the path toward full civil rights for blacks. As he told Humphrey, when the blacks get the vote, "they'll have every politician, North and South, East and West, kissing their ass, begging for support." By early 1965 the president was prepared to introduce another civil rights bill. This time, it would be *his* legislation. "He wanted something," Katzenbach explained, "that was purely Lyndon Johnson."

Soon the tragic events in a small town in central Alabama would make Johnson's bill a national priority.

Selma. An obscure town on the Alabama River in Dallas County was destined to become the civil rights battleground for 1965. Although the countywide voting-age population of 29,515 was almost 58 percent black, its voter rolls were overwhelmingly white. Of 9,877 registered voters, only 355 were black. Of the 795 blacks who attempted to register between May 1962 and August 1964, officials had enrolled only ninety-three. During that period, registrars had added 945 of 1,232 white applicants to the county voter rolls.

Its sheriff personified the county's oppression of black citizens. James Clark, a large, short-tempered, forty-three-year-old bully, would soon prove that Bull Connor was not the only inept lawman in Alabama. Clark would become to voting rights what Connor was to the 1963 civil rights debate—a vivid symbol of official southern racism and hostility toward blacks.

Dallas County had first attracted the attention of the federal government in 1961, when the Justice Department sued to prevent the county's registrars from discriminating against prospective black voters. By 1963, despite a federal injunction against that blatant discrimination, little had changed. Shortly after the passage of the Civil Rights Act of 1964, Sheriff Clark's deputies, wielding electric cattle prods, arrested fifty black citizens who appeared at the county courthouse to register to vote.

By late 1964 Selma beckoned Martin Luther King and the Southern Christian Leadership Conference. King suspected that in Selma, as in Birmingham, the authorities would be unable to respond peacefully when blacks marched and attempted to register in massive numbers. On January 2 King launched his Selma campaign, telling a crowd of seven hundred that Alabama's blacks would take their appeals for voting rights to Governor George Wallace, the state legislature, and ultimately the federal government. "We must be willing to go to jail by the thousands," he warned his audience. "We are not asking, we are demanding the ballot."

Although King depended on another overreaction by local authorities, the Selma campaign would be markedly different from his 1963 Birmingham project in one significant respect. This time he would successfully articulate one simple and distinct goal: the right to vote. While Birmingham had helped sway public opinion in the general direction of the Civil Rights Act of 1964, King's numerous objectives there had been obscure. Blacks in Birmingham had articulated a diffuse collection of demands, including better jobs and desegregation of businesses, restaurants, and public facilities. In the end, however, Birmingham produced little immediate action in Washington. Kennedy was moved to propose legislation, but Congress reacted sluggishly. Not until Kennedy died and Johnson entered the White House did civil rights gain real momentum. In the words of civil rights historian David J. Garrow, although Birmingham "deeply affected the [Kennedys], there was no widespread national outcry, no vocal reaction by the nation's clergy, and no immediate move by the administration to propose salutary legislation."

In Selma the demand was focused, forcefully expressed, and easily understood. The black citizens of Dallas County simply demanded the right to participate in the most fundamental exercise of the American democratic process.

In the weeks that followed, Sheriff Clark arrested Selma's blacks by the hundreds as they marched to the Dallas County Courthouse to register as voters. On January 19 the sheriff ordered a large group of blacks to wait in an alley near the side entrance of the courthouse. When they resisted this indignity, Clark arrested more than sixty of them on charges of unlawful assembly. Clark had walked into King's trap. The arrests energized Selma's fledgling protest movement. The next day another group of blacks appeared at the courthouse. Clark blocked their way. Armed with a billy club and a cattle prod, he stood defiantly in the courthouse doorway and issued his order: Wait in the alley! Clark promptly ordered the arrests of 150 citizens who disobeyed his order. The following week King turned up the heat again. The protests escalated. On February 1, King led 265 blacks to the courthouse, violating the city's parade permit. This time Selma's police officers arrested them all, including SCLC leaders King and Ralph Abernathy.

When almost 160 black children poured out of Selma's schools to protest the arrests, Clark played into King's hands again. With county jails already overflowing with black citizens, Clark ordered his deputies to herd the children toward the Fraternal Order of Police Lodge, six miles outside Selma. Clark's men waved billy clubs and cattle prods. They forced the terrified youngsters to march out of town at a quick trot. "You like to march so much, so we'll let you!" Clark shouted. The forced march lasted for three miles, until the deputies allowed the weary and frightened children to "escape." By week's end Clark had imprisoned more than 2,600 of Selma's black citizens. In an open letter to the *New York Times,* King pointed to the tragic irony: "There are more Negroes in jail with me than there are on the voting rolls." Meanwhile, in nearby Marion, Alabama, state troopers arrested nearly seven hundred black students who had peacefully marched to the courthouse to protest the county's voting rights and public accommodations violations.

Events in Selma unfolded before a horrified national audience. Most graphic and disturbing was an Associated Press photograph taken of Clark as he brought down his billy club on a black woman whom two deputies had wrestled to the ground. True, the woman had landed the first punch to Clark's left eye, but the photographer did not capture that blow on film. The next day the photograph ran on the front pages of newspapers across the country. As *Newsweek* observed, the picture was "worth more to Martin Luther King's registration drive than all the thousands of words" that accompanied the story. Television cameras captured another violent incident involving Clark. When a black preacher, C.T. Vivian, called the sheriff "an evil man" for forcing twenty-five blacks to stand outside the courthouse in a rainstorm, Clark punched Vivian in the face and knocked him to the ground. "One of the first things I ever learned," Clark later bragged, "was not to hit a nigger with your fist because his head is too hard." As Selma's more temperate police chief later observed, King and the SCLC were manipulating Clark "just like an expert playing a violin."

On February 5, Dallas County authorities released King from jail. He was now more defiant and determined than ever. The voting rights protests would spread across the South, he pledged, but he had particular designs on Alabama. He would work to triple the number of black voters in Alabama for the 1966 Congressional elections and would "purge Alabama of all Congressmen who have stood in the way of Negroes." The next day President Johnson's press secretary, George Reedy, announced that the administration had decided to act. Johnson would soon be sending Congress a "strong recommendation" for a voting rights bill.

King left Selma for Atlanta, but the protests continued. In nearby Marion there was more trouble. When four hundred protesters left the Zion Methodist Church to march through town, a small group of Marion policemen, backed up by fifty Alabama state troopers and a motley collection of angry white thugs, was waiting for them. Also in the group was Sheriff Clark, dressed in civilian clothes but wielding a billy club. Ordered to disperse, the marchers refused. Police and troopers tore into the crowd, beating the marchers at random. "They didn't have to be marching," recalled one witness. "All you had to do was be black." In the melee, the police and troopers injured several newspaper reporters and television cameramen. One victim was Cager Lee, an eighty-two-year-old man. Shouting "Nigger, go home," one of the troopers dragged Lee into the street and kicked him. Several state troopers assaulted Lee's daughter. Her son, Jimmie Lee Jackson, was shot in the stomach trying to save his mother. He died eight days later. The Montgomery *Alabama Journal* declared, "Alabama is, once again and worse than ever before, disgraced by mindless 'police work' and blood."

With Jackson's death, the reinvigorated Selma project had a martyr. King immediately announced a fifty-mile march to Montgomery, where blacks would stage a dramatic rally for voting rights at the State Capitol. "I can't promise you that it won't get you beaten," King told his followers. "I can't promise you that it won't get your house bombed. I can't promise you that you won't get scarred up a bit. But we must stand up for what is right!"

On the afternoon of Sunday, March 7, over six hundred blacks and a few whites gathered at the Brown Chapel African Methodist Episcopal Church. Despite orders from Governor Wallace prohibiting the march, the group was eager to begin its trek toward Montgomery. Armed with only bedrolls and knapsacks, the marchers wound their way through town and headed for the Edmund Pettus Bridge, which traversed the Alabama River. Along the way the marchers sang the Baptist hymn that had, by now, become the anthem of the civil rights movement:

We shall overcome, we shall overcome,
We shall overcome someday.
Oh, deep in my heart, I do believe,
We shall overcome someday.

As the marchers walked along U.S. Highway 80, an imposing unit of sixty state troopers blocked their way about four hundred yards short of the bridge. Headed by Colonel Al Lingo, the troopers were a menacing sight as they stood shoulder to shoulder in several rows, armed with revolvers, billy clubs, helmets, and gas masks. Nearby, spoiling for trouble, were Sheriff Clark's well-armed men, some of them on horseback. A bloodthirsty crowd of white townspeople was not far away.

As the marchers approached the phalanx of troopers, state police major John Cloud bellowed into his bullhorn: "Turn around and go back to your church! You will not be allowed to march any further! You've got two minutes to disperse!" When the marchers refused to turn back, Cloud gave the order: "Troopers—forward!" In an instant, the heavily armed troopers donned their gas masks and launched themselves into the crowd. A *Newsweek* reporter described the rest:

> The front ranks of the column fell like dominoes before the first rush of state troopers; John Lewis, national chairman of the Student Nonviolent Coordinating Committee, went down with a mild skull fracture. At a half-walk, half-run, troopers shoved and clubbed the marchers into retreat. Behind them, the sheriff's cavalry mounted a Cossack charge into the scattering column. A fresh wave of troopers laid down the first volley of tear-gas canisters. A thick, acrid, blue-gray cloud spread over the highway. Billies flailed, horses dashed in and out, Negroes sprawled and choked and wept and screamed: "Please, no! God, we're being killed!" And across the road, in front of the Chick-N-Treat cafe, a gallery of whites whooped and cheered.

By now the march had disintegrated into a frantic and bloody retreat. The terrified marchers fled toward town. But Clark's deputies fiercely pursued them. They were spared only when Selma police chief Wilson Baker ordered Clark to keep his men back. "Everything will be all right," Clark angrily told Baker. "I've already waited a month too damn long!" By day's end the troopers and deputies had beaten the marchers so badly that seventy-eight black citizens required hospital treatment.

Television and newspaper cameras captured the entire ghastly scene. On Monday morning almost every newspaper in the country played the bloody Selma incident on its front page. The national outcry was deafening. In Detroit ten thousand people—led by the city's mayor and Michigan's governor—took to the streets in a peaceful but angry protest. Marchers also turned out in Toronto, Illinois, New Jersey, California, Wisconsin, Connecticut, New York, and Washington, D.C. At the White House, Johnson said he "deplored the brutality" in Selma but urged both sides to moderate their actions.

Congress reacted viscerally to the news from Selma, in what *Newsweek*'s congressional reporter, Samuel Shaffer, called "a wave of indignation greater than any episode in the long civil rights struggle." Suddenly lawmakers appeared eager to enact tough, meaningful voting rights legislation. In the Senate, Ralph Yarborough of Texas cried, "Shame on you, George Wallace, for the wet ropes that bruised the muscles, for the bullwhips which cut the flesh, for the clubs that broke the bones, for the tear gas that blinded, burned and choked into insensibility." In the House, Ohio congressman Wayne Hays proposed cutting the number of the Alabama delegation in half. Another Ohio congressman, Charles Vanik, suggested closing all of Alabama's defense and space installations as long as the state "chooses to declare war on the U.S. Constitution." Vanik declared, "The shame of Selma is the shame of America."

In Atlanta King said that as a "matter of conscience and in an attempt to arouse the deepest concern of the nation," he would lead another march to Montgomery on Tuesday, March 9. He issued an urgent call for white clergymen from around the nation to join him. The response surprised even King. The next day more than four hundred ministers, priests, and rabbis streamed into Selma from all regions of the nation. Despite a federal court order postponing the march, King agreed to abide by a secret compromise brokered by the president's emissary, Community Relations Service chairman LeRoy Collins. Alabama authorities would permit King's followers to march, but only to the bridge where the previous trek had ended in violence. At that point they would be allowed to kneel, pray, and then turn around.

On Tuesday afternoon King led 1,500 people from Brown Chapel toward the now-infamous Edmund Pettus Bridge. As he confronted the mass of state troopers, King halted the march. Again Major Cloud stood between the marchers and the long road to Montgomery. "You can have your prayer and then return to church if you so desire," Cloud told King. The crowd knelt and prayed for fifteen minutes. "We come to present our bodies as a living sacrifice," Ralph Abernathy said. "We don't have much to offer, but we do have our bodies, and we lay them down on the altar today." As the marchers finished their prayers, Cloud issued an unexpected order: "Troopers, withdraw!" Suddenly Highway 80 was clear. Governor Wallace had hoped to bait King into violating the court order against the march. King was more disciplined than the Alabama authorities. "Let's return to church and complete our fight in the courts," he said, as the marchers slowly began to reverse course.

That night King tried to put the best face on his partial victory. "At least we had to get to the point where the brutality took place," he told the gathering at Brown Chapel. "And we made it clear when we got there that we were going to have some form of protest and worship. I can assure you that something happened in Alabama that's never happened before. When Negroes and whites can stand on Highway 80 and have a mass meeting, things aren't that bad."

The day would not be free of violence and tragedy. That night a white Unitarian minister from Boston, James J. Reeb, was attacked as he and two other ministers left a black-owned cafe near downtown Selma. "Hey, niggers!" a group of whites shouted as they pursued the three ministers. All three were beaten, but Reeb sustained the worst injuries. He died two days later in a Birmingham hospital.

To many observers, it appeared that President Johnson had been only a passive, even indifferent observer of the events in Selma. Outside the White House, six hundred demonstrators protested the administration's perceived inaction by chanting, "LBJ, just you wait. See what happens in '68" and "LBJ, open your eyes, see the sickness of the South, see the horrors of your homeland." At the Justice Department, protesters were evicted after staging two sit-ins to protest Johnson's response to events in Selma. Inside the White House, twelve demonstrators on a regular tour of the mansion began an embarrassing sit-in to protest Johnson's civil rights policies.

Johnson's indecision over Selma was mistaken for indifference. Even before Selma—and well before the protests began outside the White House—he had instructed the Justice Department to draft voting rights legislation that would attract bipartisan support in the Senate and the House. Several times Johnson had talked with prominent civil rights leaders to assure them of his commitment to congressional action on voting rights. In his State of the Union Address in early January, the president had urged Congress to pass voting rights legislation, although he had yet to decide whether he would propose a voting rights bill or a constitutional amendment.

The violence in Selma outraged Johnson, although he complained privately that King and his marchers would be more successful "if they were in Washington, working on their senators, getting a voting bill passed." Master strategist that he was, though, Johnson instinctively understood that Selma had thrown open a window of opportunity through which he could now push strong voting rights legislation. Many liberals and some civil rights leaders were not as strategic in their approach to Selma. They urged Johnson to send federal troops to restore order, a course that would only have complicated matters for the president.

Attorney General Katzenbach, despite his own initial eagerness to dispatch the military, strongly advised Johnson that he lacked authority to make such a decision unilaterally. Katzenbach's counsel was wise. Had Johnson sent troops to Alabama without a request from state or local officials, he might have provoked further violence and ruined all chances for passage of his voting rights bill. For now he would reluctantly defer to Katzenbach, even if that caused him to appear indifferent to Selma's violence. Even so, the unrelenting protests outside the White House, along with the harsh criticism by civil rights leaders and some liberals, hurt Johnson deeply. "Once again," he later said, "my southern heritage was thrown in my face."

In Selma, King demanded permission to lead a march all the way to Montgomery. The compromise trek to the Pettus Bridge had been only a temporary solution. Although Johnson wanted to avoid further violence, he would not protect King's marchers with federal troops unless Alabama officials explicitly requested them. He waited for Wallace to make the next move. "Make it clear we're not going to give an inch," he told aides. "Now that Wallace, he's a lot more sophisticated than your average southern politician, and it's his ox that's in the ditch. Let's see how he gets it out." Meanwhile, he told Katzenbach, "let's have that voting rights bill ready to go to Congress just as soon as we give the word."

On March 11 Wallace gave Johnson an opening. When the White House learned that the Alabama governor had indicated his desire to meet with the president, Johnson quickly sent word of his willingness to set up an appointment. On Saturday, March 12, Wallace entered the Oval Office for a three-hour meeting. The six-foot-three Johnson invited the diminutive governor to sit on the sofa. Johnson took a seat in a nearby rocking chair. As Wallace's small frame sank into the cushions, Johnson leaned his imposing frame forward. He almost touched Wallace's nose with his. "Well, Governor, you wanted to see me?"

For fifteen minutes Wallace anxiously explained to Johnson the need to preserve law and order, quell troublemaking by outside agitators, and keep federal troops out of his sovereign state. "I saw a nervous, aggressive man," Johnson recalled, "a rough, shrewd politician who had managed to touch the deepest chords of pride as well as prejudice among his people." When Wallace finished, it was Johnson's turn. He focused on Wallace's nervous eyes.

"Now, tell me, how come the Negroes in Alabama for the most part can't vote?"

"They can vote," Wallace replied.

"If they're registered," Johnson said.

"White men have to register, too."

"That's the problem, George; somehow your folks down in Alabama don't want to register them Negroes. Why, I had a fellow in here the other day, and he not only had a college degree, but one of them Ph.D.s, and your man said he couldn't register because he didn't know how to read and write well enough to vote in Alabama. Now, do all your white folks in Alabama have Ph.D.s?"

"Those decisions are made by the county registrars, not by me," Wallace replied.

"Well then, George, why don't you just tell them county registrars to register those Negroes?"

"I don't have that power, Mr. President, under Alabama law—"

"Don't be modest with me, George, you had the power to keep the president of the United States off the ballot [in the 1964 election]. Surely you have the power to tell a few poor county registrars what to do."

"I don't. Under Alabama law they're independent."

"Well then, George, why don't you just persuade them what to do?"

"I don't think that would be easy, Mr. President, they're pretty close with their authority."

"Don't shit me about your persuasive power, George. Why, just this morning I was watching you on television . . . And you was attacking me."

"Not you, Mr. President, I was speaking against federal intervention—"

"You was attacking me, George. And you know what? You were so damn persuasive that I had to turn off the set before you had me changing my mind. Now, ordinarily I'm a pretty strong-minded fellow, just like them registrars. Will you give it a try, George?"

Wallace, the former bantamweight boxer, emerged from the lengthy meeting looking slightly punch-drunk, as if he had gone too many rounds with a much larger heavyweight. "Hell," he said later, "if I'd stayed in there much longer, he'd have had me coming out for civil rights."*

At an impromptu press conference in the Rose Garden, Johnson strode confidently before the waiting microphones. "Never in his sixteen months in office," wrote a reporter for *Time*, "was he more in command of the situation." First Johnson announced that he would send Congress a voting rights bill early the following week. Next he forcefully condemned the violence in Selma: "It is wrong to do violence to peaceful citizens in the streets of their towns. It is wrong to deny Americans the right to vote. It is wrong to deny any person full equality because of the color of his skin." With Wallace standing somberly just behind his right shoulder, Johnson informed reporters that he had "advised the governor of my intention to press with all the vigor at my command to assure that every citizen of this country is given the right to participate in his government at every level through the complete voting process."

He was, he said, committed to maintaining law and order. "If the state and local authorities are unable to function, the federal government will completely meet its responsibilities." He had also told Wallace, he said, "that the brutality in Selma last week must not be repeated. I urged that the governor publicly declare his support for universal suffrage in the state of Alabama and the United States of America."

Despite having applied his considerable persuasive talents to Wallace, Johnson had really wanted only one concession, which he got: Several days later Wallace officially notified the president that his state was unable to bear the financial burden of protecting King's marchers on their five-day journey from Selma to Montgomery. Johnson in turn federalized the Alabama National Guard. Federal troops would be used, but not because the president had unilaterally ordered them into action; they would be mobilized because the state could not afford them. As Johnson explained, "they were not intruders forcing their way in; they were citizens of Alabama."

That, Johnson said, "made all the difference in the world."

---

*Wallace eventually did become an advocate of civil rights. Thirty years later he joined civil rights leaders in a reenactment of the Selma-to-Montgomery march.

CHAPTER TWENTY-THREE

We Shall Overcome

NINETY-SIX YEARS AFTER the states had ratified the Fifteenth Amendment, Lyndon Johnson's voting rights legislation was ready. In its simplest form, it would breathe life into Section I of the moribund constitutional amendment, which declared that "the right of citizens of the United States to vote shall not be denied or abridged by the United States or by any State on account of race, color, or previous condition of servitude."

In contrast to previous voting rights bills, Johnson's legislation would not rely on federal district courts for enforcement. Instead the president would ask Congress to establish uniform voting standards in those states with the worst histories of voting rights violations. The bill would abolish literacy and other qualification exams in states and jurisdictions where less than half the voting-age citizens had voted in or registered for the November 1964 general election. In those states, federal registrars could assume responsibility for voter registration. States that blocked federally registered voters from the polls could have their ballots impounded by the courts. Under the bill's provisions, the federal government would immediately send voting examiners into at least six southern states whose voter turnouts in the November election had been below 50 percent: Mississippi (33 percent), South Carolina (38 percent), Alabama (36 percent), Virginia (41 percent), Georgia (43 percent), and Louisiana (47 percent). Thirty-four counties in North Carolina and one county each in Arizona and Maine would qualify for voting examiners. Another important provision required states in which the bill nullified voter-qualification laws to submit all subsequent changes in voting statutes to a three-judge District of Columbia panel.

The existing voting rights laws—despite considerable litigation by the Justice Department under Kennedy and Johnson—had produced only minor progress in the seven years since the Civil Rights Act of 1957. Johnson now proposed what one Justice Department official called an "almost revolutionary" change: The Justice Department would no longer seek relief from deliberate or hostile federal district courts. Rather, the government could send federal voter registrars directly into states or jurisdictions when the attorney general certified to the U.S. Civil Service Commission that voting rights violations existed.

With the bill ready for introduction, Johnson's major concern was the manner in which he would present it to Congress. On Sunday evening, March 14, he met in the White House Cabinet Room with Humphrey and the House and Senate leadership to discuss whether he should present his bill to a joint session of Congress. Dirksen and Mansfield opposed a joint session.

"Don't panic now," Dirksen advised. "This is a deliberative government. Don't let these people say, 'We scared him into it.'"

Others—Speaker John McCormack, House Majority Leader Carl Albert, and Humphrey—urged Johnson to take his bill directly to Congress. "Logic is what you are saying," the vice president argued. "But emotions are running high. A message of what this government is doing—simply—is what is needed." Johnson, who had already decided he should personally present the bill to Congress, readily agreed. In minutes, Humphrey drafted a statement from the Congressional leaders: "The leadership of the Congress [has] invited the president to address a Joint Session of Congress on Monday evening to present the president's views and outline of a voting rights bill."

Going before Congress in this way had its risks. Johnson would be placing much of his considerable popularity and power behind a single bill whose passage was likely, but by no means assured. Since Harry Truman had appeared before a joint session in 1946 to request special legislation to end a national railway strike, no president had appeared in the House chamber to present his request for a specific bill. But the drama that the historic speech would produce was *exactly* what Johnson wanted. As Johnson later explained, "I felt I had to reassure the people that we were moving as far and as fast as we could. I knew this reassurance would not be provided by the cold words of a written message."

The next night, at nine o'clock, Johnson stood at the podium in the House of Representatives. The speech he was about to deliver was hastily prepared. Speech writer Richard Goodwin had feverishly labored since morning, under intense pressure, to produce a polished text. Even as Johnson stood before the assembled members of Congress, the speech was not yet on the TelePrompTer. Johnson would read the first twelve pages from his loose-leaf binder before aide Jack Valenti could crawl across the floor of the House well and nervously thread the speech tape onto the machine. "I almost died a thousand deaths getting it here in time," Valenti whispered to the TelePrompTer operator.

Not every member of Congress was in the House chamber as Johnson began his speech. The Mississippi and Virginia delegations staged a boycott, as did several other southern members. None of this troubled Johnson; his audience was the entire nation, not southern members of Congress.

Beginning his speech forcefully, Johnson immediately placed the voting rights issue into its larger, more significant context:

> I speak tonight for the dignity of man and the destiny of democracy. I urge every member of both parties, Americans of all religions and of all colors, from every section of the country, to join me in that cause.
>
> At times, history and fate meet at a single time in a single place to shape a turning point in man's unending search for freedom. So it was at Lexington and Concord. So it was a century ago at Appomattox. So it was last week in Selma, Alabama.
>
> There, long-suffering men and women peacefully protested the denial of their rights as Americans. Many were brutally assaulted. One good man, a man of God, was killed.
>
> There is no cause for pride in what has happened in Selma. There is no cause for self-satisfaction in the long denial of equal rights of millions of Americans.
>
> But there is cause for hope and for faith in our democracy in what is happening here tonight.
>
> For the cries of pain and the hymns and protests of oppressed people have summoned into convocation all the majesty of this great government of the greatest nation on earth.

The issue, Johnson declared, is "the harsh fact that in many places in this country, men and women are kept from voting simply because they are Negroes." Current laws, he insisted, "cannot overcome systematic and ingenious discrimination. No law that we now have on the books—and I have helped to put three of them there—can ensure the right to vote when local officials are determined to deny it." The Constitution, Johnson said, is clear: no one can be denied his voting rights because of his race or color. "We have all sworn an oath before God to support and to defend that Constitution," he declared. "We must now act in obedience to that oath."

On Wednesday, he said, he would "send to Congress a law designed to eliminate illegal barriers to the right to vote." And he noted that the last civil rights bill passed "after eight long months of debate." This time, Johnson insisted, "there must be no delay, or no hesitation or no compromise with our purpose . . . We ought not, we must not wait another eight months before we get a bill. We have already waited a hundred years and more and the time for waiting is gone. So I ask you to join me in working long hours, nights and weekends, if necessary, to pass this bill. And I don't make that request lightly."

With his next words, Johnson elevated himself and his presidency to a higher plane—linking himself inextricably and forever with the noble cause of civil rights:

> But even if we pass this bill, the battle will not be over. What happened in Selma is part of a far larger movement which reaches into every section and state of America. It is the effort of American Negroes to secure for themselves the full blessings of American life.
>
> Their cause must be our cause, too. Because it is not just Negroes, but really it is all of us, who must overcome the crippling legacy of bigotry and injustice.

Then—for one brief, dramatic moment—Johnson paused. Raising his arms like an evangelical preacher certain of the righteousness of his message, Johnson declared:

> And we shall overcome!

For a split second, the chamber was quiet. Perhaps his audience was ever so stunned that the president of the United States had, as Richard Goodwin said, "adopted as his own rallying cry the anthem of black protest, the hymn of a hundred embattled black marches." Suddenly the entire chamber exploded in spontaneous, rapturous applause. Congressmen, senators, cabinet members, Supreme Court justices leapt to their feet in an emotional, thunderous ovation. House Judiciary Committee chairman Emanuel Celler cheered wildly. Tears welled in the eyes of Majority Leader Mansfield. In the gallery, blacks and whites wept openly. Watching the speech in far-away Selma, Martin Luther King cried. Next to Harry McPherson sat a glum southern congressman, who, shocked by Johnson's words, simply sputtered, "Goddamn!"

The real hero of the civil rights struggle, Johnson continued

is the American Negro. His actions and protests, his courage to risk safety and even to risk his life, have awakened the conscience of this nation. His demonstrations have been designed to call attention to injustice, designed to provoke change, designed to stir reform. He has called upon us to make good the promise of America. And who among us can say that we would have made the same progress were it not for his persistent bravery, and his faith in American democracy.

As he ended his forty-five-minute speech, Johnson recalled for his audience his first post-college job, as a teacher at a Mexican-American school in Cotulla, Texas:

My students were poor and they often came to class without breakfast, hungry, and they knew even in their youth that pain of prejudice. They never seemed to know why people disliked them. But they knew it was so. Because I saw it in their eyes. I often walked home late in the afternoon after the classes were finished, wishing there was more that I could do. But all I knew was to teach them the little that I knew, hoping that it might help them against the hardships that lay ahead.

Somehow you never forget what poverty and hatred can do when you see its scars on the hopeful faces of a young child.

I never thought then in 1928 that I would be standing here in 1965. It never even occurred to me in my fondest dreams that I might have the chance to help the sons and daughters of those students and to help people like them all over this country.

But now I do have that chance and I'll let you in on a secret. I mean to use it. And I hope that you will use it with me.

When Johnson finished, the assembled members of Congress rose for another standing ovation. As he walked out of the chamber, down the center aisle, Johnson came face to face with the House Judiciary Committee chairman Emanuel Celler.

"Manny, I want you to start hearings tonight."

Celler was stunned. "Mr. President, I can't push that committee or it might get out of hand. I'm scheduling hearings for three days next week, beginning Tuesday."

Johnson was persistent. "Start them *this* week, Manny. And hold night sessions, too."

Then, Johnson walked away. In the words of *Time:* "He strode from the chamber a changed man, confident . . . that he had launched the U.S. itself inexorably toward a new purpose."

When Johnson delivered his historic speech, Richard Russell was a thousand miles away. Following more than a month's confinement at Walter Reed Army Hospital, Russell had left town to recuperate in Puerto Rico, then in Florida, and finally in Winder. He suffered from a pulmonary edema, a condition in which his emphysema-damaged lungs became congested with fluid and restricted his breathing. Despite intensive medical treatment, his condition had worsened. Doctors were finally forced to perform a tracheotomy to assist his breathing. "Not a day goes by that my thoughts and those of Lady Bird and the girls are not with you," Johnson wrote to Russell on February 11. Throughout Russell's hospitalization, Johnson phoned Walter Reed almost every day and received periodic reports on Russell's condition from his aides. "I lean on you so much, Dick," Johnson wrote, "and not having you where I can talk to you is an unfillable void."

Russell's extended absence from the Senate—he would not return to work in Washington until May 24—only fueled speculation that he would not run again in 1966. Rumors abounded in Washington and in Georgia that Russell might not recover, or that Governor Carl Sanders would challenge him for reelection. "I am sure you and the president are well aware of the implications of anything incapacitating happening to Senator Richard Russell," *Atlanta Constitution* editor Ralph McGill wrote to White House aide Jack Valenti on February 11. "This would immediately produce the crisis in southern political leadership that might be an opportunity to loosen it up a bit now that Strom Thurmond is out of it."* McGill hastened to add that he was not "indulging in any wishful thinking."

Although Russell would eventually recover and move aggressively to head off any challenge to his Senate seat, his impact on the voting rights debate would be negligible. His illness aside, it is difficult to imagine how even a healthy Russell could have altered the dynamics of the debate over an immensely popular bill. In truth, Russell no longer exercised a disproportionate influence on most legislative questions; his voting record on major issues now placed him outside the Senate's mainstream. In the previous two years, for example, he had voted against a host of successful Johnson administration proposals besides civil rights, including the nuclear test-ban treaty, the War on Poverty bill, the Manpower Training Act, tax reduction legislation, federal aid to higher education, and a wheat deal with Russia. In Russell's absence, southern leadership had fallen to Allen Ellender, the seventy-five-year-old senator from Louisiana who was the most senior southerner after Russell. Although colleagues respected Ellender for his intelligence and integrity, in the end he would provide the same unimaginative and purely defensive leadership that had characterized Russell's efforts in 1964.

Passage of the Civil Rights Act of 1964 had left the southerners reeling. Now, just as they had begun to recover, Johnson and the Senate's liberals came charging again with an extremely popular voting rights measure. "The Senate is like the South after Grant took Richmond," a liberal senator told the *Saturday Evening Post* in March. "The southern generals are still brilliant, but their troops are old and tired, and there simply aren't enough to go around."

The liberal Democratic ranks had grown by two seats in the 1964 elections; Democrats in the Senate now held a 68-32 advantage over Republicans, their largest margin since 1940. Unlike their aging southern conservative counterparts, the liberals had energized their ranks with the addition of young men in their 30s—Edward Kennedy of Massachusetts, 33, and Joseph Tydings of Maryland and Birch Bayh of Indiana, both 37.

A particular cause of the southerners' gloom was the cloture triumph of 1964. The filibuster's absolute failure had crippled their ability to mount another offensive against civil rights in 1965. Russell believed, in

*Thurmond had switched to the Republican party in September 1964.

the words of one friend, that once the southerners had "lost their virginity," cloture would be easily repeated in 1965. That sentiment was echoed by an aide to a southern senator, who candidly explained to the *Wall Street Journal*, "They're tired. Many of them have been sick. And the civil rights fight last year really took the heart out of most of them."

Adding to the southerners' helpless distress was the way that Johnson's brilliant speech energized the supporters of a strong voting rights bill. Typical was the review of journalists Rowland Evans and Robert Novak, who called it "the best, most genuinely moving speech" that Johnson had made as president. The speech "had been a summons and a sermon," historian Doris Kearns observed. "It had been that rare thing in politics, rarer still for Lyndon Johnson—a speech that shaped the course of events." Eloquently written and brilliantly delivered, the speech capitalized on the powerful emotions that Selma had generated. In only forty-five minutes, Johnson transformed the nation's raw outrage over violence in Alabama into an undeniable determination to secure— with powerful legislation—the voting rights of all Americans.

The guardians of the Old South were further disturbed by a growing apostasy in their own ranks. Louisiana's Russell Long, elected to succeed Humphrey as Democratic whip, signaled that he might find the courage to support the bill. On March 17, the morning after attending a private party at which Long was present, White House aide Jim Jones informed the president that Long had "spoke[n] in strong support of the Voting Rights bill (although he said he would work for some amendments)." Long suggested he could persuade eleven of twenty-two southern senators to support the bill, and, Jones reported, "he will carry these eleven votes into the Southern caucus in hopes of thwarting a big filibuster attempt." At least two other erstwhile civil rights opponents, George Smathers and J. William Fulbright, appeared to have little stomach for a spirited filibuster. Even Harry Byrd, Virginia's venerable segregationist, seemed to lose his zest for the fight. Asked by *Newsweek*'s congressional reporter, Samuel Shaffer, if he would participate in the southern filibuster, Byrd replied, "Yes, I'll have to do my part, but you know you can't stop this bill. We can't deny the Negroes a basic constitutional right to vote."

As Byrd's extraordinary statement demonstrated, the southern reflex to oppose all civil rights legislation usually overpowered their professed loyalty to the Constitution. Even though they opposed the bill—on Constitutional grounds, they argued—most southern senators were never fond of fighting voting rights legislation. "It simply was not a respectable argument to make [that blacks should not vote]," Attorney General Nicholas Katzenbach said, "and none made it." As *Newsweek* columnist Kenneth Crawford had observed, southern senators realized that "slobbish deputies have supplanted colorful orators as symbols of Dixie . . . Bad conscience about the trickery by which Negroes have been kept away from Southern polls has had a disquieting effect even on some who remain unreconciled to equal access to public accommodations and other concessions to Negroes."

On March 18 Mike Mansfield asked the Senate to refer the voting rights bill to the Judiciary Committee with instructions to report it by April 9. "That is a pitiful thing," complained John Stennis before the vote, "if we really mean to study a proposal of this magnitude." Judiciary chairman James Eastland, whose committee had never willingly reported a civil rights bill, unwittingly provided the Senate ample reason to impose Mansfield's deadline. "Let me make myself clear," Eastland declared. "I am opposed to every word and every line in the bill." Later that day senators voted 67-13 to give Eastland's committee no more than fifteen days to return with a bill. Despite its chairman's vehement opposition, there was little doubt that the committee—which now included a solid, influential bloc of nine liberals—would favorably report the legislation.

Meanwhile in the House, Attorney General Katzenbach began his testimony for the legislation, telling the Judiciary Committee that the administration bill represented a "new approach, an approach which goes beyond the tortuous, often ineffective pace of litigation . . . a systematic, automatic method to deal with discriminatory tests, with discriminatory testers, and discriminatory threats." Although some Republicans complained that the bill was too narrow to eradicate small pockets of voter discrimination, Chairman Celler was now in firm control of his committee. Applying the lessons of his near-debacle in committee the previous year, he now said he would not allow the bill to become "freighted down" with amendments that might jeopardize its passage. Despite Celler's concerns, House passage was inevitable. Following the 1964 elections, the Democrats now controlled 295 seats to the Republicans' 140—an advantage of 155 seats and the largest Democratic majority since 1938.

Three days later, on March 21, Martin Luther King and thirty-four hundred followers embarked on the first leg of a four-day, fifty-four-mile march from Selma to Montgomery. The marchers—protected by a thousand U.S. military police, nineteen hundred federalized Alabama National Guardsmen, U.S. marshals, and FBI agents—arrived in Montgomery on Thursday, March 25. As they converged on the Capitol grounds for a massive rally, Governor Wallace cowered in his office. He reneged on a promise to meet with a small group of demonstrators. Instead Wallace meekly peeked through his tightly shut Venetian blinds and muttered to aides, "That's quite a crowd." King, in his speech, reminded the marchers that they had overcome powerful odds in their trek to Montgomery. "And there were those who said that we would get here only over their dead bodies, but all the world today knows that we are here and that we are standing before the forces of power in the state of Alabama, saying 'We ain't goin' let nobody turn us around.' "

In Washington the Senate and House Judiciary committees quickly put their imprints on the voting rights bill. Remarkably, both panels approved bills that were much stronger than the original administration version. In the Senate the Judiciary Committee added a ban on poll taxes in state and local elections and an additional trigger mechanism that would authorize the appointment of federal voting registrars in states or voting districts where fewer than 25 percent of eligible minority citizens were registered. The Senate committee did, however, weaken the bill slightly in other areas. At Dirksen's behest, and with administration support, Judiciary members narrowly voted to permit states with literacy tests and low turnout to escape from the bill's automatic trigger mechanism if less than 20 percent of their voting-age population was nonwhite. Dirksen also persuaded the committee to exempt a state or locality from the bill if its voting participation in the most recent presidential election exceeded the national average *or* at least 60 percent of the voting-age residents were registered. This provision meant that the bill would not apply to any state or political district outside the South. Some liberals found this particularly bothersome. They argued—accurately, it turned out—that more crafty southern states might try to release themselves from the bill's grip simply by increasing their white registration. Another Dirksen amendment changed a provision that would have allowed states and counties to exempt themselves from the bill by persuading a three-judge court in Washington that they had not practiced discrimination during the preceding ten years. Dirksen insisted on reducing that time by half.

Dirksen's negotiations over the bill's specifics differed from his 1964 effort in one significant respect: This time, after the events in Selma, the Republican leader's ultimate support for the voting rights bill had never been in doubt. At first he had discounted the need for a voting rights bill, believing that the provisions of the 1964 act were sufficient. But the brutality of authorities in Alabama shocked and deeply offended him. After Selma he told his aides that he would support "revolutionary" legislation to guarantee the right to vote. Initially Dirksen recoiled from the idea of sending federal registrars into the South, preferring more aggressive enforcement through the federal courts. Yet he kept an open mind, conferring often with Johnson and Katzenbach while Justice Department attorneys drafted the bill in February. "My real concern," Dirksen said, "is not to put anyone in jail, but to get people to vote." Finally Dirksen acknowledged that many federal courts in the South could not be trusted to enforce the law. He reluctantly agreed to support the registrar provision, but only if the bill called them "examiners" and only if the trigger provision applied to just seven Southern states.

Dirksen's approach to voting rights was strikingly similar to his negotiating style throughout the civil rights debate of 1964. Joined by aides to Mansfield, Justice Department officials engaged in intense negotiations with several Dirksen aides, including his chief representative, Neal Kennedy. For days the group reviewed "every line of the bill" in response to the many questions that Kennedy raised for Dirksen. Ultimately the administration yielded little of substance. Rather, as one Justice Department participant observed, the tedious negotiating process primarily permitted Dirksen "to come forward with a changed bill so that he could justify to his party moving from a skeptic position, or an opposition position, to a supporting position." Attorney General Nicholas Katzenbach later remembered Dirksen's role less charitably: "He was demonstrating his power. [He believed that] he was the important guy, you needed him. It was something of an ego trip." Dirksen of course saw his own role in the most favorable, altruistic light. He quoted Abraham Lincoln to justify his evolution from civil rights opponent to one of its most vocal champions: "The dogmas of the quiet past are inadequate to the stormy present. The occasion is piled high with difficulty and we must rise with the occasion. As our case is new so must we think anew and act anew."

While he tinkered with the bill at its margins, Dirksen was genuinely concerned about two provisions. He wanted to restrain the bill's power to dispatch voting registrars to the South, and he worried about the constitutionality of its poll tax provision. On the poll tax question, John-son, Mansfield, and Katzenbach shared Dirksen's concerns. They feared the negative consequences in the South if the Supreme Court eventually ruled that Congress could ban poll taxes only by constitutional amend-ment. Congress had previously taken that route in 1962, when it passed an amendment banning poll taxes in federal elections. There were also Supreme Court precedents to consider. In 1937 and in 1951 the court had rejected the notion that poll taxes were de facto violations of the Fifteenth Amendment. In fact, not every state that imposed a poll tax (Vermont, for example) used it to exclude black voters. As Katzenbach wrote in a memorandum to Johnson:

> First, the ban is an invitation to persons not to pay these taxes. Should the Court hold the ban unconstitutional, thousands of first-time voters in Alabama, Mississippi and Virginia, who have been misled into failing to pay their taxes, may lose their vote in important State elections. The second danger is the very seriously damaging impact of a judicial declaration of unconsti-tutionality with respect to any portion of the Voting Rights Act of 1965.

On April 30 Mansfield and Dirksen offered a substitute for the Ju-diciary Committee bill. It became the Senate's pending business. Though very similar to the committee draft, the leadership proposal was different in two important respects. First, with Dirksen's reluctant approval, it eliminated the "escape clause" that would have released states from the bill's provisions when at least 60 percent of their adult residents were registered. Second, it dropped the poll tax ban. In its place, Mansfield and Dirksen inserted language authorizing the attorney general to ini-tiate "forthwith" court proceedings against enforcement of any poll taxes used in a discriminatory fashion.

The Senate's liberals generally favored the leadership bill. Michigan's Philip Hart, the only senator to have participated in the day-to-day negotiations between Justice officials and Dirksen's staff, argued that the bill "is stronger and better balanced than the original legislation sent to Congress. But it is our intention to improve it." That meant insisting on the poll tax ban, despite administration warnings that such an amend-ment might eventually render the bill unconstitutional. Even Humphrey could not reason with his former liberal colleagues; they remained de-termined to press for an amendment to restore the anti–poll tax provision. Led by Massachusetts freshman Edward Kennedy and New York's Jacob Javits, the liberals believed that the Judiciary Committee's outright ban was indeed constitutional. "There is no purpose in leaving this issue to the Supreme Court rather than seeking an act of Congress," Kennedy said, "if, admittedly, the congressional finding is to the effect that we believe, in 1965, that poll taxes have the effect of discriminating against many citizens and depriving them of their constitutional rights."

Dirksen was a notoriously flexible man. On the poll tax question, however, he refused to budge. He had already relinquished his "escape clause" provision during his negotiations over the leadership substitute. Now he declared flatly that if the bill contained a poll tax ban, "I would have difficulty going to any other senator and asking him to vote for cloture. Then it would be a fielder's choice. It would be every man for himself." Attorney General Katzenbach shared Dirksen's views on the poll tax issue and knew he could not afford to lose the minority leader's crucial support. "If we had not opposed the flat ban," he later explained to Johnson, "I believe Senator Dirksen, Senators Aiken and Prouty of Vermont, and other Republicans would probably [have been] lost for cloture. With only 45 Democratic votes, we could not prevail without these Republicans." Injecting himself into the Senate debate for the first time, Johnson announced that, although he sympathized with Kennedy and Javits, he supported Mansfield and Dirksen. "I have always been opposed to the poll tax," the president said. "I am opposed to it now. [But] I have been advised by constitutional lawyers that we have a problem in repealing the poll tax by statute."

Except for this one issue, the leadership commanded a solid majority of the Senate, as evidenced by the first vote on a southern amendment on May 6. North Carolina's Sam Ervin took direct aim at the heart of the bill—the automatic appointment of voting examiners—with an amendment to give federal district courts the power to authorize their appointment. The trigger provision, some southerners argued, invested too much power in the hands of the attorney general. "People shout about the powers of the Attorney General," Dirksen finally said in frustration. "I wish someone would tell me who in our form of government is to enforce the Constitution and the law if it is not the Attorney General. Will someone point to a law officer or to an administrator who is going to do it except the Attorney General?" The Senate rejected Ervin's amendment, 25-64. Only five southern Democrats, none from the Deep South, voted with the majority.

The vote was significant. It was an overwhelming endorsement by the Senate of the bill's toughest and most important provision. Ervin's crushing defeat meant that the southerners would have almost no hope of making substantive inroads into the bill. The absurd arguments that some of them made against the bill only worsened their dilemma. "I make the statement," Strom Thurmond solemnly declared to the Senate on May 3, "that no one in South Carolina is unconstitutionally denied the right to vote. There have been no valid complaints by anyone." Thurmond then claimed that the bill would result in "a totalitarian state in which there will be depotism and tyranny." James Eastland saw similar consequences if Congress enacted the bill. "This bill is the worst kind of tyranny," he said on May 6. "This bill and the civil rights bill passed last year are the most far-reaching acts in the history of this country. These bills are designed to destroy the culture and the civilization of a great people . . . Some say that this bill furthers democracy. The cold facts are that we are watching the sun set on human liberty and individual freedom in this country."

Little that the southerners could say, however, would hold much sway in the Senate in 1965. Although most of them would vote against Kennedy's poll tax amendment, the alternative was hardly more to their liking. After all, the issue was not *whether* Congress should completely abolish the poll tax. The only question was *how* would it do so? The irony of the southerners' situation—rejecting an outright ban in favor of an aggressive, congressionally mandated court challenge—did not escape Paul Douglas. On May 10 he wryly noted that many southerners "who would support the Mansfield-Dirksen position" were the same senators "who, in the past, have chided the Court for usurping legislative functions." These southerners, Douglas said, "are now saying that we should leave this legislative duty to the courts."

On May 11, with all but five southern Democrats voting with the leadership, the Senate rejected the Kennedy-Javits poll tax amendment, 45-49. Although Martin Luther King decried the Senate vote as "an insult and blasphemy," the matter was not yet resolved. The provision was still alive in the House. The following day the House Judiciary Committee reported a voting rights bill that included a ban on the poll tax as a voting requirement. A week later Mansfield and Dirksen moved to mollify the liberals by sponsoring an amendment, declaring that poll taxes did infringe on the constitutional right to vote. While still hoping that the final bill would contain an outright ban, Kennedy accepted the amendment. He admitted that "it does strengthen the poll tax section of the bill [and] will make the task of the Attorney General that much easier in the suits he is directed to bring." The amendment passed, 69-20.

In the Senate, at least, the way seemed clear to final passage. Yet southerners remained intransigent. Though not quite engaged in a full-fledged filibuster, they were determined to press ahead with scores of amendments—and they would take their time doing it.

On three occasions, Mansfield requested unanimous consent to speed up debate on the bill by imposing a one-hour time limit on each amendment. Each time Ellender objected. With seventy-one amendments pending or awaiting introduction, Dirksen became exasperated. "There are mountainous pieces of legislation still to come," he complained after the Senate rebuffed Mansfield's first request on May 12. His colleagues, he added, should begin preparing for a long session. In fact, he said sarcastically, senators "better start buying Christmas presents." By the time of his third request on May 19, Mansfield announced his intention to move forcefully to end debate. On May 21 he filed a cloture motion signed by thirty-eight senators. A vote was set for the following week.

On May 25, after rejecting more than a dozen weakening amendments offered by Sam Ervin and John Stennis, the Senate held a decidedly anticlimactic vote. Senators imposed cloture by a 70-30 margin. The feckless filibuster was over. It was the twenty-fifth day of debate and only the second time in the Senate's history that a filibuster of a civil rights bill had been stopped. Both had occurred within a year's time. Once cloture was assured, the southern opposition completely collapsed. "The way things are," said Ervin, one of the few southerners who had shown any enthusiasm for the debate, "I don't think I could even get a denunciation of the Crucifixion in the bill." A recuperated Russell, who had returned to the Senate on May 24, summed up the sentiment among southerners when he told *Time*, "If there is anything I could do, I would do it. But I assume the die is cast."

The next day, facing little opposition from the southerners, the Senate voted, 77-19, to send the voting rights bill to the House. Thirty Republicans joined forty-seven Democrats in support of the bill, but the South gave little ground. Three moderate southerners who had seemed ready to break with their diehard colleagues—Democratic whip Russell Long, former whip George Smathers, and J. William Fulbright—remained securely within the fold of the southern bloc. Only five marginal southerners—Ross Bass and Albert Gore of Tennessee, Fred Harris and Mike Monroney of Oklahoma, and Ralph Yarborough of Texas—supported the bill.

The House bill differed only slightly from the Senate-passed version, but there was one important difference: Liberals on the Judiciary Committee managed to restore the poll tax ban that the Senate had narrowly rejected. Although the committee formally reported the bill to the House on June 1, Rules Committee chairman Howard Smith promptly applied the brakes and delayed consideration of the bill for a month. When the House debate finally began on July 6, two prominent Republicans—Minority Leader Gerald Ford and Judiciary member William McCulloch—sparked what David Broder called "a major battle for political credit" among blacks and civil rights activists. Ford and McCulloch offered a much weaker substitute bill that did not ban the poll tax. It also replaced the automatic trigger for voting examiners with a milder provision authorizing examiners only after the attorney general received twenty-five or more complaints. Furthermore, the Republican measure did not ban literacy tests in states with low voting records, nor did it include the committee provision requiring a Washington court to approve all voting laws passed by the delinquent states. After House members rejected the Republican bill, 215-166, Johnson declared that the substitute "would have seriously damaged and diluted the guarantee of the right to vote for all Americans." In an angry response, Ford and McCulloch said that Johnson's past opposition to civil rights qualified him as a "Lyndon-come-lately" on the issue. "Lyndon Johnson," they said, "has traveled a crooked path" to become an advocate of civil rights legislation.

While moderates and conservatives had found the Republican amendment an attractive alternative to the administration bill, other House members were in no mood for the kind of protracted, bruising battle with the Senate that the Ford-McCulloch substitute threatened. Near-unanimous Republican support for the substitute bill had seemed assured until a July 7 speech by Virginia Democrat William Tuck, who argued that civil rights opponents should support the Republican bill. Fearing that the public would interpret their votes for the Ford-McCulloch bill as a vote against voting rights, at least fifteen Republicans threw their support to the Judiciary Committee bill. On July 9 the House overwhelmingly passed the voting rights bill—including the poll tax ban—by a vote of 333-85. In all, thirty-six southerners (thirty-three Democrats and three Republicans) supported the bill, including a former opponent of civil rights, Majority Whip Hale Boggs of Louisiana.

House and Senate conferees began their first meeting in an atmosphere of optimism. The only significant difference between the two bills was the poll tax question. But proposals by Dirksen and House Judiciary Chairman Celler to strengthen the Senate's poll tax provision did not satisfy House liberals. Meanwhile some House Republican conferees, hoping that the poll tax question would bring down the entire bill, were even less inclined to compromise. It was just this possibility of a bill-killing deadlock that brought liberals and civil rights leaders like Martin Luther King to their senses. Once they had derided the Senate bill as a sellout because of its weaker poll tax provision. Now reality began to set in. Disagreements over the poll tax, which was then employed to discriminate in only four states, were simply not serious enough to risk bringing down an otherwise strong and effective bill. "While I would have preferred that the bill eliminate the poll tax at this time—once and for all," King told Attorney General Katzenbach on July 28, "it does contain an express declaration by Congress that the poll tax abridges and denies the right to vote." King expressed confidence that the Senate's poll tax provision, if vigorously pursued by the attorney general, "will operate finally to bury this iniquitous device." The next day, with King's statement in hand, Katzenbach persuaded House liberals to yield to the Senate. Senate conferees responded by dropping several provisions to which the liberals objected, including one that exempted from the bill those areas whose voting-age populations were less than 20 percent nonwhite. On August 3 House members passed the conference report on the Voting Rights Act of 1965 in a lopsided vote, 328-74. The following day, after a perfunctory debate, the Senate adopted the report, 79-18. This time, six "southerners" supported the bill: Smathers, Bass, Gore, Harris, Monroney, and Yarborough. Only one Republican, Strom Thurmond of South Carolina, voted no.

Two days later, on August 6, a joyous Lyndon Johnson—"I would rarely see him happier," aide Joseph Califano later said—went to the Capitol to sign the Voting Rights Act of 1965. Speaking in the Capitol Rotunda before the signing, Johnson seized the moment to deliver another memorable and emotional speech:

Today is a triumph for freedom as huge as any victory that has ever been won on any battlefield. Yet to seize the meaning of this day, we must recall darker times.

Three-and-a-half centuries ago the first Negroes arrived at Jamestown. They did not arrive in brave ships in search of a home for freedom. They did not mingle fear and joy, in brave expectation that in this new world anything would be possible to a man strong enough to reach for it.

They came in darkness and they came in chains.

And today we strike away the last major shackle of those fierce and ancient bonds. Today the Negro story and the American story fuse and blend . . .

This law covers many pages. But the heart of the act is plain. Wherever—by clear and objective standards—states and counties are using regulations, or laws, or tests to deny the right to vote, they will be struck down. If it is clear that state officials still intend to discriminate, the federal examiners will be sent in to register all eligible voters. When the prospect of discrimination is gone, the examiners will be immediately withdrawn.

Under this act, if any county anywhere in this nation does not want federal intervention it need only open its polling places to all of its people.

Johnson told a national television audience and the assembled members of Congress that the attorney general would begin filing lawsuits the next morning. The Justice Department would challenge the constitutionality of Mississippi's poll tax and would officially begin to certify states where voting discrimination existed. By the following Monday, Johnson said, the Justice Department would begin designating "many counties where past experience clearly shows that federal action is necessary and required. And by Tuesday morning, trained federal examiners will be at work registering eligible men and women in ten to fifteen counties." On that day, he said, the Justice Department would file poll tax suits in Texas, Alabama, and Virginia.

And I pledge you that we will not delay or we will not hesitate or we will not turn aside, until Americans of every race and color and origin in this country have the same right as all others to share in the process of democracy.

But these new rights carried responsibilities, Johnson said:

Presidents and Congresses, laws and lawsuits can open the doors of the polling places, and open the doors to the wondrous rewards which await the wise use of the ballot.

But only the individual Negro, and all others who have been denied the right to vote, can really walk through those doors and can use that right and can transform the vote into an instrument of justice and fulfillment.

So, let me now say to every Negro in this country: You must register. You must vote. You must learn, so your choice advances your interest and the interest of our beloved nation. Your future, and your children's future, depend on it, and I don't believe that you are going to let them down.

Johnson directed his closing words to the nation at large:

The central fact of American civilization—one so hard for others to understand—is that freedom and justice and the dignity of man are not just words to us. We believe in them. Under all the growth and the tumult and abundance, we believe. And so, as long as some among us are oppressed—and we are part of that oppression—it must blunt our faith and sap the strength of our high purpose.

Thus, this is a victory for the freedom of the American Negro. But it is also a victory for the freedom of the American nation. And every family—across this great, entire searching land—will live stronger in liberty, will live more splendid in expectation, and will be prouder to be American because of the act that you have passed that I will sign today.

CHAPTER TWENTY-FOUR

Disillusionment and Defeat

THE EASY PART WAS OVER. Congress had finally enacted powerful legislation to guarantee the civil and voting rights of all black Americans. Enforcing those new rights would be difficult, but not as daunting as the task of creating and nurturing an economic and social environment in which black citizens could achieve the American Dream of economic independence and prosperity.

Johnson, who had long stressed the importance of economic rights for blacks, instinctively understood this. In June, even before the voting rights bill became law, he had ordered his aides to begin planning a White House Conference on civil rights, *To Fulfill These Rights*, for the following November. In a June speech at Howard University, Johnson announced plans for the conference and demonstrated the depth of his understanding of the nation's black underclass. There was, he said, "another nation" of blacks, "deprived of freedom, crippled by hatred, the door of opportunity closed to hope." Johnson declared that

> Negroes are trapped—as many whites are trapped—in inherited, gateless poverty. They lack training and skills. They are shut in slums, without decent medical care. Private and public poverty combine to cripple their capacities . . .
>
> Negro poverty is not white poverty. Many of its causes and many of its cures are the same. But there are differences—deep, corrosive, obstinate differences—radiating painful roots into the community, and into the family, and the nature of the individual.
>
> These differences are not racial differences. They are solely and simply the consequences of ancient brutality, past injustice, and present prejudice. They are anguishing to observe.

Most significant to Johnson was "the breakdown of the Negro family structure" and its dire consequences:

> For this, most of all, white America must accept responsibility. It flows from centuries of oppression and persecution of the Negro man. It flows from the long years of degradation and discrimination, which have attacked his dignity and assaulted his ability to provide for his family.
>
> This, too, is not pleasant to look upon. But it must be faced by those whose serious intent is to improve the life of all Americans.
>
> Only a minority—less than half—of all Negro children reach the age of eighteen having lived all their lives with both of their parents . . . The family is the cornerstone of our society. More than any other force it shapes the attitude, the hopes, the ambitions, and the values of the child. And when the family collapses, it is the children that are usually damaged. When it happens on a massive scale, the community itself is crippled.

Only five days after Johnson signed the Voting Rights Act, the violent, angry voice of the "other nation" of blacks was heard in Los Angeles. Six days of rioting in the city's Watts district resulted in 34 deaths, more than 856 injuries, 3,100 arrests, and $200 million in property damage. It took 15,400 California National guardsmen and 1,000 law enforcement officers to restore peace. When the mayhem died, entire city blocks were smoldering. An incredulous German reporter observed that the area resembled his native land "during the last months of World War II." The Watts riots were the worst racial disorder in American history. Meanwhile, in Chicago, two days of racial unrest resulted in 80 injuries and 123 arrests.

A minor police incident had sparked the Watts violence, but its root causes ran as deep as the geologic faults that traversed the southern California landscape. "The people don't feel so bad about what happened," one rioter later explained. "They had nothing to lose. They don't have jobs, decent homes. What else could they do?" As a heckler shouted at Martin Luther King, who came to inspect the riot's aftermath: "I had a dream, I had a dream—hell, we don't need no damn dreams. We want jobs."

At first Johnson reacted tentatively. "We must not let anger drown understanding," he pleaded. A frustrated public, however, demanded law and order. As long as helpless southern blacks were the victims of brutal white violence, they would enjoy public sympathy. Now that the angry demands of black rioters were drowning out the peaceful pleas of black protesters, widespread public support for civil rights was in jeopardy. In a matter of days, Johnson changed his tune. "Neither old wrongs nor new fears can ever justify arson or murder," he said in a speech. "A rioter with a Molotov cocktail in his hands is not fighting for civil rights any more than a Klansman with a sheet on his back and a mask on his face." Both, Johnson said, were "lawbreakers." Even as he condemned the violence, Johnson remained hopeful that his vision of a just American society would prevail. "In twenty fields or more, we have passed—and we will pass—far-reaching programs . . . that are rich in hope and that will lead us to a better day." Pounding the lectern, Johnson cried, "And we shall overcome, and I am enlisted for the duration."

In 1964 and 1965, Johnson had easily mustered a broad, bipartisan consensus to pass laws attacking what Harry McPherson called "observable cruelties"—voting and job discrimination and denied access to public facilities and accommodations. By 1965, however, the civil rights movement that Johnson had known had turned into something more volatile and dangerous. As McPherson told Johnson in June 1965, black leaders showed "more interest in discovering fresh fields for conquest than in making use of the franchise." Civil rights leaders marched "victoriously" out of the South toward new battlegrounds—the poverty-stricken tinderboxes that were the ghettos of large northern cities.

The new civil rights movement trained its eye on America's largely unobservable cruelties: poverty, joblessness, inadequate education, and poor nutrition and health care. Martin Luther King, still a giant of the movement, was challenged on his left flank by more militant leaders such as Malcolm X (assassinated in early 1965), Elijah Muhammad, Floyd McKissick, and Stokley Carmichael. Each was better attuned than King to the frustrations and rage of young urban blacks. The ascendancy of these new leaders, coupled with the success of the civil rights and voting rights acts, presented King and his movement with what one civil rights historian termed "the crisis of victory." King's movement, Adam Fairclough observed, "had no program or plan for translating the notional equality of the law into the social actuality of shared wealth and power."

The result was that the almost-magical convergence of public support and congressional will on civil rights would never be so easily duplicated. Urban riots and growing black militancy began to chill the hearts of many northern whites, once so sympathetic to the plight of southern blacks. A Gallup Poll in late 1966 showed that more than half of white Americans believed that President Johnson was moving too quickly on racial integration. By 1966 a civil rights bill that prohibited racial discrimination in the sale and rental of private housing ran into trouble in the Senate after passing the House. Erstwhile civil rights supporter Everett Dirksen, insisting that the housing provision was an unconstitutional invasion of private property rights, led the Senate opposition to the bill. Twice failing to muster enough votes to break cloture, the Senate adjourned without acting on the legislation—just one year after the overwhelming passage of the Voting Rights Act. Watts and other racial unrest, Harry McPherson later suggested, had done the damage by "justify[ing] the worst feelings of the racists in Congress and in the press."

In the South, meanwhile, the white backlash that Johnson and others had predicted began to emerge with a vengeance. Although blacks registered in record numbers and more than 150 now held elective office, the massive registration of new white voters offset much of the blacks' anticipated voting strength. Alabama's archsegregationist governor, George Wallace, was building a broad, loyal following beyond the South. As his strength in several primaries in 1964 had proved, many northern blue-collar whites shared Wallace's vehement opposition to civil rights. In Congress, meanwhile, the midterm elections of 1966 hit the Democratic party hard. The party lost forty-seven seats in the House and four in the Senate.

One Democratic victim was Paul Douglas. His distinguished Senate career ended in defeat at the hands of his youthful Republican challenger, millionaire businessman Charles Percy. Exploiting Douglas's principled support of open housing and other civil rights legislation, Percy appealed to white voters who were shocked by racial violence and fearful that their neighborhoods would be invaded and degraded by swarms of black tenants and homeowners. Refusing to modify his position on fair housing, Douglas became the only incumbent senator not reelected in 1966.

Despite the growing complexity and volatility of the nation's racial problems, Johnson remained persuaded that he could legislate a better America. "I don't think there was ever a president that was more of an activist than Johnson," Congressman Emanuel Celler declared shortly after Johnson left the White House in 1969. Like many other members of Congress, Celler believed that the nation had undergone a unique and exhausting experience during Johnson's five-year presidency. "I don't think there was any president that could have driven—I used that world advisedly—driven the Congress as hard as he did."

The legislative record of Johnson's early presidency was remarkable: Johnson presented the Eighty-ninth Congress (1965-66) with 200 legislative proposals. Congress enacted an incredible 181, including civil rights, voting rights, Medicare, aid to education, aid to Appalachia, clean air, water pollution control, aid to small businesses, a military pay increase, community health services, child nutrition, rent supplements, highway safety, mine safety, tire safety, and a minimum wage increase. "He would lie, beg, cheat, steal a little, threaten, intimidate," *Time* correspondent Hugh Sidey recalled. "But he never lost sight of that ultimate goal, his idea of the Great Society."

In the months after Johnson signed the Voting Rights Act, the administration moved decisively to enforce the law. By early 1966, federal examiners had registered more than 100,000 blacks in Alabama, Louisiana, Mississippi, and South Carolina. More than 200,000 new voters were registered in other states and districts covered by the act. In three separate decisions in 1966, the Supreme Court rejected South Carolina's constitutional challenge of the bill's formula for triggering voting examiners; prohibited all uses of the poll tax; and affirmed the bill's provision that guaranteed the vote to non-English-speaking citizens educated in schools under the American flag.

Johnson also labored to place blacks in important positions in the judiciary and in his administration. His most prominent appointment came in 1967, when he nominated Thurgood Marshall, the former NAACP lawyer and U.S. Solicitor General, as an associate justice of the Supreme Court. In all, Johnson appointed eighteen blacks to the federal bench. Black appointees to his administration included Clifford Alexander, White House deputy counsel and later chairman of the Equal Employment Opportunity Commission; Robert Weaver, secretary of Housing and Urban Development; Andrew Brimmer, assistant secretary of Commerce and member of the board of governors of the Federal Reserve System; Patricia Harris, ambassador to Luxembourg; Carl Rowan, director of the United States Information Agency; and Roger Wilkins, director of the Community Relations Service.

The ease with which the president enforced the Voting Rights Act

and appointed blacks to top government positions was not always rep-
licated in the larger civil rights arena. The daunting task of implementing and enforcing the myriad provisions of the Civil Rights Act of
1964 soon became an unmanageable burden. Unfortunately for Hubert
Humphrey, the tangled enforcement of civil rights laws would nearly
destroy his effectiveness as vice president.

Worse, it almost ruined his sixteen-year friendship with Johnson.

Humphrey believed that he would establish a new standard of usefulness and influence for the vice presidency. Johnson, after all, could
not help recalling the misery and isolation he himself had endured under
Kennedy. He knew how a vice president's valuable talents could be, and
often were, wasted. Surely, Humphrey thought, Johnson would work to
create a refreshingly different relationship with his vice president.

In the early days of the administration, at least, Humphrey's assumption proved correct. At Johnson's request, Humphrey examined the
federal government's civil rights enforcement efforts and advised the
president to consolidate them under one umbrella. Johnson agreed. In
February the president signed an executive order creating a new White
House entity, the President's Council on Equal Opportunity. The vice
president would chair the council and coordinate the administration's
civil rights and antidiscrimination policies.

Just as Humphrey appeared to have secured a vital role on Johnson's
team, he fumbled the ball. In February 1965 he lost Johnson's confidence
in an embarrassing disagreement over the president's decision to launch
a sustained bombing of military targets in North Vietnam after Viet
Cong forces had assaulted a U.S. military compound, killing nine Americans and wounding seventy-six others. As Johnson prepared to drastically escalate U.S. involvement in the Southeast Asian conflict, he
convened the National Security Council to discuss the decision. Believing he had the support of Secretary of State Dean Rusk and Secretary
of Defense Robert McNamara, Humphrey spoke up. He opposed escalating the war. And he strongly urged Johnson to delay his decision.
However, Rusk and McNamara failed to voice their support of the vice
president. Humphrey was not only isolated in his opposition to the
president's decision, but he had broken with Johnson in the presence of
others. Johnson was furious with what he believed to be Humphrey's
open betrayal. The consequences were severe. "He was frozen out,"
recalled aide Ted Van Dyk, "really sent to purgatory for a full year."
While he could not prohibit Humphrey from attending National Security

Council meetings, Johnson began to exclude him from other informal gatherings where he made the most important foreign policy decisions.

Although Humphrey was demoralized, at least he had civil rights responsibilities—thus far, the central issue of the Johnson administration—to occupy his time. Yet in August, doubting Humphrey's determination and toughness to forcefully enforce the 1964 law, Johnson cruelly stripped Humphrey of those responsibilities. Johnson "knew he had the guts, the toughness, and ability to endure the pain that a civil rights revolution would inflict," domestic policy advisor Joseph Califano explained, but the president "wasn't sure that Humphrey did." However, Attorney General Nicholas Katzenbach believed Johnson's motivation was simply an outgrowth of his personality. "He wanted to get all the credit himself," Katzenbach said later.

Almost before Humphrey knew what had happened, Johnson summarily abolished the two committees that Humphrey chaired—the Committee on Equal Employment and the Council on Equal Opportunity. Johnson transferred responsibility for enforcing the prohibition of discrimination in federally funded programs to the Justice Department. He shifted other enforcement activities to appropriate departments or agencies. To the press and the public, the whole thing was Humphrey's idea. Johnson even instructed Califano to draft a memorandum recommending the changes—and ordered him to obtain Humphrey's reluctant signature. "Johnson was really a sadist," said Humphrey's friend Edgar Berman, adding that "it was a little masochistic of Humphrey to take this." Had Humphrey enjoyed a better relationship with Johnson at the time, he might have averted what Califano viewed as a castration. Instead, aide John Stewart said, "Humphrey was left standing around looking like a damn fool." Van Dyk and Katzenbach maintained that Humphrey could have successfully challenged Johnson's decision but lacked the courage or fortitude. "Humphrey, fatally, never stood up to him," Van Dyk said.

Humphrey endured other affronts. Johnson fumed whenever Humphrey received favorable press coverage. Johnson repeatedly refused Humphrey's requests to take reporters with him when he traveled. He insisted on personally approving the manifest of Humphrey's plane before each trip. Johnson blamed most leaks from the White House on Humphrey. "That goddam Humphrey," Johnson protested to his staff, "he'll say anything to anybody." Van Dyk and others even suspected that Johnson tapped Humphrey's office phones, a consequence of the president's doubts about Humphrey's discretion. "We were never fully trusted," Van Dyk said.

Humphrey never complained to Johnson over these and other indignities. "Humphrey found it very difficult to stand up and really let fly his opinions, if they were opposed to those of Johnson," Harry McPherson observed. "In a nose-to-nose encounter, he was simply outmatched." But, as McPherson quickly added, "so was everybody else, for that matter. Very few men in our time have been able to stand up and face down Lyndon Johnson." Walter Heller, a Humphrey friend and chairman of Johnson's Council of Economic Advisors, blanched at Johnson's casual abuse of Humphrey. "LBJ treated him like a staff sergeant might treat a private. I was just appalled. I was embarrassed." Yet Johnson's brutal treatment of Humphrey was not constant. There were extended periods of harmony and friendship between the two men. And Humphrey did have Johnson's ear on several important issues. As Humphrey's chief of staff, William Connell, explained, with Johnson "it was either a bear hug or a kick in the ass."

Humphrey's banishment from the center of civil rights enforcement did not, in itself, hinder the effective administration of the Civil Rights Act's fair employment provisions. It can be argued that Humphrey—a poor administrator served by a weak staff—could never have effectively coordinated and directed the many-faceted aspects of civil rights that Johnson initially placed at his command. Yet the subsequent enforcement arrangement devised by Johnson, Califano, and other White House and Justice Department officials was far from exemplary. Civil rights enforcement was disassembled like an automobile engine; its interlocking parts were distributed among various government departments and commissions. For example, the White House gave responsibility for federal employment practices to the Civil Service Commission but then handed the oversight of contract compliance to the Labor Department. Meanwhile the President's Committee for Equal Opportunity in Housing, the Community Relations Service, and the U.S. Civil Rights Commission all fell into various states of disuse or outright irrelevance.

Almost a year after passage of the Civil Rights Act, Johnson—now preoccupied with the Vietnam War, foreign affairs, and various domestic issues—had not named a chairman for the Equal Opportunity Employment Commission. The commission foundered before it set sail. Johnson's eventual nominee, Franklin D. Roosevelt, Jr., was a monumental disappointment. Uninterested and ineffectual, Roosevelt devoted more time to yachting than to the important business of enforcing the nation's fair employment laws. A painfully long search for his successor followed his resignation in the spring of 1966. By the end of its first year, an ineffective, overworked, and underfunded EEOC had received almost nine thousand fair employment complaints and strained under the weight of a six-month backlog of three thousand cases.

In 1966 Johnson finally brought Humphrey out of the White House deep freeze and bestowed on him the dubious honor of leading spokesman for the administration's controversial Vietnam policy. To biographer Carl Solberg, the period was "the most startling chapter in Humphrey's life." In February, on a fourteen-day trip to nine Asian countries, including South Vietnam, Humphrey abruptly changed his view of the war and overcame his previous doubts about U.S. involvement. By the time he returned to the warmth of Lyndon Johnson's embrace, Humphrey had become one of the loudest, most enthusiastic supporters of the president's war policies.

Having discovered that the path to Lyndon Johnson's favor went through Vietnam, Humphrey went overboard in his support of the war. "We went through almost a full year from mid '66 to mid '67 in which he would make the most outrageous, off-the-cuff statements," said Ted Van Dyk. "It was almost as if we were going to stop the yellow communist horde in San Francisco." Suddenly Humphrey found himself more in agreement with belligerents such as Russell Long, Strom Thurmond, and Richard Russell than with his old liberal allies. His abrupt emergence as a hawk shocked many of his friends. "I never expected," Oregon's Wayne Morse remarked, "my vice president to make this plea for war." A group of liberal writers declared that Humphrey had "betrayed the liberal movement."

As much as Vietnam reinvigorated Humphrey as vice president, it eventually destroyed Johnson's effectiveness as president. Increasingly distracted by America's deadly descent into the morass of Southeast Asia, Johnson left much of his domestic program open to attacks by conservatives, many of whom—ironically—strongly supported his Vietnam policy. By the end of 1968, conservatives in Congress would scale back Johnson's poverty, rent supplement, and model cities programs and impose stringent spending restraints on much of the budget's domestic side. As Johnson insisted in a 1970 interview:

I knew from the start that I was bound to be crucified either way I moved. If I left the woman I really loved—the Great Society—in order to get involved with that bitch of a war on the other side of the world, then I would lose everything at home. All my programs. All my hopes to feed the hungry and shelter the homeless. All my dreams to provide education and medical care to the browns and the blacks and the lame and the poor. But if I left that war and let the Communists take over South Vietnam, then I would be seen as a coward and my nation would be seen as an appeaser and we would find it impossible to accomplish anything for anybody anywhere on the entire globe . . .

Once the war began, then all those conservatives in the Congress would use it as a weapon against the Great Society. You see, they'd never wanted to help the poor or the Negroes in the first place. But they were having a hard time figuring out how to make their opposition sound noble in a time of great prosperity.

Vietnam and the Great Society were, in the words of Johnson's old friend Virginia Durr, the "horror of the dichotomy" of his presidency. "All the people who were for him on the civil rights issue were against him, mostly, on the war issue. All people who were for him on the war issue were against him on the civil rights issue." This cruel dilemma ensured that Johnson's presidency, in the end, could not succeed. The tragic war that Johnson would never win robbed his domestic initiatives of vital resources and crucial public support.

On the afternoon of Sunday, March 31, 1968, Johnson dropped by Humphrey's southwest Washington apartment for an unexpected visit. The president was scheduled to deliver a nationally televised speech that night in which he would announce a peace initiative and a reduction of the bombing in North Vietnam. Although Humphrey and Muriel were preparing to leave for Mexico City, Johnson told Humphrey that he should watch the speech. Then he handed Humphrey a copy of the text. As he reached the closing lines of Johnson's address, Humphrey turned white. Johnson would announce his decision not to seek reelection.

"Mr. President, are you really going to do this?"

"As of now," Johnson replied, "I am almost certainly going to."

Humphrey protested. "You can't just resign from office. You're going to be reelected."

Johnson said he believed he might have no other choice. "Hubert, nobody will believe that I'm trying to end the war unless I do that. I just can't get them to believe that I want peace."

There was another reason, Johnson explained. "This is a terrible strain," he said, "and men in my family have died early from heart trouble. I'd like to live a little bit longer."

The news was incredible. Almost everyone had assumed Johnson would run for reelection and would win the Democratic nomination, despite the discontent of his party's liberals. In February Minnesota senator Eugene McCarthy had finished a strong second behind Johnson in the party's New Hampshire primary. Four days later New York senator Robert Kennedy announced his candidacy for the nomination. "If I ever had any doubts about Johnson's running," old friend Jim Rowe had said, "I would have lost them the day Kennedy announced, because he is not about to turn the country over to Bobby."

That night, after outlining steps to de-escalate the war, Johnson made his stunning announcement. "I shall not seek, and I will not accept the nomination of my party, for another term as your president." In Mexico City, Humphrey wept as he listened to Johnson's final words on a radio in the American Embassy. The next morning, Russell—who had been warned about the bombshell announcement—said Johnson's withdrawal "prove[d] the sincerity of his overwhelming desire to end the war in Vietnam and bring peace to the whole world."

Johnson hoped that his magnanimous decision would begin a healing process for the nation. Four days later an assassin's bullet killed Martin Luther King, who had flown to Memphis to support a labor strike by the city's sanitation workers. King's death touched off an enormous wave of riots in at least 125 cities. The worst was in Washington, D.C., where ten people died in violence sparked by the death of America's best-known proponent of nonviolence.

Humphrey announced for the Democratic nomination on April 27. He declared that his candidacy would embody "the politics of happiness, the politics of purpose, and the politics of joy." Critics, and even a few supporters, ridiculed that ebullient, cheery rhetoric at a time when war, violent protest, and assassination were tearing the nation apart. But joy and optimism remained the center of Humphrey's political philosophy, even though the grueling campaign would test his temperament as never before.

In June Humphrey became the leading, perhaps the presumptive, nominee. Robert Kennedy, celebrating victory in the California primary, was assassinated at the Ambassador Hotel in Los Angeles. With Kennedy's death, prominent liberals and labor leaders gravitated toward Humphrey with one important reservation—many Americans still viewed him as the most outspoken advocate of Johnson's Vietnam war policy. Although he eventually captured the nomination at a riot-plagued convention in Chicago, Humphrey did little to give voters an idea of how his views on the unpopular war differed from Johnson's. He offered only an occasional flimsy promise of future independence from his president.

Much of the problem rested with Johnson's insecurities and over-bearing nature. He would tolerate no criticism of his policy within the administration, even if it meant handing the election to Republican nominee Richard Nixon. Johnson believed that any open break with Humphrey on Vietnam would not only embarrass the president but would endanger the delicate peace negotiations in Paris. Johnson quashed each of Humphrey's attempts to distance himself from administration policy, even insisting that the party platform affirm unequivocal support for Johnson's conduct of the war. In the words of one observer, Humphrey's problem "was that too many Americans regarded him as a Lyndon Johnson without the Texas accent." Johnson, on the other hand, seemed alternately ambivalent about and frustrated with Humphrey's candidacy. Johnson believed, correctly, that Humphrey had surrounded himself with advisors who wanted the vice president to renounce the president's Vietnam policies. "He could not understand why Hubert didn't renounce those advisors," Max Kampelman said. "He had, therefore, frequent doubts about Humphrey, occasional anger, and some bitterness."

Russell, meanwhile, was decidedly indifferent to Humphrey's candidacy. He would vote, as always, for the Democratic ticket, although he privately favored Nixon. Perhaps Russell's attitude was like that of his Louisiana Senate colleague, Russell Long, who confessed that when he pulled the lever for Democratic nominee George McGovern in 1972, he muttered a simple prayer: "Dear God, please don't let this man win."

Low on money and suffering from a poor campaign organization, Humphrey was locked in a tight race with Nixon and an increasingly popular independent candidate, former Alabama governor George Wallace. Down in the polls by as much as fifteen points, Humphrey and his advisors knew that he really had but one option. Calling for an end to the bombing in North Vietnam, his advisors believed, was the only way Humphrey could prevent the election from becoming a disastrous referendum on Lyndon Johnson's presidency. On September 30 Humphrey's financially strapped campaign scraped together $100,000 for a half hour of network television time in which Humphrey finally put some distance between himself and his president. While the statement was a separation from Johnson's policy, it was not a clear break. He did not say he would absolutely end the bombing; he was "willing" to consider it. "Hubert still wasn't willing to turn around far enough," said Utah senator Frank Moss. "He moved a bit—enough that the press could say he'd taken a step away." But the announcement was a far cry from total repudiation.

The result was that Nixon and Humphrey—both driving their campaigns down the political center lane—were virtually indistinguishable on the major issues, foreign and domestic. Humphrey was willing to stop the bombing. Nixon alluded to a secret plan to end the war. According to George Wallace, there was not "a dime's worth of difference" between them. Although Nixon beat Humphrey by less than half a million votes out of more than 71 million cast, Humphrey lost badly in the Electoral College. Wallace, in one of the strongest showings ever for a third-party candidate, carried five southern states: Arkansas, Louisiana, Mississippi, Alabama, and Georgia. Nixon carried every other southern or border state except Texas, which went for Humphrey by the narrowest of margins. In the Senate, Republicans were on the march. The party picked up five seats for a total of forty-two, their largest number since 1956.

Only four years earlier, Johnson had won in the largest landslide in presidential history. Now the American electorate turned its back on his would-be successor. Fifty-seven percent of voters cast ballots for Nixon or Wallace. Viewed in that light, the election was a deafening repudiation of Lyndon Johnson's administration. The dissolution of the solid Democratic South—which had begun in 1948 after Humphrey's civil rights platform plank sent many southerners into the arms of Strom Thurmond and the Dixiecrats—was now complete. How ironic that Humphrey, the ideological and legislative father of the Civil Rights Act of 1964, would fall victim to the very forces that he had unleashed twenty years earlier. Analyzing the returns in the South with astonishing prescience, journalist Theodore White saw nothing but doom and despair for the Democrats. "If the trend line continues, the Democratic Party may disappear as a national party which can rouse loyalties in every section of the nation," White wrote in *The Making of the President—1968.* "If the Democrats shrink to a ghetto vote in the South, they could become a party dominated by Northern labor unions, big-city minority blocs, and ideologues who control the new campus proletariat."

On election night, at least, Humphrey's "politics of joy" became the politics of despair. "Edgar," he said to his close friend Edgar Berman in the early morning hours of November 6, "I let so many people down." Now, he confessed, he understood how two-time Democratic nominee Adlai Stevenson must have suffered.

"But, Jesus," he sighed, "at least Stevenson lost to Eisenhower. I lost to Nixon."

Over the objections of a weakened southern bloc, Congress enacted the Civil Rights Act of 1968 in April. It was, Russell said, "another in a long line of legislation designed to apply almost exclusively to the South." Although the Senate had refused to end a southern-led filibuster in three successive votes in February and March, a compromise between liberals and Republican leader Dirksen led to a narrow vote for cloture on March 4.

The most important provision of the bill, and the major obstacle for southern conservatives, was its open housing provision. When the law was fully in effect by 1970, the federal government would prohibit discrimination in the sale or rental of about 80 percent of all housing units. Only private home owners who sold their dwellings without the services of a real estate agent were exempted from the law. The act also included criminal penalties for those who injured or interfered with someone exercising a specified civil right: voting, jury duty, participation in a government program, school or college attendance, or the enjoyment of a public accommodation. The bill's major nod to southern conservatives, sponsored by Strom Thurmond, was its antirioting provisions, which imposed criminal penalties for those who used interstate commerce, including the telephone, to incite or participate in a riot. Throughout the debate, Russell was only a minor figure. North Carolina's Sam Ervin led the southern opposition by offering an unsuccessful substitute amendment to the housing provision.

Still opposed to civil rights legislation, the seventy-year-old Russell had lost his enthusiasm for the fight. It was futile, he believed, to wage another bruising, all-out battle against the bill's almost-inevitable passage. He understood that most Republicans, eager to recapture the White House in the fall election, would support whatever compromise Minority Leader Dirksen might negotiate with the liberals. Once that compromise was reached, the small band of southerners could do little beyond advancing a handful of antirioting amendments.

For Russell, still chairman of the Armed Services Committee, the most pressing issue in his world became Lyndon Johnson's disastrous Vietnam war policy. Since 1954 Russell had strenuously opposed U.S. involvement in the former French Indo-China, convinced "that we would be bogged down in the jungle fighting the Chinese in their kind of war for the next 25 years." Once the war was on, Russell supported his president—although he urged Johnson to abandon his gradual approach to the conflict in favor of a massive military effort aimed at a quick resolution. "I started out as what they call a 'dove,'" he told *Reader's Digest* in 1966, "but history has turned me into a screaming hawk. I think we should bomb any and all targets in North Vietnam that contribute to the communist campaign of tyranny and aggression."

Russell delivered that advice to Johnson repeatedly: Win the war or get out! But his influence with the president was outweighed by Johnson's military advisors at the Pentagon, chiefly Defense Secretary Robert McNamara. "I know from experience," he wrote, "that when my advice is in conflict with McNamara's, it is no longer considered." To one of his sisters, Russell complained that Johnson "won't pay any attention to me." Even Johnson admitted that he sometimes disregarded Russell's counsel. "I don't always follow Dick Russell's judgment," the president told *Atlanta Constitution* reporter Wayne Kelley in 1968, "but I always get it." Unable to affect the outcome of the conflict, Russell—as de facto chairman of the Appropriations Committee—devoted himself to ensuring the war's proper funding. In time Russell's disillusionment over Johnson's embrace of civil rights only exacerbated his disgust over Johnson's war policies. According to aides, friends, and family, Russell became increasingly disillusioned with his old friend and protégé throughout the 1960s. At the heart of that disappointment was

Johnson's passionate embrace of civil rights, which culminated in 1965 when Johnson proclaimed, "We shall overcome!"

Russell told aides that Johnson had "stultified his convictions" on civil rights. Had he believed that Johnson's support for civil rights was the result of a genuine change of heart, he might have accepted the transformation. But, as Russell's old friend Luke Austin recalled, Russell maintained that "Johnson did this for political gain." (Russell must have forgotten that he helped Johnson enact the Civil Rights Act of 1957 precisely for the political purpose of helping his protégé win the Democratic presidential nomination.) Despite their many years of friendship, civil rights became a stumbling block in their relationship. Russell never told Johnson of his disenchantment. There was never so much as an argument over civil rights. Instead, Russell's affection for Johnson was gradually supplanted by his deep disappointment over the president's approach to civil rights, the Great Society, and the Vietnam War.* Nonetheless, Johnson apparently perceived Russell's disillusionment. According to Sam Ervin, Johnson once confessed to Russell, "I know I have been a disappointment to you." Russell, said Ervin, "didn't know what to say." Russell's discontent manifested itself in the manner he began withdrawing from Johnson toward the end of his presidency. Russell grew to dread his private visits with Johnson, complaining to aides that during private meetings Johnson often cried. "He just couldn't stand to be subjected to that kind of emotionalism," his press secretary, Powell Moore, recalled. When he could not avoid an Oval Office meeting with Johnson, Russell often invited a colleague, usually John Stennis, to accompany him.

Angered by something Johnson did or said, or disgusted with Johnson's refusal to heed his advice, Russell sometimes refused to speak to his old friend. "There were times when he just wouldn't take phone calls from Johnson," Proctor Jones recalled, explaining that Russell instructed his receptionist to tell the White House that Russell was out of his office. "In many ways," said Powell Moore, "they were like a couple of children who are close playmates. There would be times when they would be on the outs with each other, they'd hardly speak for ninety-

---

*In a 1970 television interview, Russell discussed the Great Society programs that he opposed. He complained that Johnson "made every conceivable mistake, almost, from the standpoint of administration and organization . . . Nobody can quarrel with the abolition of poverty, but instead of having just two or three organizations, with a minimum of components . . . every time he had a new thought, he created an entirely new organization" (*Richard Russell: Georgia Giant,* Cox Broadcasting, 1970).

day periods. And there were other times, I think, when he was going down there [to the White House] every week and that the president was calling him frequently."

Nothing, however, hastened the disintegration of Russell's friendship with Johnson more than a personal dispute that erupted in February 1968. The rift began innocently when Russell recommended an old family friend, Alexander Lawrence of Savannah, for nomination to the federal bench from Georgia's Southern District. The sixty-two-year-old Lawrence had sound professional credentials. A practicing lawyer for thirty-seven years, he was the former president of the Georgia Bar Association, current president of the Georgia Historical Society, and author of several books. But Lawrence's most useful credential was his friendship with Russell. Or so it seemed.

Trouble developed shortly after Russell sent his recommendation to Johnson. A speech that Lawrence had delivered to a women's group in November 1958 quickly returned to haunt him. In that speech, which had so impressed Russell that he later inserted it into the *Congressional Record*, Lawrence attacked the justices of the Supreme Court as threats to liberty for usurping their constitutional authority in school desegregation and other cases. Black and white civil rights activists in Georgia seized upon the speech as evidence of Lawrence's unwillingness to uphold the Constitution in civil rights cases. Said two Georgia NAACP officials in early April, "Mr. Lawrence clearly demonstrated his inability to accept or interpret the Constitution and Supreme Court decisions which are the law of the land." They urged Russell not to "unleash Mr. Lawrence on South Georgia." Concerned that the opposition to Lawrence might influence Attorney General Ramsey Clark's recommendation, Russell went directly to Johnson on May 4. He urged the president to send the nomination promptly to the Senate.

The situation placed Johnson in a quandary. He had given his attorney general wide latitude in the nomination process; moreover he did not wish to offend civil rights groups by nominating someone who might undermine the enforcement of civil rights laws in Georgia. "The president didn't want to cause any problem," recalled White House aide Larry Temple, "but he also valued the judgment and friendship of Senator Russell." Johnson told Clark, "If we come to the final conclusion that we can't appoint him, then we'll come to that conclusion. We'll cross that bridge. But if there's any way at all that we can posture this man in a way that he can be appointed without hampering the judiciary, without doing anything to undermine the judiciary, I want to do it. I want to appoint this man." Clark was doubtful that Lawrence's segregationist reputation could be rehabilitated, but he continued his investigation. Johnson, meanwhile, quietly met with the chairman of the American Bar Association committee that reviewed judicial nominees. He made an unusual request, asking the chairman to personally investigate Lawrence's qualifications.

On May 11 Russell's fears were realized. Clark informed him that he would oppose Lawrence's nomination. "To say that I was surprised, distressed and disappointed when the Attorney General told me he would not recommend Mr. Lawrence is expressing it mildly," Russell wrote in a four-page letter to Johnson on May 20. Lawrence was no racist, Russell argued. In fact, he said, Lawrence had vigorously attacked the Ku Klux Klan in 1950 when he headed the Georgia Bar Association. The opposition to Lawrence, Russell explained, came from "the extreme left." Then Russell made a rare personal appeal: Rejecting Lawrence "would, of course, be extremely embarrassing to me" because the recommendation "has been publicized and discussed over the entire state." As Russell reminded Johnson, "I have never made a personal appeal to you for a presidential appointment since you have occupied the exalted position of president of the United States." Now he was. He awaited Johnson's decision.

Showing little sympathy for Johnson, Russell complained privately to an *Atlanta Constitution* reporter that "Clark was running the president and that the president was holding up on an appointment that should have gone through." Russell's distaste for Clark had predated the controversy over Lawrence. When Russell had urged Johnson to arrest and prosecute militant civil rights activist H. Rap Brown for his open advocacy of violence, Johnson replied that Clark would not do so. Russell was disgusted. "Who is president? Are you president or is Ramsey Clark president?" Johnson may have shared Russell's low assessment of Clark. But his friendship with Clark's father, former Supreme Court Justice Tom Clark, complicated matters. In Russell's mind, the matter was simple: Johnson should override Clark's opposition and send Lawrence's nomination to the Senate. To bolster his case, Russell sent Johnson a list of prominent attorneys throughout the Southern District of Georgia who attested to Lawrence's qualifications. Several weeks later he mailed Clark a letter of endorsement signed by the former presidents of the Georgia Bar Association. "These men represent many different political philosophies and opinion," Russell said, "but they are unanimous in their opinion that Mr. Lawrence is peculiarly well qualified to serve as judge."

In early June Russell was still hopeful that Johnson would overrule Clark, but the attorney general continued to stall. He was, Larry Temple suspected, "intentionally dragging his feet." He knew that without more evidence than the 1958 speech, Johnson would eventually send Lawrence's name to the Senate. "I think Ramsey was sort of playing for another day," Temple suggested, "hoping that something would happen that would help him to persuade the president not to nominate this man. He felt very keenly about it."

By July, after a month of inaction on the nomination, Russell's hope turned to disgust. Clark's position, Russell wrote his friend Judge Griffin Bell of the Fifth Circuit Court of Appeals, "is unreasonable to the point of being vicious." As for the president, Russell said, "I have never been as disappointed in a man as I am in Johnson for being frightened by the prospect" of opposition from Georgia's civil rights activists. By now the controversy over Lawrence threatened not only Russell's friendship with Johnson, but the future of Johnson's two nominees to the Supreme Court.

On June 13 Earl Warren resigned as chief justice. Johnson quickly nominated a reliable liberal, his old friend Associate Justice Abe Fortas. He submitted the name of another longtime friend to fill the vacancy created by the elevation of Fortas—Homer Thornberry, a judge on the Fifth Circuit Court of Appeals and a former Texas congressman. Anticipating a certain amount of southern and conservative opposition to Fortas, Johnson obtained what he thought were commitments of support from Russell and Everett Dirksen.

But now Russell had second thoughts about his commitment to Johnson. Could it be, Russell wondered, that Johnson was holding up the Lawrence nomination as a form of blackmail to ensure his support for Fortas and Thornberry? On July 1 Russell sent Johnson an unusually spiteful letter reminding him that his recommendation of Lawrence was now more than four and a half months old. "From our conversations," Russell said, he was convinced that despite the attorney general's opposition "you would name Mr. Lawrence." Then he added:

> To be perfectly frank, even after so many years in the Senate, I was so naive I had not even suspected that this man's nomination was being withheld from the Senate due to the

changes expected on the Supreme Court of the United States until after you sent in the nominations of Fortas and Thornberry while still holding the recommendations for the nomination of Mr. Lawrence either in your office or in the Department of Justice.

Whether it is intended or not, this places me in the position where, if I support your nominees for the Supreme Court, it will appear that I have done so out of my fears that you would not nominate Mr. Lawrence.

Johnson, he suggested, was treating him "as a child or a patronage-seeking ward heeler." He now advised Johnson "that in view of the long delay in handling and the juggling of this nomination, I consider myself released from any statements that I have made to you" regarding the Supreme Court nominations. Furthermore, Russell said, "you are at liberty to deal with the recommendations as to Mr. Lawrence in any way you see fit." Russell ended the three-page letter with the over-wrought assertion that Lawrence and his family "have already been humiliated beyond what decent and honorable people should be required to bear at the hands of a motley collection of fanatics, mystics and publicity seekers." Before he mailed the letter, Russell summoned his Georgia colleague, Herman Talmadge, to his office. "He read me a hell of a mean letter," recalled Talmadge, who volunteered to cosign it. Although Russell declined his offer, Talmadge assured him, "Well, it will get results."

As expected, the letter shocked Johnson. Outraged, he immediately phoned Clark. "I think your foot dragging on this has destroyed one the great friendships I've had with one of the great men that has ever served this country," he said, adding, "Ramsey, I want to go ahead and nominate him." Strangely, Johnson did not immediately contact Russell. Instead he dispatched his assistant Tom Johnson, a Georgia native whom Russell admired. Tom Johnson reported that Russell believed Johnson was holding Lawrence until Russell announced his support of Fortas and Thornberry. Several days later, Johnson finally phoned Russell.

"Dick," Johnson began, "I have your letter here in my hand. I don't think this letter reflects creditably upon you as a statesman. I don't think it reflects very well on me as your president. I don't think it reflects very well on our long friendship." Johnson said he would not keep the letter in his files and would return it to Russell. "I hope you destroy it."* Furthermore, Johnson said, there was never a connection between the Supreme Court nominees and the Lawrence nomination. Johnson added that while he would nominate Lawrence, "it's not a quid pro quo. It wasn't when I first told you I was going to. It isn't now, and it isn't going to be." Regarding the Fortas nomination, Johnson advised, "You do whatever you want to on that, and I know it'll be the right decision."

Several weeks later, after the American Bar Association determined that Lawrence was highly qualified for the position, the White House forwarded his name to the Senate, which later confirmed him. Meanwhile the Fortas nomination fell on hard times. Hit with accusations of financial impropriety, Fortas saw his southern and Republican support evaporate. On September 26 Russell wrote to tell Johnson that "with deep regret" he would not support Fortas. In October, facing certain defeat in the Senate, Fortas withdrew his nomination.

From Russell's standpoint, the Lawrence incident destroyed his friendship with Johnson. Later that year, as Johnson prepared to leave the White House, Russell refused to join dozens of colleagues who paid tribute to the president. Only when urged by his staff did he approve a routine, lifeless statement about his old friend. About that time, Russell even refused to grant an interview to historians who were gathering reminiscences of Johnson for an ambitious oral history project sponsored by the Johnson presidential library.

Almost twenty years of friendship between two of America's most influential and talented public servants was lost in a cloud of mistrust and misunderstanding. On Johnson's part, vacillation and miscommunication were at fault. As for Russell, his pride, racial insensitivity, and an overactive imagination allowed a routine dispute to balloon to enormous proportions. For another two and a half years, until Russell's death in January 1971, Johnson tried to rebuild the remnants of their relationship. Russell rebuffed each of Johnson's attempts at reconciliation.

Shortly before Johnson left town in January 1969, he traveled to Capitol Hill one last time to deliver his State of the Union address. He took a moment in the speech to praise Russell, who had just been elected president pro tempore of the Senate. He had "avoided many pitfalls," Johnson told the Congress, by following Russell's "good common sense

---

*Despite Johnson's orders and his suggestion to Russell, copies of the letter were kept on file in the White House and by Russell's staff.

counsel." Although Russell was flattered, he refused to acknowledge Johnson's gesture. The kind remark, it seemed, had done nothing to repair their shattered friendship. As the two men parted, Russell's heart remained colder than the January nighttime air.

Their paths would never cross again.

Three men—their lives inextricably intertwined over several decades by politics, friendship, and civil rights—now shared something else in common. As they approached the ends of their extraordinary political careers, each endured the pain of rejection and defeat.

Russell, his thirty-five-year fight against civil rights at an end, mourned the passing of his beloved Old South and the disappearance of the Democratic party as he knew it. Humphrey's immense satisfaction with the passage of legislation he had championed for so long was transcended by the bitter sting of his defeat at Richard Nixon's hands. And Johnson, although largely responsible for the most important social legislation of the century, left the White House in dishonor—not in the bright sunshine of human rights, but under the dark clouds of a disastrous foreign war.

This Dynamic Symbol of Hope

DESPITE HIS CHRONIC EMPHYSEMA, Russell was an active man. By the late 1960s, however, his persistent health problems began to take their toll. In March 1969, doctors found a malignant tumor on his left lung. Although radiation treatments proved successful, his emphysema remained a constant affliction. Press secretary Powell Moore noted "a real deterioration" in his energies by 1970. "He started losing weight and just didn't have much motivation during that time." Sometimes Russell would dissolve into two- or three-minute coughing fits. "His face would turn purple," Herman Talmadge said, "and you'd think he was about to have a heart attack." Weakened by his failing health, Russell resorted to walking with the aid of a cane and finally began to move around the Senate in a motorized wheelchair. Oxygen tanks to help him breathe were on standby in his office and apartment.

On December 8, 1970, doctors admitted Russell to Walter Reed Army Hospital for the last time. Hoping to lift his spirits, President Richard Nixon came to give Russell a briefing on Vietnam. "He didn't want to talk about his sickness," Nixon recalled. "He didn't talk about himself. He never talked about himself; he talked about the country." As Nixon left, Russell told him, "I only wish I could get back down there so I could work."

On the morning of January 21, 1971, Russell's condition was grave. Yet his presence in the Senate was still powerfully felt. One of his last official acts had been to sign a proxy giving his vote for Democratic whip to Robert Byrd of West Virginia. Byrd believed that he had a tenuous hold on a majority of the Senate's fifty-five Democrats in his effort to unseat the incumbent whip, Edward Kennedy. The proxy might be crucial. If his Georgia colleague died before the vote, Byrd would run instead for reelection as secretary of the Democratic Conference. Shortly before the vote, Byrd got the word. Russell was still alive. Byrd nodded to his West Virginia colleague, Jennings Randolph, who rose to nominate Byrd for whip. Russell's proxy was cast, but Byrd had not needed his vote after all. He beat Kennedy in a 31-24 vote.

That afternoon at two twenty-five—conscious almost to the last minute of life and surrounded by several brothers and sisters—Russell died. He was seventy-three. He had served in the Senate for thirty-eight years.

The next morning a black hearse carrying Russell's body left for Andrews Air Force Base. His final trip to Winder would be aboard *Air Force One*. En route the hearse took a slight detour, turning onto the U.S. Capitol Plaza on the East Front. As the hearse halted at the Senate steps, Russell's sisters, Mary Green and Ina Stacy, were astounded and deeply moved by what they saw: Standing at attention on the marble steps, hands over their hearts, were at least sixty members of the U.S. Senate. It was an impressive and poignant farewell. When the hearse paused again in front of the House steps, Green and Stacy watched as the members of Georgia's House delegation stood in another silent tribute.

The next day, as Russell's body lay in state in the Georgia Capitol, President Nixon arrived to pay homage to his former Senate colleague. From Texas, Johnson expressed his sympathy in a telegram to Russell's nephew, Richard B. Russell III: "He was an uncommon man with an uncommon devotion to duty. He will be sorely missed. To quote a poet on another great leader, 'He fell like a kingly cedar tree and left a lonesome place against the sky.' "

Rain and heavy fog marred Russell's funeral the next day. The weather forced a large contingent of congressmen and senators led by Vice President Spiro Agnew to land their plane in Charleston, South Carolina. John Stennis and others delivered their eulogies in a hastily arranged television transmission. In a wooded area just behind the family home, Russell was buried in the family plot, near his father and mother.

On that cold, rainy afternoon, only two of Russell's former colleagues made it through the forbidding weather to pay their respects in person. One was Florida's freshman Democratic senator, Lawton Chiles, who had barely known Georgia's fallen giant. The other senator had known Russell well. Almost twenty-two years earlier to the day, Russell had ridiculed "that damn fool" from Minnesota. Now, with their many civil rights battles behind them, Hubert Humphrey came to honor his fallen adversary.

Johnson adapted to retirement slowly. Depressed at first—he was, after all, out of the limelight for the first time in more than thirty years—he gradually began to enjoy himself. He took great interest in the daily operations of his ranch, down to the number of eggs his hens laid each week. He worked on his memoirs and supervised the construction of his presidential library on the University of Texas campus in Austin. Meanwhile, according to his friend Abe Feinberg, he began smoking cigarettes again—"like a fiend."

In the spring of 1972, Johnson suffered another heart attack while attending the funeral of former Tennessee governor Buford Ellington. For the rest of his life, every day would be a constant battle with angina—intense chest pains that beset him most afternoons.

Johnson's last public appearance came in December 1972 at a civil rights symposium sponsored by the LBJ Library. Undeterred by an ice storm, the former president defied the orders of Lady Bird and his doctor and drove from the ranch to Austin. The gathering was a virtual Who's Who of civil rights: Hubert Humphrey, Earl Warren, Roy Wilkins, Clarence Mitchell, and Burke Marshall all attended.

But the spirit of unity that brought the participants to Johnson's symposium was soon threatened. Several black leaders demanded equal time to address the gathering and condemn the racial policies of the Nixon administration. As chairman of the meeting, Burke Marshall balked at their demands but worried that a threatened demonstration might mar the event. Johnson overruled Marshall. "Burke, I'm not really afraid of that demonstration. I've seen lots of them. I just don't want anybody to think that they haven't had a chance to speak."

When it came Johnson's turn at the podium, he startled delegates with his appearance. He walked slowly to the podium. His hair was long in back. He looked old and haggard.

"I do not want to say that I have always seen this matter—in terms of the special plight of the black man—as clearly as I came to see it in the course of my life and experience and responsibility," Johnson said. "Even if I could have known what lay ahead, I am not sure now that I could have believed at that time that the progress which has been won in these past ten years is a fact. Black Americans are voting now where they were not voting at all ten years ago." Blacks now had greater opportunities, Johnson said. "Black Americans are working now where they were not working ten years ago. Black Americans, Brown Americans—Americans of every color and every condition—are eating now and shopping now and going to the bathroom now and riding now and spending nights now and obtaining credit now and giving now and attending classes now and coming and going in dignity where and as they were never able to do in years before."

Nevertheless, Johnson insisted, the nation's work on civil rights had only begun. "So let no one delude themselves that our work is done," he said. "By unconcern, by neglect, by complacent beliefs that our labors in the field of human rights are completed, we of today can seed—can seed our future with storms that would rage over the lives of our children and our children's children."

Later, after some black attendees began fighting over whether they should endorse the National Urban League's call for a black summit with Nixon, Johnson unexpectedly went to the podium again. This time he appeared energized and stronger. He urged the delegates to give Nixon a chance. "I believe every man elevated to that high office, where he can go no farther, wants to do what he thinks is right," Johnson insisted. "And it's a lot easier to want to do what's right than to *know* what's right. That's the big problem. And some—some presidents, and I speak of myself particularly, had a learning process and we knew more when we left Washington than when we went there. And some of you men were patient and understanding and tolerant of me, as you feel people have not been tolerant of you." Johnson argued that Nixon "doesn't want to leave the presidency feeling that he's been unfair or unjust or unequal to his fellow man. *But knowing what's right is important . . .* So, get your priorities. See that what we've done, we don't lose."

Lyndon Johnson died less than six weeks later, on January 22, 1973. Alone in his bedroom at the ranch, he suffered a fatal heart attack. He was sixty-four.

Before his funeral at Washington's National City Christian Church, his body lay in state in the Capitol Rotunda, where thousands of mourners, most of them black, slowly filed past in silent tribute. A black woman accompanying her daughter paused for a moment in front of Johnson's flag-draped casket. "People don't know it," the mother quietly told her daughter, "but he did more for us than anybody, any president, ever did."

Defeat in the 1968 presidential election had sent Humphrey reeling. He had come *so* close. "My dreams and hopes," he later said, "were smashed in a year when so much more in America was destroyed." Returning home to Minnesota, Humphrey tried to keep busy. He taught political science at Macalester College and the University of Minnesota. The Encyclopaedia Britannica made him chairman of its education division and paid him a grand sum—$75,000 a year. He began writing a syndicated newspaper column and went on the speaking circuit, where he earned as much as $2,500 per speech.

Yet he was restless. He had not been in private life since 1945. Though he had declined Richard Nixon's offer to name him U.S. ambassador to the United Nations, Humphrey yearned to occupy public office again. In 1970 he got his chance. When Eugene McCarthy announced his retirement from the Senate, Humphrey jumped in the race—and won big. He was back. Despite his status—sixteen years in the Senate, four years as vice president, and his party's nominee for president—Humphrey was again a mere freshman in a body where seniority was king. He had influence but no power. He was an acknowledged expert on foreign affairs but was denied a seat on the Foreign Relations Committee.

Humphrey actually yearned for another shot at Richard Nixon. In 1972, sensing that the campaign of his 1968 running mate, Edmund Muskie, was faltering, Humphrey entered the race for the Democratic nomination. Although he won several primaries, the demons of 1968 remained too vivid. His loyalty to Lyndon Johnson and the Vietnam War haunted him, and he was no longer viewed as an authentic liberal. As Mel Elfin, *Newsweek*'s Washington bureau chief, later explained: "For the 'cool' generation of the '60s, Humphrey's frenzied pace, his sentimentality and, above all, his support of Lyndon Johnson's war in Vietnam turned him into an object of derision. He became 'The Hump,' the warmonger who put loyalty to LBJ above loyalty to principle. Forgotten were his service to civil rights, his creation of the Peace Corps, and his espousal of an agenda full of liberal causes." The nomination went instead to his Senate colleague, South Dakota's George McGovern, who later lost to Nixon in a landslide. Although Humphrey flirted with the idea of another run in 1976, he ultimately shrank from the prospect of a grueling primary schedule. His White House dream was, finally, over. He would run for reelection to the Senate.

Just when it appeared that he had no more battles to fight, fate presented Humphrey another daunting challenge. Shortly before the 1976 election, Humphrey learned that he had bladder cancer. The diagnosis was not an absolute surprise; doctors had treated him for precancerous polyps on his bladder since 1967. While the first signs of the disease had appeared in 1973, radiation treatments staved its growth. But this was different. Now doctors would remove his bladder. For a short while, Humphrey seemed to recover. As usual, his optimism was undimmed. "Oh, my friend," he explained, "it is not what they take away from you that counts, it's what you do with what you have left."

Returning to Washington with renewed spirit, Humphrey was eager to challenge incumbent Robert Byrd for majority leader. But when he tested the waters, Humphrey quickly determined that he could not win. Sensing that the cancer would soon claim his life, Humphrey's Democratic colleagues presented him with a consolation prize: He would serve as deputy president pro tempore of the Senate, a position created just for him. Besides the small perks of the office, the post gave Humphrey what he most wanted—a position in the Democratic leadership. President Carter would invite him to attend all congressional leadership meetings at the White House. Only a year earlier, as Humphrey contemplated another run for the White House, Jimmy Carter had disparaged his potential rival as a "has-been." In time Carter realized that he was nothing of the sort. Humphrey became one of the president's most valued advisors and supporters in the Senate.

In the late summer of 1977, an emaciated Humphrey returned to Minnesota for much-needed rest as the relentless cancer steadily destroyed his body. Surgery on an intestinal blockage revealed that the disease had now spread to his pelvis. His condition, the doctors told him, was terminal. The best medicine, they advised, was to surround himself with friends and colleagues.

On October 23, President Carter stopped in Minneapolis on *Air Force One* to bring Humphrey back to Washington. As his family said good-bye at the airport, Carter hugged his new friend. "Hubert Humphrey," the president said, fighting back tears, "is the greatest American that I know." After riding on the presidential jet, Humphrey joked, "Well, for at least twenty years I have been trying to get on *Air Force One*. I realize it was not a prolonged experience, but just the thought of it, the vibrations, gave me new hope and new strength."

Washington welcomed him back like the hero he was. The House and Senate unanimously passed legislation renaming the Health, Education and Welfare Department building after Humphrey. The House of Representatives invited him to deliver an address—the first time House members had ever so honored a sitting senator. To much laughter, he explained that he never ran for the House because "I found out that they have a two-minute or five-minute [speech] rule." Afterward, House members praised him generously. "You are," said Speaker Tip O'Neill, "the most genuine liberal this country has ever produced."

On October 25, as a dying Humphrey entered the Senate chamber for a final tribute, senators rose in five minutes of sustained, emotional applause. Even his old nemesis Strom Thurmond embraced him. "Some men attempt to alter the course of history or bend the direction of their era through thunder and threat," Majority Leader Robert Byrd said in the first of several tributes. "They launch armies, marshal forces, and foster plots. Hubert Humphrey has changed our own time through the impact of his personality, the exertion of his energy, the vibrance of his spirit, the exercise of his intellect, and the compassion of his heart. Consequently, he is a man whose influence will reverberate for generations, in America and around the world."

When it came Humphrey's moment to speak, his words moved many in the chamber to tears. Herman Talmadge later called it "the most emotional scene I would witness in my twenty-four years in Washington." As usual Humphrey laced his speech with humor and optimism. On this day, however, his weak voice also cracked with emotion. His eyes were misty. "My good friend, Senator [Dale] Bumpers, sitting alongside of me here said, 'This is just a little too much, isn't it, Hubert?' And I said: 'Hush. I like it.' " Then Humphrey turned serious:

Gentlemen, most of you know me as a sentimental man, and that I am. Today is a very special day in my life, not only because I feel strong enough to come to this historic Chamber, back to the U.S. Senate, the greatest parliamentary body in the world, but more significantly because of the genuine friendship and warmth that has been exhibited here today by my colleagues.

The greatest gift in life is the gift of friendship, and I have received it. And the greatest healing therapy is friendship and love, and over this land I have sensed it. Doctors, chemicals, radiation, pills, nurses, therapists, are all very, very helpful, but without faith in yourself and in your own ability to overcome your difficulties, faith in divine providence and with the friendship and the kindness and the generosity of friends, there is no healing. I know that.

Reminding his colleagues that detractors had often labeled him a "foolish optimist," Humphrey reaffirmed his confidence in America's future. "History is on my side," he said. "More people today are enjoying more of what we call, at least in the material sense, the good things of life in every form." Most important, he said,

> we are a heterogeneous population, and we are trying to demonstrate to the world what is the great moral message of the Old and New Testament; namely, that people can live together in peace and in understanding, because really that is the challenge. That is what peace is all about.
>
> It is not a question of whether we pile up more wealth; it is a question of whether or not we can live together, different races, different creeds, different cultures, different areas, not as a homogeneous people but rather in the pluralistic society where we respect each other, hopefully try to understand each other, and then have a common bond of devotion to the Republic . . .
>
> Now, my plea to us is, in the words of Isaiah, as a former president [Johnson] used to say—and I mean it very sincerely—"Come, let us reason together." There are no problems between the different points of view in this body that cannot be reconciled, if we are willing to give a little and share a little and not expect it all to be our way. Who is there who has such wisdom that he knows what he says is right? I think we have to give some credence to the fact that majority rule, which requires the building of an understanding and the sharing, at times the compromising, is the best of all forms of rule.

As Humphrey ended, he apologized to his colleagues. "Well, I got wound up," he said. "I did not intend to be that long, but that has been the story of my life."

On December 22, Humphrey returned to his Waverly, Minnesota, home for the last time, hitching a ride with his friend and protégé, Vice

President Walter Mondale. He spent his last days reaching out to friends and mending fences with old adversaries. On January 13, 1978, the cancer he fought so valiantly finally claimed his life. He was sixty-six.

Tributes poured in from all political corners. Richard Nixon called Humphrey a "dedicated patriot" who "commanded the genuine respect and affection of his political opponents and allies alike." Majority Leader Byrd said, "During any era, only a few men through their own efforts affect a profound and lasting change on human society. Hubert Humphrey was one of those men." Democratic congressman Paul Simon of Illinois added, "The life of every American—no matter how lowly or lofty his or her station—has been enriched by this dynamic symbol of hope who walked among us." *Newsweek* said, "Humphrey was the latest in a distinguished line of Senators, from Henry Clay and Daniel Webster to Robert La Follette and Arthur Vandenberg, whose impact on public life was greater than that of most presidents. He did not achieve his lifelong dream of the presidency, but he inspired and sustained the dreams of many others for a better America."

"He became the conscience of his country," Mondale said at the tearful memorial ceremony in the Capitol Rotunda attended by President Carter and former presidents Ford and Nixon. Later, at Humphrey's funeral service in Minnesota, the Reverend Calvin Didier prayed: "If he seems loquacious, be patient with him, Lord, as we have always been, because he most always has a good point."

Perhaps President Carter characterized Humphrey best of all: "From time to time, our nation is blessed by the presence of men and women who bear the mark of greatness and who help us see a better vision of what we can become. Hubert Humphrey was such a man."

Civil Rights Act of 1957
Summary of Major Provisions

TITLE I

Created a six-person executive Commission on Civil Rights whose members are appointed by the president subject to Senate confirmation.

Established rules for the commission, empowering it to investigate allegations of voting discrimination against U.S. citizens by reason of their color, race, religion, or national origin; study and collect information concerning legal developments constituting a denial of equal protection of the laws under the Constitution; and appraise the laws and policies of the federal government with respect to equal protection of the laws under the Constitution.

TITLE II

Authorized the president to appoint an additional assistant attorney general in the Justice Department subject to Senate confirmation.

TITLE III

Extended the jurisdiction of district courts to include any civil action begun to recover damages or secure equitable relief under any act of Congress providing for the protection of civil rights, including the right to vote.

Repealed a statute of 1866 giving the president power to employ troops to enforce or to prevent violation of civil rights legislation.

TITLE IV

Prohibited intimidation or coercion of persons attempting to vote in general or primary elections for Federal offices.

Empowered the attorney general to seek an injunction when an individual is deprived or about to be deprived of his right to vote. Gave district courts jurisdiction in such proceedings without requiring that administrative remedies be exhausted.

Ensured any person cited for contempt the right to counsel and to compel witnesses to appear.

TITLE V

Mandated that any person convicted in a criminal contempt case arising from the act's provisions be punished by fine or imprisonment or both.

Set the maximum punishment for individuals under the act's provisions at a $1,000 fine or six months in jail.

Permitted judges to determine whether defendants in criminal contempt cases involving voting rights could be tried with or without a jury.

Provided that in the event a criminal contempt case was tried before a judge without a jury and sentence upon conviction was more than three hundred dollars or forty-five days in jail, the defendant could demand and receive a jury trial; this section would not apply to contempts committed in the presence of the court or so near as to directly interfere with the administration of justice, nor to the behavior or misconduct of any officer of the court in respect to the process of the court.

Established standards for service on federal juries: Any U.S. citizen over twenty-one who resided for one year within a judicial district would be competent to serve as a federal grand or petit juror unless he or she (1) had been convicted of a crime punishable by imprisonment for more than one year and civil rights had not been restored; (2) was unable to read, write, speak, and understand the English language; or (3) was incapable, either physically or mentally, to give efficient jury service.

(Sources: *CR,* 8/2/57, 13473–74; *CQ Almanac,* 1957, 553–54.)

APPENDIX 2

Civil Rights Act of 1960
Summary of Major Provisions

TITLE I

"Whoever, by threats or force, willfully prevents, obstructs, impedes, or interferes with, or willfully attempts to prevent, obstruct, impede, or interfere with, the due exercise of rights or the performance of duties under any order, judgment, or decree of a court of the United States, shall be fined not more than $1,000 or imprisoned not more than one year." Obstructive acts could also be prevented by private suits seeking court injunctions.

TITLE II

Criminalized the crossing of state lines to avoid prosecution or punishment for, or providing evidence regarding, the bombing or burning of any building, facility, or vehicle, or the attempt to do so. Penalties not to exceed $5,000 and/or five years in prison.

Criminalized the transportation or possession of explosives with the knowledge or intent that they would be used to blow up any vehicle or building.

Outlawed the use of interstate facilities, such as telephones, to threaten a bombing; punishable by a $1,000 fine and/or one year in prison.

TITLE III

Required that voting records and registration papers for all federal elections be preserved for twenty-two months, and be relinquished to the attorney general or his representative upon written request.

TITLE IV

Empowered the Civil Rights Commission, extended for two years in 1959, to administer oaths and take sworn statements of witnesses.

TITLE V

Authorized arrangements to provide for the education of children of members of the armed forces on active duty, if the schools in which free public education is usually provided are closed, and the U.S. Commissioner of Education has determined that no other local educational agency can provide their schooling.

TITLE VI

Authorized the attorney general, after winning a civil suit brought under the 1957 Civil Rights Act, to ask the court to hold another adversary proceeding and make a separate finding of a "pattern or practice" of depriving blacks of the right to vote in the areas covered by the suit.

Should a court declare a "pattern or practice," permitted any black citizen living in the area to ask the court to issue an order declaring him qualified to vote if he had proved that (1) he was qualified under state law to vote; (2) he had attempted to register after the "pattern or practice" finding; (3) he had been prevented from registering or found unqualified by someone acting "under color of law."

Declared that state officials, subject to contempt of court proceedings, must permit that person to vote.

To enforce these provisions, authorized courts to appoint voting referees, who must be qualified voters in the judicial district. These referees would receive applications and take evidence, without cross examination by opponents, and then report their findings to the court.

State officials may challenge the referee's report. If the state's objections are denied, the court or the referee could issue the aggrieved person a certificate declaring him or her qualified to vote.

(Sources: *CR*, 4/8/60, 7811–13; *CQ Almanac*, 1960, 186.)

APPENDIX 3

Civil Rights Act of 1964
Summary of Major Provisions

TITLE I

Required election officials to apply uniform standards in registering voters; prohibited them from disqualifying persons for minor errors or omissions on applications for voting in federal elections.

Created, in voting rights suits, a rebuttable presumption that a person who has completed a sixth-grade education in a predominantly English-language school is sufficiently literate or intelligent to vote.

Required that any literacy tests must be in writing unless an agreement with the attorney general provides otherwise.

If the attorney general has requested the court to find a pattern or practice of discrimination in a voting rights suit, authorized the attorney general or any defendant to request a three-judge court to hear the case.

TITLE II

Prohibited discrimination on account of race, color, religion, or national origin in public accommodations if discrimination or segregation in such accommodation is supported by state laws or official action, if lodgings are provided to transient guests or interstate travelers are served, or if a substantial portion of the goods sold or entertainment presented moves in interstate commerce.

Business considered "public accommodations" under the act: restaurants, cafeterias, lunchrooms, lunch counters, soda fountains, gasoline stations, motion picture houses, theaters, concert halls, sports arenas, stadiums, or any hotel, motel, or lodging, except owner-occupied units with five or less rooms for rent. Also covered were any public establishment within or containing an accommodation otherwise covered (for example, a store containing a lunch counter or a barbershop in a hotel). Specifically exempted were private clubs, except to the extent that they offer their facilities to patrons of covered establishments (such as hotels).

Authorized any aggrieved person to bring suit in a federal court for injunctive relief and gave the court discretion to waive payments of fees, costs, and security; appoint an attorney for the plaintiff; and permit the attorney general to intervene if he certifies that the case is of general public importance.

Authorized the attorney general to initiate an action for preventive relief and request a three-judge court whenever he finds a pattern or practice intended to deny full exercise of Title II rights.

TITLE III

Authorized the Justice Department to bring suits, upon written complaints of individuals, to secure desegregation of state or locally owned, operated, or managed public facilities when aggrieved persons cannot initiate or maintain legal proceedings because of financial limitations or potential economic or other injury to themselves or their families.

TITLE IV

Authorized the attorney general to initiate and intervene in public school desegregation suits when aggrieved persons are unable to sue and provides technical and financial assistance, when requested by school boards, to assist in problems arising out of school desegregation.

Stipulated that nothing in the title is intended to prohibit classification and assignment of students for reasons other than race, color, religion, or national origin.

Stipulated that desegregation does not mean assigning of students to schools in order to overcome racial imbalance, and nothing in the title shall authorize a court or any official to order the transportation of students from one school district to another in order to achieve racial balance.

TITLE V

Extended the life of the U.S. Civil Rights Commission for four years, through January 31, 1968.

Added two new duties to the commission: to serve as a national clearinghouse for civil rights information and to investigate voting frauds.

Changed the rules of procedure for hearings to make them more like those in effect for other federal administrative agencies.

TITLE VI

Prohibited discrimination under any program or activity receiving federal assistance against any person because of race, color or national origin. Stipulated that before enforcing provisions of the title, federal agencies must first seek voluntary compliance.

TITLE VII

Prohibited certain employers, labor unions, and employment agencies whose actions affect interstate commerce from discriminating against employees or members on the basis of race, color, religion, sex, or national origin. Stipulated that when religion, sex, or national origin is a bona fide occupational qualification, an employer may discriminate on those bases.

Created a five-member Equal Employment Opportunity Commission, appointed by the president and confirmed by the Senate.

Authorized the commission to investigate written charges of unlawful employment practices and to attempt to resolve the problem by informal methods of conference, conciliation, and persuasion. Failing voluntary resolution of the complaint, after sixty days, the aggrieved individual could bring a civil suit. Authorized the courts, at their discretion, to appoint an attorney for the complainant and permit the attorney general to intervene.

Authorized courts to order cessation of the unlawful practice and to order reinstatement or hiring of employees with or without back pay.

TITLE VIII

Directed the Census Bureau to compile statistics of registration and voting by race, color, and national origin in areas of the country recommended by the Civil Rights Commission.

TITLE IX

Authorized the attorney general to intervene in private suits where persons have alleged denial of equal protection of the laws under the Fourteenth Amendment and where he certifies that the case is of "general public importance."

TITLE X

Established a Community Relations Service in the Department of Commerce to help communities resolve disputes relating to discriminatory practices based on race, color, or national origin.

TITLE XI

Required that in any criminal contempt case arising under the act, except voting rights cases, defendants are entitled to demand a jury trial, subject to no more than a $1,000 fine and six months in prison.

(Source: *CR*, 7/29/64, 17243–44.)

APPENDIX 4

Voting Rights Act of 1965
Summary of Major Provisions

1. Declared that "no voting qualification or prerequisite to voting, or standard, practice, or procedure shall be imposed or applied by any State or political subdivision to deny or abridge the right of any citizen of the United States to vote on account of race or color."

2. Authorized the Civil Service Commission to appoint federal voting "examiners," or registrars, responsible for determining an individual's qualification to vote. Examiners would require registration of qualified persons by state and local officials for all elections—federal, state, and local—including party caucuses and state political conventions.

Appointment of voting examiners would be made when:

a. A federal court, hearing a suit filed by the attorney general, determined the need for examiners to guarantee voting rights in a state or political subdivision.

b. The attorney general certified that he had received meritorious complaints from twenty or more residents of a political subdivision alleging that officials had denied them the right to vote under color of law on account of race or color, or that he determined that general discrimination existed in that subdivision. Examiners would be appointed in such cases only if the area qualified statistically and otherwise as one practicing massive discrimination as defined under the triggering formula provided in the bill and had not exempted itself through the act's provision for judicial relief.

c. The attorney general determined that a literacy test or similar device was used as a qualification for voting on November 1, 1964; *and* the Director of the Census determined that less than 50 percent of the persons of voting age residing in the area were registered on November 1, 1964, or that less than 50 percent of such persons voted in the 1964 presidential election.

Provided that the appointment of examiners under the automatic triggering formula (c) would be terminated by the attorney general or a three-judge federal district court in the District of Columbia when a state or a political subdivision proved that no literacy tests or similar device had been used during the preceding five years for the purpose or with the effect of discriminating.

3. Declared that states or subdivisions could free themselves from the appointment of federal examiners:

a. By successfully petitioning the attorney general that state and local election officials had enrolled all persons listed by federal examiners as qualified to vote and that there was no reasonable cause to believe that the right to vote would be denied or abridged on account of race or color.

b. In the case of political subdivisions in which a Census Bureau survey demonstrated that more than 50 percent of the subdivision's nonwhite voting-age population was registered to vote, by proving in a three-judge federal district court in the District of Columbia that the same voting condition existed as political subdivisions petitioning the attorney general had to show existed in their areas.

4. Stated that new voting laws enacted by state or local governments whose voter qualification laws were nullified under the bill could not take effect until approved by the Attorney General or a District of Columbia Federal court.

5. Suspended literacy tests or similar voting qualifications when the attorney general and director of the census determined that a state or political subdivision came within the scope of the act's automatic triggering formula.

6. Declared that no person who demonstrated that he had successfully completed the sixth grade in a private or accredited public school could be denied the right to vote in any federal, state, or local election, except in states in which state law determined that a different level of education is presumptive of literacy.

Stipulated that a person could not be denied the right to vote because of inability to read or write in English if he had demonstrated that he had successfully completed the sixth grade in a school under the American flag where instruction was conducted in a language other than English.

7. Declared that the constitutional right of U.S. citizens to vote is denied or abridged in states that impose the payment of a poll tax as a voting requirement. Directed the attorney general to challenge "forthwith," in the appropriate Federal district courts, such poll taxes or any substitute for such taxes, enacted after November 1, 1964.

(Sources: *CR*, 5/26/65, 11752–55; *CQ Almanac*, 1965, 534–36.)

APPENDIX 5

Excerpts of Relevant Rules
of Procedure of the U.S. Senate

CLOTURE MOTION

RULE XXII (1917–49)

If at any time a motion, signed by sixteen Senators, to bring to a close the debate upon *any pending measure* is presented to the Senate, the presiding officer shall at once state the motion to the Senate, and one hour after the Senate meets on the following calendar day but one, he shall lay the motion before the Senate and direct that the Secretary call the roll, and, upon the ascertainment that a quorum is present, the presiding officer shall, without debate, submit to the Senate by an aye-and-nay vote the question:

"Is it the sense of the Senate that the debate shall be brought to a close?"

And if that question shall be decided in the affirmative by a *two-thirds vote of those voting*, then said measure shall be the unfinished business to the exclusion of all other business until disposed of.

Thereafter no Senator shall be entitled to speak in all more than one hour on the pending measure, the amendments thereto, and motions affecting the same, and it shall be the duty of the presiding officer to keep the time of each Senator who speaks. Except by unanimous consent, no amendment shall be in order after the vote to bring the debate to a close, unless the same has been presented and read prior to that time. No dilatory motion, or dilatory amendment, or amendment not germane shall be in order. Points of order, including questions of relevancy, and appeals from the decision of the presiding officer, shall be decided without debate.

RULE XXII (1949–59)

". . . any time a motion signed by sixteen Senators, to bring to a close the debate upon *any measure, motion, or other matter* pending before the Senate, or the unfinished business, is presented to the Senate, the Presiding Officer shall at once state the motion to the Senate, and one hour after the Senate meets on the following calendar day but one, he shall lay the motion before the

Senate and direct that the Secretary call the roll, and, upon the ascertainment that a quorum is present, the Presiding Officer shall, without a debate, submit to the Senate by a yea-and-nay vote the question:

"Is it the sense of the Senate that the debate shall be brought to a close?"

And if that question shall be decided in the affirmative by *two-thirds of the Senators duly chosen and sworn,* then said measure, motion, or other matter pending before the Senate, or the unfinished business, shall be the unfinished business to the exclusion of all other business until disposed of.

RULE XXII (1959–75)

. . . "Is it the sense of the Senate that the debate shall be brought to a close?"

And if that question shall be decided in the affirmative by *two-thirds of the Senators present and voting,* then said measure, motion, or other matter pending before the Senate, or the unfinished business, shall be the unfinished business to the exclusion of all other business until disposed of.

QUORUM CALLS AND MOTION TO ADJOURN

RULE V, SECTION 3

During a quorum call ". . . and pending its execution, and until a quorum shall be present, no debate nor motion, except to adjourn, shall be in order."

LIMIT OF TWO SPEECHES PER DAY

RULE XIX, SECTION 1

". . . no Senator shall speak more than twice upon any one question in debate on the same day without leave of the Senate, which shall be determined without debate."

COMMITTEE REFERRAL OF HOUSE-PASSED BILLS

RULE XIV, PARAGRAPH 4

". . . every bill and joint resolution of the House of Representatives which shall have received a first and second reading without being referred to a committee shall, if objection be made to further proceeding thereon, be placed on the calendar."

(Source: *Senate Manual Containing the Standing Rules and Orders of The United States Senate.* Washington: U.S. Government Printing Office, 1921, 1951, and 1961.)

ACKNOWLEDGMENTS

IT IS PERHAPS A TIRED EXPRESSION, but it is true: No work of nonfiction is the product of any one person. A book such as this would be impossible to research, write, and edit without the support and assistance of others. Many people deserve my wholehearted gratitude:

My agent, Clyde Taylor, for his friendship, his wise counsel, and his aggressive advocacy; my editor at Harcourt Brace, John Radziewicz, for his encouragement, his help in improving the manuscript, and his commitment to the project; and Dan Hammer, who copyedited the book with great skill and care.

For their unfailing support and forbearance, Senator John Breaux and my colleagues on Senator Breaux's staff in Washington and in Louisiana, particularly Norma Jane Sabiston, Fred Hatfield, Judy Siegel, Ashley Wall, Michael Jefferson, Suzy Sonnier, Bette Phelan, and Karen Gravois. And my friends and colleagues at the Louisiana Democratic party: Jim Brady, Jim Nickel, Missy Broussard, Pat Hoffman, Hal Kilshaw, Mark Tiner, Wendy Wilson, and Edward Wisham.

The staff of the Lyndon Baines Johnson Library in Austin, Texas, including Allen Fisher, Linda Hanson, and E. Philip Scott; the staff of the Richard B. Russell Library for Political Research and Studies in Athens, Georgia, particularly Pam Hackbart-Dean and Sheryl B. Vogt; the staff of the Moorland-Spingarn Research Center at Howard University in Washington; the staff at the Minnesota Historical Society in Saint Paul; and the staff of the U.S. Senate Library.

For research assistance, Sue Kerr and Marci Lichtl, who were both graduate students in the political science department at Louisiana State University.

For their cheerful help and guidance, I wish to give special recognition to the many librarians and students at the Middleton Library at Louisiana State University and to the staff of the East Baton Rouge Parish Library. Although a fine research facility, the Middleton Library, like other university libraries in

Louisiana, is inadequately funded. Despite that handicap, inflicted by decades of Louisiana's nearsighted political leadership, the Middleton Library was an invaluable resource in my research.

Several people helped me immensely with their honest and insightful scrutiny of the manuscript, in whole or in part. They are Dave Norris, George E. Reedy, Max Kampelman, Wayne Parent, Paul Mann, Vincent Marsala, George Brazier, Clyde Taylor, and Raymond Wolfinger. While these people improved the manuscript with their thoughtful and careful critiques, any errors of fact or any flawed conclusions are the fault of no one but the author. Those wishing to inform me of errors may write to me in care of my publisher.

I must pay tribute to the many journalists and historians whose written works proved helpful to me. In chronicling the broader civil rights movement, I benefited from several excellent sources: *Parting the Waters* by Taylor Branch, *Bearing the Cross* by David J. Garrow, *To Redeem the Soul of America* by Adam Fairclough, *The Civil Rights Era* by Hugh Davis Graham, and *Before the Mayflower* by Lerone Bennett, Jr. I also owe debts of gratitude to Gilbert C. Fite for his excellent biography, *Richard B. Russell, Jr.;* Robert A. Caro for his monumental biographies of Lyndon Johnson, *The Path to Power* and *Means of Ascent;* the late Merle Miller for the invaluable oral history interviews contained in his biography, *Lyndon;* the late Hubert H. Humphrey for his refreshingly candid autobiography, *The Education of a Public Man;* Denton L. Watson for his exhaustive biography of Clarence Mitchell, *Lion in the Lobby*. Four books, in particular, helped me understand the culture of the Senate in the 1950s: *U.S. Senators & Their World* by Donald R. Matthews, *Citadel* by William S. White, *Deadlock or Decision: The U.S. Senate and the Rise of National Politics* by Fred R. Harris, and *The U.S. Senate* by George E. Reedy.

For those who wish to delve more deeply into the history of the Civil Rights Act of 1964, I highly recommend the fine work by Charles and Barbara Whalen, *The Longest Debate*. David J. Garrow provides an excellent recounting of the origins of the Voting Rights Act of 1965 in his book *Protest at Selma*. Both works were indispensable in my research.

I wish to thank the firsthand witnesses to many of the events described in this book for generously sharing their experiences and insight: Ellen Brown, Clark Clifford, the late J. William Fulbright, Theodore Hesburgh, Hubert H. Humphrey III, Proctor Jones, Max Kampelman, Nicholas Katzenbach, Anthony Lewis, Russell Long, Harry McPherson, Burke Marshall, George Reedy, Herman Talmadge, Strom Thurmond, Ted Van Dyk, Harris Wofford, and Raymond Wolfinger. In addition, I relied on hundreds of oral history interviews compiled by the John F. Kennedy Library, the Lyndon B. Johnson Library, the Library of Congress, Columbia University, the Minnesota Historical Society, the U.S. Senate Historical Office, the Richard B. Russell

Library for Political Research and Studies, and the Moorland-Spingarn Research Center.

I must also acknowledge that some people declined or did not respond to my requests for interviews. They include Russell Baker, Herbert Brownell, Robert Byrd, Joseph Califano, Ramsey Clark, Muriel Humphrey Brown, Edward Kennedy, Eugene McCarthy, Mike Mansfield, William Proxmire, George Smathers, Theodore Sorenson, and Jack Valenti. Although I did obtain recollections by some of these people from other sources—including oral histories—their firsthand accounts were greatly desired and would have been valuable.

In describing legislation, I relied heavily on *Congressional Quarterly*'s yearly almanacs and weekly reports. Since 1945 *Congressional Quarterly* has covered the day-to-day activities of Congress with unsurpassed skill, insight, and accuracy. Its various publications are vital tools for anyone writing about the Congress in the post–World War II era. For my description of debates, I primarily used the *Congressional Record*. As the most accurate record of the minute-by-minute proceedings of both houses, the *Congressional Record* has its shortcomings. Members routinely edit, and sometimes expunge, their remarks at the conclusion of a debate. While I have no reason to doubt that the quotations in this book were actually spoken in debate, it is impossible to assure the reader of the *Record*'s absolute accuracy.

For their support, friendship, and love: my parents, Robert and Charlene Mann; my mother-in-law and father-in-law, Alfred and Gerry Horaist; my brother, Paul Mann (who helped me overcome periodic frustrations with my computer); my sister, Sarah Luker; my friend and pastor, Chris Andrews; and my good friends John Copes, Jim Oakes, Ross Atkins, Jerry Johnson, Ron LeLeux, Kyle France, Roger Guissinger, Chris Peacock, and Harvill Eaton.

Finally, my wife, Cindy, cheerfully abided my absences while I researched and wrote this book. She never once protested when I abandoned her and retreated to my office to write. Far from complaining, she zealously defended me against all intrusions and distractions. No one gave me more support and reassurance. Cindy continues to fill every day of my life with enormous love and happiness. I cannot imagine life without her. This book is dedicated to her with all my love.

BIBLIOGRAPHY

ABBREVIATIONS USED
IN BIBLIOGRAPHY AND SOURCE NOTES

CQ   *Congressional Quarterly*

CR   *Congressional Record*

CUOHC   Columbia University Oral History Collection

FMOC   Association of Former Members of Congress, Oral History Project, Library of Congress

HHH   Hubert H. Humphrey

JFKL   John F. Kennedy Library, Boston, Massachusetts

LBJ   Lyndon B. Johnson

LBJL   LBJ Library, Austin, Texas

MHS   Minnesota Historical Society, Saint Paul, Minnesota

MSRC   The Moorland-Spingarn Research Center, Howard University, Washington, D.C.

NYT   *New York Times*

RBR   Richard B. Russell

RBRL   Richard B. Russell Library for Political Research and Studies, University of Georgia, Athens, Georgia

USSHO   Senate Staff Oral History Program, U.S. Senate Historical Office

WP   *Washington Post*

WSJ   *Wall Street Journal*

SELECTED ARTICLES

"A Barrier Falls: The U.S. Negro Moves To Vote." *Newsweek.* 8/16/65, 15–16.

"A Man Who Takes His Time." *Time.* 4/25/60, 20–24.

"A Round for the South." *Time.* 7/22/57, 12–13.

" 'A Salable Piece of Work.' " *Time.* 6/5/64, 22.

"About That 'Political Revolt' in the South." *U.S. News & World Report,* 9/27/57, 69–70.

"Ahead of the Wind." *Time.* 11/17/58, 21–22.

"All Over? Or Just Starting?" *Time.* 9/4/64, 19–19A.

" 'An American Tragedy,' " *Newsweek.* 3/22/65, 18–23.

"Another Tragic Era?" *U.S. News & World Report.* 10/4/57, 33–36, 42, 48, 50–51, 64.

"As the Senate Voted." *The New Republic.* 6/20/64, 6.

"At Last, a Vote." *Time.* 5/15/64, 32.

Baker, Russell. "Humphrey: Thunder! . . . Lightning?" *NYT Magazine.* 1/11/59, 12, 34, 36, 39, 42.

————. "Master of 'The Art of the Possible.' " *NYT Magazine.* 12/1/63, 26, 130–133.

Bennett, Lerone, Jr. "What Negroes Can Expect From President Lyndon Johnson." *Ebony.* 1/64, 81–83, 86–88.

Bickel, Alexander M. "After a Civil Rights Act." *The New Republic.* 5/9/64, 11–15.

————. "Amending the Voting Rights Bill." *The New Republic.* 5/1/65, 10–11.

————. "The Voting Rights Bill Is Tough." *The New Republic.* 4/3/65, 16–18.

"Big Guns of Southern Revolt: Strategist Byrnes, Organizer Byrd, Canny Russell, Careful George." *U.S. News & World Report.* 11/16/51, 46–49.

Boney, F. N. " 'The Senator's Senator': Richard Brevard Russell, Jr., of Georgia." *The Georgia Historical Quarterly.* Fall 1987, 477–490.

Briggs, Robert L. "A Man with Southern Connections." *The New Republic.* 11/14/55, 8–9.

Busch, N. F. "Senator Russell of Georgia." *Reader's Digest.* 12/66, 150–52.

Cater, Douglass. "How the Senate Passed the Civil Rights Bill." *The Reporter.* 9/5/57, 9–13.

————. "What Makes Humphrey Run." *The Reporter.* 3/5/59, 15–20.

"Challenge from the South." *Time.* 3/10/52, 23–24.

"Civil Rights—Backstage Drama." *Newsweek.* 8/12/57, 25–26.

"Civil Rights—Best Chance?" *Newsweek.* 7/15/57, 23–24.

"Civil Rights Bill: 'It Will Not Be Denied.' " *Newsweek.* 6/29/64, 17–18.

"Civil Rights: Can They Satisfy Ike?" *Newsweek.* 8/19/57, 23–24.

"Civil Rights—Civil Strife?" *Newsweek.* 9/2/57, 17–19.

"Civil Rights. Now—Or Never." *Newsweek.* 8/5/57, 24–25.

"Civil Rights: Shape of Compromise." *Newsweek.* 7/29/57, 23–24.

"Civil Rights: That New Feeling." *Newsweek.* 6/1/64, 19.

Clark, Joseph S. "With All Deliberate Delay: Some Thoughts on Streamlining the Senate." *The New Republic,* 4/18/64, 13–15.

"Clerical Lobbyists." *America.* 5/9/64, 624.

"Close to Kingship." *Time.* 5/29/64, 22–23.

Coffin, Tris. "How Lyndon Johnson Engineered Compromise on Civil Rights Bill." *The New Leader.* 8/5/57, 3–4.

Collins, Frederic W. "Senator Russell in the Last Ditch." *NYT Magazine.* 10/20/63, 16.

"Commander of the Filibuster." *U.S. News & World Report.* 3/14/60, 25.

Conn, Harry. "How Right Is Russell?" *The New Republic.* 5/12/52, 9–11.

"Crack in Dike—Ike?" *Newsweek.* 5/12/52, 28–29.

"Cracking the Whip for Civil Rights." *Newsweek.* 4/13/64, 26–28, 31–32.

Crawford, Kenneth. "Second Appomattox." *Newsweek.* 5/3/65, 35.

"Crisis in Civil Rights." *Time,* 6/2/61, 14–18.

"Curtain Goes Up on Another North vs. South Debate." *U.S. News & World Report.* 7/26/57, 96–106.

"Days of Violence in the South." *Newsweek.* 5/29/61, 21–23.

"Debate in the Senate: A Meeting in Birmingham." *Time,* 4/10/64, 21–22.

"Debate on the Doctrine." *Time.* 3/11/57, 15–16.

"Dirksen Amendments." *The New Republic.* 6/6/64, 3–4.

Drew, Elizabeth Brenner. "The Politics of Cloture." *The New Republic.* 7/16/64, 19–23.

"Education of a Senator." *Time.* 1/17/49, 13–16.

"Electric Charges." *Time.* 3/26/65, 19–23.

"Everybody's Getting Fat." *Time.* 5/18/62, 16.

"Explosion in Alabama." *Newsweek.* 5/20/63, 25–27.

"Ev's Law." *Time.* 5/22/64, 23.

"Firebrand Senator Cools Down." *Business Week.* 6/1/63, 29–30.

"Freedom—Now." *Time.* 5/17/63, 23–25.

" 'Freedom Riders' Force a Test." *Newsweek.* 6/5/61, 18–23.

Greenfield, Meg. "The Man Who Leads the Southern Senators." *Reporter.* 5/21/64, 17–21.

"How Senate Dean Judges Six Presidents." *U.S. News & World Report.* 2/23/70, 18.

"How the Rights Vote Was Engineered." *The New Republic.* 2/29/64, 17–19.

"If a Filibuster Comes, Russell Will Be the Manager." *U.S. News & World Report.* 7/1/63, 18.

Jarman, Rufus. "The Senate's Gabbiest Freshman." *The Saturday Evening Post.* 10/1/49, 30, 120–122.

"Kefauver Keeps Rolling." *Newsweek.* 5/19/52, 28.

"Kefauver's Stake." *Newsweek.* 5/5/52, 25–26.

Kempton, Murray. "Dirksen Delivers the Souls." *The New Republic.* 4/2/64, 9–11.

———. "Mr. Humphrey's Conquering Hosts." *The New Republic.* 4/4/64, 6–8.

Kiker, Douglas. "Russell of Georgia: The Old Guard at Its Shrewdest." *Harper's Magazine.* 9/66, 101–104.

Kopkind, Andrew. "Birth of a Bill: The Labored Progress of Voting Rights." *The New Republic.* 5/15/65, 11–13.

"LBJ—Half the Way." *The New Republic.* 7/25/60, 5.

"LBJ: 'I Ask for a Mandate to Begin.' " *Newsweek.* 16–22.

Leuchtenburg, William E. "The Old Cowhand from Dixie." *The Atlantic Monthly.* 12/92, 92–97, 100.

Lindley, Ernest K. "Statesmanlike." *Newsweek.* 8/12/57, 35.

Lisagor, Peter. "Ask Not 'What Became of Hubert Humphrey?' " *NYT Magazine.* 7/25/65, 6–7, 42–47.

Lloyd, David Demarest. "Figuring the Early Odds on the Democratic Candidates." *The Reporter.* 1/23/58, 24–29.

Manfred, Frederick. "Hubert Horatio Humphrey: A Memoir." *Minnesota History,* Fall 1978, 87–101.

Martin, Harold H. "The Man Behind the Brass." *The Saturday Evening Post.* 6/2/51, 22–23, 42, 45, 47.

"Mississippi: The Sound and the Fury." *Newsweek.* 10/15/62, 23–29.

"Mississippi versus the United States." *Newsweek.* 10/8/62, 32–37.

Oberdorfer, Don. "Filibuster's Best Friend." *The Saturday Evening Post.* 3/13/65, 90.

"One-Man Show." *Time.* 1/19/59, 15–16.

Peterson, Evelyn. "Sen. Humphrey Goes to Washington." *The Pathfinder.* 1/26/49, 28–31.

"Political Leaders and Editors Size Up the Little Rock Crisis." *U.S. News & World Report.* 10/4/57, 58–61.

"Politics—The Impact: Losses, Gains, Outlook." *Newsweek.* 10/7/57, 28–29.

"Protest on Route 80." *Time.* 4/2/65, 21–22.

"Pulling Lightning." *Newsweek.* 5/25/64, 33.

"Quizzing Russell." *U.S. News & World Report.* 6/13/52, 54–62.

"Rearguard Commander." *Time.* 7/22/57, 12.

"Richard Russell, RIP." *National Review.* 2/9/71, 129.

Rovere, Richard H. "Letter from Washington." *The New Yorker.* 8/31/57, 72–82.

"Russell Defends Filibuster." *NYT Magazine.* 3/15/64, 20.

"Russell Sounds Call for Civil-Rights Fight." *U.S. News & World Report.* 2/3/64, 8.

"Senator Russell of Georgia: Does He Speak for the South?" *Newsweek.* 8/19/63, 20–24.

"Shades of Bull Connor." *Newsweek.* 2/1/65, 21–22.

Shaffer, Samuel. "Hubert Humphrey Comes on Strong." *NYT Magazine.* 8/25/63, 11, 62–63.

Shannon, William V. "Why Humphrey Gets Taken for Granted." *The New Republic.* 7/4/64, 10–12.

Shore, William B. "One City's Struggle Against Intolerance." *The Progressive.* 1/49, 24–26.

"South in the Saddle." *Newsweek.* 3/10/52, 27–28.

"Southern Negroes & The Vote: The Blot Is Shrinking, But It Is Still Ugly." *Time,* 7/29/57, 12.

"Surprising Defeat." *Time,* 8/12/57, 11–16.

Stern, Mark. "Lyndon Johnson and Richard Russell: Institutions, Ambitions and Civil Rights." *Presidential Studies Quarterly.* Fall 1991, 687–704.

"The Bill as Amended." *The New Republic.* 6/20/64, 5.

"The Central Point." *Time.* 3/19/65, 23–28.

"The Controversy over Federal Civil Rights Legislation." *Congressional Digest.* 4/8/57, 99–128.

"The Edge of Violence." *Time.* 10/5/62, 15–17.

"The Final Vote." *Time.* 6/26/64, 17–18.

"The Great Issue." *Newsweek.* 9/16/57, 33–36.

"The Historic Vote: 71 to 29." *Newsweek.* 6/22/64, 25–26.

"The Minuet." *Newsweek.* 6/15/64, 30, 35.

"The South Knows Better." *The Nation.* 7/20/57, 21–22.

"The South States Its Case." *U.S. News & World Report.* 6/24/63, 78–80.

"The Starry Heavens—The Moral Issue." *Newsweek.* 3/29/65, 19–22.

"Though the Heavens Fall." *Time.* 10/12/62, 19–22.

"Truman's Won't-Run Bombshell Sets Off Democratic Campaign." *Newsweek.* 4/7/52, 29–31.

"Veteran Spokesman for the Old South." *Business Week.* 4/18/64, 28–29.

" 'Vicious Stuff.' " *Time.* 7/29/57, 13.

"Victory in Jail." *Time.* 2/12/65, 16–17.

"Warm-up for the Fight Against Civil-Rights Bill." *U.S. News & World Report.* 7/12/57, 70–75.

"When Is a Majority a Majority?" *Time.* 3/20/64, 22–26.

White, William S. "Democrats' Board of Directors." *NYT Magazine.* 7/10/55, 10–11.

———. "The 'Club' That Is the U.S. Senate." *NYT Magazine,* 11/7/54, 9, 30, 32–34.

————. "The Southern Democrat Now Takes Over." *NYT Magazine.* 1/9/55, 9, 34, 37–38.

"Why the South Took Rights Law Quietly." *Business Week.* 7/11/64, 28.

Wicker, Tom. "L.B.J. In Search of His New Frontier." *NYT Magazine.* 3/19/61, 29, 123–24.

————. "Winds of Change in the Senate." *NYT Magazine.* 9/12/65, 52–53, 119–20, 122, 124.

Wieck, Paul R. "Dirksen's Double Play." *The New Republic.* 4/17/65, 13–14.

"Will South End Negro Schools?" *U.S. News & World Report.* 5/28/54, 21–25.

LIBRARIES AND MANUSCRIPT COLLECTIONS

Columbia University Oral History Collection, Manuscript Division, Library of Congress, Washington, D.C.

Hubert H. Humphrey Collection, Minnesota Historical Society, Saint Paul, Minnesota.

Hubert H. Humphrey Oral History Project, Minnesota Historical Society, Saint Paul, Minnesota.

LBJ Library Oral History Collection, LBJ Library, Austin, Texas.

Oral History Department, Moorland-Spingarn Research Center, Howard University, Washington, D.C.

Oral History Interviews, Richard B. Russell Collection, Richard B. Russell Library for Political Research and Studies, University of Georgia, Athens.

Oral History Program, John F. Kennedy Library, Boston, Massachusetts.

Papers of Lyndon B. Johnson, LBJ Library, Austin, Texas.

Records of the JFK Assassination, Tapes and Transcripts of Telephone Conversations and Meetings, National Archives, Washington, D.C.

Richard B. Russell Collection, Richard B. Russell Library for Political Research and Studies, University of Georgia, Athens.

Senate Staff Oral History Program, Manuscript Division, Library of Congress, Washington, D.C.

The Modern Congress in American History, Oral History Collection, Association of Former Members of Congress, Manuscript Division, Library of Congress, Washington, D.C.

INTERVIEWS AND ORAL HISTORIES

Alexander, Clifford, 11/1/71, LBJL.

Allen, Ivan, Jr., 2/17/71, RBRL.

Allen, Ivan, Jr., 5/15/69, LBJL.

Anderson, Clinton P., 4/14/67, JFKL.

Anderson, Clinton P., 5/20/69, LBJL.

Anderson, Eugenie Moore, 7/14/78, MHS.

Attig, Francis J., 4/5/78, USSHO.

Auerbach, Carl, 7/13/78 &
  7/24/78, MHS.
Austin, John Rich, 4/14/71, RBRL.
Austin, Luke, 3/13/71, RBRL.
Backstrom, Charles, 7/21/78, MHS.
Barrow, Allen E., 6/11/72, LBJL.
Bates, William M., 2/25/71, RBRL.
Berry, Levette J. "Joe," 12/10/85,
  LBJL.
Bentley, James Lynwood, Jr.,
  2/18/71, RBRL.
Bennett, Wallace, 12/1/78, FMOC.
Berman, Edgar, 8/31/78, MHS.
Bernard, Berl, 6/17/68, JFKL.
Bible, Alan Harvey, 4/30/71, RBRL.
Biemiller, Andrew, 7/25/78, MHS.
Birdwell, W. Sherman, Jr., 10/20/70,
  LBJL.
Boggs, Hale, 5/10/64, JFKL.
Boggs, Hale, 3/13/69 & 3/27/69,
  LBJL.
Bolling, Richard, 11/1/65, JFKL.
Bolling, Richard, 2/27/69, LBJL.
Branton, Wiley, 1/16/69 &
  10/20/69, MSRC.
Brooks, David William, 3/25/71,
  RBRL.
Brown, Ellen, 1/3/94, author
  interview.
Bryant, C. Farris, 3/5/71, LBJL.
Burns, James MacGregor, 5/14/65,
  JFKL.
Byrd, Robert, 4/29/71, RBRL.
Calhoun, Lawton Miller, 2/26/71,
  RBRL.
Caplan, Marvin, 11/14/67, MSRC.
Carlton, John Thomas, 3/5/71,
  RBRL.
Carter, Clifton C., 10/15/68 &
  10/30/68, LBJL.
Carter, James Earl, 2/22/71, RBRL.
Carter, Hodding, 11/8/68, LBJL.

Cater, Douglas, 4/29/69 &
  5/26/74, LBJL.
Case, Clifford P., 3/1/79, LBJL.
Cellebrezze, Anthony J., 1/26/71,
  LBJL.
Celler, Emanuel, 4/3/78, FMOC.
Celler, Emanuel, 4/11/72, JFKL.
Celler, Emanuel, 3/16/69, LBJL.
Church, Frank, 5/1/69, LBJL.
Clark, Joseph, 10/2/78, FMOC.
Clark, Ramsey, 4/16/69, LBJL.
Clements, Earle, 10/24/74 &
  12/6/77, LBJL.
Clifford, Clark, 3/17/69 & 7/2/69,
  LBJL.
Clifford, Clark, 3/24/94, author
  interview.
Cocke, Earl Jr., 1/28/85, RBRL.
Cohen, Wilbur, 9/4/69, MSRC.
Collins, LeRoy, 12/15/72, LBJL.
Colmer, William M., 5/5/74, LBJL.
Connell, William, LBJL.
Connell, William, 2/15/78, MHS.
Cook, Donald C., 6/30/69, LBJL.
Cronin, John, 8/18/67, MSRC.
Darden, George W. "Buddy" III,
  2/12/71, RBRL.
Darden, William H., 12/6/74,
  RBRL.
Darden, William H., LBJL.
Davis, James, 12/3/83, LBJL.
D'Ewart, Wesley, CUOHC.
Diggs, Charles, 3/13/69, LBJL.
Dirksen, Everett M., 5/8/68 &
  6/30/69, LBJL.
Douglas, Paul H., 6/6/64, JFKL.
Douglas, Paul H., 11/1/74, LBJL.
Dunahoo, R. Mark, 2/19/71, RBRL.
Durr, Virginia, 3/1/75, LBJL.
Dwoskin, Harry, 3/26/71, RBRL.
Eastland, James O., 2/19/71, LBJL.
Eastland, James O., 4/21/71, RBRL.

Ellender, Allen, 8/29/67, JFKL.

Ellender, Allen, 6/30/69, LBJL.

Ellender, Allen, 4/30/71, RBRL.

Ervin, Sam J., Jr., 4/28/71, RBRL.

Farmer, James, 10/69, LBJL.

Freeman, Orville, 2/14/69, LBJL.

Freeman, Orville, 1/16/78, MHS.

Fulbright, J. William, 3/5/79, FMOC.

Fulbright, J. William, 6/19/89, author interview.

Fulbright, J. William, 4/19/71, RBRL.

Gartner, David, MHS.

Glickstein, Howard, 11/10/69, MSRC.

Goldsmith, John, 3/6/71, RBRL.

Goldstein, Abe, 2/17/71, RBRL.

Gomez, Millard, 4/23/71, RBRL.

Grayson, Spence Moore, 2/25/71, RBRL.

Green, Mary Willie Russell, 7/29/73, RBRL.

Hartt, Julian, 7/7/78, MHS.

Hall, Walter, 6/30/69, LBJL.

Halleck, Charles, 9/19/68, LBJL.

Hawkins, Augustus F., 2/28/69, MSRC.

Hays, Brooks, 10/5/71, LBJL.

Heller, Walter, 8/9/78, MHS.

Henry, Aaron, 9/12/70, LBJL.

Hesburgh, Theodore, 3/2/95, author interview.

Hesburgh, Theodore, 1971, JFKL.

Hesburgh, Theodore, 2/1/71, LBJL.

Hildenbrand, William F., 3/20/85, USSHO.

Hill, Lister, 2/1/71, LBJL.

Horwitz, Solis, 6/9/69, LBJL.

Howard, Francis Humphrey, 2/20/78, MHS.

Humphrey, Hubert H., 8/17/71, 6/20/77 & 6/21/77, LBJL.

Humphrey, Hubert H. III, 1978, MHS.

Humphrey, Hubert H. III, 4/12/94, author interview.

Hyneman, Charles, 8/16/78, MHS.

Jackson, Henry, 3/13/78, LBJL.

Jenkins, Walter, 9/22/83, LBJL.

Johnson, Alfred T. "Boody," 11/27/79, LBJL.

Johnson, Lady Bird, 6/28/77, RBRL.

Johnson, Paul B., 9/8/70, LBJL.

Jones, Luther, 6/13/69, LBJL.

Jones, Proctor, 11/8/93, author interview.

Kampelman, Max, 1/1/78, MHS.

Kampelman, Max, 2/3/94, author interview.

Katzenbach, Nicholas, 11/16/64, JFKL.

Katzenbach, Nicholas, 11/12/68, LBJL.

Katzenbach, Nicholas, 3/29/95, author interview.

Keating, Kenneth, 2/2/68, CUOHC.

Kelly, Harry, 6/20/78, MHS.

Kelley, Wayne P., Jr., 3/16/71, RBRL.

Kennedy, Robert F., 12/4/64, 12/6/64 & 12/22/64, JFKL.

King, Martin Luther, Jr., 3/9/64, JFKL.

Krock, Arthur, 11/21/69, LBJL.

Lawson, Belford V., 1/11/66, JFKL.

Leonard, Earl T., 2/15/71, RBRL.

Lewis, Anthony, 7/23/70, JFKL.

Lewis, Anthony, 4/1/94, author interview.

Long, Russell B., 4/23/71, RBRL.

Long, Russell B., 2/22/77 & 6/26/78, LBJL.

Long, Russell B., 2/2/91, 8/28/91, 11/6/94, author interviews.

Long, Russell B., 3/8/93 correspondence with author.

McGee, Gale, 6/8/79, 6/11/79 & 9/17/79, FMOC.

McGee, Gale, 2/10/69, LBJL.

McGill, Ralph, 1/6/66, JFKL.

McGovern, George, 7/29/78, MHS.

McPherson, Harry, 7/26/78, MHS.

McPherson, Harry, 11/9/93, author interview.

Magnuson, Warren, 3/14/78, LBJL.

Manatos, Mike, 7/10/69, LBJL.

Mankiewicz, Frank, 4/18/69, LBJL.

Mansfield, Mike, 6/23/64, JFKL.

Mansfield, Mike, 12/9/93 correspondence with author.

Marshall, Burke, 6/13/64, 6/20/64, 12/4/64, 12/6/64 & 12/22/64, JFKL.

Marshall, Burke, 10/28/68, LBJL.

Marshall, Burke, 2/27/70, MSRC.

Marshall, Burke, 6/30/94, author interview.

Marshall, Thurgood, 7/10/69, LBJL.

Martin, Louis, 5/14/69, LBJL.

Martin, Ruby G., 2/24/69, LBJL.

Minow, Newton, 3/19/71, LBJL.

Mitchell, Clarence, 4/30/69, LBJL.

Mitchell, Clarence, 12/6/68, MSRC.

Mitau, G. Theodore, 8/22/78, MHS.

Monroney, A. S. "Mike," 3/20/69, LBJL.

Mooney, Booth, 4/8/69 & 3/10/77, LBJL.

Moore, Powell, 3/6/71, RBRL.

Moore, Powell, 1/23/76, LBJL.

Moss, Frank, 9/20/78, FMOC.

Mudd, Roger, 3/4/71, RBRL.

Mundt, Karl, 9/21/68, LBJL.

Muskie, Edmund, 8/4/78, MHS.

Nathan, Robert, 8/31/78, MHS.

Nixon, Richard, 4/13/78, RBRL.

O'Donnell, Kenneth, 7/23/69, LBJL.

Pearson, Drew, 4/10/69, LBJL.

Peterson, Patience Russell, 9/19/73, RBRL.

Pickle, J. J. "Jake," 3/2/72, LBJL.

Pollak, Stephen, 1/30/69, LBJL.

Proxmire, William, 2/4/86, LBJL.

Rauh, Joseph, 1965, JFKL.

Rauh, Joseph, 7/30/69, LBJL.

Rauh, Joseph, 6/22/78, MHS.

Rauh, Joseph, 8/28/67, MSRC.

Raesly, Barboura, 6/16/75, RBRL.

Reedy, George, 12/12 & 12/20/68, 2/14/72, 6/7/75, 6/21/77, 5/21/82, 6/2/82 letter to Gillette, 10/27/82, 5/23 & 5/24/83, 8/16 & 8/17/83, 12/20 & 12/21/83, 6/22/84, LBJL.

Reedy, George, 1/7/94, author interview; 2/11 & 2/12/95 correspondence with author.

Riddick, Floyd, 3/5/71, RBRL.

Riddick, Floyd, 6/78–2/79, USSHO.

Rowe, James, 9/16/69, LBJL.

Russell, Fielding, 9/5/74, RBRL.

Russell, Henry Edward "Jeb," 6/21/74, RBRL.

Rustin, Bayard, 6/17/69, LBJL.

Ryan, Ed, 7/11/78, MHS.

Saltonstall, Leverett, 1976, FMOC.

Sanders, Harold Barefoot, 11/3/69, LBJL.

Shore, William, 6/27/78, MHS.

Shuman, Howard, 6–10/87, USSHO.

Sidey, Hugh, 4/7/64, JFKL.

Sidey, Hugh, 4/7/64, LBJL.

Siegel, Gerald, 5/26/69, 2/11/77 & 6/17/77, LBJL.

Smathers, George, 7/10/64, JFKL.

Smathers, George, 8–10/89, USSHO.

Sorenson, Theodore, 5/3/64, JFKL.

Spain, Jack Holland, 4/28/71, RBRL.

Sparkman, John J., 6/9/77, LBJL.

Sparkman, John J., 4/28/71, RBRL.

St. Claire, Darrell, 12/16/76, USSHO.

Stacy, Ina, 4/5/71, RBRL.

Stennis, John C., 6/17/72, LBJL.

Stennis, John C., 4/21/71, RBRL.

Stewart, John, 6/21/78, MHS.

Talmadge, Herman E., 3/10/66, JFKL.

Talmadge, Herman E., 7/17/69, LBJL.

Talmadge, Herman E., 4/21/71, RBRL.

Talmadge, Herman E., 1/13/95, author interview.

Tames, George, 1/13/88, USSHO.

Taylor, Hobart, 2/1/69, LBJL.

Thomas, Modine, 2/10/71 & 9/3/80, RBRL.

Thornberry, Homer, 12/21/70, LBJL.

Temple, Larry, 6/12/70, 8/7/70 & 8/11/70, LBJL.

Thurmond, Strom, LBJL.

Thurmond, Strom, 4/27/71, RBRL.

Thurmond, Strom, 8/10/89, author interview.

Troutman, Robert B., Jr., 3/4/71, RBRL.

Tully, Grace, 10/1/68, LBJL.

Udall, Morris, 2/22/73, MSRC.

Underwood, Norman, 2/12/71, RBRL.

Van Dyk, Frederick "Ted," 6/21/78, MHS.

Van Dyk, Frederick "Ted," 3/29/95, author interview.

Vander Zee, Rein J., 1/28/92, USSHO.

Warren, Earl, Jr., 9/21/71, LBJL.

Waters, Herbert J., 3/31/78, MHS.

Weisl, Edwin, Jr., 10/30/68, LBJL.

White, William S., 3/5/69 & 3/10/69, LBJL.

Wicker, Tom, 6/16/70, LBJL.

Wilkins, Roy, 1960, CUOHC.

Wilkins, Roy, 8/13/64, JFKL.

Wilkins, Roy, 4/1/69, LBJL.

Williams, Eugene and Helen, 10/27/74, LBJL.

Williams, John, 5/12/79, FMOC.

Wofford, Harris, 11/29/65, JFKL.

Wofford, Harris, 11/10/93, author interview.

Wolfinger, Ray, 4/25/95, author interview.

Wright, Zephyr, 12/5/74, LBJL.

Young, Milton, 4/23/71, RBRL.

Young, Whitney, Jr., 6/18/69, LBJL.

Zeidman, Philip, 7/25/78, MHS.

BOOKS AND OTHER PUBLICATIONS

Abernathy, Ralph David. *And The Walls Came Tumbling Down*. New York: HarperPerennial, 1989.

Adams, Sherman. *Firsthand Report: The Story of the Eisenhower Administration*. New York: Harper, 1961.

Ambrose, Stephen E. *Eisenhower: The President, Vol. II*. New York: Simon & Schuster, 1984.

Amrine, Michael. *This Is Humphrey: The Story of the Senator.* New York: Doubleday, 1960.

Anderson, Clinton. *Outsider in the Senate.* New York: World, 1970.

Anderson, J. W. *Eisenhower, Brownell, and the Congress: The Tangled Origins of the Civil Rights Bill of 1956–1957.* University: University of Alabama, 1964.

Anderson, William. *The Wild Man from Sugar Creek: The Political Career of Eugene Talmadge.* Baton Rouge: Louisiana State University, 1975.

Ashmore, Harry. *Civil Rights and Wrongs: A Memoir of Race and Politics, 1944–1994.* New York: Pantheon, 1994.

Baker, Bobby. *Wheeling and Dealing: Confessions of a Capitol Hill Operator.* New York: W. W. Norton, 1978.

Barnett, Richard and Garai, Joseph. *Where the States Stand on Civil Rights.* New York: Bold Face, 1962.

Bartley, Numan V. and Graham, Hugh D. *Southern Politics and the Second Reconstruction.* Baltimore: Johns Hopkins, 1975.

Bartley, Numan V. *The Rise of Massive Resistance: Race Politics in the South During the 1950s.* Baton Rouge: Louisiana State University, 1969.

Bennett, Lerone, Jr. *Before the Mayflower: A History of Black America.* New York: Penguin, 1984.

Berman, Daniel M. *A Bill Becomes Law: Congress Enacts Civil Rights Legislation.* New York: Macmillan, 1966.

———. *It Is So Ordered: The Supreme Court Rules of School Segregation.* New York: W. W. Norton, 1966.

Berman, Edgar. *Hubert: The Triumph and Tragedy of the Humphrey I Knew.* New York: Putnam, 1979.

Berman, William C. *The Politics of Civil Rights in the Truman Administration.* Ohio State University Press, 1970.

Bernstein, Barton J. and Matusow, Allen J. *The Truman Administration: A Documentary History.* New York: Harper & Row, 1966.

Bowles, Chester. *Promises to Keep: My Years in Public Life, 1941–1969.* New York: Harper & Row, 1971.

Branch, Taylor. *Parting the Waters: America in the King Years, 1954–63.* New York: Simon & Schuster, 1988.

Brinkley, Douglas. *Dean Acheson: The Cold War Years, 1953–71.* New Haven: Yale University, 1992.

Brownell, Herbert. *Advising Ike: The Memoirs of Attorney General Herbert Brownell.* Lawrence: University of Kansas, 1993.

Burk, Robert Fredrick. *The Eisenhower Administration and Black Civil Rights.* Knoxville: University of Tennessee, 1984.

Burns, James MacGregor. *The Crosswinds of Freedom.* New York: Knopf, 1989.

————. *John Kennedy: A Political Profile*. New York: Harcourt, Brace & Company, 1960.

Byrd, Robert C. *The Senate, 1789–1989: Addresses on the History of the United States Senate*. Washington: U.S. Government Printing Office, 1989.

Califano, Joseph A., Jr. *The Triumph and Tragedy of Lyndon Johnson: The White House Years*. New York: Simon & Schuster, 1991.

Caro, Robert A., *The Years of Lyndon Johnson: Means of Ascent*. New York: Knopf, 1990.

————. *The Years of Lyndon Johnson: The Path to Power*. New York: Knopf, 1982.

Carothers, Leslie A. *The Public Accommodations Law of 1964: Arguments, Issues and Attitudes in a Legal Debate*. Northampton, Massachusetts: Smith College, 1968.

Chandler, David Leon. *The Natural Superiority of Southern Politicians*. New York: Doubleday, 1977.

Chappell, David L. *Inside Agitators: White Southerners in the Civil Rights Movement*. Baltimore: Johns Hopkins, 1994.

Chester, Lewis, et al. *An American Melodrama: The Presidential Campaign of 1968*. New York: Viking, 1969.

Clark, Joseph S. *Congress: The Sapless Branch*. New York: Harper & Row, 1964.

Clifford, Clark. *Counsel to the President: A Memoir*. New York: Random House, 1991.

Cohen, Dan. *Undefeated: The Life of Hubert Humphrey*. Minneapolis: Lerner Publications, 1978.

Cohodas, Nadine. *Strom Thurmond and the Politics of Southern Change*. New York: Simon & Schuster, 1993.

Congress and the Nation, Vol. I. Washington: Congressional Quarterly.

Connally, John. *In History's Shadow: An American Odyssey*. New York: Hyperion, 1993.

Conway, Alan. *The Reconstruction of Georgia*. Minneapolis: University of Minnesota, 1966.

Cooper, William J. and Terrill, Thomas E. *The American South: A History*. New York: Knopf, 1990.

Cotton, Norris. *In the Senate: Amidst the Conflict and the Turmoil*. New York: Dodd, Mead & Company, 1978.

Dabney, Dick. *A Good Man: The Life of Sam J. Ervin*. Boston: Houghton Mifflin, 1976.

Dallek, Robert. *Lone Star Rising: Lyndon Johnson and His Times, 1908–1960*. New York: Oxford, 1991.

Douglas, Paul H. *In the Fullness of Time: The Memoirs of Paul H. Douglas*. New York: Harcourt Brace Jovanovich, 1972.

Dugger, Ronnie. *The Politician: The Life and Times of Lyndon Johnson—The Drive for Power, from the Frontier to Master of the Senate.* New York: Norton, 1982.

Dulles, Foster Rhea. *The Civil Rights Commission: 1957–1965.* Michigan State University Press, 1968.

Duram, James C. *A Moderate Among Extremists: Dwight D. Eisenhower and the School Desegregation Crisis.* Chicago: Nelson-Hall, 1981.

Eisele, Albert. *Almost to the Presidency: A Biography of Two American Politicians.* Minnesota: Piper, 1972.

Eisenhower, Dwight D. *Waging Peace, 1956–1961.* New York: Doubleday, 1965.

Engelmayer, Sheldon D. and Wagman, Robert J. *Hubert Humphrey: The Man and His Dream.* New York: Methuen, 1978.

Ervin, Sam J., Jr. *Preserving the Constitution: The Autobiography of Senator Sam J. Ervin, Jr.* Charlottesville: Michie, 1984.

Evans, Rowland and Novak, Robert. *Lyndon B. Johnson: The Exercise of Power.* New York: New American Library, 1966.

Face the Nation: The Collected Transcripts from the CBS Radio and Television Broadcasts. New York: Holt Information Systems, 1972.

Fairclough, Adam. *To Redeem the Soul of America: The Southern Christian Leadership Conference and Martin Luther King, Jr.* Athens: University of Georgia, 1987.

Filvaroff, David B. and Wolfinger, Raymond E. *The Origin and Enactment of the Civil Rights Act of 1964.* Presented at the Conference on the Civil Rights Act of 1964: A Thirty Year Perspective, The Federal Judicial Center, Washington, D.C., November 11–12, 1994.

Findlay, James F., Jr. *Church People in the Struggle: The National Council of Churches and the Black Freedom Movement, 1950–1970.* New York: Oxford, 1993.

Fite, Gilbert C. *Richard B. Russell, Jr., Senator from Georgia.* Chapel Hill: University of North Carolina, 1991.

Fleming, Dan B., Jr. *Kennedy vs. Humphrey, West Virginia, 1960: The Pivotal Battle for the Democratic Presidential Nomination.* Jefferson, North Carolina: McFarland & Co., 1992.

Foley, Michael. *The New Senate: Liberal Influence on a Conservative Institution, 1959–1972.* New Haven: Yale University, 1980.

Friedman, Leon. *Southern Justice.* New York: Pantheon, 1965.

Garrow, David J. *Bearing the Cross: Martin Luther King, Jr., and the Southern Christian Leadership Conference.* New York: Vintage, 1988.

———. *Protest at Selma: Martin Luther King, Jr., and the Voting Rights Act of 1965.* New Haven: Yale University, 1978.

Goldman, Roger with Gallen, David. *Thurgood Marshall: Justice for All*. New York: Carroll & Graf, 1992.

Goldsmith, John A. *Colleagues: Richard B. Russell and His Apprentice, Lyndon B. Johnson*. Washington, D.C.: Seven Locks, 1993.

Goodwin, Richard N. *Remembering America: A Voice from the Sixties*. New York: Harper & Row, 1988.

Gore, Albert. *Let the Glory Out: My South and its Politics*. New York: Viking, 1972.

Graham, Hugh Davis. *The Civil Rights Era: Origins and Development of National Policy, 1960–1972*. New York: Oxford, 1990.

Greene, John Robert. *The Crusade: The Presidential Election of 1952*. Lanham, Maryland: University Press of America, 1985.

Griffith, Winthrop. *Humphrey: A Candid Biography*. New York: Morrow, 1965.

Halberstam, David. *The Fifties*. New York: Villard, 1993.

Harris, Fred R. *Deadlock or Decision: The U.S. Senate and the Rise of National Politics*. New York: Oxford, 1993.

Harvey, James C. *Civil Rights During the Kennedy Administration*. Jackson: University and College Press of Mississippi, 1971.

———. *Black Civil Rights During the Johnson Administration*. Jackson: University and College Press of Mississippi, 1973.

Hesburgh, Theodore M. *God, Country, Notre Dame*. New York: Doubleday, 1990.

Humphrey, Hubert H. *The Education of a Public Man: My Life and Politics*. Minneapolis: University of Minnesota, 1991.

Javits, Jacob K. *Javits: The Autobiography of a Public Man*. Boston: Houghton Mifflin, 1981.

Johnson, Lyndon. *The Vantage Point: Perspectives of the Presidency, 1963–1969*. New York: Holt, Rinehart & Winston, 1971.

Johnson, Sam Houston. *My Brother Lyndon*. New York: Cowles, 1969.

Kampelman, Max M. *Entering New Worlds: The Memoirs of a Private Man in Public Life*. New York: HarperCollins, 1991.

Kearns, Doris. *Lyndon Johnson and the American Dream*. New York: Harper & Row, 1976.

Kennedy, Stetson. *Jim Crow Guide: The Way It Was*. Boca Raton: Florida Atlantic University, 1990.

Loevy, Robert D. *To End All Segregation: The Politics of the Passage of the Civil Rights Act of 1964*. Lanham, Maryland: University Press of America, 1990.

Lord, Walter. *The Past That Would Not Die*. London: Hamish Hamilton, 1966.

MacNeil, Neil. *Dirksen: Portrait of a Public Man*. New York: World, 1970.

McCullough, David. *Truman*. New York: Simon & Schuster, 1992.

McPherson, Harry. *A Political Education: A Journal of Life with Senators, Generals, Cabinet Members and Presidents*. Boston: Little, Brown, 1972.

Maclear, Michael. *The Ten Thousand Day War, Vietnam: 1945–1975*. New York: Avon, 1981.

Mann, Robert. *Legacy to Power: Senator Russell Long of Louisiana*. New York: Paragon House, 1992.

Martin, Harold H. *Georgia: A Bicentennial History*. New York: Norton, 1977.

Matthews, Donald R. *U.S. Senators and Their World*. New York: Vintage, 1960.

Matthews, Donald R. and Prothro, James W. *Negroes and the New Southern Politics*. New York: Harcourt, Brace & World, 1966.

Matusow, Allen J. *The Unraveling of America: A History of Liberalism in the 1960s*. New York: Harper & Row, 1984.

Miller, Merle. *Lyndon: An Oral Biography*. New York: Putnam, 1980.

Mooney, Booth. *LBJ: An Irreverent Chronicle*. New York: Thomas Y. Crowell Co., 1976.

Morison, Samuel Eliot. *The Oxford History of the American People*. New York: Mentor, 1972.

Myrdal, Gunnar. *An American Dilemma: The Negro Problem and Modern Democracy*. New York: Harper, 1944.

Nearing, Scott. *Black America*. New York: Vanguard, 1929.

Nevins, Allan and Commager, Henry Steele. *A Pocket History of the United States*. New York: Washington Square, 1986.

Nolen, Claude H. *The Negro's Image in the South: The Anatomy of White Supremacy*. Lexington: University of Kentucky, 1967.

O'Donnell, Kenneth P., et al. *"Johnny, We Hardly Knew Ye": Memories of John Fitzgerald Kennedy*. Boston: Little, Brown, 1970.

O'Neill, William L. *American High: The Years of Confidence, 1945–1960*. New York: Free Press, 1989.

Origins and Development of Congress. Washington: Congressional Quarterly, 1976.

The Oxford Dictionary of Quotations. Oxford: Oxford, 1980.

Parmet, Herbert S. *JFK: The Presidency of John F. Kennedy*. New York: Dial, 1983.

Pollack, Jack Harrison. *Earl Warren: The Judge Who Changed America*. Englewood Cliffs: Prentice-Hall, 1979.

Potter, David M. *The South and the Concurrent Majority*. Baton Rouge: Louisiana State University, 1972.

Reedy, George E. *Lyndon B. Johnson: A Memoir*. New York: Andrews and McMeel, 1982.

————. *The U.S. Senate: Paralysis or a Search for Consensus?* New York: Crown, 1986.

Reeves, Richard. *President Kennedy: Profile of Power*. New York: Simon & Schuster, 1993.

Ripley, Randall B. *Power in the Senate*. New York: St. Martin's, 1969.

Ross, Irwin. *The Loneliest Campaign: The Truman Victory of 1948*. New York: New American Library, 1968.

Rowan, Carl T. *Breaking Barriers: A Memoir*. New York: HarperPerennial, 1991.

Ryskind, Allan H. *Hubert: An Unauthorized Biography of the Vice President*. New Rochelle: Arlington House, 1968.

Viorst, Milton. *Fire in the Streets: America in the 1960s*. New York: Simon & Schuster, 1979.

Safire, William. *Safire's Political Dictionary*. New York: Ballantine, 1978.

Schlesinger, Arthur M., Jr. *A Thousand Days: John F. Kennedy in the White House*. Boston: Houghton Mifflin, 1965.

————. *Robert Kennedy and His Times*. Boston: Houghton Mifflin, 1978.

Shaffer, Samuel. *On and Off the Floor: Thirty Years as a Correspondent on Capitol Hill*. New York: Newsweek, 1980.

Simon, Rita James. *Public Opinion in America: 1936–1970*. Chicago: Rand McNally, 1974.

Sorenson, Theodore C. *Kennedy*. New York: Harper & Row, 1965.

Solberg, Carl. *Hubert Humphrey: A Biography*. New York: W. W. Norton, 1984.

Sprigle, Ray. *In the Land of Jim Crow*. New York: Simon & Schuster, 1949.

Strober, Gerald S. and Deborah H. *"Let Us Begin Anew": An Oral History of the Kennedy Presidency*. New York: HarperCollins, 1993.

Talmadge, Herman E. *Talmadge: A Political Legacy, A Politician's Life*. Atlanta: Peachtree, 1987.

Understanding Congress: Research Perspectives [The Papers and Commentary from "Understanding Congress: A Bicentennial Research Conference," February 9–10, 1989, Washington, D.C.]. Washington: U.S. Government Printing Office, 1991.

Valenti, Jack. *A Very Human President*. New York: W. W. Norton, 1976.

Warren, Earl. *The Memoirs of Earl Warren*. New York: Doubleday, 1977.

Watson, Denton L. *Lion in the Lobby: Clarence Mitchell, Jr.'s Struggle for the Passage of Civil Rights Laws*. New York: Morrow, 1990.

Whalen, Charles and Barbara. *The Longest Debate: A Legislative History of the 1964 Civil Rights Act*. Cabin John, Maryland: Seven Locks, 1985.

White, Theodore H. *The Making of the President 1960*. New York: Atheneum, 1961.

————. *The Making of the President 1964*. New York: Atheneum, 1965.

————. *The Making of the President 1968*. New York: Atheneum, 1969.

White, William S. *Citadel: The Story of the U.S. Senate.* New York: Harper & Brothers, 1957.

————. *The Professional: Lyndon B. Johnson.* Boston: Houghton Mifflin, 1964.

Wicker, Tom. *JFK and LBJ: The Influence of Personality Upon Politics.* New York: Morrow, 1968.

Wilson, Woodrow. *Congressional Government: A Study in American Politics.* Cleveland: World, 1956.

With Liberty and Justice for All: An abridgement of the Report of the United States Commission on Civil Rights, 1959. Washington, D.C.: U.S. Government Printing Office, 1959.

Wofford, Harris. *Of Kennedys and Kings: Making Sense of the Sixties.* New York: Farrar, Straus & Giroux, 1980.

The World Almanac and Book of Facts. New York: World Almanac, 1992.

Woodward, C. Vann. *The Strange Career of Jim Crow.* New York: Oxford, 1974.

SOURCE NOTES

CHAPTER ONE

1 *As he approached the massive podium:* Solberg, 17; *New York Herald Tribune,* 7/15/48; *WP,* 7/15/48.

1 *"Hubert was like a whirlwind":* Minnesota History, Fall 1978.

2 *Truman's men hoped to strike this clever:* WP, 7/15/48.

3 *"crackpots":* Ross, 120; Humphrey, 76; McCullough, 640.

3 *Though concerned about the prudence:* Humphrey, 76; WP 7/15/48; Biemiller and Rauh OH, MHS; Solberg, 14.

3 *plotting their next move:* Solberg, 14; NYT, 7/15/48.

4 *had little confidence:* Clifford, 196; Solberg, 124.

4 *"There was no question":* Rauh OH, MHS.

5 *"This may tear the party apart":* Humphrey, 77.

6 *"an intellectual prober":* Eisele, 14–15; Humphrey, 8; Amrine, 35; Solberg, 43.

6 *"Dad set high standards for me":* Solberg, 42; Howard OH, MHS; Humphrey, 8.

6 *Like many children:* Cohen, 28–31; Solberg, 35; Humphrey, 8.

7 *Hubert learned more than generosity:* Humphrey, 10.

7 *"It is something I've never forgotten":* Humphrey, 15; Cohen, 34; Griffith, 53; Time, 1/17/49.

7 *Humphrey's university studies:* Eisele, 21, 24; Cohen, 43–44.

8 *Humphrey returned:* Amrine, 37; Humphrey, 27–28.

8 *Muriel Buck:* Humphrey, 30–32.

8 *While visiting his sister in Washington:* Pathfinder 1/26/49; Griffith, 59.

9 *Humphrey's ambitions:* Griffith, 61; Solberg, 53; Eisele, 26.

9 *Humphrey fulfilled his dream:* Humphrey, 42.

10 *Humphrey soon befriended:* Eisele, 50; Time, 1/17/49.

10 *his first full-time job:* Eisele, 52.

10 *he jumped into the race:* Cohen, 95; *Minnesota History,* Fall 1978; Eisele, 52–53; Humphrey, 50.

11 *For the next two years:* Time, 1/17/49; Humphrey, 57.

11 *Humphrey's next political opportunity:* Eisele, 57.

11 *the right to appoint the police chief:* Ryan OH, MHS; Cohen, 120; Solberg, 104; Eisele, 58.

12 *With his official powers limited:* Survey Graphic, June 1948; Solberg, 107; Humphrey, 65; *Time,* 1/17/49; Eisele, 58.

12 *nothing characterized Humphrey's tenure as mayor:* Humphrey, 67; Solberg, 105–6; *Progressive,* 1/49.

13 *Humphrey's vigorous support for civil rights:* Humphrey, 71–72.

13 *Americans for Democratic Action:* Solberg 12; Rauh & Anderson OH, MHS; Humphrey, 69–74.

14 *"The Democratic Party is responsible":* NYT, 7/15/48.

14 *Rayburn assured both sides:* Humphrey, 77; Biemiller OH, MHS.

15 *Back at his hotel:* Solberg, 15–16; Rauh OH, MHS.

15 *"We highly commend President Harry Truman":* NYT, 7/15/48.

15 *"The good phrases were his":* Solberg, 16.

15 *"You want to build a [Henry] Wallace movement?"* Rauh OH, MHS.

16 *Ed Flynn:* Humphrey, 78.

16 *As Humphrey waited his turn to speak:* Solberg, 17.

16 *"I realize that in speaking":* The Official Report of the Democratic National Convention, Philadelphia, Pennsylvania, July 12 to July 14, inclusive 1948, Local Democratic Political Committee of Pennsylvania, 189–92; Solberg, 17.

19 *"cheering like madmen":* CR, 6/19/63, 11167; *WP,* 7/15/48.

19 *To Illinois delegate Paul Douglas:* Eisele, 68; Shore OH, MHS.

19 *In the* Minneapolis Star: *Minneapolis Star,* 7/15/48; Engelmayer and Wagman, *xxxi.*

20 *"Even though I feared":* Humphrey, 78.

20 *After eight minutes:* Solberg, 19.

20 *The conservative states' rights plank:* Humphrey, 78; *The Official Report of the Democratic National Convention, Philadelphia, Pennsylvania, July 12 to July 14, inclusive 1948,* Local Democratic Political Committee of Pennsylvania, 195–210; Solberg 19; *NYT,* 7/15/48; Talmadge, 148.

20 *Rayburn moved quickly:* Hardeman and Bacon, 337; *NYT,* 7/15/48; *U.S. News & World Report,* 7/23/48; *WP,* 7/15/48; *New York Herald Tribune,* 7/15/48.

CHAPTER TWO

23 *"Any attack on Georgia":* Fite, 94.

23 *In this atmosphere:* Martin, 116–118; Conway, 22, 39; Bennett, 484.

24 *"emblazoned in the white Southern memory"*: Gore, 20.

24 *"the only victor in the South"*: Conway, 219.

24 *By the 1890s:* Morison, 107.

25 *laws and customs that made up Jim Crow:* Sprigle, 53; Kennedy, 58–71.

25 *"The churches and lodge rooms"*: Nearing, 59, 63.

26 *Gunnar Myrdal:* Myrdal, 600; *NYT*, 4/23/56.

26 *"Discrimination against the Negro"*: Sprigle, 7–9.

27 *cruel social customs:* Cooper and Terrill, 544–47.

27 *Lynchings rarely occurred:* Kennedy, 150–55.

27 *"When I was growing up in the South"*: Talmadge, 200.

28 *the purity of the "white race"*: Myrdal, 107.

28 *In 1947 a special committee:* Bernstein and Matusow, 95–99.

29 *"It's a mistake"*: McPherson, author interview; McPherson OH, LBJL.

29 *What he saw as liberal attempts:* Fite, 225.

30 *"someone for whom they could vote"*: Ibid., 239.

30 *Russell was born:* Green OH, RBRL; Fite, 1; *Reader's Digest*, 12/66.

30 *R.B.'s father was prosperous: Richard Russell: Georgia Giant,* Cox Broadcasting 1970; Peterson OH, RBRL.

31 *"Be a man"*: Fite, 20.

31 *"If he ever wants to go into politics"*: Peterson OH, RBRL.

31 *R.B. was a devoted son:* Green OH, RBRL; Fite, 22.

31 *"I guess you'd say I was quiet": Richard Russell: Georgia Giant,* Cox Broadcasting 1970; Fite, 30–34.

32 *"I will appreciate the support"*: Fite, 39–40.

32 *a political base within the House: Ibid.,* 43–46.

32 *Russell agonized:* Green & Henry Russell OH, RBRL; *Ibid.,* 49.

32 *the Senate campaign behind him: Ibid.,* 50–53, 58.

33 *Russell accurately sensed:* Ibid., 60; Dunahoo OH, RBRL.

33 *"I would stop my car": Richard Russell: Georgia Giant,* Cox Broadcasting 1970.

33 *"Dick had a wonderful knack"*: Dunahoo OH, RBRL.

34 *"When I get to be governor"*: Green OH, RBRL.

34 *On election day:* Fite, 73, 76.

34 *He rarely used the term:* Fite, 74.

35 *Chief Justice Richard Russell:* Fite, 84.

35 *In almost every way: Reader's Digest,* 12/66; Fite, 89, 90, 100.

36 *Crisp fought back:* Fite, 115–16.

36 *Russell arrived: Reader's Digest,* 12/66; *Saturday Evening Post,* 6/2/51.

37 *"Senator Harris was on the Appropriations Committee": Richard Russell: Georgia Giant,* Cox Broadcasting 1970.

37 *"If there ever was anyone"*: Talmadge & Fulbright OH, RBRL.

37 *Russell was once engaged:* Stacy & Dunahoo OH, RBRL; *Richard Russell, Georgia Giant,* Cox Broadcasting 1970.

37 *When he was not at work:* Darden OH, RBRL.

38 *books by the bundle:* Talmadge & Raesly OH, RBRL.

38 *"If the country's in bad shape":* Fite, 127.

38 *With his reelection in 1936: Ibid.,* 145; Anderson, *The Wild Man from Sugar Creek,* 161.

39 *To some northern observers:* Fite, 163.

39 *"Just carve on my tombstone":* Bennett, 365.

40 *a sputtering rage:* Fite, 183; Graham, 14.

40 *Their opening:* Watson, 148; Graham, 15.

41 *"the difference between A and Z":* Long, author interview. The South, McGill wrote in 1946, is "a [news] story, whether we like it or not. And, while the rest of the nation has its share of crime, ours [violence against blacks] is different and it too often is un-American." (*Atlanta Constitution,* 8/3/46.)

41 *there was Harry Truman:* Raleigh, N.C. *News & Observer,* 11/03/91.

41 *Relying on the 1947 report:* Bernstein and Matusow, 104–8; McCullough, 586–88.

42 *Truman's agenda:* RBR to H. T. Dearing, 3/12/48, Civil Rights X, RBRL; RBR news release, 2/5/48, Speech/Media, RBRL; RBR to Mrs. John A. Strausbaugh, 3/8/48, Civil Rights X, RBRL.

42 *Truman's bold attempt:* Fite, 232.

42 *"the big bear":* Chandler, 263; Fite, 232; *Atlanta Constitution,* 3/9/48.

43 *Allied with conservative Republicans: Congress and the Nation,* Vol. I, CQ, 1617; RBR news release, 9/20/48, Speech/Media, RBRL.

43 *With Truman heading the national ticket:* Fite, 239.

43 *tough new platform language: Ibid.,* 240.

44 *"He has fought courageously":* The *Official Report of the Democratic National Convention, Philadelphia, Pennsylvania, July 12 to July 14, inclusive 1948,* Local Democratic Political Committee of Pennsylvania, 230–34.

44 *"You shall not crucify": Ibid.* 280–81.

44 *"a shining beacon": Ibid.,* 263–64, 270–80; *New York Herald Tribune,* 7/15/48.

44 *Truman won the nomination:* McCullough, 641.

45 *"the South will not be crucified":* The *Official Report of the Democratic National Convention, Philadelphia, Pennsylvania, July 12 to July 14, inclusive 1948,* 280–81.

45 *"Everybody knows": Ibid.,* 300–306; Bernstein and Matusow, 150–53.

45 *"My left flank":* Burns, *The Crosswinds of Freedom,* 237.

46 *"The chips are down":* WP, 6/16/48.

CHAPTER THREE

47 *"over long bones"*: Dallek, 326.

47 *"I am opposed"*: LBJ speech, 5/22/48, Legislative Files, House papers, LBJL.

48 *"I will say"*: Kearns, 232; Caro, *The Path to Power*, 407.

48 *"His part of Texas"*: White OH, LBJL; Johnson, *The Vantage Point*, 155.

48 *In pursuit of the Senate seat*: White OH, LBJL; Miller, 533; *Time*, 1/1/65.

48 *His temper was legendary*: Reedy, *Lyndon B. Johnson*, 158; Miller, 534.

48 *entirely one dimensional*: Durr & Birdwell OH, LBJL.

49 *This passion for politics*: Caro, *Means of Ascent*, 128–29.

49 *a dogged, effective advocate*: Caro, *The Path to Power*, 527–28.

49 *"utmost enthusiasm"*: Miller, 118.

49 *spreading rumors*: Ibid., 121; Caro, *Means of Ascent*, 270–77.

50 *Taft-Hartley hurt the most*: Pickle OH, LBJL; Dallek, 325.

51 *"There were no 'darkies' "*: Johnson, *The Vantage Point*, 155.

51 *"straight as a shingle"*: Caro, *The Path to Power*, 48.

51 *reputation for honesty*: Miller, 10.

52 *Rebekah's favor*: Dugger, 61.

52 *a quick mind*: Caro, *The Path to Power*, 101; Dallek, 41–44.

52 *"I would sit in the gallery"*: Kearns, 36–37.

52 *Soon after his return*: Caro, *The Path to Power*, 80.

53 *Ku Klux Klan*: Dallek, 55; Johnson, *My Brother Lyndon*, 30–31.

53 *Mounting debts*: Caro, *The Path to Power*, 93, 97.

53 *"how Lyndon acted"*: Ibid., 153, 160; Berry OH, LBJL.

54 *techniques of flattery*: Miller, 28; Alfred Johnson OH, LBJL.

54 *Johnson had always tried*: Dallek, 69–71, 73; Caro, *The Path to Power*, 199.

54 *By the summer of 1928*: CQ Almanac, 1965, 1367.

55 *By all accounts*: Miller, 34.

55 *Johnson returned*: Luther Jones OH, LBJL; Miller, 35–36.

55 *his first political speech*: Miller, 36–37; Caro, *The Path to Power*, 202–3.

55 *Kleberg needed a secretary*: Miller, 39; Jones OH, LBJL; Caro, *The Path to Power*, 234.

56 *Johnson soon set his sights*: Miller, 48.

56 *Johnson stampeded*: Ibid., 48; Dugger, 173–74; Caro, *The Path to Power*, 263.

57 *When he met Lady Bird*: Miller, 44; Dugger, 176; from Lady Bird Johnson interview on 20/20, ABC, 3/24/95.

57 *He now fawned*: Hardeman and Bacon, 236–37; Caro, *The Path to Power*, 333–34.

57 *a new challenge:* Dugger, 185.

58 *Johnson attacked his new job:* Miller, 56.

58 *"a fair break":* Ibid., 56.

58 *Johnson's willingness:* Dugger, 187–88; Miller, 56.

58 *"He fought for those kids":* Dugger, 189.

59 *"Don't you remember":* Caro, *The Path to Power*, 416.

59 *Johnson was the youngest:* Pickle OH, LBJL.

59 *"He was energetic":* Birdwell OH, LBJL.

59 *"mix up a little mud":* Dugger, 195.

60 *courtship of the black vote:* Caro, *The Path to Power*, 407; Dugger, 197.

60 *When Johnson returned to Washington:* Dugger, 207.

60 *his chance to meet Roosevelt:* Beautiful Texas, American Experience, PBS, 9/30/91.

60 *The next morning:* Caro, *The Path to Power*, 448; Dugger, 202–3.

61 *"He was smiling":* Caro, *The Path to Power*, 449.

61 *was shameless:* Caro speech, *Understanding Congress: Research Perspectives*, 102; Long, author interview.

61 *Rayburn's inner circle:* Dallek, 166.

62 *Another authority figure:* Ibid., 164–66.

62 *fight with Rayburn:* Miller, 75.

62 *fealty to Roosevelt:* Evans and Novak, 13.

62 *a special election:* Miller, 79–83; Caro, *Means of Ascent*, 19–53; Pickle OH, LBJL.

63 *O'Daniel beat Johnson:* Miller, 86–88; Evans and Novak, 14.

63 *Johnson could have responded:* Evans and Novak, 8, 13, 18, 22; Caro, *Means of Ascent*, 80–118.

64 *Truman's coolness:* Caro, *Means of Ascent*, 122–24.

64 *drifted toward the right:* Beautiful Texas, American Experience, PBS, 9/30/91.

64 *"a misnomer":* Caro, *Means of Ascent*, 126.

64 *never supported one piece:* CQ, 8/7/64, 1691–93.

65 *never played on racial fears:* Miller, 73.

65 *"far more liberal":* Connally, 53; Miller, 73.

65 *his silence was not enough:* Clifford and Virginia Durr OH, LBJL.

65 *As Johnson prepared:* Rowe OH, LBJL.

65 *abundant caution:* Connally, 66.

66 *Johnson proudly posed:* Dugger, 209–11; Miller, 73; Connally, 67.

66 *Shortly after his election:* Miller, 66.

67 *"I've always felt":* Hall OH, LBJL.

67 *Truman's civil rights program:* LBJ speech, 5/22/48, Legislative Files, House papers, Box 333, LBJL.

67 *Stealing the election:* Caro, *Means of Ascent,* 312.

67 *202 citizens: Ibid.,* 303–50.

CHAPTER FOUR

69 *tempting offers:* Fite, 239.

69 *harbored no desire: Ibid.,* 241.

70 *Ideally cast for the role:* Cohodas, 177, 179; McCullough, 645; *Atlanta Constitution,* 7/21/48.

70 *In Washington:* McCullough, 651; Cohodas, 181; Burns, *The Crosswinds of Freedom,* 238.

71 *"the damnedest tramp":* Caro, *Means of Ascent,* 373.

71 *Several weeks later:* McCullough, 695–96.

72 *Struggled to draw:* Cohodas, 181–82.

72 *On election day:* McCullough, 710, 694–95.

72 *Truman carried: Ibid.,* 710–11; *World Almanac and Book of Facts,* 396–424.

73 *"the lesson seemed":* Talmadge, 149.

73 *"The gutsy little man":* Burns, *The Crosswinds of Freedom,* 238.

73 *Black voters:* McCullough, 713; Ross, 6.

73 *Truman's fiery attacks:* Byrd, 603.

74 *a radical proposal:* RBR statement, 1/27/49, RBRL.

74 *In Russell's view:* Fite, 244.

75 *Daniel Webster:* Webster quoted by Woodrow Wilson in *Congressional Government,* 135.

75 *their de facto commander:* Reedy, author interview.

75 *this informal but effective coalition:* Fulbright, author interview; White, *Citadel,* 87; Anderson, *Outsider in the Senate,* 96; Reedy, *The U.S. Senate,* 31; Chandler, 263.

76 *"I used to wonder":* HHH OH, LBJL.

76 *Idealistic liberals such as Douglas:* Douglas, 206.

77 *"a little band of liberals":* HHH OH, LBJL.

77 *"On the surface":* Douglas, 205; White, *Citadel,* 76.

78 *survival, not southern heritage:* Ripley, 69.

78 *Greater than even seniority:* Safire, 226.

79 *"little group of willful men": Ibid.,* 226.

79 *Since 1917:* White, *Citadel,* 60.

80 *"the walls of Jericho":* Douglas, 269.

80 *sown the seeds:* Berman, *The Politics of Civil Rights in the Truman Administration,* 147; Anderson, *Insider in the Senate,* 95.

80 *"I now repeat to the Eighty-First":* Berman, *The Politics of Civil Rights in the Truman Administration,* 139, 140; Fite, 244.

81 *liberal faction fell strangely silent:* Berman, *The Politics of Civil Rights in the Truman Administration,* 143.

82 *While the liberals rested:* Dallek, 367; Evans and Novak, 32.

82 *"the last citadel":* Fite, 245.

82 *a "gag rule":* Anderson, *Outsider in the Senate,* 134.

83 *begin the battle over cloture:* CR, 2/28/49, 1583, 1593–94.

83 *his first formal remarks:* Ibid., 3/9/49, 2042–49.

84 *Johnson's words struck:* LBJ legislative files, Senate Papers, Box 214, LBJL; Hall OH, LBJL.

85 *eloquent and stinging criticism:* Rowe to LBJ, 2/23/49, Legislative Files, Senate Papers, Box 214, LBJL.

85 *Johnson responded to Rowe:* LBJ to Rowe, 3/15/49, Legislative Files, Senate Papers, Box 214, LBJL.

85 *a repudiation of the New Deal:* Miller, 144.

86 *a sign to Russell:* LBJ to Rowe, 3/15/49, Legislative Files, Senate Papers, Box 214, LBJL; Reedy, author interview; Hall OH, LBJL.

86 *two responsibilities:* Jenkins OH, LBJL.

86 *"I ran against a caveman":* Baker, 40.

87 *injured his own cause:* Berman, *The Politics of Civil Rights in the Truman Administration,* 147–48.

87 *On March 10:* Ibid., 149–51.

87 *Russell's victory:* Ibid., 152.

88 *sudden vacuum:* Minutes of 3/14/49 meeting, HHH Senate Files, Box 625, MHS.

88 *the product of that compromise:* Berman, *The Politics of Civil Rights in the Truman Administration,* 151–53; CR, 3/17/49, 2721–22.

88 *"tightens the rule of cloture":* CR, 3/17/49, 2721; 3/16/49, 2610; 3/14/49, 2419.

89 *Despite warnings from liberals:* Berman, *The Politics of Civil Rights in the Truman Administration,* 155–56; White, *Citadel,* 64. Oregon's Wayne Morse later charged that crucial Republican support for the rule had been secured by a "deal" in which unnamed Republicans supported Russell in exchange for southern opposition to the extension of electrical power lines in the Northwest.

89 *"not like the Democratic convention":* Douglas, 269.

CHAPTER FIVE

91 *watched from above:* Humphrey, 87; HHH OH, LBJL.

91 *attitude of his new colleagues:* Humphrey, 112, 87.

92 *"that damn fool":* HHH OH, LBJL; Humphrey, 87, 88; Solberg, 136; CBS News Special Report: *Some Friends of President Johnson,* 1/24/73.

92 *Humphrey's arrival in Washington:* Time, 1/17/49; Solberg, 133–34; HHH

speech to Civil Rights Symposium, 1/72; CBS Interview, The Last Interview, Box 3, LBJL.

93 *When Humphrey called on Truman:* Humphrey, 88.

93 *Humphrey took his oath of office:* Life, 9/27/68; Humphrey, 88–89.

93 *Before he left town:* Humphrey, 89.

93 *It is difficult:* Connell OH, LBJL; Vander Zee OH, USSHO; Nathan OH, MHS.

94 *As he arrived in Washington:* Kampelman, author interview; Shore OH, MHS.

94 *Paul Douglas:* Douglas, 231.

95 *He talked too much:* Connell & Nathan OH, MHS; Life, 9/27/68.

95 *"The long custom of the place":* White, *Citadel,* 82; Fulbright, author interview; Anderson, *Outsider in the Senate,* 98.

96 *No formal rites of passage:* White, *Citadel,* 83.

96 *Like elder members:* Matthews, *U.S. Senators and Their World,* 92–101.

97 *Perhaps most important:* Ibid., 101; *NYT Magazine,* 11/7/54; Wilson, 145.

97 *Howard Shuman:* Shuman OH, USSHO.

98 *when he arrived in Washington:* Life, 9/27/68; Humphrey, 85.

98 *he never stopped:* Solberg, 138–40; *Saturday Evening Post,* 10/1/49.

99 *He introduced legislation:* HHH press releases, 3/25 & 4/28/49, Senate Files, Box 625, MHS; *CR Index,* 1949; Solberg, 141.

99 *By contrast:* CR Index, 1949.

99 *Andrew Biemiller:* Biemiller OH, MHS; Kampelman, author interview.

99 *raised more than a few eyebrows:* Solberg, 139; *Newsweek,* 6/27/49; *Saturday Evening Post,* 10/1/49.

100 *"He liked to be liked":* Kampelman OH, MHS.

100 *"Is there any reason":* Rauh to HHH, 10/7/49, Senate Files, Box 625, MHS.

100 *Harry Byrd:* McPherson, 21; Chandler, 263.

101 *Humphrey first learned:* Solberg, 143.

101 *Humphrey believed:* Kampelman, author interview; Humphrey, 91.

102 *"a full and complete study":* CR, 2/24/50, 2328–29.

102 *"egregious error":* Humphrey, 92; Kampelman, author interview; Ryskind, 162.

103 *Byrd held his fire:* White, *Citadel,* 75; CR, 3/2/50, 2610–12.

103 *"As the senator from Minnesota":* Ibid., 2611–12.

103 (footnote) *Many of the committee's recommendations:* CR, 3/2/50, 2613.

104 *orchestra of praise:* Ibid., 2615–19.

104 *This humiliating parade:* Ibid., 2620–22; Solberg, 144.

104 *Humphrey was typically unbowed:* CR, 3/2/50, 2622–26.

105 *"I know when I've been licked":* Humphrey, 92.

105 *"when one attacks the old-guard coalition"*: CR, 3/2/50, 2627; Humphrey, 92.

CHAPTER SIX

106 *"Johnson 'came to the Senate' "*: Miller, 141; HHH OH, LBJL.

106 *a serious, hardworking representative:* St. Claire OH, USSHO; Ellender & Carter OH, LBJL.

107 *"the most important two hands"*: McPherson, author interview.

108 *"Johnson learned"*: Kearns, 104; Evans and Novak, 33; Donald Cook & HHH OH, LBJL.

108 *"Richard Russell found"*: Kearns, 105.

108 *"Lyndon was smart"*: Hill & Lady Bird Johnson OH, RBRL; John Connally, 121.

109 *In those early months:* Miller, 142; Dallek, 380; Darden & Hill OH, LBJL; Goldsmith, 14.

109 *Johnson's intense courtship: Richard Russell: Georgia Giant,* Cox Broadcasting, 1970; Fulbright & Darden OH, LBJL; Long, author interview.

110 *"only one way to see Russell"*: Kearns *Dream,* 103; *Richard Russell: Georgia Giant,* Cox Broadcasting, 1970.

110 *Donald Cook:* Cook OH, LBJL.

110 *attack on Leland Olds:* Evans and Novak, 35–39; Dallek, 375–77.

111 *"I was in with Paul Douglas"*: HHH OH, LBJL.

111 *Felix Longoria:* Miller, 144–45; Jenkins OH, LBJL.

112 *"I don't think Lyndon"*: Jones & HHH OH, LBJL; Miller, 148.

112 *"trying to be a captain"*: HHH OH, LBJL.

112 *his own private exile: Ibid.;* Humphrey, 104.

112 *"They had friends"*: Eisele, 93; Humphrey, 104.

112 *his easy humor:* Humphrey, 105.

113 *lunch in the senators' private dining room:* Long, author interview.

113 *"these men accepted me"*: Life, 9/27/68.

113 *Humphrey made friends:* Humphrey, 112–13; Solberg, 161.

114 *It is ironic:* Kampelman, author interview.

114 *wartime tax bill:* Heller OH, MHS.

114 *"I wanted to know"*: Solberg, 145–46; Humphrey, 105–6.

115 *a team of tax experts:* Solberg, 146; Humphrey, 106; Kampelman, author interview.

115 *no foolhardy surprise:* Humphrey, 106.

115 *"big pork barrel"*: CQ Almanac, 1950, 591; CR, 8/29/50, 13704, 13671.

115 *"I was on the floor"*: Kampelman, author interview; Kampelman, 101.

116 *"David and Goliath"*: Heller OH, MHS.

116 *"Their gesture"*: Kampelman, author interview; Kampelman, 101.

116 *"What ultimately saved the day"*: Life, 9/27/68.

117 *"That young fellow"*: Humphrey, 107; Kampelman, author interview.

117 *"or he found me"*: *Life*, 9/27/68.

117 *little personal contact*: Humphrey, 116; *Some Friends of President Johnson*, 1/24/73, CBS News.

117 *Humphrey was not alone*: Darden & Stennis OH, LBJL.

118 *"his own private FBI"*: HHH OH, LBJL.

118 *threw the door wide open*: RBR to Sparkman, 12/1/50, Dictation Series I, Box 7, RBRL; Darden OH, LBJL; *Atlanta Constitution*, 11/13/50.

119 *Ernest McFarland*: White, *Citadel*, 106.

119 *The real intrigue*: Barrow OH, LBJL; Clark OH, FMOC. "Bob Kerr was not Jesus Christ," Clark added. "Anything that Bob said went down with Lyndon. It shouldn't have, because [Kerr] wasn't that good."

119 *Johnson was much more*: Fite, 268; Darden OH, LBJL.

119 *Russell probably saw in Johnson*: Reedy OH, LBJL; Dallek, 390–91; Fite, 266; Evans and Novak, 42–43.

120 *"You'll destroy me"*: Dugger, 367.

120 *"an honorary degree"*: Miller, 150.

CHAPTER SEVEN

121 *reason for confidence*: CQ Almanac, 1950, 375–81; *Congress and the Nation*, Vol. I, 1618.

121 *elections of 1950*: Berman, *The Politics of Civil Rights in the Truman Administration*, 179; *CQ Almanac*, 1951, 333–34.

122 *"In his view"*: Reedy, *The U.S. Senate*, 91.

122 *By 1952*: Stern, Mark, "Lyndon Johnson and Richard Russell: Institutions, Ambitions and Civil Rights," *Presidential Studies Quarterly*, Fall 1991, 690.

123 *"In Russell's eyes"*: Ibid., 92.

123 *"in some place like Kalamazoo"*: Ervin OH, RBRL; Fite, 290.

123 *Russell made up his mind*: *Time*, 3/10/52; *Newsweek*, 4/28/52.

124 *Many of Russell's friends*: Long & Eastland OH, RBRL; RBR to Robert H. Bailey, 9/27/68, Dictation Series I, Box 7, RBRL; *Richard Russell: Georgia Giant*, Cox Broadcasting, 1970.

124 *a reluctant campaigner*: Smathers OH, USSHO; Greene, 135–36; Fite, 285.

125 *"In thirteen Southern states"*: *Newsweek*, 5/12/52.

125 *In Florida*: Fite, 286; *Time*, 5/19/52; *Newsweek*, 5/19/52.

126 *two immediate problems*: U.S. News & World Report, 3/7/52; *Time*, 5/19/52.

126 *Great White Hope*: *Richard Russell: Georgia Giant*, Cox Broadcasting, 1970.

126 *"I am an American"*: *Time*, 6/23/52.

126 *southerner couldn't be elected president*: Reedy OH, LBJL.

127 *an obvious sectional candidate*: Fite, 295.

127 *"personal vindication"*: Kampelman OH, MHS; *CQ Almanac,* 1952, 501.

127 *"held no allure"*: Fite, 296; Dallek, 417–18; Darden OH, LBJL; Watson, 216.

128 *"a middle-of-the-road candidate"*: Fite, 297–98; Talmadge, 154.

128 *The defeat of Senate Democratic Leader:* Eastland OH, LBJL; Stennis OH & Talmadge OH, RBRL.

129 *largely alone:* Reedy OH, LBJL; Reedy, author interview.

129 *Accounts differ:* Reedy, author interview; Evans and Novak, 51; McFarland OH, LBJL.

129 *The next morning:* Baker, 60–61.

130 *John "Jake" Carlton:* Carlton OH, RBRL.

130 *a dinner party:* Kearns, 107.

130 *"How are you going to vote"*: HHH OH, LBJL.

131 *Russell nominated Johnson:* Minutes of Democratic Conference, 1/2/53 & RBR notes, Papers of the Democratic Leader, Box 364, LBJL; *Atlanta Journal and Constitution Magazine,* 6/30/68.

132 *overwhelmingly for Johnson:* HHH OH, LBJL; Evans and Novak, 57; Dallek, 425.

132 *to chastise him:* HHH OH, LBJL.

132 *Shortly after his election:* Dallek, 429–30.

133 *Democratic minority was split:* Time, 6/22/53; White, *Citadel,* 102; Reedy memorandum, 11/6/52, Office Files of George Reedy, Box 413, LBJL; Sparkman & Cater OH, LBJL.

133 *The Democrats' cooperation:* Reedy to Mann, 2/11/95.

133 *the image of Democratic unity:* Miller, 156; Baker, 65.

134 *Johnson's tenure:* McPherson OH, LBJL; McPherson OH, MHS; Rauh OH, LBJL.

134 *his first day as leader:* Riddick OH, USSHO; *Time,* 6/22/53.

135 *energetic work habits:* Rowe, Long, McGee & HHH OH, LBJL; Miller, 174.

135 *"Watching him go"*: NYT Magazine, 12/1/63.

135 *Besides his imposing physical presence:* Shuman OH, USSHO; Jackson & Clements OH, LBJL.

136 *his only passions:* Reedy OH, LBJL.

136 *"an area of compromise"*: Talmadge OH, LBJL.

136 *acute sense of timing:* Smathers OH, USSHO.

137 *increase the minimum wage:* Miller, 176.

137 *late 1954: Ibid.,* 163.

137 *A united Democratic party: Ibid.,* 173.

138 *pragmatic vote counts:* Watson, 216.

138 *The "continuing body" principal: Ibid.,* 357.

138 *In early January:* Anderson, *Outsider in the Senate,* 130–32; Rauh OH, LBJL.

139 *"the art of the possible":* Mitchell OH, LBJL; Mitchell OH, MSRC; Rauh OH, LBJL.

139 *Johnson's cooperative relationship: Beautiful Texas,* PBS, The American Experience, 9/30/91; Connally, 130; Weisl Jr. OH, LBJL.

140 *Constant grumbling: NYT Magazine,* 12/1/63.

140 *Timing, votes, and Democratic unity:* Shuman OH, USSHO; *Atlanta Journal and Constitution Magazine,* 6/30/68.

140 *"admiring patronage":* White, *Citadel,* 102; Smathers OH, USSHO; Smith OH, LBJL.

141 *Johnson's domineering leadership:* Douglas, 234; Long OH, LBJL.

141 *"gain all the power":* Thurmond OH, LBJL.

141 *"a back-alley job":* Kearns, 122.

142 *"cowboy making love":* HHH OH, LBJL.

142 *Jim Rowe:* Rowe OH, LBJL.

142 *bridge to the liberals:* Vander Zee OH, USSHO; Kearns, 133.

143 *"a big old reed":* Kearns, 133; McPherson OH, MHS; Solberg, 163.

143 *"the first man": Some Friends of President Johnson,* 1/24/73, CBS News.

143 *"I always felt":* HHH OH, LBJL; Solberg, 161, 163.

144 *"a second value":* Humphrey, 115.

144 *"early in the game":* Biemiller & McPherson OH, MHS.

144 *"did a great deal":* HHH OH, LBJL; *New Republic,* 11/14/55; Mooney & Siegel OH, LBJL.

145 *By 1953:* HHH to RBR, 12/31/52, Civil Rights X, Box 99; HHH to RBR, 1/26/53; & RBR to HHH, 1/28/53, Civil Rights X, Box 22, RBRL.

145 *Johnson was seducing him:* HHH OH, LBJL; Kearns, 132.

145 *"The liberals are very independent":* HHH OH, LBJL.

146 *"get shot down in flames":* Muskie OH, MHS.

146 *"learned early": Life,* 9/27/68; Douglas OH, LBJL; HHH to Thomas L. Stokes, 1/23/53, HHH Senatorial Files, Correspondence (legislative), Box 104, MHS.

146 *"beachhead among Southern conservatives": New Republic,* 11/14/55; HHH to Cecil Newman, 1/18/55; HHH to Walter White, 1/13/55; HHH to Walter White, 2/8/55, HHH Papers, Correspondence (legislative), Box 117, MHS.

147 *Humphrey often urged:* Muskie OH, MHS; Shuman OH, USSHO.

147 *"On the basic things":* HHH OH, LBJL.

148 *"I don't know about you":* Kampelman, author interview.

148 *"persuade both sides":* McPherson, author interview.

148 *"chemistry of the body":* Kampelman, 99.

CHAPTER EIGHT

150 *In support of these measures:* Bennett, 260.

150 *"fragile legal props":* Ibid.

151 *"Sir, it is no secret":* Nolen, 87.

151 *clever roadblocks:* Matthews and Prothro, 13–14.

151 *advocate for the white man:* Morison, 108; Matthews and Prothro, 15; Bennett, 274.

152 *Lynching was common:* Bennett, 352.

152 *In 1940:* Matthews and Prothro, 17–18.

152 *"formless and shapeless mass":* Bennett, 277.

152 *Frustrated at every turn:* Myrdal, 503; Wilkins OH, CUOHC.

153 *Federal employment opportunities:* Myrdal, 319, 338–39.

154 *"The question":* WP, 7/7/87.

154 *Supreme Court's imprimatur:* Burns, *The Crosswinds of Freedom*, 321; Bennett, 376; Nevins and Commager, 534; O'Neill, 249; Halberstam, 423.

154 *Perhaps no group:* Cohodas, 254; Pollack, 176.

155 *In a letter to Judge:* LBJ to Wilson, 5/28/54, U.S. Senate Legislative Files, 1953–54, Box 252, LBJL; Stern, *Presidential Studies Quarterly*, Fall 1991; Dallek, 445.

155 *"We say to the Supreme Court":* Bennett, 376.

156 *its initial Brown decision:* Goldman, 112; Berman, *It Is So Ordered*, 123; Bartley and Graham, 53.

157 *Parks's arrest:* Garrow, *Bearing the Cross*, 13.

157 *Like Parks:* Ibid., 16; Branch, 146.

157 *"more like a boy":* Garrow, *Bearing the Cross*, 20.

157 *"We are not here":* Ibid., 24.

158 *boycott enjoyed greater success:* Branch, 162; Garrow, *Bearing the Cross*, 58.

158 *Three nights later:* Branch, 196.

158 *"We have just started":* Garrow, *Bearing the Cross*, 83.

159 *"It is disturbing":* CQ Almanac, 1956, 51.

159 *a cautious moderate:* Duram, 54, 61.

159 *"cordial relations":* O'Neill, 253; Ambrose, 189–92.

159 *Any real progress:* Watson, 226–27.

160 *"interposition":* U.S. News & World Report, 5/28/54.

161 *A controversial document:* Cohodas, 283–84.

161 *"to head off":* Reedy OH, LBJL.

162 *Initially, Russell obtained:* Fite, 333; RBR to M. Hayes Mizell, 4/30/62, RBRL.

162 *"civil rights act was inevitable":* Reedy OH, LBJL.

162 *"I took one quick look":* Gore, 104.

162 *"The unwarranted decision":* CR, 3/12/56, 4460.

163 *Moments after George finished: Ibid.*, 4461.

163 *Morse fumed: Ibid.*, 4462.

164 *"If we persist": Ibid.*, 4463.

164 *"We live in a world": Ibid.*, 4463.

164 *The most significant aspect: Ibid.*, 4464; LBJ statement, 3/10/56, U.S. Senate, Office Files of George Reedy, Box 423, LBJL.

164 *Johnson had struggled:* Baker, 70.

165 *Russell never pressured Johnson:* Reedy OH, LBJL; Stennis OH, LBJL.

165 *his refusal to sign: Ibid.*

165 *reasons not to sign:* Reedy OH, LBJL; Reedy memorandum, June 9, 1955, Papers of George Reedy, Box 415, LBJL.

165 *broader vision:* Dallek, 490–91; Hays OH, LBJL; H OH, LBJL.

CHAPTER NINE

167 *an informal White House dinner:* Warren, 291.

167 *Eisenhower's clumsy attempt:* Eisenhower, 149; Burk, 157–58; Ambrose, 303; *CQ Almanac*, 1956, 51.

168 *dizzying series of events: CQ Almanac*, 1956, 458.

168 *Brownell's idea: NYT*, 7/18/57; Brownell, 199.

169 *Brownell's real strategy:* Reedy to Mann, 2/11/95.

169 *Brownell's early drafts:* Adams, 335–39; *CQ Almanac*, 1956, 459.

169 *generated more scorn:* Brownell, 203; *NYT*, 4/10/56.

170 *By late April: CQ Almanac*, 1956, 459–60.

170 *On the other side of the Capitol:* Reedy to LBJ, 7/24/56, Office Files of George Reedy, Box 420, LBJL.

170 *"regular and orderly procedure":* HHH to Pearson, 12/31/56, Senatorial Files, 1949–64, HHH Papers, MHS.

171 (footnote) *"drive the South out":* Minutes of Democratic Policy Committee, 6/27/56, Papers of the Democratic Leader, Box 364, LBJL.

171 *"a symbol of racism":* New Orleans *Times-Picayune*, 3/3/56.

171 *"respect for Douglas":* Mooney OH, LBJL.

171 *Unlike Johnson:* Shuman OH, USSHO; Sydney H. Schanberg, *Newsday*, 11/4/94; Mooney OH, LBJL; McPherson, 30.

172 *"For the first time":* Douglas, 285.

172 *The Douglas-Lehman plan: CR*, 7/23/56, 13937; Douglas, 281; *CR*, 6/17/57, 9348; Anderson, *Eisenhower, Brownell, and the Congress*, 100.

173 *Douglas was furious: CR*, 7/23/56, 13996, 14163.

173 *a parliamentary minefield:* Shuman OH, USSHO.

174 *"If every resort is to be made": CR*, 7/24/56, 14163.

174 *Douglas kept his word: Ibid.*, 14191, 14194, 14198, 14201–2, 14216, 14220.

174 *Douglas escalated the hostilities: Ibid.*, 14216; Watson, 346; Rauh OH, MSRC.

175 *the Senate upheld its leader:* CR, 7/24/56, 14229.
175 *a crushing blow:* CQ Almanac, 1956, 464; Douglas, 281; Shuman OH, USSHO.

CHAPTER TEN

176 *"sitting firmly in the lap":* New Republic, 11/14/55.
177 *"ashes and sackcloth":* Solberg, 173–74.
177 *"his vice-presidential running mate":* Humphrey, 136.
177 *another cruel disappointment:* Ibid., 136–37; Eisele, 103–04; Solberg, 173–76.
178 *"all proposals for the use of force":* Congress and the Nation, Vol. I, 1620.
178 *"worst" defeat:* Solberg, 176; LBJ to HHH, 9/18/56, HHH Papers, Senatorial Files, Correspondence (legislative), Box 225, MHS.
178 *Johnson's wake-up call:* Watson, 355.
178 *Democrats were most alarmed:* Ibid., 354–55; Anderson, *Eisenhower, Brownell, and the Congress,* 134; Eisenhower, 154.
180 *"to go along with Eisenhower":* Minow OH, LBJL.
180 *Humphrey had assured Johnson:* Dallek, 507–8; HHH to LBJ, 9/10/56, HHHH Papers, Senatorial Files, Correspondence (legislative), Box 225, MHS; Eisele, 104; Solberg, 178.
180 *An anonymous memorandum:* Undated memo, Senate Papers, Office Files of George Reedy, Box 420, LBJL; Solberg, 178.
180 *liberal revolt in his ranks:* Kearns, 147.
181 *"You're crazy":* Siegel OH, LBJL; Douglas OH, LBJL; Marshall OH, LBJL; Henry OH, LBJL.
181 *"he believed in civil rights legislation":* Mitchell OH, LBJL.
182 *"for civil rights from the very beginning":* Reedy, author interview; Weisl Jr. OH, LBJL.
182 *The real Johnson:* Watson, *Lion in the Lobby,* 338; Miller, *Lyndon,* 177.
182 *"in any way anti-Semitic":* Shuman OH, USSHO; Rauh OH, LBJL; Mitchell OH, LBJL.
182 *No longer content to wait:* Anderson, *Outsider in the Senate,* 144–45; Shuman OH, USSHO; Congress and the Nation, Vol. I, 1427.
183 *The strong-arm tactics Johnson employed:* Anderson, *Outsider in the Senate,* 145.
183 *portended their ultimate success:* CQ, 8/7/64, 1694; Rauh OH, MSRC; Reedy to LBJ, undated, Senate Papers, Legislative Files, 57–58, Box 291, LBJL; Reedy to LBJ, undated, U.S. Senate, 1949–61, Office Files of Solis Horwitz, Box 408, LBJL.
184 *a NATO conference in Paris:* Reedy to Michael Gillette, 6/2/82, LBJL.
184 *House passed Eisenhower's civil rights bill:* CQ Almanac, 1957, 557.
185 *"throb to flood control":* Reedy, *Lyndon Johnson,* 113.

185 *the new coalition:* CR, 6/18/57, 9506; Mooney, Jackson, Humphrey & Hagerty OH, LBJL; Smathers OH, USSHO; Ambrose, 164.

186 *Douglas had grown wiser:* CQ Almanac, 1957, 561; CR, 6/17/57, 9348; CQ Almanac, 1957, 561; Shuman OH, USSHO; CR, 6/20/57, 9827.

186 *a curious collection of Republicans and Democrats:* Eisenhower, 155.

186 *"working to prevent the passage":* LBJ to Johnny Cooner, 7/10/57, U.S. Senate Papers, 1949–61, Box 289, LBJL.

187 *"to blame the Democrats for its defeat":* Anderson, *Outsider in the Senate,* 146.

187 *Another, more intriguing motivation:* CR, 6/20/57, 9827.

187 *a sudden, "unexplained" about-face:* Congress and the Nation, Vol. I, 946–54.

188 *Douglas felt particularly betrayed:* Douglas, 286–87; Congress and the Nation, Vol. I, 954.

188 *nothing short of brilliant:* Long OH, LBJL; Kearns, 149.

CHAPTER ELEVEN

189 *an ambitious program:* Friedman, 64; *Congressional Digest,* 4/57, 108, 110; NYT, 10/20, 10/24 & 10/25, 1956; *Time,* 7/29/57; Monroe (Louisiana) *Morning World,* 10/19/56; U.S. Commission on Civil Rights, *With Liberty and Justice for All,* 76.

191 *There was much about the administration bill:* Miller, 206; Newsweek, 7/15 & 7/22, 1957.

191 *southerners particularly abhorred Part IV:* Watson, 362.

192 *found Part III weak:* Douglas, 285.

192 *the bill had remained virtually intact:* Ibid., 288.

192 *Russell rose on the floor of the Senate:* CR, 7/2/57, 10771–75; WP, 7/3/57; U.S. News & World Report, 7/12/57.

194 *a major news event:* WP, 7/3/57; NYT, 7/3/57; U.S. News & World Report, 7/12/57.

194 *At a press conference the next day:* CQ Almanac, 1957, 562.

194 *"I am not enough of a lawyer":* Public Papers of the Presidents of the United States, Dwight D. Eisenhower, 1/1 to 12/31/57, 357.

194 *"time, diligence, and some legal training":* NYT, 7/13/57.

195 *In the wake of Russell's assault:* CR, 7/11/57, 11350; Time, 7/22/57.

195 *"We were sunk":* Douglas, 288; Shuman OH, USSHO; Time, 7/22/57.

195 *The irony of Russell's life:* NYT, 7/3/57.

195 *"just fighting a delaying action":* Time, 8/12/57.

196 *Russell did not attempt to force his views:* Long, author interview; Stennis OH, RBRL.

196 *South Carolina's Strom Thurmond:* Transcript of RBR phone conversation with Carter Pittman, 9/2/57, RBRL; Fite, 338; Time, 7/22 & 8/12/57; Newsweek, 7/15/57.

197 *A compromise bill:* Burns, *John Kennedy*, 205.

197 *After the southern meeting:* Time, 8/12/57.

197 *Thirty years later:* Thurmond, author interview.

197 *As the Senate approached: Richard Russell: Georgia Giant*, Cox Broadcasting, 1970.

197 *Nixon told a group of House freshmen:* WP, 7/11/57; Newsweek, 8/5/57.

198 *Emanuel Celler knew better:* WP, 7/11/57.

198 *"wouldn't twist anybody's arm":* D'Ewart OH, CUOHC.

198 *Johnson exhorted his colleagues:* CR, 7/12/57, 11442.

198 *Johnson had known what it would take:* Eisenhower, 159.

199 *"one side cannot vote for anything":* Reedy to LBJ, undated, Senate Papers, Legislative Files, 1957–58, Box 291, LBJL.

199 *"Armageddon for Lyndon Johnson":* Rowe to LBJ, 7/3/57, Office Files of George Reedy, Box 421, LBJL.

199 *When he did speak in the Senate:* New Leader, 8/5/57; CR, 7/9/57, 11057, 7/10/57, 11176, 7/11/57, 11307, 7/12/57, 11500 & 7/15/57, 11623.

200 *Russell, too, exhorted his troops:* Time, 8/12/57.

200 *split his troops into sectors: Ibid.*

200 *Johnson broke new ground:* CR, 7/16/57, 11826.

200 *the decades-old coalition:* Newsweek, 7/29/57; NYT, 7/15/57.

201 *southerners were massively outnumbered:* CQ Almanac, 1957, 562.

201 *"I think there is a way":* Anderson, *Outsider in the Senate*, 147.

202 *"glued" himself to his desk:* Anderson OH, LBJL. Most published accounts have given Johnson credit for persuading Anderson to spearhead the amendment to strike Part III. "He didn't at all," Anderson insisted.

202 *" 'Beware of the Greeks' ":* CR, 7/26/57, 12825.

202 *"If you were going to filibuster":* Reedy, author interview.

203 *Eisenhower's weak, faltering defense: Public Papers of the Presidents of the United States, Dwight D. Eisenhower*, 1/1 to 12/31, 1957, 555.

203 *"At two successive press conferences":* CQ Almanac, 1957, 566; WP, 7/19/57.

203 *Johnson quickly moved:* White, *The Professional*, 217.

203 *Humphrey offered an amendment:* CR, 7/23/57, 12429.

204 *"The vote on Part III": Ibid.,* 7/24/57, 12564 & 7/24/57, 12565.

204 *"the bill was strengthened": Ibid.,* 7/25/57, 12714.

204 *Such a scheme:* Reedy to Michael Gillette, 6/2/82, Reedy OH, LBJL; Reedy, author interview.

204 *"These Negroes":* Kearns, 148; *Beautiful Texas*, PBS, American Experience, 9/30/91.

205 *"Hubert, it don't take any genius": Beautiful Texas*, PBS, American Experience, 9/30/91.

205 *"Paul, be ready":* McPherson, author interview.

205 *"the liberals, unfortunately, closed the line":* Miller, *Lyndon,* 209.

206 *"routine acquittals of white offenders":* Reedy, *Lyndon B. Johnson,* 116.

206 *"full scope of the dilemma":* Ibid.

206 *After a spirited struggle:* CQ Almanac, 1957, 557.

207 *Douglas began building the case:* Ibid., 6/10/57, 8606.

207 *"we fully support trial by jury":* CQ Almanac, 1957, 567.

208 *"Running all through our Constitution":* CR, 7/10/57, 11197; Open Hearing, ABC, 6/14/57, reprinted in CR, 7/22/57, 12290.

208 *Johnson worked furiously:* Church & Tully OH, LBJL.

208 *"may well have justified his entire career":* Reedy, *Lyndon B. Johnson,* 117.

209 *the means to cut the jury trial knot:* Auerbach article reprinted in CR, 7/29/57, 12873–74; Auerbach OH, MHS; *The Reporter,* 9/5/57; Church OH, LBJL; Reedy OH, LBJL.

210 *Johnson's challenge now:* Evans and Novak, 134; Brinkley, 205.

210 *"Senator O'Mahoney kept on introducing":* Horwitz OH, LBJL; *Face the Nation,* 7/28/57.

210 *While Johnson's staff labored:* Horwitz OH, LBJL; CQ Almanac, 1957, 565.

210 *Green was particularly crucial:* Evans and Novak, 135–37.

211 *"haven't got the votes":* Reporter, 9/5/57.

211 *a powerful new ally:* Reporter, 9/5/57; CR, 8/1/57, 13234; Newsweek, 8/12/57; Evans and Novak, 137.

212 *Another important vote:* Evans and Novak, 128; CR, 8/2/57, 13356.

213 *"I was* persona non grata": Church OH, LBJL.

213 *he had considered two options:* Time, 8/12/57.

213 *Johnson persuaded Church:* Horwitz OH, LBJL.

213 *With the Senate in rapt attention:* CR, 7/31/57, 13153–54.

214 *"the little Italian dancing master":* Ibid., 7/31/57, 13157–62; Horwitz OH, LBJL; Reedy, *Lyndon B. Johnson,* 119.

214 *"I consider it a mistake":* CR, 8/1/57, 13306.

215 *Humphrey's was another vote:* Auerbach OH, MHS.

215 *"Johnson seemed to have his number":* Shuman OH, USSHO; CR, 8/16/57, 14996.

215 *Humphrey played a minor role:* Solberg, 180; HHH to Reuther, 1/22/57, HHH Senatorial Files, 49–64, MHS.

216 *On the evening of August 2:* Time, 8/12/57.

216 *Johnson received additional assurance:* Evans and Novak, 138; Reporter, 9/5/57.

216 *As the debate began to lose its steam:* CR, 8/1/57, 13356.

217 *When voting ended:* Time 8/12/57; CR, 8/1/57, 13356 & 8/2/57, 13422; Congress and the Nation, Vol. I, 1957, 1624; NYT, 8/2/57.

217 *Johnson deserved credit:* CR, 8/12/57, 14401; Washington Evening Star, 8/5/57.

217 *"largely ineffective"*: CQ Almanac, 1957, 564, 568; *Washington Evening Star*, 8/2 & 8/5/57; *CR*, 8/2/57, 13485.

217 *Johnson inserted a fusillade*: *CR*, 8/5/57, 13539–40.

218 *Eisenhower's veiled veto threats*: *Washington Evening Star*, 8/9/57.

218 *philosophical resignation of pragmatic liberals*: *CR*, 8/6/57, 13698–99.

218 *"no Johnny-come-lately"*: *Ibid.*, 8/7/57, 13851.

219 *"the implications of my vote"*: *Ibid.*, 13898.

219 *the Senate made history*: *CQ Almanac*, 1957, 563.

219 *a last-minute endorsement*: Rauh OH, MSRC.

220 *Martin briefly suggested*: *CR*, 8/14/57, 14726 & 8/12/57, 14361–62.

220 *Two weeks of negotiations*: Eisenhower, 161; *CR*, 8/23/57, 15793; *CQ Almanac*, 1957, 568.

221 *"I rise to speak"*: Cohodas, 294; *NYT*, 8/30/57.

221 *a "cold fury"*: Reedy OH, LBJL. *NYT*, 8/30/57; Long, author interview.

221 *the Senate passed the Civil Rights Act*: *NYT*, 8/30/57; *CQ Almanac*, 1957, 569; Ambrose, 412; transcript of RBR phone conversation with Carter Pittman, 9/2/57, RBRL.

221 *Johnson received rave reviews*: Douglas, 290; *NYT*, 8/25/57; White & Clifford OH, LBJL; Reedy to Michael Gillette, 6/2/82, LBJL; Webb B. Joiner to LBJ, 8/23/57 & E.B. Sloss to LBJ, 9/23/57, Legislative Files, Senate Papers, Box 289, LBJL.

222 *The bill had political implications*: Wicker OH, LBJL; Burns, *John Kennedy*, 204; Rauh OH, JFKL.

222 *initial judgments of the bill itself*: *Beautiful Texas*, PBS, American Experience, 9/30/91; Marshall OH, LBJL; Wofford, author interview; Thurmond, author interview.

223 *southern senators quickly noted*: Text of 10/8/57 RBR speech, Speech Files, Box 31, RBRL.

223 *"Maybe I voted wrong"*: Miller, 212.

224 *"a genuine defeat for racism"*: Anderson, *Outsider in the Senate*, 148.

CHAPTER TWELVE

225 *Eisenhower initially refused to intervene*: Ambrose, 421.

226 *Mann wired Eisenhower*: Branch, 224. Other sources on the Little Rock crisis: Duram, 143–159; Ambrose, 413–23; Bartley, 251–69; *U.S. News & World Report*, 10/4/57.

227 *loath to send troops into the South*: *U.S. News & World Report*, 10/4/57; RBR statement, 10/24/57; RBRL; Goldsmith, 66.

227 *a lengthy, passionate telegram*: RBR to Eisenhower and Wilson, 9/26/57, RBRL; Eisenhower, 173.

228 *rhetoric of other southerners*: *U.S. News & World Report*, 10/4/57.

228 *not the only ones critical of the president*: *Ibid.*, 10/4/57.

228 *"Even the moderates":* Newsweek, 10/7/57.

229 *"profane the name":* RBR speech draft, 2/17/58, Dictation Series I, RBRL.

229 *the Supreme Court upheld:* Morison, 457; RBR statements, 9/12/58, RBRL.

229 *Russell's growing despair:* Fite, 346; *Congress and the Nation*, Vol. I, 1497–1501.

230 *"a more equitable distribution":* RBR statement, 12/22/58, Dictation Series I, RBRL.

231 *a series of controversial court rulings:* McPherson, 131; Case OH, LBJL.

231 *The results were several measures: Congress and the Nation*, Vol. I, 1442; *CQ Almanac*, 1958, 287–91; Watson, 411.

232 *On August 20:* McPherson, author interview; *CQ Almanac*, 1958, 287, 291.

232 *no reason for concern:* McPherson, author interview; McPherson, 133.

232 *unwisely provoked the Senate's conservatives: CQ Almanac*, 1958, 291–95.

233 *The liberals were aghast:* McPherson, author interview; Humphrey OH, LBJL.

233 *Sitting alongside Johnson:* McPherson, author interview.

233 *At Russell's gentle prodding:* CR, 8/20/58, 18750.

233 *demanded a roll call vote: Ibid.,* 18750; Lewis, author interview.

233 *Johnson stormed over to Humphrey:* McPherson, author interview.

233 *For more than an hour:* Lewis, author interview.

234 *Johnson's performance: Ibid.;* McPherson, 134.

234 *Johnson needed was a different approach:* McPherson, author interview; Lewis, author interview; Evans and Novak, 166.

235 *On the afternoon of August 21:* CR, 8/21/58, 18928; Dallek, 537; *NYT,* 8/25/58.

235 *a period of disappointment:* Goldsmith, 69–70; Jones, author interview; McPherson, 167.

235 *chain-smoking caught up with Russell:* Dunahoo, Darden & Leonard OH, RBRL; Jones, author interview.

236 *"The responsibility for this disaster":* Time, 11/17/58.

236 *Southerners were especially despondent: Ibid.;* RBR speech text, 2/10/59, Speech Files, RBRL; Foley, 27.

237 *transformed the ideological complexion: CQ Almanac*, 1958, 713–15, 739–46; Foley, 25–27.

237 *liberals were ecstatic:* Clark, 9; Connell OH, LBJL.

237 *restive majority to lead:* McPherson OH, LBJL; Evans and Novak, 196.

238 *a dynamic new leader:* Bennett OH, FMOC; MacNeil, 167.

238 *Johnson moved forcefully: Business Week*, 5/2/59.

239 *leftward, westward shift:* Time, 1/19/59; Fite, 347.

239 *"meaningless gesture": CQ Almanac*, 1959, 213.

239 *On January 12: Face the Nation,* 1/18/59, CBS News, 16, 17; *Time,* 1/19/59.

240 *absolute sway over committee assignments:* Shuman OH, USSHO; *CQ*

Almanac, 1959, 212–14; Evans and Novak, 200–202; Dallek, 547; *Face the Nation*, 1/18/59, 18.

240 *Despite the liberals' harsh judgment:* Horwitz OH, LBJL; *CQ Almanac*, 1959, 213.

241 *Another fissure in Johnson's leadership: CR*, 2/23/59, 2814–17.

241 *a growing sentiment among Democrats:* Proxmire OH, LBJL; McPherson, 169.

241 *Proxmire's attack outraged and offended Johnson:* Shaffer, 217; Foley, 31.

242 *Publicly, Johnson responded: CQ*, 6/5/59, 766; *Face the Nation*, 1/18/59, 19.

242 *avoid the divisive and tiring issue:* Dallek, 549.

243 *"dragging his feet on that right to vote": Face the Nation*, 9/27/59, 309.

243 *On January 20: CQ Almanac*, 1959, 291.

243 *The bill's centerpiece:* Horwitz to LBJ, 2/16/59, U.S. Senate, 49–61, Office Files of Solis Horwitz, Box 408, LBJL.

243 *Wilkins reacted coolly:* NAACP press release, 1/22/59, Legislative Files, Senate Papers, Files of Solis Horwitz, Box 408, LBJL.

243 *White House offered its own bill: CQ Almanac*, 1959, 291.

244 *The most extensive bill: Ibid.*, 291. Several of the legislative proposals in the various bills were outgrowths of investigations and recommendations from the Civil Rights Commission. After concluding that "legislation presently on the books is inadequate to assure that all our qualified citizens . . . enjoy the right to vote," commissioners offered a series of recommendations. These included a requirement that state and local registrars maintain voting records for five years (included in the administration bill), the appointment of federal registrars in the South (later incorporated into legislation by Humphrey and Douglas), and creation of "an advisory and conciliation service" to mediate local disputes over desegregation (adopted by Johnson in his legislation).

244 *Russell, predictably, opposed all of the bills: CQ*, 2/13/59, 277; *CQ Almanac*, 1959, 292.

244 *unaware of the liberals' determination: CQ*, 4/24/59, 569 & 4/6/60, 757–58.

245 *sputtering drive for a civil rights bill: Ibid.*, 2/19/60, 254.

245 *an important concession: Ibid.*, 9/18/59, 1282; *CQ Almanac*, 1959, 292; *CR*, 2/15/60, 2477; Chappell, 171.

245 *Russell regarded Johnson's move:* Russell speech excepts, Dawson (Georgia) Lions Club, 12/10/59, RBRL.

246 *authentic nature of southern race relations:* Miller, *227;* Branch, 271–75; Bennett, 383–84.

246 *brewing unrest throughout the South:* Branch, 272.

CHAPTER THIRTEEN

247 *promise to take up a civil rights bill:* Miller, 226.

247 *game of verbal gymnastics:* RBR speech text, 2/8/60, Speech Files, RBRL.

247 *Eisenhower's civil rights bill:* Miller, 227.

248 *Russell again sounded the alarms:* RBR speech text, 2/9/60, Speech Files, RBRL.

248 *alternative to Eisenhower's voting referee proposal:* CQ, 2/19/60, 255.

248 *On February 15:* CR, 2/15/60, 2444.

248 *unfinished business now before the Senate:* Ibid., 2470.

249 *Johnson's move was brilliant:* McPherson, author interview.

249 *Johnson's clever tactic:* CR, 2/15/60, 2470, 72.

249 *an acrimonious exchange:* Ibid., 2471.

250 *Johnson's sneak attack:* Siegel to LBJ, 2/2/60, Papers of the Democratic Leader, Box 374, LBJL.

250 *before the Little Rock crisis:* Talmadge, 187; RBR speech text, 2/9/60, Speech Files, RBRL; *CQ Almanac,* 1960, 197.

251 *Russell moved to postpone:* CQ Almanac, 1960, 198; CR, 2/17/60, 2727.

251 *after a week of running in place:* CR, 2/23/60, 3220.

251 *filibuster began to take life:* Ibid.

252 *concerned abut the physical strain:* Ibid., 2/26/60, 3575, 3580.

253 *"Look, Dick":* Talmadge, 185; Talmadge, author interview.

253 *Talmadge's proposal:* Talmadge, author interview; Ervin OH, RBRL.

254 *"The only way the opposition could hope":* Talmadge, 185.

254 *In a matter of days:* Javits, 339; WP, 3/3/60.

255 *"typical day":* Cotton, 120–21.

255 *fresh and well rested:* Ervin OH, RBRL; Talmadge, author interview; Sparkman OH, RBRL; Shuman OH, USSHO.

256 *constant alert for surprise attacks:* Miller, 228.

256 *By March 5:* CQ Almanac, 1960, 198.

257 *some tense moments:* NYT, 3/5/60; Atlanta Journal, 3/4/60.

257 *"Saturday-night bath":* Ervin OH, RBRL; NYT, 3/6/60.

257 *a partial southern victory seemed assured:* CR, 3/8/60, 4934 & 3/10/60, 5114, 5118; CQ Almanac, 1960, 199.

258 *the first on cloture since 1954:* NYT, 3/11/60; CR, 3/10/60, 5182.

258 *Johnson searched for a compromise:* NYT, 3/5/60.

258 *from Louisiana's Russell Long:* Douglas, 21; Shuman OH, USSHO; Long to Mann, 3/8/93; CQ Almanac, 1960, 195.

259 *On March 4:* CQ Almanac, 1960, 199.

259 *Johnson moved to abandon the Senate legislation:* CR, 3/24/60, 6452–55.

259 *In two days of hearings:* CQ Almanac, 1960, 200.

260 *satisfy only the moderates:* CR, 4/8/60, 7737; Clark, 14; Time, 4/18/60.

260 *"This is the way the world ends":* CR, 4/8/60, 7737, 7805.

260 *a virtually deserted gallery:* Newsweek, 4/11/60; CQ Almanac, 1960, 200.

260 *negotiated a fair deal:* RBR press release, 4/11/60, RBRL. George Reedy

maintained that Johnson's prospects as a presidential nominee in 1960 helped to keep "the southerners in line" and gave Johnson the "elbow room" for compromise that Russell and others would not have accorded him "if he were just another senator from Texas."

260 *satisfied no one completely: New York Post*, 3/11/60.

261 *John F. Kennedy of Massachusetts:* Chappell, 173.

262 *Stuart Symington:* White, *The Making of the President 1960*, 45.

262 *As for Humphrey:* Eisele, 107; Humphrey, 142–48.

262 *When he announced his candidacy:* White, *The Making of the President 1960*, 38.

262 *"You are just not that well known":* Humphrey, 149.

263 *another important aspect to Johnson's strategy:* McPherson, 171; Humphrey OH, LBJL.

263 *rely on* Republican *colleagues for help:* Young OH, LBJL.

264 *"I suspected":* Mooney, *LBJ*, 127.

264 *by stressing his role as Senate leader:* McPherson, 172; Shuman OH, USSHO.

264 *Johnson also waited too long:* Reedy & McFarland OH, LBJL.

265 *"He came into the bedroom carrying coffee":* Eisele, 141.

265 *the primaries were the only route:* White, *The Making of the President 1960*, 95; Humphrey, 151.

266 *Kennedy was much better organized:* Humphrey, 151.

266 *West Virginia seemed tailor-made:* Fleming, *1960*, 5–11, 14, 105; Humphrey, 157; White, *The Making of the President 1960*, 131.

266 *"Is anyone going to tell me":* Fleming, 37.

267 *"I didn't expect it to become so bitter":* Eisele, 145.

267 *Kennedy decisively won:* Humphrey, 162; White, *The Making of the President 1960*, 135.

268 *"Yet it was Kennedy's ordeal and triumph":* Wofford, 48; Goodwin, 79.

268 *The next morning:* McPherson, 174; Humphrey, 163.

268 *Bitter memories of the hard-fought race:* Eisele, 151.

268 *Kennedy invited Rauh to share a taxi:* Rauh OH, LBJL.

CHAPTER FOURTEEN

270 *Johnson had traveled to New York:* Miller, 239.

270 *"no time for the people":* Freeman OH, LBJL.

271 *Many liberals:* Miller, 240.

271 *Johnson's reluctance to sell himself aggressively:* Connally, 161.

271 *To bolster his standing among black leaders:* Wofford, 47; *CQ*, 5/13/60, 849.

272 *notable exceptions to this view:* Wofford, 47.

272 *Bowles first presented the civil rights language:* Bowles, 291.

272 *"What Bowles may not have made clear"*: Wofford, author interview; Wofford, 51. According to Bowles, he also presented the draft of the strong civil rights plank to southern members of the Platform Committee at an "off-the-record" breakfast meeting. "I stressed our determination to present a strong civil rights plank to the convention," Bowles recalled, "and added that we had the votes to do so. However, I was anxious to avoid as far as possible language that would arouse a passionately negative response in their states and force them into making bitter speeches" (Bowles, 291).

273 *"all out for the Bowles platform"*: Wofford, author interview.

273 *Imagine Bowles's surprise*: Bowles, 292; Wofford, 52; *CQ Almanac*, 1960, 772.

273 *stunning in its commitment to bold action*: *CQ*, 7/15/60, 1248.

273 *"like a child in a candy store"*: Rauh OH, MSRC.

274 *Instead of walking out*: *CQ*, 7/15/60, 1250; *CQ Almanac*, 1960, 773.

274 *Such were the declining fortunes*: *CQ*, 7/29/60, 1352.

274 *Shortly before the convention*: Talmadge OH, LBJL; Talmadge, author interview.

275 *"Most vice presidents don't do much"*: *Meet the Press*, 7/10/60.

275 *"this was absolutely impossible"*: McGee OH, LBJL; Bryant OH, LBJL.

275 *Johnson's dismissing the idea*: Dallek, 565; McGovern OH, LBJL; Miller, 241.

275 *When the end finally came*: Miller, 253; Hardeman and Bacon, 439.

276 *On the morning of July 14*: Robert Kennedy OH, JFKL.

276 *Kennedy's staff opposed*: O'Donnell et al., 217.

277 *Kennedy needed peaceful relations*: *Ibid.*, 218.

277 *Meanwhile, in Johnson's camp*: Baker, 126; Miller, 256.

277 *"Well, hell, I'm tired"*: McPherson OH, LBJL.

278 *Bob Kerr burst into the room*: Harris & Ellington OH, LBJL.

278 *"I accept"*: Miller, 262.

278 *liberals and black leaders who were outraged*: Diggs & Farmer OH, LBJL.

278 *"all hell broke loose"*: Humphrey & Monroney OH, LBJL; Strober, 21; Viorst, 238; Matusow, 16.

279 *the brilliance of Kennedy's selection*: Strober, 20; Freeman OH, LBJL; *New Republic*, 7/25/60.

279 *Voices of conservative dissent*: *Human Events*, 8/25/60.

280 *Russell had advised Johnson to reject Kennedy's offer*: Fite, 376–77; RBR statement, 9/1/60, Dictation Series I, RBRL.

280 *Russell's endorsement was crucial*: Troutman OH, RBRL. Troutman said he also called on Talmadge, who had an entirely different relationship with Johnson. Asked by Troutman if he would support the ticket, Tal-

madge agreed that "it was a perfectly proper request to be made." (Troutman OH, RBRL.)

280 *Russell indeed planned to watch:* Goldsmith, 80; RBR statement, 9/1/60,
Dictation Series I, RBRL; Fite, 378.

281 *whistle-stop tour of the South:* Miller, 262.

281 *Throughout the train trip: Time,* 10/24/60.

281 *He met the issue of civil rights: Ibid.; Newsweek,* 10/24 & 31, 1960.

281 *Johnson's southern tour: Newsweek,* 10/24/60.

282 *Besides helping blunt the issue:* Evans and Novak, 292.

282 *On October 19: Atlanta Constitution,* 10/20 & 24, 1960; Garrow, *Bearing
the Cross,* 143–45.

283 *court action to rescue King:* Garrow, *Bearing the Cross,* 146.

283 *monitored the Atlanta situation for Kennedy's campaign: Atlanta Constitution,*
10/25/60.

283 *When Wofford learned of Hartsfield's statement:* Wofford, 13–14.

283 *He urged a stronger statement: Ibid.,* 16–17.

284 *the situation in Georgia worsened:* Garrow, *Bearing the Cross,* 146; Strober,
35–36; Wofford, 19; *Atlanta Constitution,* 10/27/60.

285 *Robert Kennedy was furious:* Wofford, 21; Branch, 366.

285 *"deeply indebted to Senator Kennedy":* Garrow, *Bearing the Cross,* 148;
Time, 11/7/60; Wofford, 23; *Atlanta Constitution,* 10/28/60.

285 *With ten days left:* Wofford, 21, 24; Garrow, *Bearing the Cross,* 149.

286 *On October 30:* Wofford, 27–28.

286 *Johnson was having a rough time: Time,* 11/16/60.

286 *But in Texas: Ibid.,* 11/7/60; *Newsweek,* 10/24/60.

287 *the break his Texas campaign desperately needed: Houston Post,* 11/5/60;
Miller, 270–71; *Time,* 11/16/60.

287 *another screaming mob:* Miller, 271.

287 *The following morning:* RBR to Harvey J. Kennedy, 11/17/60, Dictation
Series I, RBRL; Miller, 271–72; Fite, 379; *Houston Post,* 11/8/60.

288 *Johnson's presence on the ticket:* Eastland OH, LBJL; Halleck OH, LBJL.

289 *southerners worried:* RBR to Harvey J. Kennedy, 11/17/60, Dictation Series
I, RBRL.

CHAPTER FIFTEEN

290 *a miserable man:* Miller, 273; Kearns, 164.

290 *When Johnson confessed:* Evans and Novak, 306; Baker, 134; Shuman OH,
USSHO; Smathers OH, USSHO; McPherson, 183. In another oral history
interview, Smathers—Johnson's whip for two years—gave his leader partial blame for the dissolution of his first marriage. "He was so insistent
that you work all night long; that you don't come home for dinner; that

you go with him, where he was; he called all during the night, at any time" (Strober, 192).

291 *very different from Johnson:* Reedy & Siegel OH, LBJL.

291 *"The way Mansfield read the Johnson years":* Vander Zee OH, USSHO.

291 *"perfectly willing to explain a bill":* Fulbright, author interview; Talmadge, author interview.

291 *reluctant to lead:* Mooney, 135.

291 *On January 3, 1961: NYT,* 1/4/61; Miller, 275–76; Evans and Novak, 306–7.

292 *the smattering of vehement opposition:* Baker, 135; Proxmire OH, LBJL.

292 *a caucus and a cactus:* Miller, 276.

292 *McPherson saw the new vice president:* McPherson OH, LBJL; McPherson, 184.

292 *greeted Johnson with even greater indifference:* Baker, 144.

293 *"Kennedy's people":* White OH, LBJL.

293 *Conscious of the "provocations":* Rowe OH, LBJL; White OH, LBJL.

293 *an uneasy, distant arrangement:* Smathers OH, USSHO; O'Donnell OH, LBJL.

293 *Kennedy rarely discussed major decisions:* Marshall, author interview; Kearns, 164; Evans and Novak, 314.

294 *refusal to use him as an administration lobbyist: WSJ,* 7/28/61.

294 *Johnson's reaction to his sudden estrangement:* Krock OH, LBJL; Smathers OH, USSHO; Pearson OH, LBJL.

295 *Humphrey went to New York:* Eisele, 177, 178; *Life,* 9/27/68.

295 *With Johnson's generous assistance:* Eisele, 178.

296 *won the whip job for several reasons:* McPherson OH, MHS.

296 *"He would spend long, long hours":* Gartner OH, MHS.

296 *Mansfield's virtual abdication:* Humphrey, 181; *WSJ,* 4/20/61.

297 *Humphrey attacked the job: WSJ,* 4/20/61; *NYT Magazine,* 8/25/63.

297 *a warm and easy friendship:* Gartner OH, MHS; *NYT Magazine,* 8/25/63.

297 *One illustration of Humphrey's usefulness: Ibid.*

297 *Humphrey firmly believed:* Eisele, 179, 181; *WSJ,* 4/20/61; Shuman OH, USSHO.

298 *standing on a Washington street corner:* Wofford, 58; Wofford, author interview; Wofford OH, JFKL.

298 *a profound* intellectual *understanding:* Wofford, 62–63.

299 *On inauguration day: Ibid.,* 98–99; Reeves, 38–39; *CQ Almanac,* 1961, 856.

300 *"Did you see the Coast Guard detachment?":* Goodwin, 4–5.

300 *he had pledged to: CQ,* 1/13/61, 42; *CQ Almanac,* 1961, 392.

301 *suddenly disavowed the bills introduced: CQ Almanac,* 1961, 392; Wilkins OH, JFKL.

302 *southerners continued to chair:* Burns OH, JFKL; *NYT*, 3/6/61.

302 *a disappointed Roy Wilkins:* Wilkins OH, LBJL.

302 *Kennedy's reluctance on civil rights:* Strober, 277; Celler OH, JFKL; Marshall, author interview.

302 *Kennedy's tentative approach to civil rights:* Hesburgh, author interview.

303 *"Nobody needs to convince me any longer":* Schlesinger, *A Thousand Days*, 931.

303 *"He had a very early conviction":* Wofford, author interview.

303 *described Kennedy's reluctance to prod the Congress:* Cohen OH, MSRC; Ellender OH, JFKL.

304 *Another, more compelling explanation:* Wofford, author interview; Marshall, author interview; Smathers OH, USSHO; Burns essay, *Remembrances of John F. Kennedy*, from Burns OH, JFKL.

304 *"Everyone down in Congress":* Marshall OH, MSRC.

304 *the president issued an executive order:* CQ Almanac, 1961, 860; Celebrezze OH, LBJL; Schlesinger, *A Thousand Days*, 933.

305 *Johnson was not hesitant:* CQ, April 21, 1961, 668; Graham, 47–49.

305 *Kennedy's own hiring policy:* CQ, 2/10/61, 218.

305 *Kennedy appointed other blacks:* Harvey, *Civil Rights During the Kennedy Administration*, 22–23; Wilkins OH, JFKL.

306 *"You tell your brother":* Carl Rowan in *The* (Newark) *Star-Ledger*, 11/24/93.

306 *"We will enforce the law":* NYT, 5/7/61.

306 *first voting rights suit:* Schlesinger, *A Thousand Days*, 934–35; CQ Almanac, 1961, 393.

306 *As for school desegregation:* CQ, 1/20/61, 69 & 4/21/61, 668; *NYT*, 10/15/61; Marshall, author interview.

307 *"I don't believe we do have that power":* CQ, 4/21/61, 668.

307 *"You did get more vigorous action":* King & Rauh OH, JFKL.

307 *Rauh joined a group of ADA board members:* Rauh OH, JFKL.

308 *"Oh, shit":* Reeves, 63.

308 *Looking back:* Rauh OH, JFKL; Strober, 278.

308 *Another visitor to Kennedy in 1961:* Hesburgh OH, JFKL.

309 *the importance of a strong Civil Rights Commission:* NYT, 10/15/61.

309 *more aggressive action:* Time, 6/2/61.

310 *As they made their way:* NYT, 5/21/61.

310 *"a total breakdown of law enforcement":* Newsweek, 5/29/61.

311 *Throughout the crisis:* Time, 6/2/61.

311 *The brutal response:* Newsweek, 6/5/61; *NYT*, 5/2/61; *Time*, 6/2/61.

311 *The Freedom Riders hoped:* Strober, 294.

311 *Whatever encouragement:* Ibid.

312 *"Tell them to call it off":* Wofford, 153; Wofford, author interview.

312 *federal marshals into Montgomery:* Newsweek, 6/5/61.

312 *more violence threatened to erupt:* Time, 6/2/61.

312 *King demanded aggressive federal intervention:* Garrow, *Bearing the Cross,* 157.

313 *"We'll get those niggers":* Time, 6/2/61; NYT, 5/22/61; Garrow, *Bearing the Cross,* 158.

313 *Freedom Riders were even more determined:* Wofford, 155; Time, 6/2/61; Newsweek, 6/5/61 & 5/29/61; Branch, 412–91; Fairclough, 77–79.

313 *In the Senate, reaction to the violence:* CR, 5/22/61, 8498, 8531.

313 *Southern conservatives condemned the violence: Ibid.,* 5/23/61, 8616–17, 8648.

314 *Russell objected: Ibid.,* 5/24/61, 8712–13.

314 *shameful and hysterical response: Ibid.,* 5/25/61, 8956–57.

314 *Kennedy responded to the Freedom Rides:* CQ Almanac, 1961, 393; NYT, 9/23/61.

315 *his second State of the Union address:* Wofford, 157; CQ Almanac, 1961, 922.

315 *Congress had little to show:* CQ Almanac, 1961, 393.

315 *As the session came to a close:* CQ, 9/22/61, 1617; CQ Almanac, 1961, 393–94.

316 *"Americans might well wonder":* CQ Almanac, 1961, 398.

CHAPTER SIXTEEN

317 *"out of step":* Presidential Studies Quarterly, Fall 1991, 698; Jones, author interview.

318 *"my leadership has lost inspiration":* Fite, 382–83.

318 *the rule change died:* NYT, 1/5/61; Harvey, *Civil Rights During the Kennedy Administration,* 16.

318 *"Hey, boy":* Darden OH, RBRL.

319 *Demands for progress on civil rights:* CR, 1/18/62, 434–35.

319 *Javits's frustrations boiled over: Ibid.,* 3/8/62, 3642.

319 *Humphrey bravely defended: Ibid.,* 5/29/62, 9512.

320 *the times were finally catching up:* CQ, 3/16/62, 428; CR, 3/27/62, 5083–87.

320 *the poll tax was only "misunderstood":* CR, 3/16/62, 4410.

321 *Russell's arguments against the amendment: Ibid.,* 3/14/62, 4153.

321 *a ten-day quasifilibuster:* CR, 3/27/62, 5105; CQ, 8/31/62, 1443.

322 *another civil rights measure that Kennedy supported:* CQ Almanac, 1962, 371–75; CR, 5/2/62, 7607. The bill did not contain an outright ban on literacy tests, but those who used such tests would have been required to accept a sixth-grade education as proof of literacy. States could have also established any education level as a voting requirement so long as it was applied equally to all citizens, regardless of race.

323 *"They would go down to the courthouse":* CR, 5/2/62, 7590.

323 *despite liberal protests:* CQ Almanac, 1962, 372.

323 *Mansfield's move:* Ibid., 1962, 375.

323 *a spiteful attack on the Supreme Court:* CR, 5/2 & 3, 1962, 7599–7607, 7639–40; CQ, 5/11/62, 790–91; CQ Almanac, 1962, 377; Time, 5/18/62.

324 *Mansfield's legislative judgment:* CR, 5/1/62, 7365 & 5/14/62, 8294; CQ, 5/11/62, 790–91; Time, 5/18/62.

325 *the Senate leadership had bungled the bill:* CQ Almanac, 1962, 377; Mansfield OH, JFKL.

325 *"People are speaking up for their rights":* CR, 5/8/62, 7917.

326 *The failure to muster the votes:* Marshall OH, JFKL.

327 *filibuster thrived in the Senate:* Harvey, *Civil Rights During the Kennedy Administration,* 37; Garrow, *Bearing the Cross,* 161.

327 *gradual desegregation of public schools:* CQ, 8/3/62, 1297.

328 *The crisis began:* CQ Almanac, 1962, 244; Time, 10/5/62.

328 *Barnett placed himself squarely in the middle:* Time, 10/5/62; Branch, 649.

328 *Meredith was thwarted again:* CQ Almanac, 1962, 244.

329 *On September 26:* Branch, 651.

329 *an agitated crowd:* Lord, 191; Paul Johnson OH, LBJL.

329 *as Meredith and his escorts drove:* CQ Almanac, 1962, 244.

330 *willingness to back down:* Lord, 196; CQ Almanac, 1962, 245.

330 *Barnett released the alarming news:* Time, 10/12/62; Newsweek, 10/15/62; Branch, *Parting the Waters,* 662–67; Lord, 207–9.

331 *Choking and cursing:* Newsweek, 10/15/62; Paul Johnson OH, LBJL.

331 *" 'squirrel hunting' that night":* Branch, 667; USA Today, 6/9/88; Time, 10/12/62; Newark Star-Ledger, 11/1/92.

332 *rioters had gone:* Branch, *Parting the Waters,* 668; Newark Star-Ledger, 11/1/92; Strober, 304; Newsweek, 10/15/62.

332 *As the campus emerged:* Newsweek, 10/15/62; Time, 10/12/62; Branch, 670; CQ Almanac, 1962, 245.

332 *Among southern members of Congress:* CR, 9/29/62, 21282 & 10/1/62, 21415; Thomasville Times Enterprise, 9/28/62.

333 *More responsible leaders:* CQ Almanac, 1962, 244; CQ, 10/5/62, 1809; CR, 10/1/62, 21415.

333 *another human rights embarrassment:* CQ, 10/5/62, 1809; NYT, 10/3/62.

333 *The consequences of the Oxford riot:* Time, 10/12/62.

334 *President Kennedy's pledge:* Wofford & Wilkins OH, JFKL.

334 *several persuasive reasons:* Burke Marshall & Sorenson OH, JFKL.

334 *There were more reasons:* Kennedy OH, JFKL.

335 *the order's exact wording:* Sorenson & Burke Marshall OH, JFKL.

335 *On November 20:* Sorenson, 482; CQ, 11/23/62, 2203.

336 *welcome news to liberals:* King OH, JFKL.

CHAPTER SEVENTEEN

337 *"couldn't buy a bill":* Vander Zee OH, USSHO.

337 *"Freedom to the Free":* CQ, 2/15/63, 190–91; *Atlanta Constitution,* 11/21/93.

338 *touted the administration's achievements:* CQ, 2/15/63, 190–91.

338 *a fire chief:* Clark OH, LBJL.

338 *federal courts were not always reliable:* Katzenbach OH, JFKL; *NYT,* 7/19/63.

339 *During his first voting rights case:* Reeves, 466; Friedman, 188–91; Wilkins OH, JFKL.

339 *"dry tinder":* Reedy to LBJ, undated, Civil Rights, Confidential Memos —Reedy, Vice Presidential Papers, LBJL.

339 *The biennial clash over cloture:* Clark, 123; CQ, 2/8/63, 139.

340 *liberal entreaties for a ruling:* CR, 1/23/63, 1219; *NYT,* 1/29/63.

340 *"Russell, old as he was":* McPherson, 188; CQ, 2/8/63, 139.

341 *Russell could see his ultimate defeat:* *Newsweek,* 8/19/63; *NYT,* 2/1/63.

341 *shifting political sands:* Simon, 62–69.

341 *surprisingly strong civil rights bill:* CQ, 2/15/63, 191; Rauh OH, MSRC.

342 *Kennedy finally joined the legislative debate:* CQ, 3/8/63, 292.

342 *The president's acknowledgment:* *Ibid.;* Garrow, *Bearing the Cross,* 233; Rauh OH, JFKL; Wilkins OH, JFKL.

342 *In a relatively mild attack:* RBR statement, 2/28/63, RBRL; CQ, 3/8/63, 293.

343 *the most damning criticism of the bill:* CQ, 3/8/63, 293.

343 *restlessness in the Democratic ranks:* Smathers OH, JFKL; Solberg, 221; Watson, 544.

344 *King's followers prepared to take to the streets:* Bennett, 388–89; Fairclough, 108.

345 *King's choice of Birmingham:* *Time,* 5/10/63.

345 *On April 3:* Garrow, *Bearing the Cross,* 237.

346 *"riding around in big cars":* Fairclough, 118.

346 *Connor came to its rescue:* Garrow, *Bearing the Cross,* 239; Fairclough, 121.

346 *On April 12:* Bennett, 391.

347 *his movement was in crisis:* *Ibid.,* 392; Garrow, *Bearing the Cross,* 244–45.

347 *"We had run out of troops":* Garrow, *Bearing the Cross,* 247; Bennett, 393.

348 *On Thursday, May 2:* *Time,* 5/10/63; *Los Angeles Times,* 5/4/63; Garrow, *Bearing the Cross,* 249; *NYT,* 5/3/63; *Boston Globe,* 5/4/63.

349 *That night at a church rally:* *Time,* 5/10/63; *NYT,* 5/4/63.

349 *Some of the worst violence:* *Time,* 5/17/63.

349 *Later that night:* *Newsweek,* 5/20/63; Bennett, 399.

350 *sensational news on television and in newspapers:* *Boston Globe,* 5/4/63; *NYT,*

5/4/63; Los Angeles Times, 5/4/63; Time, 5/17/63; Newsweek, 5/20/63; New York Herald Tribune, 5/13/63.

350 *segregationists loudly decried perceived violations:* CR, 5/21/63, 9115, 9140.

351 *resulting media coverage:* Garrow, *Bearing the Cross,* 251; Strober, 284.

351 *urged Birmingham's white leaders to give some ground:* Newsweek, 5/20/63.

351 *From the beginning:* King & Wilkins OH, JFKL.

352 *"shuffle along the dark side":* Udall OH, MSRC.

352 *By the end of May:* CQ, 5/31/63, 838; Reedy to LBJ, 5/24/63, Civil Rights, Confidential memos, Vice Presidential Papers, LBJL; Burke Marshall OH, JFKL.

352 *most of the president's advisors were far from enthusiastic:* Burke Marshall OH, JFKL; Schlesinger, *Robert Kennedy and His Times,* 357; Robert Kennedy OH, JFKL. Burke Marshall, author interview.

353 *"I'll give you fifteen to one":* Hesburgh, author interview.

353 *the president had no choice:* Burke Marshall OH, JFKL; Glickstein OH, MSRC.

353 *No other attorney general:* Whalen, 5; WP, 5/23/63.

353 *several provisions quickly emerged:* WP, 5/24/63; Katzenbach OH, LBJL.

354 *Perhaps the bill's most controversial section:* Burke Marshall & Sorenson OH, JFKL; *U.S. News & World Report,* 6/24/63.

355 *the constitutional basis for such a provision:* Burke Marshall OH, JFKL.

355 *the most hotly debated aspect: Hearings Before the Committee on Commerce, United States Senate, 88th Congress, First Session, on S. 1732, A Bill to Eliminate Discrimination in Public Accommodations Affecting Interstate Commerce.* Washington: U.S. Government Printing Office, 1963, 1295–1300.

355 *at Burke Marshall's urging:* Burke Marshall OH, MSRC; RFK OH, JFKL; CQ, 6/21/63, 998; Berman, *A Bill Becomes A Law,* 40; Carothers, 79.

356 *One other aspect of the bill:* Stewart OH, MHS; Katzenbach OH, JFKL; *CQ Almanac,* 1963, 351.

357 *On May 24:* Evans and Novak, 376.

357 *"One hundred years ago":* LBJ speech, 5/30/63, LBJL.

358 *At first Johnson had wanted to decline:* CBS Interviews, The Last Interview, Box 1, LBJL; LBJ speech, 5/30/63, LBJL.

358 *the disuse of Lyndon Johnson:* Miller, 305; Thornberry OH, LBJL; RFK OH, JFKL.

CHAPTER EIGHTEEN

359 *Johnson had strong feelings:* Graham, 76–77.

359 *sending over Burke Marshall:* Burke Marshall OH, LBJL; Marshall, author interview. Marshall said it was possible that Johnson and Kennedy *never* directly discussed what would be the most important and controversial social legislation ever submitted to Congress. "This [the Congress] was

Lyndon Johnson's turf, in a way," he said, "and, so, the president wanted to have his advice . . . But whether the president himself had a one-on-one conversation with the vice president, I don't know."

360 *again pressed O'Donnell for an audience:* Graham, 77.

360 *lengthy conversation with Sorenson:* Transcript of LBJ/Sorenson phone conversation, 6/3/63, LBJL.

363 *In his 1965 memoir:* Sorenson, 499; Sorenson & RFK OH, JFKL.

364 *Johnson was not the only member:* Marshall, author interview.

364 *On June 11:* Sorenson, 493; Burke Marshall OH, JFKL; Videotape of *The Civil Rights Act of 1964: A Conference at the John F. Kennedy Library,* 4/25/94, author's files.

365 *Kennedy began his historic speech:* U.S. News & World Report, 6/24/63.

366 *the cold-blooded murder:* Bennett, 401–2; Branch, 824–25.

366 *Russell reacted to Kennedy's speech:* U.S. News & World Report, 6/24/63.

366 *Russell knew that he was fighting:* NYT Magazine, 11/20/63; Newsweek, 8/19/63.

367 *"Russell can summon":* WSJ, 6/19/63.

367 *The whole matter:* RBR to Eugene Kelly, 8/16/63, Dictation Series I, RBRL.

367 *Kennedy's bill would encounter many skeptics:* McGill OH, JFKL; Jones, author interview; NYT, 11/20/63.

368 *Few northerners who despaired:* Allen, Carter & Mudd OH, RBRL.

368 *Whatever his motives:* NYT Magazine, 10/20/63; Newsweek, 8/19/63.

368 *The prospects for Kennedy's bill:* Baker to Mansfield, 6/27/63, Manatos: Civil Rights, 63–65, WHCF, Aides Files, Box 6, LBJL; CQ Almanac, 1963, 344.

369 *Republicans held the key:* Whalen, 13; Katzenbach OH, JFKL.

369 *a full-court press:* Cronin OH, MSRC; CQ Almanac, 1963, 344.

370 *On June 22:* Katzenbach OH, JFKL; Garrow, *Bearing the Cross,* 271–72.

370 *Kennedy pulled a piece of paper:* Branch, 839; Rauh OH, JFKL.

371 *Kennedy made another effective point:* Garrow, *Bearing the Cross,* 272; Robert Kennedy OH, JFKL.

371 *The unusual debut of Kennedy's program:* CQ, 6/21/63, 999–1000.

371 *As the legislation began its deliberate pilgrimage:* Farmer OH, LBJL; Sorenson OH, JFKL.

372 *"If I had to pick one day":* Humphrey, 201.

372 *"There is no sense of threat":* CR, 8/27/63, 15917.

372 *joined marchers in their walk:* Humphrey, 202.

373 *"Pass the bill":* Rustin OH, LBJL.

373 *In the House, meanwhile:* RFK OH, JFKL; Whalen, 38.

373 *In an ironic twist:* CQ Almanac, 1963, 348–49; Whalen, 39.

374 *After lengthy negotiations:* CQ Almanac, 1963, 349; Marshall OH, MSRC.

374 *"rather lose the whole bill":* RFK OH, JFKL.

374 *Russell knew that the coming debate over civil rights:* Newsweek, 8/19/63.

375 *Some observers applauded Russell: Ibid.; U.S. News & World Report,* 6/24/63.

376 *Two of the nation's most prominent Georgians:* CQ Almanac, 1963, 355; Allen OH, LBJL; *Hearings Before the Committee on Commerce, United States Senate, 88th Congress, First Session, on S. 1732, Part I, Serial 26.* Washington: U.S. Government Printing Office, 1963, 861–66.

377 *"the real sense of Johnson's commitment":* McPherson OH, LBJL.

378 *to drive his car and his beagle:* Eugene Williams OH, LBJL; Johnson, 154–55.

378 *"there was nothing I could say":* Johnson, 155.

CHAPTER NINETEEN

379 *The news of President Kennedy's murder:* Mudd OH, RBRL.

379 *Russell's thoughts turned to his friend:* Leonard OH, RBRL.

379 *Across town:* Humphrey, 191; *Life,* 9/27/68.

380 *when* Air Force One *touched down:* Humphrey, 191–92.

380 *the most overwhelming day of Johnson's life:* Saturday Evening Post, 3/13/65; Riddick OH, USSHO.

380 *In the days following the assassination:* Evans and Novak, 345–46; Records of the JFK Assassination, Box 85, Tapes and Transcripts of Telephone Conversations and Meetings, National Archives.

381 *From the moment of John F. Kennedy's death:* Notes of Troika meeting, The President's Appointment File, Diary Backup, 11/25/63, Box 1, LBJL; Whalen, 77; Valenti, 117.

381 *Johnson telephoned several civil rights leaders:* LBJ-King phone transcript, 11/25/63, Records of the JFK Assassination, Box 85, Tapes and Transcripts of Telephone Conversations and Meetings, National Archives.

382 *"I want that bill passed":* Whalen, 81.

382 *Johnson's demeanor:* Notes of Troika meeting, The President's Appointment File, Diary Backup, 11/25/63, Box 1, LBJL; Burke Marshall OH, LBJL.

382 *"Some of the liberals":* Notes of Troika meeting, The President's Appointment File, Diary Backup, 11/25/63, Box 1, LBJL.

382 *Johnson had a speech of his own:* Miller, 337; Humphrey, 196–97.

383 *"All I have I would have given":* Miller, 338–39; *Public Papers of the Presidents, Lyndon B. Johnson, 1963–1964,* 11/27/63, 8–10; Wicker, 169.

384 *When Johnson finished his speech:* Fite, 408.

384 *The speech was enormously reassuring:* Miller, 340; Douglas, 295.

384 *the most dubious liberals:* Ruby Martin OH, LBJL.

385 *Many southern conservatives were not as doubtful:* Paul Johnson OH, LBJL; Wicker, 175.

385 *In the days and weeks after Kennedy's death:* Heller OH, MHS; Evans and Novak, 351; Miller, 341.

385 *On the opposite end of the civil rights spectrum:* RBR statement, 11/27/63, Dictation Series I, RBRL.

386 *Though disappointed in his old friend:* LBJ-RBR phone transcript, 11/29/63, Records of the JFK Assassination, Box 85, Tapes and Transcripts of Telephone Conversations and Meetings, National Archives.

387 *"You destroyed me":* Ibid., LBJ-RBR phone transcript, 12/7/63.

387 *Russell attended only a few:* Fite, 406; *Richard Russell: Georgia Giant,* Cox Broadcasting, 1970; Transcript of WSB-TV appearance, 6/23/64, Speech/ Media, News Releases, RBRL.

388 *Johnson's immediate concern:* LBJ-Anderson phone transcript, 11/30/63, Records of the JFK Assassination, Box 85, Tapes and Transcripts of Telephone Conversations and Meetings, National Archives.

388 *"If we could ever get that signed":* Ibid., LBJ-Graham phone transcript, 12/2/63.

388 *Although he quietly pushed:* Ibid.

389 *Johnson wisely handed over tactical control:* Graham, 141.

389 *In the end:* Whalen, 91.

389 *On January 30:* CQ Almanac, 1964, 344; CQ, 2/14/64, 293.

389 *The bill that passed the House:* CQ, 2/14/64, 293.

390 *"When we got the bill through the House":* Mitchell OH, LBJL.

391 *With precious little hope:* Johnson, 157–58; CQ, 1/24/64, 157.

391 *"When you have the responsibility":* Transcript of CBS Interview: The Last Interview, Box 1, LBJL.

392 *"I knew that if I didn't get out in front":* Kearns, 191.

392 *Russell offered no advice:* RBR speech to Peachtree Christian Church, 1/5/64, Dictation Series I, RBRL; RBR statement, 1/8/64, Dictation Series I, RBRL.

392 *Despite their disagreement over the issue:* Miller, 369; *Business Week,* 4/18/64; *Reporter,* 5/21/64.

393 *For the first time:* Katzenbach OH, JFKL; Katzenbach OH, LBJL.

393 *Johnson endorsed the Justice Department's cloture strategy:* Time, 3/20/64; Manatos to O'Brien, 2/13/64, Office Files of Harry McPherson, Box 21, LBJL; Katzenbach, author interview.

394 *Mansfield was rarely a headstrong man:* MacNeil, 231.

394 *"We would win":* Johnson, 158.

394 *he remained a reluctant leader:* Katzenbach, author interview; HHH to file, 1964, HHH Vice Presidential Papers, Civil and Human Rights, Box 821, MHS.

394 *"What is going to be important":* Vander Zee to HHH, 12/2/63, HHH Senatorial Files, 1949–64, MHS.

394 *Johnson gave Humphrey little or no advice:* Humphrey, 204; Miller, 368; Humphrey OH, LBJL.

395 *Humphrey took Johnson's advice:* Meet the Press, 3/8/64; Humphrey OH, LBJL.

395 *Johnson's White House well understood:* Katzenbach remarks to *The Civil Rights Act of 1964: A Conference at the John F. Kennedy Library,* 4/25/94, videotape in author's files; Wolfinger, author interview.

396 *Humphrey meant to alter that equation:* Loevy, 147; HHH to file, 1964, HHH Vice Presidential Papers, Civil and Human Rights, Box 821, MHS.

396 *Humphrey appointed a floor captain:* CR, 2/17/63, 2882; HHH to file, 1964, HHH Vice Presidential Papers, Civil and Human Rights, Box 821, MHS.

396 *Each morning:* New Republic, 4/4/64.

397 *To build solidarity:* Humphrey, 206–7.

397 *The April 9 newsletter:* CR, 4/18/64, 8369.

397 *sophisticated system for answering quorum calls:* Loevy, 144.

397 *Humphrey addressed the quorum problem:* CQ, 6/19/64, 1205–6; New Republic, 1/1/65; CR, 4/18/64, 8369.

398 *In the early weeks of the debate:* HHH Senatorial Files, Correspondence, Legislative, Box 224, MHS; Whalen, 164–65; Christian Century, 5/13/64.

398 *organized as never before:* Hildenbrand OH, USSHO.

399 *"I had to make up my mind":* HHH to file, 1964, HHH Vice Presidential Papers, Civil and Human Rights, Box 821, MHS.

399 *"carried more on his shoulders":* Washington Star, 3/15/64.

399 *Russell's strategy for the coming debate:* RBR statement, 1/24/64, WHCF, Name File, Richard Russell, Box 344, LBJL; Face the Nation, 3/1/64; Talmadge, 195.

400 *Russell had nineteen soldiers:* NYT, 2/23/64.

400 *Russell was in serious trouble:* Humphrey, 206.

401 *"That black vote was getting to be":* Long, author interview.

401 *"age resisting youth":* The New Republic, 4/4/64.

401 *Giving Russell even more reason for distress:* Reporter, 5/21/64; Face the Nation, 3/1/64.

402 *In April:* Reporter, 5/21/64.

402 *Russell believed his cause was just:* Washington Star, 3/15/64; Business Week, 4/18/64.

402 *Russell lost his first skirmish:* CQ, 2/28/64, 385.

402 *On March 9:* CR, 3/9/64, 4754; CQ Almanac, 1964, 356–57.

403 *Eastland told Humphrey:* CR, 3/21/64, 5865.

403 *Eastland was not alone:* Ibid., 3/25/64, 6429.

403 *"This is mere socialism":* Ibid., 4/20/64, 8443.

403 *There* were *substantive arguments: Ibid.*, 1/29/64, 1338 & 3/9/64, 4753.

404 *basing the bill's public accommodations section: Ibid.*, 3/10/64, 4855. For an excellent discussion of the southerners' constitutional objections to the public accommodations section, see *The Public Accommodations Law of 1964: Arguments, Issues and Attitudes in a Legal Debate*, 2–10.

404 *"I state unhesitatingly": CR*, 3/9/64, 4744.

404 *"if Mr. Jones wishes to go out to dinner": Ibid.*, 3/9/64, 4766.

404 *On March 26: Time*, 4/10/64; *CQ Almanac*, 1964, 357–58.

405 *Oregon's Wayne Morse: Ibid.; Time*, 4/3/64.

405 *"This is no longer a battle":* White, *The Making of the President 1964*, 213.

CHAPTER TWENTY

406 *Shortly after noon on Monday: CQ*, 4/3/64, 655; *CQ Almanac*, 1964, 358; *CR*, 3/30/64, 6552–53.

407 *an embarrassing setback: CQ*, 4/10/64, 682.

408 *The situation elated the southerners: NYT*, 4/5/64; Humphrey, 207.

408 *By April 11:* HHH to file, 1964, HHH Vice Presidential Papers, Civil and Human Rights, Box 821, MHS; *Time*, 4/24/64; *Newsweek*, 4/27/64; *CQ*, 4/17/64, 717.

408 *"This made them all the more unhappy":* HHH to file, 1964, HHH Vice Presidential Papers, Civil and Human Rights, Box 821, MHS.

409 *Republican version of Lyndon Johnson:* MacNeil, 167; Talmadge, 197; *Reporter*, 7/16/64.

409 *Dirksen's importance to the bill's passage: WP*, 2/20/64; MacNeil, 230.

410 *plenty of compelling reasons:* Whalen, 155–56; Talmadge, 196.

410 *candidly acknowledged his qualms about the bill:* Whalen, 159–60; *CQ Almanac*, 1964, 359; *Time*, 4/24/64; *Reporter*, 7/16/64.

411 *amendments sparked a vigorous debate: Face the Nation*, 4/19/64; *Time*, 4/24/64.

411 *Dirksen cautiously waded into the debate: CQ*, 4/17/64, 717.

411 *Humphrey responded to Dirksen:* Whalen, 160.

411 *"You're manager of the bill":* Humphrey OH, LBJL.

412 *As the southern filibuster droned:* Findlay, 55; White, *The Making of the President 1964*, 215.

412 *Humphrey not only understood the potential:* Whalen, 165; Watson, 601; *CQ Almanac*, 1964, 360; *New Republic*, 4/64.

412 *some religious groups had been laboring:* NCCC letter, 3/6/64, HHH Senatorial Files, Correspondence (Legislative), MHS; *New Republic*, 4/4/64; Findlay, 51–54.

412 *During the House debate:* Rauh OH, MSRC.

413 *The clerical network was effective: Reporter*, 7/16/64; Cronin OH, MSRC; Rauh OH, MSRC.

413 *"the great and cheering fact":* America, 5/9/64.

413 *Russell complained:* Face the Nation, 3/1/64; CR, 5/8/64, 10416.

414 *By late April:* Face the Nation, 4/26/64.

414 *undercutting the bill's support:* Time, 4/24/64.

414 *National civil rights groups:* Ibid., 4/24; HHH-Kuchel statement, 4/15/64, HHH Papers, Senatorial Files (Correspondence/legislative), MHS.

414 *If such protests continued:* Face the Nation, 3/1/64.

415 *Thirty-seven days after they began their filibuster:* CQ, 5/1/64, 863.

416 *The importance of Dirksen's amendment:* Time, 4/24/64.

416 *Humphrey and Mansfield's increasing impatience:* CQ, 5/1/64, 863.

416 *While taking his first tentative steps:* Kearns, 190; Johnson, 159.

417 *his special relationship with Johnson:* Whalen, 172.

417 *Johnson's refusal to negotiate:* HHH to file, 1964, HHH Vice Presidential Papers, Civil and Human Rights, Box 821, MHS.

417 *By Tuesday, May 5:* Whalen, 174; CQ Almanac, 1964, 361–62; Time, 5/15/64 & 5/22/64; Reporter, 7/16/64.

418 *inched toward a deal:* CQ, 5/8/64, 901.

418 *Russell's turnabout infuriated Humphrey:* Time, 5/22/64; CR, 5/12/64, 10616; NYT, 5/12/64.

419 *exhausted Mansfield's abundant patience:* NYT, 5/12/64; Time, 5/22/64.

419 *Off the Senate floor:* The (Newark, N.J.) Star-Ledger, 10/1/92.

419 *On the fair employment changes:* Whalen, 182–83.

420 *Standing before the assembled reporters:* Newsweek, 5/25/64; Time, 5/22/64.

420 *The major changes to the House bill:* CQ Almanac, 1964, 362–65.

420 *Dirksen was satisfied:* Rauh OH, MSRC; New Republic, 7/16/64 & 5/2/64.

421 *an instant hero:* Time, 5/22/64 & 6/5/64; MacNeil, 236; CR, 5/26/64, 11943; CQ, 5/29/64, 1032.

422 *At a May 19 meeting with reporters:* CQ Almanac, 1964, 365; Oxford Dictionary of Quotations, 267; Reporter, 7/16/64.

422 *On May 26:* CQ, 5/29/64, 1032 & 6/5/64, 1077; Time, 6/5/64; Whalen, 190.

423 *Most of the Senate's thirty-three Republicans:* Hildenbrand OH, USSHO; CQ, 5/22/64, 987.

423 *"Where the hell else can they go?":* Newsweek, 5/25/64.

423 *a minor mutiny:* HHH to file, 1964, HHH Vice Presidential Papers, Civil and Human Rights, Box 821, MHS.

423 *On Friday, June 5:* CQ Almanac, 1964, 366–67; HHH to file, 1964, HHH Vice Presidential Papers, Civil and Human Rights, Box 821, MHS.

424 *Humphrey's bargaining with Hickenlooper:* HHH to file, 1964, HHH Vice Presidential Papers, Civil and Human Rights, Box 821, MHS.

424 *Now Humphrey knew:* Ibid.; Newsweek, 6/22/64; NYT, 6/11/64.

424 *That evening at 7:38:* CQ *Almanac,* 1964, 367.

424 *"At night, when I kiss my children":* CR, 6/10/64, 13308.

425 *Russell was next:* Whalen, 198; CR, 6/10/64, 13308–9.

425 *yielded two minutes to Humphrey:* CR, 6/10/64, 13310.

426 *it was Dirksen's moment:* Whalen, 198; MacNeil, 236; CQ *Almanac,* 1964, 367; *Time,* 6/19/64.

426 *Before Dirksen could complete his speech:* Whalen, 199.

426 *Before a packed gallery:* NYT, 6/11/64; *Time,* 6/19/64; *Newsweek,* 6/22/64; Whalen, 199.

426 *As the clerk reached the name:* NYT, 6/11/64; WP, 6/11/64; *Life,* 6/19/64.

427 *Hayden emerged from the Democratic cloakroom:* Time, 6/19/64.

427 *By the time the roll call ended:* CQ, 6/12/64, 1169.

427 *Russell was a sore loser:* CR, 6/10/64, 13329.

427 *While Russell fumed:* Humphrey, 211–12; *Life,* 9/27/68.

428 *Humphrey was torn:* Life, 9/27/68.

428 *On June 19:* CQ *Almanac,* 1964, 371–72.

428 *After a brief debate:* Ibid., 377; CQ, 7/3/64, 1331.

428 *"the culmination":* Humphrey, 210–11; CQ, 6/19/64, 1206; Watson, 620.

429 *Humphrey may have been the big winner:* Newsweek, 6/29/64; HHH to file, 1964, HHH Vice Presidential Papers, Civil and Human Rights, Box 821, MHS; *Reporter,* 7/16/64.

429 *Russell's strategy:* Humphrey, 211; Mitchell OH, LBJL.

430 *If Russell was putting on a show:* Reader's Digest, 12/66; LBJ to RBR, 7/23/64, WHCF, EX HU 2, Box 3, LBJL.

430 *not the only losers in the debate:* Newsweek, 6/29/64; *Time,* 6/26/64; Califano, 55.

431 *many credited Dirksen and Humphrey:* NYT, 6/11/64; Shuman OH, USSHO.

431 *Johnson had made the most arduous:* Johnson, 160.

CHAPTER TWENTY-ONE

433 *"Most of the southerners":* LBJ-Smathers phone conversation, 11/23/63, Records of the JFK Assassination, Tapes and Transcripts of Telephone Conversations and Meetings, Box 85, National Archives.

433 *entertaining thoughts of the vice presidency:* Humphrey, 214; *Time,* 9/4/64; *Newsweek,* 9/7/64; Kampelman, 150.

433 *In an unsolicited memorandum:* Eisele, 197–98; Van Dyk, author interview; Clifford OH, LBJL.

434 *his friends were not at all shy:* Newsweek, 9/7/64; Eisele, 200; White, *The Making of the President 1964,* 327.

434 *a Johnson-Humphrey ticket made perfect sense:* Kampelman, 150.

435 *From the earliest days of 1964:* Humphrey, 218; Eisele, 200.

435 *Another strong indication:* Humphrey, 221–22; Van Dyk OH, MHS; Eisele, 204.

435 *Heeding Johnson's instructions:* Humphrey, 218–20; *Time,* 9/4/64; Van Dyk OH, MHS.

435 *Humphrey's effort was working:* Forbes, 8/1/64.

436 *Throughout the spring:* Humphrey, 221.

436 *cast a wide net:* Newsweek, 9/7/64; Miller, 387.

436 *For a brief while:* O'Donnell OH, LBJL.

437 *when Humphrey arrived:* Humphrey, 222.

437 *another potential obstacle:* Miller, 392; Harvey, *Black Civil Rights During the Johnson Administration,* 23; Van Dyk OH, MHS; Eisele, 212.

438 *Johnson sent Humphrey White House aide:* Humphrey, 222–23; Miller, 392–93; Eisele, 214.

439 *"Five times I saw him":* Rauh OH, MSRC; *New Republic,* 7/4/64.

439 *"Is Tom Dodd being considered, too?":* Humphrey, 223; Monroney OH, LBJL.

439 *When the two men arrived:* Newsweek, 9/7/64; White, *The Making of the President 1964,* 342–43.

439 *"do you want to be vice president?":* Humphrey, 224–26.

440 *Johnson was frank:* Van Dyk, author interview.

440 *"happier than a bouncing beagle":* Christian Science Monitor, 8/28/64.

440 *"During the last few weeks":* CQ, 8/28/64, 2014–15.

441 *By his own admission:* Humphrey, 229; Van Dyk OH, MHS; Van Dyk, author interview.

441 *whistle-stop tour: Public Papers of the Presidents, Lyndon B. Johnson, 1963– 1964,* 1285–86.

442 *many in the audience were stunned:* Valenti, 161; Miller, 398.

443 *"I do not intend to take any part":* Fite, 419.

443 *"I do not believe that even he would ask me":* RBR to Carter, 9/1/64, RBRL.

443 *"The political wounds":* Fite, 420–21.

CHAPTER TWENTY-TWO

445 *The passage of the Civil Rights Act of 1964 proved:* CQ, 7/10/64, 1454–55, 7/24/64, 1545 & 12/18/64, 2812; *CQ Almanac,* 1964, 378; *Business Week,* 7/11/64.

447 *public accommodations provision had sharp teeth:* Pollak OH, LBJL; Katzenbach, author interview.

447 *The voting rights provisions:* CQ, 3/26/65, 557.

448 *This deplorable state: Ibid.;* Garrow, *Protest at Selma,* 20–21; Ashmore, 172.

448 *From the White House:* Miller, 371; Katzenbach, author interview.

449 *the countywide voting-age population:* CQ Almanac, 1965, 538.

449 *Its sheriff personified the county's oppression:* Ibid.; Garrow, *Protest at Selma,* 34.

449 *By late 1964:* Fairclough, 229.

450 *"deeply affected the [Kennedys]":* Garrow, *Protest at Selma,* 144.

450 *In the weeks that followed:* Fairclough, 230–31; *Time,* 1/29, 2/19 & 2/12, 1965.

451 *Events in Selma unfolded:* Newsweek, 2/8/65; *Time,* 2/26/65.

451 *On February 5:* CQ Almanac, 1965, 538; CQ, 2/19/65, 270.

451 *In nearby Marion:* Fairclough, 238–39; *Time,* 2/26/65.

452 *"I can't promise you":* Time, 3/19/65.

452 *On the afternoon of Sunday, March 7:* Ibid.

453 *"The front ranks of the column fell":* Newsweek, 3/22/65.

453 *the march had disintegrated:* Ibid.

453 *the entire ghastly scene:* Time, 3/19/65.

453 *Congress reacted viscerally:* Shaffer, 98; Newsweek, 3/22/65.

454 *"matter of conscience":* Garrow, *Protest at Selma,* 85–87; Newsweek, 3/22/65; *Time,* 3/19/65.

454 *King tried to put the best face on":* Time, 3/19/65.

455 *To many observers:* Garrow, *Protest at Selma,* 89–93; Johnson, 162.

455 *Johnson's indecision:* NYT, 1/5/65; Katzenbach to O'Brien, 1/11/65, Reports on Legislation, Box 8, LBJL.

455 *The violence in Selma outraged Johnson:* Evans and Novak, 494.

455 *Many liberals and some civil rights leaders:* Goodwin, 320; Garrow, *Protest at Selma,* 90–94; Johnson, 161–62; Katzenbach, author interview.

456 *Johnson wanted to avoid further violence:* Johnson, 162.

456 *"Make it clear":* Goodwin, 320.

456 *"Well, Governor:"* Johnson, 162; Goodwin, 321.

457 *"Now, tell me":* Goodwin, 322–23.

457 *"if I'd stayed in there much longer":* Johnson, 163.

458 *an impromptu press conference:* Time, 3/19/65.

458 *"they were not intruders forcing their way in":* Johnson, 163.

CHAPTER TWENTY-THREE

459 *uniform voting standards:* CQ, 3/19/65, 434–35.

459 *The existing voting rights laws:* Pollak OH, LBJL.

460 *"Don't panic now":* Valenti Notes, 3/14/65, CBS Interview, The Last Interview, Box 2, LBJL; Johnson, *The Vantage Point,* 163–64; Goodwin, 324–25.

460 *Going before Congress in this way:* Time, 3/26/65; Johnson, *The Vantage Point,* 164.

460 *The next night, at nine o'clock:* Newsweek, 3/29/65; Shaffer, 100.

461 *Not every member of Congress:* CQ Almanac, 1965, 1365–67; Johnson, *The Vantage Point,* 165–66.

461 *"I speak tonight for the dignity of man":* CQ Almanac, 1965, 1365–67.

462 *For a split second:* Goodwin, 334; Garrow, *Bearing the Cross,* 408; Kearns, 229; Califano, 56.

463 *The real hero of the civil rights struggle:* CQ Almanac, 1965, 1365–67.

464 *"Manny, I want you to start hearings tonight":* Newsweek, 3/29/65.

464 *"He strode from the chamber":* Time, 3/26/65.

464 *Russell was a thousand miles away:* WHCF, Name Files, Box 344, "Richard Russell," LBJL; Fite, 426.

464 *Russell's extended absence:* McGill to Valenti, 2/11/65, WHCF, Name Files, Box 344, "Richard Russell," LBJL.

465 *Although Russell would eventually recover:* Saturday Evening Post, 3/13/65.

465 *Passage of the Civil Rights Act: Ibid.*

465 *A particular cause of the southerners' gloom:* Mudd OH, RBRL; *WSJ,* 8/6/65.

466 *Adding to the southerners' helpless distress:* Evans and Novak, 497; Kearns, 230.

466 *apostasy in their own ranks:* Jones to Marvin Watson, 3/17/65, LE HU 2–7, Executive, LBJL; *Newsweek,* 5/3/65; Miller, 434.

466 *"It simply was not a respectable argument":* Katzenbach OH, LBJL.

467 *"slobbish deputies":* Newsweek, 5/3/65.

467 *On March 18:* CR, 3/18/65, 5390, 5388; CQ, 3/26/65, 558; Graham, 166.

467 *Meanwhile in the House:* CQ, 3/26/65, 556–57; Graham, 166.

467 *Three days later:* Time, 4/2/65.

468 *In Washington the Senate and House Judiciary committees:* CQ, 4/16/65, 685–86.

468 *Dirksen's negotiations over the bill's specifics:* MacNeil, 252–53.

469 *Dirksen's approach to voting rights:* Pollak OH, LBJL; Katzenbach, author interview; CR, 4/21/65, 8205.

469 *While he tinkered with the bill:* Katzenbach to LBJ, 5/21/65, LE HU 2–7, LBJL.

470 *On April 30:* CR, 4/30/65, 9072; CQ, 5/7/65, 857–59; MacNeil, 255.

470 *The Senate's liberals:* CQ, 5/7/65, 857 & 4/30/65, 824; Pollak OH, LBJL CR, 4/30/65, 9077.

471 *a notoriously flexible man:* MacNeil, 255; Katzenbach to LBJ, 5/21/65, LE HU 2–7, LBJL; *Newsweek,* 5/10/65.

471 *Except for this one issue:* CR, 5/6/65, 9805.

472 *The vote was significant: Ibid.,* 5/3/65, 9242–43 & 5/6/65, 9830–31.

472 *Little that the southerners could say: Ibid.,* 5/10/65, 10034.

472 *On May 11:* CQ, 5/14/65, 899–900 & 5/21/65, 962–63; CR, 5/19/65, 11015.

473 *On three occasions:* CQ, 5/21/65, 963; CR, 5/19/65, 11018–19 & 5/21, 1965, 11188.

473 *On May 25:* Time, 6/4/65.

473 *The next day:* CQ, 5/28/65, 1007.

474 *The House bill differed:* NYT, 7/13/65; CQ, 6/4/65, 1052, 6/11/65, 1123–24, 7/2/65, 1299, 7/9/65, 1324 & 7/16/65, 1361.

474 *While moderates and conservatives had found:* CQ Almanac, 1965, 561; NYT, 7/13/65; CQ, 7/16/65, 1361.

475 *House and Senate conferees began:* Garrow, *Protest at Selma*, 130–32; CQ Almanac, 1965, 562–563; Graham, 173.

475 *On August 3:* CQ, 8/6/65, 1539.

475 *Two days later, on August 6:* Califano, 57.

476 *"Today is a triumph for freedom":* LBJ speech, 8/6/65, Reports on Enrolled Legislation (PL 89-110), Box 22, LBJL; Newsweek, 8/16/65.

CHAPTER TWENTY-FOUR

478 *"Negroes are trapped":* CQ Almanac, 1965, 571. Most of the speech, but particularly the passages decrying the disintegration of the black family, was influenced by the research of a Department of Labor official, Daniel Patrick Moynihan. When Moynihan's more detailed and straightforward conclusions about the black family were leaked to the news media, they sparked a firestorm of criticism among liberals and civil rights leaders. Johnson refused to defend him, and Moynihan resigned. Many years later Moynihan's controversial thesis became widely accepted as fact.

479 *the violent, angry voice:* Bennett, 422.

479 *A minor police incident:* Newsweek, 8/30/65.

479 *At first Johnson reacted tentatively:* Ibid.

480 *something more volatile and dangerous:* McPherson to LBJ, 6/17/65, WHCF, HU 2, Box 3, LBJL; McPherson, 343.

480 *The new civil rights movement trained its eye:* Fairclough, 253.

480 *almost-magical convergence of public support:* CQ Almanac, 1966, 450–51; McPherson OH, LBJL.

481 *One Democratic victim:* Douglas, 577–94; CQ Almanac, 1966, 1394–95; Newsday, 11/4/94.

481 *Despite the growing complexity:* Celler OH, LBJL.

482 *The legislative record:* Miller, 408.

482 *after Johnson signed the Voting Rights Act:* Garrow, *Protest at Selma*, 185, 187; CQ Almanac, 1965, 564–65.

482 *Johnson also labored:* Memorandum: Black Appointees of the Johnson Administration, CBS Interview, The Last Interview, Box 2, LBJL.

483 *Humphrey believed:* Van Dyk, author interview.

483 *In the early days of the administration:* Solberg, 267; Humphrey, 307; *CQ Almanac,* 1965, 565–66.

483 *he fumbled the ball:* Maclear, 123; Van Dyk, author interview; Van Dyk & Connell OH, MHS; Solberg, 274.

484 *Humphrey was demoralized:* Van Dyk, author interview; Califano, 65; Katzenbach, author interview.

484 *Almost before Humphrey knew what had happened:* Califano, 65–69.

484 *Had Humphrey enjoyed a better relationship:* Califano, 67; Eisele, 236; Katzenbach and Van Dyk, author interviews. It is not entirely clear who conceived of the plan to strip Humphrey of his civil rights authority— Johnson or Califano. Califano blamed Johnson. Humphrey blamed Califano. In his memoirs, Humphrey wrote that "Joe was smart and able, liked power, and did not want to share it. He convinced the President that direction of federal civil rights efforts should flow from him." According to Ted Van Dyk, Califano "was one of the few people Humphrey ever actively disliked, and I always thought it was with good reason." Califano, Van Dyk maintained, "was power mad." (Humphrey, 307; Van Dyk OH, MHS; Van Dyk, author interview.)

484 *Humphrey endured other affronts:* Reedy, author interview; Connell OH, LBJL; Solberg, 279; Van Dyk, author interview.

485 *Humphrey never complained:* McPherson & Connell OH, LBJL; Heller OH, MHS.

485 *the subsequent enforcement arrangement:* Graham, 180–86.

485 *The commission foundered: Ibid.,* 189–90, 201–3.

486 *In 1966:* Solberg, 285; Eisele, 240–44.

486 *Humphrey went overboard:* Eisele, 245; Solberg, 293.

486 *destroyed Johnson's effectiveness:* Kearns, 251–52.

487 *"horror of the dichotomy":* Durr OH, LBJL; Miller, 458.

487 *On the afternoon of Sunday, March 31:* Miller, 508–9.

488 *"You can't just resign":* Eisele, 323.

488 *"If I ever had any doubts":* Kearns, 338.

488 *"I shall not seek":* Miller, 512–13.

488 *In Mexico City: Ibid.,* 511; RBR statement, 4/1/68, Dictation Series I, RBRL.

488 *an assassin's bullet:* Burns, *The Crosswinds of Freedom,* 413; Miller, 514.

488 *Humphrey announced for the Democratic nomination:* Chester, et al., 145–46.

489 *In June:* Eisele, 334.

489 *Much of the problem: Ibid.,* 335; Kampelman, 169. When Humphrey first announced for the Democratic nomination, Johnson ordered his cabinet officers to remain neutral in the race between Humphrey, Kennedy, and McCarthy (Califano, 291–92).

489 *decidedly indifferent to Humphrey's candidacy:* Fite, 462; Mann, 304.

489 *Low on money:* Chester, et al., 421; Moss OH, FMOC.

490 *virtually indistinguishable: CQ Almanac,* 1968, 945, 955.

491 *"If the trend line continues":* White, *The Making of the President 1968,* 464, 468.

491 *On election night:* Berman OH, MHS.

491 *Over the objections of a weakened southern bloc: CQ Almanac,* 1968, 152–62.

492 *the most pressing issue in his world:* Fite, 437; *Reader's Digest,* 12/66.

492 *Russell delivered that advice repeatedly:* Fite, 441; Green OH, RBRL; *Atlanta Journal and Constitution Magazine,* 6/30/68.

492 *Unable to affect the outcome:* Fite, 461.

492 *Russell's disillusionment:* Jones, author interview; Austin, Lady Bird Johnson & Ervin OH, RBRL.

493 *Russell's discontent:* Moore OH, RBRL.

493 *Angered by something Johnson did or said: Ibid.;* Jones, author interview.

494 *Nothing, however, hastened the disintegration:* RBR and Talmadge to LBJ, 2/13/68, Dictation Series I, RBRL.

494 *Trouble developed shortly after Russell sent his recommendation: Jacksonville Times-Union,* 4/4/68; Fite, 477–78.

494 *The situation placed Johnson in a quandary:* Temple OH, RBRL.

495 *On May 11:* Russell to LBJ, 5/20/68, Southern District Judgeship, RBRL.

495 *Showing little sympathy:* Kelly OH, RBRL; Fite, 478; Jim Jones to Tom Johnson, 5/24/68, WHCF, Name Files (Richard Russell), Box 344, LBJL; RBR to Clark, 6/14/68, Dictation Series I, RBRL.

496 *Russell was still hopeful:* Temple OH, RBRL.

496 *after a month of inaction:* RBR to Griffin Bell, 6/7 & 7/2, 1968, Dictation Series I, RBRL.

496 *an unusually spiteful letter:* Russell to LBJ, 7/1/68, Office Files of Larry Temple, Box 1, LBJL; Talmadge, author interview.

497 *the letter shocked Johnson:* Temple OH, RBRL.

498 *"with deep regret":* RBR to LBJ, 9/26/68, Dictation Series, RBRL.

498 *From Russell's standpoint:* Powell Moore OH, LBJL.

498 *Shortly before Johnson left town:* Fite, 481.

EPILOGUE

500 *persistent health problems began to take their toll:* Fite, 482–83; Moore OH, LBJL; Talmadge, 163; Calhoun OH, RBRL; Proctor Jones, author interview.

500 *"He didn't want to talk about his sickness":* Nixon OH, RBRL.

500 *On the morning of January 21: Washington Star,* 1/22/71.

501 *Russell died: Atlanta Journal,* 1/21/71.

501 *a black hearse carrying Russell's body:* Green & Stacy OH, RBRL.

501 *as Russell's body lay in state:* Fite, 492; LBJ to RBR III, 1/22/71, Post Presidential File, Box 141, LBJL.

501 *Rain and heavy fog:* Fite, 492–93.

501 *only two of Russell's former colleagues:* Talmadge, 164.

502 *Johnson adapted to retirement slowly:* Miller, 543–45; Kearns, 360.

502 *In the spring of 1972:* Miller, 551.

502 *"Burke, I'm not really afraid of that demonstration":* Ibid., 560–61.

502 *Johnson's turn at the podium:* Transcript of Civil Rights Symposium, CBS Interview, The Last Interview, Box 3, LBJL.

503 *black attendees began fighting:* Miller, 562–63; Transcript of Civil Rights Symposium, CBS Interview, The Last Interview, Box 3, LBJL.

503 *"People don't know it":* Miller, 556.

504 *Defeat in the 1968 presidential election:* Humphrey, 305.

504 *Yet he was restless:* Ibid., 324–25.

504 *Humphrey actually yearned for another shot:* Newsweek, 1/23/78.

505 *Humphrey learned that he had bladder cancer:* Solberg, 308, 448–49; Newsweek, 1/23/78.

505 *Returning to Washington:* Boston Globe, 10/31/93; CR, 10/25/77, 34897.

506 *Washington welcomed him back:* Newsweek, 1/23/78.

506 *On October 25:* WP, 10/26/77; NYT, 10/26/77; CR, 10/25/77, 34897.

506 *Humphrey's moment to speak:* Talmadge, 174; CR, 10/25/77, 34897–98.

507 *On December 22:* NYT, 1/14/78; Newsweek, 1/23/78.

508 *"He became the conscience of his country":* NYT, 1/16 & 1/17, 1978.

508 *"From time to time":* NYT, 1/14/78.

INDEX